Oscar Wilde's Chatterton

OSCAR WILDE'S CHATTERTON

Literary History, Romanticism, and the Art of Forgery

Joseph Bristow and Rebecca N. Mitchell

Yale

UNIVERSITY
PRESS

New Haven & London

Published with the assistance of Furthermore: a program of the J. M. Kaplan Fund.

Published with assistance from the foundation established in memory of
Philip Hamilton McMillan of the Class of 1894, Yale College.

Yale University Press books may be purchased in quantity for educational, business, or
promotional use. For information, please e-mail sales.press@yale.edu (U.S. office) or
sales@yaleup.co.uk (U.K. office).

Set in Electra type by Integrated Publishing Solutions.
Printed in the United States of America.

Library of Congress Cataloging-in-Publication Data
Bristow, Joseph.
Oscar Wilde's Chatterton : literary history, romanticism, and the art of forgery / Joseph
Bristow and Rebecca N. Mitchell.
pages cm
Includes bibliographical references and index.
ISBN 978-0-300-20830-6 (hardback)
1. Wilde, Oscar, 1854–1900 — Knowledge — Literature.   2. Wilde, Oscar, 1854–1900 —
Criticism and interpretation.   3. Criticism — Great Britain — History — 19th
century.   4. Chatterton, Thomas, 1752–1770 — Criticism and interpretation.
5. Chatterton, Thomas, 1752–1770 — Influence.   I. Mitchell, Rebecca
N. (Rebecca Nicole), 1976–.   II. Title.
PR5824.B85 2015
828'.809 — dc23
2014028495

A catalogue record for this book is available from the British Library.

This paper meets the requirements of ANSI/NISO Z39.48-1992 (Permanence of Paper).

10 9 8 7 6 5 4 3 2 1

CONTENTS

ILLUSTRATIONS

PREFACE

Oscar Wilde's Chatterton: Literary History, Romanticism, and the Art of Forgery developed from research that began in the imposing Oscar Wilde archive housed at the William Andrews Clark Memorial Library (University of California, Los Angeles) in the summer of 2012. At the time, we were participating in the National Endowment for the Humanities summer seminar "Oscar Wilde and His Circle," which focused on the wealth of materials held in the Clark Library's collections. Our thanks go to librarian Gerald Cloud, together with his colleagues Jennifer Bastian, Scott Jacobs, Rebecca Fenning Marschall, Nina Schneider, and Shannon K. Supple. During the seminar, we also benefited from Justine Pizzo's invaluable research assistance.

At UCLA, the Center for Seventeenth- and Eighteenth-Century Studies kindly administered all arrangements for the seminar. We remain grateful to its staff members: Myrna Ortiz, Kathy Sanchez, Candis Snoddy, and Suzanne Tatian. The center generously offered additional research assistance during the 2012–13 academic year. We appreciate the acumen with which Amy Gordanier and Grace Ballor identified sources for the present book. Lynda Tolly of the English Reading Room, UCLA, assisted with obtaining copies of books we needed urgently. Jennifer Osorio of the Young Research Library, UCLA, provided us with copies of several important periodical articles. Maximillian E. Novak kindly shared his recent research on Herbert Croft's *Love and Madness*. At the University of Texas–Pan American, we received much-appreciated support from three student assistants: Seham Obaid, Justin Escobedo, and Jose Flores.

Many other administrators, librarians, and researchers have given us valuable advice. Chris Terrey, Jackie Madden, and Laurel Brake checked to see if the college records at Birkbeck contained any information about the lecture on

Thomas Chatterton that Wilde delivered there in November 1886. The editors of Wilde's journalism, Mark W. Turner and John Stokes, shared their extensive knowledge of the periodicals in which Wilde published his reviews. Simon Reader kindly offered his thoughts on Wilde's habit of maintaining notebooks, as well on Wilde's visit to Toronto in 1882. Grant F. Scott offered us guidance on John Keats's correspondence and poetry. Helen Deutsch pointed us in the direction of reliable editions of several eighteenth-century works. Richard Sha directed us to sources that we would not otherwise have found. Michael Nicholson alerted us to recent scholarship on John Clare and Chatterton. Eric Johnson and Rebecca Jewett of the Rare Books and Manuscript Library at the Ohio State University provided us with copies of the marked-up proofs of the *Century Guild Hobby Horse*. Rebecca Russell, Special Collections Librarian at the Woodsen Research Center of Rice University, assisted us in securing the prospectus for the Vale Press edition of Chatterton's Rowley poems. In Bristol, Clays Underdown, verger at St. Mary Redcliffe Church, provided access to the Muniment Room, and the staff of the Bristol Record Office offered assistance in locating information on the city's Chatterton memorials. Ronjaunee Chatterjee took several photographs of the memorials to John Keats at the Protestant Cemetery, Rome. Daniel Cook made available to us his detailed research on the reception of Chatterton's poetry. Jane Aaron and Gregory Dart informed us of the best editions of Charles Lamb's writings. Fiona Stafford threw helpful light on sources that explained the controversies surrounding the reception of James Macpherson's *Works of Ossian*. Colin Jones and Josephine McDonagh alerted us to an important source about Herbert Croft's fiction. Lois Woods, Local History Librarian at the Poole History Centre, very kindly copied for us a review of Wilde's lecture on Chatterton, which took place at Bournemouth in April 1888. Susan Odell Walker, head of Public Services at the Lewis Walpole Library, Yale University, helped us trace the provenance of the "Chatterton" notebook. Richard B. Watson, head of Reference Services, Harry Ransom Center, University of Texas, Austin, kindly responded to our query about the estate of James F. Drake, Inc. Robert Seiler directed us to an important source relating to Walter Pater. The two anonymous readers for Yale University Press made many useful observations about the shape and structure of our discussion, and we remain grateful for the generosity of their insights.

Parts of chapter 5, on Wilde's essay "Pen, Pencil and Poison," have appeared in the *Pater Newsletter*. Short sections of chapters 1 and 2 were delivered as papers at the conference entitled "Romanticism at the Fin de Siècle," which took place at Trinity College, Oxford, on 15 and 16 June 2013. Our thanks go to Luisa Calè and Stefano Evangelista for hosting this invaluable symposium. Aspects of chapter 4 were presented at the conference of the North American Victorian Studies Association, held in Pasadena, 23–27 October 2013. Aspects of our research were presented at a public lecture at the William Andrews Clark Memorial Library on 16 January 2014. A presentation on sections of chapter 3 was made at the North American Society for the Study of Romanticism, Washington, D.C., 10–13 July 2014.

The British Library kindly granted us permission to quote from several unpublished sources. The Tate Britain Museum generously permitted us to reprint Henry Wallis's *Chatterton*. Portraits of Wilson Barrett are reproduced thanks to the kind permission of the Victoria and Albert Museum, London. The illustration for "Ossian (With Variations)" appears with the permission of Punch Cartoon Library, London. At the William Andrews Clark Memorial Library, Jennifer Bastian and Scott Jacobs graciously assisted in reproducing images from the library's holdings, including those of Wilde's "Chatterton" notebook and the Vale Press's edition of the Rowley poems.

In our documentation, we have of course referred to authoritative editions. In the case of Wilde's works, we have made reference, wherever possible, to the Oxford English Texts Edition volumes that contain Wilde's critical essays, prose, journalism, the 1890 and 1891 texts of *The Picture of Dorian Gray*, and the English and French texts of *Salome*. For Wilde's society comedies, we have referred to the New Mermaids editions. For the expanded version of "The Portrait of Mr. W.H.," which Wilde drafted (but never published) not long after the shorter text appeared in *Blackwood's Edinburgh Magazine* in 1889, we have used Linda Dowling's Penguin edition of *The Soul of Man under Socialism and Selected Critical Prose* (2001). For the remainder of Wilde's oeuvre, we have referred to the *Collected Works*, ed. Robert Ross, 14 vols. (London: Methuen, 1908), which still retains greater authority than several more recent editions. Our references to Chatterton's writings are taken from the *Complete Works*, ed. Donald S. Taylor and Benjamin B. Hoover, 2 vols. (Oxford: Oxford University Press, 1971), which corrects errors in previous editions. On occasion, it has proved important to identify the earliest publication in which a work appeared. Frequently, we have given both the first publication of a work and then the reprinting in a widely available, reliable source. Since eighteenth- and nineteenth-century critics did not always reach consensus on the spelling of Shakespeare's name, we have preserved their chosen orthography.

The Office of Faculty Affairs at the University of Texas—Pan American generously provided funds to cover the costs of permissions clearance and photographic reproduction of several of the figures we reproduce here. UCLA's Friends of English and Department of English kindly assisted with the costs of permissions for both published and unpublished materials by Wilde that remain in copyright. Our thanks go to Ali Behdad for supporting us with this arrangement.

At Yale University Press, Eric Brandt, Christopher Rogers, Erica Hanson, and Dan Heaton provided tremendous editorial support. We are especially grateful to Otto Bohlmann for expert copyediting. Nancy Wolff completed the exceptionally detailed index. Our thanks go to Joan K. Davidson, president of Furthermore grants in publishing, for a much-appreciated award to support the final stages of production. We are grateful to Dean David Schaberg, Division of the Humanities, UCLA, for providing a grant from the Dean's Discretionary Fund to assist in defraying the costs of indexing.

We are especially grateful to Merlin Holland for granting permission for the reproduction of Wilde's "Chatterton" notebook and the notes on Dante Gabriel Rossetti's *Ballads and Sonnets* (1881); these documents appear in Appendix A and B, respectively. Mr. Holland has also kindly granted permission to reproduce quotations from Wilde's correspondence that remain in copyright in the United States through 2039.

OSCAR WILDE'S CHATTERTON

INTRODUCTION

O Chatterton! how very sad thy fate!
Dear child of sorrow—son of misery!
How soon the film of death obscured that eye,
Whence Genius mildly flashed, and high debate.

—JOHN KEATS (1815)

On the evening of Wednesday, 24 November 1886, the thirty-two-year-old
Oscar Wilde made his way through the London fog in order to deliver a lecture
about the largely self-educated eighteenth-century poet Thomas Chatterton.
For more than a century, Chatterton's extraordinary reputation as a brilliant
young forger from Bristol who committed suicide at the age of seventeen had
made him into one of English literary history's most intriguing subjects. The
venue of Wilde's presentation was the Birkbeck Literary and Scientific Institution. Established in 1823 as the Mechanics' Institute, the college had provided working people with a rich array of evening classes, including ones that
led to degrees from the University of London. Wilde featured in a series of
distinguished speakers, including explorer Henry Morton Stanley, war correspondent Archibald Forbes, and editor Charles Dickens Jr. (Dickens Jr. was
well known for the "Dickens dictionaries" about his father's illustrious career.)
When Wilde reached the Breams Building on Fetter Lane, this thriving place

Epigraph: John Keats, "O Chatterton! how very sad thy fate," first published in *Life, Letters, and Literary Remains*, ed. Richard Monckton Milnes, 2 vols. (London: Moxon, 1848),
1:12–13; reprinted, with a slightly different text, in *Complete Poems*, ed. Jack Stillinger
(Cambridge, MA: Harvard University Press, 1978), 5–6.

1

of learning served the needs of more than three thousand students. Yet he was taken aback at the number of men and women in the audience, not least because they had traveled through bad weather to listen to him. As Wilde explains in a letter to his friend, the poet and designer Herbert P. Horne: "I was very nearly coming to fetch you the night of the fog to come and hear my lecture on Chatterton at Birkbeck, but did not like to take you out on such a dreadful night. To my amazement I found 800 people there! And they seemed really interested in the marvellous boy."[1] Wilde's reference to the "marvellous Boy" drew on the very well known phrase that William Wordsworth had used to immortalize Chatterton in "Resolution and Independence" (1807).[2] Wordsworth's image of a precocious poet forever suspended in his glorious youth fueled an already widely known legend about a brilliant young man's tragic self-murder. By and large, Victorians followed their predecessors in assuming that Chatterton killed himself because distinguished author Horace Walpole callously declined to offer the aspiring poet much-needed patronage that would prevent starvation. It was true that when Chatterton presented the aristocratic Walpole with poems supposedly written by a fifteenth-century Bristol priest, Walpole eventually refused to believe that they were anything other than the teenager's own false-hearted handiwork (though in later years Walpole disclaimed any responsibility for the young man's death). The devastating end to Chatterton's promising career proved all the more moving to his Victorian readers because he arguably stood for them as a misunderstood Romantic genius: a prodigy of immeasurable artistic gifts who in abject desperation freed himself from a merciless and patrician literary world.[3]

If the remarkable turnout at the Birkbeck lecture on Chatterton was due in part to fascination with the young poet's legend, it was also probably fueled by

1. Oscar Wilde, "To Herbert P. Horne," 7 December 1886, *The Complete Letters of Oscar Wilde*, ed. Merlin Holland and Rupert Hart-Davis (London: Fourth Estate, 2000), 289–90.

2. William Wordsworth, "Resolution and Independence," in Poems, in Two Volumes *and Other Poems, 1800–1807*, ed. Jared Curtis (Ithaca, NY: Cornell University Press, 1983), 125. On occasion, nineteenth-century critics referred to Wordsworth's poem as "The Leech-Gatherer." On the relations between the prosody of Wordsworth's poem and Chatterton's verse, see chapter 1 (58).

3. Julie Crane describes the Victorian appropriation of the Chatterton figure in "'Wandering between Two Worlds': The Victorian Afterlife of Thomas Chatterton," in *Romantic Echoes in the Victorian Era*, ed. Andrew Radford and Mark Sandy (Aldershot: Ashgate, 2008), 27–37. We discuss a wide range of Victorian pictorial and literary renditions of the Chatterton legend in chapter 2 (85–108).

Wilde's well-established celebrity, which originated in the late 1870s when he graduated from Oxford and moved to London, where he mingled with members of the artistic elite. In his mid-twenties, when he boldly presented himself as a "Professor of Aesthetics" at fashionable social gatherings, Wilde frequently donned outré buttonholes in the form of lilies and sunflowers, earning him attention in the press. His most notable entrée to exclusive metropolitan circles occurred at the opening of the elegant Grosvenor Gallery in April 1877, at which he reputedly wore a coat that was cut in the shape of a cello. Such antics magnetized newspaper journalists and social commentators. As Wilde's name circulated ever more widely, writers for the London stage took the opportunity to exploit the eccentric image that this young aesthete presented to his transfixed public. Popular dramatic works, especially F. C. Burnand's *The Colonel* (1881) and W. S. Gilbert and Arthur Sullivan's comic opera *Patience; or, Bunthorne's Bride!* (1881), enjoyed poking fun at this particular aspect of Wilde's mannered aestheticism, which made itself evident not just in his striking attire but also his gushing poems.

In Edmund Yates's widely noted magazines *Time* and *World*, Wilde came to attention through his poetic devotion to leading actresses. In "The New Helen," for example, he apostrophizes society beauty Lillie Langtry, who turned to the stage in 1876, in these unrestrained lines: "Lily of love, pure and inviolate! / Tower of ivory! red rose of fire!"[4] Equally enthusiastic in its comparison with a mythical figure from antiquity is Wilde's paean to Sarah Bernhardt, who had played the leading role in Racine's *Phèdre* (1677) at London's Gaiety Theatre in the summer of 1879: "surely once some urn of Attic clay / Held thy wan dust."[5] And when he was declaring his adoration of these celebrities, his longer poems made their affiliations with writers such as John Keats patently clear: "Cease, Philomel," his speaker asserts in "The Burden of Itys," "thou dost the forest wrong / To vex its sylvan quiet with such wild impassioned song."[6] Such verses drew several less-than-kind notices when he collected them in his first major volume, *Poems* (1881). It is not surprising that this rather pretentious volume received mostly negative reviews, because much of its contents, which enthu-

4. Wilde, "The New Helen," *Time: A Monthly Miscellany of Interesting and Amusing Literature* 1 (1879): 400–402; *Poems and Poems in Prose*, ed. Bobby Fong and Karl Beckson, *The Complete Works of Oscar Wilde* (Oxford: Oxford University Press, 2000), 1:109.

5. Wilde, "To Sarah Bernhardt," *World: A Journal for Men and Women* 10 (1879): 18; reprinted as "Phèdre," in *Poems* (London: David Bogue, 1881), 168; in *Poems and Poems in Prose*, 1:116.

6. Wilde, "The Burden of Itys," in *Poems and Poems in Prose*, 1:64. "The Burden of Itys" first appeared in *Poems* (1881), 61–82.

siastically followed Percy Bysshe Shelley's idealistic lead to honor the "Spirit of Beauty," echoed the works of many influential forebears.[7] The *Saturday Review*, for example, claimed that Wilde had attentively "read Messrs. Tennyson, Swinburne, Arnold, and Rossetti with great pleasure, and he has paid them the compliment of copying their mannerisms very naively."[8] By the autumn of 1881, Wilde therefore had earned a reputation as an eccentrically dressed young poet who made sensational appearances in the art world. At this stage of his changeful career, Wilde had not yet attempted giving talks about his thoughts on aesthetics, although he assuredly informed his followers about his passion for *l'art pour l'art*. Even if Wilde's intimates recognized his unrivaled gifts as an engaging dinner-party raconteur, few would have imagined that he would soon make his mark as one of the most widely advertised public speakers to fill large lecture halls on both sides of the Atlantic.

In the concluding months of 1881, the sharp criticisms that Wilde suffered at the hands of a mostly unsympathetic English press strangely worked to his advantage. It was exactly his notoriety as an outlandish lover of art that made him the perfect candidate to develop a remunerative career as a modern arbiter of taste. Theatrical entrepreneur Richard D'Oyly Carte seized on the idea that Wilde could serve as the ideal vehicle to advertise the American production of *Patience*: the comic opera that satirized this young man's unconventional image and the art-for-art's-sake philosophy he advocated. Carte, who managed Gilbert and Sullivan's affairs, issued a contract to the inexperienced Wilde, who agreed to offer presentations on aestheticism at North American venues where *Patience* was likely to tour. Wilde's lectures aimed to introduce an American public to the fashionable aestheticism that the operetta lampooned. To attract large audiences, Wilde agreed to don a bizarre aesthetic garb: a comical outfit, with one or two faintly medieval touches. This lecture costume, which featured velvet knee breeches, silken hose, and patent leather pumps, was partly based on the attire that George Grossmith—in a magnificent performance as the broodingly pretentious poet Bunthorne—sported on stage in *Patience*. Correspondingly, Bunthorne's preposterous apparel amplified to the point of absurdity some of the details of the flamboyant fashions that Wilde had worn at exclusive occa-

7. Oscar Wilde, "The Garden of Eros," in *Poems and Poems in Prose*, 1:133. "The Garden of Eros" first appeared in *Poems* (1881), 17–34. Shelley's phrase appears in "Hymn to Intellectual Beauty" (1817) (*Shelley's Poetry and Prose*, ed. Donald H. Reiman and Neil Fraistat, 2nd ed. [New York: Norton, 2002], 94).

8. [Anon.,] Review of Wilde, *Poems*, in *Saturday Review*, 23 July 1881: 118; reprinted in Karl Beckson, ed., *Oscar Wilde: The Critical Heritage* (London: Routledge and Kegan Paul, 1970), 37.

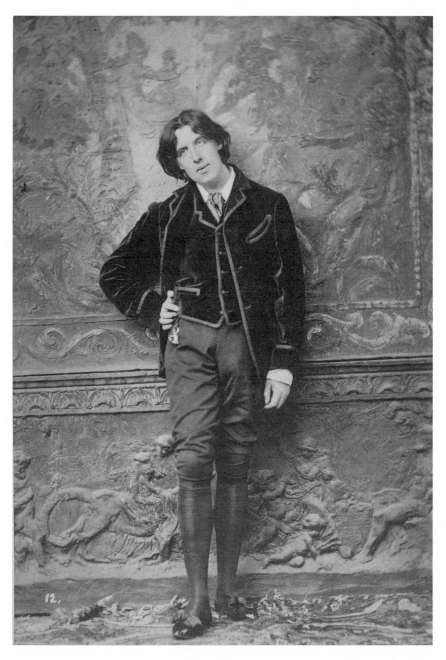
Figure 1. Napoleon Sarony, full-length portrait of Oscar Wilde in knee breeches, 1882. Photograph, 17 × 11 cm. Image courtesy of William Andrews Clark Memorial Library, University of California, Los Angeles. Box Wildeiana 19, Folder 4.

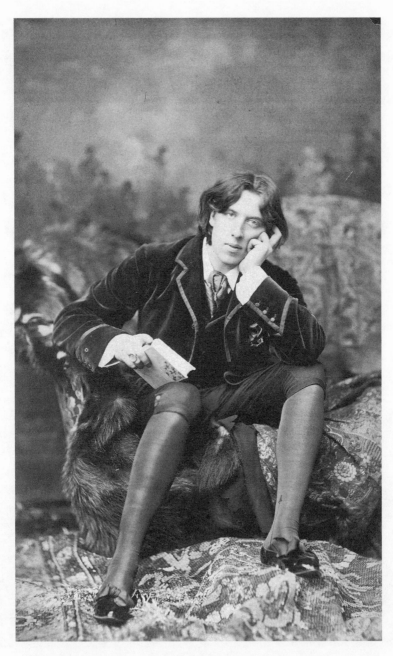

Figure 2. Napoleon Sarony, portrait of seated Oscar Wilde holding a book, 1882. Photograph. Image courtesy of William Andrews Clark Memorial Library, University of California, Los Angeles. Box Wildeiana 20, Folder 33.

sions, especially his penchant for reviving long-outmoded styles. From start to finish, *Patience* takes great delight in mocking Bunthorne's lily-clutching affectations as "An ultra-poetical, super-aesthetical, / Out-of-the-way young man!"[9]

Dressed accordingly, Wilde made his debut as a public speaker in New York City on 9 January 1882: the date that marked the beginning of a demanding ten-month lecture tour that transformed Wilde into a renowned icon on a larger scale than he had ever enjoyed in London. From coast to coast, Wilde traveled to cities large and small on a well-paid mission, enlightening American audiences on "The English Renaissance of Art," "The Decorative Arts," and "The House Beautiful." In the most ambitious of these talks, Wilde elevated the "supreme æsthetic faculty" as the phenomenon at the heart of what he interchangeably termed "the great English Renaissance of Art in this century" and "our romantic movement," since both phrases aptly characterized "our most recent expression of beauty."[10] Just before Wilde delivered his first lecture, the staff at Napoleon Sarony's famous studio took twenty-seven photographs (in three different sizes) of Wilde in a variety of carefully orchestrated poses that drew attention to his remarkable coats, hats, and shoes (see Figures 1 and 2). Sarony's striking images, whose copyright restrictions ensured that no other photographs could be taken of Wilde during the tour, feature the aesthete in suitably effete and languid poses that bear passing resemblance to those that Grossmith hilariously adopted as Bunthorne. American caricaturists were quick to exaggerate and ridicule such mannerisms, just as their British counterparts had done. Even though Wilde, by most accounts, performed rather poorly as a public speaker ("He began to speak in a voice that might have come from the tomb," as the *New York Times* unkindly put it), people flocked to see him in his extraordinary costume: "He wore a low-necked shirt with a turned-down collar, and large white necktie, a black claw-hammer coat and low shoes with bows. A heavy gold seal hung to a watch-guard from a fob-pocket."[11] Wilde's style of dress, as opposed to his literary or artistic bona fides, received the closest attention from the outset.

After his return to England at the beginning of 1883, Wilde remained a popular presenter of public talks, and he appears to have adopted a more sober manner of dress and refined his lecturing technique when he spoke on such matters as his "Personal Impressions of America." One report of his presenta-

---

9. W. S. Gilbert, *Patience; or, Bunthorne's Bride!* (London: Chappell, 1882), 37.

10. Oscar Wilde, "The English Renaissance of Art," in *The Collected Works of Oscar Wilde*, ed. Robert Ross, 14 vols. (London: Methuen, 1908), 14:243–44.

11. [Anon.,] "Oscar Wilde's Lecture: A Large Audience Listens to the Young Æsthete," *New York Times*, 10 January 1882: 5.

tion on American culture at Wandsworth Town Hall states that he appeared "in ordinary costume, and carried an orange-coloured silk handkerchief in his breast. He spoke with great fluency, in a voice now and then singularly musical, and only once or twice made a scarcely perceptible reference to notes."[12] In Dublin, he made a favorable impression on one audience member, Nannie Robinson, who became known, after her marriage to Robert Dryhurst, for her deep involvement with anarchist politics. This politically motivated woman, who attended Wilde's talk on "The House Beautiful" at the Gaiety Theatre on the afternoon of 22 November 1883, reported in a letter to her future husband: "He speaks well, and he told us many things about art worth having, and many that were the reverse."[13] She took special note of Wilde's sage advice: "Buy nothing that is not absolutely useful and truly beautiful." Wilde cannily parlayed his public renown on matters relating not only to home decoration but also to fashion into successful lectures on the serious subject of dress and dress reform, which were also warmly welcomed. The *Bath Chronicle and Weekly Gazette*, for example, observed that a "lecture, which lasted about an hour and a quarter, was listened to by the greater proportion of the audience with much interest, and all were amused at the witticisms and good-humoured criticisms respecting the absurdities of much of the fashionable dress of to-day."[14] Much of his time during 1884 was devoted to presenting talks in provincial towns such as Bath, while in 1885 he also visited more than twenty venues in his native Ireland, where "his plain commonsense arguments" about modern attire proved that he was no longer "the eccentric apostle of a momentarily fashionable craze, to be seen, heard, and laughed at."[15] By the mid-1880s, Wilde had effectively cultivated

12. Quoted in Stuart Mason [Christopher Sclater Millard], *Impressions of America* (Sunderland: Keystone Press, 1906), 17. Mason does not provide details of this source.

13. Nannie Robinson, "To Alfred Robert Dryhurst," 22 November 1883, Clark Library, MS. 2013 010. (After her marriage, Nannie Florence Dryhurst, as she became known, had important links with Peter Kropotkin, George Bernard Shaw, and W. B. Yeats.) She also observes that "a goodly sprinkling of Philistine youths . . . evidently hoped for an opportunity of disconcerting the lecturer." The "glare" of Wilde's "glorious eye" managed to subdue them.

14. [Anon.,] "Mr. Oscar Wilde's Lecture on Dress," *Bath Chronicle and Weekly Gazette*, 23 October 1884: 7.

15. [Anon.,] "Mr. Oscar Wilde on Dress," *Freeman's Journal and Daily Commercial Advertiser*, 6 January 1885: 7. Wilde's talk took place at the Gaiety Theatre, Dublin, the previous day. The report noted that Wilde attracted an audience of five hundred people, and observed: "He was plainly attired, and one sought in vain to discover any extravagances in his manner."

his celebrity into a solid reputation as an auspiciously received public speaker. Moreover, when he arrived at Birkbeck to present his talk on Chatterton, he was familiar to the audience. Two years previously, he had made a well-received presentation there. As the *Morning Post* reported in November 1884: "Last evening Mr. Oscar Wilde delivered a lecture on 'The Value of Art in Modern Life' at the Birkbeck Institution. There was an unusually large attendance of members and their friends, and the lecture was followed with great interest. Mr. Wilde, who was frequently applauded, illustrated his remarks by a series of costumes expressive of his views on the correct principles of dress."[16]

Yet the impressive attendance at Birkbeck for the talk on Chatterton in November 1886, as Wilde could tell, was attributable not just to his reputation as a public speaker but also to the Victorians' enduring fascination with Chatterton. In the 1880s, seemingly more than ever before, British audiences would have been familiar with Chatterton's legend—especially the brilliant poems this prodigy composed in the guise of an imaginary fifteenth-century priest from Bristol he called Thomas Rowley—through countless kinds of cultural works, including stage plays, elegiac lyrics, critical essays, and biographical studies. During the Victorian era, the number of periodical articles and reviews about the young Bristol poet ran into the hundreds, and such publications were complemented by a ready supply of illustrations and paintings that sought to capture the wretched, suicidal end of a promising poet. Not surprisingly, given this overwhelming mass of material, Wilde was hardly alone in selecting Chatterton as an appealing lecture topic. Members of wealthy circles could hear the well-known literary editor Edmund Gosse speak on Chatterton at the society hostess Lady Audrey Buller's drawing rooms, not long after Wilde had withstood the fog on his way to Birkbeck.[17] Beyond the metropolis, too, there was plenty of interest in this precocious eighteenth-century writer. The Rev. J. W. Dawson discussed Chatterton at the Ryde Young Men's Christian Association of the Isle

16. [Anon.,] "Notice of Lecture," *Morning Post*, 20 November 1884: 2. The Birkbeck Literary and Scientific Institution is now known as Birkbeck, University of London.

17. Gosse's talk, which belonged to a series titled "The Poets of the Eighteenth Century," took place during the summer of 1888 ("From Our London Correspondent," *Manchester Guardian*, 14 June 1888: 5). In his *History of Eighteenth Century Literature, 1660–1780* (London: Macmillan, 1889), Gosse remarks: "Chatterton is—let us say it boldly—the most extraordinary phenomenon of infancy in the literature of the world. To an intellect so untrammelled, to a taste so mature, to an art so varied and so finished at the age of seventeen, twenty years more of life might have sufficed to put the possessor by the side of Milton and perhaps of Shakespeare" (334).

of Wight, as did H. S. Pearson at the Midland Institute, Birmingham.[18] In the poet's hometown, a group of ardent Chattertonians including Wilde actively campaigned to establish a museum at the poet's birthplace in Pile Street (sometimes spelled Pyle Street), Bristol, located next to the imposing Church of St. Mary Redcliffe, where several of the teenage writer's ancestors had served as sexton. So popular was Chatterton as an inspiring topic on the lecture circuit that Wilde's last recorded public talk, which took place at Bournemouth on 7 April 1888, focused on the young Bristol poet.

To his Victorian enthusiasts such as Wilde, Chatterton was best known for the works he ingeniously crafted in Rowley's idiosyncratic, faux-medieval orthography: a bizarrely archaic style that at times resembles, if only indistinctly, the language of Geoffrey Chaucer's *Canterbury Tales* (1387–1400). The Rowley poems had first come to public attention through the editorial labors of Thomas Tyrwhitt, a Chaucer scholar of renown, in 1777. Even though the poems that Chatterton claimed were Rowley's failed to secure his literary fame during his lifetime, they possessed such metrical verve and rhetorical authority that from the 1770s onward they held generations of readers in awe. "'Tys songe bie mynstrelles," begins the dedication of Rowley's verse-drama *Ælla* (1769), "thatte yn auntyent tym, / Whan Reasonn hylt herselfe in cloudes of nyghte, / The preeste delyvered alle the lege yn rhym."[19] At the start of this ambitious "Tragycal Enterlude, or Discoorseynge Tragedie," whose sources include a 1722 edition of William Camden's *Britannia* (1586), Chatterton inhabits Rowley's commanding poetic voice to retell the romantic tale of the lovelorn ninth-century king of Northumbria. As these lines from Rowley's dedicatory "Epistle" to his patron show, Chatterton's work advanced the firm belief that poetry had from the ancients onward maintained the greatest spiritual sway over the "lege" (i.e., law). Such poetry, as the subject matter suggests, was deeply rooted in Anglo-Saxon, Anglo-Norman, and English history. Throughout his oeuvre, Chatterton addressed events that were either significant in the development of his native Bristol or crucial in defining the modern English nation. With great confidence, he imitated complex verse forms, such as variations on the Spenserian stanza.

18. The Rev. W. J. Dawson delivered his presentation, "The Marvellous Boy," on 30 November 1886 ("Ryde," *Portsmouth Evening News*, 3 December 1886: 2). H. S. Pearson's lecture, "Thomas Chatterton: A Torn Page of English Poetry," took place on 31 January 1887 ("News of the Day," *Birmingham Daily Post*, 31 January 1887: 4).

19. Thomas Chatterton, *Ælla: A Tragycal Enterlude or Discoorseyne Tragedie, wrotenn bie Thomas Rowleie; Plaiedd before master Canynge, atte his howse nempte the Rodde Lodge; [and also before the Duke of Norfolck, Johan Howard]* in *The Complete Works of Thomas Chatterton*, ed. Donald S. Taylor and Benjamin B. Hoover, 2 vols. (Oxford: Clarendon Press, 1971), 1:175.

Take, for example, the rhetorical boldness that we find at the start of the second of the two poems he titled "Battle of Hastings." As its title indicates, this work focuses on the demoralizing Norman invasion of England. Chatterton, in Rowley's guise, observes that the poem is "by Turgotus, Translated by Roulie for W. Canynge Esq." Dating from the later part of 1768, this 720-line poem purports to be Bristol parish priest Rowley's verse translation of an "Ancient poem . . . by Turgot a Saxon Monk of the *Tenth* Century," which was supposedly written for a real personage, Sir William II Canynges (c. 1399–1474), a wealthy merchant who had served many times as both mayor and a member of Parliament for Bristol.[20] As researchers have discovered, there was a historical Turgot (who scholars believe might have been the author of Simeon of Durham's *Historia Dunelmensis Ecclesiæ* [*History of the Church of Durham*, c. 1104–1108]), although Chatterton's placing of Turgot in the tenth century, as the author of an event that occurred in 1066, is of course a glaring anachronism. Despite this error, Chatterton cleverly incorporated real people and historical events with his own inventions: a strategy that helped sustain the illusion that his poems were veracious, especially to the somewhat gullible Bristol citizens who expressed delight when they thought he had discovered previously unknown works by a gifted poet who had received the famous Canynges's patronage. In both of the poems titled "Battle of Hastings," Chatterton ensured that his imaginary Bristol priest had translated a work that recorded a foundational national event. This famous military conflict at Hastings occurred on 14 October 1066, when William the Conqueror's well-trained cavalry and bowmen defeated King Harold's ill-prepared and outnumbered infantry. "Battle of Hastings [II]," which emulates Matthew Prior's skillful adaptation of the Spenserian stanza in "Ode, Humbly Inscrib'd to the Queen" (1706), as well as Prior's novel commitment to echoing Spenser's archaisms, shows Chatterton's exceptional talent for learning complicated verse forms and understanding some of the finer points of English poetic history.[21]

20. "Battle of Hastings [I]," in *Complete Works of Thomas Chatterton*, ed. Taylor and Hoover, 1:26. (This is the first of two poems with the same title.) These words come from the headnote that Chatterton furnished for the first of these two poems on the Battle of Hastings. The historical record states that Canynges's last name ended in an "s," although Chatterton always omits this final consonant. Canynges's tomb is in the Church of St. Mary Redcliffe, Bristol, with which Chatterton's family had a very close association.

21. The full title of Prior's work is "Ode, Humbly Inscrib'd to the Queen: On the Glorious Success of Her Majesty's Arms, 1706," which—as its subtitle states—is "Written in Imitation of Spenser's Stile." The ten-line stanzas are composed of nine decasyllabic lines and a final alexandrine (following a *ababcdcdee* rhyme scheme). Prior's speaker declares:

On this occasion, Chatterton adeptly deploys a stanza of nine decasyllabic lines with a concluding flourish in an alexandrine, combined with a demanding rhyme scheme (*ababbcbcdd*), all of which he renders in Rowley's antiquated locutions:

> OH Truth! immortal daughter of the skies,
> Too lyttle known to wryters of these daies,
> Teach me, fayre Saincte! thy passynge worthe to pryze,
> To blame a friend and give a foeman prayse.
> The fickle moone, bedeckt wythe sylver rays,
> Leadynge a traine of starres of feeble lyghte,
> With look adigne the worlde belowe surveies,
> The world, that wotted not it coud be nyghte;
> Wythe armour dyd, with human gore ydeyd,
> She sees Kynge Harolde stand, fayre Englands curse and pryde.[22]

As these lines show, Chatterton is not content merely to adopt either Spenser's or Prior's form but instead devises a stanza all of his own by blending a Spenserian rhyme scheme with Prior's addition of the rhymed couplet and a final line of hexameter. Beyond its structure, the verse sings with internal rhyme and clever repetition: the first quatrain contrasts hard alliterative "truth" with "teach" and with softer assonance—an effect heightened through the repeated substitution of "y" for "i." This is a quirk of Chatterton's Rowleyese that he uses with exceptional finesse. Note, too, the seventh and eighth lines of the stanza, where the stressed syllables lull sleepily, amplifying the impact of the final foot. Throughout the second quatrain, the repeated use of "with" (or "wythe") intensifies the stanza's consonance and also links phrases ending with *b*-rhymes with the final couplet.

Brilliantly, Chatterton's refined technique lends rhetorical force to his speaker's account of the devastating carnage that King Harold—who will soon die at the hands of the overpowering invaders—witnesses on the blood-strewn battlefield. The scene is clearly one of tragedy for Harold's beleaguered troops. Yet the poem also communicates that the devastated monarch, as he surveys the loss of his land, occupies a contradictory position in English history. On the one hand, he has surrendered his country to the foreign power. On the other hand, Harold's defeat has created the conditions for exactly the type of modern

---

that in praising Her Majesty he will "follow HORACE with impetuous Heat, / And cloath the Verse in SPENSER's Native Style" (*The Literary Works of Matthew Prior*, ed. H. Bunker Wright and Monroe K. Spears, 2 vols. [Oxford: Clarendon Press, 1959], 1:233).

22. "Battle of Hastings [II]," in *Complete Works of Thomas Chatterton*, ed. Taylor and Hoover, 1:68.

English in which the imaginary Rowley writes. Chatterton was almost alone among poets of his generation to look back on the significance of this crushing military downfall for English poetry. The invasion instantiated the massive linguistic shifts that resulted, three centuries later, in Chaucer's English: precisely the idiom that Chatterton aims to contrive for Rowley. In other words, "Battle of Hastings [II]" proceeds in an English style that stood at the head of the distinguished poetic tradition that found some of its greatest examples in Chaucer's rhyme royal, the intricate stanza that Spenser devised for *The Faerie Queene* (1590–1596), and Prior's early eighteenth-century elaboration of that verse form in the ode that clearly inspired Chatterton's work. Still, Chatterton's ingenuity lies in his ambition to create through Rowley a dignified synthesis of Chaucer's language, Spenser's form, and Prior's position in this decidedly English poetic genealogy.

Chatterton's greatness as a distinctly English poet had become familiar to Victorian readers through several editions of his works. In 1842, C. B. Willcox brought out two volumes that comprehensively covered the poet's life, writings, and letters. Willcox concludes his highly favorable assessment of Chatterton's verse on an exultant note that places the young poet's astonishing creativity alongside Shakespeare: "It is not unlikely that, had he lived, we might have had another Midsummer Night's Dream; and though Shakspere must ever remain unapproachable, still we should have read the rich and exquisite faery poetry with delight, and returned to it again and again, as to a fountain of joy whose waters would well freshly and inexhaustibly."[23] Almost thirty years later, the well-known philologist Walter W. Skeat took the bold step of modernizing the idiosyncratic orthography that Chatterton had devised for the Rowley poems. Although those who came to regard Chatterton's invented Rowleyese as an integral part of the boy's genius ultimately questioned this approach, Skeat's edition nonetheless proved to be popular, and it was the source from which many of Chatterton's mid-Victorian acolytes came to know the young poet's work. These publications, which also include John Richmond's modernized edition of 1885, reveal that there was an ever-broadening interest in not just the tragic biography but also the very substantial oeuvre that the wunderkind produced in a prolific career that spanned less than two whole years.

At the same time, the enduring debate about Chatterton's career focused

---

23. [C. B. Willcox], "The Life of Chatterton," in *The Poetical Works of Thomas Chatterton, with Notices of His Life, History of the Rowley Controversy, a Selection of His Letters, and Notes Critical and Explanatory*, ed. Willcox, 2 vols. (Cambridge: W. P. Grant, 1842), 1:cl. Willcox's volumes came out in an enlarged edition in 1857.

on whether his Rowley forgeries disclosed his abiding criminality or his abundant brilliance. When faced with evidence that suggested the Rowley writings were Chatterton's own work, some readers on occasion remained baffled at how such a poorly educated young man could ever have composed them. Yet, as Nick Groom has ably chronicled, in the decades that followed Chatterton's death, when everyone recognized that he had invented Rowley, countless poets grieved the loss of his remarkable genius.[24] In his 1815 sonnet on Chatterton, for example, Keats bemoans the poet's "sad fate," since the young man died alone in a shabby London garret, his talent ignored by an unappreciative public and skeptical would-be patrons. As Keats's reverent sonnet shows, at the time when this Romantic poet wrote in praise of this piteous "son of misery" Chatterton remained a figure of mortifying grief because he had gone to his grave wholly unacknowledged. Chatterton's poetry—which extends to many works that he composed in a modern eighteenth-century idiom that differs entirely from the antiquated Rowley poems—inspired nearly every major poet whose writings became associated with the literary movement that Victorians labeled English "Romanticism." Samuel Taylor Coleridge and Percy Bysshe Shelley acknowledged the greatness of this literary ancestor. By 1803, Robert Southey and Joseph Cottle—both of whom were closely linked with Bristol—issued the first comprehensive edition of Chatterton's works; this edition reprinted George Gregory's *Life of Thomas Chatterton, with Criticisms on His Genius and Writings, and a Concise View Concerning Rowley's Poems*, the first sustained biography, which had originally appeared in 1789. By the 1840s, Robert Browning, who still had to make his mark as a major poet of the time, contributed a singularly affirmative critical account of Chatterton to a leading magazine. In the following decade, the most famous Victorian critic of John Milton's works, David Masson, published articles that ultimately formed the basis for his monograph on Chatterton published in 1874. Meanwhile, in 1869 Daniel Wilson—a formidable Scottish polymath who held the first chair in English literature at the University of Toronto—brought out his hefty, book-length study that provided the most accomplished inquiry to date into the history of the poet. In essence, by the Victorian era both Chatterton's biography and poetry had become an ongoing source of critical discussion and cultural inspiration. We revisit all of these materials and their role in strengthening Chatterton's reputation in much greater detail throughout chapter 2.

24. See Nick Groom, *The Forger's Shadow: How Forgery Changed the Course of Literature* (London: Picador, 2002); and Groom, ed., *Thomas Chatterton and Romantic Culture* (New York: St. Martin's, 1999).

Since there is no known record of Wilde's talk on Chatterton at Birkbeck, it remains impossible to tell whether this famous lecturer dwelled primarily on Chatterton's engaging creative forgeries or the tragedy of the young poet's untimely death. Yet one thing is certain. Wilde had researched his subject thoroughly and drawn an informed and uplifting picture of the young Bristol poet. The detailed "Chatterton" notebook that Wilde compiled in the mid-1880s reveals the considerable lengths to which he went to collate information about the Bristol poet. This substantial document, which is held at the William Andrews Clark Memorial Library, reveals that Wilde's fascination with Chatterton relates to his unwavering interest—one that he established during his undergraduate days at Oxford—in the most influential authors associated with the recently named "Romantic movement." Close to the start of the notebook, Wilde comments on Chatterton's illustrious position in English literary history:

> Thomas Chatterton the father of the
> Romantic movement in literature, the
> precursor of Blake, Coleridge and
> Keats, the greatest poet of his time,
> was born on the 20th November
> <u>1752</u>· in the house adjoining the
> Pyle Street School in Bristol. the
> house is still standing—
> A posthumous child. his father having
> died three <u>months</u> previously.—
> His father not the sexton—though
> that office for some centuries had
> been hereditary in his family (Appendix A, f.5^r [338])

As this passage demonstrates, the notebook—which is reproduced in Appendix A (333–409)—provides the earliest evidence we have of Wilde's enthusiastic participation in a widespread late Victorian commitment to revering Chatterton: a figure of such prodigious gifts that he managed to become nothing less than the presiding spirit of English Romanticism. This claim, as we show in the present book, was an assertion that originated in the 1870s and 1880s. By tracing Chatterton's powerful legacy through the Romantic tradition, Wilde formed part of an impassioned generation of artists and writers who established the conviction that Chatterton's works had positively redirected the course of English poetry. On this view, Chatterton's forgeries—along with James Macpherson's *Works of Ossian* (1765) and Thomas Percy's *Reliques of English Poetry* (1765)—played a formative role in the Romantics' decisive reaction against neoclassicism. In each case, Chatterton, Macpherson, and Percy gathered together poems that celebrated the spirit of romance in both authentically and spuriously ancient works that were deeply rooted in the English and Scottish past.

This view of late eighteenth-century English literary history, in which Romanticism broke with a predominant neoclassical tradition, remained a vital source of debate in many publications that appeared during the final quarter of the nineteenth century. Yet through his exhaustive notes on Chatterton's life and works, Wilde does more than simply record the young poet's position as the inspirer of leading Romantics such as Keats. Especially at the beginning and end of the "Chatterton" notebook, Wilde's astute observations and selection of materials reveal that he himself strongly identified with the literary tradition that stemmed from the Romantic poets' knowledge of the Chatterton legend. Not only do Wilde's notes revere the memory of his favorite late Romantics, they also mention the work of several members of the Pre-Raphaelite movement who saw in Chatterton—as Wilde readily acknowledged—an important forebear. At the conclusion of "Chatterton" notebook, Wilde reproduces, for example, Rossetti's fine sonnet about Chatterton that first appeared in *Ballads and Sonnets* (1881) (f.82ʳ [408–9]). That Wilde read Rossetti's 1881 volume attentively is evident in the detailed notes he took on this collection, which we reproduce for the first time in Appendix B (411–15).

Wilde's observant framing of Romantic literary history and artistic heritage through Chatterton's legacy should have made this substantial notebook the focus of intense scholarly interest. Yet, for reasons that require careful investigation, this has regrettably not been the case. Certainly, during the past forty years scholars have on several occasions discussed Wilde's lengthy notes on the Bristol poet. These critics, however, have often relegated this sizable manuscript to the margins of Wilde studies, a decision based on almost uniformly dismissive judgments about its contents. Disappointingly, it has not so much been the copious information that the notebook contains as Wilde's apparently questionable method of note taking that has driven the largely negative critical interpretations of this important document. The "Chatterton" notebook has prompted scornful responses because it features many pages where Wilde has dutifully cut and pasted sections of printed text from the two best-known Victorian sources on Chatterton's fleeting career: Masson's *Chatterton: A Story of the Year* 1770 and Wilson's *Chatterton: A Biographical Study*. Nowhere does Wilde acknowledge these sources. He has simply taken a blade to those pages that interested him and accordingly glued and inserted each one into his notebook. The sheer quantity of these cut-and-pasted passages—some of which Wilde variously annotated and emended—has startled those scholars who have looked closely at this long-unpublished record of Wilde's reading. For reasons we discuss below, these researchers have assumed that Wilde's ample cutting and pasting from unnamed critical authorities is an indisputable sign of his predilection to commit a criminal act: to steal, furtively and unapologetically, from other people's works.

To say that Wilde's clippings from both Masson's and Wilson's book-length studies of Chatterton have caused an affront to those literary historians who have consulted the notebook (as well as several critics who have evidently never looked at it at all) would be an understatement. As we explain in chapter 4, several commentators have jumped to the bleak conclusion that the excerpts from the aforementioned critical volumes remain incontrovertible evidence of his supposedly habitual, and thoroughly shameful, plagiarism.[25] Paul K. Saint-Amour, in a sophisticated analysis of the manuscript, has asserted that Wilde's "notes are a pastiche of clippings and handwriting," which "plagiarize page upon page from other writers' books."[26] Josephine M. Guy has gone so far as to suggest that the notebook is the "smoking gun" of Wilde's literary larceny.[27] Modern critics have often drawn such damaging judgments because they have inferred that the notebook is the verbatim basis of Wilde's lecture at Birkbeck.[28] On occasion, they have also suggested that this lengthy document could have

25. Works that discuss the Chatterton notebook as evidence of Wilde's plagiarism include Merlin Holland, "Plagiarist, or Pioneer?" in *Rediscovering Oscar Wilde*, ed. George Sandulescu (Gerrards Cross: Colin Smythe, 1994), 193–213; Lawrence Danson, *Wilde's Intentions: The Artist in His Criticism* (Oxford: Oxford University Press, 1997); Josephine M. Guy and Ian Small, *Oscar Wilde's Profession: Writing and the Culture Industry in the Late Nineteenth Century* (Oxford: Oxford University Press, 2000); K. K. Ruthven, *Faking Literature* (Cambridge: Cambridge University Press, 2001); Robert Macfarlane, *Original Copy: Plagiarism in Nineteenth-Century Literature* (Oxford: Oxford University Press, 2007); Florina Tufescu, *Oscar Wilde's Plagiarism: The Triumph of Art over Ego* (Dublin: Irish Academic Press, 2008); and Thomas Wright, *Oscar's Books* (London: Chatto and Windus, 2008). We discuss several of these sources in detail in chapter 4 (208).

26. Paul K. Saint-Amour, *The Copywrights: Intellectual Property and the Literary Imagination* (Ithaca, NY: Cornell University Press, 2003), 97. Saint-Amour dismisses the idea that "such clippings might be pardoned as overzealous scrapbook-keeping" on the grounds that Wilde evidently edited the cuttings (99).

27. Josephine M. Guy, "Self-Plagiarism, Creativity and Craftsmanship in Oscar Wilde," *English Literature in Transition, 1880–1920* 41, no. 1 (1998): 7.

28. Ruthven, *Faking Literature*, 140; Danson, *Wilde's Intentions*, 90; Wright, *Oscar's Books*, 176–77; Tufescu, *Oscar Wilde's Plagiarism*, 13–16; and Josephine M. Guy, "Introduction," in *Criticism: Historical Criticism, Intentions, The Soul of Man*, vol. 4, *The Complete Works of Oscar Wilde* (Oxford: Oxford University Press, 2007), 4:xxx–xxxi.

served as a draft, or even the finished text, of an essay Wilde planned to (but finally did not) publish in an avant-garde magazine devoted to the unity of the arts, the *Century Guild Hobby Horse*.[29] These views, we contend, are entirely mistaken, not least because they misrepresent the content, structure, and objectives of the "Chatterton" notebook.

From one angle it may initially appear that Wilde was taking lazy shortcuts in his research because he pasted clippings from both Masson's and Wilson's respective studies in such voluminous quantities, and some phrasing in the notebook suggests that its contents were composed in preparation for a future project. Moreover, the very idea that Wilde vandalized and defaced copies of printed books in the name of organizing his knowledge of Chatterton's life and works may seem a reprehensible practice. Especially in our own times, when dishonesty in the scholarly world arises when students and colleagues reproduce sources word for word without due acknowledgment, Wilde's method of arranging information from respected Victorian experts on Chatterton may suggest he was bent on thieving from other critics' works. In some respects, the fact that several of Wilde's contemporaries—most famously, the American painter James McNeill Whistler and various theater critics of the 1890s—repeatedly accused Wilde of plagiarism might also lead one to suspect that the "Chatterton" notebook simply confirms these critics' accusations. Yet if we clear our minds of the recurrent charges of plagiarism that dogged Wilde at many points in his busy literary career, the shape and structure of the "Chatterton" notebook begin to look altogether different. The document emerges before our eyes as what it simply is: a well-researched notebook.

Keeping notebooks was one of Wilde's professional habits, and, as we explain, the numerous notebooks he kept took different forms, depending on their purpose. Besides featuring pasted excerpts from Masson's and Wilson's volumes, the notebook he dedicated to Chatterton—which we believe served as a work of detailed reference for Wilde—contains quotations from the writings of Ralph Waldo Emerson, Dante Gabriel Rossetti, and Percy Bysshe Shelley, all of whom counted prominently among the literary sources that influenced his thinking at this time. An arguably more significant point of reference, and one that has only recently been acknowledged in scholarship on Wilde's "Chatterton" notebook, was the respected reviewer and essayist Theodore Watts's thoughtful essay about Chatterton that appeared in T. Humphry Ward's four-volume anthol-

29. Josephine M. Guy, "'Trafficking with Merchants for His Soul': Dante Gabriel Rossetti among the Aesthetes," *Proceedings of the British Academy* 105 (1999): 176; and Danson, *Wilde's Intentions*, 90.

ogy of *The English Poets: Selections, with Critical Introductions* (1880).[30] Watts, whom Wilde knew from mutual social contacts, had become the closest of friends with Swinburne and Rossetti: two of the major Pre-Raphaelite authors whose writings (as reviewers quickly observed) Wilde had eagerly emulated in his earliest poetry. It was Watts, an esteemed critic of poetry in his day, who first claimed that Chatterton was governed by "an artist's yearning to represent," and that "if perfect representation seemed to him to demand forgery, he needs must forge": Wilde transcribed these important lines in his notebook and was not, as has some critics have assumed, their author.[31] It was also from Watts that Wilde gleaned the idea that Chatterton was "the father of the | Romantic movement in literature," as well as the "precursor of Blake, Coleridge and | Keats." Watts worded the claim about the influence that Chatterton exerted on the English Romantics as follows: "And when we consider the influence Coleridge himself had upon the English romantic movement generally, and especially upon Shelley and Keats, and the enormous influence these latter have had upon subsequent poets, it seems impossible to refuse to Chatterton the place of the father of the New Romantic school."[32] In many different parts of the "Chatterton" notebook, one can find several correspondences like these between Wilde's comments and Watts's fine essay.

Yet it would be incorrect to presume that Wilde was brazenly lifting Watts's bold assertions without appropriate acknowledgment from an established source, simply because Wilde failed to record the origins of these comments in his notebook. His note taking, we need to remember, was a private affair, and there is no evidence to suggest that he intended to publish or present the sources he had assembled in this document as his own work. Instead, Wilde's variations on Watts's phrasing reveal that he was fully engaged with an important critical essay in a significant anthology, one that was reshaping the ways in which readers thought about the most influential figures in the history of English poetry. Fur-

30. Geoff Dibb observes that some of the notes on f.75^r of the "Chatterton" notebook comprise "a fairly exact annexation of part of Theodore Watts' *Critical Introduction* to the Chatterton chapter of *The English Poets*" (*Oscar Wilde, a Vagabond with a Mission: The Story of Oscar Wilde's Lecture Tours of Britain and Ireland* [London: Oscar Wilde Society, 2013], 208). Dibb also points to this source in the annotations to his transcription of the "Chatterton" notebook (see 370, 371). We discuss Dibb's transcription in our Editorial Introduction to Appendixes A and B (325–30).

31. Theodore Watts, "Thomas Chatterton," in *The English Poets: Selections with Critical Introduction by Various Writers*, ed. T. Humphry Ward, 4 vols. (London: Macmillan, 1880), 3:405.

32. Watts, "Thomas Chatterton," *The English Poets*, 3:401.

ther, Watts's discussion, as Wilde surely understood, belonged to a contentious debate about the significance that the "New Romantic School" (a movement that the Victorians dated from the late eighteenth century) had come to hold for critics of differing stripes at the time he was delivering his Chatterton lectures. In drawing these comments from Watts—a commentator who had thought long and hard about the Romantic tradition—Wilde was taking notes from a leading critical voice linked with the Pre-Raphaelites, with whose works he felt a close literary allegiance. Our analysis therefore seeks to lay to rest the idea that Wilde's appropriation of sources such as Watts's essay in the notebook remains a sign of Wilde's inculpating plagiarism: a word whose modern sense, as the classically trained Wilde knew well, derived from Martial's metaphorical use of it to describe a feckless writer who abducted another's literary works.[33] The critical focus on Wilde's apparent plagiarism has distracted attention from what truly matters about this important document, which throws extensive light on a pivotal moment when Wilde's creative output and intellectual life underwent several astounding shifts.

The only known account of the Birkbeck lecture dwells nostalgically on Wilde's appearance, the subject that had long held the strongest public interest in Wilde. In a passing comment in his memoir *Twenty Years in Paris* (1925), journalist Somerville Story recalls hearing "Wilde lecture on Chatterton with his hands in pockets and a lily in his buttonhole leaning against a table."[34] Since it recollects not the Chatterton content but Wilde's inimitable personal manner of dress, Story's memory is perhaps tinted with some wistfulness for the flamboyant young Wilde whose aesthetic mannerisms and daring attire had made him the talk of the town. As the reports of his earlier lectures in England and Ireland revealed, Wilde had for some time discarded the costumes he wore as "Professor of Aesthetics" by dressing in an altogether more conventional style for a public speaker. The English *Agricultural Journal* observed just weeks before his Birkbeck lecture: "The Bard of Beauty no longer wears breeches of picturesque cut, but he is, nevertheless, the most popular lecturer of our time."[35]

Yet even as he met with success on the lecture circuit, Wilde was simulta-

33. See M. Valeriusi Martialis, "Epigrammaton Liber I, 52," in *Epigrammata*, ed. D. R. Shackleton Bailey (Stuttgart: Teubner, 1990), 31.

34. Somerville Story, *Twenty Years in Paris* (London: Alston Rivers, 1925), 156–57.

35. [Anon.,] 'The Country Gentleman," *Agricultural Journal*, 13 November 1886: 1464. The writer may well have had some acquaintance with Wilde, since he declares more than a week before the event took place: "His lecture on Chatterton is fine." Alfred Thompson famously caricatured Wilde as "The Bard of Beauty" in Edmund Yates's magazine, *Time* (3 [September 1880]: 97).

neously changing his career path. By late 1886, he was gradually moving away from a hectic professional life as an itinerant lecturer and jobbing reviewer for well-regarded newspapers such as the *Pall Mall Gazette* to a livelihood based on his two-year editorial stint at *The Woman's World* (1887–1889): a magazine that, under Wilde's direction, provided a serious outlet for women intellectuals of the time. Wilde's own writing was similarly turning to more scholarly topics. In the summer preceding the Chatterton lecture, Wilde wrote on Keats's poetry in two periodicals: the finely printed *Century Guild Hobby Horse* (closely linked with the emergent Arts and Crafts movement) to which he contributed a brief scholarly essay on "Keats' Sonnet on Blue," and the less well known *Dramatic Review*, where he published "Sonnet: On the Recent Sale by Auction of Keats's Love Letters," which offers a critical perspective on the unseemly commercialism of an auction that exposed intimate details about the Romantic poet's amatory affairs.[36] In other words, when he presented his lecture on Chatterton in 1886, Wilde was transforming into a writer who demanded to be taken more seriously than ever before. The "Chatterton" notebook elucidates the ways in which he was reshaping his career as a successful journalist and authoritative writer who would soon excel in many different literary genres: the essay, short fiction, novel, and society play.

In the chapters that follow, we maintain that the "Chatterton" notebook inspired many of the remarkable shifts that took place during the mid and late 1880s in Wilde's evolving emergence as a major fin-de-siècle author. Chatterton's life and works not only presented Wilde with a body of splendid literary forgeries that had stimulated the greatest Romantic poets; Chatterton also served as a stirring example of a gifted artistic maverick whose previous disrepute as a seemingly duplicitous faker of fifteenth-century poems signified his immense creativity rather than despicable criminality. As a consequence, Chatterton offered Wilde the opportunity to deepen his understanding of the history of English Romanticism as well as the independence of artistic creativity from moral prescriptions of any kind. By devoting such energy to Chatterton, Wilde was hardly idolizing the young Bristol poet as a figure who sought to get away with underhanded wrongdoing. Wilde grasped instead that, at its finest, literary forgery could be the sign of supreme artistry, in ways that enabled him defiantly to link the imagination with the most inventive forms that might express, not empirical truths, but inspired lying.

---

36. Oscar Wilde, "Keats' Sonnet on Blue," *Century Guild Hobby Horse* 1, no. 3 (July 1886): 82–86; Wilde, "Sonnet: On the Recent Sale by Auction of Keats's Love Letters," *Dramatic Review* 2, no. 52 (January 1886): 249. We discuss the sale of Keats's letters and Wilde's response in chapter 1 (142–45).

This point emerges most forcefully in many of Wilde's later works, especially the exceptional critical dialogue, "The Decay of Lying" (1889, revised 1891), which he regarded as the finest essay in his volume of critical prose, *Intentions* (1891), as well as his short fiction written in the years immediately following the Chatterton lecture. Arguably, the greatest impact that Wilde's deep knowledge of Chatterton had on his storytelling appeared in "The Portrait of Mr. W.H." (1889, revised c. 1891): his brilliant novella about the mysterious identity of the "onlie begetter" to whom Shakespeare dedicated his sonnets. At the opening of this ingenious narrative, whose earliest version appeared in *Blackwood's Edinburgh Magazine*, Wilde's narrator recalls a conversation that he had with a friend about "the question of literary forgeries," which prompted them to talk of various forgers, including Chatterton.[37] As we explain in chapter 6, this remarkable tale elaborates a theory about the identity of the cryptic "W.H." that had, not coincidentally, stood at the center of a debate between Thomas Tyrwhitt and Edmond Malone: two of the most significant eighteenth-century scholars who engaged thoroughly with Chatterton's works. More broadly, Wilde's fascination with Chatterton's genius for fabricating imaginary personae informs many of Wilde's subsequent writings that explore connections between art and crime, including "Lord Arthur Savile's Crime" (1887), "The Canterville Ghost" (1887), and his only novel, *The Picture of Dorian Gray* (1890, revised 1891), in which a beautiful portrait bears an intimate connection with the morally ugly hero's recklessness. In Chatterton's writings, as Jerome J. McGann has observed, we enter into the "brainy world of an artist whose delight lies in hoaxing and masking. The line to Oscar Wilde is direct."[38] Wilde's Chatterton—his conception of the poet, his research on the poet, and his creative works inspired or informed by the poet—thus marked a formative moment in his career. After the "Chatterton" notebook, more than ever before, Wilde's works became consumed with variously assumed and forged identities, whether playfully, as in *The Importance of Being Earnest* (1895) ("my name is Ernest in town and Jack in the country") or terrifyingly, as in "C.3.3." (the number of Wilde's cell that he

37. Oscar Wilde, "The Portrait of Mr. W.H.," in *The Soul of Man under Socialism and Selected Critical Prose*, ed. Linda Dowling (Harmondsworth: Penguin Books, 2001), 33. Dowling takes her text of this work from the extended version of "Mr. W.H." that Wilde most likely completed in the early 1890s; this revised text appeared posthumously in Mitchell Kennerley's 1921 edition (New York: privately printed, 1921).

38. Jerome J. McGann, "The Infatuated Worlds of Thomas Chatterton," in Thomas Woodman, ed., *Early Romantics: Perspectives in British Poetry from Pope to Wordsworth* (Basingstoke: Macmillan, 1998), 241. McGann's essay first appeared as "Infatuated Worlds," *London Review of Books* 16, no. 18 (22 September 1994): 6–7.

used in place of his own name to sign the earliest editions of his protest against capital punishment, *The Ballad of Reading Gaol* [1898]).[39]

As every reader interested in Wilde knows, the momentous success that he eventually enjoyed in the early 1890s resulted from a series of four well-received society comedies, beginning with *Lady Windermere's Fan* (1892) and ending with *The Importance of Being Earnest*. But no sooner did Wilde firmly preside over London's West End stage than he embarked on a hazardous libel suit against the father of Lord Alfred Douglas, his male lover. The suit arose because the Marquess of Queensberry objected strongly to Wilde's intimacy with his youngest son. After months of harassing Wilde, both in public venues such as the Café Royal and the sanctity of Wilde's family home, at the end of February 1895 the marquess delivered an insulting visiting card that accused the successful dramatist (in an infamous misspelling) of "Posing as Somdomite." The events that took place in court are extremely well known. At the very point when Wilde's success as a writer had reached its pinnacle, Queensberry's defense team rallied such unexpected amounts of inculpating evidence—including Wilde's close involvement with many different types of young men, some of them male prostitutes and blackmailers—that Wilde's counsel, Sir Edward Clarke, withdrew the prosecution. Sir Edward had no wish for the proceedings to last any longer, since he wished to do "something to save, to prevent, what would be a most terrible task."[40] In the two subsequent trials that the Crown aggressively pursued against Wilde, knowledge about his acquaintance with London's homosexual underworld eventually led a somewhat baffled jury to send him down for two years in solitary confinement (with hard labor) for committing acts of "gross indecency" with other men.

Yet, toward the end of his brutal prison sentence, when he had access to reading materials as well as pencil and paper, Wilde found succor in the many literary works that had for years given him the greatest creative sustenance. In this context, Chatterton never ceased to inspire him. Wilde's earliest biographer, his sometime friend Robert Harborough Sherard, recalled that Wilde "used frequently to recommend the reading and study of Chatterton to people who wrote to him for advice on literary study."[41] During his final months in jail, Wilde contemplated the presence of God in the greatest literary artworks:

39. Wilde, *The Importance of Being Earnest*, ed. Russell Jackson, New Mermaids edition (London: Ernest Benn, 1980), 12.

40. Merlin Holland, *Irish Peacock and Scarlet Marquess: The Real Trial of Oscar Wilde* (London: Fourth Estate, 2003), 281.

41. Robert Harborough Sherard, *The Real Oscar Wilde* (London: T. Werner Laurie, 1916), 252–53.

"Wherever there is a romantic movement in art there somehow, and under some form, is Christ, or the soul of Christ. He is in *Romeo and Juliet*, in the *Winter's Tale*, in Provençal poetry, in the *Ancient Mariner*, in *La Belle Dame sans Merci*, and in Chatterton's *Ballad of Charity*."[42] And, slightly later, when he anticipated his release, Wilde gave his close friend Robert Ross (who became his literary executor) a list of writers whose works he wished to relish when he walked free: "You know the sort of books I want: Flaubert, Stevenson, Baudelaire, Maeterlinck, Dumas *père*, Keats, Marlowe, Chatterton, Coleridge, Anatole France, Gautier, Dante and all Dante literature."[43] The "Chatterton" notebook shows why, in Wilde's personal canon of great writers, the "marvellous Boy" stood as an equal in this most distinguished company.

Oscar Wilde's Chatterton: Literary History, Romanticism, and the Art of Forgery is organized around six main topics that Wilde's "Chatterton" notebook occasions. We first show that Wilde compiled his extensive notes when Chatterton's cultural legend and literary reputation had reached their apogee. By the 1880s, the cult of personality surrounding the young Bristol poet had undergone many transformations since the years that immediately followed his untimely death. Chapter 1, "Thomas Chatterton: Writing the Life, Editing the Poetry," explains the unfolding of Chatterton's biographical background before exploring the complex publication and reception history of his verse, the bulk of which came to public attention in the decade after his suicide. After detailing Chatterton's brief life, we consider the debate about the authenticity of Chatterton's "Rowley" forgeries, and the generations of editorial approaches that shaped his verse in print. In the second chapter, "The Chatterton Legend: Tributes, Adaptations, Memorials," we follow the evolution of the myth of Chatterton, from his haunting influence in the verse of the poets of the early nineteenth century, to the revivals of interest in Chatterton's life and works evidenced in the mid-century—as in, for example, Henry Wallis's enormously popular 1856 painting that movingly depicts the young poet's death—and to the fin-de-siècle efforts to establish a museum in honor of Chatterton's memory in his hometown of Bristol. Wilde's eager dedication to honoring the young poet has relevance not only to his own literary development but also—as we explore in the following

42. Wilde, "To Alfred Douglas," January to March 1897, *Complete Letters*, 747. Wilde's own title for the long, often philosophical document from which this passage is taken was "Episotla: In Carcere et Vinculis" ("Letter: In Prison and in Chains"). In 1905, when Robert Ross published a carefully selected extract from this letter, he named it (after Psalm 130) *De Profundis*.

43. Wilde, "To Robert Ross," 6 April 1897, *Complete Letters*, 791.

chapter—to the broader Victorian consolidation of an identifiable "Romantic" movement.

Chapter 3 inquires into the critical background that informs Wilde's bold assertion that Chatterton was "the father of the | Romantic movement in literature." As we demonstrate, the Victorian conceptualization of Romanticism as a distinct movement (one that emerged from the time of Chatterton) remained a source of considerable contestation among late nineteenth-century critics whose political allegiances were often diametrically opposed. Writers such as Watts who championed Romanticism met with opposition from antiliberal voices that believed that the tradition that began with Chatterton had exerted a deleterious influence on English literary history. In order to elucidate the reasons why Wilde's discovery of Chatterton meant so much to him in the mid-1880s, we consider how it developed from his fascination with Romanic poets such as Keats and Shelley during his undergraduate days at Oxford.

Chapter 4, "Wilde's 'Chatterton' Notebook: The Art of Forgery and the Charge of Plagiarism," turns to the form and content of Wilde's notebook itself. Notebooks had long formed a central part of Wilde's writing practice. He used them as repositories not only for germinating critical ideas and philosophical insights but also for taking record of inspiring quotations and memorable turns of phrase that he collected from cherished literary sources. Frequently, he preserved drafts of his aphorisms—ones that infused such incisive wit in his later writings—in notebooks. That notebooks served him such an urgent purpose is especially evident during his prison sentence. In jail he took refuge in his notebook once he had access to the range of books he successfully requested from J. O. Nelson, the prison governor who also kindly granted him the pen and paper that enabled Wilde to compose the long letter that posthumously appeared, in carefully edited form, in 1905 as *De Profundis*. As he informed his close friend More Adey: "I have tried to remember and write down the *Florentine Tragedy*: but only bits of it remain with me, and I find that I cannot invent: the silence, the utter solitude, the isolation from all humane and humanising influences, kill one's brain-power: the brain loses its life: becomes fettered to monotony of suffering. But I take notes of books I read, and copy lines and phrases in poets: the mere handling of pen and ink helps me: the horror of prison is the horror of complete brutalisation: that is the abyss always in front of one, branding itself on one's face daily, and the faces of those one sees. I cling to my notebook: it helps me: before I had it my brain was going in very evil circles."[44]

44. Wilde, "To More Adey," 25 September 1896, *Complete Letters*, 666. Wilde appears to have started work on *A Florentine Tragedy* in 1893, and the work was still not finished before he went to jail on 25 May 1895.

While our editorial introduction to the manuscript (317–32) attends to the material qualities and provenance of this document as well as our editorial practices, in chapter 4 we consider Wilde's use of notebooks in his writing practice before examining in extensive detail the composition and structure of the "Chatterton" notebook. In addition to identifying the sources on which Wilde drew, we trace Wilde's use of ideas or phrases from the notebook in his later writing, especially in a number of his thoughtful reviews for the *Pall Mall Gazette*. We also evaluate the problems that have arisen when scholars have misattributed Wilde's sources; among these, we argue, are rather implausible interpretations of the notebook's contents. Instead, we contend that Wilde's engagement with sources about Chatterton's career enabled him to grasp that the Rowley forgeries stemmed, not from a despicably immoral impulse, but from an immensely powerful imagination. The Rowley poems, as Wilde came to realize, were the product of a superb creativity that fabricated brilliant fictions about an entrancing literary history that never could have possibly existed. We discuss, too, Wilde's plentiful editorial marks on the "Chatterton" notebook, which suggest much about the keen editorial eye that he took to the passages that he had carefully cut and pasted from both Masson's and Wilson's studies. In particular, Wilde's sustained engagement with Wilson's sophisticated 1869 book draws into question Daniel Cook's claim that in the post-Romantic period, which began in the 1830s, "little substantial progress was made towards a full appreciation of [Chatterton's] merits on his own terms."[45] Both here and in chapter 3 our discussion reveals that significant late Victorian writers, including the Pre-Raphaelite poet and artist Rossetti, approached Chatterton's oeuvre with exceptional seriousness. Wilde's "Chatterton" notebook remains a document of central importance in the concerted Victorian reassessment of the revered position that the "marvellous Boy" held for several influential commentators in English literary history.

The remainder of chapter 4 looks closely at the extant critical literature on this document, which—as we mentioned above—largely assumes that the manuscript testifies to Wilde's inexcusable predisposition to purloin other writers' ideas, insights, and phrases. Our approach to the "Chatterton" notebook differs from those scholars who have inferred that it formed the basis of the lecture Wilde delivered at Birkbeck. We likewise depart from those researchers who have readily surmised that the "Chatterton" notebook contains the text of the essay that Wilde intended to publish in the *Century Guild Hobby Horse*. In any

45. Daniel Cook, *Thomas Chatterton and Neglected Genius, 1760–1830* (Basingstoke: Palgrave Macmillan, 2013), 196.

case, the considerable length of the notebook indicates that any attempt Wilde might have made to report its contents in public would have resulted in a rather fragmented presentation that lasted several or more hours. More to the point, it is doubtful that Wilde aimed to pass off well-known sources, with diction that varied so dramatically from his own well-known voice, as his own original work. This observation has important bearing on the early attacks that Wilde endured when his peers denounced him as a plagiarist, and on the similar charges that persist in scholarly assessments of Wilde's work to this day.

In chapter 5, "Wilde, Forgery, and Crime: 'Pen, Pencil and Poison,' 'The Decay of Lying,' and the Short Fiction," we explore the influence that Wilde's inquiries into Chatterton exerted on his later essays and fiction. We look first at the two remarkable pieces of criticism, "Pen, Pencil and Poison" and "The Decay of Lying"; taken together, these astute discussions show Wilde's development of the idea that fine art might arise even from criminal instincts. In "Pen, Pencil and Poison," Wilde concentrates on the legendary life of the dandyish criminal Thomas Griffiths Wainewright, who fueled his extravagant lifestyle with money he collected from the exorbitant life insurance policies he had taken out on family members he later murdered. But, as Wilde knew from his research on this Regency scoundrel, Wainewright also carved out an impressive career as one of the most accomplished art critics of his time, whose connections with the esteemed *London Magazine* placed this lover of art at the center of a gifted circle whose members belonged to the Romantic tradition that absorbed Wilde's interest. By comparison, "The Decay of Lying" argues in favor of the counterintuitive belief that telling patent untruths and weaving deceptive fiction constitutes the finest imaginative creativity.

Both of these essays challenge those readers who might assume that any kind of artwork should impart instructive wisdom; in light of these works, Wilde's short fictions that he collected in *Lord Arthur Savile's Crime and Other Stories* (1891) resonate anew. In his amusing depiction of cultural conflicts that arise when an American family moves into an ancient English home, "The Canterville Ghost" (1887) features a protagonist who rewrites an ancestral past—complete with mock-medieval diction—to relieve a centuries-old ghost of his pain. Similarly funny is the title story, "Lord Arthur Savile's Crime" (1887), which first appeared in the *Court and Society Review*. In this adroit short fiction, a young man who is about to marry has his hand read by a cheiromantist. To rid himself of the burden of a future that, he is told, will include murder, he kills the palm reader in a chance encounter on the Embankment in London, only to be told that the cheiromantist was a fake. This homicide not only happily seals Lord Arthur's altogether unexpected fate: a blissful wedding and a delightful family life; it also renders true what was a blatant lie. In these and other stories, the traces of Wilde's deepening understanding of Chatterton's creative drive can be glimpsed.

In chapter 6, we discuss at length Wilde's most finely researched and carefully sustained fictional engagement with forgery. In "The Portrait of Mr. W.H.," Wilde leads readers through an intriguing tale in which a series of young men strive to believe that the cryptic "W.H." in the dedication to Shakespeare's Sonnets refers to the young Willie Hughes, a boy actor in the King's Men. Wilde knew from the extensive sources he used that the first proponent of the Willie Hughes theory was none other than Tyrwhitt, whose outstanding editorial work brought Chatterton's poetry to notice seven years after the young poet's death. Very few Victorian commentators on Shakespeare's Sonnets—which feature the competing affections between the older male speaker, the enigmatic Dark Lady, and the attractive young man—pledged much (if any) faith in the idea of Willie Hughes. But Wilde took Tyrwhitt's proposition and transformed it into a complex narrative in which each male character works strenuously to prove, or at least to create a compelling illusion, that Shakespeare's adored "W.H." was a beautiful boy who performed brilliantly on stage; one character goes so far as to forge a painted portrait of "W.H." As it unravels its many unexpected turns, Wilde's narrative discloses its implicit knowledge of the intense debates that attended two of the best-known forgers of Shakespeare's works—William-Henry Ireland and John Payne Collier—whose energetically executed literary fakes became as legendary as those of Chatterton. This fine story left its own legacy to several of Wilde's later works, such as *The Picture of Dorian Gray* and the society comedies, in which various kinds of forged identities—to greater and lesser degrees—generate intricate plots.

In our Conclusion, we consider the destinies of the two related phenomena that have arisen from Wilde's "Chatterton" notebook. First, we consider the impact of Wilde's Chatterton inquiries in the writings he produced after "Mr. W.H." We discuss the manner in which the deceptive portrait of Wilde's ostensibly ageless Dorian Gray relates to the concepts of forgery, lying, and fiction-making that inform many of his finest essays. We then examine Wilde's most amusing foray into the invention of false identities in the last of his society comedies to enjoy success on the London stage, *The Importance of Being Earnest*. The second half of our Conclusion considers Chatterton's presence in English culture and the study of English literature after Wilde's own terrible death, which took place—in the most straitened of circumstances—in a shabby hotel room in the Latin Quarter of Paris at the end of November 1900.

Chatterton catalyzed Wilde's interest in the thematic and psychological links between creative agency and criminality, originality and artifice. As some of his friends would go on to note, Wilde's own too-early demise at the age of forty-six recalled Chatterton's. Wilde passed away, after suffering meningoencephalitis, with few friends and many debts, his genius woefully underappreciated. In the decades following Wilde's untimely death, Chatterton continued to inspire other artists, particularly young poets, who regularly honored the "marvellous Boy" in verse, as generations before them had done. Despite the production of Chatterton stage plays, novels, and biographies throughout the early twentieth century, by 1930, when E. H. W. Meyerstein's fine biography presented a sophisticated and accurate record of Chatterton's life, fascination with the poet had steadily begun to wane. Assuredly, in 1971 Donald S. Taylor's magisterial edition of Chatterton's work provided a definitive account of the poet's ambition and achievement. Yet by the very point when scholars had at last a fine textual edition to consult, Chatterton's name had already slipped to the edges of academic inquiries into English Romanticism: the trailblazing literary movement that, according to Victorians, this suicidal teenager had by and large inspired.

Wilde's own reputation, by contrast, underwent a noticeable upturn in the scholarly world during the latter half of the twentieth century, after many years when his works languished in the margins of literary studies.[46] Despite its many errors, Richard Ellmann's imposing biography, *Oscar Wilde* (1987), remains the definitive study of its kind in an increasingly busy field of inquiry.[47] Yet Ellmann's influential volume perpetuates many misconceptions about Wilde's engagement with Chatterton's life and work. Even the steadily appearing Oxford English Texts edition, which provides more comprehensively than ever before insights into Wilde's methods of composition, his interaction with editors, and his publication practices, has not yet reached a firm decision about including Wilde's "Chatterton" notebook among its many volumes.

46. For an account of Wilde's critical reception in Britain after his death in 1900, see Joseph Bristow, "Picturing His Exact Decadence: The British Reception of Oscar Wilde, 1900–1987," in Stefano-Maria Evangelista, ed., *The Reception of Oscar Wilde in Europe* (London: Continuum, 2010), 20–50.

47. It is difficult to overestimate the influence that Ellmann's biography has exerted over both general and scholarly interest in Wilde's importance in fin-de-siècle literary culture. The numerous errors in Ellmann's scholarship are recorded in Horst Schroeder, *Additions and Corrections to Richard Ellmann's Oscar Wilde*, 2nd ed. (Braunschweig: privately published, 2002). It is worth reading Schroeder's "additions and corrections" in relation to J. D. Murphy, "Additions and Corrections to Horst Schroeder's *Additions and Corrections to Richard Ellmann's* Oscar Wilde," *The Wildean* 24 (2004): 72–75. Murphy suggests that that Schroeder is not always fair when criticizing Ellmann's scholarship.

As part of a comprehensive effort to mitigate these misconceptions and omissions, our six chapters are followed by annotated transcriptions of two manuscripts, ones that complement the authoritative textual editing that has thrown increasing light on Wilde's wide-ranging canon: first, we present an edition of the substantial "Chatterton" notebook (Appendix A); and second, we reproduce and annotate the five pages of notes that Wilde made on Rossetti's *Ballads and Sonnets* (Appendix B). In Appendix A, our transcription includes not only all of Wilde's handwritten entries but also the clippings from both Wilson's and Masson's studies. Wilde's cut-and-pasted excerpts from these volumes make up a reasonably thorough biography of Chatterton in their own right. We cross-reference all of these contents with Wilde's sources, including Watts's essay, as well as the many noted allusions in the work. We also identify those passages that Wilde repurposed in his later periodical writings, which draw frequently on turns of phrase and ideas he refined in the notebook. Meanwhile, our transcription of the notes on Rossetti's *Ballads and Sonnets* shows Wilde to be a highly attentive reader, since it records lines of Rossetti's verse that are particularly striking. In these notes, Wilde also uses diction similar to his writing on Chatterton to describe Rossetti's individuality and genius, and he situates Rossetti in relation to the "Romantic movement" (f.1^v, f.5^r [333, 338]). Here, too, we offer thorough annotations, thus allowing readers a fuller picture of Wilde's detailed engagement with Chatterton than has previously been possible.

Thomas Chatterton:
Writing the Life, Editing the Poetry

In November 1886, when Wilde presented his lecture at the Birkbeck Literary and Scientific Institution, Chatterton had been the stuff of legend for well over a hundred years. His fame had become so assured that schoolchildren could be expected to know the life story of the once-obscure poet whose career came to public light only in the 1780s. In his 1883 handbook for elementary schoolteachers, Frederick William Hackwood holds up Chatterton as an example of "those who openly mutiny at their fate, who are constantly discontented and frequently grumbling, who view life and its duties lugubriously."[1] A life such as Chatterton's, Hackwood sternly intones, is not to be "enjoyed but endured"; students, he asserts, should strictly observe—in stark contrast to Chatterton's woe-begotten case—that it is their "duty to derive from [life] as much *reasonable* pleasure as possible."[2] Hackwood elaborates the limits of *"reasonable"* pleasure, since he suggests that teachers should "strongly caution against excess in every shape"; he closes this punishing section of the lesson with yet another striking admonition: *"Further insist* that our enjoyment must be real and NOT ASSUMED, **as some modern Æsthetes pretend to have an affection for art, Nature, Mediævalism, etc.**"[3] In this undisciplined decade, then, Hackwood expected his potentially insubordinate charges to link the late Victorian "Aesthete" with the thoroughly remiss Chatterton so that that these two figures appear as similarly deceitful types. Both sorts of men, in his view, had no appreciation of life's true blessings. Yet, as Hackwood almost grudgingly implies, the

1. Frederick William Hackwood, *Notes of Lessons on Moral Subjects: A Handbook for Teachers in Elementary Schools* (London: T. Nelson and Sons, 1883), 181.
2. Hackwood, *Notes of Lessons on Moral Subjects,* 182.
3. Hackwood, *Notes of Lessons on Moral Subjects,* 182. Emphasis in original.

modern aesthete's affectations and Chatterton's discontent were all too likely to absorb an ordinary schoolchild's restless imagination.

The fact that Hackwood went out of his way to make an example of Chatterton's perturbing biography gives a firm impression of the attention that the "marvellous Boy" had attracted by the 1880s. During this decade, Wilde— whose credentials as an aesthete remained unparalleled—worked to strengthen the already popular appreciation of Chatterton, which was not always as unsettling as Hackwood's cautionary wisdom might suggest. Accounts of Chatterton's life could be readily found in nonjudgmental articles such as J. M. Ingram's 1884 feature in *Harper's Monthly Magazine,* one of the popular transatlantic literary monthlies. Yet the story of Chatterton's brief career not only proved to be a source of moral contention; it also remained open to some factual debate, since the biographical record contained various inaccuracies that Victorians such as Ingram sought to contest and correct. There were, for example, such fundamental difficulties with aspects of Chatterton's life story that, even a century after his demise, no reliable depiction of his face and features had emerged. Ingram concludes by stating that it "is questionable whether any authentic portrait of the boy-poet exists," even though several likenesses that supposedly resembled the poet had been either published or exhibited.[4]

Similar problems beset the record of Chatterton's ancestry. In 1881, the *Athenæum*—a well-respected literary weekly that often welcomed articles that threw fresh light on historical authors' lives—focused attention on Chatterton's relatives. A dispute began with a letter from a librarian at the Bristol Museum, John Taylor, who claimed that he had recently studied a history of the Bible that the Chatterton family once owned. The volume, Taylor declared, contained inscriptions that recorded the births of the young poet and his two older siblings: "The firm, round, schoolmaster's style of penmanship shows the hand of the poet's father, who conducted the Pile-street school" where the poet was born.[5]

4. John H. Ingram, "Chatterton and His Associates," *Harper's New Monthly Magazine* 67 (1883): 240. Ingram mentions three portraits that mistakenly appeared before the public as depictions of Chatterton: first, the portrait that features opposite the title page of John Dix's unreliable biography, *The Life of Thomas Chatterton, Including His Unpublished Poems and Correspondence* (London: Hamilton, Adams, 1837); second, a picture exhibited at the South Kensington museum in 1867 and wrongly attributed to William Hogarth; and third, an unspecified "print said to be 'from a picture belonging to his sister.'" Dix's biography, which we discuss later in this chapter (48), was reprinted in 1851.

5. John Taylor, "To the Editor," *Athenæum* 2824 (10 December 1881): 780; reprinted in *New Facts Relating to the Chatterton Family, Gathered from Manuscript Entries in a "History of the Bible," which Once Belonged to the Parents of Thomas Chatterton the Poet and from Parish Registers,* ed. William George (Bristol: W. George, 1883), 5.

As Ingram swiftly pointed out, it would have been impossible for Chatterton's father to record the birth of his third child, since he died several months before his son was born. To Ingram, this presumed discovery simply amounted to yet another saddening imposture that showed how "poor Chatterton . . . has been made the victim of unscrupulous fabricators."[6] This was also the case with the attribution to Chatterton of works that he never composed. "I could point," Ingram continues, "to a large *quantum* of rubbish foisted on the public as by the 'marvellous boy' that is not his work at all."[7] In particular, Ingram draws attention to Walter W. Skeat's 1871 popular Aldine edition of *The Poetical Works of Thomas Chatterton*, whose contents—although Ingram declines to specify this fact—include the spurious poem "To Horace Walpole," which is written in a hand (as the manuscript in the British Museum shows) that does not look like any of the ones Chatterton used.[8] In response, Taylor stated that the inscription in the history of the Bible that Ingram claimed had been fabricated was in handwriting different from that of the others. Someone apart from Thomas Chatterton Sr. had recorded the birth. Meanwhile, the owner of this family volume, William George, professed the authenticity of the document by stating that it contained fresh information about the marriage of Chatterton's parents, the birth date of the poet's sister, and the name that the poet's older brother (who passed away at four months) had at his christening. George ends his discussion by stating that such "fresh details" will assist a "future biographer" in producing "a more adequate understanding of the local family connections of one who has excited so much interest in the literary world."[9]

Such details evidently interested Oscar Wilde, who took heed of these controversies about Chatterton's life. Besides consulting both David Masson's *Chatterton: A Story of the Year 1770* (1874) and Daniel Wilson's *Chatterton: A Biographical Study* (1869), he owned a copy of the pamphlet that gathered the trenchant exchanges between Taylor, Ingram, and George from the pages of the *Athenæum*.[10] Clearly, the complications involved in obtaining an accurate

6. John H. Ingram, "To the Editor," *Athenæum* 2825 (17 December 1881): 813; reprinted in *New Facts Relating to the Chatterton Family*, 7.

7. Ingram, "To the Editor," 813; in *New Facts Relating to the Chatterton Family*, 7.

8. Nick Groom contends that the manuscript of these lines suggests that the poem is a forgery; see "The Case against Chatterton's 'Lines to Walpole' and 'Last Verses,'" *Notes and Queries* 50 (2003): 278–80. For an opposite (and questionable) view, see *The Complete Works of Thomas Chatterton*, ed. Donald S. Taylor and Benjamin B. Hoover, 2 vols. (Oxford: Clarendon Press, 1971), 2:986. The poem first appeared in Dix, *Life of Thomas Chatterton*, 102.

9. William George, in *New Facts Relating to the Chatterton Family*, 13.

10. In the Clark Library's photocopy of the *Catalogue of the Library of Valuable Books, Pictures, Portraits of Celebrities, Arundel Society Prints, Household Furniture, Carlyle's*

account of Chatterton's career, his literary output, and even his visage were urgent matters when Wilde explored the developing opinion that the young Bristol poet stood at the head of the English Romantic tradition. In this chapter, we begin with an early entry in Wilde's "Chatterton" notebook to trace the extraordinary legacy of Chatterton's despairing life and brilliant works during the hundred and fifteen years following his untimely death. We follow Wilde's lead by exploring the various accounts of Chatterton's somewhat checkered life story, ones that reveal by turns the poet's impetuousness, ambitiousness, and immense creative talent. As we show here, Chatterton's early embattled reputation was eventually replaced with his ascendant fame in literary circles, which ensured that Victorian schoolchildren had to be cautioned about his troubling biography, even if they did not necessarily recite the amazing forgeries that testified to his greatness. Thereafter, we explore where the biographical sources that Wilde used in his notebook stand in relation to the upsurge of cultural interest in Chatterton's life, poetic canon, and literary legacy, especially in the young poet's hometown of Bristol.

"A BOY OF LEARNING AND A BARD OF TROPES": THE LIFE OF THOMAS CHATTERTON, 1752–1770

In the opening pages of his notebook on Chatterton, Wilde observed that it was impossible to divorce the poet's life from his work:

> Without a full
> comprehension of his life the secret
> of his literature is not revealed.
> And so in going over the details
> of the life of this marvellous
> boy I do so not to mar the
> perfect joy and loveliness of his
> song by any overemphasis of the
> tragedy of his death, but simply
> to enable us to understand

Writing Table, Chippendale and Italian Chairs, Etc., Which Will Be Sold by Auction, by Mr. Bullock . . . on Wednesday, April 24th 1895 (London: Bullock, 1895), which is based on a copy held in the Eccles Bequest, there is typewritten entry pasted onto one of several additional leaves at the back that appears to come from an auction house or bookseller's catalogue; this entry states that there was a *New Facts* pamphlet that William George inscribed "To Oscar Wilde Esq., with the Editor's Respects." Clark Library, PR5828 C357.

the curious form he used, and to
appreciate an art that to many
    may seem an anachronism. (f.4^r [337])

It is clear that understanding the specific circumstances of Chatterton's upbringing in Bristol, together with the four months the poet spent busily in London before his suicide, was essential to appreciate the unique nature of the antiquarian Rowley forgeries upon which his reputation rested. Further, the telling
and retelling of Chatterton's life served as a bellwether for both the reception
and the regard of his poetry.

Yet, until a century after Chatterton's death, gaining an accurate sense of
his biography had been a difficult pursuit, not least because information about
his brief career initially emerged in the oddest of sources: a best-selling novel
that was ostensibly based on a much-publicized murder case. In 1780, Herbert
Croft published his sensational epistolary novel about forgery and homicide,
Love and Madness. This work of fiction focuses attention on the Rev. James
Hackman's 1779 murder of Lord Sandwich's mistress, actress Martha Ray. Time
and again, Croft's homicidal Hackman endorses Chatterton's "extraordinary genius."[11] "My mind," the fictionalized "Mr. H." asserts, "does not now harbour
a doubt that Chatterton wrote the whole" of the Rowley canon.[12] That a novel
should have brought the Rowley controversy into the midst of Hackman's murderous history says much about the prominence Chatterton's career enjoyed
just ten years after his early demise in an obscure garret at Holborn. Croft,
as John Brewer has shown, counted among the earliest researchers who went
eagerly "to Bristol in search of Rowley," where he "visited Chatterton's family" and "persuaded Chatterton's sister to write a short memoir of her brother":
"Obviously Croft was preparing to intervene in what was fast becoming the
most fashionable literary controversy of the day."[13] Yet Croft's researches yielded
only a threadbare account of the poet's life: Chatterton's meager education at a
bluecoat charity school ("reading, writing, and accounts, composed the whole
circle of sciences" that Chatterton learned); the fact that in July 1767 the young
man was "articled clerk to an attorney of Bristol"; and the questionable patronage that the poet received from two Bristol gentlemen ("Mr. Catcott and
Mr. Barrett, a pewterer and a surgeon"), who appear to have made "no incon-

---

11. [Herbert Croft,] *Love and Madness: In a Series of Letters, One of Which Contains the
Original Account of Chatterton, a New Edition, Corrected* (London: G. Kearsley, 1786), 148.

12. [Croft,] *Love and Madness,* 141.

13. John Brewer, *Sentimental Murder: Love and Madness in the Eighteenth Century*
(London: HarperCollins, 2004), 174–75.

siderable sum" from selling the Rowley manuscripts they obtained from Chatterton's family following his premature death.[14] Apart from these details, *Love and Madness* concentrates on Chatterton's formidable literary achievements that mostly spanned the tender ages of fifteen to seventeen.

Through its blended genre, which couples studied research with wild supposition, Croft's novel foregrounded the link between the fictions that Chatterton invented and the role of narrative in securing his fame. It was, however, left to others to produce the first full-length, fact-based account of Chatterton's career. Although there remained plenty of gaps to fill after his volume appeared in 1789, George Gregory's biography enabled readers to grasp not only Chatterton's huge literary ambitions but also the poet's unquestionable accomplishment. Gregory's *Life* recounts a fairly straightforward narrative about the gifted young man's bold attempts to gain a foothold in a literary world that did not easily open its doors to one of such humble origins. The poet, he tells us, was his father's posthumous child. This parent, who did not reach the age of thirty, had served in succession as a school usher, as a "singing man" at Bristol cathedral, and finally as a master at the free school at Pile Street, where the son was born.[15] Though the young Chatterton was thought to be "a dull boy, and incapable of improvement," his interest was piqued by an illuminated manuscript (with which, according to his mother, he *"fell in love"*) and a black-letter bible.[16] By the age of ten or eleven, after having received two years of modest education as a boarder at Colston's bluecoat school, Chatterton "wrote a Catalogue of the Books he had read, to the number of seventy."[17] Such wide reading

14. [Croft,] *Love and Madness*, 144, 146, 147.

15. G[eorge] Gregory, *The Life of Thomas Chatterton, with Criticisms on His Genius and His Writings, and a Concise View of the Controversy Concerning Rowley's Poems* (London: G. Kearsley, 1789), 2. Gregory's volume, which at times draws on *Love and Madness*, is a revised version of the text that appeared in the *Biographia Britannica; or, the Lives of the Most Eminent Persons Who Have Flourished in Great Britain and Ireland from the Earliest Ages, to the Present Times*, 2nd ed. (London: Rivington, 1789), 4:573–619. Originally, Croft planned to write this biography. Croft passed up this opportunity to the editor of the *Biographia Britannica*, Andrew Kippis, who then handed it over to Gregory. Michael Lort, the historian who researched Chatterton's life through the poet's family and contacts at Bristol in the 1770s, advised Gregory on the content on this biography. "As an eighteenth century unsentimental view of the poet," E. H. W. Meyerstein writes in what remains to this day the definitive biography, "Gregory's Life, short and restricted as it is, must always command respect" (*A Life of Thomas Chatterton* [New York: Charles Scribner's Sons, 1930], 485).

16. Gregory, *Life of Thomas Chatterton*, 4. Emphasis in the original.

17. Gregory, *Life of Thomas Chatterton*, 11.

was unusual in a boy whose training prepared him for low-level positions in law and commerce, which was exactly where his schooling led. In John Lambert's tedious office, where Chatterton was apprenticed to "copy precedents," not all was lost for the young man; the occupation gave him access to a library of law books, as well as copies of literary and historical works that he devoured. Most important among these was a 1695 English-language edition of William Camden's *Britannia* (1586): the antiquarian chorography, initially published in Latin, which provided the first detailed national history of all parts of England from the period of the Roman Empire onward.[18]

Around this time, Chatterton made visits to the Muniment Room (also known as the Treasury Room) at St. Mary Redcliffe, the architecturally imposing church that the famous mayor of Bristol, known to Chatterton as William Canynge, rebuilt in the fifteenth century.[19] This room had for centuries held several locked chests. The authorities, Gregory says, broke them open in 1727 because it was assumed that they might contain deeds of some value relating to the church. (Daniel Wilson states that the date was somewhat later.)[20] For the most part, Gregory recalls, the vellum manuscripts they found there were deemed worthless. Chatterton's ancestors adapted them for covering books that children used at the Pile Street School. Very soon, Chatterton plundered these parchments, removed their old ink, and inserted new script in antiquated handwriting to convince potential patrons that they were the work of Thomas Rowley, the late medieval priest he conjured from his tremendously fertile imagination.

Gregory provides us with a good sense of the range of reading that Chatterton undertook once he made contact with local men whose sponsorship the determined young poet pursued. Among the books he borrowed from these contacts were John Kersey's *Dictionarium Anglo-Britannicum; or, a General English Dictionary* (1708) and an edition of Thomas Speght's *Workes of Our Lerned and Antient Poet, Geffrey Chaucer*, which first came out in 1598. Apparently inspired by this reading, Chatterton began composing, and several of his works appeared

18. Gregory, *Life of Thomas Chatterton*, 26. Some argue that Chatterton's dissatisfaction with the position and his eventual suicide served as a model for the title character of Herman Melville's "Bartleby the Scrivener." See Maryhelen C. Harmon, "Melville's 'Borrowed Personage': Bartleby and Thomas Chatterton," *ESQ: A Journal of the American Renaissance* 33, no. 1 (1987): 35–44.

19. Strictly speaking, the historical figure that Chatterton calls William Canynge is properly known as William II Canynges. We discuss the reasons why Chatterton made this distinguished Bristol citizen the patron of Thomas Rowley on 57–59.

20. Daniel Wilson states that "the date should probably be 1735" (*Chatterton: A Biographical Study* [London: Macmillan, 1869], 21).

(under the initials "D.B.") in the opening numbers of the London-based *Town and Country Magazine*, a journal that eventually became associated with sexual controversies, as we know from Richard Brinsley Sheridan's biting comedy, *The School for Scandal* (1777).[21] Gregory mentions that Chatterton placed there "some extracts from Rowley's manuscripts; and . . . some pieces called Saxon poems, written in the style of Ossian," the ancient Celtic poet whose verses James Macpherson in the 1760s claimed he had translated into prose from a range of Scottish sources.[22]

No sooner had Chatterton secured this success than he took the initiative to send a packet of his Rowley forgeries to Horace Walpole's bookseller in London. It was a brave step. According to Gregory, Chatterton informed the renowned Whig politician, art historian, and author of the famous Gothic romance *The Castle of Otranto* (1764) that he "was the son of a poor widow, who supported him with great difficulty; that he was apprentice to an attorney, but had a taste for more elegant studies."[23] This was, in other words, a bid for patronage.

21. In Sheridan's *School for Scandal*, Snake informs Lady Teazle about Mrs. Clackitt: "I have more than once traced her causing a *tête-à-tête* in the *Town and Country Magazine*, when the parties perhaps had never seen each other's faces before in the course of their lives" (*The School for Scandal*, ed. F. W. Bateson [London: Ernest Benn, 1979], 10). Chatterton signed his works in the *Town and Country* "D.B.," which stood for "Dunhelmus Bristoliensis."

22. Gregory, *Life of Thomas Chatterton*, 48. The works Chatterton placed in the *Town and Country* in 1769 alone were "The Court Mantle" (the transcript of Rowley's prose piece on this item of dress), "Ethelgar: A Saxon Poem" (which followed the trend for producing "Ossianic" pieces in the prose style of Macpherson's *Ossian*), "Elegy I" ("Haste, haste! ye solemn messengers of night"), the Ossianic "Kenrick," "Saxon Atchievements" (a prose piece, with illustrations, of Saxon heraldry), the Ossianic "Cerdick," Rowley's "Elinoure and Juga," "To Mr. Holland" (a poem in honor of the actor Charles Holland), the Ossianic "Godred Crovan," "Elegy to the Memory of Mr. Thomas Phillips, of Fairford" (the senior boy and usher who was at Colston's during Chatterton's time there), "Elegy II" ("Joyless I seek the solitary shade"), the Ossianic "The Hirlas I," a short historical essay called "Antiquity of Christmas Games," the poem "The Copernican System," "The Advice" (a poem that takes, among other things, a stab at Walpole), and "The Hirlas II." This is, by any account, a formidable amount of poetry for an unknown sixteen-year-old to have placed in a London journal. We address the significance of Macpherson's *Ossian* in relation to Chatterton's writings in chapter 2 (110–15).

23. Gregory, *Life of Thomas Chatterton*, 50. The words come from Walpole, in his *Letter to the Editor of the Miscellanies of Thomas Chatterton* (Strawberry Hill: privately published, 1779), 33; we discuss the context of Walpole's document later in this chapter (45–47). This letter does not appear in the *Complete Works of Thomas Chatterton*. Taylor and Hoover print a letter dated 8 April 1769, in which Chatterton informs Walpole: "I am not able to dispute with a person of your literary character . . . I am but sixteen years of

And initially, until he realized the works were impostures, Walpole showed interest in them. Diplomatically (since he had been told that he had to exercise sensitivity toward Walpole), Gregory remarks that this immensely wealthy gentleman's curt response to the young scrivener from Bristol was "rather too much in the common-place style of Court replies," though Walpole insisted that his letter to Chatterton was kind.[24] In any case, Chatterton received the brush-off badly, and he sent what Walpole deemed to be a "singularly impertinent" epistle, in which the poet—who demanded that Walpole return the packet of poems—contended that the aristocrat "would not have *dared* to use him so ill, had he not been acquainted with the narrowness of his circumstances."[25] As Gregory observes, the "the disappointed poet" wreaked his revenge on Walpole in "a ridiculous portrait" in prose that appeared in the *Town and Country*.[26] In words that Walpole was appalled to read, Chatterton characterized his enemy as "the redoubted baron Otranto, who has spent his whole life in conjectures."[27] Still, Gregory concludes his discussion of the affluent aristocrat's "frigid reception"

---

age." Since it had become clear that Walpole had no interest in the Rowley poems, Chatterton proceeded to declare: "I am obliged to you, sir, for your advice, and will go a little beyond it, by destroying all my useless lumber of literature, and never using my pen again but in the law" (1:271).

24. Gregory, *Life of Thomas Chatterton*, 51; Gregory suggested that Walpole himself characterized his response to Chatterton as a "court-reply," but in a letter to Hannah More, Walpole protested: "Now my own words, and the truth, as they stand in print in the very letter of mine which this author [Gregory] quotes, were, '*I wrote him a letter with as much kindness and tenderness as if I have been his guardian.*' Is this by my account a court-reply?" "To Hannah More," c. 10 September 1789, *Letters of Horace Walpole, Earl of Orford* (London: Richard Bentley, 1840), 6:353; reprinted in *The Yale Edition of Horace Walpole's Correspondence*, ed. W. S. Lewis, 48 vols. (New Haven: Yale University Press, 1937–1983), 31:326.

25. Gregory, *Life of Thomas Chatterton*, 53. Gregory has changed Chatterton's letter from first to third person and interpolated some of the phrasing; the text should read: "I think myself injured, sir; and, did not you know my circumstances, you would not dare to treat me thus" ("To Horace Walpole," 24 July 1769, in *Complete Works of Thomas Chatterton*, ed. Taylor and Hoover, 1:340).

26. Gregory, *Life of Thomas Chatterton*, 53. Such was the biting force of Chatterton's letter to Walpole that someone composed a bitterly resentful poem based on the text: "Had I the Gifts of Wealth and Lux'ry shar'd / Not poor and Mean—Walpole! thou hadst not dared / Thus to insult" (*Complete Works of Thomas Chatterton*, ed. Taylor and Hoover, 1:341). The poem first appeared in John Dix's unreliable *Life of Thomas Chatterton* (102); several subsequent commentators, including Robert Browning, believed it to be Chatterton's own work.

27. "Memoirs of a Sad Dog," quoted in Gregory, *Life of Thomas Chatterton*, 53; and in *Complete Works of Thomas Chatterton*, ed. Taylor and Hoover, 1:658.

by stating that for anyone "to ascribe to Mr. Walpole's neglect . . . the dreadful catastrophe [i.e., the poet's suicide], which happened at a distance of nearly two years after [i.e., in August 1770, seventeen months after Chatterton's earliest letter to Walpole], would be the highest degree of injustice and absurdity."[28]

That Chatterton remained angry and distressed for many months after Walpole's rejection emerges when Gregory reports that the young man had declared himself an infidel to a friend in Bristol. Chatterton, it appears, was contemplating committing suicide on Easter Sunday, 1770: an intention he disclosed in the intimidating "Last Will and Testament" (composed of a headnote, sixty lines of couplets, and a will) that he left for his panicked employer to read. In the verse that prefaces his instructions for the tomb to be raised in his memory, Chatterton characterizes himself proudly as "A Boy of Learning and a Bard of Tropes."[29] He follows these remarks by stating that he recognizes it will remain for the coroner and jury to assess his "Soundness of . . . Mind," and he understands that they may well deem him a "Mad genius."[30] In this histrionic mode, Chatterton proceeds to make stipulations about his monument, which he states should feature a "Flat stone on the Top and adding six Tablets," with inscriptions in "old English Characters" and "Roman Characters."[31] This frenzied document, regardless of its pretentiousness, nonetheless did the trick. Promptly released from his indentures, the headstrong Chatterton embarked on a career in London, where he hoped to find work with a bookseller.

By May 1770, Chatterton was installed in the home of a plasterer at Shoreditch in the East End, where one of his relatives, Mrs. Ballance, resided. By this time, he had already circulated "Kew Gardens"—a political verse satire in the style of Charles Churchill—to George Edmunds, who edited the *Middlesex Journal*. Edmunds's politics were allied with radical John Wilkes, who led a famous campaign in the county of Middlesex so that voters, rather than the House of Commons, could select their representatives. An English patriot, Wilkes had already gained a fierce reputation for making a seditious libel against George III for entering into the Paris Peace Treaty (1763), which ended the Seven Years' War. In particular, Wilkes, who was consequently ousted from Parliament and became an exile in France for several years because of his challenge to the monarch, objected to the power that John Stuart, 3rd Earl of Bute, exercised

28. Gregory, *Life of Thomas Chatterton*, 52, 56.

29. ["Will"], in *Complete Works of Thomas Chatterton*, ed. Taylor and Hoover, 1:502. The editors have supplied this title. This document is generally known as Chatterton's "Last Will and Testament."

30. ["Will"], in *Complete Works of Thomas Chatterton*, 1:502, 503.

31. ["Will"], in *Complete Works of Thomas Chatterton*, 1:503.

as head of government (until 1763) over the young king. Wilkes exploited what he alleged were the earl's Jacobite sympathies, which recalled the rising of 1745 when "Bonnie Prince Charlie" (Charles Edward Stuart) sought to regain the throne for the exiled Scottish house of Stuart. Chatterton, in recognition of this attack, satirized what he believed were the political manipulations that took place in 1770 at Kew Gardens, the home of the Dowager Princess of Wales, mother of George III and rumored mistress of the Earl of Bute. Chatterton is not slow to impugn what he sees as Bute's treacherous Jacobite interests, and how these exert influence on the widowed princess: this seductive political leader like a "happy Genius comes along / Humming the music of a highland song."[32]

Gregory's portrait depicts Chatterton striving to find a niche in the radical literary culture of the metropolis, and his biography accentuates the poet's politically motivated works in order to show the young man's honorable literary aspirations. Especially significant to the young poet in the radical political circle in which he wished to move was William Beckford, Lord Mayor of London, a divisive figure who remained one of Wilkes's ardent supporters. After challenging Parliament's rejection of Wilkes's election, Beckford applied directly to George III; when the indignant monarch offered only a curt reply, Beckford responded by suggesting that anyone encouraging the king to alienate himself from his people and from the city of London was "a betrayer of our happy constitution, as it was established at the glorious revolution."[33] The threat was clear. In Beckford's view, George III stood on the same path that had led to James II's loss of the crown in 1688. Chatterton instantly touted his support for Beckford's defiance toward the Crown. Under the name of "Probus" in both the *Middlesex Journal* and the *Political Register,* he published a letter in which he championed Beckford's "perseverance in the glorious cause [that] will check the rapid progress of oppression."[34] As Gregory notes, Chatterton's letter proved success-

32. "Kew Gardens," in *Complete Works of Thomas Chatterton,* ed. Taylor and Hoover, 1:513.

33. [Anon.,] *City Petitions, Addresses, and Remonstrances &c., Commencing in the Year MDCCLXIX, and Including the Last Petition for the Burial of the Rt. Hon. the Earl of Chatham in St. Paul's Cathedral with his Majesty's Answers, also Mr. Alderman Beckford's Speech to the King, on the Twenty-Third of May,* 1770 (London: David Steel, 1778), 23. Beckford alludes to the deposition of James II, which occurred in light of his arrest of seven bishops for seditious libel after they had questioned the monarch's right to impose his religious policies upon them. Members of the Protestant aristocracy invited William of Orange to invade; the invasion resulted in James II's fleeing to the court of Louis XIV.

34. "Probus" [Chatterton], "To The Lord Mayor: For the Middlesex Journal," in *Complete Works of Thomas Chatterton,* ed. Taylor and Hoover, 1:580.

ful in currying the Lord Mayor's favor: "His Lordship," Chatterton told his sister, Mary, "received me as politely as a citizen could, and warmly invited me to call on him again."[35]

Yet Beckford's sudden death in June 1770 made Chatterton "almost frantic," especially because of the financial consequences.[36] Although the Wilkite journal ironically named the *North Briton* (the reference to Scotland in the title aimed to insult Bute's followers) set in type a second letter from "Probus" that praises Beckford's challenge to Parliament, the publisher rejected it once the rebellious Lord Mayor unexpectedly died. Simultaneously, Chatterton was also hedging his bets on winning the favor of the prime minister, Lord North, to whom he wrote "an encomium on Administration for rejecting the City Remonstrance."[37] Without passing judgment on the apparent inconsistency in Chatterton's opportunism through writing for both opposing parties in this political rift, Gregory simply states that that the poet "was serious in his intention of writing on both sides."[38] Chatterton held out hope that he would take up a central position in London's political circles: "My company," he boasted to Mary Chatterton, "is courted every where; and, could I humble myself to go into a compter [debtor's prison], could have had twenty places before now; but I must be among the great; state matters suit me better than commercial."[39]

Perhaps for this reason Chatterton moved from Shoreditch to Holborn. Unannounced, he took lodgings in the home of Mrs. Angel at Brooke Street. At this point, although he had little money, he nonetheless sent his family members "a number of little unnecessary presents . . . while perhaps he himself was almost in want of the necessaries of life."[40] Desperate for funds, "his towering ambition" was quickly "reduced to the miserable hope of securing the very ineligible appointment of a surgeon's mate to Africa": a journey that would have taken the poet to the major hubs of the slave trade—the "dreary shore / Where Gambia's rapid billows roar."[41] Yet Gregory is eager to show that, even in these cir-

35. Gregory, *Life of Thomas Chatterton*, 87; this letter, dated 30 May 1770, is in *Complete Works of Thomas Chatterton*, ed. Taylor and Hoover, 1:588.

36. Gregory, *Life of Thomas Chatterton*, 67.

37. Gregory, *Life of Thomas Chatterton*, 88. We discuss Chatterton's approach to Lord North later in this chapter (47).

38. Gregory, *Life of Thomas Chatterton*, 88.

39. Gregory, *Life of Thomas Chatterton*, 91, 263; in *Complete Works of Thomas Chatterton*, ed. Taylor and Hoover, 1:650. This letter is dated 20 July 1770.

40. Gregory, *Life of Thomas Chatterton*, 97.

41. Gregory, *Life of Thomas Chatterton*, 96. These lines appear in "To Miss B— —sh, of Bristol," which was first published under the name of "Celorimon" in the *Town and*

cumstances, Chatterton was "not . . . without the consolations of his muse."[42] The thought of Africa, it seems, inspired two of the poet's highly admired African eclogues, "Narva and Mored" and "The Death of Nicou," which—with the earlier "Heccar and Gaira," which appeared in the *Court and City Magazine*— indicate the influence of William Collins's *Oriental Eclogues* (1759). Yet this prospect of employment came to nothing, since William Barrett, to whom Chatterton applied for a recommendation, refused to supply the letter. Even though Chatterton completed one of his finest Rowley poems, "An Excelente Balade of Charitie," in the weeks that followed, these two eclogues—published in the *London Magazine*—are the last works that Gregory mentions before he reaches the desperate moment when Chatterton took his life. "Whatever unfinished pieces he might have," Gregory observes, Chatterton "cautiously destroyed them before his death; and his room, when broken up, was found covered with little scraps of paper."[43] The poet died because he had, "as appears by the Coroner's Inquest, swallowed arsenick in water."[44] His body, we learn, was "buried in a shell, in the burying ground of Shoe-lane work-house."[45]

Chatterton's suicide, which occurred in obscurity, startled the public as information about him began to circulate. His self-murder became such a cultural preoccupation that a Chatterton handkerchief with a print depicting his demise appeared around 1782 (Figure 3).[46] Surrounding an illustration of the poet in his garret is a short account of his career, which ended, as we discover at the end of the printed text, in "wretchedness, despair, and suicide." For almost a hundred years, hardly anyone questioned that Chatterton's self-murder was deliberate. The only noticeable dissenting voice in the debate about Chatterton's suicide was Ingram's, and it took until 1883 before Ingram drew attention to certain difficulties in the belief that hunger, poverty, and rejection had driven Chatterton to the grave: "For over a century no one appears to have doubted the assertion that Chatterton committed suicide, and yet some of his contemporaries appear to have been skeptical on that point."[47] He adds that there were no signs of self-mutilation, and even if there was some probability in the idea

---

Country Magazine 2 (1770): 327; reprinted in *Complete Works of Thomas Chatterton*, ed. Taylor and Hoover, 1:605.

42. Gregory, *Life of Thomas Chatterton*, 96.

43. Gregory, *Life of Thomas Chatterton*, 100.

44. Gregory, *Life of Thomas Chatterton*, 100.

45. Gregory, *Life of Thomas Chatterton*, 100.

46. The "Chatterton Handkerchief" was first reproduced in Meyerstein, *A Life of Thomas Chatterton*, opp. 476.

47. Ingram, "Chatterton and His Associates," 239.

Figure 3. Chatterton handkerchief, circa 1782. British Library shelf mark C.39.h.20.
© British Library Board.

that Chatterton was famished, he was not impecunious, since "at the time of his death he was owed ten pounds by various publishers."[48] To this day, the debate about exactly what made Chatterton take his life remains unresolved.[49] Richard Holmes observes that nineteenth-century scholarship remained "prudishly silent" on the fact that the "distemper" to which Chatterton refers in a letter to his

48. Ingram, "Chatterton and His Associates," 240. Many years later, Ingram concluded that Chatterton was "heart-broken and starving," and thus "the poor boy deemed his only escape was by death and he killed himself" (*The True Chatterton: A New Study from Original Documents* [London: T. Fisher Unwin, 1910], 281).

49. In 1930, Meyerstein, having sifted through masses of documentation, cast doubt that starvation mixed with emotional distress drove the young poet to his grave; he provided an alternative reason for Chatterton's self-murder: "A complete explanation of the

sister, dated 19 June 1770, "is almost certainly some form of venereal disease."[50] Holmes cites the only early source that threw light on the fact that Chatterton had consulted with a local pharmacist to treat this "Foul Disease." This was historian Michael Lort, who researched the poet's life with great thoroughness in the 1770s.[51] On the basis of this information, Holmes concludes that he thinks Chatterton's demise "was a mistake": an accidental overdose of a mixture of arsenic and opium (the one a drastic cure for venereal disease, the other a painkiller).[52]

Yet, as Holmes says, seldom did commentators dwell on the suggestion that Chatterton used these drugs as palliatives. Instead, critics argued whether the adverse effects of Walpole's rejection prompted Chatterton's suicide. In 1782, Walpole had to defend himself against humiliating charges that his unwillingness to offer Chatterton support made him responsible for the young man's death. "I shudder," he wrote in response to harsh remarks that one of Chatterton's editors made in public, "at having that dismal catastrophe imputed to my cruelty and arrogance."[53] "I am accused," he stated indignantly, "of blasting this promising genius, and of depriving the world of the lord knows what Iliads

---

suicide, from sheer physical torment, with no mental complex whatever, is afforded by the hypothesis that he had severe gonorrhœa, for the calomel which Cross [an apothecary] gave him would act as a purgative only, unless it were an ointment, which would not relieve the pain to any extent" (*A Life of Thomas Chatterton*, 441–42). By the mid-twentieth century, as Groom observes, there was some consensus among several commentators—including Donald Taylor—who agreed with Ingram and Meyerstein that Chatterton's death appeared accidental. Subsequent critics, such as Tom Paulin, however, rebutted such views. The debate about the poet's death remains unresolved. Groom persuasively concludes that the available evidence points in two possible directions: "either Chatterton was mad [an idea that Romantic poets such as Lord Byron upheld] (or desperate, or starving, and so forth) and poisoned himself with arsenic laced with opium, or he was treating himself with arsenic for the pox, and either deadening its pain with opium or simultaneously taking opium recreationally" ("The Death of Chatterton," in Alistair Heys, ed., *From Gothic to Romantic: Thomas Chatterton's Bristol* [Bristol: Redcliffe Press, 2005], 124).

50. Richard Holmes, "Thomas Chatterton: The Case Re-Opened," *Cornhill* 178 (1970): 243. The letter Holmes mentions appears in *Complete Works of Thomas Chatterton*, ed. Taylor and Hoover, 2:598–99.

51. The manuscript in which Lort records Cross's remark about Chatterton's "Foul Disease" was held at the Avon County Reference Library, Bristol (BRL 11457, f.137), and is quoted in Louise J. Kaplan, *The Romance of the Impostor-Poet Thomas Chatterton* (New York: Atheneum, 1988), 193.

52. Holmes, "Thomas Chatterton," 244.

53. Walpole, *A Letter to the Editor of the Miscellanies of Thomas Chatterton*, 9.

and Lost Paradises, which this youth might have procreated in his own or any other name—for in truth he was fonder of inventing great bards, than of being one."[54] To some readers' eyes, Walpole protested too much. His defensiveness looked hypocritical, since he had presented the first edition of his most famous work, *The Castle of Otranto*, as itself the translation of a 1529 Italian manuscript that had surfaced in an English library. (Only later, after the novel had enjoyed wide circulation, did Walpole "ask pardon" of his audience for "having offered his work to them under the borrowed personage of a translator.")[55] More damning, though, was Walpole's patronizing characterization of Chatterton's abased literary position among literary counterfeiters: "All of the house of forgery are relations; and though it is just to Chatterton's memory to say, that his poverty never made him claim kindred with the richest, or more enriching branches, yet his ingenuity in counterfeiting styles, and I believe, hands, might easily have led him to those more facile imitations of prose, promissory notes."[56] As Paul Baines has observed, no one apart from Walpole "makes quite so explicit a connection—here a *narrative* and causal connection—between literary and criminal forgery."[57] Although Walpole, in the same paragraph, proceeded to qualify this remark by stating that Chatterton "never attempted to defraud, cheat, rob, unpoetically," it proved hard for succeeding generations to forgive his harsh suggestion that the poet might as well have forged banknotes.[58] Victorians, in particular, rarely exonerated Walpole's superciliousness, and, in vigorous defense of the "marvellous Boy," they frequently quoted his bitter words of contempt.[59]

In 1806, Chatterton had a strong advocate in John Davis, who pointed a finger directly at the man who had denied patronage to the young poet from

54. Walpole, *A Letter to the Editor of the Miscellanies of Thomas Chatterton*, 13.

55. Horace Walpole, *The Castle of Otranto: A Gothic Story*, 3rd ed. (London: William Bathoe, 1766), xiii.

56. Walpole, *A Letter to the Editor of the Miscellanies of Thomas Chatterton*, 24.

57. Paul Baines, *The House of Forgery in Eighteenth-Century Britain* (Aldershot: Ashgate, 1999), 162.

58. Walpole, *A Letter to the Editor of the Miscellanies of Thomas Chatterton*, 24.

59. Walpole's remark infuriated many of Chatterton's Victorian readers; see, for instance, [Robert Browning,] "Review of *Conjectures and Researches Concerning the Love Madness and Imprisonment of Torquato Tasso* by Richard Henry Wilde," *Foreign Quarterly Review* 29, no. 58 (1842): 476–77; and C. B. Willcox, "The Life of Thomas Chatterton," in *The Poetical Works of Thomas Chatterton, with Notices of His Life, History of the Rowley Controversy, a Selection of His Letters, and Notes Critical and Explanatory*, ed. Willcox, 2 vols. (Cambridge: W. P. Grant, 1842), 1:xcvii.

Bristol: "Walpole very gravely descants upon the literary coinage and forgery of Chatterton, as if he could wash [h]is own hands of the sin. But was not Walpole himself an egregious literary impostor?"[60] Davis reinforces his censure toward the aristocrat with unbounded praise for the "exalted genius" that he finds everywhere in Chatterton's life and poetry. According to Davis, "The Minstrel's song" in *Ælla*, which constitutes Rowley's longest work, "is unrivalled for its pathetic tenderness."[61] Yet there was still resistance to the greatness that many critics discerned. The dismissive life that Alexander Chalmers included in his *Works of the English Poets* (1810) depicts Chatterton as anything but marvelous. Chalmers claims that Walpole "fairly and elegantly appreciated" the aspiring poet, and he pours scorn on this "undisciplined young man" for demonstrating such inconsistency in his politics.[62] In particular, Chalmers follows Walpole by observing that even before Beckford died, Chatterton vacillated in his political affiliations, and to this effect Chalmers draws attention to a document—one that we know about only through Lort's research—in which Chatterton, under the guise of "The Moderator," wrote to Lord North denouncing Wilkes as the "Epitome of the faction, Selfinterested, Treasonable and Inconsiderable."[63] Such changeability, in Chalmers's view, demonstrates "how unsafe it would be for any party to trust" Chatterton.[64] This negative image forms part of Chalmers's larger perception that everything about the poet—"his noblest flights, his

---

60. John Davis, *The Life of Thomas Chatterton* (London: T. Tegg, 1806), 51. The attack on Walpole's hypocrisy was commonplace. In 1829, Cottle stated: "Horace Walpole had no *right* to feel very indignant at a literary forgery, after the deception he had practised on the public, in affirming that his *'Castle of Otranto'* was a translation from the Italian" ("On Rowley's Original Manuscripts," in *Malvern Hills: With Minor Poems and Essays*, 4th ed., 2 vols. [London: T. Cadell, 1829], 2:404).

61. Davis, *The Life of Chatterton*, 137, 51.

62. Alexander Chalmers, "The Life of Chatterton," in Samuel Johnson, *The Works of the English Poets, from Chaucer to Cooper; Including the Series Edited with Prefaces, Biographical and Critical, by Dr. Samuel Johnson; the Additonal Lives, by Alexander Chalmers*, 21 vols. (London: J. Johnson, 1810), 15:374. Walpole comments that in London Chatteron was "vainly hoping to gratify his ambitions by adultation to and or satires on all ranks and parties of men" (*Letter to the Editor of the Miscellanies of Thomas Chatterton*, 11).

63. Lort provided Walpole with a large amount of information on Chatterton: see, for example, Lort, "To Horace Walpole," 20 July 1779, and "Appendix I: Walpole's Collection of Chattertoniana," in *Horace Walpole's Correspondence*, 16:174–77 and 331–63. Taylor and Hoover provide documentation of "A Briton. To Lord North" in *Complete Works of Thomas Chatterton*, 2:774–76. Lort, as Meyerstein points out, was among the first critics to deduce "Chatterton was the author of Rowley" (*A Life of Thomas Chatterton*, xvi).

64. Chalmers, "The Life of Chatterton," 15:374.

sweetest strains, his grossest ribaldry, and his most common-place imitations of
the productions of magazines"—stemmed from "the same ungovernable impulse, which, cameleon-like, imbibed the colours of all it looked on."[65] He
concludes by remarking: "It will not be possible to perpetuate the fame of an
author, who has concealed his best productions under the garb of a barbarous
language"; as a consequence, Chalmers declares that the Rowley "controversy
is no longer interesting."[66] Chalmers, though, held a minority opinion. For the
most part, it was Walpole, not Chatterton, who emerged from subsequent biographies in an unfavorable light. John Dix, in his 1837 study, condemned outright Walpole's *"singularly insolent"* treatment of the poet.[67]

Dix's biography is also significant because it recuperated the image of Chatterton in the fanciful spirit that Croft evoked in *Love and Madness.* To this end,
Dix conjured a magical portrait of the poet's upbringing through sources that
were complete, if enticing, fabrications. In 1872, Walter Thornbury pointedly
redressed the many errors and inconsistencies in Dix's work, but even Thornbury confessed that at one time he relished the anecdotes Dix had compiled to
paint a captivating picture of the poet's youth. Especially appealing to Thornbury had been the story about the way "the boy forger" would "lock himself in
a back room and in Redcliffe church with old parchments, and reappear with
hands and face begrimed with ochre and charcoal."[68] Though some of Dix's
inaccuracies would be unfortunately perpetuated in later works on Chatterton's
life, by 1857 the bogus nature of this biography had been exposed.[69] Further,
much more reliable sources had begun to emerge. In 1842, C. B. Willcox, who
consulted the Chatterton manuscripts housed at the British Museum, plentifully praised the poet's ambition. In the most thorough account to appear since
Gregory's *Life,* Willcox put in perspective the age-old claims and counterclaims
connected with Chatterton's character as a forger. "The fabrication of the
poems," he says, "the mere poems of Rowley, must be forgiven him. No one was
injured, no one was defrauded."[70] Willcox applies the same balanced treatment
to Walpole. Even though Willcox avers that "Chatterton, indeed, had no right

65. Chalmers, "The Life of Chatterton," 15:377.

66. Chalmers, "The Life of Chatterton," 15:379.

67. Dix, *Life of Thomas Chatterton*, 100. Emphasis in the original.

68. "John Dix, the Biographer of Chatterton," *Notes and Queries* 4, no. 9 (13 April 1872):
295. For this episode, see Dix, *Life of Thomas Chatterton*, 14–15. The most noteworthy
of Dix's inventions appear in "Appendix A" (299–319), which purports to be a document
by George Cumberland.

69. See W. Moy Thomas, "The Inquest on Chatterton," *Athenæum* 1571 (5 December
1857): 1518.

70. Willcox, "The Life of Thomas Chatterton," in *The Poetical Works*, 1:lxx.

to expect patronage at the hands of Horace Walpole," and states that it would be most unfair to inculpate Walpole for Chatterton's fate, this biographer suggests that the aristocrat proved uncivil, especially when Chatterton petitioned his correspondent for the return of his Rowley materials: "The silence which Walpole continued to preserve towards Chatterton—notwithstanding the importunity with which the latter had urged the return of his manuscripts—does not tell much in his favour."[71] Willcox, however, concludes by quoting Lord Byron's derogatory comment: "Chatterton, *I* think was mad."[72] "In charity, if not from conviction," Willcox states in hurried agreement, "let the reader think so too."[73] On this note, Willcox takes his cue to sermonize about the piteous young creature: "Poor Chatterton!" he pronounces, "had he learnt to confide in the wisdom and the love of God . . . the marvellous Boy would have been the perfect man, and instead of a record of sorrow and a death of madness, we should have to commemorate the history of a happy poet and a Christian philosopher."[74]

Willcox's moralizing proved too much for Robert Browning. Soon after reading this somewhat high-minded account of the life, Browning stressed that Chatterton did not suffer in any way from the "habitual insincerity" that even the forger's strongest proponents believed lay at the young poet's core.[75] Instead, Browning maintained, Chatterton was a true genius whose "capabilities were of the highest class."[76] In Chatterton's career, he says, we see how such great talent "begins to develop itself by imitation"; on this view, the inventor of Rowley was on the brink of gaining faith in his own immense creative gifts.[77] Particularly

71. Willcox, "The Life of Thomas Chatterton," in *The Poetical Works*, 1:cvii, xcix, cii.

72. Willcox, "The Life of Thomas Chatterton," in *The Poetical Works*, 1:cxi. Byron's letter to Leigh Hunt had appeared in a footnote in Thomas Moore's editions of the poet's works; see, for example, *The Works of Lord Byron: With His Letters and Journals, and His Life*, ed. Moore, 17 vols. (London: John Murray, 1832–1833), 3:241.

73. Willcox, "The Life of Thomas Chatterton," in *The Poetical Works*, 1:cxi.

74. Willcox, "The Life of Thomas Chatterton," in *The Poetical Works*, 1:cxli.

75. [Browning,] Review of Wilde, *Torquato Tasso*: 468. This work is reprinted in *Browning's Essay on Chatterton*, ed. Donald Smalley (Cambridge, MA: Harvard University Press, 1948). Smalley observes that Browning drew on several well-known sources, including John Dix's unreliable *Life of Thomas Chatterton*, Croft's *Love and Madness*, and Jacob Bryant's *Observations upon the Poems of Thomas Rowley, in which the Authenticity of Those Poems is Ascertained* (London: T. Payne, T. Cadell, and P. Elmsley, 1781). Browning also looked critically at Willcox's anonymously edited *Poetical Works of Thomas Chatterton*. Willcox's biography, Smalley states, was among the accounts that in Browning's view "foully outraged" Chatterton's reputation (*Essay on Chatterton*, 135).

76. [Browning,] Review of Wilde, *Torquato Tasso*: 469.

77. [Browning,] Review of Wilde, *Torquato Tasso*: 469.

important to Browning is Chatterton's decision to depart from Bristol so that he could liberate his individual imagination in the metropolis. The well-considered move to London, Browning observes, enabled Chatterton to "disengag[e] himself from the still increasing trammels of his daily life of enforced deceit."[78] In no way can Browning accept the detrimental belief that "Chatterton gave to the very last, occasional symptoms that the fabricating, falsifying spirit was far from extinct in him."[79] In other words, Chatterton "had come to London to produce works of his own. . . . *No more Rowley.*"[80] Browning therefore goes out of his way to rewrite the story of the young poet's final weeks, which he believes featured "the one exception" that was "An Excelente Balade of Charitie," to claim that Chatterton had almost freed himself entirely from the forgeries: "The plastic and co-ordinating spirit which distinguishes Chatterton so remarkably, seems perhaps stronger than ever in these few last days of his existence."[81] Browning regarded the forgery as merely one step in the development of a full poetic artistry, one that would later be abandoned; on that note, Browning withdraws from passing any judgment on the death of Chatterton, whom he conclusively asserts wrote "the finest poetry."[82] In every respect, Chatterton emerges from Browning's essay as an impeccable, if not exemplary, poetic genius who was set to establish himself as one of the nation's leading—because uniquely gifted—literary men.

Browning's efforts to esteem Chatterton's verse emerged as newer biographical studies started to draw on the increasing wealth of information about the Bristol poet. Readers and writers of Wilde's generation could turn to several useful sources that went some way toward correcting the rather erratic and sometimes judgmental biographical record. The first was Masson's *Chatterton: The Story of a Year* 1770, parts of which initially appeared in the *Dublin University Magazine* in 1851, and which was later reprinted in his *Essays Biographical and Critical: Chiefly on English Poets* (1856).[83] In a testament to Chatterton's increasing popularity, Masson published a book-length edition of his 1856 essay in 1874. At the time, Masson, who wrote authoritatively about the English Ro-

---

78. [Browning,] Review of Wilde, *Torquato Tasso*: 475.

79. [Browning,] Review of Wilde, *Torquato Tasso*: 480.

80. [Browning,] Review of Wilde, *Torquato Tasso*: 480–81, 482. Emphasis in the original.

81. [Browning,] Review of Wilde, *Torquato Tasso*: 482.

82. [Browning,] Review of Wilde, *Torquato Tasso*: 483.

83. David Masson, "Chatterton: A Story of the Year 1770," in *Essays Biographical and Critical: Chiefly on English Poets* (Cambridge: Macmillan, 1856), 178–345. The first iteration appeared in the *Dublin University Magazine*: part I, chapter I, 38 (1851): 1–17; part I, chapter II, 38 (1851): 178–92; and part II, chapters I and II, 38 (1851): 420–35. Masson issued a revised edition of his study in 1899.

mantics whom Wilde revered, had served as professor of rhetoric and English literature at the University of Edinburgh for nine years. He ranked among the most noted biographers of his time; his massive seven-volume *Life of John Milton*, which began publication in 1859, took almost fifty years to complete. Altogether slender by comparison, his nonetheless substantial commentary on Chatterton, which Wilde used sparingly in the notebook, reworked much of the material that was already available in the succession of biographies that began with Gregory's *Life*. More than any of his predecessors, however, Masson took care to strengthen our knowledge of Chatterton's bibliography, which he reveals to have been extraordinarily prolific, especially after the poet moved to London. He shows, for example, that between April and June 1770 Chatterton completed no fewer than thirteen pieces of writing.[84]

Although Masson asserts that the Rowley poems show how Chatterton "had but obeyed the proper instinct of his genius," his study advances the belief that Chatterton was a forward-looking, aspiring intellectual, a "thinking young Englishman of the early part of the reign of George III."[85] To be sure, Chatterton's "*forte* was," Masson admitted, "the antique."[86] But Masson suggests that the career that Chatterton developed during his final months in London not only displays extraordinary productivity but also suggests (mistakenly, as it turns out) that the poet had outgrown his Rowley forgeries. "It will have been observed," Masson states somewhat in the manner of Browning, "in his ceaseless efforts to become known in London, Chatterton made no use of his antiques."[87] Immediately, Masson embarks on a speculation about what would have happened to Chatterton had the young man tried to market his Rowley poems in the capital: "Who can tell? On the one hand, by refraining from it, he moved to a fate sad enough; on the other, he might have lived on a hardened literary liar."[88] Once he has reached this discouraging conclusion, Masson dwells on Chatterton's avowed infidelity ("I am no Christian," the poet told George Catcott in August 1770) before lamenting that the Bristol poet suffered from "hereditary insanity."[89] Masson ends his narrative with a Gothic touch. On the night of Chatterton's suicide, he says, "the Devil was abroad . . . in the sleeping

84. David Masson, *Chatterton: A Story of the Year 1770* (London: Macmillan, 1874), 190–92.

85. Masson, *Chatterton: A Story of the Year 1770*, 50, 54.

86. Masson, *Chatterton: A Story of the Year 1770*, 50.

87. Masson, *Chatterton: A Story of the Year 1770*, 204.

88. Masson, *Chatterton: A Story of the Year 1770*, 205.

89. Masson, *Chatterton: A Story of the Year 1770*, 235, 242. An expurgated version of Chatterton's letter to Catcott, which Masson uses, first appeared in the *European Magazine* 21 (1792): 265, and the letter is reprinted in restored form, including Chatterton's

city."[90] Even though Masson tried to show that Chatterton sought to supersede the antiquated forgeries through writing poems that "possess little interest," he paradoxically ends by lauding the Rowley poems as the works that demonstrate that, among his generation, Chatterton "was, with all his immaturity, almost solitary in the possession of the highest poetic gift."[91] Masson's study is inconsistent, reflecting perhaps the changeable nature of Chatterton's life story in both public and critical regard during the past hundred years. In sum, Masson's inquiry capitulates to the belief that Chatterton's greatness, even if the poet might have remained a "hardened liar," nonetheless depends on the Rowley poems.

To Daniel Wilson, in what was by far the finest Victorian intervention into the history of the "marvellous Boy," Masson's "appreciation of the poet's genius [was] adequate," and he similarly affirmed that Masson's "estimation of [Chatterton's] writings" proved "discriminating and just."[92] But in his altogether superior *Chatterton*, Wilson unforgivingly observed that Masson's study, since it repeated some of Dix's doubtful findings, was more suited to a "magazine article" than a "careful biography."[93] Wilson, a Scotsman raised in Edinburgh, earned his considerable reputation as the first professor of English and history at University College, Toronto, and his publications ranged across topics as wide as Puritan history and Native American ethnography. Prior to *Chatterton*, his major publication was *Prehistoric Man: Researches into the Origin of Civilisation in the Old and New Worlds* (1862). Exactly what drew Wilson to the young Bristol poet remains unclear from the current scholarship on this formidable polymath.[94] Perhaps it was Chatterton's fascination with an ancient past that inspired Wilson to pursue this detailed study, which for many years stood as the definitive critical work on the subject. A practiced historian, Wilson undertook to set the record of Chatterton's life straight.

---

comments on his sexual assignations with a prostitute, in *Complete Works of Thomas Chatterton*, ed. Taylor and Hoover, 1:668–70. It is probable that Masson had seen the complete text of this letter in the British Museum, since he clearly consulted the Chatterton MSS housed there (see *Chatterton: A Story of the Year 1770*, 90). The reference to Chatterton's "hereditary insanity" originated with Robert Southey, a claim that we discuss in chapter 2 (84).

90. Masson, *Chatterton: A Story of the Year 1770*, 248.

91. Masson, *Chatterton: A Story of the Year 1770*, 269, 284.

92. Wilson, *Chatterton: A Biographical Study*, xii.

93. Wilson, *Chatterton: A Biographical Study*, xii.

94. The most substantial research on Daniel Wilson's achievements is Robert Stacey and Elizabeth Hulse, *Sir Daniel Wilson: Ambidextrous Polymath* (Toronto: University of Toronto Press, 2001); this volume concentrates mostly on Wilson's career as "an artist of modest but genuine gifts" (131).

More deeply researched than any preceding work on Chatterton, Wilson's monograph repeatedly draws attention to the young poet's exceptional gifts. He reminds readers, for example, that Walpole believed that Chatterton's earliest Rowley poem, the "Bristowe Tragedie," was the work of Thomas Percy, since it brilliantly imitated the popular *Reliques of English Poetry*: a volume that Joseph Ritson, himself an antiquarian of great repute, ventured was a work of forgery.[95] To Wilson, Chatterton's "fine ballad . . . as a genuine specimen of the homely epic muse . . . is wonderful as the production of a boy."[96] As he recounts the disputes that developed around Chatterton's reputation in the late eighteenth century, Wilson constantly exposes the unthinking manner in which moralists had readily condemned this young man: "It was far easier," Wilson contends, "to believe him a 'forger,' a 'liar,' and a cheat, than to discern in the poor charity-boy, or attorney's clerk, a poet of rare genius and strange creative power."[97]

Not surprisingly, to Wilson it makes perfect sense that the young poet approached no less a figure than Walpole for patronage, since in many respects the wealthy author "had [also] his dream of mediæval art, and realized it in costly, if not very tasteful fashion, by converting his cottage at Strawberry Hill, Twickenham, into a pseudo-Gothic Aladdin's palace"; Walpole's extravagant pile, in Wilson's view, bore striking resemblance to the "Cabynet of auntyaunte monumetis" that Chatterton ascribed to Rowley's supposed benefactor, "Master Canynge."[98] As Wilson sees it, the "Rowley romance"—including the invented monk, the invented pseudo-medieval orthography, the invented poems purport-

---

95. Ritson's *Select Collection of English Songs* (1783) drew heavily on Percy's *Reliques of Ancient English Poetry* (London: J. Dodsley, 1765); nonetheless, in the preface to this collection, Ritson accused Percy of having composed *Reliques* through dishonest means: "It will be, here, sufficient to observe, that frequent recourse has, in compiling materials for the present volumes, been necessarily had to many of the originals from which the *Reliques* are professedly printed; but not one has, upon examination, been found to be followed with either fidelity or correctness. That the above work is beautiful, elegant, and ingenious, it would be ridiculous to deny; but they who look into it to be acquainted with the state of ancient poetry, will be miserably disappointed or fatally misled. Forgery and imposition of every kind, ought to be universally execrated, and never more than when they are employed by persons high in rank or character, and those very circumstances are made use of to sanctify the deceit" (Ritson, *Select Collection of English Songs*, 3 vols. [London: J. Johnson, 1873], 1:x).

96. Wilson, *Chatterton: A Biographical Study*, 84, 86.

97. Wilson, *Chatterton: A Biographical Study*, 109.

98. *Wilson, Chatterton: A Biographical Study*, 170. For Rowley's collection of ancient monuments for Canynge (including an image of the parchments Chatterton fabricated), see *Complete Works of Thomas Chatterton*, ed. Taylor and Hoover, 1:117–18 and Plate V (opp. 1:117).

edly from Rowley's pen, and Chatterton's enterprising attempts to secure patronage through those poems—remained of much greater value to Chatterton
than the political works that the young man started writing opportunistically
at the end of 1769 "when his successive efforts to find a patron or publisher
for his antique poems had failed."[99] As a Scot, Wilson found little to praise
in Chatterton's desire to support the "notorious demagogue" Wilkes, and he
reminds his readers that "on every Fifth of November, when protestant English
boys are kindling their bonfires for Guy Fawkes, those of presbyterian Scotland
take advantage of the occasion to make an *auto-da-fé* of Johnny Wilkes!"[100] Yet,
ultimately, Wilson cannot hold against Chatterton those "chameleon" qualities
that Chalmers, in particular, had deplored: "Chameleon-like, he catches the
satiric vein of Churchill; the envenomed prejudice of Wilkes; the lofty-toned,
yet narrow, bitterness of Junius. He assumes, not unsuccessfully, the rough vigour of Smollett; apes at times the r[h]ythmical niceties and the antithesis of
Pope, or the polished grace of Gray and Collins; or, in the guise of a Saxon
monk, rivals the Gaelic Ossian, in his heroic affectations. But, all the while,
this versatile mocking-bird had his own genuine song, in virtue of which those
imitative echoes of contemporaries have still a value for us."[101] In conclusion,
Wilson asserts that only "after a century of confused and blundering controversies" can we "clearly discern how wonderful was that genius that wrapped itself
in such quaint disguise to tempt the credulity of that faithless age."[102]

Wilson's comprehensive discussion received generous praise, with Margaret
Oliphant in *Blackwood's* observing that this "sympathetic study of [Chatterton's]
short sad life" treated its subject "with more painstaking labour or truer feeling"
than any study before it.[103] Particularly admirable for Oliphant was Wilson's
refusal to indulge in "elaborate discussions about the comparative wickedness
of literary forgeries."[104] Evidently, Wilson wished to share his enthusiasm with
Thomas Carlyle, to whom he gave a presentation copy of *Chatterton*. Yet his

99. Wilson, *Chatterton: A Biographical Study*, 246.

100. Wilson, *Chatterton: A Biographical Study*, 254, 55.

101. Wilson, *Chatterton: A Biographical Study*, 261. Junius, the pen name of an unknown writer who published in the *Public Advertiser* from 21 January 1769 to 21 January
1772, was a critic of Lord North's government. Tobias Smollett was well known for his
defenses of fellow Scotsman the Earl of Bute. See the "Chatterton" notebook, f.76ʳ (ooo),
for Wilde's notes on this excerpt.

102. Wilson, *Chatterton: A Biographical Study*, 302.

103. [Margaret Oliphant,] Review of Wilson's *Chatterton*, *Blackwood's Edinburgh Magazine* 107 (1870): 476.

104. [Oliphant,] Review of Wilson's *Chatterton*: 476.

Scottish compatriot, even though he praised Wilson's "clear and concise" study, drew the conclusion that Chatterton was "incapable of being saved"; there was, for Carlyle, "a considerable want of *reverence*, and an enormous overplus of ambition and egoism."[105] Clearly, the poet's life remained too volatile for some readers to tolerate. Still, Carlyle found it hard to deny that Chatterton produced "marvellously precocious Poetry." There is no doubt Carlyle took Wilson's scholarly efforts seriously, and it is evident that Wilson's 1869 monograph reinforced the young poet's strong literary reputation, which rose higher than ever before. In 1887, just a year after Wilde's lecture, Charles Kent's detailed contribution to the newly established *Dictionary of National Biography* grabbed the attention of one reviewer, who remarked: "Chatterton is handsomely treated, receiving almost as much attention as Chaucer."[106]

THE ROWLEY CONTROVERSY:
AUTHENTICATING CHATTERTON

Chatterton's rise to prominence as a leading English poet relied of course on much more than his increasingly detailed and stabilized biography. By the 1880s, his poetry had undergone more than a century's worth of extensive editorial scrutiny. Yet the editing of the poet's large oeuvre remained a topic of enduring disputation. The textual editing of Chatterton's works kept returning to several related questions that originated in the 1770s and 1780s. On the one hand, his editors had to contend less with the issue of attributing the Rowley poems to Chatterton than with establishing the best way of presenting the young poet's antiquated orthography. Was it the case that Chatterton initially composed his Rowley poems in modern English before transposing it, courtesy of his antiquarian sources, into a faux-medieval style? On the other hand, these scholars had to adjudicate which of the many manuscripts that had made their way into libraries at Bristol and London warranted publication. Sometimes it proved hard for researchers to determine if a manuscript conformed to one of several hands that Chatterton used. Should they reprint the lewd poetry whose obscenity was startling? Might the mere mention of these bawdy works destroy the widely touted legend that Chatterton took his life because he was a piteous victim of circumstance? Both the Rowley and the non-Rowley writings could and did generate different types of controversy.

105. Thomas Carlyle, "To Daniel Wilson," 10 January 1870, British Library, Add. MS 47867. Emphasis in the original. This document forms part of the Meyerstein Bequest.
106. [Anon.,] "Minor Notices," *The Literary World* 18, no. 8 (April 1887): 123.

The status of Rowley's writings, which account for only a portion of Chatterton's output, first came to widespread public attention in 1777, when the distinguished scholar Thomas Tyrwhitt (famous for his 1775 edition of Geoffrey Chaucer's *Canterbury Tales*) published his widely noted edition of *Poems, Supposed to Have Been Written at Bristol by Thomas Rowley, and Others, in the Fifteenth Century*. This important volume, the first (though not complete) collection of Chatterton's Rowley poems, emerged from the researches that Thomas Fry, president of St. John's College, Oxford, initially undertook to locate the Rowley manuscripts in the month that Chatterton died. By 1772, when transcripts of the Rowley poems began to circulate, a well-received edition of the earliest Rowley poem, the "Bristowe Tragedie," appeared.[107] Given the great interest that Rowley inspired, it soon became clear that Rowley's works required the attention of an experienced editor such as Tyrwhitt. In no respect does Tyrwhitt jump to conclusions about either the authenticity or the inauthenticity of the twenty-six pieces he edited. As Daniel Cook has observed, "Tyrwhitt sought to present these texts as part of an authorial collection of literary curiosities, however fragmentary, so that, whether attributed to a fifteenth-century priest or an eighteenth-century scrivener's apprentice," the judgment about their origins will be left to the reader's discretion.[108] Tyrwhitt thus concentrates his considerable editorial skills on presenting the Rowley poems in accordance with the numerous glosses that the young poet added to the ancient "compositions, which he professed to have copied from antient MSS."[109] At the start of the volume, Tyrwhitt provides notes on the sources for all his texts, many of which come from manuscripts or transcriptions that William Barrett and George Catcott owned. Tyrwhitt, however, at times emended the peculiar orthography to create

---

107. "The Execution of Sir Charles Baldwin" (London: privately printed, 1772). The entry for this work in F. A. Hyett and W. Bazeley's bibliography *Chattertoniana* reads: "This is the first of the Rowley Poems that was separately printed. It will be found, under the title of 'The Bristowe Tragedie,' in the several editions of Chatterton's collected works. It was probably suggested by the death of Sir Baldwin Fulford, a Lancastrian, who was executed in Bristol in 1461" (*Chattertoniana* [Gloucester: John Bellows, 1914], 10).

108. Daniel Cook, "Tyrwhitt's Rowley and Authorial Editing," *The Library: The Transactions of the Bibliographical Society* 11, no. 4 (2010): 449.

109. [Thomas Tyrwhitt,] "Preface," in [Chatterton,] *Poems, Supposed to Have Been Written at Bristol, by Thomas Rowley, and Others, in the Fifteenth Century; the Greatest Part Now First Published from the Most Authentic Copies, with an Engraved Specimen of One of the MSS, to which Are Added, A Preface, an Introductory Account of the Several Pieces, and a Glossary* (London: T. Payne, 1777), xii. This volume went into a third edition by 1778.

—as Cook points out—a "more palatable medievalism."[110] Such changes involved removing the final "e" from certain words, since Tyrwhitt remained under the impression that this vowel would have been pronounced in Middle English, and thus its presence in Chatterton's Rowley poems would unintentionally disturb the decasyllabic lines. Elsewhere, as Cook observes, Tyrwhitt departs from an authoritative text—such as the published version of "Elinoure and Juga" in the *Town and Country Magazine*—and readily transforms, for example, Rowley's "languyshmente" into modern "languishment."[111]

Tyrwhitt's editorial work immediately sparked a heated debate about the genuineness of the antiquated poems that Chatterton had declared were Rowley's. In creating his inventive conception of Rowley, Chatterton located his imaginary priest in a historical context that was well known to those citizens of Bristol from whom he sought patronage. Rowley, into whom Chatterton projected much of his literary ambition, had his own patron: no one less than William Canynge, who served as both mayor and M.P. to what had been England's second city and was a major patron of the Church of St. Mary Redcliffe, where he was buried in 1474. Chatterton managed to place in *Felix Farley's Bristol Journal* what he stated was the transcript of a fifteenth-century document, which contained Rowley's report on the opening of the city's Old Bridge. The publication of the prose "Bridge Narrative" in October 1768 was timely, since it coincided with the opening of the New Bridge to foot traffic, and was therefore likely to arouse local interest. Indeed, it did, as Barrett and Catcott, both of them Bristolians who shared strong (if amateur) antiquarian interests, approached the young man to find out more about the origin of this short prose work. Chatterton, in response to Barrett's inquiries, then entrusted the antiquarian with some of the fake manuscripts of Rowley's works. The self-serving Catcott, meanwhile, obtained several of Chatterton's carefully engineered notebooks that contained samples of Rowley's poetry.

The only Rowley poem that Chatterton published during his lifetime was "Elinoure and Juga: Written Three Hundred Years Ago by T. Rowley, a Secular Priest." Composed in a technically demanding version of rhyme royal (the stanza that Chaucer exploited in several poems, including *Troilus and Criseyde*), this dialogue adopts the elaborate "Rowleyese" that integrates its quirky late me-

---

110. Cook, "Tyrwhitt's Rowley and Authorial Editing," 456.

111. See Cook, "Tyrwhitt's Rowley and Authorial Editing," 456. Cf. [Chatterton,] *Poems, Supposed to Have Been Written at Bristol, by Thomas Rowley, and Others*, 17; and in *Complete Works of Thomas Chatterton*, ed. Taylor and Hoover, 1:292. Cook suggests that some of Tyrwhitt's emendations appear a little inconsistent, since on some words this editor adds a final "e." As Cook remarks, it appears that Tyrwhitt is simultaneously "modernizing and antiquating freely" (456).

dieval orthography with finely controlled meter. Here we discover "twa pynynge maydens," "Echone bementynge [lamenting] for her absente mate," who had been fighting near St. Albans during the Wars of the Roses.[112] No matter how eccentric its orthography may appear, the poem derives its idiom from widely available sources. The outmoded vocabulary of "Elinoure and Juga," like many of the lines attributed to Rowley, comes from Chatterton's precocious reading of Speght's edition of Chaucer's writings. Other crucial sources included Nathan Bailey's early eighteenth-century historical dictionary, which broadened Chatterton's knowledge of Middle English. The prosody, too, owes much to Thomas Gray. As Taylor has observed, one of the finest lines appears at the start of the fourth stanza: "No mo the miskynette shalle wake the morne."[113] "It would," he says, "be difficult to imagine a poet catching the essence of Gray's 'Elegy' [1751] more closely and yet turning it so completely to his own purposes."[114] Such was the far-reaching influence of this poetic dialogue that its form left a deep impression on Wordsworth's "Resolution and Independence," which not only acknowledges the greatness of the "marvellous Boy" but also follows Chatterton's deft adaptation of the Chaucerian stanza.

The Rowley poems form only part of a larger body of verse that displays Chatterton's remarkable ability to adapt and perfect the prosodic demands of complex forms. Besides the satires such as "Kew Gardens," most of Chatterton's other poetry is *in propria persona*, and it includes ballads modeled on Thomas Percy's then-recent (and immediately popular) national collection of this well-established genre, *Reliques of English Poetry*. There are one or two exceptions. Chatterton wrote an antiquated poem on his hometown of Bristol for one

112. "Elinoure and Juga: Written Three Hundred Years Ago by T. Rowley, a Secular Priest," in *Complete Works of Thomas Chatterton*, ed. Taylor and Hoover, 1:291.

113. "Elinour and Juga," in *Complete Works of Thomas Chatterton*, ed. Taylor and Hoover, 1:292. Chatterton glosses "miskynette" as a "small bagpipe."

114. Donald S. Taylor, *Thomas Chatterton's Art: Experiments in Imagined History* (Princeton: Princeton University Press, 1978), 292. Jeremiah Milles, who defended Rowley's authenticity, compared the meter to Gray's in [Chatterton,] *Poems, Supposed to Have Been Written at Bristol, by Thomas Rowley, and Others* (London: T. Payne, 1782), 417. (We discuss Milles's misguided defense of Rowley's authenticity later in this chapter [62–64].) Gray's famous line from "Elegy Written in a Country Churchyard" reads: "The curfew tolls the knell of parting day" (*The Poems of Thomas Gray, William Collins and Oliver Goldsmith*, ed. Roger Lonsdale [London: Longman, 1969], 117). Susan Stewart offers an important clue to the memorability of this meter: "We might note its perfect iambic pentameter that washes against the trochaic pull of the compound syllables (*curfew* and *parting*) and the elision of 'tolls the' and 'knell of'' (*Poetry and the Fate of the Senses* [Chicago: University of Chicago Press, 2002], 117). Chatterton adroitly imitates these remarkable effects.

"Raufe Chedder, Chappmanne, 1356," who preceded Rowley by a century. In "A Chronycalle of Brystowe," this individual—whose identity Chatterton seems to have based on the man who served as the city's mayor in 1361 and 1363—proceeds in the common meter familiar to Percy's *Reliques*: "Ynne whilomme daies, as Storie saies / Ynne famous Brystowe towne / Dhere lyved Knyghtes, doughtie yn fyghtes / Of marvellous renowne."[115] Among the eminences Chedder recalls is William Canynge's ancestor, the equally successful Bristol mayor and M.P. who bore the same name: "Canynge grete of fayre Estate / Bryngeth to Tradynge Londe."[116] Moreover, Chatterton composed impressive elegies in a modern idiom, which he dedicated to Thomas Phillips, the usher at Colston's school. In these works, the phrasing draws on the poetry of such eighteenth-century contemporaries as Collins, William Cowper, and Gray. One of these finely arranged poems contains these striking lines: "When golden Autumn, wreathed in rip'ned Corn, / From purple Clusters prest the foamy Wine."[117] It does not take much to see how Chatterton's legacy echoes in the famous ode "To Autumn" (1820) by one of his closest nineteenth-century readers, Keats.[118]

Many of the poet's non-Rowley writings appeared in John Broughton's edition of *Miscellanies in Prose and Verse, by Thomas Chatterton, the Supposed Author of the Poems Published under the Names of Rowley, Canning, &c.* (1778). In his preface, Broughton insists that the author was "a person whose genius and abilities, exercised at a very early period of life, will no less command the respect of posterity" than the forgeries ascribed to Rowley.[119] Broughton de-

115. "A Chronycalle of Brystowe Wrote bie Raufe Chedder, Chappmanne. 1356," in *Complete Works of Thomas Chatterton*, ed. Taylor and Hoover, 1:268.

116. "A Chronycalle of Brystowe," in *Complete Works of Thomas Chatterton*, ed. Taylor and Hoover, 1:269.

117. "Elegy to the Memory of Mr. Thomas Phillips, of Fairford," in *Complete Works of Thomas Chatterton*, ed. Taylor and Hoover, 1:384.

118. Keats's poem noticeably amplifies the fruitfulness of Chatterton's lines; Keats's personified "Autumn" conspires with the sun "to load and bless / With fruit the vines that round the thatch-eves run" (*Complete Poems*, ed. Jack Stillinger [Cambridge, MA: Harvard University Press, 1978], 360). Keats himself said: "I always somehow associate Chatterton with Autumn" ("To J. H. Reynolds," 21 September 1819, in *The Letters of John Keats, 1814–1821*, ed. Hyder Edward Rollins, 2 vols. [Cambridge, MA: Harvard University Press, 1958], 2:16. Echoes of Chatterton's poetry in Keats's writings are explored in Robert Gittings, "Keats and Chatterton," *Keats-Shelley Journal* 4 (1955): 47–54; and Nai-Tung Ting, "The Influence of Chatterton on Keats," *Keats-Shelley Journal* 5 (1956): 103–8.

119. "J.B." [John Broughton], "Preface," in *Miscellanies in Prose and Verse by Thomas Chatterton: The Supposed Author of the Poems Published under the Names of Rowley, Canning, &c.* (London: Fielding and Walker, 1778), ix–x.

plores the "very cold reception" that "a gentleman well known in the republic of letters" (i.e., Walpole) gave to this "prodigy of genius."[120] Yet, during the years immediately following Chatterton's death, it was principally the truly distinctive but much-disputed Rowley canon that made the young Bristol poet the focus of impassioned literary discussion. To the first cohort of Chatterton's most attentive readers, who were aware of the Rowley poems long before Tyrwhitt brought them to public attention, it remained a wholly open question whether the young poet had devised these extraordinary works. Soon after Chatterton's death, Barrett and Catcott stood the most to gain materially from the publication of Rowley's purported works, and they remained steadfast in their public avowals—whatever private doubts they may have harbored—that the antiquated parchments in their hands were genuine. Catcott, who kept the trove of Rowley manuscripts and transcriptions that Chatterton entrusted to him, apparently wanted a handsome sum for this cache of documents. "It is said," wrote the Rev. John Chapman in December 1771, that Catcott "has refused two hundred pounds for them. But I believe it has never been offered to him."[121] Later, the Rev. John Whitaker, a respected historian of Manchester, also had the opportunity to speak with Barrett, who possessed "several of Rowley's MSS., and particularly a part which exhibited, in Rowley's drawing, several Roman and inscribed stones, that Rowley said were found in and about Bristol."[122] As Whitaker could tell, however, these were "errant forgeries"—ones that suggested that either somebody had practiced a trick upon a gullible medieval priest or that the fabled Rowley himself was simply a "knave."[123]

Barrett eventually included his Rowley materials in his detailed *History and Antiquities of the City of Bristol* (1789), where he made a staunch defense of the by now controversial works that Chatterton had given him: "The critics may contend about the originality of all or any of the manuscripts, about alterations

120. Broughton, "Preface," xix, xviii, xx. In his use of the phrase "prodigy of genius," Broughton is quoting Thomas Warton, *The History of English Poetry*, 3 vols. (London: Dodsley, 1775–1778), 2:157.

121. Revd. John Chapman, "To Dr. Ducarel," 15 December 1771, in John Nichols, *Illustrations of the Literary History of the Eighteenth Century: Consisting of Authentic Memoirs and Original Letters of Eminent Persons, and Intended as a Sequel to the Literary Anecdotes*, 8 vols. (London: Nichols, Son, and Bentley, 1817–1858), 4:572. Chapman was vicar of the parish of Weston, Bath, near Bristol.

122. Revd. John Whitaker, "To Dr. Ducarel," 13 June 1772, in Nichols, *Illustrations of the Literary History of the Eighteenth Century*, 4:857.

123. Whitaker, "To Dr. Ducarel," 13 June 1772, in Nichols, *Illustrations of the Literary History of the Eighteenth Century*, 4:857.

or additions made, about the usage of old and obsolete words and the language of the time, suffice it for the author of this history that he has faithfully and honestly transcribed and printed them. If it offends, and what will not offend, the 'genus irritabile vatum' [the irritable race of poets], he shall leave them to amuse themselves at their leisure in the way they like best, but wishes nothing but an enquiry after the truth would direct their pens."[124] Aware that the some readers might judge Chatterton harshly as a sinner, Barrett cautiously adds that he "cannot but lament the unhappy fate of the misguided youth," who forgot "he was a being accountable for his actions to his Maker and his Judge."[125]

It took some time before the public concurred that the works Chatterton had entrusted to Barrett and Catcott were forgeries. At the first annual banquet held at the newly established Royal Academy in 1771, Oliver Goldsmith, in the face of several skeptics, declared that the Rowley poems were genuine. Disbelievers, however, especially Lort, were quick to challenge such staunch defenses of Rowley's existence. Meanwhile, Thomas Warton, editor of the compendious *History of English Poetry* (1774), had adopted a middle stance, which later readers increasingly embraced. Warton was willing to include in his anthology several poems attributed to Rowley. But, as he admitted, even if there were "some circumstances that incline us to suspect these pieces to be a modern forgery," it remained the case that they possessed "considerable merit."[126] Several years later, Tyrwhitt's timely edition of the Rowley poems appeared at a juncture that he hoped would encourage "the unprejudiced and intelligent Reader" to decide if "the Poems be really ancient, or modern; the compositions of Rowley, or the forgeries of Chatterton"; either way, such writings, he believed, "must always be considered as a most singular literary curiosity."[127] Others, such as Henry Dampier, remained unconvinced that Warton, in particular, had produced sufficient evidence to uphold the belief that the Rowley poems were forgeries or that Chatterton had made them. Dampier could not accept that there was any comparable quality between Chatterton's non-Rowley poems that Broughton gathered in *Miscellanies* and the ones ascribed to Rowley that appeared in Tyrwhitt's edition the previous year. "There cannot," Dampier observed, "be any two collections of poems more essentially different than Chat-

124. William Barrett, *The History and Antiquities of the City of Bristol; comp. from Original Records and Authentic Manuscripts, in Public Offices or Private Hands; Illustrated with Copper-Plate Prints* (Bristol: W. Pine, 1789), 646.

125. Barrett, *The History and Antiquities of the City of Bristol*, 646.

126. Warton, *The History of English Poetry*, 2:139.

127. [Tyrwhitt,] "Preface," in [Chatterton,] *Poems, Supposed to Have Been Written at Bristol, by Thomas Rowley, and Others*, xii.

terton's and Rowlie's. The former have every imperfection one might expect from the author's age; and excel in those points only, which are more within the reach of a boy."[128] Samuel Johnson, who was surprised to hear Goldsmith assert Rowley's authenticity at the Royal Academy, made a visit to Bristol, where he and his biographer James Boswell met Barrett and Catcott. Both of these Bristol guardians of Chatterton's memory declared, as they did to everyone else, that the young man had without question found the Rowley manuscripts in a trunk stored at St. Mary Redcliffe. Since he had received *"ocular demonstration"* of these documents, Johnson instantly recognized the imposture; he concluded that Chatterton was indeed a forger, though at the same time Chatterton remained for Johnson the "most extraordinary young man" that he had ever come across: "It is wonderful," Johnson exclaimed, "how the whelp has written such things."[129]

Approaches to Chatterton's verse began to shift from the ocular assessment upon which Johnson relied to linguistic or prosodic analysis. In 1781 Jacob Bryant undertook the daunting task of placing Chatterton's invented fifteenth-century idioms under such scrutiny that he managed (despite his misgivings about some mistaken transcriptions) to determine that there were "many convincing proofs of their genuine antiquity."[130] A contemporary defender of Warton subjected many of the presumed Rowley's works to exacting analysis, including a passage from the interlude called "The Tournament": "The Lyonncel from sweltrie Countries broughte, / Coucheynge binethe the sheltre of the Briere."[131] "What lines," this anonymous commentator asks, "can be smoother than these?"[132] Yet it is clear to him that "they have the air of modern poetry," since in his view prosody before the Reformation looks "very rugged compared with the above."[133] Meanwhile, supporters of Rowley's authenticity also included Dean Jeremiah Milles (president of the Society of Antiquaries), who declared in no

128. [Henry Dampier,] *Remarks upon the Eighth Section of the Second Volume of Mr. Warton's History of English Poetry* (London: T. Payne, 1778), 25.

129. Boswell, *Boswell's Life of Johnson, together with Boswell's Journal of a Tour of the Hebrides and Johnson's Diary of a Journey into North Wales*, ed. George Birkbeck Hill, revised by L. F. Powell, 6 vols. (Oxford: Clarendon Press, 1934–1950), 3:51.

130. Bryant, *Observations upon the Poems of Thomas Rowley*, iii.

131. "The Tournament: An Interlude," in *Complete Works of Thomas Chatterton*, ed. Taylor and Hoover, 1:285.

132. [Anon.,] *An Examination of the Poems Attributed to Thomas Rowley and William Canynge with a Defence of the Opinion of Mr. Warton* (Sherborne: R. Goadby; London: R. Baldwin, 1782), 17.

133. [Anon.,] *An Examination of the Poems Attributed to Thomas Rowley and William Canynge*, 17.

uncertain terms that "the supposition of a forgery . . . is irreconcilable with every idea of rational conduct, and much more so with the genius and disposition of this extraordinary youth."[134] Even though Milles admitted that Chatterton was by all accounts an "extraordinary youth," he also took pains to note that the young man was "illiterate"—and thus wholly incapable of creating forgeries of this scale and ambition.[135] Walpole, who had good reason to take interest in these debates about Chatterton, made extensive critical notes on the inconsistencies and wrongheadedness of Milles's volume that was full of contradictory reasoning.[136]

As Louise J. Kaplan has pointed out, Milles counted among several researchers who gleaned as much information as they could from Chatterton's adoring mother and sister, and their findings certainly presented them with a challenge: although eager to defend Chatterton's honesty in transcribing Rowley's verse, they were obliged to maintain that it was also impossible for the young man to have written them. "The Rowleyans" such as Milles, Kaplan observes, "had to demonstrate Chatterton too untutored and unskilled to have written such beautiful poetry, but then again he had to have been at least clever enough to recognize the worth of the ancient documents and sufficiently literary to transcribe them."[137] As one can see, Chatterton's gifts tested both these hostile critics' credulity and their sense of decency. How could they, in this delicate situation, dare to insult the poet's closest relatives by suggesting that the dearly departed young man had lacked the necessary education to devise such well-crafted works?

In many respects, the most level-headed assessments to emerge from these contending justifications and denunciations of Rowley's authenticity arose when Edmond Malone, best known for his astonishing labors as the founder of the modern tradition of editing Shakespeare's works, stepped into the fray of what he rightly described as the veritable "*Rowleiomania*" that struck the literary world in the early 1780s.[138] In his fair-minded estimations of "this in-

---

134. Milles, "Preliminary Dissertation," in [Chatterton,] *Poems Supposed to Have Been Written at Bristol, by Thomas Rowley, and Others*, 13.

135. Milles, "Preliminary Dissertation," 4.

136. Walpole's notes on Milles's edition of [Chatterton,] *Poems Supposed to Have Been Written at Bristol, by Thomas Rowley, and Others*, and other sources, such as Bryant's *Observations upon the Poems of Thomas Rowley*, appear in "Appendix: Walpole's Collection of Chattertoniana," in *The Yale Edition of Horace Walpole's Correspondence*, 16:331–63.

137. Kaplan, *The Family Romance of the Impostor-Poet Thomas Chatterton*, 254.

138. [Edmond Malone,] *Cursory Observations on the Poems Attributed to Thomas Rowley, A Priest of the Fifteenth Century, with Some Remarks on the Commentaries on those Poems, by the Rev. Dr. Jeremiah Milles, Dean of Exeter, and Jacob Bryant, Esq; and a Salutary Proposal Addressed to those Gentlemen* (London: J. Nichols, 1782), 1.

genious boy," Malone—as his biographer Peter Martin comments—attacks "Bryant and Milles rather than Chatterton": "What irked Malone was that two men [Bryant and Milles] could use such authority as they had, with inadequate literary-historical knowledge, to mislead."[139] Malone patiently looks in turn at four sets of evidence that in his view expose the indisputable reasons why the Rowley poems are nothing other than forgeries: the versification is too modern; there are traces of imitated modern authors; there are abundant anachronisms; and, in particular, the style of the handwriting on the manuscripts is incongruous, since—as Malone immediately recognized—it could hardly have derived from the fifteenth century.[140] In his thoughtfully argued discussion, Malone bases his measured conclusion that the Rowley poems are forgeries on several judicious inferences, ones that noticeably refrain from passing moral censure on the fakes that this gifted young man had manufactured. Even as he itemizes this telltale evidence, Malone cannot help but pay homage to the brilliance with which Chatterton, who clearly lacked the advantage of the finest education, conjured these amazing faux-medieval poems:

> Although I have as high an opinion of [Chatterton's] abilities as any person whatsoever, and do indeed believe him to have been the greatest genius since the days of Shakspeare, I am not ready to acknowledge that he was endued with any miraculous powers. Devoted as he was from his infancy to the study of antiquities, he could not have been so conversant with ancient language, or have had all the words necessary to be used to present to his mind, as to write antiquated poetry of any considerable length, offhand. He, without doubt, wrote his verses in plain English, and afterwards embroidered them with such old words as would suit the sense and metre. With these he furnished himself, sometimes probably from memory, and sometimes from glossaries; and annexed such interpretations as he found or made. When he could not readily find a word that would suit his metre, he invented one.[141]

In a similar spirit, Malone proceeds to observe dispassionately that it is easy to show why "Chatterton's acknowledged productions" (that is, the non-Rowley poems) contain—as some critics had maintained—"a little inferiority."[142] According to Malone, such works were simply exercises in which Chatterton did not emulate the best models. "The verses that he wrote for Rowley," Malone

139. Peter Martin, *Edmond Malone, Shakespearean Scholar: A Literary Biography* (Cambridge: Cambridge University Press, 1995), 76.

140. [Malone,] *Cursory Observations*, 11.

141. [Malone,] *Cursory Observations*, 41–42.

142. [Malone,] *Cursory Observations*, 49.

contends, "are *perhaps* better than his others, because they contain the thoughts of our best poets often in their own words."[143] Moreover, Malone begs his reader to take into consideration that the Rowley poems were also written at Chatterton's leisure, while the others were composed expeditiously "to gain bread for the day."[144]

Despite its disinterested approach, Malone's *Cursory Observations on the Poems Attributed to Thomas Rowley* scarcely settled the controversies that had arisen from impassioned discussions of Chatterton's brief career. Very promptly, in the pamphlet wars that characterized the tenor of much eighteenth-century literary exchange, Edward Burnaby Greene attacked *Cursory Observations* for producing specious arguments that attributed entirely mistaken distinction to the poet he condescendingly called "the Lad"; Malone, Greene maintains, wrongly "glories in behalf of the *thief*, at the time he turns informer against *him*, without a blush to pronounce the character a road to reputation."[145] Yet it is clear from a 1797 tourist guide to Bristol that Malone's astute assessment had helped guide public opinion toward a positive evaluation of Chatterton's unique achievement. The young Bristol poet, it declared, was "one of the greatest human Geniuses in the World."[146] Subsequently, Chatterton's poetic brilliance became evident through the increasingly authoritative editions of his work that soon began to appear.

CHATTERTON'S OEUVRE: EDITING THE "MARVELLOUS BOY"

Once Robert Southey and Joseph Cottle's three-volume edition of *The Works of Thomas Chatterton* appeared in 1803, it reprised another unsettled quarrel about the poet's legacy. This significant edition, which included a reprint of Gregory's *Life* and expanded well beyond the twenty-six pieces that Tyrwhitt identified and the materials in Broughton's *Miscellanies*, emerged from its editors' desire to right what they believed was the considerable injustice that Chatterton's relatives had suffered after his premature death. Four years earlier in the *Monthly Magazine*, Southey reiterated Croft by restating the fact

143. [Malone,] *Cursory Observations*, 49.

144. [Malone,] *Cursory Observations*, 49.

145. Edward Burnaby Greene, *Strictures upon a Pamphlet Intitled, Cursory Observations on the Poems Attributed to Rowley, a Priest of the Fifteenth Century, with a Postscript* (London: J. Stockdale, 1782), 16. Emphasis in the original.

146. George Heath, *The History of Antiquities, Survey and Description of the City and Suburbs of Bristol; or Complete Guide* (Bristol: W. Matthews, 1797), 169.

that both Barrett and Catcott had gained financially from using Chatterton's writings without offering any substantial benefit to the poet's family. Yet, with piercing irony, Southey reserves most of his ire for the "clergyman" only named as "Mr. H——C——" as the most exploitative of all. Southey reveals that Croft had called upon Chatterton's now-married sister, Mary Newton, with the request that he might borrow her correspondence from her brother *"for one hour."*[147] The letters never came back. Southey claims that two weeks later, on 27 July 1778, Croft wrote to Mrs. Newton, assuring her that "all the little treasure shall be faithfully returned."[148] The following month he wrote asking for more information about Chatterton. By July 1779, both Chatterton's mother and sister were astonished to find that the items they had loaned to Croft were published in *Love and Madness*. It appears that the only sum with which Croft parted for the family, apart from the "the guinea given to Mrs. Chatterton, and half guinea to her daughter," was £10.[149] Southey concludes by stating that the profits from the comprehensive edition of Chatterton's work for which he is raising a subscription will assist the impoverished poet's mother "to render her old age comfortable."[150] In his blustering response, where he attacks Southey's egalitarian *"pantisocratical"* politics, Croft offers this disingenuous defense: "If Mrs. N.'s memory were stronger, she might perhaps recollect that that I *was* at liberty to do what I pleased with the *originals*, in return for what I gave her and her mother. Had ten pounds more been demanded for them, or even another guinea, I imagine that I should have refused."[151]

In the 1803 edition, Southey sought to bring an end to the "emolument of strangers"—namely, those individuals who had unfairly profited from "the productions of the most extraordinary young man that ever appeared in this country."[152] Despite his disdain for Croft's tactics in procuring Chatterton's manu-

---

147. Southey, "To the Editor of the *Monthly Magazine*," *Monthly Magazine* 8 (1799): 771.

148. Southey, "To the Editor of the *Monthly Magazine*," 771.

149. Southey, "To the Editor of the *Monthly Magazine*," 772.

150. Southey, "To the Editor of the *Monthly Magazine*," 772.

151. Herbert Croft, "A Letter from Denmark to Mr. Nichols, Printer of the *Gentleman's Magazine*, by the Rev. Sir Herbert Croft, Respecting an Unprovoked Attack Made upon Him during his Absence from England," *Gentleman's Magazine* 79 (1800): 103, 104. Croft's letter, which appears in three parts of this volume of the magazine, ultimately claims that Southey has set Chatterton's mother and sister against him, who remains their "best friend" (323). In 1793, Southey and Coleridge devised plans to establish an egalitarian "pantisocracy" in the United States. The plans eventually dissolved.

152. Robert Southey, "Preface," in *The Works of Thomas Chatterton*, ed. Joseph Cottle and Robert Southey, 3 vols. (London: T. N. Longman and O. Rees, 1803), 1: n.p.

scripts, Southey included several works that had first been printed in *Love and Madness*. The edition includes "Sly Dick," which Croft had transcribed from a manuscript that he claimed had been "written by Chatterton at about eleven," along with two other works—both from Croft's transcriptions—that date from this period.[153] When discussing "Apostate Will," a satire on Methodism, Southey and Cottle observe that it remains impossible to believe that anyone instructed Chatterton in the composition of such accomplished verse: "He knew no tutor, no friend, no parent—at least no parent who could correct or assist him."[154] The edition, too, contains more than thirty poems that had not previously appeared, including ones based on manuscripts at the British Museum, which by the turn of the nineteenth century held many materials relating to the poet's career. Moreover, the first volume ends with a wholly modernized version of "Elinour and Juga" (by "S.W.A. Aged Sixteen").[155] Already, it seems, there was an interest in making Rowley more intelligible for a modern readership. Other additions to Chatterton's oeuvre involve a modernized version of "The Romaunte of the Cnyghte," which forms part of one of the poet's most elaborate forgeries: a fabricated account of Henry Burgum's family history, which appealed to Burgum's ego; he was a pewterer and also Catcott's trading partner. Among their selections from the extensive prose that Chatterton produced, the editors brought to special attention his correspondence with Walpole, including the epistle in which the young poet writes that he has "lived long enough to see that poverty attends literature."[156]

The 1803 edition not only served the practical purpose of remunerating the poet's sister but, since it brought together every piece of writing that was known to have been Chatterton's, also fortified the poet's standing and helped to balance out his oeuvre. Yet, as those who researched Chatterton's papers knew, Cottle and Southey's edition was not truly complete, as they had omitted the "indecent satirical poem" that Gregory had discreetly mentioned in passing.[157]

153. Chatterton, *Works*, ed. Cottle and Southey, 1:1.

154. Chatterton, *Works*, ed. Cottle and Southey, 1:7.

155. This version had appeared in the *Town and Country Magazine* a month after Chatterton's original version was published. "Eleanora and Juga," *Town and Country Magazine* (June 1769): 328. Bertrand Bronson writes that "S.W.A." was Robert Nares ("Thomas Chatterton," in *The Age of Johnson* [New Haven: Yale University Press, 1949], 252). Other modernized versions of "Elinour and Juga" appeared in the *European Magazine and London Review* (18 [September 1790]: 224–25) and the *Bath Chronicle* (10 October 1872: 4).

156. Chatterton, *Works*, ed. Cottle and Southey, 3:297.

157. Gregory, *Life of Thomas Chatterton*, 79, 80. The style of this indecent work did not discourage Gregory from quoting one of its inoffensive "descriptive passages" that showed "great merit" (80).

Eighteenth- and early nineteenth-century critics might have grappled with Chatterton's penchant for forgery and the relative merits of his poetic faculties, but it was left for much later commentators to contend with his obscenity. On this sensitive topic, the intimate connections between Chatterton's biography and his poetry are especially pronounced. Since these obscene writings had been excluded entirely from published editions, Wilson's and Masson's studies were among the first to assess the value of the poet's more salacious works. In 1869, Wilson wrestled with the unfinished and (at the time) unpublished "Exhibition. A Personal Satire," which speaks, as the opening lines explain, not of "miserable daubings" in the Royal Academy but of those "infamous" erotic ones that aim "To please the modest Virgin's Eyes and Ears."[158] Wilson declares that it "would have been well had" this satire "perished" because it provided dismaying "evidence that youthful purity had been sullied, and [that] the precocious boy was only too conversant with forbidden things."[159] Determined not to judge Chatterton's "hasty effusions" too harshly, and thus deny readers the opportunity to judge for themselves, Wilson classes this work with two expressly political satires, "Kew Gardens" and "The Whore of Babylon."[160] Together with "The Exhibition," these two poems share many lines in common. In forgiving tones, Wilson claims that these productions "rank with the loose after-dinner gossip and scandal, rather than with the earnest thoughts, of ordinary men."[161]

The sexual contents of Chatterton's writings certainly threatened to taint his otherwise sanctified image as a mistreated genius. As Kaplan observes, "The Exhibition" was kept out of public view until 1910, when Ingram included an expurgated version of it in an appendix to his biography; even then, Ingram had to receive "permission by the British Art Gallery Committee, who had possession of the manuscript, to publish" this work.[162] More troubling was "The Letter Paraphras'd," which Masson (though not Wilson) dwelt on at some length, since he was clearly shocked by what he found among the Chatterton manuscripts. Masson alludes to a "dingy piece of letter-paper . . . containing a very ugly scrawl in an uneducated female hand."[163] This half-literate missive appears to be a young woman's reproach to Chatterton for failing to show sexual interest in her. Translated into Standard English, the document declares: "I'll not be

---

158. "The Exhibition: A Personal Satire," in *Complete Works of Thomas Chatterton*, ed. Taylor and Hoover, 1:546. This poem dates from May 1770.

159. Wilson, *Chatterton: A Biographical Study*, 201.

160. Wilson, *Chatterton: A Biographical Study*, 195.

161. Wilson, *Chatterton: A Biographical Study*, 195.

162. Kaplan, *The Family Romance of the Impostor-Poet Thomas Chatterton*, 155.

163. Masson, *Chatterton: A Story of the Year 1770*, 91.

courted by boys and knaves. I'll have a man and a man shall have me. If I want a fool, I'll send for thee." To impress her point, this correspondent concludes by stating: "If you are going to the Devil, I wish you a good Gonery" (in which the final word might mean trip or, less innocently, gonorrhea).[164] In Masson's view, these were evidently the words of "some obscure female, avenging herself, with all the energy of feminine malice, for the *spretæ injuria formæ* [the insult of beauty being slighted]."[165] Though he quotes the woman's letter in full, Masson had no wish to reproduce "the extremely impolite and not at all quoteable Hudibrastic lines" that Chatterton had composed on the reverse of this epistle.[166] One can see why he omitted the following representative obscene lines from the verse spoken in the voice of an "Unknown Girl":

> My loving Dear I send thee this
> To tell thee that I want to piss
> Pray let me speak the matter blunt
> I want to stretch my narrow Cunt[.][167]

Splenetic in tone, these couplets echo the Earl of Rochester's vivid poetic depictions of genitalia. Their strident vulgarity has struck Chatterton's modern editors to be so extreme that they make "our previous notions of C[hatterton] . . . inadequate."[168] Many years after Masson consulted it, this document was removed from its folio at the British Museum, where it had been preserved for decades under lock and key. It remained unpublished until 1971. Both Masson and Wilson, in their distinct ways, thus strove hard to preserve an appealing image of Chatterton, even though it was difficult for them to hold back from intimating that the precocious young man's most personal sentiments were not always dignified.

Yet it would be misleading to characterize Wilson's authoritative study as purely an exercise in negotiating his way around those aspects of Chatterton's oeuvre that threatened to make the young man seem sexually tainted. What emerges most powerfully from this fine monograph is Wilson's entirely fresh approach to Chatterton's creation of Thomas Rowley. He has no interest in re-

---

164. This translation is given in *Complete Works of Thomas Chatterton*, ed. Taylor and Hoover, 2:1135.

165. Masson, *Chatterton: A Story of the Year 1770*, 91. The Latin tag comes from Virgil Aeneid, 1.27.

166. Masson, *Chatterton: A Story of the Year 1770*, 92.

167. "The Letter Paraphras'd," in *Complete Works of Thomas Chatterton*, ed. Taylor and Hoover, 1:686.

168. *Complete Works of Thomas Chatterton*, ed. Taylor and Hoover, 2:1135.

hearsing once again what had become outdated arguments about Chatterton's guilt as a literary fraud. (Willcox, for one, had already laid out the whole debate for the first generation of Victorian readers.)[169] Instead, Wilson builds a strong case that shows that, while it was clear to the young man's "loving friends" that the "possible identity" of Chatterton and Rowley might have been one and the same, the legal apprentice astutely understood that if he unmasked "his 'Rowley' to its Barretts, Catcotts, Thistlethwaites, and Smiths" in his hometown of Bristol, he would "simply expose himself to insult and contempt."[170] In Wilson's view, the most outstanding feature of Chatterton's astounding imagination was that Rowley emerged from what had since the poet's time at Colston's been a remarkable "phantasy, nurturing associations which thenceforth became a part of his being."[171] As Wilson points out, Rowley turned into an inspiring vehicle through which Chatterton could imagine a remunerative poetic career that would prove very hard for a recent schoolboy with a modest education to attain in modern Bristol. Wilson demonstrates that even to Milles—who wrongheadedly pledged his faith in Rowley's existence—the figure of William Canynge served the fifteenth-century priest "as a parallel to Mæcenas": the classical patron of Horace, Propertius, and Varius.[172] "To him," Wilson observes, "Rowley sends his verses from time to time, ever sure of some liberal acknowledgment in return."[173] In other words, through Rowley the young Chatterton projected his developing poetic identity into a historical universe where he could enjoy successful authorship: "In the antique romance as a whole, there is no difficulty in recognising, through its transparent disguise, the modern Bluecoat boy fondly imagining, in some fancied schoolmate among the Bakers and Thistlethwaites of his own day, the sympathising friend and future patron, whose wealth was to be generously shared with the poet."[174] Wilson extends this thoughtful view of Chatterton's capacity for self-projection—one that plausibly presents Rowley as Chatterton's alter ago—to other aspects of the young man's antiquated poetry. In the visionary poem "The Storie of Wyllyam Canynge," which Wilson slightly modernizes, the tableau that features Canynge as an infant ("the fate-marked babe . . . / . . . eager gasping after light") suggests to Wilson that this

169. See Willcox, "The History of the Rowley Controversy" and "Appendix to the Rowley Poems," 1:cli–clxvii, 313–20.

170. Wilson, *Chatterton: A Biographical Study*, 126, 128.

171. Wilson, *Chatterton: A Biographical Study*, 16.

172. Wilson, *Chatterton: A Biographical Study*, 139. Milles, in [Chatterton,] *Poems, Supposed to Have Been Written in Bristol, by Thomas Rowley, and Others*, 191–92.

173. Wilson, *Chatterton: A Biographical Study*, 139.

174. Wilson, *Chatterton: A Biographical Study*, 140.

"beautiful picture of . . . the ideal patron of Rowley is in reality that of the poet himself."[175] Since the Rowley poems exhibit for Wilson such a strong element of poetic self-fashioning, it is not surprising that he concludes: "Thomas Rowley was no mere *nom de plume,* but a genuine reality to Chatterton."[176]

Wilson's *Chatterton* remains one of the finest inquiries into the "marvellous Boy." Undoubtedly, Wilson may appear to concede too much to a Victorian readership skeptical of the sexual licentiousness of the previous generations of poets. Similarly, his decision to update the spellings of Rowley's lines appears to stem from a comparable desire to make Chatterton's poetry digestible for his audience. But while Wilson indulged in emending Rowley's English slightly for modern tastes, he never went so far as philologist Walter W. Skeat, who completely recast the priest's poetry so that it matched the current idiom of Victorian readers. Skeat's edition of the *Poetical Works,* first published in 1871 and reissued in 1875 and 1890 as part of the well-known Aldine Edition of the British Poets, marks the most significant edition to appear since Willcox's two-volume set in 1842. To complement Skeat's endeavors, Edward Bell furnished a fresh account of Chatterton's life. Bell holds the Bristol poet in high esteem: "In originality of thought (notwithstanding some evident plagiarism), Chatterton, if the early age at which he began to compose be taken into account, stands before any poet on record."[177] But Skeat's effort to unveil such originality had mixed consequences. As his detailed footnotes and essay on the Rowley poems demonstrate, Skeat traced Chatterton's etymological sources; such research sought to settle beyond question whether Chatterton had written the Rowley poems. Once he concluded that the Rowleian dialect was Chatterton's invention, and, more important, a variation applied to the poems after they had been composed in Chatterton's natural phrasing, Skeat took the bold step of transforming the faux-antiquated spellings of the Rowley poems into blunt modern English. Such modernization had previously been attempted only on a small scale, as in "Eleanora and Juga (Modernised)," in Wilson's minor emendations, and in a privately printed edition of selected Rowley poems, edited by James Glassford.[178] None of these efforts, however, matches Skeat's more comprehen-

175. Wilson, *Chatterton: A Biographical Study,* 146. The lines, in their original, read: "the Fate mark'd Babe . . . / . . . eager gaspeynge after Lyghte" (*Complete Works of Thomas Chatterton,* ed. Taylor and Hoover, 1:245).

176. Wilson, *Chatterton: A Biographical Study,* 157.

177. [Edward Bell,] "The Life of Thomas Chatterton," in *The Poetical Works of Thomas Chatterton,* ed. Walter W. Skeat, 2 vols. (London: Bell and Daldy, 1871), 1:cii.

178. James Glassford, *Chatterton's Ella, and Other Pieces Interpreted: Or, Selection from the Rowley Poems, in Modern Reading* (Edinburgh: privately printed, 1837). This rare edi-

sive modernizations. Here, for example, is Skeat's translation of the opening lines of *Ælla*, which we quote in our Introduction: "'Tis sung by minstrels, that in ancient time, / When Reason hid herself in cloud of night, / The priest delivered all the law in rhyme."[179] Such textual changes, Skeat argued, rendered the Rowley poems more authentic: "Indeed," he writes in his preface to the Rowley poems, "we really thus approximate more closely to the true original text, viz. to the text as first conceived in the author's brain before it was translated into the Rowleian dialect."[180] Skeat cast his authority for the changes in Chatterton himself, using the footnotes that Chatterton provided as direct substitutions for Rowleian words, thus justifying his editorial confidence in his ability to intimate accurately Chatterton's "true original text."

Further, Skeat insists that his editorial practices belong to a "very necessary method" that ensured the Rowley poems became "accessible *for the first time* to the general public."[181] Skeat seems to regard the interpretive faculties of that public readership with some skepticism. He suggests that Chatterton's original Rowley poems ensured that the reader was "continually pulled up, sometimes three times in a line, by hard words which no amount of acquaintance with early MSS. will enable him to solve."[182] Nevertheless, Skeat assigns blame not to readers but to Chatterton, who "sometimes crowded his pages with hard words so mercilessly and unsparingly," in some cases undertaking "a special effort" to make understanding difficult through obscure vocabulary that "often come[s] in clotted masses."[183]

Some critics agreed with Skeat's editorial procedures. *Tinsley's Magazine*, an illustrated monthly, expressed its appreciation for his heavily footnoted editorial work, since it divested the Rowley poems of "the wretched pseudo-antique word-forms wherein Chatterton was led to dress them," through a dubious impulse that was—as this anonymous reviewer proceeds to observe—"led by an uncontrollable desire to deceive."[184] Moreover, this commentator found Skeat's

---

tion received little attention; the only mention of the work we were able to locate is in a review of Glassford's 1846 collection *Lyrical Compositions*: "Several years ago [Glassford] printed privately, with a critical preface, a modernized version of the 'Ella,' and some other pieces of the ill-fated Chatterton" ([Anon.,] *"Lyrical Compositions Selected from the Italian Poets; with Translations* by James Glassford," *Edinburgh Review* 84, no. 169 [July 1846]: 104).

179. Chatterton, "Epistle to Mastre Canynge on Ælla," *Poetical Works*, ed. Skeat, 2:21.

180. Skeat, "The Rowley Poems," in *Poetical Works*, 2:xxxix.

181. Skeat, "Preface," in *Poetical Works*, 1:xi. Emphasis in the original.

182. Skeat, "The Rowley Poems," in *Poetical Works*, 2:xxxix.

183. Skeat, "The Rowley Poems," in *Poetical Works*, 2:xl.

184. [Anon.,] "Chatterton: Or, the Rowley Romance," *Tinsley's Magazine* 14 (1874): 389.

exposure of Chatterton's apparent etymological errors especially satisfying, since the philologist revealed that the Bristol poet simply repeated mistakes from his sources. Kersey's dictionary had misled the author of Rowley's works in such lines as the following one from the "Entroductionne" to *Ælla*: "Somme cherisaunei 'tys to gentle mynde."[185] As Skeat points out, "cherisaunei" is Kersey's misprint for "cherisaunce" (meaning comfort) in *The Romaunt of the Rose*.[186] But, even though he proved scrupulous in detailing such mistakes, Skeat's unembellished rendition of this line — "Some comfort must it be to gentle mind" — obliterated the historical sources that Chatterton used to create an air of authenticity in Rowley's idiom.[187] Many early reviewers who approved of his changes did so on the grounds noted by Skeat himself, employing Skeat's own words by insisting that the modernization of the antiquated spelling made these at times hard-to-decipher works accessible.[188]

The *Saturday Review*, in a commentary on the 1875 reissue of Skeat's edition, allowed that "the modernizing of real old poems is a thing which can hardly ever be justified, and, for the most part, can hardly be too much condemned," but agreed that the "same process applied to the false Rowley is not only an improvement, but is, in truth, a restoration."[189] A critic in the *Athenæum* praised Skeat while noting that his editorial work laid bare not only the strengths of Chatterton's verse but also its weaknesses: "With the hindrances of the old spelling and sham antiquarianism cleared out of the way by Mr. Skeat's knowledge and diligence, the reader of Chatterton's poems can now settle more easily whether the editor's estimate of his author . . . is right or not."[190] In such readings, just as in Skeat's edition, Chatterton's medievalisms were thought to distract attention from the value of his poetry.

With the passage of time, however, there was a critical reaction against these textual modernizations that Tyrwhitt (in a much more measured manner) had

---

185. "Entroductionne" to *Ælla*, in *Complete Works of Thomas Chatterton*, ed. Taylor and Hoover, 1:178.

186. Chatterton, *Poetical Works*, ed. Skeat, 2:27.

187. Chatterton, *Poetical Works*, ed. Skeat, 2:27. Skeat, in a manner that seems inconsistent with his editorial practice, preserves Chatterton's idiosyncratic spelling of "Entroductionne."

188. See "Current Literature," *Daily News* (London), 27 March 1875: 2; "Bell and Skeat's Chatterton," *Saturday Review*, 3 April 1875: 447–48; and "Literature," *Bristol Mercury, and Western Counties Advertiser*, 9 December 1871: 6.

189. "Bell and Skeat's Chatterton," *Saturday Review*, 447–48.

190. "The Poetical Works of Thomas Chatterton, with an Essay on the Rowley Poems," *Athenæum* 2302 (9 December 1871): 749.

initiated more than a century before. Dante Gabriel Rossetti, one of the found-ing members of the Pre-Raphaelite Brotherhood, admitted that the "best way of getting at" Chatterton was through Skeat's edition; but at the same time Ros-setti also believed that Skeat's "readable rendering of the Rowley dialect" was not "by any means as well done" as it might have been.[191] Rossetti's respect for Chatterton's poetic gifts was never in question. Although Rossetti had been ac-quainted with Chatterton's works since the late 1840s, his fascination with the Rowley poems flourished during the final years of his career. At no point did Rossetti ever contend that Chatterton, as several critics were quick to suggest, had traded in literary deceit and historical inaccuracy. Instead, his admiration for Chatterton soared above even that of Wordsworth. In a sonnet dating from the spring of 1880 that Wilde would transcribe in his notebook, Rossetti placed Chatterton alongside no one less than the Bard: "With Shakespeare's manhood at a boy's wild heart."[192] This line confirms what Rossetti had already confided to the young man who would soon become his factotum, Hall Caine: "[Chatter-ton] was as great as any English poet whatever, and might absolutely, had he lived, have proved the only man in England's theatre of imagination who could have bandied parts with Shakespeare."[193]

Despite Rossetti's measured endorsement, appreciation for the moderniza-tion of Rowley's poetry was on the wane. Only a few years later, when Roden Noel agreed that Skeat's modernized edition enabled the public to "now *read* Chatterton; for he has long been to the majority a mere name," his was a lonely voice, and one that Wilde sharply criticized.[194] In a pointed review of Noel's *Essays on Poetry and Poets* (1886), Wilde took this writer to task for following Skeats's lackluster updating of Chatterton's antiquated spelling in the Rowley

191. Rossetti, "To Thomas Henry Hall Caine," 23 May 1880, in *The Correspondence of Dante Gabriel Rossetti*, ed. William E. Fredeman, 9 vols. (Cambridge: D. S. Brewer, 2002–2010), 9:186.

192. Dante Gabriel Rossetti, "Five English Poets: I. Thomas Chatterton," in Rossetti, *Ballads and Sonnets* (London: Ellis and White, 1881), 313. During the spring of 1880, Rossetti was rapidly acquiring detailed knowledge of Chatterton. We discuss Rossetti's fascination with Chatterton, which indirectly spurred Wilde's interest in the "marvellous Boy," in chapter 3 (154–57).

193. Rossetti, "To Thomas Henry Hall Caine," 23 May 1880, *Correspondence*, 9:186. Hall Caine quoted from this item of correspondence in *Recollections of Dante Gabriel Rossetti* (London: Elliot Stock, 1882), 184–85. Rossetti was firm on this point, since, on 2 June 1880, he reiterated to Caine: "Chatterton's work is replete with wisdom & nobility worthy of Shakespeare himself" (*Correspondence*, 9:198).

194. Roden Noel, *Essays on Poetry and Poets* (London: Kegan Paul, Trench, 1886), 36.

poems. He insisted: "Chatterton's archaisms were an essential part of his in-spiration and his method."[195] He dwelt at some length on Noel's lack of judg-ment: "Mr. Noel in one of his essays speaks with much severity of those who prefer sound to sense in poetry, and no doubt this is a very wicked thing to do; but he himself is guilty of a much graver sin against art when, in his desire to emphasize the meaning of Chatterton, he destroys Chatterton's music. In the modernized version he gives of the wonderful 'Songe to Ælla' he mars by his corrections the poem's metrical beauty, ruins the rhymes, and robs the music of its echo."[196] Even more than Rossetti before him, Wilde remained committed to the accurate representation of Chatterton's antiquarianism.

Wilde was not alone in valuing Chatterton's pseudo-medieval orthography. The final edition of Chatterton's works to appear in the nineteenth century would celebrate the artistry and visual texture of the poet's invented Rowleyese more than any previous edition. Edited by Robert Steele, and limited to only 210 copies, the Vale Press's 1898 two-volume set features striking "wild briony," "lau-rel leaf," and "rose and nightingale" decorations designed by Charles Ricketts, cofounder of the Vale Press (Figure 4). Wilde and Ricketts were well known to each other and shared a common aesthetic philosophy; Ricketts had designed the bindings and decorations of the 1891 edition of *The Picture of Dorian Gray*, *Lord Arthur Savile's Crime and Other Stories* (1891), *A House of Pomegranates* (1891), the reissue of *Poems* (1892), and *The Sphinx* (1894).[197]

In addition to the volume's exquisite production values, the selection of text was significant. The edition follows the text that Tyrwhitt established in his 1777 volume, reprinting Chatterton's original spellings and including many of the textual glosses that Chatterton himself had provided. Maintaining the original orthography, as we can see in the prospectus for the set, counted among the most important aspects of the edition: Steele stated that a fresh generation of readers would be able to "appreciate a text of the Rowley Poems wherein each word stands as its author gave it to the world," and further noted the "influence

195. Wilde, "A 'Sentimental Journey' through Literature," *Pall Mall Gazette*, 1 De-cember 1886: 5; in *Journalism Part I*, ed. John Stokes and Mark W. Turner, *The Complete Works of Oscar Wilde*, 7 vols. to date (Oxford: Oxford University Press, 2000 and continu-ing), 6:112.

196. Wilde, "A 'Sentimental Journey' through Literature," in *Journalism Part I*, ed. Stokes and Turner, 6:112. Noel had remarked in his chapter on Walt Whitman: "Words can never be mere sound, but always must remain symbolic sound with a determined meaning" (*Essays on Poetry and Poets*, 309).

197. As we note in our Conclusion (293), Wilde encouraged Ricketts to take on Chat-terton.

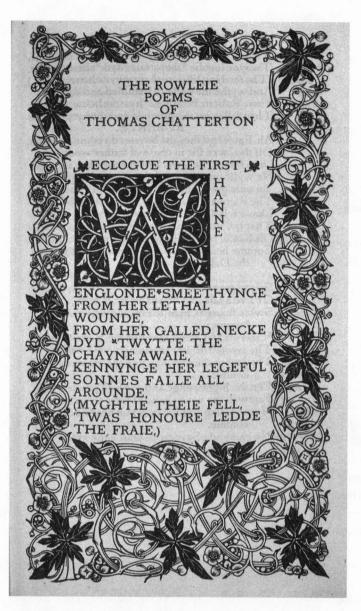

Figure 4. Charles Ricketts, title page of "Eclogue the First," from *The Rowley Poems of Thomas Chatterton*, 2 vols. (London: Vale Press, 1898), 1:5. Image courtesy of William Andrews Clark Memorial Library, University of California, Los Angeles. Press Coll. Vale.

[the Rowley Poems] exerted on the founders of the modern romantic school."[198] Steele's foreword reiterates this sentiment, noting that the poems warrant interest because they were a source "of Coleridge's inspiration and, through him, of the modern romantic school," and insisting that "the form of the words is one of the æsthetic elements which give value to Chatterton's work."[199]

With few copies in circulation, contemporary reviews of the Vale Press edition are scarce. Those that exist tend to offer high praise for Steele's and Ricketts's efforts, are fiercely critical of Skeat's modernizing editorial practice, and refer to Chatterton unequivocally as a founder of the Romantic school. By 1899, the *Saturday Review*—which had in 1875 praised Skeat's edition—questioned Skeat's authority even to comment on poetry, citing his work on Chatterton as a singular example that demonstrated that "a real gift for philology may exist entirely apart from any sense of the qualities which go to determine the arts of literature."[200] The critic asks: "Did the colour, the music . . . form no part of this verse in its original conception? Surely, any competent critic of poetry would not for a moment doubt that the artistic worth of these Poems consists largely in these very qualities?" The critic notes that Skeat's treatment of Chatterton is of a piece with the general view of the poet at the start of the nineteenth century. But since then, "time has wrought its changes; and now every year brings to Chatterton a more assured place in the history of English letters, as one of the fathers of our modern romantic poetry."[201] Even more significant, the writer traces a direct line from Chatterton and the Romantics to aesthetic poetry: "Chatterton anticipates, by nearly a century, that peculiar phase of our more recent verse which Mr. Pater has designated 'the Aesthetic School of Poetry.' Indeed, what that fine critic has somewhere said of such verse might be said with equal truth of Chatterton's verse: that it is no 'mere reproduction' of mediaeval poetry, but 'a finer ideal, extracted from what in relation to any actual world is already an ideal.'"[202] The Vale Press edition, the reviewer concluded, finally did justice to Chatterton's works. In many ways, Steele's editorial labors and Ricketts's fine printing marked the most remarkable tribute that Chatterton received in the world of nineteenth-century publishing. At this point in the fin de siècle, Ricketts had arguably triumphed more than any of his peers in en-

---

198. Robert Steele, "Prospectus for *The Rowley Poems of Thomas Chatterton*" (London: Vale Press, n.d. [c. 1898]). Reprinted in Maureen Watry, *The Vale Press: Charles Ricketts, a Publisher in Earnest* (New Castle, DE: Oak Knoll Press, 2004), 141.

199. Robert Steele, "Foreword," *The Rowley Poems of Thomas Chatterton*, 2 vols. (London: Vale Press, 1898), 1:n.p.

200. [Anon.,] "Chatterton," *Saturday Review* (21 January 1899): 85–86.

201. "Chatterton," *Saturday Review*: 85–86.

202. "Chatterton," *Saturday Review*: 85–86.

suring that his beautifully produced books were artworks in their own right. As we explain later, the twentieth-century world never embraced the "marvellous Boy" with such aesthetic passion on the page. That was because there were distinctly nineteenth-century reasons for retelling the story of Chatterton's life, his frustrations, and his forgeries in such visually powerful detail, as we can see in the numerous tributes, adaptations, and memorials in his name that we discuss in chapter 2.

2

THE CHATTERTON LEGEND: TRIBUTES, ADAPTATIONS, MEMORIALS

ROMANTICIZING CHATTERTON: MYTH AND MUSE

Just as biographical and editorial inquiries into Chatterton's career flourished over the course of more than a century, so too did Chatterton come to hold an iconic place in the late eighteenth- and nineteenth-century cultural imagination. Herbert Croft's *Love and Madness* marks a starting point in the rapid myth-making that quickly came to surround the indigent Chatterton's early death, as Croft used his bully pulpit to feature others' works inspired by the young poet. In the second edition of his best-selling novel, Croft reprinted Hannah Cowley's monody on the "Bright Star of Genius" who suffered from "haggard Poverty."[1] (As Andrew Bennett has pointed out, Cowley's fine tribute probably exerted some influence on Keats's famous sonnet about the "still stedfast, still unchangeable" celestial body that takes as its title her reference to the Bristol poet's "Bright Star.")[2] Such poetic accolades became so numerous that Gregory inserted into his biography a short anthology of eulogistic lines on Chatterton

1. Hannah Cowley, "A Monody," *Morning Post and Daily Advertiser*, 24 October 1778: 9; reprinted in [Herbert Croft,] *Love and Madness: In a Series of Letters, One of Which Contains the Original Account of Chatterton, a New Edition, Corrected* (London: G. Kearsley, 1786), 235–36. Gregory reprinted Cowley's poem in *The Life of Thomas Chatterton, with Criticisms of his Genius and Writings, and a Concise View of the Controversy Concerning Rowley's Poems* (London: G. Kearsley, 1789), 124–26.

2. Andrew Bennett, *Romantic Poets and the Culture of Posterity* (Cambridge: Cambridge University Press, 1999), 146. Keats, "Keats's Last Sonnet," in *Life, Letters and Literary Remains of John Keats*, ed. Richard Monckton Milnes, 2 vols. (London: Edward Moxon, 1848), 2:306; and "Bright star, would I were stedfast as thou art," in *Complete Poems*, ed. Jack Stillinger (Cambridge, MA: Harvard University Press), 247.

that had appeared in the years since Croft's volume. These eulogies include John Scott's ode, "Written after a Journey to Bristol," in which the poetic voice mourns the "wondrous tuneful youth, / The bard" of this city, "whose boasted ancient store / Rose recent from his own exhaustless mine!"[3] Equally touching in its praise is Helena Maria Williams's "Sonnet to Expression," where she refers to Chatterton as the one "the muses lov'd—when hope forsook / His spirit."[4] In the same publication that printed Williams's sonnet, Mary Robinson observed that "Penury, e'en made CHATTERTON her own."[5] Meanwhile, gifted working-class poet Ann Yearsley, who also came from the Bristol area, produced a moving elegy in Chatterton's honor, in which the distressed poet recalls his torment at discovering that death would satisfy him more than a life of undeserved misery: "Scorning to fawn at Insult's knee, / My woes were doubled, deeper rais'd my groan; / More sharp, more exquisite came Agony; / And latent Anguish seal'd me for her own."[6] Such laudatory poetry furthered blurred the distinction between the basic facts and the romantic idealization of Chatterton's life.

To many members of the generation that came to admire the Rowley poems, the idea that Chatterton had forged them in a fraudulent manner was simply beside the point when they considered his redoubtable imaginative gifts. Among the steadfast supporters of Chatterton's antiquarianism was George Hardinge, solicitor-general to the queen, who anonymously published *Rowley and Chatterton in the Shades* (1782). In this "new Elysian interlude," the spirit of Rowley informs the audience: "There is something in the wildness of his port and the lightning of [his interlocutor Chatterton's] eye, which marks superior intelligence."[7] Six years later, Hardinge championed the precocious forger in a poetic tribute, "The Genius of Chatterton" (1788), which concludes with this high-flown rhetorical flourish: "Come, Pierian powers, MY bold Design, / And stamp

3. John Scott, "Written after a Journey to Bristol," in *Poetical Works* (London: J. Buckland, 1782), 224–25; reprinted in Gregory, *Life of Thomas Chatterton*, 126. Scott also mourns Chatterton as "that poor Youth, whose tales relate / Sad JUGA's fears and BAWDIN's fate," in "The Muse; or, Poetical Enthusiasm," in *Poetical Works*, 206.

4. Helena Maria Williams, "Sonnet to Expression," *Morning Herald and Daily Advertiser*, 17 September 1782: 18; reprinted in Gregory, *Life of Thomas Chatterton*, 129–30.

5. Mary Robinson, "The Poet: A Fragment," *Morning Herald and Daily Advertiser*, 11 October 1785: 10.

6. Ann Yearsley, "Elegy on Mr. Chatterton," in *Poems on Various Subjects, by Ann Yearsley, Milkwoman of Clifton, near Bristol; Being Her Second Work* (London: G. G. J. and J. Robinson, 1787), 147.

7. [George Hardinge,] *Rowley and Chatterton in the Shades: or, Nugæ Antiquæ et Novæ—A New Elysian Interlude in Prose and Verse* (London: T. Becket, 1782), 3.

with ROWLEY'S name each consecrated line."[8] Similar tributes followed. William Hayley, for example, urged his readers to denounce luxury and prevent a future Chatterton from enduring unnecessary poverty in the name of pursuing his great poetic vocation: "Too oft the wealthy," Hayley's speaker declares, "to proud follies born / Have turn'd from letter'd Poverty with scorn"; as he sees it, the time has come to "Search the dark scenes where dropping Genius lies," since it is imperative that "Our generous nation ne'er may weep to see, / A future CHATTERTON by poison dead."[9] Meanwhile, Henry Pye, who became poet laureate in 1790, acknowledged the greatness of many English poets, including several of his peers, such as Hayley, whose voice he heard "sailing on the rainbow-tinctur'd wings / Of chaste Imagination"; it is in this context that Pye witnesses the "streaming eye" with which "the sorrowing Muse / Pale Chatterton's untimely urn bedews."[10]

The British Romantics were not slow to put their distinctive stamp on Chatterton's image as an incomparable genius whose deserving ambitions had been cruelly dashed. Samuel Taylor Coleridge's first published poetic work appeared in 1790: "Monody on the Death of Chatterton," a contemplation of poetic creativity, which he continued to revise six times until the 1820s. In the earliest version, Coleridge's ode addresses the high price Chatterton paid for his great ambition to earn renown: "Chatterton! methinks I hear thy name, / For cold my Fancy grows, and dead each Hope of Fame."[11] Those critics such as Walpole and Milles who had denied Chatterton's gifts seemed to Coleridge, in the prefatory note he drafted for this poem, to resemble a predatory "Owl mangling a poor dead Nightingale!"[12] During this period, as opinion continued to shift, there was increasing acclamation for Chatterton's poetic brilliance. William-Henry Ireland, who found the Rowley poems an inspiration for the infamous Shakespearean forgeries he produced during the 1790s, applauded "Apollo's child,

8. Hardinge, *The Genius of Chatterton: An Irregular Ode, Written on the Supposition of His Being the Author of the Poems Attributed to Thomas Rowley in the Fifteenth Century* (London: T. Becket, 1788), 11.

9. William Hayley, *An Essay on Epic Poetry; in Five Epistles, to the Revd. Mr. Mason with Notes* (London: J. Dodsley, 1782), 86, 87.

10. Henry James Pye, *Poems on Various Subjects*, 2 vols. (London: J. Stockton, 1787), 2:159, 160.

11. Coleridge, "Monody on the Death of Chatterton," in *The Collected Works of Samuel Taylor Coleridge, Poetical Works II, Poems (Variorum Text): Part 1*, ed. J. C. C. Mays, Bollingen Series LXXV, 16 vols. (Princeton: Princeton University Press, 2001), 16.1.2:172. These lines, which date from 1790, were removed from the 1794 and succeeding texts of the poem.

12. Coleridge, "Monody on the Death of Chatterton," in *Collected Works*, 16.2.1:172.

Great Chatterton," in a volume titled *Neglected Genius* (1812).[13] Perhaps more powerfully responsive than any of his devoted contemporaries, Keats remained dazzled by the overpowering "flash" of "Genius" that manifested itself in this desolate "child of sorrow."[14] Keats's admiration for this predecessor was so great that he dedicated one of his most ambitious poems, *Endymion*, to "THE MEMORY OF THOMAS CHATTERTON." Keats attended William Hazlitt's lectures on the English poets, and when Hazlitt questioned the value of his fellow critics' equating Chatterton's precocity with genius, Keats protested. In a letter to his brother, he complains that he "was very disappointed at [Hazlitt's] treatment of Chatterton."[15] Perhaps Keats expressed this opinion to Hazlitt, or perhaps other admirers of Chatterton did so, because Hazlitt's next lecture opened with an apology: "I am sorry that what I said in the conclusion of the last Lecture respecting Chatterton, should have given dissatisfaction to some persons, with whom I would willingly agree on such matters."[16] Hazlitt went on to discuss in greater detail his objections, which center on the "learned rhapsodists" whose hyperbolic assessments of the young Bristol poet placed him on equal footing with Shakespeare and Homer; yet "of [Chatterton's] actual productions," Hazlitt writes, "one may think as highly as he pleases."[17] Keats seems to have been

13. William-Henry Ireland, "The Foregoing Stanzas, in the Modern Style of Versification," in *Neglected Genius: Illustrating the Untimely and Unfortunate Fate of Many British Poets, from the Period of Henry the Eighth to the Era of the Unfortunate Chatterton* (London: G. Cowie, 1812), 70. This poem is a modernized translation of the preceding one, "The Tourneie," which cleverly imitates Chatterton's "Rowleian Style"; this homage to Chatterton contains no fewer than eighty-five glosses (62–67). Ireland's volume contains several other apostrophes to Chatterton's name. We discuss Ireland's forgeries in relation to Wilde's "Portrait of Mr. W.H." in chapter 6 (257–67).

14. John Keats, "O Chatterton! how very sad thy fate," in *Complete Poems*, 32. Keats's sonnet dates from 1815, and it first appeared in *Life, Letters, and Literary Remains*, ed. Milnes, 1:12. Keats also referred to the pleasure of being able to "sit, and rhyme and think on Chatterton" in his early poetic epistle "To George Felton Matthew," written in November 1815 (*Complete Poems*, 15).

15. Keats, "To George and Tom Keats," 21 February 1818, in *The Letters of John Keats*, ed. Hyder Edward Rollins, 2 vols. (Cambridge, MA: Harvard University Press, 1958), 1:237.

16. William Hazlitt, "On Burns, and the Old English Ballads," *Lectures on the English Poets* (London: Taylor and Hessey, 1818), 245. As H. E. Rollins notes in his annotations to *The Letters of John Keats* (1:237), biographers of both Keats and Hazlitt suggest that Hazlitt's apology was offered in response to Keats's feedback. See Dorothy Hewlett, *A Life of John Keats* (New York: Hurst and Blackwell, 1949), 139ff.; P. P. Howe, *The Life of William Hazlitt* (New York: George H. Doran, 1922), 243; and Nicholas Roe, *John Keats: A New Life* (New Haven: Yale University Press, 2012), 214.

17. Hazlitt, "On Burns, and the Old English Ballads," in *Lectures on the English Poets*, 246.

unmoved by such cautions against the possibility of exaggerating Chatterton's merits. Two years later, not long before his own untimely death, Keats commented on the distinctly national qualities he cherished in this revered poetic forebear: "Chatterton . . . is the purest writer in the English language. He has no French idiom, or particles like Chaucer; 'tis genuine English Idiom in English words."[18]

Percy Bysshe Shelley was equally impressed. In his famous memorial to Keats, "Adonais" (1821), Shelley counts Chatterton among the English poetic "inheritors of unfulfilled renown."[19] Chatterton provided a melancholy example of the forestalled ambitions to laboring poet John Clare, who in his earliest surviving letter expressed his "great . . . Expectations" about poetic fame, knowing full well that he might "be building 'Castles in the Air.'"[20] During this period, Southey—who had done such important editorial work, and had acted as steward of the Chatterton family name—dedicated some of his bold hexameters in A *Vision of Judgement* (1821) to recalling Chatterton's name as first among "the youths whom the Muses / Mark'd for themselves at birth."[21] These lines were the culmination of many years of reading Chatterton: a figure who, as Nick Groom observes, "haunted Southey's imagination and dreams," reveries in which the young poet—as Southey informed Grosvenor Charles Bedford—represented a human form that troublingly lacked "the due mixture of Piety."[22] Indubitably, Chatterton inspired not only awe but also anxiety in

18. Keats, "To J. H. Reynolds," 21 September 1819; in *The Letters of John Keats*, ed. Rollins, 2:167.

19. Percy Bysshe Shelley, "Adonais," in *Shelley's Poetry and Prose*, ed. Donald H. Reiman and Neil Fraistat, 2nd ed. (New York: W. W. Norton, 2002), 423.

20. "To J. B. Henson," in *The Letters of John Clare*, ed. Mark Storey (Oxford: Clarendon Press, 1985), 3; quoted in John Goodridge, *John Clare and Community* (Cambridge: Cambridge University Press, 2013), 12. Goodridge provides a detailed account of Clare's extensive engagement with Chatterton's writings (11–35).

21. Robert Southey, *The Vision of Judgement* (London: Longman, Hurst, Rees, Orme, and Brown, 1821), 42.

22. Nick Groom, "Love and Madness: Southey Editing Chatterton," in Lynda Pratt, ed., *Robert Southey and the Contexts of English Romanticism* (Aldershot: Ashgate, 2006), 19–20. Southey, "To Grosvenor Charles Bedford," 1 June 1793, in *New Letters of Robert Southey*, ed. Kenneth Curry, 2 vols. (New York: Columbia University Press, 1965), 1:25. In a memoir, Southey recalls that in the mid-1780s, when he was twelve or thirteen, he came across Rowley's poem; it was a time when "Chatterton's history was in fresh remembrance, and that story . . . acted upon me with all the force of local associations" (*The Life and Correspondence of Robert Southey*, ed. Charles Cuthbert Southey, 6 vols. [London: Longman, Brown, Green, and Longmans, 1849–1850], 1:118).

Southey. Even though in A *Vision of Judgement* Southey's speaker acclaims the "Marvellous boy, whose antique songs and unhappy story / Shall, by gentle hearts, be in mournful memory cherish'd" in Bristol, Southey nonetheless injected a new element into the debate about Chatterton's mental disposition. He remarks—in a revealing parenthesis—on the "act of madness innate" that led to the young man's suicide.[23] In an explanatory note, Southey clarifies this line: "In the case of Chatterton," he says, self-murder "was the manifestation of an hereditary disease. There was a madness in the family. His only sister, during one part of her life, was under confinement."[24] Taken together, these Romantic tributes produce an image of a distinctly English, if tragically afflicted, genius who died well before his time.

These English poets' praise of Chatterton's significance in the national pantheon hardly alienated his name from other European traditions. Further afield, in the world of French Romanticism, Alfred de Vigny's *Chatterton* (1835)—which departs considerably from the record of the forger's life—enjoyed increasing success on the Parisian stage (where it has remained in repertory ever since). Vigny's drama, in which the suicidal poet is a sensitive, despairing misfit, would in turn inspire countless viewers and readers, many of whom would become important to Wilde. Théophile Gautier, whose poetry Wilde quotes in *The Picture of Dorian Gray*, was entranced by the play upon its premiere, describing it as making "une des vives impressions" ("one of the strong impressions") of his youth.[25] When he saw the play again some twenty years later, that impression was equally strong. Gautier bemoaned that Chatterton "veut forcer sa pensée vierge à se donner pour de l'argent comme une courtisane" ("had to force his virgin thought to sell itself for money like a courtesan").[26] Many writers in the audience "a pu reconnaitre là le tableau . . . de ses luttes intérieures et de ses abattements" ("were able to recognize the picture . . . of their inner struggles and their dejections").[27] "En somme," he concludes, "la poésie est un don fatal, une

23. Southey, *The Vision of Judgement*, 42.

24. Southey, *The Vision of Judgement*, 64.

25. Théophile Gautier, "Reprise de Chatterton (en Décembre 1857)," in *Histoire du romantisme* (Paris: Bibliothèque Charpentier, 1905), 152. His original impressions were recorded in *Histoire de l'art dramatique en France depuis vingt-cinq ans* (Brussels: Librarie Universelle, 1859), 41–42. Unless otherwise indicated, all translations from the French are our own. For Wilde's quotations from Gautier's poetry, see Wilde, *The Picture of Dorian Gray*, ed. Joseph Bristow, *The Complete Works of Oscar Wilde*, 7 vols. to date (Oxford: Oxford University Press, 2005), 3:142–44, 304–5, and 421–22.

26. Gautier, *Histoire du romantisme*, 159.

27. Gautier, *Histoire du romantisme*, 159.

sorte de malédiction pour celui qui le reçoit en naissant" ("in sum, poetry is a fatal gift, a sort of curse for him who received it at birth").[28] Flaubert similarly expressed his esteem for Vigny in a letter to Louise Colet: "Je lui suis reconnaissant de l'enthousiasme que j'ai eu autrefois en lisant Chatterton" ("I am grateful to him for the enthusiasm I once had reading Chatterton").[29] Baudelaire, too, was well versed in Vigny's writing, and he drew on Chatterton as an example of the genial author fated to misery in his first published work, *La Fanfarlo* (1847).[30] The reach of Vigny's *Chatterton* extended beyond France and through the rest of the century. For example, Italian composer Ruggero Leoncavallo's opera *Chatterton*, which adapted Vigny's drama, was composed in 1876 and premiered four years before the *fin* of the *siècle*. The eighteenth-century poet's legend had become a European sensation.

POPULARIZING CHATTERTON: IMAGE AND STAGE

The ensuing decades witnessed several additional developments in the cultural understanding of Chatterton's significance as either an intrinsically mad or formidably gifted genius. Arguably, the most noteworthy event was the exhibition of Henry Wallis's arresting painting of Chatterton's suicide at the Royal Academy in 1856 (Figure 5). This great work, which enjoyed an instantaneous impact, was the first portrayal of the poet's death to make the misery of the garret, in which he took his life, appear wholly unsuited to a figure of such poetic grace. Even if the setting of the poet's chambers in Holborn is grimly realistic, Wallis's depiction of Chatterton's body could not be more romantic in the broadest sense of the term. His model, the twenty-seven-year-old George Meredith, lies elegantly draped on a shabby couch. The exquisitely pale corpse, which occupies much of the horizontal axis, has a right arm drooping onto the floor, while the left one rests delicately upon his unbuttoned shirt. The right fist clutches the remains of one of his torn-up manuscripts, which are strewn around a chest containing the young poet's papers. All of these elements—the

28. Gautier, *Histoire du romantisme*, 150.

29. Flaubert's appreciation is all the more striking since, at the time of the letter (March 1854), he likely would have suspected that Colet had begun an affair with Vigny. Gustave Flaubert, *Correspondance, deuxième série (1850–1854)* (Paris: Charpentier, 1889), 389.

30. "La mortalité s'abattait joyeusement sur les hôpitaux, et les Chatterton et les Savage de la rue Saint-Jacques crispaient leurs doigts gelés sur leurs écritoires" ("mortality was falling happily on hospitals, and the Chattertons and Savages of the Rue Saint-Jacques clenched their fingers frozen on their writing desks"). Charles Baudelaire, *La Fanfarlo*, in *Petits poems en prose: Les paradis artificiels* (Paris: Michel Lévy Frères, 1869), 421.

Figure 5. Henry Wallis, *Chatterton*, 1856. Oil on canvas, 62.2 × 93.3 cm. No1685.
© Tate, London, 2013.

alluring richness of Meredith's brushed-back auburn hair, his purple crushed velvet breeches, and the lush crimson robe cast upon a chair—conjure Chatterton as an icon of aesthetic luxuriance: one whose physical attractiveness was unfairly at odds with the wrongful circumstances in which he died. Wallis's distinguished painting certainly contrasted with earlier, often sentimental depictions of the poet, which included John Flaxman's *Chatterton Drinking from the Cup of Despair* (dating from the mid-1770s), where the young man from Bristol animatedly takes the poison from an allegorical representation of death. Yet, as William L. Pressly has suggested, Wallis's painting derived some of its inspiration from Henry Singleton's 1794 *The Death of Chatterton* (Figure 6), which Edward Orme engraved for a widely circulated print.[31] Wallis appears to have rearranged for his own purposes from Singleton not only the setting of a lowly garret but also the model's open shirt, knee breeches, and supine position on an unkempt bed.

31. Pressly, *The Artist as Original Genius: Shakespeare's "Fine-Frenzy" in Late-Eighteenth-Century British Art* (Newark: University of Delaware Press, 2007), 168. Pressly comments that in 1795 the painter John Cranch depicted the same scene; J. T. Smith engraved Cranch's painting of Chatterton's death.

Figure 6. Edward Orme, after Henry Singleton, *Death of Chatterton*, 1794. Stipple engraving, 40.0 × 50.2 cm. NPG D32498. © National Portrait Gallery, London.

Not surprisingly, both the striking pathos and intense color of Wallis's art-work evoked impassioned responses among his contemporaries. Charles Dickens, for example, thought Wallis's *Chatterton* "a painful [i.e., moving] picture of a great deal of merit."[32] John Ruskin, too, found Wallis's arresting painting to be "faultless and wonderful."[33] Similarly, the *Art Journal* stood in awe of its "marvellous power," and asserted that *Chatterton* "may be accepted as a safe

32. Charles Dickens, "To Georgina Hogarth," 5 May 1856, in *The Letters of Charles Dickens*, ed. Graham Storey and Kathleen Tillotson, The Pilgrim Edition, 12 vols. (Oxford: Clarendon Press, 1965–2002), 8:111. Groom contends that the scene in Dickens's *Bleak House* depicting the impoverished copyist Nemo's death amid a "wilderness marked with a rain of ink" inspired Wallis's painting: see Groom, "'I Am Nothing": A Typology of the Forger form Chatterton to Wilde," in Francis O'Gorman and Katherine Turner, eds., *The Victorians and the Eighteenth Century: Reassessing the Tradition* (Aldershot: Ashgate, 2004), 215; and Dickens, *Bleak House*, ed. George Ford and Sylvère Monod (New York: Norton, 1977), 120.

33. John Ruskin, *Notes on Some of the Principal Pictures Exhibited in the Rooms of the Royal Academy and the Society of Painters in Water-Colours: No. II—1856*, 6th ed. (London: Smith, Elder, 1856), 26.

augury of the artist's fame."[34] William Holman Hunt, who maintained careful records of the Pre-Raphaelite movement, recognized the value that Wallis's portrait had in maintaining Chatterton's memory: "The cruelty of the world towards poor Chatterton . . . will never henceforth be remembered without recognition of Henry Wallis . . . who first so pathetically excited pity for his fate in his picture of the death of the hapless boy."[35] Little wonder that Wallis's fine painting was copied and plagiarized on several occasions.[36] By 1871, John Addington Symonds acknowledged the amazing legacy of Wallis's portrait. As he reflected on Chatterton's impact across the years, Symonds observed: "We do not wonder that Chatterton should . . . have inspired such a picture as that of his death by Wallis," since the poet's "pungent genius" transmitted to other artists nothing less than "an atmosphere surcharged with electricity."[37] In his own poetry, Symonds himself appeared to be highly responsive to Wallis's painting in 1884, when he wrote adoringly of the "nut brown tresses / Thrown" from Chatterton's "recumbent head"; on this occasion, the sensual image of Chatterton captivated Symonds's decidedly homoerotic gaze, as it lingered on the young poet's ivory-colored flesh, which looked "like sculptured marble / Fashioned from some Grecian's brain / For a young Adonis sleeping / Till the zephyrs wake again."[38] The intense drama of Chatterton's suicide had become a common topos in Victorian poetry. In 1885, for example, Evelyn Pyne published her dramatic monologue "A Poet's Death (Chatterton, August 1770)." Once he has swallowed his phial of poison, Pyne's Chatterton defiantly cries out to the world that has cruelly misunderstood him: "I *am* a genius!"[39]

Elsewhere in the imaginative writing of the Victorian age, Chatterton's life

34. [Anon.,] "The Royal Academy: Exhibition the Eighty-Eighth," *Art Journal* 18 (1856): 169.

35. William Holman Hunt, *Pre-Raphaelitism and the Pre-Raphaelite Brotherhood*, 2 vols. (London: Macmillan, 1905), 2:417.

36. In 1859, the Dublin photographer James Robinson produced a stereoscopic photograph that employed props and a model to reproduce each and every detail in Wallis's panting; a court injunction against Robinson failed in 1860. John Thomas Peele's *Prayer for Health*, shown at the Royal Academy in 1871, reproduced the setting of Wallis's painting. See Krzystof Z. Cieskowski, "The Legend Makers: Chatterton, Wallis and Meredith," *History Today* 32, no. 11 (November 1982): 34.

37. John Addington Symonds, Review of *The Poetical Works of Thomas Chatterton* (1871), *Academy* 15 (December 1871): 549–50.

38. Symonds, "For a Picture of the Dead Chatterton," in *Fragilia Labilia* (Portland, ME: Thomas B. Mosher, 1902), 30. Symonds's volume originally appeared in 1884.

39. Evelyn Pyne, "A Poet's Death (Chatterton, August 1770)," in *A Poet in May* (London: Kegan Paul, Trench, 1885), 61.

and works became prominent points of reference. In Wilkie Collins's sensation novel *The Woman in White* (serialized in 1859–1860), the scheming Count Fosco poses the following question in his invidious contemplation of crime: "Who is the English poet who has won the most universal sympathy—who makes the easiest of all subjects for pathetic writing and pathetic painting."[40] The answer of course is "that nice young person who began life with a forgery, and ended it by a suicide—your dear, romantic, interesting Chatterton."[41] Thomas Hardy, too, became absorbed in Chatterton's legend. Besides celebrating Chatterton's greatness in two of his novels, *A Pair of Blue Eyes* (1872–1873) and *The Wood-landers* (1886–1887), Hardy's reading of Masson's *Chatterton: A Story of the Year 1770* prompted him to conjure this tableau in his notebooks, which appears in Emma Hardy's hand: "A scene—39 Brooke Street Holborn—Chatterton looking out of the Attic window past midnight and hearing a street woman singing joined by a costermonger with bass & a hulking fellow standing by."[42] It was also during this period that the famous nonsense poem "Jabberwocky" appeared in Lewis Carroll's *Through the Looking-Glass and What Alice Found There* (1871). On this occasion, however, it was the memory of Rowley rather than the Bristol poet's time in London that shaped the idiosyncratic humor of

40. Collins, *The Woman in White*, ed. Maria K. Bachman (Peterborough, Ontario: Broadview Press, 2006), 259. Julie Crane addresses this connection in "'Wandering be-tween Two Worlds': The Victorian Afterlife of Thomas Chatterton," in Andrew Radford and Mark Sandy, eds., *Romantic Echoes in the Victorian Era* (Aldershot: Ashgate, 2008), 27–37.

41. Collins, *The Woman in White*, 259. As Bachman points out, Collins's good friend, Augustus Egg, owned Wallis's *Chatterton* (259).

42. There is an allusion to Chatterton in *A Pair of Blue Eyes* in the serial version (*Tins-ley's Magazine*, 12 [1873]: 501), and in the first edition: "Stratford has her Shakespeare . . . Bristol has her Chatterton" (*A Pair of Blue Eyes*, 3 vols. [London: Tinsley, 1873], 3:184), although the reference was deleted for the Osgood, McIlvaine (1895) and later editions. In *The Woodlanders*, Hardy's narrator quotes four lines from *Ælla* (taken from Skeat's mod-ernized edition): "When the fair apples, red as evening sky, / Do bend the tree unto the fruitful ground, / When juicy pears, and berries of black dye / Do dance in air, and call the eyes around." The narrator comments on the relevance of these lines to the scene set at Sherton Abbas in the fictional region of Wessex: "The landscape confronting the window might indeed have been part of the identical stretch of country which the youthful Chatter-ton had in his mind" (Hardy, *The Woodlanders*, *Macmillan's Magazine* 54 [1886]: 474, and *The Woodlanders*, 3 vols. [London: Macmillan, 1887], 2:147, and *Ælla*, in *The Poetical Works of Thomas Chatterton*, ed. W. W. Skeat, 2 vols. [London: Bell, 1875], 2:38. Hardy owned Skeat's 1875 edition.) Hardy's notebook entry appears in *The Literary Notebooks of Thomas Hardy*, ed. Lennart A. Björk, 2 vols. (New York: New York University Press, 1985), 1:15.

Carroll's much-recited stanzas. "Jabberwocky" contains more than a handful of Chatterton-like touches, especially in the memorable opening lines: "'Twas brillig and the slithy toves / Did gyre and gimble in the wabe."[43] Such phrasing puzzles Carroll's Alice, who admits that "it seems very pretty"; but, as she quickly observes, "it's rather *hard* to understand."[44] Many readers would have instantly grasped Carroll's joke, since the absurdity of this ingenious verse more than obviously satirized the bizarre vocabulary that Chatterton had furnished for the fictitious Rowley. Take, for instance, Chatterton's "An Excelente Balade of Charitie," where we discover that "bretful" means "filled with," and "chelandri" is a "pied goldfinch."[45] "Brillig" and "toves" occupy a parallel register. Carroll's whimsy was not lost on *Macmillan's Magazine*, which promptly published an article by one "Thomas Chatterton," who claimed that during a séance spirits had communicated to him that "Jabberwocky" was a translation of an original German work, "Der Jammerwoch."[46]

Importantly for Wilde, in 1884 the much-elaborated story of Chatterton's wretched demise inspired Henry Arthur Jones and Henry Herman's histrionic one-act curtain-raiser, *Chatterton*, which opened at the Princess's Theatre, London, with Wilson Barrett (whom Wilde knew) in the lead (Figure 7). The action takes place at Mrs. Angel's home at Holborn, and it creates a wholly imaginary scene that transforms Gregory's observation that it was "by no means improbable," given Chatterton's "strong passions" and lack of "religious principles," that the young man "might frequently be unprepared to resist the temptations of a licentious metropolis."[47] Jones and Herman envision their eminently attractive protagonist as a wholly deserving, if deeply misunderstood, romantic lover. Two well-heeled young cousins of the playwrights' invention, Lady Mary and Cecelia, ask the landlady if they might see where the absent Chatterton resides. Once these visitors beg to know when Chatterton might return, Mrs. Angel divulges that he often "wanders about the streets for days and nights together, without anything to eat, and then he comes in and sits at that table and writes away for

43. Carroll, *Through the Looking-Glass and What Alice Found There*, in *The Annotated Alice: Alice's Adventures in Wonderland and Through the Looking-Glass*, ed. Martin Gardner, Definitive ed. (New York: W. W. Norton, 2000), 148.

44. Carroll, *The Annotated Alice*, 150.

45. Chatterton, "An Excelente Balade of Charitie: As Writen by the Prieste Thomas Rowley, 1464," in *Complete Works of Thomas Chatterton*, ed. Donald S. Taylor and Benjamin B. Hoover, 2 vols. (Oxford: Clarendon Press, 1971), 1:645.

46. "Thomas Chatterton," "The Jabberwock Traced to Its True Source," *Macmillan's Magazine* 25 (1872): 337.

47. G[eorge]. Gregory, *The Life of Thomas Chatterton, with Criticisms of His Genius and Writings, with a Concise View of the Controversy Concerning Rowley's Poems* (London: G. Kearsley, 1789), 109.

Figure 7. H. R. Barraud, Wilson Barrett as Chatterton in *Chatterton*, Princess's Theatre, 1884. Photograph, 13.9 × 10.3 cm. Guy Little Collection. © Victoria and Albert Museum, London.

hours like a madman."[48] Mrs. Angel, however, admits that she cannot make Chatterton out, a remark that prompts Lady Mary to declare: "That's what the world always says of genius."[49]

The action continues frenetically. Before Chatterton returns, Lady Mary remains for an instant in his room and discreetly slides among his papers a letter from her father that offers him a secretarial position at Whitehall. In the ensuing scene, his friend Boaden enters. A distraught Chatterton begs to know whether the headmaster known to this companion will offer him a position. The answer is negative. "Is it money?" Chatterton wishes to know.[50] The dialogue hurtles toward the terrible conclusion that everyone knowledgeable about the poet's life suspected:

> BOADEN: It's not money.
> CHATTERTON: What then?
> BOADEN: The Walpole business. He [the headmaster] happened to have
>   heard about those verses you sent to Walpole. — [CHATTERTON *winces.*]
>   and he said he couldn't forgive you.[51]

Soon after, Chatterton learns from the only letter he has received that his friends at Bristol, whom he petitioned for support, have largely disowned him as well. In response, Boaden encourages the abstemious Chatterton to drown his sorrows in liquor. But the young poet will not comply. Left alone on the stage, he decides to swallow the poison he has kept in a cabinet, and he proceeds to tear up his manuscripts. Yet once the arsenic begins to flow through his veins, he discovers the letter that Lady Mary has placed among his papers. In the end, Chatterton vainly struggles for his life: "Mary," he cries out, "my goddess, my star, my hope beyond my hope. I come to thee."[52] Such resolve of course arrives too late. Chatterton, tearing open his shirt, staggers across the floor and drags himself to his bed, where he collapses in a tableau similar to the one immortalized in Wallis's painting. "Death," he exclaims heroically, "you have not conquered me. I shall live. World who denied me bread, you shall give me fame, my name shall be upon your lips and my words graven upon your heart forever."[53] No matter how much of the plot of this single-act drama has been conjured from Jones and Herman's wild imagination, the outcome of the

48. Henry Arthur Jones [and Henry Herman], *Chatterton,* in *One Act Plays for Stage and Study,* ed. Zona Gale (New York: Samuel French, 1943), 21.

49. Jones [and Herman], *Chatterton,* 21.

50. Jones [and Herman], *Chatterton,* 31.

51. Jones [and Herman], *Chatterton,* 31.

52. Jones [and Herman], *Chatterton,* 36.

53. Jones [and Herman], *Chatterton,* 36.

play is clear: on the London stage Chatterton's tragedy had reached a fevered pitch.

Victorian audiences relished *Chatterton*. Barrett included the drama in tours of England and the United States to great acclaim. What the play lacked in historical accuracy it more than compensated for in poetic fervor and pathos for the plight of the tortured genius; the speech on the value of Chatterton's art, which one review described as "rhapsodies on the blessings and glories of poesy," was held up for special praise.[54] "One of Chatterton's speeches, where he describes the uses of poetry," waxed the *Sunday Times*, "was actually sublime in its expression, and elicited the fervent applause of the audience from the magnificent way in which it was delivered."[55] The monologue was not only a vehicle for Barrett's theatrical tour de force; it also helped to align Chatterton's artistic philosophy with the aesthetic movement. In one of his frenzied responses to Mrs. Angel's Philistine question, "What's the use of poetry?" Chatterton proclaims: "To live upon when one can't get bread and cheese."[56] By the time the play premiered, this had become an archetypal image of the fanatical modern poet who would starve for his art. (Aesthetes had been satirized on the stage only a few seasons before, in Burnand's *The Colonel* [1881], for finding "nourishment in contemplating a dew-drop on a rose leaf.")[57] "To give more beauty to beauty," Chatterton continues, "more grace to grace, more truth to truth, to deck the flowers of the field, to rain perfume on the rose, and music on the nightingale."[58] The excursus ends with a Wildean paradox: "There is nothing useful but poetry, and nothing real but the poet."[59]

Barrett's old-fashioned costume of black knee breeches and jacket also vividly call to mind Wallis's painting: a connection amplified through publicity stills replicating the painting's setting and pose exactly (Figure 8). Moreover, these photographs resemble Napoleon Sarony's studio portraits of Wilde donning aesthetic costume at the start of his exhaustive lecture tour of North America in January 1882. Since Wilde's tour was in part a venture that aimed to draw attention to the American production of Gilbert and Sullivan's *Patience* (1881), these photographs of Wilde similarly generated interest in this comic opera's leading

54. "Wilson Barrett as Chatterton," *The Era*, 7 June 1884: 11; originally printed in the *Winning Post*.

55. "Wilson Barrett as Chatterton," *The Era*, 31 May 1884: 10; originally printed in the *Sunday Times*.

56. Jones [and Herman], *Chatterton*, 28.

57. F. C. Burnand, *The Colonel*, ed. Pierre Marteau (2004; http://www.xix-e.pierre-mar teau.com/ed/colonel.html), n.p.

58. Jones [and Herman], *Chatterton*, 29.

59. Jones [and Herman], *Chatterton*, 29.

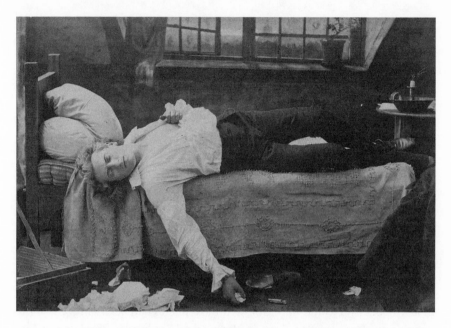

Figure 8. H. R. Barraud, Wilson Barrett as Chatterton in *Chatterton*, Princess's Theatre, 1884. Photograph, 10.2 × 14.8 cm. Guy Little Collection. © Victoria and Albert
Museum, London.

characters, especially the aesthetic poet Bunthorne and the faux-medieval costumes of the rival dragoons. But, unlike the aesthete Lambert Stryke in *The
Colonel*, Bunthorne in *Patience*, and Wilde on his American lecture tour, commentators had no reason to poke fun at Barrett's depiction of a medievalized
Chatterton; the young genius's position as a presiding spirit over English poetry
had become incontestable. Moreover, Barrett's adept delivery ensured that the
resonance between the poet's early demise at the end of the eighteenth century and burgeoning aesthetic philosophies of the late nineteenth century was
rendered sincerely, without the slightest irony or hint of satire. Notably, Wilde
took an eager interest in Barrett's performance. He acted as chairman at the
banquet held in Barrett's honor at the Criterion Restaurant on 12 August 1886;
this dinner celebrated Barrett and his theatrical company before they departed
for the United States.[60] It also took place three months before Wilde's lecture
on Chatterton at the Birkbeck Literary and Scientific Institute. The ongoing
success of Wilson's curtain-raiser continued for several years. In an 1889 letter

    60. See "The Banquet to Mr. Barrett," *The Era*, 14 August 1886: 13. Barrett's repertoire
during his tour of America included *Hamlet*, W. G. Wills and Herman's *Claudian* (1883),
and Barrett and Sydney Grundy's *Clito* (1886), as well as three curtain-raisers, Jones and

to the critic and poet Richard Le Gallienne, who at the time served as Barrett's literary secretary, Wilde regretted that he could not attend the matinee performance of *Chatterton* at the Princess's Theatre: "I admire both the play and the players extremely," he declared.[61]

MEMORIALIZING CHATTERTON: WILDE, CHATTERTON, AND THE CENTURY GUILD

A desire to commemorate the tragic life and death of Chatterton, regardless of its mechanism or motivation, formed the basis of a constellation of attachments that shaped Wilde's work in the late 1880s. The young Bristol poet served as a nexus of interest for a group of "ardent Chattertonians," including the young architect, designer, and poet Herbert P. Horne, with whom Wilde began sharing his enthusiasm.[62] Wilde's developing friendship with Horne is significant because this recent acquaintance belonged to the circle of accomplished artists and writers associated with the avant-garde Century Guild, whose name echoed the Guild of St. George: an educational charity that Ruskin founded in 1871 in order to promote preindustrial values of beauty and purity in the face of ugly capitalist modernity. The Century Guild, which believed it had a distinctly nineteenth-century responsibility for extending Ruskin's project, brought together a small group of three men—Arthur Heygate Mackmurdo, Selwyn Image, and Horne—whose creed was to honor the unity of the arts: "Credo in unam Artem, multipartitam, indivisibilem" ("I believe in one art, manifold, indivisible").[63] The Century Guild's aims were evident in their impressive, finely printed jour-

---

Herman's *Chatterton*, Brandon Thomas's *The Colour-Sergeant* (1885), and Jones's *A Clerical Error* (1879). See James Thomas, *The Art of the Actor-Manager: Wilson Barrett and the Victorian Theatre* (Ann Arbor: UMI Research Press, 1984), 91–97. Chatterton's life also attracted attention in regional theater; George Marsh's *Life and Death and Chatterton* opened at the Rotunda Theatre, Liverpool, on 21 July 1885 with Gertrude Norman in the leading role of Chatterton ([Anon.,] "New Pieces Produced at the Provincial Theatres, from December 1884, to End of November, 1885," *The Era Almanack and Annual* [1886]: 72). In 1887, the poet's life attracted attention in Continental Europe when the German author Heinrich Blau, a London resident who may have seen Jones and Herman's drama, published his own play in blank verse, *Thomas Chatterton: Tragödie in vier Akten* (London: Hirschfeld Bros., 1887).

61. Wilde, "To Richard Le Gallienne," 17 May 1889, in *The Complete Letters of Oscar Wilde*, ed. Merlin Holland and Rupert Hart-Davis (London: Fourth Estate, 2000), 399.

62. Wilde, "To Herbert P. Horne," 7 December 1886, in *Complete Letters*, 289.

63. Selwyn Image, "On the Unity of Art," *Century Guild Hobby Horse* 1, no. 5 (January 1887): 2. Wilde quoted this Latin creed when discussing Image's lecture at Willis's Rooms,

nal, initially named the *Century Guild Hobby Horse* (issued first in 1884, and then, after a two-year gap, continuously from 1886 to 1892) and later simply called *The Hobby Horse* (1893–1896).[64] "This was," as Ian Fletcher observes, "perhaps the most complete example of an English 'Total Art' periodical with its hand-made paper, specially designed initials, borders and typography, and programmatic content."[65]

To Charles Ricketts, Mackmurdo's venture took its inspiration from the Pre-Raphaelite publication *The Germ: Thoughts towards Nature in Poetry, Literature, and Art*, which appeared in four numbers in 1850.[66] (Dante Gabriel Rossetti's early prose and poetry were especially prominent in *The Germ*.) Ricketts was not alone in detecting that inspiration. In a notice of the forthcoming inaugural 1884 issue of the *Century Guild Hobby Horse*, a writer for the *Edinburgh Evening News* named the Century Guild "a patent imitation of the pre-Raphaelite Brotherhood, whose short-lived organ, 'The Germ,' was indeed a germ of great things."[67] After offering a sarcastic benediction—"May its hobby-horse, like the wooden steed of Troy, serve to introduce, within the ramparts of Philistinism, a new Rossetti, a new Burne-Jones, a new William Morris!"—this writer suggests that the journal will be short-lived. Even while acknowledging the Pre-Raphaelite influence on the Century Guild, this commentator also linked Mackmurdo's early efforts in advancing aestheticism, quipping that "for quaint humour" the new journal's prospectus "may almost be called unrivalled even in this age of Postlethwaitism."[68] Contemporary readers would instantly have recognized the name of Jellaby Postlethwaite, the consummate aesthetic poet of George Du Maurier's mocking *Punch* cartoons, whose mannerisms and physiognomy at times recalled Wilde's. Readers would likely also have understood the application of the term "mutual admiration society" to the Century

---

in late 1887: "The Unity of the Arts: A Lecture and a Five O'Clock," *Pall Mall Gazette*, 12 December 1887: 13; in *Journalism Part II*, ed. John Stokes and Mark W. Turner, *The Complete Works of Oscar Wilde*, 7 vols. to date (Oxford: Oxford University Press, 2000 and continuing), 7:33–34.

64. Mackmurdo launched the *Century Guild Hobby Horse* in 1884. The volume numbers of the journal date from its relaunch in 1886. There is some overlap in the contents of the initial issue from 1884 and the first volume of 1886.

65. Ian Fletcher, *Rediscovering Herbert Horne: Poet, Architect, Typographer, Historian* (Greensboro, NC: ELT Press, 1990), 1.

66. See Temple Scott, "Mr. Charles Ricketts and the Vale Press," *Bookselling* 2 (1896): 508.

67. [Anon.,] "Occasional Notes," *Edinburgh Evening News*, 20 March 1884: 2.

68. [Anon.,] "Occasional Notes," 2.

Guild; Du Maurier used this phrase to describe his group of regularly caricatured aesthetes in *Punch*.[69] Once published, the first number of the journal met
with a similar reaction. The *Liverpool Mercury* hardly minced words when it
scorned the "most ludicrously feeble yet foolishly pretentious exhibition of the
kind of literary affectation which is now associated with the idea of Mr. Ruskin's
later admirers."[70] While this particular reviewer refrains from overt aesthetic
descriptors, it remains clear that such calumny against "literary affectation" extends to Mackmurdo's journal the same kind of mockery that made Wilde a
figure of satirical fun in the late 1870s and early 1880s.

By 1886, when the magazine was relaunched under Herbert P. Horne's direction, the link with the aesthetic movement—and therefore with Wilde—came
more explicitly into view. Although Wilde's contribution to the journal would
not appear until the third issue in July of that year, and despite the fact that he
was not a member of the Century Guild and played no part in the development
of this publication, one writer surmised that the periodical was "fearfully and
wonderfully aesthetic," and that all aspects of its production "suggest[ed] Mr.
Oscar Wilde and the school of which he aspire[d] to be chief."[71] To portray
Wilde in 1886 as an aspiring leader of "Postlethwaitism," of course, was misguided. Moreover, the Century Guild's aesthetic philosophy had little in common with the aestheticism that Du Maurier derided in *Punch*.

With Horne at the editorial helm, the *Century Guild Hobby Horse*'s emphasis on celebrating the interconnections between the most revered forms of
art, as well as handicrafts and furnishings, became even more prominent in its
expanded number of pages.[72] To begin with, the contributions by Image, Mackmurdo, and Horne give a good sense of the Century Guild's cultural and intellectual orientation, which frequently considered great art's intricate relations
with spirituality, politics, and tradition. Image, a radical Anglican, focused his
discussion of the growing presence of nude figures in modern art on the tension

69. [Anon.,] "Occasional Notes," 2. The *Edinburgh Evening News* critic opens his notice with this cutting remark: "A mutual admiration society, known, or rather unknown,
as 'The Century Guild,' proposes to publish a periodical. . . ." The *Pall Mall Gazette*
previews the *Hobby Horse* by describing the Century Guild as a "small but fervent set of
mutual admirers." The notice also explicitly links the group's efforts with Ruskin's work;
it concludes that "the 'Hobby Horse' is to be turned out of Mr. Ruskin's own particular
stable" ([Anon.,] "Literary Notes," *Pall Mall Gazette*, 6 March 1884: 6).

70. [Anon.,] "Art Notes," *Liverpool Mercury*, 3 June 1884: 5f.

71. [Anon.,] "January Magazines," *Leeds Mercury*, 30 December 1884: 6c.

72. Aymer Vallance, "Mr. Arthur H. Mackmurdo and the Century Guild," *Studio* 16,
no. 73 (April 1899): 183–92.

between aesthetics and religion: where "Art," he says, demands that we "cultivate the joyous and exuberant life of the senses," the New Testament states "*Qui sunt Christi carnem suam crucifixerunt*" ("those who are Christ's have crucified the flesh"); these "two doctrines," he contends, "remain irreconcilable."[73] Meanwhile, Mackmurdo reminded readers of the exquisite examples of early Florentine art that belong to the National Gallery, London. Particularly impressive for Mackmurdo is Giotto, whose thoughtful works served as "a powerful instrument in counselling rulers and a safe agent in teaching the people the limit and power of political government."[74] Horne, by the far the most prolific contributor, offered finely crafted lyrics, such as "A—Further—Meditation for His Mistress," which combines an 1880s trend for reviving the idioms of seventeenth-century lyric (especially those of Robert Herrick) with the refrains that Dante Gabriel Rossetti favored in some of his "Art-Catholic" poems: "You are the treasury that God / (O blessed Lord!) / Made of gold light and ivory dew."[75]

Elsewhere in this 1886 volume, Horne commented at length on seventeenth-century architect and painter Inigo Jones's commitment to the highest principles of art: "His was too true a sense of what Art is to allow him to imagine that even in the depths of Nature alone, much less in her more superficial appearances, as so many of our painters, sculptors, and even poets, seem to think, would he find the Alpha and Omega of Art."[76] (Such sentiments find an extreme echo in Wilde's "Decay of Lying" [1889, revised 1891], where his spokesman, Vivian, declares: "The more we study Art, the less we care for Nature.")[77] Horne, too, shared his passion for architectural history in a short piece

73. Selwyn Image, "On the Representation of the Nude," *Century Guild Hobby Horse* 1, no. 1 (January 1886): 12.

74. Arthur H. Mackmurdo, "Notes on the National Gallery: Giotto" *Century Guild Hobby Horse* 1, no. 1 (January 1886): 39.

75. Herbert Horne, "A—Further—Meditation for His Mistress," *Century Guild Hobby Horse* 1, no. 2 (April 1886): 47. Herrick was one of Horne's poetic models; see Robert Herrick, *Hesperides*, ed. Horne (London: Walter Scott, 1887). On the Victorian poetic revival of Herrick's works, see Rebecca N. Mitchell, "Robert Herrick, Victorian Poet: Christina Rossetti, George Meredith, and the Victorian Recovery of *Hesperides*," *Modern Philology* 113, no. 1 (August 2015).

76. Herbert Horne, "A Study of Certain Buildings Designed by Inigo Jones and yet Remaining in London," *Century Guild Hobby Horse* 1, no. 4 (October 1886): 137.

77. Wilde, "The Decay of Lying," in Wilde, *Criticism: Historical Criticism, Intentions, The Soul of Man*, ed. Josephine M. Guy, *Complete Works of Oscar Wilde*, 7 vols. to date (Oxford: Oxford University Press, 2000 and continuing), 4:73. Horne records Wilde visiting his home while he was at work on the Jones article: "In the evening while I was work-

on the modern improvements at the original site of Charterhouse, the distinguished private school established in 1611 at Smithfield, East London. As Horne observes, Charterhouse, which was built on the site of a Carthusian monastery, is where many great writers—Addison, Crashaw, Steele, and Thackeray—had been educated. At the vanguard of those who wished to preserve historic buildings, Horne looked with horror on the modern "practical age" whose newfangled "offices and warehouses" threatened to "sweep away much and mar the rest of this builded record of Saints and Poets."[78] Read alongside one another, the writings of these founding members of the Century Guild reveal that they had taken upon themselves the task of both venerating and sustaining England's national cultural heritage, whether in painting, poetry, or architecture.

In the Century Guild's company, several much more established figures voiced comparable opinions on English art and artists in the *Hobby Horse*. William Michael Rossetti, Dante Gabriel Rossetti's brother and the leading critical advocate of Pre-Raphaelitism, contributed an assessment of his close associate, the painter Ford Madox Brown: "Mr. Brown," he declares, "bears an obvious resemblance to our Elizabethan playwrights, with Shakespear as the sun in their solar system; from this point of view, his art might be called Elizabethan art, and as such essentially English."[79] At the same time, however, William Michael Rossetti stresses Brown's equally prominent modernity, since he finds a "touch of the Carlylean in Mr. Brown's interpretation of history."[80] Frederic Shields, whose own art bore the influence of Dante Gabriel Rossetti, Brown, and Blake, writes enthusiastically about the posthumous exhibition of Dante Gabriel Rossetti's works, which had taken place at the Royal Academy in 1883; this event showcased "the great sun whose glory the Art world had heretofore only partially inferred from transient gleams."[81] Seldom, as Shields acknowledges, had the public previously had access to Dante Gabriel Rossetti's exqui-

---

ing on the I. Jones article O. Wilde looked in and had a talk. I afterwards went round with him to his house and smoked cigarettes. He gave me an autotype of Burne Jones." Diary entry 5 July 1886 (Museo Horne, Inv.2600/29; segn. H.VII.4), quoted in Edward Chaney and Jane Hall, "Herbert Horne's 1889 Diary of His First Visit to Italy," *The Volume of the Walpole Society* 64 (2002): 81, n. 34.

78. Herbert Horne, "Nescio quæ nugarum, No. I: At the Charterhouse," *Century Guild Hobby Horse* 1, no. 2 (April 1886): 78.

79. W. M. Rossetti, "Ford Madox Brown: Characteristics," *Century Guild Hobby Horse* 1, no. 2 (April 1886): 50.

80. Rossetti, "Ford Madox Brown," 52.

81. Frederic Shields, "Some Notes on Dante Gabriel Rossetti," *Century Guild Hobby Horse* 1, no. 4 (October 1886): 140.

sitely executed oils and watercolors. Especially important to Shields is Dante Gabriel Rossetti's admiration for other artists, notably Blake, whose workroom Rossetti memorialized in a fine sonnet that Shields reprints in this article. Not surprisingly, Blake's reputation, which both Dante Gabriel Rossetti and Swinburne did much to recover in the 1860s, looms large in these pages. Herbert H. Gilchrist, the son of Blake's most significant nineteenth-century biographers, contributed a short note on Blake's ballad, "Little Tom the Sailor," which also reappears in the journal in a facsimile of Blake's original broadsheet—with its striking script and etchings—that was first published in 1800.

Besides these contents, there are advertisements for the furnishings, wallpapers, silks, cretonnes, picture frames, wrought iron, and chased brass and copper work that were available through the guild's designers and manufacturers. These particular commodities marked a decisive movement in English art and design. Historians acknowledge that one of the lasting influences of the Century Guild was to foster the development of the Arts and Crafts movement. In 1888, Wilde took great interest in this movement when it held its first exhibition at the New Gallery, Regent Street, London. Such was his attentiveness to this celebration of the united arts that he reviewed in the *Pall Mall Gazette* all five of the lectures that accompanied the Arts and Crafts exhibition.[82]

In 1886, though, Wilde's burgeoning connections to the Century Guild circle were evidenced in his first contribution to the guild's journal: a short article entitled "Keats' Sonnet on Blue," which discusses the composition of the sonnet, appeared in the third (July) number of the 1886 *Century Guild Hobby Horse*, alongside a reproduction of a manuscript of the sonnet that an American relative of Keats had given to Wilde after she met the young lecturer during his 1882 tour of the United States. The article drew positive notices, with one newspaper suggesting that it "should be read by all students" of Keats.[83] Prior to this work, Wilde's most impressive publication to date was arguably his long essay "Shakespeare and Stage Costume" (1885), in the *Nineteenth Century*. It seems that Wilde intended to continue his work on the Romantics for the *Hobby*

---

82. Wilde, "Mr. Morris on Tapestry," *Pall Mall Gazette*, 2 November 1888: 6; "Sculpture at the 'Arts and Crafts,'" *Pall Mall Gazette*, 9 November 1888: 3; "Printing and Printers: Lecture at the Arts and Crafts," *Pall Mall Gazette*, 16 November 1888: 5; "The Beauties of Bookbinding: Mr. Cobden-Sanderson at the Arts and Crafts," *Pall Mall Gazette*, 23 November 1888: 3; and "The Close of the 'Arts and Crafts': Mr. Walter Crane's Lecture on Design," *Pall Mall Gazette*, 30 November 1888: 3; reprinted in *Journalism Part II*, ed. Stokes and Turner, 7:96–99, 103–8.

83. [Anon.,] "Literary, Music, and Drama," *Sheffield and Rotherham Independent*, 24 July 1886: 3.

Horse by publishing an essay on Chatterton in the first volume.[84] In the October issue a note appended to the table of contents regretted that "Mr. Oscar Wilde's article on Chatterton has been unavoidably postponed until the January number."[85] The genesis of the article is murky: the note was a late addition, inserted after the page proofs had been prepared, and we have not been able to locate any record that suggests that the journal had, at an earlier point, advertised the news that Wilde's discussion of Chatterton was forthcoming. As it turned out, the essay never appeared, and no mention was made of an essay on Chatterton in the January issue. The reasons why it did not materialize remain puzzling, because in 1886 Wilde had done much in the name of honoring Chatterton besides delivering a lecture and compiling plentiful notes and reflections in his notebook on the young Bristol poet's career.

Wilde's correspondence reveals that he had recently expressed to Horne his "ardent enthusiasm" to devise a "scheme for a Chatterton memorial" at the Pile Street School in Bristol, where the poet was born.[86] In August 1886, when Horne had dined with him at his family home, Wilde had succeeded in persuading this young acquaintance to collaborate on this scheme. Horne, it seems, had drafted a letter, presumably to attract subscribers who wished to support the renovation of the school building where Chatterton was raised. Horne's proposal, however, expressed even more ambition than Wilde had in mind, a point that becomes clear in Wilde's gentle admonition: "The more I think of that little grey building the more I feel we should proceed cautiously."[87] "Perhaps after all," he continues, "cleaning, repairing, and a tablet would be enough."[88] In his letter, Wilde fears it would be unwise to give the impression that they planned to remodel the whole building: "We must not," he says wryly, "have William Morris down upon us to begin with."[89] The very thought that

84. It is worth observing that the *Century Guild Hobby Horse* published a review of Lady Jane Wilde's *Ancient Legends of Ireland* (1887).

85. [Anon.,] "Contents of No. IV," *Century Guild Hobby Horse* 1, no. 4 (October 1886): 122. This notice of the delay in publishing Wilde's essay on Chatterton was added in handwriting at the last minute to the proofs of the third issue of the first volume in October 1886. We are grateful to the Department of Special Collections, Ohio State University, which owns the proofs, for this information. SPEC.RARE.CMS.59.

86. Wilde, "To Herbert P. Horne," 13 December 1886, in *Complete Letters*, 290.

87. Wilde, "To Herbert P. Horne," 16 August 1886, in *Complete Letters*, 284.

88. Wilde, 16 August 1886, in *Complete Letters*, 284.

89. Wilde, 16 August 1886, in *Complete Letters*, 284. It is worth noting that Mackmurdo had expressed some hostility to Morris's social activism, especially his involvement in the Socialist Democratic Federation, in the first 1884 number of the *Century Guild Hobby*

this venture might involve designers such as Morris, who cofounded the Society for the Protection of Ancient Buildings in 1877, encouraged Wilde to remark the following week: "We must not spoil by new gauds the ancient spirit of the place."[90] In principle, he wished to restore the birthplace that Mrs. S. C. Hall, in her *Pilgrimages to English Shrines* (1850), counted among modern national tourist sites, even though to her mind it seemed that "if he had lived through a long age of prosperity, Chatterton could never have been trusted or esteemed, *from his total want of truth*."[91] "Of course the whole place," Wilde commented to Horne of the school building, "should be a Chatterton museum."[92]

Two weeks after he spoke at the Birkbeck Literary and Scientific Institution, Wilde's plans for the museum at Pile Street were falling more fully into shape. "Of course we will have the tablet," he assured Horne. "Do you think we should have a bas-relief of T.C.?"[93] In the same correspondence, he suggests a "simple inscription" that concludes: "One of England's greatest poets and sometime pupil at this school."[94] Later that month, Wilde's correspondence reveals that he and Horne had visited the Pile Street School together. Yet, at the same time, it appears that Horne's interest was waning, perhaps because this designer and poet in his early twenties did not respond kindly to Wilde's suggestion that Horne had "overstep[ped] . . . the limits of right judgement."[95] In order to rekindle Horne's enthusiasm, Wilde adds that he planned to hold a "small meeting" with Mackmurdo, and he said to Horne that his absence "would be the absence of one of Chatterton's best lovers."[96] In his letter, Wilde also remarks that he has recruited Theodore Watts, whose 1880 essay on Chatterton had inspired him. Another guest, Wilde suggests, might be the radical preacher and literary critic Stopford Brooke, who had for several years served as a Unitarian minister at Clifton (close to Chatterton's hometown); like Wilde, Brooke had recently

---

Horse; although he praised Morris for "rais[ing] the tone and character of industrial art to the high rank it attains in this country," he disliked Morris's socialist politics for "advocating what we believe to be dangerously narrow-sighted remedies to existent evils" (Arthur H. Mackmurdo, "The Guild Flag's Unfurling," *Century Guild Hobby Horse,* no. 1 [1884]: 11).

90. Wilde, "To Herbert P. Horne," 23 August 1886, in *Complete Letters,* 285.

91. Mrs. S. C. Hall, *Pilgrimages to English Shrines* (London: Arthur, Hall, Virtue, 1850), 109. Emphasis in the original.

92. Wilde, 23 August 1886, in *Complete Letters,* 285.

93. Wilde, 7 December 1886, in *Complete Letters,* 289.

94. Wilde, 7 December 1886, in *Complete Letters,* 289.

95. Wilde, "To Herbert P. Horne," 13 December 1886, in *Complete Letters,* 290.

96. Wilde, 13 December 1886, in *Complete Letters,* 290.

attended the Shelley Society's production of the verse drama *Hellas* (1822) at St. James's Hall, London.[97]

The scheme clearly appealed to the Century Guild, which had already sponsored similar plans for a memorial to the poets of the Lake District, taking over a scheme that the Wordsworth Society had originally proposed. In January 1887, when it announced that project in the *Hobby Horse*, the Guild noted parenthetically that it was currently "aiding a Chatterton Memorial, at Bristol"—this would be the only mention of Chatterton in the January number.[98] Almost a year later, when Wilson Barrett performed the lead in Jones and Herman's *Chatterton* in Bristol, the actor made an appeal to his audience in which he said that special encouragement should be given to pupils at the Pile Street School who displayed aptitude in literature and the arts. Barrett's call to honor Chatterton's birthplace prompted the *Bristol Mercury* to comment on the recent flurry of activity by various well-known figures, including Wilde, as the famous actor urged the city authorities to set about creating a museum. The *Mercury* indicated that the Century Guild's plans were still under way, and the newspaper suggested revisions of its own to Barrett's scheme:

> Last year Dr. Garnett, of the British Museum; Mr. Oscar Wilde, and other members of the Century Guild of Art in London, corresponded with a well-known citizen on the subject, offering to repair and decorate the building and plant the ground in front. Photographs and sketches of the premises have been prepared for the purpose, and Mr. Havard Thomas, a Bristol sculptor, has promised a marble medallion. There being a complete set of graded schools in the parish, it is not thought that Mr. Wilson Barrett's educational suggestion is feasible in connexion with the Pyle street school, but his object might be gained by founding a Chatterton scholarship for Redcliff boys at the Bristol Grammar School, or offering local prizes for composition in poetry or prose. In such a movement hearty cooperation would no doubt be given by Mr. J. T. Francombe, headmaster of Redcliff Endowed Schools, and formerly of the Pyle street school. Chatterton literature now forms a fairly large collection, and our enthusiastic bibliophile, Mr. William George—whose exertions

97. Thomas J. Wise, "The Performance of Hellas," *Note-Book of the Shelley Society* (London: Reeves and Turner, 1888), 134. Brooke also delivered a lecture at the inaugural meeting of the Shelley Society, 10 March 1886 (see 1–7).

98. [Anon.,] "The Memorial to the Men of Letters of the Lake District," *Century Guild Hobby Horse* 1, no. 5 (January 1887): 42. On 25 November 1886, the *Daily News* reported that a meeting to discuss such a memorial to the Lake Poets had taken place the previous day at Burlington House ([Anon.,] Untitled, *Daily News* [London], 25 November 1886: 6).

in this particular cause are beyond all praise—possesses the most complete library on the subject, including the Chatterton family bible, discovered a few years ago, which contains the original entries up to the birth of the poet.[99]

The *Mercury* added that each year as many as one hundred visitors made the literary pilgrimage to the school on Pile Street in the name of Chatterton's memory. It noted, too, that serious protests had met proposals to demolish and rebuild the premises.

Such information shows that Wilde and his friends at the Century Guild, as well as the star of the one-act *Chatterton*, sought to pay much greater tribute to the poet than the existing monument, which had emerged after many years of fraught discussion between supporters of the project and the church authorities. As early as 1780, John Flaxman had exhibited at the Royal Academy a design for a memorial to Chatterton to be installed at St. Mary Redcliffe. Yet this project was never realized in stone. In 1784, the *Lady's Magazine* discussed a design for a cenotaph in Chatterton's honor, since the poet's remains had been laid to rest in a pauper's burying ground at Shoe Lane, London.[100] Almost forty years later, Wordsworth expressed his readiness to "assist, according to [his] means, in erecting a Monument to the memory of Chatterton, who with transcendent genius was cut off by his own hand while he was yet a Boy in years."[101] But these plans, too, were frustrated. In 1829, Joseph Cottle recorded that the dean of Bristol, believing that the young poet was nothing more than a sinner, had stated categorically that the "circumstance of Chatterton's *death* would operate as an effectual bar to any such monument being placed in the *Cathedral*."[102]

99. "Chatterton Memorials," *Bristol Mercury*, 4 November 1887: 3. Richard Garnett was Assistant Keeper of Printed Books at the British Museum. Several sources refer to Pile Street with the alternative spelling, Pyle Street. James Havard Thomas, who trained at the Bristol School of Art, eventually became professor of sculpture at the Slade School of Fine Art, University College London, in February 1915. Thomas, notably, attended the opening of Shelley's *Hellas* (*Note-Book of the Shelley Society*, 134). The journalist in the *Bristol Mercury* is also referring to the recent debate about the volume on the history of the Bible that the Chatterton family owned (see our discussion on 32–33).

100. Pressly, *The Artist as Original Genius*, 168.

101. Wordsworth, "To J. Forbes Mitchell," 21 April 1819, in *The Letters of Dorothy and William Wordsworth*, edited and arranged by Ernest de Selincourt, 2nd ed., ed. Mary Moorman and Alan G. Hill, 8 vols. (Oxford: Clarendon Press, 1967–1993), 3:535. Wordsworth's editors note that Mitchell was already the treasurer of the fund for erecting a monument to Robert Burns.

102. Cottle, *Malvern Hills, with Minor Poems and Essays*, 4th ed., 2 vols. (London: T. Cadell, 1829), 1:168. On this page, Cottle, who owned several of Chatterton's manuscripts,

Eventually, in 1839, the foundation stone for a cenotaph in Chatterton's honor, based on local architect S. C. Fripp's design, was laid next to the north porch of the Church of St. Mary Redcliffe. Completed in April 1840, this towering memorial, which was more than thirty feet high, placed a statue of Chatterton as a schoolboy, with one hand placed on his chest, atop a series of Gothic pillars and arches (Figure 9).[103] The vicar, who appears to have sensed that this memorial stood in honor of an unbeliever, stipulated that the most prominent panel facing St. Mary Redcliffe should contain the following admonitory lines from Edward Young's *Night Thoughts* (1742–1745): "Know all; know infidels: unapt to know; / 'Tis immortality your nature solves."[104] Supporters of the monument had wished instead to include Chatterton's apostrophe from his "Last Will and Testament": "Reader—Judge not: if thou art a Christian, believe that he shall be Judged by a Superior Power; to that Power only is he now answerable— ."[105] But the authorities would not budge, most likely because Chatterton's firmly worded lines came from a scandalous document threatening self-murder.

Like many matters associated with Chatterton's name, the controversy surrounding the 1840 cenotaph did not die down. Six years later, M. R. Whish, the vicar of the church, contended that the structure had been erected, without his permission, on consecrated ground, and he duly ordered it to be taken down and stored in the crypt. Just more than a decade after it had been removed, members of the parish raised funds to restore the monument, this time on an unhallowed area near the church, close to Chatterton's birthplace in Pile

---

prints his "Epitaph for a Proposed Monument to Chatterton, at Bristol." In 1837, Dix commented that "prejudice has paralyzed the several efforts which have been made to erect some tribute to [Chatterton's] genius" (John Ross Dix, *The Life of Thomas Chatterton, Including His Unpublished Poems and Correspondence* [London: Hamilton, Adams, 1837], 294).

103. "Chatterton Memorials," 3.

104. The lines should read: "Know all; Know Infidels,—unapt to Know! / 'Tis Immortality your Nature solves" ("Night VII," in *Night Thoughts*, ed. Stephen Cornford [Cambridge: Cambridge University Press, 1989], 191). Wilson draws attention to this inscription in *Chatterton: A Biographical Study* (London: Macmillan, 1869), 323.

105. "[Will]," in *Complete Works of Thomas Chatterton*, ed. Taylor and Hoover, 1:503. Wilson comments on this request from Chatterton's supporters (*Chatterton: A Biographical Study*, 324). The inscription from Chatterton's "Last Will and Testament" was finally entered on the monument. In 1865, Frederick Martin observed: "Close to the church of St. Mary Redcliffe the poet stands, in the dress of Colston's charity school, with a roll of parchment in hand, and the inscription underneath" ("Memoir," in *Poems of Thomas Chatterton* [London: Charles Griffin, 1865], xlvi).

Figure 9. F. W. Fairholt, illustration of the Chatterton cenotaph,
Bristol, from Mrs. S. C. Hall's *Pilgrimages to English Shrines* (London:
Arthur Hall, Virtue, 1850), p. 124. Image courtesy of William Andrews
Clark Memorial Library, University of California, Los Angeles.

Street. In 1869, Wilson observed that, even though the monument had stood on the different site for more than twenty years, "no inscription ha[d] been placed on it," and he hoped that the installation of a new vicar might mean that "better taste will be allowed to prevail in refilling the panels."[106] Meanwhile, little care had been taken to preserve the dwelling where Chatterton was an infant. By the time Wilde and members of the Century Guild were working to restore the original charm of the "little grey building," the only markers that showed that the modest structure was the poet's birthplace were a "rustic oak-framed pen-and-ink copy of Chatterton's portrait as a child," which hung in the sitting room, and a "heavy mahogany-framed portrait of the late Dante Gabriel Rossetti," which decorated the bedroom.[107] Rossetti, as the *Mercury* noted, was "a warm admirer of Chatterton," but it protested that the presence of the portrait of Rossetti was an intolerable anachronism. Even in the 1880s, the portrait of Chatterton as a child was known to be inaccurate.[108]

No further record suggests Wilde's meeting to raise funds for the museum ever took place. Nor is there information that shows that Wilde or other members of the Century Guild pursued transforming the Chatterton birthplace any further in 1887. Possibly, Wilde discovered that the city authorities responded unfavorably to his scheme. In a much longer historical view, his efforts to create this kind of memorial to Chatterton's memory marked the pinnacle of the immense biographical research, editorial labor, and cultural activity that made the Bristol poet appear greater in literary stature than ever before. But the collapse of the museum did not mean that Wilde lost interest in the "marvellous Boy." The last lecture Wilde ever delivered, on 7 April 1888, at the Shaftesbury Hall, Bournemouth, was titled "Thomas Chatterton: The Boy-Poet of the Eighteenth

106. Wilson, *Chatterton: A Biographical Study*, 324.

107. "Chatterton Memorials," 3.

108. "Chatterton Memorials," 3. The only possible candidate for a true likeness of Chatterton is a painting by Una Taylor. Theater critic William Archer commented in an article about Robert Louis Stevenson's family home, "Skerryvore," at Bournemouth that among the artworks that hung in the drawing room was "a copy by Miss Una Taylor (a daughter of Sir Henry) of what purports to be an authentic portrait of Chatterton" (*Critic*, 5 November 1887: 226). Taylor (1857–1922) was a novelist and artist. There is no record that this painting has survived. In her memoirs, Taylor records the "ties of close affection that sprang to life between Skerryvore" and her parents' home at the Villa, Bournemouth (*Guests and Memories: Annals of a Seaside Villa* [London: Humphrey Milford and Oxford University Press, 1924], 362). See our discussion on 187–88 for Dante Gabriel Rossetti's views on the inauthenticity of what appears to be the same portrait.

Century."[109] Even though the group of writers and artists (some of them linked with the Century Guild) who promoted the idea might not have succeeded in securing a museum that honored Chatterton at Bristol, Wilde had already sought to secure the poet's legacy in a different way: by positioning the "marvellous Boy," through creative and critical means, not merely as an icon of the Romantics but also as their major poetic ancestor. It is to Wilde's interest in the canonization of Chatterton within the literary history of Romanticism that we turn in the next chapter.

109. Wilde was in contact with members of the Richards family about the lectures he delivered at Bournemouth, where they organized a series of weekly entertainments at Shaftesbury Hall. On 19 March 1888, he addressed a brief letter to "Miss Richards," informing her that he would lecture on Thomas Chatterton (*Complete Letters*, 344). He was also in touch with S. Wall Richards, at the same Bournemouth address, on 16 June 1887 and 16 March 1888 (Clark Wilde MS Box 74 Folder 8). Under the Richards's auspices, Wilde had given a lecture titled "Dress" at Bournemouth on 28 January 1887, and stayed with them at their boarding house, The Grange, on West Cliff Gardens. Wilde appears to have had the intention of delivering a lecture on Irish art at Toynbee Hall, London, in late 1889, although there is no record of this event having taken place (see "To Henrietta Barnett," November 1889, in *Complete Letters*, 415).

3

WILDE'S DISCOVERY OF CHATTERTON: THE "FATHER OF THE ROMANTIC MOVEMENT"

At the time he delivered his lecture on Chatterton, Oscar Wilde's career was transforming. He was transitioning from the performances he had honed during four solid years of addressing countless audiences and was developing, with greater energy than ever before, his profile as an accomplished author, critic, and editor. His discovery of Chatterton stands at the center of these changes. Paying close attention to Chatterton enabled Wilde to understand that the astonishing inventiveness of the Rowley forgeries evinced the creative impulse that inspired the finest forms of imaginative literature. Exploiting the links between imagination, authenticity, and truth, Chatterton's artistic originality arose in fabrications that conjured a literary past that historically never existed. Such fakes, Wilde knew from his reading about Chatterton, might strike some interpreters as the result of ungovernable, if not immoral, motivations. In the critical essays and shorter fiction that Wilde wrote from the mid-1880s onward, he radically inverted such interpretations. Throughout these essays, shorter fiction, and dramas, generous artistic license, lying, and even criminal intent become—as we explain in later chapters—the foundation for great art.

Understanding Chatterton's artistry not only informed Wilde's creative work; it also shaped his knowledge of the Romantic poets, whose works he had long admired. If Wilde's interest in Keats and Shelley stemmed from his university days, through Chatterton he grasped the mechanisms with which their verse made its impact. This deepening comprehension enriched Wilde's aesthetic philosophy. No longer would he merely mimic Keats and Shelley, as his attention turned increasingly to the stakes of the creative process. Through studying Chatterton, he saw that the category of "the Romantic" had a constructed and a contested history, one that involved an imaginative conjuring of the past.

Wilde's newfound interest in Chatterton was a natural extension of his long-standing fascination with the writings of Keats and Shelley; but Chatterton was also connected to several writers and artists—past and present—with whose tradition Wilde wished to be affiliated. Chatterton revered, and in some ways modeled his work on, Scottish poet James Macpherson's *Works of Ossian* (1765), a collection that Macpherson claimed were his prose translations of orally transmitted poems of the Highlands and the Hebrides. Like Chatterton's Rowley poems, Macpherson's *Ossian* not only inspired subsequent generations of poets—Wilde's parents chose his names from Macpherson's narratives—but it also stood at the heart of arguments about their supposed authenticity. Despite the questions of authenticity and forgery that their writings raised, these great forerunners' influence remained for Wilde unimpeachable. In his view, just as Chatterton drew from Macpherson, Keats drew from Chatterton. This was a point articulated by the Pre-Raphaelite poet and painter Dante Gabriel Rossetti and Rossetti's exceptionally close friend Theodore Watts (better known, when he won fame through his novel about Gypsy life, *Aylwin* [1898], as Theodore Watts-Dunton). Wilde's bold declaration in the notebook that Chatterton was "the father of the Romantic movement" (f.5^r [338]) originated in Watts's outstanding contribution to Thomas Humphry Ward's noteworthy 1880 anthology, *The English Poets*. Watts's essay, which stands alongside contributions from Matthew Arnold, Walter Pater, and Algernon Charles Swinburne, counts among the earliest documents in English literary criticism to locate Chatterton as the "father of a New Romantic School."[1] This claim, which strikes Daniel Cook as a "historical absurdity," may look remarkably skewed from our modern perspective, regardless of the impact Chatterton's legacy exerted on Coleridge, Keats, Shelley, and Southey.[2] As Nick Groom observes, had Chatterton survived Shelley's death by several months in 1822, he would have qualified—at the grand old age of seventy—as anything but the "marvellous boy."[3] Only a premature death permitted Chatterton to become for the Victorians both the first and the youngest Romantic poet. But the claim that Chatterton fathered English Romantic poetry was an implicitly politicized one by the time Wilde started compiling his notebook. The very idea that Chatterton was the founder of a new literary movement in England formed part of a particular type of period-oriented literary

1. Theodore Watts, "Thomas Chatterton," in Thomas Humphry Ward, ed., *The English Poets: Selections with Critical Introductions by Various Writers, and a General Introduction by Matthew Arnold*, 4 vols. (London: Macmillan, 1880), 3:401. *The English Poets* was reprinted and expanded through the 1920s.

2. Daniel Cook, *Thomas Chatterton and Neglected Genius, 1760–1830* (Basingstoke: Palgrave Macmillan, 2013), 202.

3. See Nick Groom, "Introduction," in *Thomas Chatterton and Romantic Culture*, ed. Groom (Basingstoke: Macmillan, 1999), 9.

history that not only developed during the early stages of Wilde's career but also affected Wilde's sense of his place as an heir to the Romantic cultural tradition.

WILDE, CHATTERTON, AND "THE SPIRIT OF MODERN ROMANCE"

The adjective "Romantic," itself hardly a transparent term, had of course been a staple of European literary criticism for the larger part of the nineteenth century, and it is instructive to consider how its development in Britain eventually identified Chatterton as one of the earliest poets who should be associated with the term. Friedrich Schlegel's *Dialogue on Poetry* (1799–1800) broadly summoned a tradition discernible in "Shakespeare, Cervantes, in Italian poetry, in that age of knights, love, and fairytales in which the thing itself and the word for it originated."[4] Later, English critics most often placed the Romantic in opposition to the classical: an approach that enjoyed wide circulation in Germany before it became fully intelligible in the English-speaking world. Probably the earliest English source that explores this distinction is Coleridge's series of lectures on literature, which date from 1809, although an English translation of Madame de Staël's *De l'Allemagne* (1813) appears to have popularized the epithet as a clearly apprehensible concept.[5] By the 1830s, the opposition between the Romantic and the classical was well established. The school of Wordsworth, according to the *European Magazine and London Review* (1822), disdained the "critical" rules of poets like Pope and promoted instead a poetry written "as the *spirit moveth*."[6] In his 1837 essay, "The American Scholar," Emerson—whose works Wilde knew well and whom Wilde would cite in his "Chatterton" notebook—developed a model of cultural succession in which "Romantic" came between the older "Classic" and the modern "Reflective."[7] And by 1852, in his theoretical treatise on poetics, E. S. Dallas could readily assume that "every one must be

4. Friedrich Schlegel, *Dialogue on Poetry and Literary Aphorisms*, trans. Ernst Behler and Roman Struc (University Park: Pennsylvania State University Press, 1968), 101.

5. René Wellek first made this point in "The Concept of 'Romanticism' in Literary History," *Comparative Literature* 1, no. 1 (1949): 8–9. These sources have been discussed at length by other scholars, including George Whalley, "England: Romantic—Romanticism," in Hans Eichner, ed., *"Romantic" and Its Cognates: The European History of a Word* (Toronto: University of Toronto Press, 1972), 157–262.

6. ["M.M.D.,"] "On the Genius of Spenser, and the Spenserian School of Poetry," *European Magazine and London Review* 82 (1822): 436. Emphasis in the original.

7. Ralph Waldo Emerson, "The American Scholar," in *Nature, Addresses, and Lectures*, ed. Robert E. Spiller and Alfred R. Ferguson, *The Collected Works of Ralph Waldo Emerson*, 10 vols. (Cambridge, MA: Belknap Press of Harvard University Press, 1971–2013), 1:66.

more or less acquainted with that distinction between romantic and classical poesy."[8] The coupling of the two terms had therefore become commonplace during the midcentury, and for the most part critics used them in a largely neutral, descriptive manner.

The "Romantic" did not simply signify an opposition to the "classical," however. Commentators also applied the idea of the Romantic to authors whose writings appealed to archaic forms or oral traditions, especially those of long-lost Northern European cultures, as when in 1839 the *Athenæum* noted: "What has been called the Romantic school, revived by Ossian, Percy &c., being essentially northern in its spirit, genial to our clime, kin to our very elements, must extinguish the Classic."[9] Noticeably, in this commentary the Romantic revival owes much to the works of two antiquarians, Macpherson and Thomas Percy. Percy's *Reliques of English Poetry* (1765) presented to the public a vast canon of largely forgotten ancient verse—mostly comprising variants of ballads such as "Chevy Chase"—and subsequently enjoyed great influence on Coleridge and Wordsworth's *Lyrical Ballads.* The transformation of English poetry inspired by *Reliques* proved hard to ignore. Vicesimus Knox observed in 1782 that the "popular ballad," once deemed to have been the work of some "illiterate minstrel," had been "rescued from the hands of the vulgar" and placed in the library "of the man of taste."[10]

Chatterton counted among the earliest writers to respond enthusiastically to Percy's energetic antiquarianism, which—as Groom shrewdly puts it—collected "exhibits in the cultural museum of Englishness and choice examples of the Gothic temperament," in ways that helped to "defuse the explosive revolutionary politics of ballads" that were (to use the words of one 1760s commentator) "sung in the streets by the vulgar."[11] In addition, then, to resuscitating and valuing forgotten verse, Percy's collection challenged ossified assumptions about class and taste, or even class and genre; as Knox noted, no longer was the ballad unpalatable to the "man of taste." A stable notion (however outmoded or inaccurate) of English nationalism also emerged in Percy's ballads, a sentiment that appeared to transcend class lines. As Chatterton's modern editors have shown,

8. E. S. Dallas, *Poetics: An Essay on Poetry* (London: Smith, Elder, 1852), 84.

9. [Anon.,] "The Regeneration of Our National Poetry," *Athenæum* 627 (2 November 1839): 825.

10. Vicesimus Knox, "On the Prevailing Taste for the Old Poets," in *Essays Moral and Literary: A New Edition*, 2 vols. (London: Charles Dilly, 1782), 1:214.

11. Nick Groom, *The Making of Percy's* Reliques (Oxford: Clarendon Press, 1999), 25, 23. Thomas Dyche, *A New General English Dictionary*, rev. William Pardon (1765), quoted in Groom, *The Making of Percy's* Reliques, 23.

the opening lines of Rowley's nationalist "Battle of Hastings [I]" echo one of the several versions of "Chevy Chase" that feature in the first volume of Percy's *Reliques*. Percy's version relied on a simple common meter: "O Christ! it was a grief to see, / And likewise for to heare, / The cries of men lying in their gore, / And scatter'd here and there."[12] In Chatterton's supposed translation of Saxon poet Turgot's account of the carnage in 1066, Rowley begins on this saddened note: "O Chrieste it is a Greefe to me to telle, / How manie noble Erle and valorous Knyghte, / In Fyghtynge for Kinge Harrolde noblie felle."[13] Naïve though the poem might be, its decasyllabic, ten-line stanzas advanced Percy's model.

Percy was not the only modern author whose anticlassical interests captured Chatterton's vibrant imagination. Chatterton also responded, like many of his peers, to a historically parallel but nationally discrete tradition of ancient poetry that had remained unknown to the larger proportion of English readers. In the same decade as Percy's *Reliques* was published, the gifted twenty-three-year-old James Macpherson created a sensation by issuing a short collection, *Fragments of Ancient Poetry, Collected in the Highlands of Scotland, and Translated from the Galic or Erse Language* (1760). In the preface to this volume, Macpherson asserts that he assembled these "genuine remains of ancient Scottish poetry" from unspecified sources in the Highlands before translating them into English prose.[14] Macpherson, an Aberdeen graduate who was trained in classics and was fluent in Gaelic, expanded the public's knowledge of this record of Celtic history (the period when the Romans occupied England) with *Fingal: An Ancient Epic Poem, in Six Books* (1762), which he followed in turn with *Temora: An Ancient Epic Poem, in Eight Books* (1763) and, as the culmination of these volumes, *The Works of Ossian, the Son of Fingal* (1765). As Macpherson explains, these volumes, which recount the heroic fortitude of Fingal, his son the blind poet Ossian, and his grandson Oscar, were the result of a "peregrination of six months" in the Highlands and the Hebrides, where he gathered these precious poetic materials; and he adds that if he had not transcribed and translated

12. Percy, *Reliques of Ancient English Poetry: Consisting of Old Heroic Ballads, Songs, and Other Pieces of Our Earlier Poets (Chiefly of the Lyric Kind), together with Some Few of Later Date*, 3 vols. (London: J. Dodsley, 1765), 1:240.

13. "Battle of Hastings [I]," in *The Complete Works of Thomas Chatterton*, ed. Donald S. Taylor and Benjamin B. Hoover, 2 vols. (Oxford: Clarendon Press, 1971), 1:27.

14. [Anon.,] "Preface," in [James Macpherson,] *Fragments of Ancient Poetry, Collected in the Highlands of Scotland, and Translated from the Galic or Erse Language* (Edinburgh: J. Hamilton and G. Balfour, 1760), iii; reprinted in Macpherson, *The Poems of Ossian and Related Works*, ed. Hugh Gaskill (Edinburgh: Edinburgh University Press, 1996), 51. Gaskill suggests that Hugh Blair was the author of this preface (415).

this poetry, it "would have still remained in the obscurity of a lost language."[15] Macpherson maintains that the public must respect his admission that the "imperfect semblance" of the English prose cannot do justice to "an original, which contains what is beautiful in simplicity, and grand in the sublime."[16]

Macpherson's most urgent point is that the cultural authority of this poetry lies in its artistic power to bear witness to a noble national tradition that English audiences had seldom appreciated: "When virtue in peace, and bravery in war, are the characteristics of a nation, their actions become interesting, and their fame worthy of immortality."[17] These poems addressed the historical roots of a Scottish nation that had resented its recent dependence on England to fend off the threat of French invasion during the Seven Years' War. Yet, while Macpherson and Hugh Blair (the Regius Professor of Rhetoric at Edinburgh who staunchly supported Macpherson's labors) stressed the national importance of this ancient oeuvre, neither revealed much in the way of sources that would endorse the authority of these poems. The only original document that Macpherson ever put into print was "A Specimen of the Original of *Temora*: Book Seventh," which presented the Gaelic text as a complement to part of the epic that appeared in 1763.[18] With only this single sample of Gaelic verse, *Ossian*'s readership had to put its faith in Macpherson's largely unsupported claim that his unaffected prose transposed a "species of composition [that] was not committed to writing, but delivered by oral tradition" across the centuries.[19] Enthusiasts as well as naysayers wanted further proof of the originals. Thomas Jefferson, for instance, found himself so captivated by *Ossian* that he corresponded with Macpherson's brother Charles in hopes of obtaining copies of the Gaelic manuscripts so that he could enjoy them in their complete cultural purity.[20]

15. Macpherson, "A Critical Dissertation on the Poems Ossian, the Son of Fingal," in Macpherson, *The Works of Ossian, the Son of Fingal*, 3rd ed., 2 vols. (London: T. Becket and P. A. De Hondt, 1765), 1:xxi; reprinted in Macpherson, *The Poems of Ossian and Related Works*, 51.

16. Macpherson, "Critical Dissertation," 1:xxiv, reprinted in Macpherson, *The Poems of Ossian and Related Works*, 52.

17. Macpherson, "Critical Dissertation," 1:xvi, reprinted in Macpherson, *The Poems of Ossian and Related Works*, 49.

18. Macpherson, "A Specimen of the Original of *Temora*: Book Seventh," in *Temora, An Ancient Epic Poem, in Eight Books: Together with Several Other Poems, Composed by Ossian, the Son of Fingal* (London: T. A. Becket and P. A. De Hondt, 1763), 227–47.

19. Macpherson, "Critical Dissertation," 1:xix, reprinted in Macpherson, *The Poems of Ossian and Related Works*, 50.

20. Jefferson contacted Scots merchant Charles Macpherson, who resided in Virginia, writing that *Ossian* was "source of daily and exalted pleasure," and that he was "desirous of

The reclamation of the Gaelic epic in *The Works of Ossian* proved just as popular as Percy's recovery of the ballad tradition. Yet the growing fame of *Ossian* developed hand in hand with a bitter dispute—one that resonates with the Rowley controversy—about its genuineness: a contention that lay at the heart of Victorian theorizations of Romanticism. For Macpherson's harshest critics, it appears that if the poet Ossian historically existed, then the poem *Ossian* would prove acceptable. The same might be said of the relationship between Rowley and Chatterton. Had someone been able to prove Rowley's biography at Bristol, Chatterton's transcriptions of this fifteenth-century priest seem unlikely to have met with such hostility. We can see this line of thinking in a 1763 letter that David Hume sent to fellow Scotsman Blair. Hume, who originally expressed great enthusiasm for Macpherson's project, wrote from London about the deepening suspicion that *Ossian* was an imposture: "I live in a place where I have the pleasure of frequently hearing justice done to your dissertation, but never heard it mentioned in a company, where some one person or other did not express his doubts with regard to the authenticity of the poems which are its subject, and I often hear them totally rejected, with disdain and indignation, as a palpable and most impudent forgery."[21] In an effort to "[satisfy] the world that they [the poems] are not the compositions of Mr. Macpherson himself," Blair, who treated Macpherson as a protégé, compiled a lengthy appendix to the *Works of Ossian*, in which he lists testimonies from various residents of the Highlands and Hebrides who verified the genuineness of the poetry, even as he notes that few can be found who know the orally transmitted poems.[22] Meanwhile, Macpherson, clearly insulted by the growing allegations in England that he was a forger, refused to defend in public the authenticity of *Ossian*.

Accusations of Macpherson's fraudulence persisted, as if such imaginative works only displayed criminal intent because they failed to provide elaborate authentication. In the following decade, Samuel Johnson undertook a tour of the Hebrides, which left him with no doubt about the spuriousness of Macpher-

---

learning the language in which he sung and of possessing his songs in their original form" ("To Charles Macpherson," 25 February 1773, in *Jefferson's Literary Commonplace Book*, ed. Douglas L. Wilson [Princeton: Princeton University Press, 1989], 172). See also Dumas Malone, *Jefferson the Virginian*, in *Jefferson and His Time*, 6 vols. (Boston: Little, Brown, 1938–1981), 1:392.

21. David Hume, "To Hugh Blair," 19 September 1763, in Henry Mackenzie, *Report of the Committee of the Highland Society of Scotland Appointed to Inquire into the Nature and Authenticity of the Poems of Ossian* (Edinburgh: A. Constable, 1805), 4.

22. Blair, "Appendix," in *The Works of Ossian*, 2:447; reprinted in Macpherson, *The Poems of Ossian and Related Works*, 402.

son's translations: "I believe they never existed in any other form than that which we have seen. The editor, or author, never could shew the original; nor can it be shewn by any other; to revenge reasonable incredulity, by refusing evidence, is a degree of insolence, with which the world is not yet acquainted; and stubborn audacity is the last refuge of guilt."[23] Johnson's memorable disdain, which prompted Macpherson to retort that "such expressions ought not to be used by one gentleman to another," echoed down the decades.[24] It inspired Hume to compose a disparaging essay that bemoaned *Ossian* as a "tiresome, insipid performance" whose tedious "regularity" and "uniformity" "betrays a man without genius."[25] (Hume withheld this piece from publication during his lifetime.) In response to skeptics, Macpherson's publisher insisted that "the original of *Fingal* and other poems of Ossian lay in my shop for many months during the year 1762, for the inspection of the curious."[26] No one, it seemed, looked at them. In the noisy pamphlet war that followed, nationalism was pitted against veracity: Gaelic scholar William Shaw supported Johnson, declaring that "*truth* has always been dearer to me than my *country*."[27] In response, John Clark, a member of the Scottish Society of Antiquaries, questioned Shaw's competence in Gaelic and accused him of having "an avowed intention of publishing falsehoods and

23. Samuel Johnson, *A Journey to the Western Islands of Scotland* (London: W. Strahan and T. Cadell, 1775), 273–74. As James Boswell recounted at length, Johnson remained indignant at the thought that Ossian's poetry had any claim on authenticity; Boswell recalls Johnson declaring during his stay on the Isle of Skye: "I look upon M'Pherson's *Fingal* to be as gross an imposition as ever the world was troubled with" (*Boswell's Life of Johnson*, ed. George Birkbeck Hill and L. F. Powell, 6 vols. [Oxford: Clarendon Press, 1934–1950], 5:241).

24. Macpherson, "To William Strahan," 15 January 1775, in Thomas Bailey Saunders, *The Life and Letters of James Macpherson, Containing a Particular Account of His Famous Quarrel with Dr. Johnson, and a Sketch of the Origin and Influence of the Ossian Poems* (London: Swan Sonnenschein, 1894), 246. This letter first appeared in "Dr. Johnson and Macpherson," *Academy*, 19 October 1878, 383. Macpherson tendered this letter to Johnson's publisher.

25. David Hume, "Essay on the Genuineness of the Poems," in John Hill Burton, *Life and Correspondence of David Hume: From the Papers Bequeathed by His Nephew to the Royal Society of Scotland, and Other Original Sources*, 2 vols. (Edinburgh: W. Tait, 1846), 1:471, 473.

26. T. Becket, "To the Public," 19 January 1775, in Saunders, *Life and Letters of James Macpherson*, 249. Saunders does not provide details of the newspaper where Becket placed this announcement.

27. William Shaw, *An Enquiry into the Authenticity of the Poems Ascribed to Ossian* (London: J. Murray, 1781), 37. Emphasis in the original.

imposing on the English, in the hope of acquiring some interest there; being sensible you were universally hated and despised in this country."[28] Finally, in 1805, the Highland Society produced an exhaustive report on the subject, in which scholars and antiquarians testified that Macpherson had access to manuscript sources.[29] Nevertheless, in England it proved almost impossible to shake the conviction that Macpherson had perpetuated an extravagant hoax. As the *Athenæum* observed in 1839, Macpherson's "very forgeries were prompted by an over-ambitious enthusiasm, akin to Chatterton's, which we pity and praise."[30] The sentiment holds to this day. Even though, as Fiona Stafford has pointed out, in 1952 Derick S. Thomson identified the Gaelic poems that Macpherson used, at least one Johnson scholar still believes that Ossian's authenticity remains "a nagging question . . . that refuses to go away."[31]

If one sets aside the niggling questions about Macpherson's source material, it is possible to focus instead on his considerable skill in fashioning finely cadenced English prose that distills the mood of ancient Celtic legend, which is clear from the very first fragment that appeared in 1760:

> My love is a son of the hill. He pursues the flying deer. His grey dogs are panting around him: his bow-string sounds in the wind. Whether by the fount of the rock, or by the stream of the mountain thou liest; when the rushes are nodding with the wind, and the mist is flying over thee, let me approach

28. John Clark, *An Answer to Mr. Shaw's Inquiry into the Authenticity of the Poems Ascribed to Ossian* (London: T. Longman and T. Cadell, 1781), 9–10.

29. Lord Bannatyne, for example, wrote to Henry Mackenzie—the report's editor— stating that one of two "'manuscripts' belonging to the family of Clanranald or the descendants of their bard, had got into the hands of Mr. M'Pherson. . . . Dr. Hugh M'Leod, professor of church history at Glasgow . . . assured me he had seen or examined several Gaelic manuscripts, partly written upon vellum, and apparently of great antiquity, in the possession of Mr. M'Pherson" (Mackenzie, *Report of the Committee of the Highland Society of Scotland Appointed to Inquire into the Nature and Authenticity of the Poems of Ossian* [Edinburgh: A. Constable, 1805], 281). The *Report* also includes Donald Smith's English translation of Gaelic poems that were in the possession of the Highland Committee, which he juxtaposes with Macpherson's renditions (189–269). There are strong correspondences between the two translations.

30. [Anon.,] "The Regeneration of Our National Poetry," 824.

31. Fiona Stafford, *Sublime Savage: James Macpherson and the Poems of Ossian* (Edinburgh: Edinburgh University Press, 1988), 3. Derick S. Thomson, *The Gaelic Sources of Macpherson's Ossian*, Aberdeen University Studies, 130 (Edinburgh: Oliver and Boyd, 1952). Thomas M. Curley believes the "nagging question" of Macpherson's prose renditions remains unsettled: *Samuel Johnson, The Ossian Fraud, and the Celtic Revival in Great Britain and Ireland* (Cambridge: Cambridge University Press, 2009), 3.

my love unperceived, and see him from the rock. Lovely I saw thee first by the aged oak of Branno, thou wert returning tall from the chace; the fairest among thy friends.[32]

Certainly, this poetic fragment originates in a pagan world. Yet its well-judged rhythms partly evoke the glory of the King James Version of the Psalms as well as the Song of Solomon. The declarative sentences at the start of this passage share three strong stresses, which give way to increasingly expansive clauses that accelerate the speaker's yearning to witness at close range her lover as he hunts the deer. As the lengthening syntax unravels her desire, the grammar becomes even more animated through the "flying," "panting," and "nodding" that intensifies her wish to move unseen toward him. Moreover, the archaic touches, including the pronoun "thee," the verb form "liest," and the subjunctive "let," strengthen the illusion that this scene belongs to time immemorial. Elsewhere, Macpherson's lucid and rhythmic prose exalts in simile. Turn to practically any part of *Fingal*, for example, and this rhetorical device springs from the page. When Cuchullin, protector of Irish King Cormac II, faces Swaran, King of Lochlin's invasion, Macpherson derives great resonance from a pair of carefully balanced comparisons: "So Cuchullin shaded the sons of Erin, and stood in the midst of thousands. Blood rises like the fount of a rock, from panting heroes around him. But Erin falls on either wing like snow in the day of the sun."[33] It was perhaps because such fine writing was expertly crafted that English critics doubted that it transcribed original Gaelic poems—ones, in any case, that remained unseen by disbelievers.

Like Chatterton's contemporaneous production of the Rowley poems, the intense debate about the sources of *Ossian* filled many printed pages through the end of the nineteenth century, and both the Bristol poet and his peer from Scotland remained at the center of enduring furors about literary forgery. Nevertheless, the quality of the continually popular *Ossian* gained increasing recognition, and a more balanced view of Macpherson's creative process steadily emerged. In 1805, even as Malcolm Laing admitted that *Ossian* was "full of falsehood" he still acknowledged that Macpherson's volumes had earned Ossian "the rank of a classical poet,"[34] and in 1818, William Hazlitt compared the work with nothing

32. First appeared in Macpherson, "Fragment I: Shilric, Vinvela," in *Fragments of Ancient Poetry*, 9; revised in Macpherson, *The Works of Ossian*, 1:272; reprinted in *The Poems of Ossian and Related Works*, 7.

33. Macpherson, *Fingal*, in *The Works of Ossian*, 1:41; reprinted in *The Poems of Ossian and Related Works*, 68.

34. Malcolm Laing, "Preface," in *The Poems of Ossian, &c., Containing the Poetical Works of James Macpherson, Esq.* (Edinburgh: A. Constable, 1805), vi.

less than the Bible and the poetry of Homer and Dante.[35] Inspired by a new edition of *Ossian* issued more than half a century later, Scottish critic John Campbell Shairp declared: "Ossian is alive again. Knocked down and trampled on by the dogmatic and domineering Johnson . . . thenceforth scouted by the literary world as a byword for impostor, here once more stands the old blind bard resurgent."[36] In a fair-minded spirit, Shairp admitted that in the 1760s the "Highlanders . . . were likely enough to make too unguarded and undiscriminating statements" in support of Macpherson's handiwork, though he noted "the ludicrous spectacle" of Johnson's clumsy and uninformed efforts.[37] Shairp concluded that Macpherson had without question collected "some considerable amount of ancient MS. poetry, [and] also large quantities of poetry taken down from recitations."[38] In 1888, George Eyre-Todd, in his review of the century-long polemic about Macpherson, shared much the same opinion, although what mattered for him most of all were those "passages unsurpassed in majesty and beauty."[39] The public, whatever qualms it might have had about Macpherson's purported fakery, had long concurred. Such was the ever-broadening fame of Macpherson's translations that several prominent European artists found them a source of potent creative stimulus. The legacy of *Ossian* can be found, for instance, in Goethe's Werther, in whose heart Ossian overtook Homer; in Ingres's stunning *Ossian's Dream* (1813); in ten of Schubert's youthful *Lieder* (1815–1817); and in Mendelssohn's famous *Hebrides Overture* (best known as "Fingal's Cave") (1830).[40] As Groom has shown, the distinctive rhythms, paratactic phrasing, and atmospheric settings that connect Ossian's terrestrial world with celestial bodies also make their way into the poetry of Blake, Wordsworth, Coleridge, and Keats.[41]

Wilde was the inheritor of these developments. Macpherson's influence proved

35. William Hazlitt, "On Poetry in General," in *Lectures on the English Poets: Delivered at the Surrey Institution* (London: Taylor and Hessey, 1818), 31; reprinted in *The Selected Writings of William Hazlitt,* ed. Duncan Wu, 9 vols. (London: Pickering and Chatto, 1998), 2:11.

36. J. C. Shairp, "Ossian," *Macmillan's Magazine* 24 (1871): 113.

37. Shairp, "Ossian," 113.

38. Shairp, "Ossian," 123.

39. George Eyre-Todd, "Introduction," in *Poems of Ossian, Translated by James Macpherson,* ed. Eyre-Todd (London: Walter Scott, 1888), lxvii.

40. "Ossian hat in meinem Herzen den Homer verdrängt" ("Ossian has superseded Homer in my heart"). Johann-Wolfgang von Goethe, *Die Leiden des jungen Werthers* (1774; Leipzig: Weygand, 1775), 151.

41. Nick Groom, *The Forger's Shadow: How Forgery Changed the Course of Literature* (London: Picador, 2002), 115–39.

inescapable, and not just because of the impact of *Ossian* on some of Wilde's favorite writers. At one point in *Fingal*, the poem that opens the 1765 *Works*, the great Celtic king looks to his grandson as the warrior who will defend his people justly:

> Son of my son, begun the king, O Oscar, pride of youth, I saw the shining of thy sword and gloried in my race. Pursue the glory of our fathers, and be what they have been; when Trenmor lived, the first of men, and Trathal the father of heroes. They fought the battle in their youth, and are the song of bards. — —O Oscar! bend the strong in arms: but spare the feeble hand. Be thou a stream of many tides against the foes of thy people.[42]

Throughout *Ossian*, Oscar proves himself a fearless warrior. But his sudden death in *Temora*, which follows quickly upon his killing of the enemy Cairbar, forces the great stoical king to weep because he sees at last that his dynasty has gone with his grandson to the grave:

> My sons fall by degrees: Fingal shall be the last of his race. The fame which I have received shall pass away: my age will be without friends. I shall sit like a grey cloud in my hall: nor shall I expect the return of a son, in the midst of his sounding arms. Weep, ye heroes of Morven! never more shall Oscar rise![43]

Oscar remained by far the bravest warrior in this gallant history, and such legendary valor clearly had great resonance for Wilde's parents, since they took both his first and second names from Macpherson's prose. "He is to be called Oscar Fingal Wilde," Jane Wilde wrote enthusiastically to a friend. "Is not that grand, misty, and Ossianic?"[44] This highly poetic choice was not surprising, since both of Wilde's parents were experts on Celtic lore and legend, and his father participated in the activities of Dublin's literary Ossianic Society (1853–1863), whose transactions published "Fenian poems, tales, and romances, illustrative of the Fenian period of Irish history, in the Irish language and character, with literal translations and notes explanatory of the text."[45] All of these ancient Fenian writings recorded the history of Fingal, Ossian, and Oscar in their dis-

---

42. Macpherson, *Fingal*, in *The Works of Ossian*, 1:64–65; reprinted in *The Poems of Ossian and Related Works*, 77.

43. Macpherson, *Temora*, in *The Works of Ossian*, 1:254; reprinted in *The Poems of Ossian and Related Works*, 230.

44. Richard Ellmann, *Oscar Wilde* (New York: Alfred A. Knopf, 1988), 17. Ellmann states that this letter is held at the University of Reading; Jane Francesca Wilde's correspondent is unknown.

45. [Anon.,] "Report," in *Transactions of the Ossianic Society, for the Year 1853* (Dublin: Printed under the Direction of the Council, 1854–1864), 1:6.

tinctly Irish form. As Nicholas O'Kearney states in its opening volume, the society acknowledged that the time had "come when the remnants of the history of Ireland found in the poems of Fionn, Oisin, Caoilte, Fergus, and other minor bards of antiquity shall not remain in oblivion,"[46] and the society represented the first concerted effort to gather the whole canon of ancient poetry in the Irish language. One of its aims was to refocus the debate about the degree to which the Irish had "full as good a Title to the Honour of this Poem as the Caledonian Britons,"[47] a question taken up as early as 1789, with Charlotte Brooke's verse adaptations of the Irish version of the legends of Finn. She reminded readers that "Oisin, the father of Osgur, was as much celebrated for his valour, as much for his poetical talents."[48] Brooke's volume, which is partly modeled on Percy's *Reliques*, presides over an Irish tradition that culminated in William Butler Yeats's early poetry. Yeats's well-known poem "The Wanderings of Oisin" turns to the story of the fairy princess Niamh who enchants the Celtic hero to live for hundred years as a Sidhe upon her magical islands. Yeats further derived his knowledge of Oisin from Standish Hayes O'Grady, a prominent member of the Ossianic Society. Assuredly, Wilde's resplendent birth names "Oscar Fingal" were Celtic, but it is noticeable that their origins lay in the widely recognized grandeur of the Caledonian source that inspired concerted scholarly inquiries into ancient Irish poetry.

This intimate link with the legacy of *Ossian* might have inspired the attention Wilde gave to Chatterton's seven "Ossianics," works that demonstrate Chatterton's responsiveness to those contemporary styles of writing that marked signal shifts and changes in eighteenth-century literature. "He loved," Wilde observed in the notebook, following Daniel Wilson, "to let | his intellect play— to separate | the artist from the man—this | explains his extraordinary | versatility —he cd. write polished | lines like Pope, satire like | Churchill—Philippics like | Junius—fiction like Smolletts. | Gray, Collins, Macphersons | Ossia[n]" (f.76ʳ [405]).[49] By retaining Macpherson's prose idiom, Chatterton's "Ossianics" re-

46. Nicholas O'Kearney, "Introduction" to "The Battle of Gabhra: Garristown in the County of Dublin, Fought in A.D. 283," in *Transactions of the Ossianic Society*, 1:10.

47. Ferdinando Warner, *Remarks on the History of Fingal, and Other Poems of Ossian: Translated by Mr. Macpherson* (London: H. Payne and W. Cropley, 1762), 6.

48. Charlotte Brooke, "War Ode to Osgur, the Son of Oisin, in the Front the Battle of Gabhra," in *Reliques of Irish Poetry, Consisting of Heroic Poems, Odes, Elegies, and Songs, Translated into English Verse, with Notes Explanatory and Historical; and the Originals in the Irish Character, to which is Subjoined an Irish Tale by Miss Brooke* (Dublin: George Bonham, 1789), 151.

49. Cf. Daniel Wilson, *Chatterton: A Biographical Study* (London: Macmillan, 1869), 261.

main distinct from the numerous adaptations that several writers produced in the years that immediately followed Macpherson's *Fragments of Ancient Poetry*, most of which transformed Ossian's prose into verse or drama.[50] These "Ossianics" began with "Ethelgar," dating from early 1769, which appeared in the *Town and Country Magazine*. Its story, which is set in Bristol, features protagonists who bear common Saxon names: Ethelgar and Egwina, we learn, embark on a romance, which results in marriage. Sadly, their son Ælgar perishes during a hunt, while Egwina is struck by lightning. As a consequence, Ethelgar contemplates suicide. But his road to redemption becomes clear when the spirit of the famous Saxon monk St. Cuthbert appears before him in the air: "Know, O man! said the member of the blessed, to submit to the will of God."[51] Ethelgar obliges, and joins a monastery. Macpherson's vivid similes, as well as his cadences, find strong echoes in Chatterton's imitation: "Comely as the white rocks; bright as the star of the ev'ning; tall as the oak upon the brow of the mountain; soft as the showers of dew, that fall upon the flowers of the field, Ethelgar arose, the glory of Exanceastre."[52] One further point is equally evident in the approach Chatterton takes in these "Ossianics": they are, though stylistically faithful to their source, imaginative adaptations of ancient Scottish works that English commentators already suspected of fakery.

The influence of *Ossian* on Wilde's life and work extended well beyond his "grand" and "misty" birth names. In April 1882, almost halfway through his North American lecture tour, Wilde spoke enthusiastically about *Ossian* to a largely Irish-American audience in San Francisco. This tour, which reporters recorded in considerable detail, aimed at drawing American and Canadian audiences' attention to the impact that the Aesthetic Movement had made on British culture. Among his lectures were "The House Beautiful," "The Decorative Arts," and—the lecture for which he became best known at the beginning of his tour—"The English Renaissance of Art," in which the leading term characterizes "a sort of new birth of the spirit of man" in the nineteenth century, an idea of cultural rebirth deeply informed by Pater's influential *Studies in the His-*

50. In many respects, the most ambitious of these early contributions to Ossianism was John Wodrow's 1771 translation of *Fingal* "into English Heroic Verse." Wodrow's verse translations, together with numerous other examples of literary Ossianism from 1760 onward, are collected in Dafydd Moore, ed., *Ossian and Ossianism*, 4 vols. (London: Routledge, 2004), 4: passim.

51. "Ethelgar: A Saxon Poem," in *Complete Works of Thomas Chatterton*, ed. Taylor and Hoover, 1:255.

52. "Ethelgar: A Saxon Poem," in *Complete Works of Thomas Chatterton*, ed. Taylor and Hoover, 1:253. "Exanceastre" is presumably Chatterton's antiquated spelling of Exeter.

tory of the Renaissance (1873).[53] At Platt's Hall in San Francisco, Wilde based his first talk on "The English Renaissance of Art." Later, he made an appearance at that venue to deliver to a five-hundred-strong audience a talk entitled "The Irish Poets and Poetry of the Nineteenth Century." He recalled the achievements of the poets linked with the nationalist Young Ireland movement of the 1840s, including Charles Gavan Duffy and his mother, Jane Francesca Wilde (whose early poetry appeared under the pseudonym "Speranza"). These Irish writers' works, he maintained, belonged to a distinguished Celtic tradition.

It was in this context that Wilde observed that Macpherson's *Ossian* was part of an eminent Celtic body of literature that had transformed English poetry. As he told his listeners, he took enormous pride in Macpherson's impact on later Victorian verse. In his view, such modern writing was a welcome reaction against the "dreadfully prosaic character" of most eighteenth-century poetry; Macpherson, as Wilde saw it, supplied the "strain of romance" that had "revolutionized the whole of Europe . . . influencing the work of every poet from Byron to Keats and Lamartine."[54] In the rest of the presentation, he stressed that "those chords of penetrating passion and melancholy"—what he termed the "spirit of modern romance"—that "swept over Europe with the publication of Macpherson's Ossian . . . still linger . . . in the work of every poet of our day."[55] Here again, Jane Francesca Wilde's name is important: she encouraged the idea of a direct line of influence linking Celtic literary tradition and the Romantic poets in her 1887 study *Ancient Legends, Mystic Charms, and Superstitions of Ireland*. In a laudatory review of the work for the April 1887 *Century Guild Hobby Horse*, Arthur Galton (after a small digression in which he disparages Harry Quilter's *Sententiæ Artis*, which had also earned a scathing review from Wilde) writes that the Irish folk stories described by Lady Wilde evince "emotions . . . which find their utterance in Shelley."[56] The vision of the Irish mystic defined in Lady Wilde's work resonates with the Romantic nature Oscar Wilde had detailed only a few years before in his lecture: Galton notes the "profound melancholy" and "yearning pathos" that define the Celtic myths in her account. Irish music, in Lady Wilde's words, "is the utterance of a Divine sorrow; not stormy

53. Wilde, "The English Renaissance of Art," in *The Collected Works of Oscar Wilde*, ed. Robert Ross, 14 vols. (London: Methuen, 1908), 14:243.

54. Wilde, *Irish Poets and Poetry of the Nineteenth Century: A Lecture Delivered at Platt's Hall on Wednesday April Fifth, 1882*, ed. Robert D. Pepper (San Francisco: Book Club of California, 1972), 29.

55. Wilde, *Irish Poets and Poetry of the Nineteenth Century*, 28.

56. Arthur Galton, "Ancient Legends of Ireland by Lady Wilde," *Century Guild Hobby Horse* 1, no. 6 (April 1887): 69. We discuss Wilde's review of Quilter's volume in chapter 4 (168–71).

or passionate, but like that of an exiled spirit, yearning and wistful, vague and unresting."[57]

Uniting Lady Wilde's and her son's work was the intent to detail the immense Celtic contribution to literary history. Wilde's San Francisco lecture was in part a rebuttal of Matthew Arnold's demeaning remarks about Wilde's national heritage in "On the Study of Celtic Literature" (1866). In his essay, Arnold had asserted that where "in material civilisation he has been ineffectual, so has the Celt been ineffectual in politics."[58] To uphold his questionable belief, Arnold ironically quoted a line from Macpherson's epic to represent the dismal plight of Celtic peoples within ancient and modern history: "'They went forth to the war,' Ossian says most truly, '*but they always fell*.'"[59] For Wilde, it was, to the contrary, the case that "the Celtic sentiment" informed much of the greatest nineteenth-century poetry, including Alfred Tennyson's *Idylls of the King* (1856–1885) and William Morris's *Earthly Paradise* (1868–1870).[60] He glossed the point in an interview with the *San Francisco Examiner*: "There is no lack of culture in Ireland, but it is nearly all absorbed in politics."[61] "Had I remained there," he added, mindful of ongoing campaigns for Home Rule, "my career would have been a political one."[62] The immediate turmoil in Ireland underscored this sentiment. A month after Wilde delivered his talk praising *Ossian* at Platt's Hall, his mother informed him of

57. Jane Francesca Wilde, *Ancient Legends, Mystic Charms, and Superstitions of Ireland* (Boston: Ticknor, 1888), 30; quoted in Galton, "Ancient Legends," 69.

58. Matthew Arnold, "On the Study of Celtic Literature," in *Lectures and Essays in Criticism, The Complete Prose Works of Matthew Arnold*, ed. R. H. Super, 11 vols. (Ann Arbor: University of Michigan Press, 1960–1977), 3:346.

59. Arnold, "On the Study of Celtic Literature," 3:346. Macpherson, "Cath-Loda," in *The Works of Ossian*, 2:258; reprinted in *The Poems of Ossian and Related Works*, 314. This line from *Ossian* also serves as the epigraph to Arnold's essay; the mocking emphasis is Arnold's. In his preface to *Culture and Anarchy*, Arnold again turned to Ossian, this time to mock Oscar Browning (London: Smith, Elder, 1869), iv.

60. Wilde, *Irish Poets and Poetry of the Nineteenth Century*, 28. The only other known record of Wilde's discussion of Celtic art is in a report on the lecture titled "The Value of Art in Modern Life," which he delivered, to a disappointingly small audience, at the Gaiety Theatre, Dublin, on 6 January 1885. In this lecture, Wilde, according to a newspaper report, spoke broadly about decorative art in the home, and various traditions of ornamental beauty; he mentioned to applause that there was a "far greater sense of beauty evinced in the early Celtic work than in old English art, which was deficient in delicacy and sense of proportion" ([Anon.,] "Value of Art in Modern Life," *Freeman's Journal and Daily Commercial Advertiser*, 7 January 1885: 5).

61. "Oscar Wilde: An Interview with the Apostle of Aestheticism," *San Francisco Examiner*, 27 March 1882: 2; in *Oscar Wilde in America: The Interviews*, ed. Matthew Hofer and Gary Scharnhorst (Champaign: University of Illinois Press, 2010), 101.

62. "Oscar Wilde: An Interview with the Apostle of Aestheticism," 101.

the Phoenix Park murders at Dublin: the assassination of the chief secretary and permanent undersecretary for Ireland by the Irish National Invincibles, a splinter group of the Irish Republic Brotherhood that, in 1916, staged the Easter Rising. "No one," Speranza wrote from London to her son, "knows what will be next. Some people think there will be a general massacre & smash."[63]

While Speranza maintained a salon in London that brought together Irish expatriates to discuss Home Rule, Oscar Wilde pursued a literary career whose engagement with his national background—though never indifferent—was for the most part indirect. Even though there is no circumstantial evidence that might confirm that Wilde intended to emulate the *Works of Ossian* in his own writings, it may be possible to hear echoes (as Bernard Beatty has done) of "a style—Ossian's—just like Wilde's" in the French-language one-act tragedy *Salomé*, which Wilde completed in 1892.[64] As Beatty suggests, both the original French and the different English translations that Alfred Douglas and Robert Ross created feature "metrically paired very short sentences" and an "abundance of similes" that bear traces of Macpherson's finely cadenced and strongly figurative language.[65] This suggestive connection looks plausible when we reflect upon the opening of *Salomé*, where the Page of Herodias declares to the Young Syrian: "Regardez la lune. La lune a l'air très étrange. On dirait une femme qui sort d'un tombeau. Elle ressemble à une femme morte. On dirait qu'elle cherche des morts."[66] In Douglas's somewhat mannered but well-known rendition, which evokes the rhythms of the King James Bible, this speech unfolds as follows: "Look at the moon! How strange the moon seems! She is like a dead woman rising from a tomb. She is like a dead woman. One might fancy she was looking for dead things."[67] Perhaps behind these lines we hear Macpherson's resonant parataxis at the start of the second book of *Fingal*, where the face of Crugal—"a chief that lately fell"—"is like the beam of the setting moon; his

63. Jane Francesca Wilde, "To Oscar Wilde," 8 May 1882, in *Lady Jane Wilde's Letters to Oscar Wilde, 1875–1895: A Critical Edition*, ed. Karen Sasha Anthony Tipper (Lewiston, PA: Edwin Mellen Press, 2011), 75–76.

64. Bernard Beatty, "The Form of Oscar: Wilde's Art of Substitution," *Irish Studies Review* 11 (2003): 41.

65. Beatty, "The Form of Oscar," 41.

66. Wilde, *Salomé: Drame en un acte* (Paris: Librairie de l'art independent; London: Elkin Mathews and John Lane, 1893), 9, reprinted in *Plays I: The Duchess of Padua; Salomé: Drame en un acte; Salome: Tragedy in One Act*, ed. Joseph Donohue, *The Complete Works of Oscar Wilde*, 7 vols. to date (Oxford: Oxford University Press, 2000 and continuing), 5:509.

67. Wilde, *Salome*, trans. Alfred Douglas (London: Elkin Mathews and John Lane, 1894), 1. The most complete set of Ross's emendations to Douglas's translation appears in the edition of the play that John Lane published in 1912. Ross sought to create greater alignment with Wilde's French text.

robes are of the clouds of the hill: his eyes are like two decaying flames. Dark is the wound of his breast."[68] Whether Ossian should count among the many sources that critics have identified in the somewhat stilted, percussive language of *Salomé* will perhaps remain an open question for some readers.

One teasing point, however, remained clear about the link between Wilde and *Ossian* to some of his contemporaries: the automatic association between "Oscar Fingal" and Macpherson's writings presented the satirical magazine *Punch* with the perfect opportunity to make the young Irishman's American lecture tour look like a pretentious, because Ossianic, fraud. In the first of two pieces, Wilde appears in an unearthly pose as a moonlit "Ossian (with Variations)" (Figure 10). The subtitle characterizes him as "The Son of Ia-Cultcha," mocking not only the names of several Celtic characters in Macpherson's epic but also Arnold's much-touted and widely criticized advocacy of "Culture" ("the best which has been thought and said in the world").[69] *Punch*, which mercilessly parodies Macpherson's prose, depicts this modern-day Ossian as the "car-borne Son of Erin" who has undertaken an absurdly Homeric odyssey to the "Land of Strangers."[70] On his arrival in America, he encounters a flock of followers who express unthinking devotion to his aesthetic creed, according to the narrator's *Ossian*-like intonations:

> THE Chief steps on the stranger's shore. Soon the feast of shells is spread. The joy of the hero is great. Again he resumes his soul. He forgets the dark-rolling ocean. It is in Fila-Delfia's Hall. The strangers come like a stream. His fame has reached their shores. They fill the hall. Sixty youths come in. Each bears the Flower of the Sun. The robe of each descends to his knees. They fill the foremost seats. Behold! he comes, the Son of Fame! He bears the long, bending Lily. His face is like the broad, blank moon in the skirt of a cloud, before the storms arise![71]

As one might expect, a storm does indeed break suddenly upon the lecture room. It resembles one that Wilde had already experienced at the Music Hall,

68. Macpherson, *Fingal*, in *The Works of Ossian*, 1:32; reprinted in *The Poems of Ossian and Related Writings*, 65.

69. Arnold, "Preface" (1869), in *Culture and Anarchy with Friendship's Garland and Some Literary Essays, The Complete Prose Works of Matthew Arnold*, ed. Super, 5:233.

70. [Anon.,] "Ossian (with Variations): The Son of Ia-Cultcha," *Punch*, 11 March 1882: 117. The illustration is signed "W.P." We have not been able to identify the illustrator. The association of Wilde with *Ossian* recurred in the following decade. In 1893, an Oxford student magazine, *The Ephemeral*, launched an attack on "Ossian Savage's New Play" (a reference to *A Woman of No Importance*), 1 (18 May 1893): 3–4.

71. [Anon.,] "Ossian (with Variations)," 117.

OSSIAN (WITH VARIATIONS).
THE SON OF IA-CULTCHA.

IS THIS THE SON OF CULTCHA'S SHADOWY FORM?

Figure 10. Illustration for "Ossian (with Variations)" from *Punch* (11 March 1882), p. 117. Used with permission. © Punch Limited.

Boston, in January 1882, when sixty Harvard students occupied the front two rows, each of them donning a version of Wilde's aesthetic costume. (Since someone let Wilde know about this prank in advance, he partly thwarted it by appearing in fairly conventional attire, and pronouncing: "As I look around me, I am impelled for the first time to breathe a fervent prayer, 'Save me from my disciples.' But let me, as Wordsworth says, 'Turn from these bold, bad men.'"[72] Apparently, the Harvard undergraduates applauded loudly each time he sipped from his water glass.) But where Wilde managed to exert some measure of control over these boisterous students, his satirical counterpart in *Punch* fails miserably. No sooner has "Ossian (with Variations)" begun to espouse his views on art and beauty than an impatient voice quips: "O, cut it, Son of Cultcha!"[73] At that point, everybody deserts the lecture hall, apart from one man, who pronounces in stern tones drawn directly from *Ossian:* "Son of a distant land, where thy dwellest in a field of fame, there let thy song arise, but visit us no more." All that the narrator can do is implore the aesthete to come back to those acolytes in London who "sit in the Dadoed Hall and the Chamber of Yallery-green."[74]

The following month, *Punch* published a sonnet, "Impression de Gaiety Théâtre," which it attributed to "Ossian Wilderness." Although the subject matter of the poem is obscure, it echoes the French title of Wilde's "Impression du Matin," which had first appeared in the *World* in June 1879, and was reprinted in the 1881 volume *Poems.* The sonnet refers to an actress who does not conform to the "common Continental art": a reference to the success that impresario John Hollingshead, manager of the Gaiety Theatre, enjoyed when he brought the entire Comédie Française to perform on the London stage in 1879.[75] Wilde's sonnet "Phèdre" directly celebrates Sarah Bernhardt's performance in the French company's production of Racine's drama; in the poem, he honors Bernhardt as a quasi-divine, in whom the greatest achievements of classical and Renaissance culture—from Homer's *Odyssey* to Pico della Mirandola's enlightened philosophy—are enshrined. The plaudits do not end there. His sonnet pronounces that Bernhardt's spirit dwelt among the mythological

72. The episode is recorded in great detail in Lloyd Lewis and Henry Justin Smith, *Oscar Wilde Discovers America* (1882) (New York: Harcourt, Brace, 1936), 125–26; the coauthors derive their discussion reports from several Boston newspapers. Wordsworth's phrase—"But turn we from these 'bold, bad' men"—comes from his poem "To the Lady——, on Seeing the Foundation for the Erection of——Chapel, Westmoreland" (composed 1822–1823), in *Wordsworth, Last Poems, 1821–1850,* ed. Jared Curtis, The Cornell Wordsworth (Ithaca, NY: Cornell University Press, 1999), 31. Arnold made the phrase well known in his essay "Wordsworth" (1879), in *English Literature and Irish Politics, The Complete Prose Works of Matthew Arnold,* ed. Super, 9:50.

73. [Anon.,] "Ossian (with Variations)," 117.

74. [Anon.,] "Ossian (with Variations)," 117.

75. [Anon.,] "Impression de Gaiety Théâtre (by Ossian Wilderness)," *Punch,* 8 April 1882: 168. Hollingshead records the success that the Comédie Française had from 2 June to 12 July 1879 in *Gaiety Chronicles* (London: Archibald Constable, 1898), 360–72.

streams where lyric poetry was born: "Thou should'st have gathered reeds from a green stream / For goat-foot Pan's shrill piping."[76] In contrast, *Punch* applauds "A sweet new Salome of our English land," whose "neatly fitting skirt of satinette" delights the poetic observer. Captivated by this seductress, the speaker declares that he would willingly offer her the head of radical politician Charles Bradlaugh. Enchanted, he characterizes her distinctly English demeanor as a "JOHN-KEATS-like poem of sweet motion."[77] *Punch* parodied Wilde's hyperbolic praise for Bernhardt, but the allusion to Keats suggests that Wilde's affinity for the Romantic poet was, by this point, well established. Whatever his Continental predilections, the cosmopolitan "Ossian Wilderness"—like Wilde himself —held Keats and his legacy in the highest esteem. Wilde's understanding of Keats's position in the history of English poetry explains the circumstances that led him to grasp the powerful influence that Chatterton exerted not only on the major Romantics but also their most recent heirs, the Pre-Raphaelite poets, especially Dante Gabriel Rossetti.

WILDE AND THE "GREAT ROMANTIC MOVEMENT": FROM KEATS TO ROSSETTI

Although Irish-American communities welcomed Wilde at Boston and St. Paul, he elaborated Macpherson's presiding influence over the "spirit of romance" only in his San Francisco lecture. Elsewhere on his tour, he related his thoughts about the "strain of romance" in relation to a decidedly English, not Celtic, genealogy. In its report on Wilde's lecturing debut, the *New York Tribune*, for instance, provided a transcript of "The English Renaissance of Art." Wary that "expressions such as 'classical' and 'romantic' [were] . . . often apt to become the mere catchwords of schools," Wilde nonetheless adverted to talking about "the great romantic movement" that lay at the heart of the tradition he wished to unfold.[78] In his history of this "new birth of the spirit of man," Wilde traced its origins not to *Ossian* but to Keats: "It is in Keats that one discerns the beginning of the artistic renaissance of England."[79] "Keats," he added, was "the forerunner of the pre-Raphaelite school," whose cultural significance he went on to explain, emphasizing that the Pre-Raphaelites embodied "this great romantic

---

76. Wilde, "Phèdre," in *Poems and Poems in Prose*, ed. Bobby Fong and Karl Beckson, *The Complete Works of Oscar Wilde*, 1:116. The mistaken circumflex—instead of a grave accent—is preserved in the title of Wilde's poem.

77. [Anon.,] "Impression de Gaiety Théâtre (by Ossian Wilderness)," 168.

78. Wilde, "The English Renaissance of Art," in *Collected Works*, 14:249.

79. Wilde, "The English Renaissance of Art," in *Collected Works*, 14:243, 249.

movement of ours."[80] Wilde observes: "In Rossetti's poetry and the poetry of Morris, Swinburne and Tennyson a perfect precision and choice of language, a style flawless and fearless, a seeking for all sweet and precious melodies and a sustaining consciousness of the musical value of each word are opposed to that value which is merely intellectual. In this respect they are one with the romantic movement of France of which not the least characteristic note was struck by Théophile Gautier's advice to the young poet to read the dictionary every day, as being the only book worth a poet's reading."[81] Such formulations had so much impact that within months Walter Hamilton, in *The Aesthetic Movement in England* (1882), quoted these lines from an American press report.[82]

Wilde made similar claims in his various interviews with American journalists. His championing of Keats as a member of a distinctive "romantic school" extended Leigh Hunt's famous 1816 assertion that there was an identifiable "new school" of poets, which included Keats and Shelley.[83] In San Francisco Wilde went even further by boldly associating his own poetry with a Romantic tradition that for him began with the author of *Endymion*:

> REPORTER: "Mr. Wilde, do your admirers believe that you have created a new school of poetry?"
> OSCAR WILDE: "They certainly should not—that is if I have any admirers. The Pre-Raphaelite School, to which I belong, owes its origin to Keats more than to anyone else. He was the forerunner of the school, as was Pheidias' of Grecian art, Dante of the intensity of passion, and color of Italian painting. Later, [Edward] Burne-Jones in painting and Morris, Rossetti, and Swinburne in poetry represent the fruit of which Keats was the blossom."[84]

That Wilde felt free to insert himself into the Pre-Raphaelite school was presumptuous, since he had by this time enjoyed minimal contact with Swin-

80. Wilde, "The English Renaissance of Art," in *Collected Works*, 14:249.

81. Wilde, "The English Renaissance of Art," in *Collected Works*, 14:258, 253–54.

82. Hamilton's study remains significant because it is the earliest critical work to place Wilde, as he wished to be understood, as an heir to Ruskin, popular aestheticism (such as Gilbert and Sullivan's comic opera *Patience* [1881]), and the Pre-Raphaelites. In his account of Wilde's lecture at Chickering Hall, Hamilton quotes from the *New York World*; see *The Aesthetic Movement in English* (London: Reeves and Turner, 1882), 105.

83. [Leigh Hunt,] "Young Poets," *Examiner*, 1 December 1816: 761.

84. "Oscar Wilde: An Interview with the Apostle of Aestheticism," in *Oscar Wilde in America*, ed. Hofer and Scharnhorst, 102.

burne. Meanwhile, Rossetti—whose home on Cheyne Walk was close to the rooms Wilde had taken at his friend Frank Miles's Keats House on nearby Tite Street—remained wholly unknown to him. Watts later recalled that Wilde "never saw Rossetti in his life," adding that Rossetti "bitterly resented the way in which Oscar's name was linked with him and his circle."[85] To be sure, after Wilde sent Swinburne a presentation copy of *Poems*, the Pre-Raphaelite poet arranged for Wilde to receive a copy of his *Studies in Song* (1880) inscribed with a dedication and compliments ("Amitié et remerciements") to the younger man, adding that his companion Watts sent "his best remembrances."[86] But this polite exchange hardly resulted in a friendship. Swinburne knew next to nothing about Wilde. As he informed the American critic Edmund Clarence Stedman, in response, it appears, to a query about the young lecturer who was busily traveling across the United States: "The only time I ever saw Mr. Oscar Wilde was in a crush at our acquaintance Lord Houghton's. I thought he seemed a harmless young nobody, and had no notion he was the sort of man to play the mountebank as he seems to have been doing."[87] Nor was Wilde friendly with Morris; it took until 1891 before he confessed to the older man: "I have loved your work since boyhood."[88] Despite this real-world distance, for years Wilde venerated these idols in his poetry. In "The Garden of Eros," as the speaker repeatedly exclaims his praise (echoing one of Shelley's most famous poems) for the "Spirit of Beauty," he traces a history of English poetry that connects Chaucer, Spenser, and Keats before making allusions that celebrate Swinburne's *Poems and Ballads* (1866), Morris's *Story of Sigurd the Volsung and the Fall of the Niblungs* (1876), and the one who "bears his name / From Dante and the seraph Gabriel."[89] With his admiration so documented, Wilde fully understood how strongly the Pre-Raphaelites respected Keats's legacy. Keatsian echoes in

85. Thomas Hake and Arthur Compton-Rickett, *The Life and Letters of Theodore Watts-Dunton*, 2 vols. (London: T. C. and E. C. Jack, 1916), 1:175.

86. Algernon Charles Swinburne, "To Oscar Wilde," 2 February 1882, in *The Swinburne Letters*, ed. Cecil Y. Lang, 6 vols. (New Haven: Yale University Press, 1959–1962), 4:255. Ellmann records the dedication in Swinburne's presentation copy to Wilde (*Oscar Wilde*, 32); the French translates as "with friendship and thanks."

87. Swinburne, "To E. C. Stedman," 4 April 1882, in *The Swinburne Letters*, 4:266.

88. Wilde, "To William Morris," March to April 1891, in *Complete Letters*, 476.

89. Wilde, "The Garden of Eros," in *Poems and Poems in Prose*, 1:133. "The Garden of Eros" first appeared in Wilde, *Poems* (London: David Bogue, 1881), 17–34. For the allusions to Swinburne and Morris, see 1:132. The phrase "Spirit of Beauty" originates in Shelley, "Hymn to Intellectual Beauty" (1817) (*Shelley's Poetry and Prose*, 2nd ed., ed. Donald H. Reiman and Neil Fraistat [New York: Norton, 2002], 94).

Wilde's own writing would ballast the links between his verse and that of the Pre-Raphaelites whom he worshipped.

Wilde's fashioning of himself as a de facto Pre-Raphaelite—especially when he had no established connection with that circle—certainly looks strained. But, in the broader context of literary debate in the 1870s and 1880s, his identification with Rossetti, Swinburne, and Morris was not merely an act of aspirational fandom: the association also had a political edge. This point comes into focus when we look at William John Courthope's inimical criticisms of Pre-Raphaelite poetry that appeared in the *Quarterly Review*, an old-style Tory journal that had arguably become politically entrenched in the face of the largely liberal monthlies that prospered during this period. Courthope, an Oxford-educated critic who became professor of poetry at the university in 1895, and whose imposing six-volume *History of English Poetry* began publication in the same year, relied heavily on the Romanticism/classicism binary, overtly aligning the Romantic with Liberalism. He made his own Tory radicalism clear in an exasperated review of Swinburne's *Songs before Sunrise* (1871), Rossetti's *Poems*, and Morris's *The Earthly Paradise* (1871). From Courthope's indignant perspective, these volumes were the clearest modern expressions of the detrimental "spirit of Keats": a spirit that "manifests itself more or less in the works of almost every poet who has succeeded him."[90] Courthope links what he deems Keats's deleterious "spirit" with the essence of almost all "post-revolutionary poetry of England."[91] This was, as R. V. Johnson observes, a somewhat familiar polemic, which formed part of a conservative "reaction against a poetry in which imagination took precedence over intelligence and good sense [that] had begun in the thirties."[92] Yet Courthope carries this older, conservative antipathy toward the nonrational powers of the imagination into a charged debate about these modern poets' indulgence in sensual pleasure. In particular, he characterizes "the soft and sensuous" aspects of Keats's poetry with an antisocial impulse that dispenses with "the conflict of modern opinions" in favor of the "love of beauty."[93] Courthope argues that, in the most outspoken atheist and Republican works in *Songs before Sunrise*, Swinburne "has chosen his themes not so much under the influence of political enthusiasm as from a keen literary perception of the advantages they offered to his peculiar rhetoric."[94]

90. [William John Courthope,] "The Latest Development of Literary Poetry: Swinburne—Rossetti—Morris," *Quarterly Review* 132 (1872): 61.

91. [Courthope,] "The Latest Development of Literary Poetry," 61.

92. R. V. Johnson, "Pater and the Victorian Anti-Romantics," *Essays in Criticism* 4 (1964): 43. Johnson's essay builds on R. G. Cox's important discussion "Victorian Criticism of Poetry: The Minority Tradition," *Scrutiny* 18 (1951): 2–17.

93. [Courthope,] "The Latest Development of Literary Poetry," 61.

94. [Courthope,] "The Latest Development of Literary Poetry," 66.

Meanwhile, in his response to Rossetti's ambitious poetic sequence, "The House of Life," Courthope stigmatizes those sonnets that present "a deification of the animal instincts as emasculate obscenity"; this view bolsters Robert Buchanan's infamous 1871 attack in the *Contemporary Review* on Rossetti's leadership of a "Fleshly School of Poetry," where Buchanan contemptuously states that the poet's works revel in an adult male's "mere animal sensations" in all their "shameless nakedness."[95] Besides the moral contempt he expresses toward Rossetti's poetry, Courthope voices frustration at Morris's "incurable habit of gossipping [*sic*]" because it causes Morris "to loiter in his narratives, when he should be swift and stirring."[96] "If," Courthope writes of Morris's decided lack of poetic virility, "one of his heroes, say the man born to be a King, sets out on a journey of life and death, we are told all he thought about, whether the apples he saw were ripe, and how many old women he passed, going to market."[97] Certainly, this body of Pre-Raphaelite poetry appalls Courthope because of its spineless masculinity. Yet it also tests his patience because Swinburne, Rossetti, and Morris prove immensely antisocial, purely rhetorical, emphatically secular, repeatedly distracted, and decorative in the extreme.

In the years leading up to Wilde's matriculation at Oxford, Courthope began to characterize postrevolutionary poetry even more aggressively. In his review of *Our Living Poets* (1872) by H. Buxton Forman—whose editorial labors on the works of both Keats and Shelley helped strengthen the reputations of these poets during the fin de siècle—Courthope finally complains about the one term that Forman never uses in his far-reaching study: Romanticism. According to Courthope, "the great obstacle to the production of plain and direct poetry is the almost invincible prejudice that all poetry must be necessarily embodied in a romantic form."[98] He uses "Romanticism" to denote "not so much the love of purely fanciful images of liberty and marvel, as the encroachment of

95. [Courthope,] "The Latest Development of English Poetry," 71; Thomas Maitland [Robert Buchanan], "The Fleshly School of Poetry," *Contemporary Review* 17 (1871): 336. Rossetti's fired back with "The Stealthy School of Criticism," *Athenæum* 2303 (16 December 1871): 792–94. On the controversy, which extended over many years, see John A. Cassidy, "Robert Buchanan and the Fleshly Controversy," *PMLA* 67 (1952): 65–93, and *Robert W. Buchanan* (New York: Twayne, 1973), 36–63; and Christopher D. Murray, "D. G. Rossetti, A. C. Swinburne and R. W. Buchanan: The Fleshly School Revisited, I and II," *Bulletin of the John Rylands Library* 65, no. 1 (1982): 206–32 and 65, no. 2 (1983): 176–207.

96. [Courthope,] "The Latest Development of Literary Poetry," 79.
97. [Courthope,] "The Latest Development of Literary Poetry," 79.
98. [Courthope,] "The State of English Poetry," *Quarterly Review* 135 (1873): 36.

the imagination on the domain of experience, and the application to establish a society of ideas springing out of a sentimental desire for a lawless and primitive freedom."[99] Romanticism's revolutionary origins are clearly problematic for Courthope, but equally concerning is its modern incarnation in English Liberalism: "In the present day, when the foreign politics of England are expressed in the doctrine of non-intervention, when at home society itself acknowledges no standard but that of competition, it is hard for the individual to recognise any interests which are higher and wider than his own."[100] Elsewhere, Courthope characterizes Liberalism as moral relativism coupled with knowledge based solely "on pure sensation."[101] In Courthope's view, one evident symptom of this inexcusable tendency is Matthew Arnold's recent advocacy of "Culture": a term Courthope equates with a despicable "self-cultivation" in an article that condemned Arnold's major prose writings of the 1860s and 1870s, John Addington Symonds's *Studies of the Greek Poets,* and Pater's *Studies in the History of the Renaissance.*[102] In the latter, Courthope finds a prime example of the way that the "the art of spiritualizing language" enabled the objectionable phenomenon of "culture" to "turn . . . poetry into criticism" and "transform criticism into poetry." As a result, Courthope recoils from what he rudely characterizes as Pater's "epicene style."[103]

In January 1876, Courthope turned again to Pater's work, where he found the most debilitating results of the Romantic movement. As we have noted, the opposition between Romanticism and classicism was, by the 1870s, schematic. For Courthope, the classicism of Thomas Gray, for whom imagination remained "restricted by sense and subject to reason," was superior to the Romanticism of Wordsworth and his ilk, for whom imagination—which strayed into not only revolutionary sentiment but also antisocial individualism—remained "absolutely paramount."[104] To Courthope, this unbridled "philosophical imagination" —one that he loosely traces to both Rousseau and Girondism—set such a premium on individual liberty that it had transmogrified into a "subtle form of self-flattery," which he characterizes as "the symptom of that disease which we call Romanticism."[105] And in Courthope's telling, Pater was "the most thoroughly representative critic of the romantic school," who embodied the dread-

99. [Courthope,] "The State of English Poetry," 36.
100. [Courthope,] "The State of English Poetry," 38.
101. [Courthope,] "Modern Culture," *Quarterly Review* 137 (1874): 409.
102. [Courthope,] "Modern Culture," 391.
103. [Courthope,] "Modern Culture," 411.
104. [Courthope,] "Wordsworth and Gray," *Quarterly Review* 141 (1876): 128.
105. [Courthope,] "Wordsworth and Gray," 132.

ful outcome of the cultural pathology.[106] It is unsurprising that Pater's championing of Wordsworth's "impassioned contemplation" and this great Romantic poet's withdrawal from moral teaching provoked some of Courthope's most incensed commentary on Romanticism's pernicious qualities.[107]

Pater's discerning essay "Romanticism" (1876) was an indirect but judicious response to Courthope's Tory polemic; the piece held particular resonance for Wilde, who had always maintained a close eye on Pater's publications, the controversial nature of which attracted attention at Oxford, just before Wilde entered the university. In 1873, the "Conclusion" of *Studies in the History of the Renaissance* proved contentious because it placed such emphasis on the "passion" involved in aesthetic experience—the greatest of which was "the poetic passion, the desire of beauty, the love of art for its own sake."[108] As the strongest critical voice advocating aestheticism in his time, Pater's famous dictum that in order to live life to the full, our sensorium labors "to burn always with this hard, gem-like flame" startled some of his contemporaries, who sensed that a respectable educator might be well advised to show restraint and not advance such a boldly hedonistic claim.[109] Aware that he was the target of hostility and unwilling to provoke any gratuitous attacks, Pater's "Romanticism" deftly refocuses the debate about the origins of the long-standing opposition between the Romantic and the classical. Deeply knowledgeable about German Romantic thought and French literary tradition, Pater ranks among the earliest English writers to speak of Romanticism as an identifiable quality detectable in many literary works that were not necessarily produced within a discernible period, which his contemporaries increasingly confined to the later eighteenth century. One of the main works against which Pater defines his position is Stendhal's *Racine et Shakespeare* (1823–1825), where the French novelist defends the modernity of "*le romanticisme*" against the superannuated traditionalism enshrined

106. [Courthope,] "Wordsworth and Gray," 132.

107. Walter H. Pater, "On Wordsworth," *Fortnightly Review* 15, no. 88 (1874): 463, 465.

108. Pater, *Studies in the History of the Renaissance* (London: Macmillan, 1873), 219; reprinted in *The Renaissance: Studies in Art and Poetry, The 1893 Text*, ed. Donald L. Hill (Berkeley: University of California Press, 1980), 190.

109. Pater, *Studies in the History of the Renaissance*, 210; reprinted in *The Renaissance*, ed. Hill, 189. Perhaps the most infamous attack on Pater's *Renaissance* was the the pamphlet by the bishop of Oxford, John Fielder Mackarness, "A Charge Delivered to the Diocese of Oxford," in which he identifies Pater's resistance to "abstract morality" and "what is only conventional," with a dangerous form of instruction: "So sceptics teach?:—can you wonder that some who played an honorable part in Oxford life a generation since, refuse to let their dons imbibe lessons so alien from the lore they learned." Reprinted in R. M. Seiler, ed., *Walter Pater: The Critical Heritage* (London: Routledge and Kegan Paul, 1980), 96.

in "le *classicisme*." In Pater's English translation, Stendhal pursues this idea as follows: "*Romanticism* . . . is the art of presenting to people the literary works which, in the actual state of their habits and beliefs, are capable of giving them the greatest possible pleasure; classicism, on the contrary, of presenting them with that which gave the greatest possible pleasure to their grandfathers."[110]

Yet, as he reflected on the generational difference that Stendhal upheld, Pater remained unconvinced in the belief that the "*romantic*" had historically superseded the "*classical*" through an onward march of cultural progress. From his perspective, the "romantic spirit" was an "ever-present, an enduring principle in the artistic temperament," just like the "*classical*."[111] Where, for Pater, the "romantic character in art" adds "strangeness to beauty" and also characterizes "the desire of beauty," the "classical" persists in the "measure of what a long experience has shown will at least never displease us," since "what pleased our grandparents may at least tranquillise us."[112] By elaborating the dissimilarity between these two coexisting terms, Pater notes, with mild incredulity, that the "accidental sense" in which critics have turned to "*romantic*" has involved labeling Walter Scott as such a writer because "he loved strange adventure, and sought it in the middle age."[113] Similarly, he contends that the "*classical*," a term which conventionally refers to a "well-defined literature," has often been "used in a hard and merely scholastic sense."[114] Such comments suggest that Pater was both refining and redirecting the relations between these famously paired categories that had been subject to rather loose and inaccurate usage in the past. (This is the point that Wilde echoes in "The English Renaissance

110. Walter Pater, "Romanticism," *Macmillan's Magazine* 35 (1876): 65. Many years later, Pater collected this essay as "Postscript," with an apposite epigraph taken from Pindar's ninth Olympian ode, in *Appreciations: With an Essay on Style* (London: Macmillan, 1889), 243–64. Stendhal's text is as follows:

> Le *romanticisme* est l'art de présenter aux peuples les œuvres littéraires qui, dans l'état actuel de leurs habitudes et de leurs croyances, sont susceptibles de leur donner le plus de plaisir possible.
>
> Le *classicisme*, au contraire, leur présente la littérature qui donnait le plus grand plaisir possible à leurs arrière-grands-pères.

(Stendhal [Henri Beyle], *Racine et Shakespeare: Études sur le romantisme*, nouvelle édition [Paris: Michel Lévy Frères, 1854], 32–33).

111. Pater, "Romanticism," 64.

112. Pater, "Romanticism," 65.

113. Pater, "Romanticism," 64. Stendhal defends the value of Scott's "*romantisme*" on several occasions in *Racine et Shakespeare* (see, for example, 6 and 197–98).

114. Pater, "Romanticism," 64.

of Art" when he says that the two terms are "mere catchwords of schools.") In Pater's view, it is better to think of the manner in which the two epithets define "tendencies at work at all times in art—moulding it, with the balance sometimes a little on one side, sometimes a little on the other, generating respectively, as the balance inclines on this side or that, two principles, two traditions, the classical and romantic traditions in art."[115]

Despite Pater's attention to complicating the reductive positioning of Romanticism as the antithesis of classicism, he did not rebut Courthope directly by defending the "spirit of Keats," the poet who perhaps best typified the sensibility that Courthope deplored. It therefore was left to Wilde to undertake this task. The first prose work of Wilde's to appear in print was "The Tomb of Keats," which the Catholic *Irish Monthly* included in its July 1877 issue. Everything about the poet's gravesite in the Protestant Cemetery in Rome, which Wilde had visited during the spring, appalled him. He found both the "time-worn stone" and the "violets . . . daisies and . . . poppies" to be "poor memorials of one so great as Keats."[116] But these disappointments hardly prevented Wilde from experiencing a stirring epiphany as he pondered the injustice that this unremarkable grave did to Keats's memory: "I thought of him as of a Priest of Beauty slain before his time; and the vision of Guido's St. Sebastian came before my eyes as I saw him at Genoa, a lovely brown boy, with crisp, clustering hair and red lips, bound by his evil enemies to a tree, and, though pierced by arrows, raising his eyes with divine, impassioned gaze towards the Eternal Beauty of the opening heavens."[117] Even though the portraits of Keats (such as Joseph Severn's) that were widely known among the public depicted a handsome, boyish young man, none went so far as to relate his suffering to Guido Reni's magnificent baroque depiction of the arrow-pierced St. Sebastian, held in Genoa's Palazzo Rosso. An early Christian martyr, Sebastian was sent to his death by his lover, the pagan emperor Diocletian, for his fearless devotion to Jesus Christ. Perhaps it was the cemetery's location, inside the Porta San Sebastiano, which inspired this connection between Keats's plight and that of the agonized Christian martyr.

To impress this distinctly male homoerotic vision of Keats, Wilde appended a poem with a Virgilian title—*"Heu Miserande Puer"* ("Alas, poor boy")—in

115. Pater, "Romanticism," 67.

116. Wilde, "The Tomb of Keats," *Irish Monthly*, 5 July 1877: 476–78, in *Journalism Part I*, ed. Stokes and Turner, *Complete Works of Oscar Wilde*, 6:12.

117. Wilde, 'The Tomb of Keats," in *Journalism Part I*, ed. Stokes and Turner, 6:12.

which he depicts the Romantic poet as "Fair as Sebastian and as foully slain."[118] As he developed this sonnet, he transformed parts of the sestet so that Keats was no longer the "saddest poet that the world hath seen"; by 1881, when the poem reappeared first in January in the *Burlington: A High-Class Monthly Magazine* and then in June in *Poems*, this line had changed dramatically: "O sweetest lips since those of Mitylene!"[119] By eventually linking Keats's poetic voice with Sappho's home on Lesbos, Wilde's praise for the long-deceased "Priest of Beauty" connected the Romantic poet not only with the head of the European lyric tradition but also with her well-known desires for women. As Susan J. Wolfson has observed, Wilde's phrasing makes Keats sound sexually all-inclusive: "Wilde's 'Keats' is typecast for male as well as female love: young, beautiful, doomed— the perfect subject, the perfect object, for aesthetic rapture."[120] In another work, which also appears in *Poems*, Wilde held fast to this rapturous image. Yet on this occasion—in extravagantly long lines that accentuate a yearning for the "lovely brown boy"—Keats has become a fantasized erotic object whose very being appears to have emerged from the lush environment of his odes: "Keats had lifted up his hymenæal curls from out the poppy-seeded wine, / With ambrosial mouth had kissed my forehead, clasped the hand of noble love in mine."[121] Elsewhere in *Poems*, Keats maintains a sensual presence. In the lyric titled "Endymion," for example, Keats's beautiful lad "hast the lips that should be kissed," while in the much longer "Garden of Eros" we read that the Romantic poet himself sang so sweetly that with his death nothing less than "Song passed away."[122] Moreover, in "The Garden of Eros"—amid his praise for "Morris, our sweet and simple Chaucer's child"—Wilde's speaker identifies himself as one

118. Wilde, "The Tomb of Keats," *Journalism Part I*, ed. Stokes and Turner, 6:12–13. Wilde's Latin title comes from *Aeneid* 15.882, and it refers to the young Marcellus. Wilde praised Sir Charles Bowen's "graceful rendering" of this phrase as "Child of a nation's sorrow" in "Sir Charles Bowen's *Virgil*," *Pall Mall Gazette*, 30 November 1887: 3; reprinted in *Journalism Part II*, ed. Stokes and Turner, 7:22.

119. Wilde, "The Grave of Keats," in *Poems and Poems in Prose*, 1:36. After "Heu Miserande Puer" was published in *Irish Monthly*, the revised version appeared as "The Grave of Keats" in *Burlington: A High-Class Monthly Magazine* 1 (January 1881): 35, and in *Poems* (1881), 147.

120. Susan J. Wolfson, *Borderlines: The Shiftings of Gender in British Romanticism* (Stanford, CA: Stanford University Press, 2006), 262.

121. Wilde, "ΓΛΥΚΥΠΙΚΡΟς ΕΡΩς" ("Bittersweet Love"), in *Poems and Poems in Prose*, 1:74. "ΓΛΥΚΥΠΙΚΡΟς ΕΡΩς" first appeared in *Poems* (1881), 233–36.

122. Wilde, "Endymion" and "The Garden of Eros," in *Poems and Poems in Prose*, 1:70, 131. "Endymion" and "The Garden of Eros" first appeared in *Poems* (1881), 95–97, 17–34.

of the remaining custodians of aesthetic beauty in an age of alienating science: "Shall I, the last Endymion, lose all hope / Because rude eyes peer at my mistress through a telescope!"[123] Wilde thus understood himself to be standing at the tail end of an embattled poetic tradition, one confronted by a hostile "scientific age," whose ancestry began with Keats.[124] In an indulgent hyperbole, the prolific American writer Edgar Fawcett recognized that the spirit of the "reverenced master" was so great that Wilde was set to take on nothing less than the Romantic poet's "immortal vestiture" and ascend toward the heavens, where he would meet the "splendor that men mean when they name Keats."[125]

Wilde's avowed passion for Keats, however, went further than any of his poems might suggest. Like a number of his contemporaries, he was dismayed, not only with the state of the original tombstone, but also with the unsuitable memorial tablet that had recently been installed to accompany the restored four-foot marble gravestone that Keats's friend Joseph Severn had erected in his honor. On the original tomb (as the Romantic poet requested and Wilde's poem recorded), was written the inscription, "Here lies One / Whose Name was writ in Water."[126] On 22 February 1876, a crowd of Keats's followers witnessed the unveiling of Warrington Wood's medallion portrait of Keats on the wall that divided the old part of the cemetery. Beneath this design was a rather flat-footed acrostic poem by Vincent Eyre.[127] Wilde let his consternation at such atrocious writing be known to Lord Houghton (formerly Richard Monckton Milnes),

123. Wilde, "The Garden of Eros," in *Poems and Poems in Prose*, 1:132, 134.

124. Wilde, "The Garden of Eros," in *Poems and Poems in Prose*, 1:134.

125. Edgar Fawcett, "To Oscar Wilde: On Receiving from Him a Book of His Poems," in *Song and Story: Later Poems* (Boston: James R. Osgood, 1884), 181.

126. "Thy name was writ in water—it shall stand" ('The Grave of Keats," *Poems and Poems in Prose*, 1:36). The motto on the tombstone derives from act 4, scene 2, of Shakespeare's *King Henry VIII*: "Men's evil manners live in brass, their virtues / We write in water" (*King Henry VIII (All Is True)*, ed. Gordon McMullan [London: Arden Shakespeare, 2000], 377).

127. Eyre's poem reads as follows:

Keats, if thy cherished name be "writ on water,"
Each drop has fallen from some mourner's cheek;
A sacred tribute; such as heroes seek,
Though oft in vain—for dazzling deeds of slaughter.
Sleep on! Not honoured less for Epitaph so meek.

William Sharp's complaint about the "intolerable incongruity" of this verse represented a widespread opinion; see *The Life and Letters of Joseph Severn* (London: Sampson Low, Marston, 1892), 282.

whose company he had enjoyed in the past. In a letter dating from May 1877, Wilde insisted that "this very ugly thing ought not to be allowed to remain," and he begged the older man to use his influence to ensure that a "really beautiful monument might be erected" in Keats's honor.[128] Wilde also took the liberty of mailing an offprint of his article on Keats's gravesite—"a stray sheet from a boy's diary," as he modestly styled it—to William Michael Rossetti, by then a well-known critic, in a further attempt to ingratiate himself in Pre-Raphaelite company.[129] Yet another "stray sheet from a boy's diary" (as he once again called his piece) went to Forman, a scholar who was already well known for his biography of Shelley, for which William Bell Scott—an artist close to the Pre-Raphaelites, especially Dante Gabriel Rossetti—furnished an etching of that poet's grave, which is also in the Protestant Cemetery in Rome.[130]

By 1881, when he was preparing *Poems* for publication, Wilde's devotion to Keats's memory was so strong that planned to set on the title page a quotation from the Romantic poet's remarkable correspondence with his friend the critic John Hamilton Reynolds: "I have not the slightest feeling of humility toward the Public or to anything in existence but the eternal Being, the Principle of Beauty and the Memory of great Men."[131] Perhaps wisely, Wilde decided against the quotation, substituting in its place "Helas!": a sonnet that reads much more like his own artistic manifesto than any statement modeled on Keats.[132] If Wilde had used Keats's letter as an epigraph, his wishful identification with the Romantic poet's celebrated legacy might have given the impression that he was exploiting another writer's standpoint in order to express indifference to public opinion. Even without the Keatsian epigraph, reviewers of *Poems* found many of the poems by this self-appointed "last Endymion" unsatisfactorily derivative, sounding not so much like Keats as his Pre-Raphaelite idols, such as Swinburne, whose controversial *Poems and Ballads* offered Wilde metrical models and sen-

128. Wilde, "To Lord Houghton," 17 May 1877, in *Complete Letters*, 50. The inaugural ceremony for the monument had taken place to some fanfare on 22 February 1876.

129. Wilde, "To William Michael Rossetti," 14 July 1877, in *Complete Letters*, 55.

130. Wilde, "To H. Buxton Forman," July 1877, in *Complete Letters*, 56. Wilde wrote another sonnet, "The Grave of Shelley," which also resulted from his visit to the Protestant Cemetery at Rome. The poem first appeared in *Poems* (1881), 161; see *Poems and Poems in Prose*, 1:43.

131. Keats, "To J. H. Reynolds," 9 April 1818, in *Life Letters, and Literary Remains of John Keats*, ed., Richard Monckton Milnes, 2 vols. (London: Edward Moxon, 1848), 1:120. The letter is reprinted, in a slightly different text, in *The Letters of John Keats, 1814–1821*, ed. Hyder Edward Rollins, 2 vols. (Cambridge, MA: Harvard University Press, 1958), 1:266.

132. See Wilde, *Poems and Poems in Prose*, 1:292–93.

sual subject matter that he was keen to emulate. The *Spectator*, for example, deplored the manner in which "the spirit of poetry is conjured to tarry" in Wilde's poetry "because Keats is dead, and only Mr. Swinburne,—with whom Mr. Wilde afterwards associates the names of Mr. Morris and Mr. Rossetti,—is left to us."[133]

In many respects, though, "Helas!" emerged as Wilde's bid to forward his own distinctive comprehension of the best way of honoring the "Principle of Beauty." Here Wilde's poetic voice fears that if he "did but touch the honey of romance" he may well stand to "lose a soul's inheritance."[134] His biblical allusion to 1 Samuel 14:43, where Jonathan admits to David that he had defied his father Saul's ruling over the Israelites by eating the forbidden "little honey," suggests that he allowed his soul to "drift with every passion" only with trepidation. Yet, by imagining his soul as if it were "a stringed lute on which all winds can play," he evokes the image of the Aeolian harp, which Coleridge made famous in his poem about that instrument in 1796.[135] Moreover, the desire to drift as passion dictates implicitly resounds with Pater's memorable suggestion that experience consists of "this movement, with the passage and dissolution of impressions, images, sensations," that critical analysis cannot capture.[136] Wilde's sonnet intimates that poetic "romance," whether in Coleridge's poetics or in Pater's criticism, on the one hand, and Old Testament "wisdom," on the other hand, remain in tension in his writing.

If "Helas!" voices the fear that the "honey of romance" has turned somewhat bitter, it is worth bearing in mind that it was at this time becoming increasingly difficult for the public to imagine Keats as an icon of complete artistic perfection. The same was true of other Romantics, especially Shelley. In his famous 1888 essay on recent revelations about Shelley's personal life—which involved the abandonment of his first spouse (Harriet Westbrook), who committed suicide, in favor of Mary Godwin, with whom the poet was living at the time—

133. [Anon.,] Review of Wilde, *Poems*, *Spectator*, 13 August 1881: 1048–50; reprinted in *Oscar Wilde: The Critical Heritage*, ed. Karl Beckson (London: Routledge and Kegan Paul, 1970), 44.

134. Wilde, "Helas!" in *Poems and Poems in Prose*, 1:157. The poem first appeared before the table of contents in *Poems* (1881), v.

135. Wilde, "Helas!" in *Poems and Poems in Prose*, 1:157. Coleridge's "Eolian Harp" first appeared in *Poems on Various Subjects* (London: C. G. and J. Robinsons, 1796). The metaphor of the Aeolian harp is also associated with Novalis (Georg Philipp Friedrich Freiherr von Hardenberg) in the *Fragments* (1798), and it is present in such well-known Romantic works as Shelley's *Prometheus Unbound* (1820).

136. Pater, *Studies in the History of the Renaissance*, 210; reprinted in *The Renaissance*, ed. Hill, 188.

Arnold could not repress his frustration in discovering "the new and grave matter" about the Romantic writer's infidelity in Edward Dowden's two-volume *Life* (1886): "What a set! what a world! is the exclamation that breaks from us as we come to an end of this history of 'the occurrences of Shelley's private life.'"[137] Little wonder that Arnold remarked elsewhere that Shelley remained a "beautiful but ineffectual angel."[138] Meanwhile, he observed that Coleridge had been "wrecked in a mist of opium," while Keats "died having produced too little and being as yet too immature to rival" both Wordsworth and Byron.[139] Arnold, however, did not dare question the widespread view that Keats possessed a "more consummate poetic gift" than either of these contemporaries.[140]

Dowden's account of Shelley's marital turmoil was startling to readers, but Shelley was not the first Romantic poet whose biographical reputation underwent serious revision. In the previous decade, revelations about Keats's love life sparked similar controversy. In 1878, Forman, who emerged as Keats's foremost editor during this period, published a selection of letters that unveiled Keats's seemingly troubled devotion to his beloved Fanny Brawne (later Fanny Lindon), who had passed away in 1865. Forman's selection of these often saddening letters, which had remained in the hands of Brawne's descendants, ended with Keats's desperate farewell epistle to his beloved, just before he started for Italy, knowing full well that he would probably succumb to tuberculosis in that fairer clime: "I see life in nothing but the certainty of your Love—convince me of it my sweetest."[141] Such writing exposed Keats as a troubled man, imagining

---

137. Arnold, "Shelley," *Nineteenth Century* 23 (1888): 23–39, reprinted in *The Last Word, The Complete Prose Works of Matthew Arnold*, ed. Super, 11:320. In her 1839 edition of Percy Bysshe Shelley's poetry, Mary Shelley states: "I abstain from any remark on the occurrences of his private life" ("Preface," in *The Poetical Works of Percy Bysshe Shelley*, ed. Mary Shelley, 2 vols. [London: Edward Moxon, 1839], 1:vii). This letter is quoted in part in Edward Dowden, *The Life of Percy Bysshe Shelley*, 2 vols. (London: Kegan Paul, Trench, 1886), 1:427. Much of Arnold's commentary expresses frustration with Dowden's inept characterization of Shelley's private life.

138. Arnold, "Byron," in *Complete Prose Works of Matthew Arnold*, ed. Super, 9:237. Arnold's essay first appeared as "Preface," in *Poetry of Byron*, ed. Arnold (London: Macmillan, 1881), vii–xxxi.

139. Arnold, "Byron," *Complete Prose Works of Matthew Arnold*, ed. Super, 9:236.

140. Arnold, "Byron," *Complete Prose Works of Matthew Arnold*, ed. Super, 9:236.

141. *Letters of John Keats to Fanny Brawne Written in the Years MDCCCXIX and MD-CCCXX*, ed. Harry Buxton Forman (London: Reeves and Turner, 1878), 119. This letter probably dates from May 1820. Rollins represents the wording slightly differently: "I see *life* in nothing but the cerrtainty [*sic*] of your Love—convince me of it my sweetest" (*Letters of John Keats, 1814–1821*, 2:291).

that the object of his adoration would betray him. As some Victorian reviewers observed, Keats—no matter how much his ailing health had affected his temperament—was not an entirely satisfactory lover. Edmund Gosse, for example, sensed that Keats behaved rather unreasonably, reading Brawne's letters "again and again until each sentence attains a false importance, and all seems too cold or too reproachful."[142] It is no surprise to Gosse that Brawne "finds it hard to bear with the exacting passion of so strange a lover."[143]

Gosse was kinder to Brawne than several other commentators were. By the far the harshest criticism of the letters came from an American source, R. H. Stoddard, who could not restrain his antipathy against Brawne; in a ferocious article, he jumped to the conclusion that she had been a vain, capricious, and exploitative woman who hardly deserved Keats's vulnerable affections. "The influence of Miss Fanny Brawne," he wrote, "was the most unfortunate one to which Keats was ever subjected. She made him ridiculous in the eyes of his friends, and he hated his friends accordingly."[144] "Miss Fanny Brawne," Stoddard stated with great finality, "made John Keats ridiculous in the eyes of his friends in his lifetime, and now she (through her representatives) makes him ridiculous in the eyes of the world."[145]

In the end, Stoddard assumed that the only reason for the Lindon family's decision to publish this unbefitting correspondence was a pecuniary one: "Could there be any motive other than that of lucre?"[146] He was proved right. On 2 March 1885, when the letters went up for sale at Sotheby's, London, they fetched the imposing sum of almost £544. In a detailed discussion of recent editions of Keats's works, including the weighty four-volume set that Forman completed in 1883, the *Edinburgh Review* deplored the sale of these documents. After berating Forman for reprinting Keats's correspondence with Brawne in *The Poetical Works and Other Writings*, it proceeded to excoriate her family for dishonoring the writer's privacy: "This act of desecration—for such we hold it to be—is evidently a consequence of the publication of those feverish letters which certainly never were intended to see the light or to be sold as curiosities."[147] It took until the 1930s before the public was able to read Brawne's side

142. Edmund Gosse, Review of *Letters of John Keats to Fanny Brawne*, *Academy* (9 February 1878): 112.

143. Gosse, Review of *Letters of John Keats to Fanny Brawne*, 112.

144. R. H. Stoddard, "John Keats and Fanny Brawne," *Appleton's Journal* 4 (1878): 382.

145. Stoddard, "John Keats and Fanny Brawne," 382.

146. Stoddard, "John Keats and Fanny Brawne," 382.

147. [Alexander Napier,] "The Life and Works of John Keats," *Edinburgh Review* 162 (1885): 36.

of the story, in an exculpating volume of her letters to Keats's sister, introduced by Forman's son, where she arose from "obscurity to refute silently and with dignity the unkind things that [had been] said about her in bygone days."[148]

That the vagaries of Keats's love life should attract such outrage is testament to his lasting influence. Moreover, the impact of the episode on Wilde at a formative moment in his literary development is unmistakable. Wilde had made a point of attending the controversial Sotheby's sale, which enraged him as much as it did any of his Victorian contemporaries. His terse sonnet on this event, which he published on two occasions in 1886, opens with an attack on the "brawlers of the auction" who command a "merchant's price" for "each separate pulse of passion"; in the sestet, the focus shifts to the plight of Jesus Christ during the Crucifixion, when Roman soldiers "began / To wrangle for mean raiment" and threw "Dice for the garments of a wretched man," not heeding that they were in the presence of God.[149] Wilde's sonnet could not have made it clearer to his readers that the sale amounted to sacrilege.

The two publications where this poem appeared reflect Wilde's range at this point in his career. Besides featuring several of his most significant commentaries on modern theatrical productions, Edwin Paget Palmer's *Dramatic Review* was the venue for Wilde's poem "The Harlot's House," whose modified terza rima evokes the modish fixed forms whose demands Gosse had noted in 1877,[150] showing the writer's responsiveness to works associated with French *Symbolisme*, especially Gautier's "Bûchers et tombeaux" ("Tombs and Funeral Pyres," from *Émaux et camées* [1853]) and Charles Baudelaire's "Danse macabre" ("Dance of Death," from *Les fleurs du mal* [1857, revised 1862]). Soon after appearing in Palmer's periodical, the sonnet on the sale of Keats's letters was reprinted in William Sharp's *Sonnets of This Century* (1886). Wilde informed Sharp, who in later years gulled the public by publishing Celtic romances under the name of Fiona Macleod, that he wished he could "grave" his "sonnets on an ivory tablet."[151] "A

148. M. Buxton Forman, "Preface," in *Letters of Fanny Brawne to John Keats, 1820–1824,* ed. Fred Edgcumbe (New York: Oxford University Press, 1937), vi. The hostility toward Brawne was evident in several late Victorian publications, including William Michael Rossetti's biography of Keats: "Miss Brawne enslaved [Keats] but did not inspire that tender and boundless confidence which the accepted and engaged lover of a virtuous girl naturally feels" (*Life of John Keats* [London: Walter Scott, 1887], 148).

149. Wilde, "Sonnet: On The Sale by Auction of Keats's Love Letters," in *Poems and Poems in Prose,* 1:165–66.

150. Edmund Gosse, "A Plea for Certain Exotic Forms of Verse," *Cornhill Magazine* 36 (1877): 53–71.

151. Wilde, "To William Sharp," November to December 1885, *Complete Letters,* 271.

sonnet should always *look* well," Wilde continued, "Don't you think so?"; this wry inquiry intimates his sense that the printed word was somewhat uncouth, a sentiment especially appropriate in light of the degradation brought to Keats's memory through the sale of Brawne's letters, works of "quill pens and notepaper."[152]

Wilde's phrasing also suggests that he had limited patience with Sharp, whom Wilde felt had exerted misplaced authority over the ways future generations would regard Dante Gabriel Rossetti's reputation. Both Sharp and Hall Caine, in Wilde's view, had served Rossetti poorly in the rough-and-ready books they quickly drafted after the poet-painter's death in April 1882. "Whenever a great man dies," Wilde quipped to fellow poet Richard Le Gallienne, "Hall Caine and William Sharp go in with the undertakers."[153] By 1887, Wilde reiterated the point when he complained in a *Pall Mall Gazette* review of a new Rossetti biography that, even if Caine's and Sharp's "vulgarization of Rossetti" had paved the way for better attempts, the newer study disappointingly remained "just the sort of biography that Guildenstern might have written of Hamlet."[154] "We sincerely hope," Wilde observes, "that there will soon be an end to all biographies of this kind."[155] Yet no matter how much Wilde railed against the vulgarization of Rossetti's memory that he discerned in Caine's *Recollections of Dante Gabriel Rossetti* (1882) and Sharp's *Dante Gabriel Rossetti: A Record and a Study* (1882), he could not avoid the fact that both writers drew strong attention to the Pre-Raphaelite artist's devotion to Keats; he would also have learned from both works that Rossetti was dedicated to Chatterton. Moreover, he would have seen Caine and Sharp express their disbelief in Rossetti's admiration for the young Bristol poet.

Caine proved rather reluctant to credit Chatterton with greatness. In his 1882 study, Caine disclosed that Rossetti's 1880 sonnet on Chatterton, which Wilde duly transcribed at the end of the notebook, did not appear, as originally intended, in Watts's essay because Watts "could not go to Rossetti's length in comparing" the author of the Rowley poems to Shakespeare, as Rossetti did in the sonnet. Caine reiterated his own negative outlook on Chatterton, who did not, in his view, possess "the note of personal purity and majesty of character."[156]

152. Wilde, "To William Sharp," *Complete Letters*, 271.

153. Richard Le Gallienne, *The Romantic '90s* (New York: Doubleday, Page, 1925), 30.

154. Wilde, "A Cheap Edition of a Great Man," *Pall Mall Gazette*, 18 April 1887: 5; in *Journalism Part I*, ed. Stokes and Turner, 6:146. Wilde's review focuses on Joseph Knight's concise *Life of Dante Gabriel Rossetti* (London: Walter Scott, 1887).

155. Wilde, "A Cheap Edition of a Great Man," in *Journalism Part I*, ed. Stokes and Turner, 6:148.

156. Caine, *Recollections of Dante Gabriel Rossetti* (London: Elliot, Stock, 1882), 186, 189.

Meanwhile, Sharp sounded somewhat condescending when he voiced his surprise that Rossetti, in the 1880 sonnet, placed Chatterton among the loftiest trophies of English poetry: "The lines are generous and enthusiastic, but it is difficult to realise that Rossetti could really hold such an extreme opinion regarding Chatterton: perhaps it was engendered by a late acquaintance and the enthusiasm that comes from the sense of having discovered a treasure hitherto neglected."[157] Moreover, Sharp attributed Rossetti's newfound avidity to Watts: "I have heard Rossetti state that his knowledge of the unfortunate poet's work was of very recent growth and owing to the friend whose name must so often occur in any record of the last ten years of the poet-painter's life."[158] In other words, the blame for Rossetti's belated, and seemingly misjudged, fascination with Chatterton lay with Watts: the devoted friend to whom Rossetti had affectionately dedicated his final volume, *Ballads and Sonnets* (1881).

Watts responded diplomatically to Caine's and Sharp's respective volumes by publishing a thoughtful critical essay, "The Truth about Rossetti," where he made it plain that he wished to eliminate the "many misconceptions" about Rossetti's "art that [were] already taking root."[159] With allusions to Sharp's "full and valuable but hastily written monograph" and Caine's view that "Rossetti himself believed his plastic gift to be secondary to his poetic," Watts took pains to focus not so much on his deceased friend's notorious addiction to chloral hydrate as the artist's distinguished position within Romanticism.[160] Uninterested in recent criticisms that Rossetti's poetry and painting lapsed over time into sensual "decadence," Watts placed the artist-poet firmly in a tradition of "the weird and mysterious which we call *Romantic*" that "never appeared in English art before [William] Blake"; this was, Watts adds, the movement that readers associate with the "Romantic Revival" evident in the works of Coleridge and Scott.[161] Rossetti's project, Watts asserts in italics, was to *"eliminate asceticism from romantic art, and yet remain romantic, to retain that mysticism which alone can give life to romantic art, and yet to be as sensuous as the Titians who revived*

157. William Sharp, *Dante Gabriel Rossetti: A Record and a Study* (London: Macmillan, 1882), 401.

158. Sharp, *Dante Gabriel Rossetti*, 401.

159. Theodore Watts, "The Truth about Rossetti," *Nineteenth Century* 13 (1883): 404.

160. Watts, 'The Truth about Rossetti," 407.

161. Watts, "The Truth about Rossetti," 409. Even at the time of his death, the controversy that Robert Buchanan (under the pseudonymous guide of "Thomas Maitland") generated in his attack on the unseemly sexuality in Rossetti's *Poems* (1870) still lingered. See note 95 (133).

sensuousness at the sacrifice of mysticism, was the quest, more or less conscious, of [the poet-painter's] genius."[162] Even though he does not mention Rossetti's interest in Chatterton or Rossetti's comprehensive knowledge of Keats, Watts made the connections clear between the emergence of Romanticism in the late eighteenth century and Rossetti's Pre-Raphaelite poetry and painting one hundred years later.

Rossetti also helped shape Forman's impressive edition of Keats's *Poetical Works*, which drew heavily on the editor's correspondence with Rossetti about the textual history of Keats's poems. These conversations developed at roughly the same time Watts started discussing Chatterton with the artist, and Rossetti's advice to Forman made patently clear the degree to which Keats's poetry engaged with that of Chatterton. In his annotations, Forman points out, for example, that Rossetti informed him that he wished to preserve Keats's original dedication of *Endymion*, which initially read: "To the memory of the most English of poets except Shakespeare, Thomas Chatterton"; he remarks, too, that Rossetti believed that Keats's "Devon Maid," written at Teignmouth, Devon, in 1818, echoes one of Chatterton's songs in *Ælla*.[163]

There was a piece of important textual information about Keats's oeuvre that eluded Forman. After his tour of North America, Wilde obtained one of Keats's manuscripts from the poet's niece. As Wilde explained in the *Century Guild Hobby Horse* in July 1886, it was during his visit to Louisville, Kentucky, where he had delivered a talk over four years before, that he met Keats's niece, Emma Speed. Wilde recalled that she came up to introduce herself after his presentation, in which he had reason to quote from Keats's sonnet on blue "as an example of the poet's delicate sense of colour-harmonies."[164] He spent most of 23 February 1882 in her company, which gave him the opportunity to read Keats's letters to his brother George, several of which were at the time unpublished. Later during his lecture tour, Speed sent Wilde a letter urging him to accept the manuscript of Keats's sonnet in her possession. In his short essay for the *Hobby Horse*, Wilde disclosed that the manuscript is the earliest draft of a poem that appeared as "Answer to a Sonnet Ending Thus" in Milnes's 1854 edition of the *Poetical Works*. Wilde pointed out that the manuscript he had fortunately acquired differed from the one that A. J. Horwood presented to the

162. Watts, "The Truth about Rossetti," 412. Emphasis in the original.

163. *The Poetical Works and Other Writings of John Keats, Now First Brought together, Including Poems and Numerous Letters Not before Published*, ed. Harry Buxton Forman, 4 vols. (London: Reeves and Turner, 1883), 2:265.

164. Wilde, "Keats' Sonnet on Blue," *Century Guild Hobby Horse* 1, no. 3 (July 1886): 83; in *Journalism Part I*, 6:84.

Athenæum in 1876. In his comparison of the variants between the published text and Horwood's manuscript, on the one hand, with the version he owned, on the other hand, Wilde observed that readers can grasp in this earliest rendition "the conditions that preceded the perfected form, the gradual growth, not of the conception but of the expression, and the workings of that spirit of selection which is the secret of style."[165]

Especially important for Wilde were the ways in which these versions revealed Keats's sensitivity to punctuation. The draft in the *Athenæum*, he observed, usefully inserts a comma in the final line, so that the closing sentence of the sestet reads as follows: "But how great, / When in an Eye thou art, alive with fate!"[166] Where Milnes had omitted the comma, Forman adopted it, in what Wilde believed was a "decided improvement."[167] Later, in the *Pall Mall Gazette* Wilde expressed his dissatisfaction with William Michael Rossetti's recent study of Keats, which suffered two main problems: "When Mr. Rossetti writes of the man he forgets the poet, and when he criticises the poet he shows that he does not understand the man."[168] By this stage, Wilde was no longer projecting himself as the "last Endymion" but instead presenting himself as a textual scholar who could trace that poem's roots to a potent eighteenth-century source. The time had assuredly come for him not so much to keep extending the "the neo-romantic school" in his poetry as to articulate its ancestry. As his notes on Rossetti's *Ballads and Sonnets* (1881) make evident, Wilde had become much clearer in his thought about the writers who belonged to an evolving Romantic tradition: "Like another great leader | of the romantic school | he has become a classic | in his lifetime: and remains for | younger workers in song the

165. Wilde, "Keats' Sonnet on Blue," in *Journalism Part I*, ed. Stokes and Turner, 6:84. The "Chatterton" notebook contains a similar phrase: "the conditions that precede artistic production" (Appendix A, f.2ʳ [335]).

166. A. J. Horwood, "A Sonnet by Keats," *Athenæum* 2536 (3 June 1876): 764. Horwood states that this copy of Keats's sonnet was pasted into his volume of J. H. Reynolds's *Garden of Florence and Other Poems* (1821), where a handwritten note observes that Keats wrote the poem as an answer to Reynolds's two sonnets on Sherwood Forest.

167. Wilde, "Keats' Sonnet on Blue," in *Journalism Part I*, ed. Stokes and Turner, 6:85. Forman took note of Wilde's article in *Poetry and Prose by John Keats: A Book of Fresh Verses and New Readings—Essays and Letters Lately Found—and Passages Formerly Suppressed* (London: Reeves and Turner, 1890), 25. Stillinger retains the comma in the final line; see *Complete Poems*, ed. Jack Stillinger (Cambridge, MA: Harvard University Press, 1978), 173.

168. Wilde, "Two Biographies of Keats," *Pall Mall Gazette*, 27 September 1887, 3; in *Journalism Part I*, ed. Stokes and Turner, 6:188.

most | splendid and perfect model (Appendix B, f.1ᵛ [412]). In the mid-1880s, Wilde knew how to discuss the links between Keats's life story and his brilliant art, just as he could grasp Rossetti's position as an heir to Keats. He was also poised to acknowledge the leadership that Chatterton gave to both of these great writers as the "father of the Romantic movement."

WATTS, ROSSETTI, AND CHATTERTON: "THE NEW ROMANTIC SCHOOL"

The developing critical register that positioned Chatterton as an influential proto-Romantic poet came after both David Masson and Daniel Wilson had published their respective book-length inquiries into Chatterton's career. For Wilde, the idea that Chatterton stood at the head of the "Romantic movement" derived from another source that exerted arguably greater intellectual influence over his reflections on the Bristol poet than the other materials he consulted when compiling his notebook. In his outstanding contribution to Ward's *English Poets*, Theodore Watts viewed Chatterton as the literary forefather of the English Romantics in terms almost identical to those Wilde would adopt: "When we consider the influence Coleridge himself had upon the English romantic movement generally, and especially upon Shelley and Keats, and the enormous influence these latter have had upon subsequent poets, it seems impossible to refuse to Chatterton the place of the father of the New Romantic school."[169] Watts's shrewd essay caught Wilde's attention for several connected reasons. The most significant relates to the high regard in which Wilde held Rossetti and Swinburne. By 1880, no other man could rival the intimacy Watts enjoyed with both of these leading literary figures, and it is worth dwelling for a moment on the privileged access that he maintained, in different ways, with these writers at a time when their reputations were closely connected with scandal and ill-health. In some respects, Watts, who was on friendly terms with the Wilde family, proved to be Wilde's nearest point of possible contact with the

---

169. Watts, "Thomas Chatterton," *The English Poets*, ed. Ward, 3:401. Watts's elaboration of the modern concept of a "romantic school" had part of its origins in D. M. Moir's *Sketches of the Poetical Literature of the Past Half Century* (1851). Moir grouped many different writers of prose and poetry (including Coleridge, James Hogg, "Monk" Lewis, Anne Radcliffe, and Wordsworth) within a "romantic" school (*Sketches of the Poetical Literature of the Past Half Century* [Edinburgh: William Blackwood, 1851], 17). This information is traced in David Perkins, *Is Literary History Possible?* (Baltimore: Johns Hopkins University Press, 1992), 99.

two modern authors whose poetry left such a marked impression on his earliest poems.[170]

After he removed his legal practice from St. Ives, Cambridgeshire, to London in order to pursue a part-time literary career, Watts established himself as a knowledgeable critic of English poetry through a series of impressive reviews that he placed in the *Athenæum* from 1875 onward. Nevertheless, it was his professional work as an attorney that initially brought him into personal acquaintance with both Rossetti and Swinburne. At the time of his earliest meeting with Rossetti, whom he first assisted with a case where a woman had forged the artist's signature on a check in 1872, Watts was not known to the Pre-Raphaelite circle as a particularly accomplished literary man. He had come to Rossetti's attention through a mutual acquaintance, the physician and poet Gordon Hake, whose largely mystical verses Rossetti admired. Even though Rossetti's most recent biographer claims that during this period "Watts was aged forty, going on seventy, with a solicitor's habit of seeing worst-case scenarios," the lawyer's apparently sedate—if not fogeyish—manner scarcely repelled Rossetti, who was, by any account, a difficult man to know.[171] Given his poor state of well-being (exacerbated by his addiction to chloral), Rossetti also had to weather the mental grief that Buchanan had caused by attacking him for spearheading an unpalatable "Fleshly School of Poetry." Within months of their first acquaintance, as the editors of Watts's life and letters observe, this undemonstrative legal gentleman from East Anglia turned out to be the proverbial "'friend of friends' who came to understand those subtle and cryptic sides of Rossetti's nature which few, if any, of his other friends seemed ever able to fathom."[172] So close did the two men grow that Hake himself commented on the "brotherly intimacy" that developed between them.[173] Others in the circle also noted the bond between Watts and Rossetti. Henry Treffry Dunn documented the friendship in his famous gouache and watercolor, where the two men are seen discussing the proofs of Rossetti's final volume, *Ballads and Sonnets,* in Rossetti's home and

170. Constance Wilde's visiting book shows that Watts visited the Wilde family home on Tite Street on 6 June 1887. In addition to his signature, he penned a sweet, eight-line poem titled "Baby Smiles!" apparently inspired by the charming sight of Constance with the infant Vyvyan. Autograph Album of Constance Wilde: British Library, Eccles Bequest, Add. MS 81755, f.7.

171. Jan Marsh, *Dante Gabriel Rossetti: Painter and Poet* (London: Weidenfeld and Nicolson, 1999), 457.

172. Hake and Compton-Rickett, *Life and Letters of Theodore Watts-Dunton*, 1:68.

173. Gordon Hake, *Memoirs of Eighty Years* (London: Richard Bentley, 1892), 230.

studio at Tudor House on Cheyne Walk, Chelsea.[174] In 1904, Dunn, Rossetti's former studio assistant who had become a member of Watts's own household in South London five years before, recalled that Watts "used to be Rossetti's confidant of much that he did not speak of to his general friends."[175] In 1882, at the age of fifty-three, after he had suffered a debilitating stroke and kidney failure, Rossetti died with Watts at his side. Among Rossetti's final words was a tribute to this treasured companion: "Watts is a hero of friendship."[176]

Very probably, it was in 1872 that Watts first met the other Pre-Raphaelite poet in whose professional affairs and personal life he would play an equally decisive role. In October that year, Swinburne—who happened to take rooms on the same street in Central London where Watts was lodging—turned to the solicitor for assistance with disentangling his publications from John Camden Hotten. The publisher, whose lists included works of clandestine erotic fiction, had reissued Swinburne's controversial *Poems and Ballads* (1866) after the respectable house of Edward Moxon withdrew it in response to hostile reviews. At the time, Swinburne was eager to place his works in the hands of F. S. Ellis, whose lists included Rossetti's *Poems*. Watts soon became privy to the anger Swinburne suffered when reading Buchanan's assault on his close friend Rossetti; in 1866, Buchanan had also been one of the most vicious reviewers of *Poems and Ballads*, remarking in the *Athenæum* that Swinburne was nothing less than a vendor of pornography: "Inspired in Holywell Street, composed on the Parade at Brighton, and touched up in the Jardin Mabile."[177] In quick response, Swin-

174. This work, which is owned by the National Portrait Gallery, was originally sold to Watts. Dunn was Rossetti's studio assistant from 1867 to c. 1878. See Jan Marsh's commentary on the painting, National Portrait Gallery, accessed 8 July 2012, http://www .npg.org.uk/collections/search/portraitExtended/mw05468/Dante-Gabriel-Rossetti-Theo dore-Watts-Dunton. Wilde had some social contact with Watts (see above, 150), and thus may have had some knowledge of Dunn's work.

175. Henry Treffry Dunn, *Recollections of Dante Gabriel Rossetti (Cheyne Walk Life)* (London: Elkin Mathews, 1904), 56.

176. Hake and Compton-Rickett, *Life and Letters of Theodore Watts-Dunton*, 1:229. Hall Caine, who worked for Rossetti during the artist's final years, claimed that these were among the last words that Rossetti uttered (*Recollections of Dante Gabriel Rossetti* [London: Elliot, Stock, 1882], 75). William Michael Rossetti recalls that at the time of his brother's death Watts was "at Gabriel's right side, partly supporting him" (*Dante Gabriel Rossetti: His Family-Letters*, 2 vols. [London: Ellis and Elvey, 1895], 1:399).

177. [Robert Buchanan,] Review of Swinburne, *Poems and Ballads*, *Athenæum* 2023 (4 August 1866): 137. Each of the locations that Buchanan mentions is associated with sexual commerce. Holywell Street, London, was notorious for its booksellers' trade in erotica.

burne took Buchanan to task in *Notes on Poems and Reviews* (1866). Six years later, when he was similarly inflamed by Buchanan's assault on the "Fleshly School," Swinburne wrote another piece of extraordinary invective, *Under the Microscope* (1872). Buchanan's criticisms certainly struck a nerve, since they used to vitriolic effect the very epithet that Swinburne had employed in his own review of Rossetti's *Poems*, whose contents—especially the sonnet sequence "The House of Life"—Swinburne had praised in gushing terms, writing that "no nakedness could be more harmonious, more consummate in its fleshly sculpture, than the imperial array and ornament of this august poetry."[178]

Soon after, Watts provided much-appreciated guidance on Swinburne's accounts, royalties, and negotiations with Chatto and Windus, the company that Hotten's junior partner, Andrew Chatto, founded in 1873. At the same time, Swinburne shared his manuscripts with Watts, turned to him for advice on the essays he should reprint in volume form, and ventured his ideas on possible creative projects. Such exchanges sealed their friendship. By 1876, Swinburne informed Watts: "I do not like to be always writing to one of the best friends I ever had—or any one else ever had, for that matter—on business only."[179] Even though Cecil Y. Lang, in his edition of Swinburne's correspondence, harbors the impression that Watts exuded a "fussy dreariness," he cannot but help acknowledge that this seemingly uninspiring, "soft-spoken, [and] disciplined man" was responsible for saving Swinburne's life.[180] A confluence of circumstances in Swinburne's career made intervention necessary: his alcoholism was becoming increasingly problematic, his father died, and his mother had to sell family property after Admiral Swinburne's death. At Lady Jane Swinburne's request, Watts came to a financial arrangement with her estate, which ensured that the often excitable forty-two-year-old poet went to live at The Pines: the new house on Putney Hill, South London, into which Watts moved in 1879, with his two sisters, brother in-law, and nephew. Swinburne remained at The Pines until the end of his days. With space to write, a personal library, and Watts's professional acumen to depend upon, Swinburne's suburban environment provided him with a satisfying and stable life that was not, according to those who spent time with him there, "a monotonous, vegetating existence."[181]

178. Algernon Charles Swinburne, "The Poems of Dante Gabriel Rossetti," *Fortnightly Review* 7, no. 41 (1870): 553.

179. Algernon Charles Swinburne, "To Theodore Watts," 19 December 1876, in *The Swinburne Letters*, 3:238.

180. Lang, "Introduction," in *The Swinburne Letters*, 1:xliii.

181. Thomas Hake and Arthur Compton-Rickett, *The Letters of Algernon Charles Swinburne, With Some Personal Recollections* (London: John Murray, 1918), 173.

As Swinburne informed a correspondent in May 1880, he was now "better and stronger" than he had been "for many [months]"; he was "in the company of a friend"—"a lover of the same pursuits and studies" as himself.[182]

Shortly after Swinburne removed to The Pines, Edmund Gosse sent him an invitation to contribute essays to Ward's ambitious editorial project, *The English Poets*, for which Gosse was assisting in the commissioning of contributions: "The working editor, Mr. Ward," Gosse wrote, "has set aside four poets, with whom it is his ambition that you should deal—Chatterton, Blake, Coleridge, Keats."[183] Gosse added that he understood well if Swinburne might be disposed to decline the essays on Blake and Coleridge, since the poet had already written a monograph on the one in 1868 and a critical essay on the other in 1869. Yet it was upon Keats that Gosse had the greatest hope that Swinburne would write. "A critical study . . . from your pen," Gosse implored, "would be the jewel of any collection . . . not merely from your genius, but also from the fact that that the other luminaries of that age have found expositors, but not Keats."[184] To impress the significance of Ward's venture, Gosse observed that Matthew Arnold had agreed to write on Wordsworth, Dean Church on Edmund Spenser, and Mark Pattison on Alexander Pope. In response, Swinburne enthused, "Keats I will gladly undertake."[185] But, as Gosse predicted, Swinburne was not willing to address the two poets on whose works he had already published: "I must decline, having said my say fully on Coleridge and Blake."[186] The anomaly was Chatterton. Swinburne confessed to not "knowing enough—by any means—of Chatterton, nor—on the whole—taking interest enough in him except as a splendid *lusus naturæ*, to deal adequately—that is, cordially . . . with the subject of his peculiar genius."[187] Swinburne's disclaimer might have been disingenuous. Just months before, newspapers reported that Swinburne was consulted to authenticate a manuscript thought to be Chatterton's, which suggested that he had intimate knowledge of the Bristol poet's work and hand. One account noted that "inasmuch as Algernon Swinburne worships at the shrine of Chatterton, his opinion was sought, and Algernon, after his wont, went into ecstasies

182. Swinburne, "To Paul Hamilton Hayne," 2 May 1880, in *The Swinburne Letters*, 4:140.

183. Edmund Gosse, "To Algernon Charles Swinburne," 4 October 1879, in Evan Charteris, *The Life and Letters of Sir Edmund Gosse* (New York: Harper and Brothers, 1931), 115.

184. Gosse, "To Algernon Charles Swinburne," 4 October 1879, in *The Life and Letters of Edmund Gosse*, 115.

185. Swinburne, "To Edmund Gosse," 6 October 1879, in *The Swinburne Letters*, 4:100.

186. Swinburne, "To Edmund Gosse," 6 October 1879, in *The Swinburne Letters*, 4:100.

187. Swinburne, "To Edmund Gosse," 6 October 1879, in *The Swinburne Letters*, 4:100.

over the resurrection," while a second lists Swinburne among the men of letters who believe "that the MS. is genuine."[188] Chatterton does make the occasional appearance in Swinburne's later essays, and the prose note he furnished
in Old French to his poem "The Leper" (in *Poems and Ballads* [1866]) adopts
a pseudo-medieval style that recalls Chatterton's Rowleyese.[189] Perhaps in 1879,
the newspapers overstated Swinburne's knowledge of Chatterton, or perhaps
Swinburne demurred out of deference to Watts. In any case, the essay on Keats
went to Arnold, who supplied the general introduction to Ward's anthology.[190]
Meanwhile, Pater provided the critical discussion of Coleridge, and J. Comyns
Carr—codirector of the fashionable Grosvenor Gallery that did much to advance the cause of Pre-Raphaelite art—wrote on Blake. Eventually, Swinburne
offered a short discussion of William Collins: the *"facile principem* [unacknowl-
edged chief] in the most quintessential quality of a proper poet," as he told
Gosse.[191] The essay on Chatterton was of course left to Watts.

Watts might never have taken on the project had Swinburne not refused the
commission, but it was Rossetti who had the greatest impact on Watts's understanding of Chatterton. As Oswald Doughty and John Robert Wahl have observed:
"Watts was deeply indebted to Rossetti for the material in [Watts's] Introduction
to Chatterton and selection from his poems in Ward's *English Poets*."[192] Rossetti's
fascination seems to have been sparked by reading *Endymion*, which Keats dedicated to Chatterton's memory. Keats's poem, Rossetti wrote to Jane Morris, "is
a brilliant labyrinth—a sort of magic toy."[193] "I had never," he confesses to her
about his knowledge of this poem, "really read through [it] in my life."[194] Two

188. [Anon.,] "London Gossip," *Northern Evening Mail* (Hartlepool), 10 June 1879: 4;
[Anon.,] "Interesting Literary Discovery," *Edinburgh Evening News*, 7 June 1879: 4.

189. Swinburne, "The Leper," in Swinburne, *Poems and Ballads* (London: John Camden Hotten, 1866), 137–43. Swinburne mentions Chatterton in "Tennyson and Musset"
(*Fortnightly Review* 29, no. 170 [February 1881]: 129–53) and "Charles Lamb and George
Wither" (*Nineteenth Century* 17, no. 95 [January 1885]: 66–91). Chatterton also earns a
mention in the reprint of "Wordsworth and Byron" in Swinburne's *Miscellanies* (London:
Chatto and Windus, 1886), but not in the version published originally in *Nineteenth Century* (15 [April 1884]: 583–609 and 15 [May 1884]: 764–90).

190. There is some possibility that Swinburne's fragment from an essay on Keats, which
was published in 1949, relates to Ward's anthology; see Cecil Y. Lang, "Swinburne on
Keats: A Fragment on an Essay," *Modern Language Notes* 64 (1949): 168–71.

191. Swinburne, "To Edmund Gosse," 10 October 1879, in *The Swinburne Letters*, 4:105.

192. *Letters of Dante Gabriel Rossetti*, ed. Oswald Doughty and John Robert Wahl, 4
vols. (Oxford: Clarendon Press, 1965–1967), 4:1767.

193. Rossetti, "To Jane Morris," 4 February 1880, in *The Correspondence of Dante Gabriel
Rossetti*, ed. William H. Fredeman, 9 vols. (Cambridge: D. S. Brewer, 2002–2010), 9:38.

194. Rossetti, "To Jane Morris," 4 February 1880, in *Correspondence*, ed. Fredeman, 9:38.

days later, it was clear that Rossetti was working swiftly to understand Chatterton's career, which he hoped to share with his dear friend Watts soon at dinner: "I shall have got up Chatterton much in meanwhile & have several points to put."[195] As the next few weeks unfolded, he asked his publisher Ellis (who also served as the main book buyer for the British Museum) if Willcox's 1842 edition of Chatterton's life and works is "the best."[196] Even if Rossetti's brother found this "enormous admiration of Chatterton . . . not merely excessive but a trifle fanciful," it remained a serious preoccupation in the artist's regular meetings with Watts.[197] By April 1880, Rossetti declared that Chatterton was "a glorious creature."[198] By May, Rossetti had moved beyond praising Chatterton and was instead offering Watts explicit direction in the shaping of his selections for Ward's *English Poets*, sending him many pages of hand-transcribed excerpts of Chatterton's verse. Watts appears to have accepted this guidance wholesale, even omitting from his selections for Ward's collection the exact lines of Chatterton's poetry that Rossetti had struck in his letters.[199] There is no question that during this time, when Rossetti was deeply immersed in Masson's *Chatterton*, he was invested in grasping Keats's intense respect for the "marvellous Boy," as he searched Keats's letters to see "whether [Keats] refers at all to Chatt[erto]n."[200]

Rossetti's inquiries persisted in a highly scholarly manner. Toward the end of

195. Rossetti, "To Walter Theodore Watts-Dunton," 6 February 1880, in *Correspondence*, ed. Fredeman, 9:45.

196. Rossetti, "To Frederick Startridge Ellis," 5 March 1880," in *Correspondence*, ed. Fredeman, 9:80.

197. William Michael Rossetti, "Memoir of Dante Gabriel Rossetti," in *Dante Gabriel Rossetti: His Family-Letters*, 1:358.

198. Rossetti, "To Walter Theodore Watts-Dunton," c. 29 April 1880, in *Correspondence*, ed. Fredeman, 9:164.

199. *Letters of Dante Gabriel Rossetti*, ed. Doughty and Wahl, 4:1767. Doughty and Wahl astutely note the debt that Watts owed Rossetti as a consequence of the Chatterton-related correspondence, but their transcription does not include Rossetti's telling omissions. In a letter to Watts, Rossetti records eighteen lines from "Ecologue the Third" but strikes six of them. Watts omits the same six lines in Ward's anthology, indicating the omission with a series of asterisks. Watts does, though, diverge from Rossetti's modernizations on occasions. Letter to Theodore Watts, 13 (?) May 1880, British Library, Ashley MS 1416, ff.22–23. Transcribed in Doughty and Wahl, *Letters*, 4:1771. Watts, "Thomas Chatterton," in *The English Poets*, ed. Ward, 3:416. Fredeman does not include the enclosures that Doughty and Wahl transcribe (see *Correspondence*, 9:178–79).

200. Rossetti, "To Walter Theodore Watts-Dunton," 13 May 1880, in *Correspondence*, ed. Fredeman, 9:177. Rossetti had already asked Watts to bring along a copy of the 1874 edition of Masson's *Chatterton* ("unless cumbrous") on 7 May 1880 (*Correspondence*, ed. Fredeman, 9:170).

May that year, Rossetti had turned his focus to Chatterton's modern poetry, and in his correspondence he concludes: "Skeats's ed. is a vast improvement in this section"; in this letter, Rossetti reveals that he has tried to trace the provenance of the "Last Verses" that Dix "politely 'communicated' . . . to a Boston (U.S.) editor of 1857. Dix got them from Cottle, who got them from Chattn.'s sister, only too late for *his* (Cottle's) ed. of 1803. But where is the MS.?"[201] It is a good question. As Chatterton's modern editors have suggested, these "Last Verses," which conveniently bear the date of the poet's death, are of dubious origin. Besides the fact that the history of transmission looks implausible, the content of their rolling couplets adheres to the legend that shaped the public's general knowledge of Chatterton's brief life rather too closely: "Farewell, Bristolia's dingy pile of brick, / Lovers of Mammon, worshippers of Trick! / Ye spurned the boy who gave you antique lays."[202]

During this period, Rossetti was engaged in vigorous exchanges about Chatterton with the young Hall Caine as well as Watts. As he began to comprehend the extent of Chatterton's influence, Rossetti encouraged Caine to take careful note of Chatterton's presiding spirit in a public lecture Caine was scheduled to deliver in Liverpool in 1878. "I assure you," Rossetti informs this new acquaintance, "that Chatterton's name *must* come in somewhere."[203] "Not to know Chattn.," Rossetti insisted, "is to be ignorant of the *true* day-spring of modern romantic poetry."[204] In response, Caine set about researching Chatterton's poetry through Skeat's modernized edition, and he eventually acknowledged —just as Rossetti had informed him—that "Coleridge and Keats were both devout worshippers at the shrine of Chatterton and shewed derivative points that seemed startling."[205] In 1883, the year after Rossetti died, when Caine pub-

201. Rossetti, "To Walter Theodore Watts-Dunton," 25 May 1880, in *Correspondence*, ed. Fredeman, 9:188. Rossetti is quoting from the note that Skeat included in his edition of the *Poetical Works of Thomas Chatterton* (ed. Walter W. Skeat, 2 vols. [London: Bell and Daldy, 1871], 1:266–67). This note originally appeared in the second edition of the *Poetical Works*, ed. Willcox (see note 202).

202. "The Last Verses Written by Thomas Chatterton," in *Complete Works of Thomas Chatterton*, ed. Taylor and Hoover, 2:735. The poem first appeared, with the note from "C" (Francis James Child), in Willcox, "Life of Chatterton," in *The Poetical Works of Thomas Chatterton*, ed. C. B. Willcox, 2nd ed., 2 vols. (Boston: Little, Brown, 1857), 1:cxxvi.

203. Rossetti, "To Thomas Henry Hall Caine," 23 May 1880, in *Correspondence*, ed. Fredeman, 9:186. Emphasis in the original.

204. Rossetti, "To Thomas Henry Hall Caine," 23 May 1880, in *Correspondence*, ed. Fredeman, 9:186. Emphasis in the original.

205. Caine, "To Dante Gabriel Rossetti," 1 June 1880, in *Dear Mr. Rossetti: The Letters of Dante Gabriel Rossetti and Hall Caine, 1878–1881*, ed. Vivien Allen (Sheffield: Sheffield

lished his study of the harsh ways in which early reviewers had mistreated the "Lake School" (Wordsworth and Coleridge), the "Satanic School" (Byron), and the "Cockney School" (Leigh Hunt, Keats, and Shelley), Caine recognized that Chatterton maintained a defining role in the development of Romantic poetry. Yet, compared to Rossetti's and Watts's regard for Chatterton, Caine's opinion was tempered: "Keats had less mental strength than Chatterton, and more moral courage."[206] "Downright assault, Chatterton could have borne and returned it with tenfold bitterness," Caine continued, "but sheer neglect was killing him."[207] No matter what misgivings he may have had about Chatterton's personal integrity and poetic standing, Caine framed his discussion of all of these writers by granting the young Bristol poet a place within a "neo-romantic movement"—a term that parallels Watts's perception of "the New Romantic school."[208] Others followed suit. In the same decade, the publishing firm of Walter Scott, which featured several volumes on eighteenth-century poets (including Ossian) on its lists, issued Chatterton's poetical works in its affordable Canterbury Poets series. The editor, John Richmond, made a similar assertion about Chatterton in his "Prefatory Notice": "No poet—not even Coleridge—was ever so imbued with the romantic spirit."[209]

Rossetti's input clearly shaped Watts's understanding of Chatterton's work, but Watts's essay is a tour de force, easily exceeding Rossetti's influence. Instead of situating his discussion on the tiresome terrain of forgery, the first point he establishes is the importance of preserving, as faithfully as possible, those parts of the poet's antiquated orthography that capture "the peculiar musical movement governing Chatterton's ear."[210] While Watts believes it necessary to make the Rowley poems more accessible to a modern audience, he suggests that Skeat's

---

Academic Press, 2000), 111. Rossetti had already said, on 23 May 1880, to Caine: "Strong derivative points are to be found in Keats & Coleridge from the study of Chattn." (*Correspondence*, ed. Fredeman, 9:186). Caine reprinted this part of Rossetti's letter in *Recollections of Dante Gabriel Rossetti*, 185.

206. T. Hall Caine, *Cobwebs of Criticism: A Review of the First Reviewers of the "Lake," "Satanic," and "Cockney" Schools* (London: Elliot Stock, 1883), 184.

207. Caine, *Cobwebs of Criticism*, 184.

208. Caine, *Cobwebs of Criticism*, xx.

209. John Richmond, "Prefatory Notice," in *The Poetical Works of Thomas Chatterton*, The Canterbury Poets (London: Walter Scott, 1886), 24.

210. Watts, "Thomas Chatterton," in *The English Poets*, ed. Ward, 3:400. Watts's brief selection of poems comprises (in his spellings) "An Excellent Ballad of Charity," "Eclogue the First," "Eclogue the Third," "Minstrels' Marriage-Song (from *Ælla: A Tragical Interlude*)," "The Accounte of W. Canynge's Feast," and "Minstrel's Roundelay (from *Ælla*)."

more aggressive modernization of the Rowley poems detracts from Chatterton's "originality of ear."[211] Watts takes the Bristol poet's unique but critically neglected "metrical inventiveness" as the surest clue to "the undeniable influence that Chatterton has had, both as to spirit and as to form, upon the revival in the present century of the romantic temper," and he identifies the shaping power that the Rowley poems exerted upon "romantic form."[212] As the *Athenæum* noted, the most remarkable aspect of this discussion is that "Chatterton is exalted by Mr. Watts higher, we suppose, than was ever before done by a critic writing with an expressly critical, and not merely enthusiastic or eulogistic, aim; sundry acute remarks are made about the influence which this youthful poet may be deemed to have exerted in more than one respect upon Coleridge."[213] Especially significant here is the "new principle" that Coleridge described in his preface to "Christabel" (1816); Watts identifies this "new principle" in what he terms the "anapaestic dance" whose variable rhythms catch the ear in the famous poem.[214] Such variations, which play upon the movement of the octosyllabic line familiar to the ballad, create for Watts the "Christabel ring" that we hear in such lines as these: "Save the boss of the shield of Sir Leoline tall, / Which hung in a murky old Nitch in the Wall."[215] The origins of this substitutive movement, in which tripping anapests take the place of steady iambs, emerges for Watts in Chatterton's very early poem "The Tournament," which recalls the era of the Crusades: "But whan he threwe down his Asenglave, / Next came in Syr Botelier bold and brave, / The Dethe of manie a Saracen, / Theie thought him a Devil from Hells Black Pen."[216] Even though later historians of prosody would detect this type of metrical substitution to be much commoner

211. Watts, "Thomas Chatterton," in *The English Poets*, ed. Ward, 3:400.

212. Watts, "Thomas Chatterton," in *The English Poets*, ed. Ward, 3:400–401.

213. [Anon.], Review of *The English Poets*, ed. Ward, *Vol. III, Addison to Blake; Vol. IV, Wordsworth to Dobell*, Athenæum 2778 (22 January 1881): 128.

214. Watts, "Thomas Chatterton," in *The English Poets*, ed. Ward, 3:401. For Coleridge on the "new principle," which involves "counting in each line the accents, not the syllables," see the preface to "Christabel." *Christabel: Kubla Khan, A Vision; The Pains of Sleep* (London: John Murray, 1816), vii; reprinted in Coleridge, *Poetical Works I: Poems (Reading Text): Part I*, ed. J. C. C. Mays, *The Collected Works of Samuel Taylor Coleridge*, Bollingen Series LXXV, 16 vols. (Princeton: Princeton University Press, 1969–2002), 16.1.1:482–83.

215. Watts, "Thomas Chatterton," in *The English Poets*, ed. Ward, 3:401; Coleridge, "Christabel," in *The Collected Works of Samuel Taylor Coleridge*, 16.1.1:488; quotation corrected from Watts's essay in line with the text in *Collected Works*.

216. "The Tournament," in *Complete Works of Thomas Chatterton*, ed. Taylor and Hoover, 1:24.

after Spenser than Watts suggests, the powerful claim brought Chatterton alive for Wilde.[217] This is equally the case with the astute comparison Watts draws between Keats's "Eve of St. Agnes" (1820) and Chatterton's "Excelente Balade of Charitie." In the first poem, the beadsman appears "meagre, barefoot, wan," and the alms craver in the final Rowley poem is "withered, forwynd, deade."[218] Such observations challenged the lingering moral contempt that Chatterton's name still aroused in some quarters. Where the conservative *Quarterly Review* deemed Chatterton's overweening pride to be "something altogether unwholesome and abnormal" in such a young man (it had serious doubts about his "strange character"), Watts staunchly defended the poet's individualism, which produced such independent-minded art.[219] Besides lauding the purity of Chatterton's complete "artistic identification," Watts acclaims the poet's "egotism": "Such energy as his can only exist as the outcome of that enormous egotism which is at the heart of all lyric production."[220] Even more intensely, Chatterton possessed as well truly great "dramatic instinct."[221] As we demonstrate in our close analysis of Wilde's "Chatterton" notebook in the chapter that follows, it was exactly these kinds of insights that helped Wilde understand why the Rowley poems resounded through the history of English poetry, in ways that made Chatterton rank alongside Macpherson's *Ossian*, major Romantics such as Keats and Shelley, and the Pre-Raphaelites he believed were the heirs to the "spirit of romance."

217. See George Saintsbury, *Historical Manual of English Prosody* (London: Macmillan, 1926), 142; and Paul Fussell, *Theory of Prosody in Eighteenth-Century England* (New London: Connecticut College, 1954), 92–93.

218. Keats, "The Eve of St. Agnes," in *The Poetical Works and Other Writings of John Keats*, ed. Forman, 2:72, and in *Complete Poems*, ed. Stillinger, 229; "An Excelente Balade of Charitie," in *Complete Works of Thomas Chatterton*, ed. Taylor and Hoover, 1; 646.

219. [Morris Mowbray,] "Thomas Chatterton," *Quarterly Review* 150 (1880): 108–9. Not all of Mowbray's observations are negative, since he admits that Chatterton had the potential to become a "brilliant genius"; the problem, as Morris sees it, is that Chatterton was the "victim of his own ill-regulated and devouring passions" (106).

220. Watts, "Thomas Chatterton," in *The English Poets*, ed. Ward, 3:403.

221. Watts, "Thomas Chatterton," in *The English Poets*, ed. Ward, 3:403.

4

WILDE'S "CHATTERTON" NOTEBOOK: THE ART
OF FORGERY AND THE CHARGE OF PLAGIARISM

In an October 1886 article for the *Pall Mall Gazette*, Oscar Wilde reviewed *Astray: A Tale of a Country Town*, a novel jointly written by Charlotte M. Yonge, Mary Bramston, Christabel Coleridge, and Esmé Stuart. Wilde was unimpressed, wondering if perhaps "too many collaborators are like too many cooks, and spoil the dinner."[1] While calling the novel's dullness "premeditated and deliberate," he took issue less with the novel's plot ("the story itself is not an uninteresting one") than with its form. Consisting of an "interminable series of long letters by different people, and of extracts from various diaries," the "piecemeal" and "unsatisfactory" novel failed to produce "any unity of effect."[2] The novel contained "the rough material for a story, but it is not a completed work of art." "It is," he concluded, "in fact more of a notebook than a novel."[3] The distinction is important: the formal properties of *Astray* that qualified it as "more of a notebook than a novel"—a single volume composed of extracts compiled from various sources and authors—also describe those of Wilde's extensive notes on Chatterton.

When modern scholars consider Wilde's oeuvre, they all too often overlook the difference between the notebook and the published text that he clearly articulated in his review of *Astray*. In modern critical treatments of the "Chatterton" notebook, the oversight is especially impactful, as this generic elision has led to the acceptance of the "Chatterton" notebook not as a notebook at all

---

1. Wilde, "New Novels," *Pall Mall Gazette*, 28 October 1886: 4; in Wilde, *Journalism Part I*, ed. John Stokes and Mark W. Turner, *Complete Works of Oscar Wilde*, 7 vols. to date (Oxford: Oxford University Press, 2000 and continuing), 6:101.
2. Wilde, "New Novels," in *Journalism Part I*, ed. Stokes and Turner, 6:101.
3. Wilde, "New Novels," in *Journalism Part I*, ed. Stokes and Turner, 6:101.

but rather a barefaced example of Wilde's literary larceny: a document that he supposedly tried to pass off as his original research on Chatterton. As we noted in our Introduction, in 1998 Josephine M. Guy boldly declared that the notebook constituted the "unpublished lecture on Chatterton," a revelation that made it "perhaps the most blatant" of Wilde's borrowings; Guy proceeded to describe the "MS of that lecture"—that is, the notebook—as "the smoking gun" of Wilde's "unashamed plagiarism."[4] Five years later, Paul K. Saint-Amour, in his assessment of the "Chatterton" notebook, took it as evidence that qualified Wilde as the "nineteenth century's most famous talker and plagiarist."[5] Others, apparently under the impression that the notebook forms either the transcription of Wilde's lecture or of the essay he was preparing for the *Century Guild Hobby Horse,* have followed suit. In this chapter, we show why this judgment is flawed.

Here we look at the "Chatterton" notebook qua notebook, and not a "completed work of art." We discuss where this document stands in relation to the long tradition of notebook keeping that defined Wilde's literary productivity from his earliest college years. We then turn to the "Chatterton" notebook, examining its structure and organization, and—more important—the ways in which Wilde cut, pasted, and frequently edited the passages he had selected from his three main sources: David Masson, Daniel Wilson, and Theodore Watts. His markups and revisions to others' texts, as well as his marginalia, illustrate the ways in which Wilde viewed Chatterton's life and legacy. Further, these aspects of the "Chatterton" notebook disclose Wilde's developing role as a periodical editor. We argue that the notebook functioned like many other documents of this kind that Wilde maintained throughout his career: it served as a crucible in which he could explore new ideas that shaped his later works, a claim we substantiate in chapters 5 and 6. In the final section below, we consider why modern scholars have been disposed to believe that the "Chatterton" notebook presents irrefutable evidence of Wilde's presumed penchant for stealing other artists' ideas. Our discussion reveals the remarkable ways in which the "Chatterton" notebook served as a productive resource for the development of Wilde's subsequent writings, his ongoing scholarly practices, and his authorial persona.

4. Guy, "Self-Plagiarism, Creativity and Craftsmanship in Oscar Wilde," *English Literature in Transition, 1880–1920* 41, no. 1 (1998): 7.

5. Paul K. Saint-Amour, *The Copywrights: Intellectual Property and the Literary Imagination* (Ithaca, NY: Cornell University Press, 2003), 89. Saint-Amour's judgment echoes in later criticism. To Michèle Mendelssohn, for example, Wilde is "the century's most famous plagiarist" (*Henry James, Oscar Wilde, and Aesthetic Culture* [Edinburgh: Edinburgh University Press, 2007], 7).

"BRING YOUR BOOKS—AND SOME NOTEBOOKS FOR ME": WILDE'S NOTE TAKING

From his days as an undergraduate at Trinity College Dublin between 1871 and 1874, Wilde had employed notebooks to compile extracts from the numerous readings that formed the basis of his degree in classics. At Oxford, from 1874 to 1878, he kept no fewer than five substantial notebooks, each of which assisted him in his exacting preparations for both the Moderations and the Final Examination components of his degree in *literæ humaniores* (known as "Greats"). To judge only from Wilde's correspondence with his fellow Oxonians, one might believe that he spent his days less in devoted study than in indolent ease; Wilde's letters often include declarations of shirking, not embracing, hard work. "I have not done as much reading as I thought I would," he wrote to William Ward in 1876, an underwhelming sentiment repeated throughout his correspondence of the period.[6] After detailing a few days of tea and lawn tennis, Wilde admits to Reginald Harding that he thinks he had "missed [his] First" (the highest grade awarded at Oxford), "and will have to look cheerful under the doubtful honours of a Second."[7] A week later Wilde details, again to Harding, his miscalculation of the date of his viva voce, and thus pulling off a coup through pure luck: "I was rather afraid of being put on in Catullus, but got a delightful exam from a delightful man—not on the books at all but on Aeschylus *versus* Shakespeare, modern poetry and drama and every conceivable subject."[8] This is a story he repeats to William Ward, and to both of these college pals he expresses a mixture of assuredness and perhaps insincere self-deprecation: to Harding he claims that he doesn't "care a bit" about his class on the exam, but to Ward he writes: "Of course I knew I had got a First, so swaggered horribly."[9] In later letters, he continues to insist on his idleness and his certain failure in Greats: "I am too ridiculously easily led astray . . . I feel that if I had read I would have done well up here but I have not"; "still I intend to reform and read hard if possible"; "of Greats work I have done nothing"; "I am reading hard for a Fourth in Greats"; "my Greats work has collapsed finally for ever."[10]

6. Wilde, "To William Ward," 20 March 1876, in *The Complete Letters of Oscar Wilde*, ed. Rupert Hart-Davis and Merlin Holland (London: Fourth Estate, 2000), 15.

7. Wilde, "To Reginald Harding," 28 June 1876, in *Complete Letters*, 17.

8. Wilde, "To Reginald Harding," 5 July 1876, in *Complete Letters*, 19.

9. Wilde, "To Reginald Harding," 5 July 1876, and "To William Ward," 10 July 1876, in *Complete Letters*, 19, 20.

10. Wilde, "To William Ward," 3 March 1877, in *Complete Letters*, 40; "To William Ward," 14 March 1877, *Complete Letters*, 41; "To William Ward," August 1877, in *Complete Letters*, 60; "To William Ward," Autumn 1877, in *Complete Letters*, 42; "To Reginald Harding," April 1878, in *Complete Letters*, 65. A Fourth was the lowest possible honors degree at Oxford.

As it turned out, Wilde performed outstandingly in Greats, achieving a rare "Double First" in what contemporaries regarded as the most intellectually demanding degree course at Oxford. His protestations of laziness or doubt are belied by the existence of his many notebooks dating from the period; they provide evidence of diligent, often exacting, and laborious effort. In a letter to Ward during the thick of his preparations for his final examinations, Wilde takes pains to emphasize the importance of the notebook in his studies, even while insisting in the same sentence that he has not yet started to work: "I have not opened a book yet, I have been so bothered with business and other matters. I shall be quite alone. Will you come? I will give you fishing and scenery—and bring your books—*and some notebooks for me*. I am in despair about 'Greats.'"[11] One of the most compelling of these notebooks is his "Commonplace Book," which contains his reflections on passages relating to law, literature, natural history, and philosophy taken from a host of ancient and modern sources. Particularly attractive to Wilde in these 219 pages is the kind of pithy statement he encountered in Hegel: "The condemnation which a great man lays upon the world is to force it to explain him."[12] Not only do such carefully selected remarks identify Wilde's emerging attraction to the aphorisms that became the hallmark of his later style; they also accentuate the fact that the phrases that grabbed his greatest attention were dialectical in nature. He devotes one page, for instance, to lines drawn from Wordsworth. "We murder to dissect" and "Come forth into the light of Things / Let nature be your teacher": these count among the seven quotations from the Romantic poet in a notebook that moves easily across the centuries in its compilation of nuggets of wisdom.[13] In another notebook from his earlier days at Oxford, Wilde ruminated on non-Western philosophies of history: "The Hindus had no taste for history as chronology · their acute analytical and logical mind was devoted to grammar, criticism and

11. Wilde, "To William Ward," 19 July 1877, in *Complete Letters*, 57. Emphasis in the original.

12. Wilde, "Commonplace Book," William Andrews Clark Memorial Library, Wilde W6721M3 C734 Boxed, f.197^r; in *Oxford Wilde's Oxford Notebooks: A Portrait of Mind in the Making*, ed. Philip E. Smith II and Michael S. Helfand (New York: Oxford University Press, 1989), 147. The line from Hegel comes from William Wallace, "Prolegomena," in *The Logic of Hegel: Translated from the Encyclopaedia of the Philosophical Sciences with Prolegomena* (Oxford: Clarendon Press, 1874), xiii.

13. Wilde, "Commonplace Book," f.127^r, in *Oscar Wilde's Oxford Notebooks*, 131. The quotations come from Wordsworth, "The Tables Turned; An Evening Scene, on the Same Subject" (1798), in *Lyrical Ballads and Other Poems* (London: J. and A. Arch, 1798), 186–87. The original text of Wordsworth's poem has "Nature," not "nature." See Wordsworth, *Lyrical Ballads, and Other Poems, 1797–1800*, edited by James Butler and Karen Green, The Cornell Wordsworth (Ithaca, NY: Cornell University Press, 1992), 109.

philosophy."[14] Elsewhere, he observes: "History began in poetry and has ended in philosophy."[15]

As Philip E. Smith and Michael S. Helfand have commented, the notebooks from Wilde's undergraduate years "demonstrate the powerful synthetic impetus of humanistic education at Oxford and the consequent integration of scientific, philosophical, political, and aesthetic theories characteristic of this time."[16] In other words, these documents display the development of Wilde's grasp of a formidable range of writings across the humanities and the sciences, and they identify his attempts to make discriminations between the different thinkers whose works he had to comprehend. The following set of propositions is typical of the notes Wilde made: "Plato underrated deduction, Bacon undervalued induction, tho' the two men who cd. use either method with equal ease were Aristotle and Newton."[17] In his note taking, Wilde includes, as with most keepers of traditional commonplace books, handwritten extracts from texts, all of which he arranges for comparative purposes. Each of these notebooks accumulates knowledge in a seemingly piecemeal manner: the distinctions between Adam Smith's *Theory of Moral Sentiments* (1759) and *The Wealth of Nations* (1776) appear on one page, for example, while thoughts on asceticism ("opposed by both Greeks and moderns") appear on the next.[18] The "synthetic impetus" that such excerpts display certainly helped shape his subsequent methods of literary composition. As his career developed, Wilde maintained notebooks while developing many of his major works, from his first play, *Vera* (1880), to his society drama *An Ideal Husband* (1895). The notebook was also the place where he devised his lists of aphorisms, some of which count among the most quoted in modern literature, while others (like the following) he wisely chose not to use: "I have never sowed wild oats: I have planted a few wild orchids."[19] Any serious study of

14. Wilde, "Notebook Kept at Oxford," Clark Library Wilde W6721M3 N9111 Bound, f.35^r; in *Oscar Wilde's Oxford Notebooks*, 166, f.67.

15. Wilde, "Notebook Kept at Oxford," f.5^r; in *Oscar Wilde's Oxford Notebooks*, 155, f.7.

16. Smith and Helfand, "Preface," in *Oscar Wilde's Oxford Notebooks*, x.

17. Wilde, "Notebook Kept at Oxford," f.16^r; in *Oscar Wilde's Oxford Notebooks*, 159, f.30 (quotation adjusted).

18. Wilde, "Notebook Kept at Oxford," f.17^r–f.17^v, in *Oscar Wilde's Oxford Notebooks*, 160, f.33–f.35.

19. Wilde, "Phrases, Aphorisms and Fragments of Verse," f.1^r from rear, W6721 P576 Bound, Clark Library. As with several of his notebooks, Wilde entered this comment after turning the notebook upside down and turning open the back cover. It is difficult to date this document with precision, though the fact that it contains drafts of lines from *A Florentine Tragedy* suggests it derives from 1893 or some time slightly later.

his oeuvre therefore demands that scholars examine these carefully maintained documents. Those dating from Wilde's time at Oxford, in particular, record the role that his intensive scholarly pursuits played in shaping his later creativity, especially in the critical essays that he gathered in *Intentions* (1891). What is more, Wilde's decision to keep all of his notebooks, including ones that dated from his undergraduate years, with him as part of his permanent belongings says much about the great store that he laid by these documents. The same is true of the manuscripts of his works. At the bankruptcy sale of Wilde's household goods, which took place at Tite Street on 24 April 1895, the numerous lots included a bundle of manuscripts and typescripts, which fetched £5 15s.

The Oxford notebooks, since they list excerpts from many other authors' writings, bear the strongest resemblance to the notebook that Wilde dedicated to Chatterton, even though none of these documents from his undergraduate years features cutting and pasting from printed materials. It is, though, worth bearing in mind that this practice of incorporating cuttings from printed books into scrapbooks or notebooks dates at least from the seventeenth century, when, as Ann M. Blair observes, "early modern readers engaged in various kinds of cutting and pasting from manuscripts and printed books, for reasons that ranged from plundering pretty bits to carrying out the author's intentions to outright theft."[20] By the nineteenth century, the copiousness of inexpensive printed matter made scrapbook compilation as popular as commonplace books had once been, causing some commonplace-book enthusiasts to implore compilers to resist the ease of "pasting . . . printed cuttings" into ready-made books.[21] Others, however, happily detailed recipes for making paste that would not damage clipped articles.[22] Although perhaps unconventional, Wilde's inclusion of printed extracts was therefore not unheard of, although the arrangement of the "Chatterton" notebook looks somewhat more like a scrapbook or an album of cuttings (which also became popular in the later nineteenth century) than the exclusively handwritten notebooks that informed his early studies. Wilde's approach to Chatterton's career nevertheless continued his well-established practice of using the notebook as a site in which to compile, organize, and synthesize ideas, whether his own or those of authorities; just as he did with Hegel and Wordsworth in the notes he took when preparing for Oxford exams, he

20. Ann M. Blair, *Too Much to Know: Managing Scholarly Information before the Modern Age* (New Haven: Yale University Press, 2010), 225.

21. [Anon.,] "Commonplace-Books," *Chambers Journal*, 3 April 1880: 217.

22. E. W. Gurley, *Scrapbooks and How to Make Them* (New York: The Authors' Publishing Company, 1880), 37–38.

followed the same practice with Daniel Wilson, David Masson, and Theodore Watts when pursuing his inquiries into Chatterton.

THE "CHATTERTON" NOTEBOOK AS WILDE'S ARCHIVE

The connection between the "Chatterton" notebook and Wilde's many other notebooks is evident from its first pages. It opens, not with pasted excerpts, but with many pages in Wilde's own hand. Here he takes down, as he did in his Oxford notebooks, compelling quotations, and he sketches ideas and inchoate turns of phrase that would reappear, fully formed, in his later published works. On the first folio alone, there are lines from Emerson's famous essay "The Poet" (1840), which concentrates on the nature of genius: "A man is only half himself, | the other half is his <u>expression</u>" (Appendix A, f.1ᵛ [334]).[23] There, too, Wilde alludes to Coleridge's famous "Monody" on the Bristol poet, in which the Romantic author honors Chatterton's evocation of medieval and early modern verse: "young-eyed POESY / All deftly mask'd, as hoar ANTIQUITY."[24] Interspersed among these quotations are phrases on "Previous lectures," on Chatterton's biography ("Son of a poor widow—a | boy—who began to write at | 12—and dead at 17—| matured genius—" [Appendix A, f.1ᵛ (334)]), and on a genealogy that he would tease out later in the notebook: "Chatterton— | Coleridge—Keats" (Appendix A, f.80ʳ [407]). These notes are written in black ink—perhaps an indication that they were composed after the lines on the next pages, which are, like most of the notebook, in pencil. Yet regardless of the order in which Wilde

---

23. In "The Poet," Emerson comments on the genius of this figure: "The breadth of the problem is great, for the poet is representative. He stands among partial men for the complete man, and apprises us not of his wealth, but of the commonwealth. . . . In love, in art, in avarice, in politics, in labor, in games, we study to utter our painful secret. The man is only half himself, the other half is his expression" (*Essays: Second Series*, ed. Alfred R. Ferguson and Jean Ferguson Carr, *Collected Works of Ralph Waldo Emerson*, 10 vols. [Cambridge, MA: Belknap Press of Harvard University Press, 1971–2013], 3:4).

24. Coleridge, "Monody on the Death of Chatterton," *Poetical Works II, Poems (Variorum Text): Part 1*, ed. J. C. C. Mays, Bollingen Series LXXV, 16 vols. (Princeton: Princeton University Press, 2001), 16.1.1:181. Pater quoted these lines in the essay on Coleridge he furnished for the fourth volume of Ward's *English Poets* (*The English Poets: Selections with Critical Introductions by Various Writers, and a General Introduction by Matthew Arnold*, ed. Thomas Humphry Ward, 4 vols. [London: Macmillan, 1880], 4:102–54); although Pater did not mention Chatterton's name, he drew on these lines to state that Coleridge's "Christabel" and "Rime of the Ancient Mariner" "connect themselves with that revival of ballad literature, of which Percy's *Reliques* and, in another way, Macpherson's *Ossian*, are monuments." "Coleridge," *The English Poets*, ed. Ward, 4:110.

took these notes, the darting ideas coalesce not as a unified, legible draft with fluent logic or polished structure but rather as a series of intellectual discoveries that Chatterton's life and works have inspired. On the next page, the first under the title "Chatterton," Wilde opens with an argument that one must turn to biography to understand Chatterton's work. Here and elsewhere in the notebook, Wilde seems influenced by the powerful concept of "personality," an idea of individual distinctiveness, which any of Wilde's peers would have known he had derived from Pater.[25] Wilde's development of this idea became central in his mature essays and fiction.

Meanwhile, Wilde put the content of the notebook to more immediate use. The opening pages of the "Chatterton" notebook contain several nascent ideas and phrases that Wilde incorporated in his short reviews from the middle of 1886 to early 1887, when he contributed regularly to the *Pall Mall Gazette* and other venues. The earliest of these articles dates from July 1886, "Keats' Sonnet on Blue," his first and only contribution to the *Century Guild Hobby Horse.* In the notebook, Wilde traced a poetic genealogy from Chatterton through Coleridge to Keats and wrote that "language—expression. instrument | technical process precedes arts" (Appendix A, f.1^v [334]). Much later in this document, Wilde returns to this formulation, developing it into more fluid prose: "What seems technical | is really spiritual—" (Appendix A, f.78^r [406]). By comparison, in his essay on Keats's sonnet, Wilde remarks: "In the case of poetry, as in the case of the other arts, what may appear to be simply technicalities of method are in their essence spiritual, not mechanical."[26] Wilde thus acknowledges that for a gifted poet, form is not external but integral to the artistic process. Perhaps Wilde recalled the lines from the article, published in July, when jotting in his notebook, but it seems more likely that he sketched the idea in draft form in the notebook and then refined it for the essay. Such a process suggests that he was at work on the notebook as early as July, some four months before he would present his lecture on Chatterton at the Birkbeck Literary and Scientific Institute.

In a September 1886 review of two poetry collections, Wilde's disappointed comments on a volume of poems by the pseudonymous "Two Tramps" include

25. In his "Preface" to *Studies in the History of the Renaissance*, Pater identifies the inquiries that absorb the attention of the aesthetic critic; one of these is as follows: "What is this song or picture, this engaging personality, presented in life or in a book, to *me*?" *The Renaissance: Studies in Art and Poetry, The 1893 Text*, ed. Donald L. Hill (Berkeley: University of California Press, 1980), xix–xx. Emphasis in the original. The concept of "personality" recurs at several crucial moments in Pater's study.

26. Wilde, "Keats' Sonnet on Blue," *Century Guild Hobby Horse* 1, no. 3 (July 1886): 83–84; reprinted in *Journalism Part I*, ed. Stokes and Turner, 6:84.

the proposition that the figure of the tramp "should possess that freedom of mood which is so essential to the artist, for he has no taxes to pay, and no relations to worry him."[27] Such phrasing recalls his suggestion in the notebook that the young poet from Bristol had "claimed for the artist freedom of | mood" (Appendix A, f.76ʳ [404]). An early 1887 *Pall Mall Gazette* review saw another return to phrasing from the "Chatterton" notebook. Wilde opened "Miner and Minor Poets" with these lines: "The conditions that precede artistic production are so constantly treated as qualities of the work of art itself, that one is sometimes tempted to wish that all art were anonymous"; as he proceeded to comment on such volumes as the working-class Joseph Skipsey's *Carols from the Coal-Fields* (1886), Wilde remarked that "there are certain forms of art" that remain "so individual in their utterance" that, to appreciate them fully, it is vital to have "some knowledge of the artist's life."[28] The first part of these comments is almost identical to phrasing from the opening pages of the notebook (Appendix A, f.2ʳ–f.4ʳ [335–37]).[29] Clearly, Wilde was grappling with the ways in which biographical information might account for the unique elements that one discovers in writers, such as Keats and Chatterton, who did not share the classical education of most men of letters in their time, and whose contested biographies were inextricably bound up with their critical reception.

Yet, even as he thoughtfully recycled phrases that he devised in the "Chatterton" notebook, Wilde was fully aware at this time about the exigencies of attribution. This issue came to the fore in November 1886 when he published "A 'Jolly' Art Critic," a lightly mocking review of Harry Quilter's *Sententiæ Artis* (1886). Here, too, Wilde drew observantly from his notes on Chatterton, as might be expected, given that the ensuing fracas that took place with Quilter occurred in the same week as Wilde's lecture at Birkbeck. On the young Bristol poet, Wilde had written in his notebook: "For every true artist | [. . .] portrait painter or dramatist, | be his work absolutely objective in | presentation, still reveals himself | in his manner" (Appendix A, f.2ʳ [335]). With similar phrasing, his review remarked on Quilter's many shortcomings: "That there is a difference between colour and colours, that an artist, be he portrait-painter or

27. Wilde, "The Poets' Corner," *Pall Mall Gazette*, 27 September 1886: 5; in *Journalism Part I*, ed. Stokes and Turner, 6:95.

28. Wilde, "Miner and Minor Poets," *Pall Mall Gazette*, 1 February 1887: 5; in *Journalism Part I*, 6:120. Geoff Dibb also recognizes Wilde's use of this phrasing in the review of Skipsey's verse (*Oscar Wilde, a Vagabond with a Mission: The Story of Oscar Wilde's Lecture Tours of Britain and Ireland* [London: Oscar Wilde Society, 2013], 207).

29. The "conditions that precede" phrase also appears in the *Century Guild Hobby Horse* piece on Keats. See our discussion on page 147–48.

dramatist, always reveals himself in his manner, are ideas that can hardly be said to occur to" Quilter.[30] For Wilde, the critical problem with Quilter, who took serious offense at this unforgiving review, was that this "jolly" author "rollicks through art with the recklessness of the tourist, and describes its beauties with the enthusiasm of the auctioneer," and did so with frequent errors, to boot.[31] After Quilter's solicitors wrote to the editor of the *Pall Mall Gazette*, demanding the name of the reviewer and threatening to "take proceedings,"[32] Quilter wrote a self-important letter to the editor with a refutation of Wilde's disrespectful notice: "Such a review, Mr. Editor, is . . . a greater disgrace to journalism than many of those topics on which you have poured out the vials of your wrath."[33] To uphold this claim, Quilter listed, in painstaking detail, thirteen objections to perceived misrepresentations in Wilde's unsparing commentary.

Not to be outdone, Wilde drafted a six-page letter for E. T. Cook, W. T. Stead's assistant editor, in which he rebutted Quilter's accusations through citations (with page numbers) he had listed in his review, along with notations of additional "errors not noticed" in his article and his own editorial asides. Wilde's incredulity is palpable: he twice declares Quilter's carelessness "quite monstrous" and refers to other mistakes he enumerates as "most amusing" and "an amazing confusion."[34] Wilde's was not a passing familiarity with Quilter's book but an incisive engagement, and both his review and his draft rebuttal to it were based not on broad impressions but meticulous details. Cook's published response to Quilter's letter drew heavily from Wilde's draft, and made a strong case that Quilter was mistaken to infer that misquotation bedeviled Wilde's review. As

30. Wilde, "A 'Jolly' Art Critic," *Pall Mall Gazette*, 18 November 1886: 6; in *Journalism Part 1*, 6:109. Wilde's title mocks Quilter's admiration for William Hunt, Vermont, who had declared: "Draw firm, and be jolly"; Quilter contended that in the case of Pre-Raphaelitism, its "beardless apostles" indulged in the "worship of sorrow" (*Sententiæ Artis: First Principles of Art for Painters and Picture Lovers* [London: Isbister, 1886], 140).

31. Wilde, "A 'Jolly' Art Critic," in *Journalism Part I*, ed. Stokes and Turner, 6:108. As Anne Anderson has pointed out, Quilter, who lived close to Wilde on Tite Street, was strongly opposed to the development of aestheticism; his hostility led to public clashes with Whistler, in particular. See Anne Anderson, "Oscar's Enemy . . . and Neighbour: 'Arry' Quilter and the 'Gospel of Intensity,'" *The Wildean* 27 (2005): 39–54.

32. Letter from Last & Sons to the Editor of the *Pall Mall Gazette*, 19 November 1886, British Library, Add. MS 81648.

33. Harry Quilter, "Letter to the Editor," in [E. T. Cook,] "An Art Critic and His Sententiæ," *Pall Mall Gazette*, 23 November 1886: 11. Cook's article contains Quilter's letter to the editor.

34. Oscar Wilde, undated, previously unpublished letter to E. T. Cook. Eccles Bequest; British Library, Add. MS 81648, f.1, f.3, f.4.

Cook remarked, following one of Wilde's corrections, in which he noted that Quilter refers to Frank Holl as "Mr. Hall": "Mr. Quilter . . . does not know his own book so accurately as does his reviewer."[35] In his sedulous response to Quilter's protest, Cook defended Wilde's stance in every last detail; Cook took Quilter to task, for example, for disclaiming that he referred to the "vulgarity and snobbishness of Joshua Reynolds," when in fact Quilter had remarked on "the rather vulgar and snobbish" quality of Reynolds's works.[36] Cook did admit that Wilde had inappropriately made minor changes to short quotations from Quilter's book, and thus had very slightly distorted their source. Such infractions related to Wilde's misplaced "inverted commas" (i.e., quotation marks), which he had used to summarize Quilter's phrasing instead of quoting it accurately. In his response, Wilde thanked Cook for "holding" to him, but he took issue with the manner in which he had wrongly presented quotations: "I think however that the rule about inverted commas is a little strict."[37] Cook's main criticism was not that Wilde had omitted quotation marks; instead, his complaint was that in "A 'Jolly' Art Critic" Wilde had misused them in order to compress Quilter's original.

As a consequence, Wilde promised Cook that he would accordingly correct the proof of his unfavorable forthcoming review of Roden Noel's *Essays on Poetry and Poets*, since he had slightly reordered Noel's phrases. "For instance," he told Cook, "in Roden Noel's book there occurs this amazing sentence: 'I know not any *artist of note*, unless it be Edgar Poe, Bulwer Lytton, Disraeli, or *Mr. Alfred Austin* whom we may affiliate upon Byron'!!!! I quote it as follows: that Edgar Poe, Disraeli, and Mr. Alfred Austin are 'artists of note whom we may affiliate on Byron.' I have removed the inverted commas in my proof, but I think they might have stood."[38] Wilde's small changes to Noel's surprising statement suggest that he had trained his experienced journalist's eye on another writer's not

35. Cook, "An Art Critic and His Sententiæ," 11. See Quilter, *Sententiæ Artis*, 162.

36. Cook, "An Art Critic and His Sententiæ," 11; Quilter, *Sententiæ Artis*, 140.

37. Wilde, "To E. T. Cook," c. 23 November 1886, in *Complete Letters*, 288–89.

38. The sentence that Wilde quotes from Noel's study reads as follows: "It is remarkable that, whereas on the Continent neither of these last-named poets [Wordsworth, Keats, and Chatterton] (except in some small degree Shelley) has to any extent influenced literature, while Byron has influenced it more than any other English poet except Shakespeare and Pope, among his own Anglo-Saxon people the reverse is true; for I know not any artist of note, English or American, unless it be Edgar Poe, Bulwer Lytton, Disraeli, Joaquin Miller, Mr. Alfred Austin, whom we may affiliate upon Byron; and these very partially." Roden Noel, *Essays on Poetry and Poets* (London: Kegan Paul, 1886), 50. Wilde's emended phrasing appeared in the following sentence: "What is gained by telling us . . . that Edgar Allan Poe, Disraeli and Mr. Alfred Austin are artists of note whom we may

entirely gracious prose. His revisions forced attention on the absurdity of ranking the minor poet Austin—a much-decried figure who had inflamed the tempers of several established writers through a thoughtless polemic, *The Poetry of the Period* (1870)—with no less than Byron. In Wilde's published review of Noel's *Essays*, matters of accurate representation again came to the fore, specifically in relation to Chatterton. Noel treated Chatterton's poetry in the manner of Walter W. Skeat, stripping the Rowleian dialect from the poems to render them more accessible to the reading public.[39] Wilde protested such choices, and his critical remarks on Noel's treatment of Chatterton formed part of a much larger objection to Noel's misjudged critical approach: "The fault of his book," Wilde observes, "is that it tells us far more about his own personal feelings than it does about the qualities of the various works of art that are criticised."[40] It is Noel's "anxiety to glorify the artist . . . at the expense of the work of art" that dissatisfies Wilde; this is an "anxiety," as Wilde observes, that results in "a writer so cultured as Mr. Noel" to call "other people 'Laura Bridgmans,' 'Jackasses,' and the like."[41]

Underscoring Wilde's critiques of Quilter and Noel is his measured insistence on making authentic responses to literature and rejecting pedantry masquerading as discernment. In his "Chatterton" notebook, Wilde's commitment to extensive research is immediately apparent, as he draws from the most reputable and well documented Chatterton biographies (by Masson and Wilson) and the most nuanced analytical assessment of the Bristol poet's work to date (by Theodore Watts).

THE COMPOSITION OF THE "CHATTERTON" NOTEBOOK: CLIPPINGS AND SOURCES

Just as the "Chatterton" notebook served as a testing ground for Wilde's ideas in such reviews, so too did it serve as a repository of information gathered from

---

affiliate on Byron, and that if Sappho and Milton 'had not high genius, they would be justly reproached as sensational?'" (Wilde, "A 'Sentimental Journey' through Literature," *Pall Mall Gazette*, 1 December 1886, 5; in *Journalism Part I*, ed. Stokes and Turner, 6:113.) Wilde, "To E. T. Cook," in *Complete Letters*, 289.

39. For a full discussion of Skeat's editorial practices, see chapter 1, 71–77.

40. Wilde, "A 'Sentimental Journey' through Literature," in *Journalism Part I*, ed. Stokes and Turner, 6:113.

41. Wilde, "A 'Sentimental Journey' through Literature," in *Journalism Part I*, ed. Stokes and Turner, 6:113–14. Noel's protests against the "Laura Bridgmans" who wrongly defamed poets such as Keats and against the "nameless jackass [who] donned the lion's-skin of some ephemerally popular review" of Byron appear in *Essays on Poets and Poetry*, 66, 162. Bridgman was the first American deaf-blind girl to gain a significant education in the English language.

a carefully selected range of critical authorities. Much of the material Wilde noted on Chatterton is biographical, although he inserts extracts of Chatterton's poetry, as well as his own and others' critical assessments of the "marvellous Boy." On f.5^r, for instance, we see that Wilde's notes turned directly to Chatterton's life story in a sustained fashion, introducing the poet with the epithet "father of the | Romantic movement in literature" (f.5^r [338]). What is also evident in these early pages is the ability to distill information from multiple sources that Wilde had already shown in his Oxford notebooks. He abstracted specific details about Chatterton's background from several pages of Wilson's biography, by combining insights on the personalities and characteristics of the poet's parents in order to conclude: "Eccentricity of the father became genius | in the son, from his mother he | inherited his nervous temperament" (Appendix A, f.6^r [339]). Such statements bear out Wilde's belief that it was imperative to comprehend the circumstances that shaped Chatterton's life in order to grasp the young poet's creative drive.

It was not until f.7^r that Wilde pasted his first of many clippings from Wilson's study. On this page, however, above the printed excerpt Wilde has continued in his own hand, writing a close paraphrase of Wilson's work and transcribing the biographer's acknowledged debt to R. H. Cromek, a famous London engraver, "especially of the information | derived from Mrs. Edkins. — " (Appendix A, f.7^r [339]). In these lines, Wilde has notably changed Wilson's prepositions ("from" to "of"), a feature that recurs on several occasions in the notebook. Such actions are likely attributable either to his journalistic impulse to emend awkwardness in another writer's prose or, in the case of the "Edkins" line, to imprecise transcription. If we turn to the printed clipping that appears on the page, we can see that the excerpt Wilde has cut out begins mid-paragraph with the sentence starting "She appears," which opens far to the right of the center of the page. The cutting, which he has pared to that opening word, excises the previous sentences from the paragraph that Wilde had summarized in his own hand. This clipping ends where Wilson's page concludes (a verso in the original), and the bottom, gutter, and side margins have been carefully trimmed. In line with his practice throughout the notebook, Wilde has left the verso of his own folio blank, and on the next recto has continued with clippings from Wilson's *Chatterton*. Hereafter, Wilde constructed the remainder of the "Chatterton" notebook in a similar pattern. As one leafs through the document, it alternates between pages of clippings, handwritten pages, and pages combining both. All told, forty pages of the notebook feature pasted clippings (some of the individual pages contain multiple clippings), representing thirty-nine pages of Wilson's 324-page book. Other cut-and-pasted extracts have come from thirteen pages of Masson's substantial *Chatterton: A Story of the Year 1770*. Masson's study, in particular, provided Wilde with excerpts from the poet's correspondence. In order to create this compilation of excerpts, Wilde notably excised pages from *two* copies of Wilson's volume, since on several occasions he pasted in both the recto and verso of the same folio from *Chatterton: A Biographical Study*.[42]

Interspersed throughout the notebook is Wilde's handwritten text, which often connects many of the clippings. These linking handwritten phrases have confounded several previous scholars. Most of the recent commentators on the Chatterton notebook seem to have assumed that the two sources first identified in an auction house catalogue (Wilson's and Masson's biographies) were the only ones that Wilde drew upon.[43] Scholars have also mistakenly assumed that the connecting words and phrases in Wilde's hand are uniformly his own. They are not necessarily so. Let us give a typical example. On f.16^r (Appendix A, 351), Wilde makes the following note about Chatterton's education as a bluecoat boy: "Consciousness of aims and | power beyond those of the | other boys was even now | manifesting itself— ." This statement condenses what Wilde had already found in Wilson's study: "The consciousness of powers and aims far beyond those of his fellows was even now manifesting itself in the boy."[44] Practically all of the handwritten notes that link the clippings are derived from Wilde's sources. Yet several critics, who have not traced these remarks to their origins, claim that these handwritten links are evidence that Wilde intended to pass off the purportedly plagiarized sections as his own work in the lecture he gave at the Birkbeck Literary and Scientific Institution, a charge we explore later in this chapter. Saint-Amour, in particular, has invested some of these holograph comments with Wilde's plagiaristic designs; he suggests that "Wilde has done more than cut and paste: he has struck out irrelevant or awkward passages, added occasional words, and written transitions between Wilson's and Masson's biographical work to build a smooth narrative of purloined texts."[45] Later in his discussion, Saint-Amour contrasts the nature of these "written transitions" against the obviously excerpted passages, and the stakes of such misattributions (as opposed to the charge of plagiarism) become clearer: he writes that Wilde "graft[s]

42. See, for example, Appendix A, f.35^r (where Wilde has pasted clippings from pages 139 and 140 of Wilson, *Chatterton: A Biographical Study* [London: Macmillan, 1869]) (368–69), and f.13^r and f.14^r (where Wilde has pasted clippings from pages 21 and 22 of Wilson's study) (347–48).

43. See our discussion of this document later in this chapter (206–7).

44. Wilson, *Chatterton: A Biographical Study*, 29–30.

45. Saint-Amour, *The Copywrights*, 99.

Wilson's and Masson's biographical material onto his own more theoretical passages, so that he may both narrate and exonerate Chatterton's forgeries."[46] On the one hand, granting that the handwritten excerpts are Wilde's "own more theoretical passages" perhaps gives Wilde more credit than acknowledging that the handwritten notations linking the printed clippings were also someone else's work. On the other hand, the misattribution further obscures the true nature of the notebook by proposing that Wilde did little on his own to create a readable, "smooth narrative." Florina Tufescu, for example, has readily inferred that the holograph insertions came from Wilde's imagination; she writes that these are "sentences clipped from biographies" or "modified only as far as necessary to create the overall effect of modern, Wildean style."[47] In light of a full collation of Wilde's notebook—both the handwritten and the printed entries—with his sources, there is no evidence to support either of these claims, since the "more theoretical" links between the cut-and-pasted sections are almost always transcriptions or paraphrases of Wilson's, Masson's, or Watts's words.

Such misattribution has even more complex implications when scholars have chosen to impose biographical insights onto Wilde's interest in "the marvellous Boy." Saint-Amour, for instance, provides the following gloss on a passage that appears on f.41^r–f.42^r (Appendix A, 374–75) of the "Chatterton" notebook:

> Wilde subtly alleges homosexuality in Chatterton by eroticizing the bosom friendship between Thomas Rowley and his historical contemporary William Canynge[s] (1399?–1474), mayor of Bristol. At the end of one Rowley manuscript, Chatterton describes how the two friends had lived together in their dotage. Wilde writes, "So ended this marvellous romance which Chatterton not only wrote but lived—it is his own story—but he had not yet *found* his *Canynge* . . ." When Walpole later rejects the Rowley manuscripts as inauthentic, Wilde frames Chatterton's tragic fate as romantic defeat: "Walpole accordingly returned the MSS. Chatterton's dream of a real Canynge was over."[48]

Taken out of its precise context, this commentary has some plausibility. The year Wilde lectured on Chatterton, he also met the seventeen-year-old Robert Ross, who soon became a paying guest in the Wilde family home on Tite Street. Most biographers have concurred that Ross initiated the author into a physical homo-

---

46. Saint-Amour, *The Copywrights*, 101.

47. Florina Tufescu, *Oscar Wilde's Plagiarism: The Triumph of Art over Ego* (Dublin: Irish Academic Press, 2008), 15.

48. Saint-Amour, *The Copywrights*, 251, n. 37.

sexual encounter, which was probably Wilde's first.[49] Rodney Shewan has also thoughtfully observed the connection: "It may be coincidental that 1886, the year of Chatterton, was also the year of Robert Ross."[50] The image of Chatterton had, in any case, become a byword in the Wilde household for attractive youthful masculinity. Two years earlier, Constance Wilde had informed her brother that she and her spouse recently entertained the blond-haired, good-looking Robert Harborough Sherard, whom Wilde had first met at Paris in 1883: "We had a young Mr. Sherard here to breakfast; he has a romantic story and a romantic face: I thought Chatterton was walking in when he appeared. When I knew him a little I remarked on this resemblance and he told me he had many traits of character like him."[51] Such information might support the idea that Wilde projected not only his artistic but also his physical desires onto a particular image of Chatterton-like male beauty. Yet the material that Saint-Amour has cited to substantiate the claim that Wilde "subtly alleged homosexuality" is in fact a minor variation on a line from Wilson's biography: "So ends this ingenious romance, which Chatterton not only wrote but lived."[52] Wilson's work notably used the term "Rowley Romance" as a portmanteau covering Chatterton's invention of Rowley, the poems he composed under the Rowley name, all of the actions associated with his attempts to publish the poems, and the fall-out of those efforts. The phrase to which Saint-Amour ascribes a sense of "romantic defeat" was also drawn from Wilson's biography: Wilde wrote that Chatterton awoke from a "dream of | a real Canynge" (Appendix A, f.52^r [384]), which is a close paraphrase of Wilson's text.[53] Accurate acknowledgment of the source does not entirely undermine Saint-Amour's suggestion. Wilde, after all, chose these particular lines and not others from Wilson's biography. Thus Wilde's interest in language that described Chatterton's relationships in terms of romance still reveals to us the possibility that the author imagined the young Bristol poet

49. See Richard Ellmann, *Oscar Wilde* (New York: Alfred A. Knopf, 1988), 275–76. Ross informed Arthur Ransome that he had been Wilde's "first boy"; it is a questionable claim. There is some possibility that Wilde was sexually involved much earlier with the artist Frank Miles; for a discussion of Wilde's sexual history with other men, see Molly Whittington-Egan, *Frank Miles and Oscar Wilde: "Such White Lilies"* (High Wycombe: Rivendale Press, 2008), 36ff.

50. Rodney Shewan, *Oscar Wilde: Art and Egotism* (London: Macmillan, 1977), 72.

51. Constance Wilde, "To Otho Holland Lloyd," 3 June 1884, in Wilde, *Complete Letters*, 228.

52. Wilson, *Chatterton: A Biographical Study*, 155.

53. Wilson, *Chatterton: A Biographical Study*, 190.

as a homoerotic icon. The question of accurate attribution, though, puts some pressure on Saint-Amour's argument. In this part of the notebook, "romance" is a word that points as much to Wilson's biography as it does to the kind of same-sex intimacy that caught this modern scholar's attention, and, as we show in chapter 3, the connotations of the term "romance" or "romantic" were by the late 1880s weighted with specific artistic, literary, and political values.

Yet it is not only Wilde's holograph insertions that scholars have misattributed when studying the "Chatterton" notebook. Their critical interpretation of the final page in the document provides us with another telling example of the effect of incomplete or mistaken attributions. On this last folio, Wilde had rather inaccurately copied out Dante Gabriel Rossetti's sonnet on Chatterton from *Ballads and Sonnets* (1881), and had noted at the top: "Picture of Rossetti in the | House—" (Appendix A, f.82^r [408]). What exactly Wilde intended by this headnote remains unclear, although it might refer to Henry Treffry Dunn's well-known 1882 painting, which features—as we mention in chapter 2—Rossetti in the sitting room of his home at 16 Cheyne Walk, Chelsea, where he is reading aloud to Watts.[54] In any case, Wilde had included Rossetti's name on the page where he transcribed Rossetti's poem, a volume Wilde knew well.[55] In his widely praised and cited biography of Wilde, Richard Ellmann misidentified the sonnet; he ascribed it to Wilde, who, he said, "concluded the lecture with an unpublished poem which illustrates the complexity he relished in this new hero."[56] Even though it is evident that Ellmann should have checked Wilde's source, it was probably the case that a document from an auction house misled the biographer.[57] In 1953, James F. Drake, Inc., of New York City, described the notebook in a sale catalogue as a "very interesting and unpublished rough draft, including many notes for projected expansion of the text, of an essay on Thomas Chatterton"; "the essay," the company added, "concludes with a sonnet to Chatterton by Wilde which is also apparently unpublished."[58]

54. See chapter 3, note 174 (151).

55. See Appendix B (411–15) for the notes Wilde drafted on the volume.

56. Ellmann, *Oscar Wilde*, 269.

57. Ellmann's misattribution may also have some connection with assistance he received from Chatterton's modern textual editor, Donald S. Taylor, since in his acknowledgments Ellmann writes: "Professor Donald Taylor [and also R. E. Alton] helped with Wilde's sonnet on Chatterton" (*Oscar Wilde*, xii).

58. This text appears in a typewritten note that James F. Drake, which sold the notebook in 1952, had placed inside the "Chatterton" notebook. We discuss the sales records of the notebook in our Editorial Introduction to Appendixes A and B (317–20).

In an essay that corrected this confusing error, Roger Lewis noted the "scribbled words" at the top of the notebook page. Yet Lewis decided to characterize these "scribbled words" as a "cryptic heading which may refer to an illustration for [Wilde's] projected *Century Guild Hobby Horse* article . . . but which does not necessarily lead one to infer that the sonnet below is by Rossetti."[59] Lewis, who also assumed that the notebook must have served as a transcript of Wilde's lecture, then made a further bold speculation: "Wilde gave a verbal attribution to DGR but did not note it in his manuscript."[60] By comparison, Saint-Amour, while acknowledging Rossetti's authorship, contended that Wilde ended his lecture "with an untitled (and unattributed) Rossetti sonnet that likened Chatterton to Shakespeare and Milton."[61] Such judgments, as we can see, have depended on rejecting Wilde's note about Rossetti as a legitimate attribution of the sonnet's authorship. However, a contemporary account of Wilde's 1888 lecture on Chatterton at Bournemouth, first located by Geoff Dibb, states that Wilde "concluded by reciting the beautiful sonnet to Chatterton by D. G. Rossetti," suggesting that Wilde gave due credit to his source.[62]

This enduring problem of attribution has created still further misunderstandings of an arguably more serious aspect of the "Chatterton" notebook. The mistake of ascribing Wilde's notes to the wrong source arises most problematically in relation to Watts's 1880 essay on Chatterton. Toward the end of the notebook, Wilde's handwritten notes focus on his engagement with Watts's powerful discussion of the Bristol poet in the third volume of Ward's *English Poets* (Appendix A, f.75^r–f.79^r [403–7]).[63] Wilde's respect for Watts formed part of his much larger admiration for the major Pre-Raphaelites, who, it appears, had little time for him. Even though Watts's memoirs show that he was often in Wilde's company at dinner parties, it is clear that this established critic of poetry did not take the young man altogether seriously: "Among all the artificial

59. Roger Lewis, "A Misattribution: Oscar Wilde's 'Unpublished Sonnet on Chatterton,'" *Victorian Poetry* 28, no. 2 (1990): 167.

60. Lewis, "A Misattribution," 168.

61. Saint-Amour, *The Copyrights*, 98.

62. "Lecture by Mr. Oscar Wilde," *Poole and Dorset Herald*, 12 April 1888, 6. Dibb remarks on this source in *Oscar Wilde, a Vagabond with a Mission*, 208.

63. Theodore Watts, "Thomas Chatterton," in *The English Poets*, ed. Ward, 3:400–408. We discuss Watts's essay in chapter 3 (149–59). Dibb has also identified Wilde's use of this source; see *Oscar Wilde, a Vagabond with a Mission*, 208, 368, 369.

fibres in Wilde's constitution," Watts remarked after Wilde's death, "were three genuine strings: his affection for his mother, his admiration of Rossetti, and his worship of Swinburne."[64] The only thing that united Rossetti, Watts, and Wilde was their shared regard for Chatterton, and Wilde turned to Watts as a leading critical thinker on the "marvellous Boy."

Proper attribution of a closing section of the notebook clarifies the complicated ways in which Wilde borrowed from (and, in a later work, transformed) Watts's discussion of Chatterton. Just before his transcription of Rossetti's sonnet on the Bristol poet, Wilde left off the clipped excerpts and returned to his own hand. In this section, Wilde transcribes Watts's bold justifications for Chatterton's forgeries. By mistaking these ideas for Wilde's own, modern scholars have in turn taken these lines as clear evidence of Wilde's own distinctive theory of creative production. Yet it was Watts, not Wilde, who initially framed his understanding of Chatterton through a series of searching inquiries: Was he a downright criminal or an artistic genius? Was Chatterton an original creative force or mere imitator? Watts linked these alternatives to the "nature of the man":

> For, Chatterton, far more than with any other poet of the representative kind, the question, What was the nature of his artistic impulse? is mixed up with the question, What was the nature of the man? Do these Rowley poems show the vitalising power which only genius can give? and if they do, was Chatterton's impulse to exercise that power the impulse of the dramatic poet having "the yearning of the Great Vish'nu to create a world"? or, was it that of the other class of artists, whose skill lies in "those more facile imitations of prose, promissory notes," among whom Horace Walpole would place him? For neither the assailants nor the defenders of Chatterton's character seem to see that between these two conclusions there is no middle one. Either Chatterton was a born forger, having, as useful additional endowments, poetry and dramatic imagination almost unmatched among his contemporaries, or he was a born artist, who, before mature vision had come to show him the power and the sacredness of moral conscience in art, was so dominated by the artistic conscience—by the artist's yearning to represent, that, if perfect representation seemed to him to demand forgery, he needs must forge.[65]

64. Thomas Hake and Arthur Compton-Rickett, *The Life and Letters of Theodore Watts-Dunton*, 2 vols. (London: T. C. and E. C. Jack, 1916), 1:174.

65. Watts, "Thomas Chatterton," in *The English Poets*, ed. Ward, 3:404–5. Watts's quotation about "promissory notes" comes from Horace Walpole, *A Letter to the Editor of the Miscellanies of Thomas Chatterton* (Strawberry Hill: privately published, 1779), 24. See chapter 1 (46).

This passage from Watts's essay forms the basis of Wilde's notes under the heading "Nature of his genius":

> was he mere forger
> with literary powers or
> a great artist?
> the latter is the right view. Chatterton
> may not have had the moral
> conscience which is Truth to Fact—
> but he had the artistic conscience
> which is truth to Beauty. He
> had the artists yearning to
> represent and if perfect representation
> seemed to him to demand forgery
> He needs must forge—Still
> this forgery came from the
> desire of artistic self effacement.
> He was the pure artist—that it is
>   to say
>
> there was something in him
> of "the yearning of great
> ? <u>Vishnu</u> to create a world"—
>   ————
>
> yet a distinctive note
>   of his own— (Appendix A, f.75ʳ–f.75ᵛ [403–4])

Since several critics have failed to recognize that Watts's essay was the source for most of this passage, they have argued that here we find the genesis of Wilde's justification of forgery, often as a means to explain Wilde's apparent partiality for plagiarism. Shewan, for example, cites this excerpt as Wilde's, and then proceeds to contend that its phrasing forms the basis of the author's attitude toward the dandyish homicide and forger Thomas Griffiths Wainewright in Wilde's witty essay "Pen, Pencil and Poison."[66] By comparison, Ellmann takes this passage as evidence of Wilde's identification with Chatterton through an analogous understanding of the creative impulse: "Wilde sought eagerly for analogues to his own new mode of life, and found one in a young man who used his genius to forge Jacobean plays."[67] Saint-Amour similarly mistakes Watts for

66. Shewan, *Oscar Wilde*, 77.

67. Ellmann, *Oscar Wilde*, 284. Ellmann's suggestion that Chatterton composed works in the style of "Jacobean plays" is somewhat misguided. Ellmann's misattribution has been

Wilde. In addition to the "needs must forge" passage, he cites the lines on the Romantic use of octosyllabic forms as signs of Wilde's perception of Chatterton's poetic influence:

> lyrical octosyllabic movement
>
> ---
>
> Scott stole from Coleridge
> Coleridge got from Chatterton—

what Coleridge claimed as a
new principle in poetry—the
anapaestic variations in
correspondence with some transition
in the nature of the imagery or
passion—was in reality
Chattertons—   Influence of
Chatterton seen in Coleridges
Kubla Khan and Christabel
    in Keats Eve of St. Agnes— (Appendix A, f.78^r–f.79^r [406–7])

Saint-Amour offers a caveat about attributing these lines to Wilde: "Toward the end of the lecture, he argues (this time apparently in his 'own' words, though with Chattertonian echoes) that writers inherit *only* debt from their testators, and that English Romanticism itself is therefore a legacy of debts, even a legacy of theft."[68] But, since he has already characterized the "Chatterton" notebook as a work of plagiarism, Saint-Amour believes these sentences evince Wilde's presumed belief that literary influence remains inextricable from theft. Instead, it was Watts who claimed, in telltale parentheses, that the "lyric octo-syllabic movement of which Scott made such excellent use in *The Lay of Last Minstrel*, and which Byron borrowed from him, was originally borrowed (or rather stolen) by Scott from Coleridge."[69] Watts's point is to show that the young poet who had been maligned as a forger was in fact the originator of the "new principle" that his successors such as Coleridge adapted and adopted, one after the other.

There is no question that the "needs must forge" passage proved crucial in

---

repeated not only in relation to Wilde but also in several other works: Denis Donoghue, "One Life Was Not Enough," *New York Times*, 17 January 1988: sec. 7; Brian Finney, *English Fiction since 1984* (Basingstoke: Palgrave Macmillan, 2006), 28; and Laura Savu, *Postmortem Postmodernists: The Afterlife of the Author in Recent Narrative* (Cranbury, NJ: Associated University Presses, 2009), 120.

68. Saint-Amour, *The Copywrights*, 103. Emphasis in the original.
69. Watts, "Thomas Chatterton," in *The English Poets*, ed. Ward, 3:401.

Wilde's developing understanding of artistic creativity during the later 1880s. Moreover, Wilde's observations that "Scott stole from Coleridge" and "Coleridge got from Chatterton" point to his shrewd awareness that the history of English poetry involves unavoidable patterns of derivation and imitation. The main consequence of attributing these notes to their proper source is that it shifts the interpretive interest away from Wilde's apparent passion for the inherent criminality of artistic theft, toward the genealogy of echoes and emulation that Watts informatively traced back to its progenitor, Chatterton. Watts's observation was not that Scott's borrowing from Coleridge or Coleridge's borrowing from Chatterton was criminal in nature. By identifying Chatterton as the source of influential formal innovation, Watts elevated the young poet to his rightful position as an original genius.

WILDE AS EDITOR: REFINING OTHERS' WORDS IN THE "CHATTERTON" NOTEBOOK

Much of the "Chatterton" notebook reveals Wilde's growing skills as an editor who was especially sensitive to matters of style and points of detail. At the time, he was frequently correcting proofs of his own writing and reviewing others' work. In early 1887, he was also readying himself for his tenure as editor of *The Lady's World*, which transformed into the much more radical *Woman's World* under his direction for the next two years. Wilde brought his skilled journalist's eye to his clippings. He struck out lines that repeated information he had already transcribed. He also deleted those sentences that contained a source's speculation on (instead of verified knowledge about) Chatterton's biography (see, for example, Appendix A, f.15^r [349]). Here and there, Wilde's marginal notes continued the clipped excerpts or illegible words, where he finished sentences that he had cut off in the clipping (e.g. Appendix A, f.25^r [358–59]). In these instances, Wilde took pains to include a selection accurately. He completed sentences with precision, even though he struck through those lines of the paragraph. This action, along with the fact that many of the omissions are deleted in black ink as opposed to pencil, suggests that his deletions were added at a later point, most probably when he had looked over and reviewed the pasted materials. Wilde's copyediting impulse is also evident where his marginal comments corrected awkward phrasing. A good example appears on f.33^r (Appendix A, 365–66). This is where Wilson recounted some of the biographical details that went into Chatterton's history of the poet and priest Rowley:

> He and William, the second son of John Canynge, a youth of cunning wit, —
> as we learn from the "Lyfe of W. Canynge," one of the Chatterton MSS., —

~~improved their lear together, under the care of~~ the Carmelite brothers, in the old priory which once occupied the site of Colston's School.[70]

Once he had struck through Wilson's "improved their lear together, under the care of" (in which the Scottish English word "lear" stands for "lesson" or "education"), Wilde substituted in the margin the much more accessible "were educated by" (Appendix A, f.33ʳ). One could possibly read such corrections as evidence that Wilde was preparing the notebook to be read aloud at Birkbeck, or to be published in the *Century Guild*. But it seems as, if not more, likely—especially given Wilde's approach, for example, to Quilter's slapdash work—that Wilde's marginal gloss, which explains Wilson's Scots idiom, merely indicates the degree to which he took a careful editorial eye to everything he read.

Elsewhere, Wilde strikes through Wilson's comments on Chatterton's "Elinoure and Juga." These deletions warrant attention because they suggest Wilde had no interest in Wilson's "slightly modernised" presentation of the text.[71] Like many reviewers of his time, Wilson expressed disdain for "the affected Chaucerian character" of the "language and orthography" that Chatterton devised for his Rowley poems.[72] Wilde seems equally dismissive of Wilson's suggestion that if Chatterton's invented antiquarian words were replaced with the modern equivalents that Chatterton himself provided, "the whole would be restored to the language of the eighteenth century" (Appendix A, f.25ʳ [359]).[73] Implicitly, Wilde grasped what was obvious to some of his contemporaries in their irritation with Skeat's edition: the modernization of the Rowley poems destroyed not only their visible relation to Middle English but also their prosodic integrity. Equally noteworthy is Wilde's deletion of Wilson's somewhat belittling comments on the heraldic blazon of the De Bergham arms that Chatterton presented to Bristol shopkeeper, Henry Burgum. Taken in by Chatterton's elaborate forgery, Burgum was delighted to discover his noble ancestry. Yet where Wilson views with disdain the many "apocryphal" references in the pedigree (ones that to him were "not without some interesting traces of the unwonted range of study in which the boy delighted"), Wilde simply commented that this forgery was "a brilliant if somewhat | daring act of imagination" (Appendix A, f.29ʳ [361]).[74] Correspondingly, the fact that Wilde scored through Wilson's allusion to "the boy's heraldic jests," together with some rehashed an-

70. Wilson, *Chatterton: A Biographical Study*, 136.

71. Wilson, *Chatterton: A Biographical Study*, 42.

72. Wilson, *Chatterton: A Biographical Study*, 42. See our discussion of the critical reception of nineteenth-century editions of Chatterton's verse in chapter 2 (65–78).

73. Wilson, *Chatterton: A Biographical Study*, 43.

74. Wilson, *Chatterton: A Biographical Study*, 56.

ecdotes about the poet's maiden aunt (she appears "to have better appreciated the young scapegrace than others who were made the butts of his jests"), shows that Wilde did not regard Chatterton as either an immature or an unintelligent artist (Appendix A, f.30ʳ [363]).[75]

The larger proportion of passages that Wilde duly excised from his two copies of Wilson's Chatterton provided basic bits and pieces of information about Chatterton's family background, his schooling, his move to London, his conflict with Walpole, and his suicide. That many of the clippings include Wilson's own footnotes, which indicate that Wilson drew information verbatim from Dix (among other sources), further suggests that Wilde was compiling data rather than appropriating any argument that Wilson forwarded. Wilson's study presented in turn a resource for numerous quotations, which in the first instance come from the Rowley poems. Later, when Wilde turned to Masson's monograph, he cut out sections from some of the better-known items of the young poet's correspondence from the brief, final period spent living at Holborn. Once he had taken note of Chatterton's "Last Will and Testament" (cut from Masson) and the poem that early editors titled "Suicide" (clipped from Wilson), Wilde focused on critical assessments.[76] On the one hand, Wilde noted down from Wilson's concluding commentary on the literary "versatility" in imitating different authors that Chatterton "manifested at so early an age."[77] On the other hand, Wilde prefaced Wilson's remarks with his own insight: "He saw the realm of | the imagination differed from the | realm of fact" (Appendix A, f.76ʳ [403–5]). Wilde took heed of Watts's sharp understanding of the debt that Keats's great work paid to Chatterton's finest poetry: "It is difficult to express in words wherein lies the entirely spiritual kinship between Chatterton's *Ballad of Charity* and Keats's *Eve of St. Agnes*, yet I should be sceptical as to the insight of any critic who should fail to recognise that kinship."[78] (Pater, incidentally, made a similar passing observation when he compared the "finest 'vermeil and ivory' work of Chatterton or Keats" in a discussion of the "extraordinary refinement of intelligence and variety of piteous appeal," as well as "felicity of poetic invention," that he detected in Shakespeare's *Richard II*.)[79]

75. Wilson, *Chatterton: A Biographical Study*, 59.

76. Taylor and Hoover place the poem Wilson calls "Suicide" under the title "Sentiment"; see *The Complete Works of Thomas Chatterton*, ed. Donald S. Taylor and Benjamin B. Hoover, 2 vols. (Oxford: Clarendon Press, 1971), 1:446.

77. Wilson, *Chatterton: A Biographical Study*, 261.

78. Watts, "Thomas Chatterton," in *The English Poets*, ed. Ward, 3:402.

79. Pater, "Shakespeare's English Kings," in *Appreciations: With an Essay on Style* (London: Macmillan, 1889), 206. Pater's discussion focuses on the famous deposition scene in act 4, scene 1, of Shakespeare's tragedy *Richard II* (see *Richard II*, ed. Charles R. Forker, The Arden Shakespeare, 3rd series [London: Thomson, 2002], 383–412).

After he had absorbed these insights, Wilde started to sketch his own clear sense of the "continuity of English poetry—| Chaucer—Spenser—Chatterton | Coleridge—Keats—Tennyson— | Morris" (Appendix A, f.80ʳ [407]). "What do we learn?" Wilde asks toward the end of his notes. The answer, for him, lies with Shelley, who, in the 1819 essay "On Life," declares that the "mist of familiarity" sadly "obscures from us the wonder of our being."[80] It is, Wilde insists, the "ideal | not the realistic artist who | expresses his age" (Appendix A, f.81ʳ [408]). Fittingly enough, he finished the "Chatterton" notebook with a work that brought this sense of poetic continuity to a well-judged conclusion: Dante Gabriel Rossetti's sonnet honoring Chatterton—the poet who dedicated his passion "to the dear new bower of England's art," and who, even if killed by the "fell point" of a "dart," nonetheless left imposing works that proved his "gallant swordplay" as an artist (Appendix A, f.82ʳ [408–9]).[81] A vibrant masculine force, Chatterton, in this spectacular reckoning, presided over modern English poetry.

Besides his own observations, the cut-and-pasted passages, the interlinking sentences, and the concluding remarks and quotations, the "Chatterton" notebook features other aspects of Wilde's note-taking practices in the margins. The single word 'Plato,' for example, emerges strikingly, in large, underlined letters,

80. Percy Bysshe Shelley, "On Life," in *Shelley's Poetry and Prose*, ed. Donald H. Reiman and Neil Fraistat, 2nd ed. (New York: Norton, 2002), 505. Shelley's essay first appeared in the *Athenæum* in 1832, and was reprinted several times in the nineteenth century, including in *The Prose Works of Percy Bysshe Shelley*, ed. H. Buxton Forman, 4 vols. (London: Reeves and Turner, 1880), 2:257–63. Shelley's phrasing echoes his "Defence of Poetry," where he states that poetry "strips the veil of familiarity from the world, and lays bare the naked and sleeping beauty which is the spirit of its forms" (*Shelley's Poetry and Prose*, ed. Fraistat, 533). Fraistat takes his text from Shelley's fair copy, which the poet sent to Charles Ollier in 1821; the manuscript is held at the Bodleian Library. The earliest text of these remarks from Shelley's "Defence" appears in Shelley, *Essays, Letters from Abroad, Translations, and Fragments*, ed. Mary Shelley, 2 vols. (London: Edward Moxon, 1840), 1:51. As Susan J. Wolfson has shown, Shelley's wording derives from Samuel Taylor Coleridge's *Biographia Literaria* (1817): see *Formal Charges: The Shaping of Poetry in British Romanticism* (Stanford: Stanford University Press, 1997), 20–24.

81. Rossetti, "Five English Poets: I. Thomas Chatterton," in *Ballads and Sonnets* (London: Ellis and White, 1881), 313. Elsewhere in this volume, Rossetti's poetic voice commented on the evocative links between the tragedy of the Queen of Egypt and the suffering of distinguished poets in modern London that were suggested by the placement of the ancient Egyptian obelisk known as Cleopatra's Needle on Victoria Embankment, London, in 1878; he asks the stone monument whether she has reached "A city of sweet speech scorned,—on whose chill stone / Keats withered, Coleridge pined, and Chatterton / Breadless, with poison froze the God-fired breath" ("Tiber, Nile, and Thames" [318]).

on f.8[r], next to Wilson's lines that detail Mrs. Chatterton's anxiety at the "reveries" that occupied her young son's mind:

> These strange musings, which ere long were the precursors of his poetical activity, were incomprehensible to those among whom he moved, and only excited suspicion, or doubt of his sanity. His mother said, "he had cost her many uneasy hours, from the apprehension she entertained of his going mad; as he was accustomed to remain fixed for above an hour at a time quite motionless, and then he would snatch up a pen and write incessantly." What he did write, after such prolonged reveries, does not seem to have excited any curiosity.[82]

That the alliance of genius with madness should have provoked Platonic associations for Wilde is not surprising. His Oxford notebooks elaborated his deep familiarity with Plato's dialogues. Between the *Ion* and the *Phaedrus*, Plato had established the relationship between poetic inspiration, divine inspiration, and insanity. In his influential translation of Plato's dialogues, which first appeared in 1871, Oxford professor Benjamin Jowett claimed that Socrates believes that "a man must be mad who behaves" as the rhapsode Ion does when performing Homer.[83] "Ion is confident," Jowett continued, "that Socrates would never think him mad if he could only hear" him perform his "embellishments of Homer."[84] In the *Phaedrus*, too, Plato characterized poetic inspiration as a form of possession. Besides the "madness" that inspires prophetic visions (μαντική) and religious rites (σοφροσύνη), "there is a third kind of madness, which is a possession of the Muses; this enters into a delicate and virgin soul, and there inspiring frenzy, awakens lyric and all other numbers."[85] From this perspective, there was no room left for the poet who was not "inspired and having no touch of madness"; the "sane man," Plato had written, "is nowhere at all when he enters into rivalry with the madman."[86] As far as we can tell, in cutting and pasting this passage from Wilson's *Chatterton* Wilde was adopting his established synthetic approach, one that involved finding connections across divergent fields, in the manner he had developed as an undergraduate. In other words, the name "Plato" provided a frame of reference for understanding the poetic tradition of rhapsody.

82. Wilson, *Chatterton: A Biographical Study*, 9; Appendix A, f.8[r] (341).

83. Benjamin Jowett, "Introduction" to *Ion*, *The Dialogues of Plato Translated into English with Analyses and Introductions*, trans. Jowett, 2nd ed., 5 vols. (Oxford: Clarendon Press, 1875), 1:240.

84. Jowett, "Introduction" to *Ion*, *The Dialogues of Plato*, trans. Jowett, 1:240.

85. Plato, *Phaedrus*, in *The Dialogues of Plato*, trans. Jowett, 2:122.

86. Plato, *Phaedrus* in *The Dialogues of Plato*, trans. Jowett, 2:122. See also our discussion of Wilde's use of Plato on 234–35.

Near the conclusion of the "Chatterton" notebook, Wilde includes a cue that suggests that he was learning a great deal about the young forger from Bristol and aimed to learn still more. Here he jotted down the state of Chatterton's financial affairs shortly after the poet had moved to London in late spring 1770. Especially galling to Chatterton was the unexpected death of William Beckford, Lord Mayor of London, whom he hoped might become a patron. As we mention in chapter 1, Beckford, whose wealth came from slave-owning estates in Jamaica, had recently secured the release of the radical democrat John Wilkes. At one point, Wilde notes from Wilson's study that one of the contacts that Chatterton made in London was Mr. Fell of the *Freeholders' Magazine*. Wilde records this figure as an "ardent Wilkite," and he adds that "Wilkes . . . had desired to know | him—he gets to know | Beckford" (Appendix A, f.67^r [397]). Though it is clear from these rapid notes that Wilde was attempting to understand the radical circles in which Chatterton moved, he noticeably avoids Wilson's assumptions that Chatterton ("a versatile mocking-bird" and "young literateur," who was politically full of "bombastic foibles") had "naturally taken the popular side" in this furor.[87] More interesting to Wilde is the fact that Chatterton, as Masson recorded, immersed himself in the cultural and political vibrancy of London: "goes to theatres | Garrick acting Hamlet— | Addison's Cato—" (Appendix A, f.67^r [397]).[88]

On f.70^r (399), having noted from Wilson's study the ledger that Chatterton kept, Wilde observed: "Gets despondent in July | Ballad of Charity— | rejected by the Town and | County Magazine."[89] After these words Wilde has underlined the verb *"Read."* If we were to assume that the notebook formed the basis of Wilde's lecture, this directive would suggest that this was his prompt to read aloud Chatterton's last major poem. Yet, when considered as part of Wilde's compilation of information about the young Bristol poet, this self-addressed imperative suggests that Wilde was still acquiring knowledge about a writer whose impact on English poetry he had only begun to fathom. The directive suggests, we argue, that the time had come for Wilde to read Chatterton's outstanding "Excelente Balade of Charitie," a poem that Rossetti regarded as one of Chatterton's best.

87. Wilson, *Chatterton: A Biographical Study*, 261–62.

88. Masson observed of Chatterton's activities in London: "If he did not go to see Addison's tragedy of *Cato* at Covent Garden on the 30th of April, it is not likely that he missed the opportunity of seeing Garrick in *Hamlet* at the Drury Lane on the 2d of May" (Masson, *Chatterton: A Story of the Year 1770*, 2nd ed. [London: Macmillan, 1874], 140).

89. The rejection was precipitated by the death of William Beckford; see our discussion of the Beckford/Wilkes affair in chapter 1, 41–42.

Elsewhere, the double-underlined "<u>Appearance</u>" (Appendix A, f.9ʳ [342]) is evocative, since it suggests the tangled history of depictions of Chatterton, a history in which Rossetti, Horne, and the Century Guild, along with Wilde himself, expressed considerable interest. As we have detailed, Wilde's concern over the depiction of Keats on his memorial inspired a letter-writing campaign as well as verse.[90] Wilde's allusion to the physical appearance of the Bristol poet belonged to an ongoing discussion. Several years earlier, William Michael Rossetti and Dante Gabriel Rossetti had debated the accuracy of portraits that supposedly represented Chatterton. In response to William Michael's sketch of a purported portrait of Chatterton, Dante Gabriel provided a list of ostensible depictions of the "marvellous Boy" in an attempt to set the record (and his brother) straight: "Thanks for the sketch of the Chatterton portrait (so called), for which Chatterton never sat, and which Hogarth never painted."[91] He proceeded to elaborate a theory that someone who knew Chatterton could have produced "a *reminiscent* sketch" after the young man's demise; this possibility, Dante Gabriel argued, would account for the likeness between the ostensible "Chatterton portrait" that William Michael had sketched at Peel Park, Manchester, and the engraving that he himself had seen of the life-sized oil that Sir Henry Taylor owned. (It is not clear whether William Michael meant the portrait that Henry Taylor's daughter, Una, had produced and that Robert Louis Stevenson owned.)[92] As he pondered these similar-looking portraits, Rossetti observed that they "seem to acquire additional attraction from a certain resemblance in them to the type of Keats."[93] Yet this correspondence reveals that the lack of an authenticated painting of Chatterton proved a source of frustration to Rossetti. Rossetti concluded his sonnet on Chatterton by commenting on the Bristol's poet's "unrecorded face," which remained as "sweet for ever" as the "grave unknown."[94] These details help to explain why Wilde expressed some hesitancy about incorporating "a bas-relief of T.C." at the proposed museum he was discussing with Horne; as he said to this member of the Century Guild, "there is really no picture of the poet extant": "I prefer the inscription," he wrote, "though a symbolic design might accompany it."[95] Despite his caution on this front, Wilde seems to have maintained an interest in Chatterton's ap-

90. See chapter 2, 137–40.

91. Rossetti, "To William Michael Rossetti," 4 July 1880, *The Correspondence of Dante Gabriel Rossetti*, ed. William E. Fredeman, 9 vols. (Cambridge: D. S. Brewer, 2002–2010), 9:218.

92. See chapter 2, note 108, for additional details on Taylor's portrait.

93. Rossetti, *Correspondence*, ed. Fredeman, 9:219.

94. Rossetti, "Five English Poets: I. Thomas Chatterton," 313.

95. Wilde, "To Herbert P. Horne," 7 December 1886, in *Complete Letters*, 289.

pearance. A few years later, in his "Literary Notes" column for *The Woman's World*, he reviewed Mabel Wotton's book, *Word-Portraits of Famous Writers*, noting that according to the accounts she collected, "Chatterton and Byron were splendidly handsome."[96]

Despite Wilde's well-documented, manifold interest in researching the life and work of Chatterton, and despite the evidence throughout the notebook of Wilde's editorial approach to the materials he cut, pasted, and emended, modern scholars have reached the consensus that this archive of materials on Chatterton exhibits Wilde's unremorseful and habitual indulgence in plagiarism. In the next section, we evaluate the persistence of the claims that Wilde repeatedly engaged in acts of literary larceny and suggest that from the outset, these allegations have always stood on shaky foundations. In the specific case of the "Chatterton" notebook, such charges of plagiarism obscure the notebook's crucial role in shaping Wilde's critical understanding of the inventive position that forgery might hold in artistic creativity.

WILDE, THE "CHATTERTON" NOTEBOOK, AND PLAGIARISM

Charges of Wilde's plagiarism have their origins in his contemporaries' sharp criticism of his first published volume, *Poems* (1881). Even if his critics did not claim that any of his poetry had been stolen verbatim from the Romantics and Pre-Raphaelites, they grasped that much of his work was highly derivative. The *Saturday Review*, for example, was fairly typical of the critical reception: "The book is not without traces of cleverness, but it is marred everywhere by imitation, insincerity, and bad taste."[97] At the same time, the Oxford Union famously rejected on similar grounds the very copy of *Poems* that its secretary had solicited from Wilde. In a report on the union's decision, Oliver Elton asserted that Wilde's poems were "not by their putative father at all, but by a number of better-known and more deservedly reputed authors."[98] Modern scholars, how-

96. Wilde, "Some Literary Notes," *Woman's World* 2, no. 5 (March 1889): 280; in *Journalism Part II*, ed. John Stokes and Mark W. Turner, *The Complete Works of Oscar Wilde*, 7 vols. to date (Oxford: Oxford University Press, 2000 and continuing), 7:184. In the same column, Wilde addressed W. B. Yeats's first volume of poetry, *The Wanderings of Oisin, and Other Poems* (1889), noting: "One quality Mr. Yeats has in a marked degree, a quality that is not common in the work of our minor poets, and is therefore all the more welcome to us—I mean the romantic temper" (278; in *Journalism Part II*, ed. Stokes and Turner, 7:178).

97. [Anon.,] "Recent Poetry," *Saturday Review*, 23 July 1881: 118; in Karl Beckson, ed., *Oscar Wilde: The Critical Heritage* (London: Routledge and Kegan Paul, 1970), 37.

98. Henry Newbolt, *My World as in My Time* (London: Faber and Faber, 1932), 96.

ever, have at times rebutted Elton's claim, suggesting that disdain for Wilde's developing poetic voice or even downright jealousy motivated his outcry.[99] Nowhere, it remains vital to recall, is Elton supposed to have said that Wilde's *Poems* was the result of a kleptomaniacal impulse. Nor, when public attention increasingly focused on literary property, was there any sense that Wilde had infringed copyright. Yet, in more recent years, the stigma attached to the reception of *Poems* has stuck firmly to critical perceptions of this collection. In the late twentieth century, Wilde's presumed unoriginality appeared to one disdainful scholar as a symptom of his constitutional indolence: "One feels that Wilde was more than usually immature in his slavish regurgitation of diverse and unassimilated poetic tags; one is impatient with his lazy refusal to replace the shorthand of quotation by a carefully thought-out phrasing of his own; and one is shocked at the effrontery of a would-be literary imposter."[100] As we have shown, Wilde often encouraged the idea that his manners were unstudied and—in the case of his early Oxford correspondence—that he much preferred laziness or torpor to industrious scholarship. Seldom have modern critics reflected on the idea that Wilde's youthful identification with his Romantic and Pre-Raphaelite poetic idols was so strong that his devotion to them resulted in his apparent copying of their writings. Further, while charges of affectation were frequently applied to Wilde's aesthetic mannerisms, it seems that few took seriously the idea that the lassitude or nonchalance he embodied was itself affected; his languor was (like his Double First) the product of intense, if skillfully concealed, effort.

The charge that Wilde was to some degree a literary thief clung to his name, however. From the early 1880s onward Wilde found it hard to escape the entrenched belief that he had no scruples in filching other people's ideas. By far the most controversial conflict in Wilde's career arose from criticisms that the socially competitive painter James McNeill Whistler made about Wilde's unacknowledged appropriation of his bons mots. The rivalry between the older American artist and the younger Irish author, who moved in similar fashionable circles such as the Marlborough House set, developed through a spirited, if eventually bitter, exchange, first in the *Pall Mall Gazette* and then in two pop-

99. See Merlin Holland, "Plagiarist, or Pioneer?" in *Rediscovering Oscar Wilde*, ed. George Sandulescu (Gerrards Cross: Colin Smythe, 1994), 199. Ellmann states that the proceedings at the Oxford Union had a "Swiftian lunacy" (*Oscar Wilde*, 146). The union voted against the acceptance of Wilde's volume by a fairly narrow margin: 188 against 180 votes. Elton proceeded to a distinguished career as a university professor of English; he became best known for his *Survey of English Literature, 1780–1830*, 2 vols. (London: Edward Arnold, 1912).

100. Averil Gardner, "'Literary Petty Larceny': Plagiarism in Oscar Wilde's Early Poetry," *English Studies in Canada* 8 (1982): 52.

ular magazines: Edmund Yates's *World* and Henry Labouchere's *Truth*. On 20 February 1885, Whistler had delivered in London his notorious "Ten O' Clock Lecture," whose title indicates the attention-grabbing late-evening slot when he delivered his thoughts on art. In particular, Whistler attacked the modern critic, "the unattached writer" who "has become the middleman in this matter of Art."[101] Such an arbiter of taste, in Whistler's view, could not see the "*painter's poetry*" in the artwork, since the critic treated it as he would "a novel—a history—or an anecdote."[102] Wilde retorted by objecting to the belief that only the artist can comprehend aesthetic beauty. "An artist," Wilde commented, "is not an isolated fact; he is the resultant of a certain milieu and a certain entourage, and can no more be born of a nation that is devoid of any sense of beauty than a fig can grow from a thorn or a rose blossom from a thistle."[103] In other words, Wilde claimed that cultural traditions created the circumstances in which the finest types of art could flourish. Moreover, Wilde asserted, while mentioning Poe and Baudelaire along the way, that in these modern times "an artist will find beauty in ugliness, *le beau dans l'horrible*."[104] Challenged, Whistler responded briskly in the *World*, stating that Wilde had implied that it was left to modern poets to find "'*l'horrible*' dans '*le beau*.'"[105] In turn, Wilde sparred back that Whistler had scarcely understood his critique: "Be warned in time, James; and remain, as I do, incomprehensible. To be great is to be misunderstood."[106] Wilde drove home his point about the artist's affiliation with a cultural milieu by quoting—though not explicitly acknowledging—Emerson's famous essay "Self-Reliance" (1840).[107] Wilde thus quoted another person's wisdom to

101. James Abbott McNeill Whistler, "Mr. Whistler's 'Ten O' Clock,'" in Whistler, *The Gentle Art of Making Enemies*, new ed. (London: Heinemann, 1892), 146.

102. Whistler, *The Gentle Art of Making Enemies*, 146–47.

103. Wilde, "Mr. Whistler's Ten O'Clock," *Pall Mall Gazette*, 21 February 1885: 2; in *Journalism Part I*, ed. Stokes and Turner, 6:35.

104. Wilde, "Mr. Whistler's Ten O'Clock," in *Journalism Part I*, ed. Stokes and Turner, 6:35.

105. Whistler, "Tenderness in Tite Street," *World*, 25 February 1885: 14; in *The Gentle Art of Making Enemies*, 162.

106. Wilde, "To the Painter," *World*, 25 February 1885: 14; in *The Gentle Art of Making Enemies*, 163; and in *Complete Letters*, 250.

107. In "Self-Reliance," Emerson writes: "A foolish consistency is the hobgoblin of little minds, adored by little statesmen and philosophers and divines. With consistency a great soul has simply nothing to do. He may as well concern himself with his shadow on the wall. Speak what you think now in hard words, and to-morrow speak what to-morrow thinks in hard words again, though it contradict every thing you said to-day.—'Ah, so you shall be sure to be misunderstood.'—Is it so bad, then, to be misunderstood? Pythagoras

speak eloquently on his behalf. This was a technique that he later practiced at Whistler's expense.

Toward the end of 1886, Whistler's temper flared up once more when he detected Wilde's flagrant appropriation of some of his phrases. "What has Oscar in common with Art? except that he dines at our tables and picks from our platters the plums for the pudding he peddles in the provinces."[108] "Oscar," Whistler's barbs continued, "has the courage of the opinions . . . of others!"[109] Matters did not rest there. Years later, the American painter grew vociferous once more when he read Herbert Vivian's reminiscences, which appeared in the London *Sun* in the autumn of 1889. Vivian recalled that Wilde delivered a lecture almost seven years before for which Whistler had "in good fellowship crammed him"; in the lecture, Wilde wryly addressed Whistler as "Butterfly"—Whistler commonly signed his artwork with a stylized butterfly—and failed to give the elder artist credit for his help.[110] Vivian noted that in "The Decay of Lying," published in the *Nineteenth Century*, Wilde had incorporated without acknowledging the phrase from Whistler's letter where he stated that "Oscar has the courage of the opinions . . . of others."[111] Wilde's alleged offense occurs early his 1889 essay where his main speaker in this critical dialogue, who also happens to be named Vivian, starts reading a paper of his own aloud to his interlocutor Cyril:

> One of the chief causes that can be assigned for the curiously commonplace character of most of the literature of our age is undoubtedly the decay of Lying as an art, a science, and a social pleasure. The ancient historians gave us delightful fiction in the form of fact; the modern novelist presents us with dull facts under the guise of fiction. The Blue-Book is rapidly becoming his ideal both for method and manner. He has his tedious *"document humain,"*

---

was misunderstood, and Socrates, and Jesus, and Luther, and Copernicus, and Galileo, and Newton, and every pure and wise spirit that ever took flesh. To be great is to be misunderstood." *Essays: First Series*, ed. Joseph Ferguson, Alfred F. Carr, and Jean Ferguson, *The Collected Works of Ralph Waldo Emerson*, 10 vols. (Cambridge, MA: Belknap Press of Harvard University Press, 1971–2013), 2:33–34.

108. James McNeill Whistler, "To the Committee of the 'National Art Exhibition,'" *World*, 17 November 1886, 16; in *The Gentle Art of Making Enemies*, 164.

109. Whistler, "To the Committee of the 'National Art Exhibition,'" in *The Gentle Art of Making Enemies*, 164. Ellipsis in original.

110. Whistler, "The Habit of Second Natures," *Truth*, 2 January 1890, 4–5; in *The Gentle Art of Making Enemies*, 237; and in Wilde, *Complete Letters*, 418.

111. Whistler, "The Habit of Second Natures," in *The Gentle Art of Making Enemies*, 237; and in Wilde, *Complete Letters*, 419.

his miserable little *"coin de la création,"* into which he peers with his micro-scope. He is to be found at the Librairie Nationale, or at the British Museum, shamelessly reading up his subject. He has not even the courage of other people's ideas, but insists on going directly to life for everything, and ulti-mately, between encyclopaedias and personal experience, he comes to the ground, having drawn his types from the family circle or from the weekly washerwoman, and having acquired an amount of useful information from which never, even in his most meditative moments, can he thoroughly free himself.[112]

In Whistler's eyes, the irony could not have been more blatant. According to Whistler, Wilde had appropriated a phrase from the November 1888 letter to Yates's *World* in an essay that attacked the second-rate absorption of bare, uninteresting facts into the larger part of modern fiction. How, on this view, could Wilde have begged for artistic originality in the novel when his criti-cism of such repetitive and predictable fiction relied on words that he himself had stolen from his erstwhile master? Whistler went so far as to call Wilde the criminal "arch-imposter," the "detected plagiarist," and the "all-pervading plagiarist"—one who would have violated in America the "Law of '84."[113] Yet, to Wilde, Whistler's "shrill shrieks of plagiarism" were the pitiful sign of "silly vanity or incompetent mediocrity."[114] Wilde had, after all, made a point in his critical essays of confounding many of Whistler's boldest claims in the "Ten O' Clock Lecture." Where Whistler, for example, contended that "there was never

112. Wilde, "The Decay of Lying," in Wilde, *Criticism: Historical Criticism, Intentions, The Soul of Man,* ed. Josephine M. Guy, *The Complete Works of Oscar Wilde,* 7 vols. to date (Oxford: Oxford University Press, 2000 and continuing), 4:75–76. Zola writes of Flau-bert's *Madame Bovary,* "C'est un document humain d'une vérité universelle, une page arrachée de l'histoire de notre société" ("It is a human document of the universal truth, a page torn from the history of our society"): *Les romanciers naturalistes* (Paris: Charpentier, 1893), 143. "Une oeuvre d'art est un coin de la création vu à travers un tempérament") ("a work of art is a corner of creation seen through a temperament"): Émile Zola, "M. H. Taine, Artiste," in *Mes haines: Causeries littéraires et artistiques* (Paris: Charpentier, 1879), 229.

113. Whistler, "The Habit of Second Natures," in *The Gentle Art of Making Enemies,* 236; and in Wilde, *Complete Letters,* 418. Whistler's reference to the "Law of '84" is pre-sumably an ironic one, since it implicitly alludes to *Burrow-Giles Lithographic Co. v. Sarony* (1884), in which Napoleon Sarony, whose studio retained copyright over all of the photographs accompanying Wilde's 1882 lecture tour, sued because he believed his rights to the images had been violated by a company selling unauthorized lithographs of them. The Supreme Court judged in Sarony's favor. For more on this controversy, see Michael North, "The Picture of Oscar Wilde," *PMLA* 125, no. 1 (2010): 185–91.

114. Wilde, "In the Market Place," *Truth,* 9 January 1890, 51; in Whistler, *The Gentle Art of Making Enemies,* 239; and in Wilde, *Complete Letters,* 419.

an art-loving nation," Wilde riposted in "The Critic as Artist" (1890, revised 1891) that "the Greeks were a nation of art-critics."[115]

Yet no matter how petty Whistler's gripes may appear to us, they deserve close attention because they help focus our minds on the difficulties involved in casting Wilde in the role of a deceitful plagiarist. That Whistler described his holding forth at dinner as a type of cramming certainly positions him as the workaday instructor of the younger man. This representation of Whistler's relationship with Wilde raises a pressing question about the connection between pedagogy and plagiarism: Can the teacher accuse his student of this crime because the pupil has parroted the content of the instruction? Is not one's goal, when preparing intensively for an examination, the ability to duplicate with as much fidelity as possible the information studied? Looked at critically, Whistler's self-important accusation against Wilde may well appear as an excuse to generate a decidedly public feud, one that Whistler exploited to keep himself in the public eye. Nonetheless, Whistler's insults helped sustain the broad allegation that Wilde's was not an original mind. Much later, Frank Harris—who developed a close relationship with Wilde as editor and friend—reiterated the belief that Whistler had done more to shape Wilde's wit than any other figure: "Of all the personal influences which went into the moulding of Oscar Wilde's talent, that of Whistler was by far the most important; Whistler taught him the value of wit and the power a consciousness of genius and a knowledge of men lend to the artist." In Harris's view, Wilde eventually enjoyed great success as a writer because of his "great ability" as well as "inordinate vanity"—qualities, it would seem, that no charge of plagiarism could stifle.[116]

The allegation against Wilde's derivativeness hardly evaporated when he for the first time secured rapturous acclaim in the literary world. In early 1892, when his earliest society comedy, *Lady Windermere's Fan*, won many plaudits at the St. James's Theatre, his apparent borrowings began to incense several critics. The fairly liberal-minded A. B. Walkley, for example, claimed that the "staleness of the incidents" came "from half a dozen familiar French plays," and he observed that Wilde's female protagonist was "a guileless young bride" who resembled "M. Dumas's Françillon."[117] Meanwhile, as far as Walkley could

---

115. Whistler, "Mr. Whistler's 'Ten O' Clock,'" 139; and "The Critic as Artist," in *Criticism*, ed. Guy, 4:135.

116. Frank Harris, *Contemporary Portraits* (London: Methuen, 1915), 104.

117. A. B. Walkley, Review of *Lady Windermere's Fan*, *Speaker*, 27 February 1892: 257–58; in Beckson, ed., *Oscar Wilde: The Critical Heritage*, 120. Dumas *fils*'s *Françillon*, in which the husband consorts with a courtesan, and the young wife responds by keeping company with another man, has arguably a much more risk-taking plot than *Lady Windermere's Fan*.

tell, another of Wilde's characters, Mrs. Erlynne, appeared to have stepped out from a further play by Dumas *fils*, *L'Étrangère* (1876). Elsewhere, one commentator found the drama to be a "not too ingenious blend of the *Eden* of Mr. Edgar Saltus, with the *Idler* of Mr. Haddon Chambers," together with that other well-known drama of adultery, *Françillon* (1887), once more put in for good measure.[118] Yet, as Frederick Wedmore perceived it, such borrowings were standard fare in the theater, a comment supported by the sheer number of texts cited as sources for Wilde's play. In his view, even if the fan—Wilde's major stage prop—had a clear antecedent in Haddon's *Idler* (1890), it had "hardly . . . occurred to the least intelligent to suggest plagiarism."[119]

This minor controversy paved the way for an unsparing burlesque, *The Poet and the Puppets* (1892), in which the comic actor Charles Brookfield and composer Jimmy Glover focused attention on Wilde's supposed disposition for stealing scenes, characters, and plots. At one point in this satire, the eponymous Poet expresses his plans for writing a play that is "long enough": "I'll introduce some delightful successful character from some long-forgotten standard drama."[120] The work in question, as far as Brookfield and Glover can see, is Sheridan's *School for Scandal* (1777), which they believe provided Wilde with the basic structure of *Lady Windermere's Fan*. Yet even this burlesque was obliged to admit that for all his unoriginality, Wilde had enjoyed extraordinary success, initially at Oxford ("I took every prize") and later in London ("I soon made a

118. [Anon.,] Review of *Lady Windermere's Fan*, *Black and White*, 27 February 1892: 264; in Beckson, ed., *Oscar Wilde: The Critical Heritage*, 127. Edgar Saltus's novella, *Eden: An Episode*, which features a young woman's suspicions that her husband might be unfaithful, appeared in 1888. There is no question that Wilde appropriated the fan from Chambers's drama as his central prop. *The Era*, much later in the year, claimed that there was a "serious accusation" against "the cleverest play of the season" (*Lady Windermere's Fan*) because its plot came from Sydney Grundy's *Glass of Fashion* (1883). "Imaginary Plagiarism," *The Era*, 22 October 1892: 15.

119. Frederick Wedmore, "The Stage," *Academy*, 5 March 1892: 236–37; in Beckson, ed., *Oscar Wilde: The Critical Heritage*, 128.

120. Charles Brookfield and James Glover, *The Poet and the Puppets: A Travestie Suggested by "Lady Windermere's Fan,"* in Richard W. Schoch, ed., *Victorian Theatrical Burlesques* (Aldershot: Ashgate, 2003), 228. The title of this burlesque derives from a report in the *Daily Telegraph* on Wilde's comment at the Playgoers' Club, in early February 1892, that "the stage is only 'a frame furnished with a set of puppets'"; Wilde responded by stating that "the stage is to a play no more than picture-framing is to a painting" ("The Drama of the Day," *Daily Telegraph*, 12 February 1892; Wilde, "Puppets and Actors," *Daily Telegraph*, 20 February 1892: 3; in *The Collected Works of Oscar Wilde*, ed. Robert Ross, 14 vols. (London: Methuen, 1908), 14:164; and in *Complete Letters*, 519).

renown / I dazzled folk with my variety").[121] His brilliance was indisputable. The same admission was evident in the reviews. Even if, as one critic observed, *Lady Windermere's Fan* was "scarcely a play at all," the very fact that all of the characters "serve as mouths to enunciate the author's exquisitely funny remarks on society" ensured everyone admired Wilde for his intelligence and wit.[122] Significantly, not a word in his society comedy appeared to have come from Chambers, Dumas, or Saltus. What had obviously been taken were the familiar character types, the well-worn situations, and—most glaringly of all—the fan.

Over the years, the amassing scholarly research on Wilde's later works showed that many passages in them echo writings that were essential to his intellectual growth. These inquiries disclosed that parts of "The Critic as Artist," for example, repeat ideas in Pater's *Studies in the History of the Renaissance*.[123] The same might be said of many sections of the dialogue where Lord Henry Wotton speaks in *The Picture of Dorian Gray*.[124] Yet Wilde scarcely concealed the influence that Pater's *Renaissance* had exerted on him since his "undergraduate days at Oxford," as he freely stated in his review of Pater's *Appreciations* (1889): "Mr. Pater's essays became to me 'the golden book of spirit and sense, the holy writ of beauty.' They are still this to me. It is possible, of course, that I may exaggerate about them. I certainly hope that I do; for where there is no exaggeration there is no love, and where there is no love there is no understanding."[125]

121. Brookfield and Glover, *The Poet and the Puppets*, 217. The coauthors mockingly refer to Wilde as "neighbour O'Flaherty": a reference to Wilde's (implicitly inferior and untrustworthy) Irish origins.

122. [Anon.,] Review of *Lady Windermere's Fan*, *Westminster Review* 137 (1892): 478; in Beckson, ed., *Oscar Wilde: The Critical Heritage*, 129.

123. See, for example, the main text and the editorial commentary on a passage from 'The Critic as Artist," in Wilde, *Criticism*, ed. Guy, 4:176 and 4:499–500. The first critic to explore the parallels between Pater's *Renaissance*, on the one hand, and Wilde's 1882 lecture "The English Renaissance of Art" and passages from his essays collected in *Intentions*, on the other hand, was Ernest Bendz, *Notes on the Literary Relationship between Walter Pater and Oscar Wilde* (Helsinki: Aktiebolaget Handelstryckeriet, 1912). Bendz does not discuss the similarity of Wilde's ideas to Pater's as plagiarism.

124. On the echoes of Pater's writings in Wilde's novel, see *The Picture of Dorian Gray*, ed. Joseph Bristow, *The Complete Works of Oscar Wilde*, 7 vols. to date (Oxford: Oxford University Press, 2000 and continuing), 3:359–62.

125. Wilde, "Mr. Pater's Last Volume," *Speaker*, 22 March 1890: 319; in *Journalism Part II*, ed. Stokes and Turner, 7:243. Wilde's quotation is taken from the opening lines of Algernon Charles Swinburne, "Sonnet (with a Copy of *Mademoiselle de Maupin*)," which first appeared in *Poems and Ballads: Second Series* (1878) (*The Collected Poems of Algernon Charles Swinburne*, 6 vols. [London: Chatto and Windus, 1904], 3:66).

As Wilde suggested, to be impassioned about another writer's work created for him the possibility of understanding his source of inspiration critically. In any case, Wilde's frequent evocations of Paterian phrases hardly resembled theft.[126] Consider the many echoes of Pater's *Renaissance* that we can readily detect in Wilde's novel. It would be difficult to claim that Lord Henry's advocacy of the "New Hedonism," for example, evinced the author's intent to steal surreptitiously from what was a fully recognizable source. In any case, the advice Lord Henry gives to Dorian Gray about the need to pursue pleasure, which sounds similar to sentences in Pater's "Conclusion" of his 1873 study, has terrible consequences—ones that are entirely contrary to Pater's insistence on the "desire for beauty" as the "fruit of a quickened, multiplied consciousness."[127] If critics were to level any charge of authorial filching in *The Picture of Dorian Gray*, the areas most vulnerable to this allegation would be the extensive sections that paraphrase entries from South Kensington Museum catalogues, a French book on embroidery and lace, and information gleaned from John Addington Symonds's five-volume *Renaissance in Italy* (1875–1886).[128] These exhaustive lists—which detail the artifacts, instruments, and vestments that capture Dorian Gray's attention—also evoke the kinds of objets d'art that recur in J.-K. Huysmans's antirealist novel about an aesthetic collector, *À rebours* (1884): a well-known work of fiction that counted among several French sources that at least one indignant reader believed Wilde had plundered.[129] Significantly, in one of the later sections of *The Picture of Dorian Gray*, Wilde clearly transplanted

126. For more on parsing the distinction between allusion and plagiarism, see Christopher Ricks, *Allusion to the Poets* (Oxford: Oxford University Press, 2002), and Harold Bloom, *The Anxiety of Influence* (New York: Oxford University Press, 1973).

127. Pater, "Conclusion," in *The Renaissance*, ed. Hill, 190.

128. For Wilde's adaptation of these and other sources in his novel, see Wilde, *The Picture of Dorian Gray*, ed. Bristow, 4:398–419.

129. Several months after the first edition of *The Picture of Dorian Gray* had appeared in the July 1890 issue of *Lippincott's Monthly Magazine*, a reader commented on Wilde's borrowings from French sources; this letter appeared as part of a protracted controversy about Wilde's novel, which took place in the *Scots Observer*. Besides indicating the borrowings from *À rebours*, this reader claims that the character Sibyl Vane's "inability to act . . . is conveyed from an obscure story of Balzac's entitled *Massimilla Doni*" (1837); this reader adds that the ending of Wilde's narrative owes much to Nathaniel Hawthorne's *Prophetic Pictures* (1837): "G," 'The Long Arm of Coincidence," *Scots Observer*, 6 October 1890: 410–11; reprinted in Mason [Millard], *Art and Morality: A Record of the Discussion Which Followed the Publication of "Dorian Gray*," 2nd ed. (London: Frank Palmer, 1912), 129–34. Mason's valuable study covers the full extent of the attacks on Wilde's novel that took place in the press, and later at the Old Bailey in April 1895.

comments from a review that he published in *The Woman's World.*[130] Guy has viewed Wilde's tendency to recycle some of his finer aphorisms, which he plucked from works as early as *Vera*, as a sign of his so-called "self-plagiarism": a term that can imply that he was stealing from and then mischievously reutilizing his own property.[131]

These various allegations of Wilde's fearless thieving of other writers' ideas, phrases, and situations, as well as his own, stand in sharp contradistinction to his carefully elaborated ideas on literary borrowing, criminality, and creative expression. In his reviews from the 1880s, for example, Wilde addressed uninspired borrowing as a demonstration not of an author's artistic integrity or work ethic but as an indication of poor taste. That is to say, both the writers whom an author chooses to plagiarize and the finesse with which he commits the act create the proper grounds for assessing this type of theft. We can grasp Wilde's point by returning to his commentary on two volumes of poetry, the one ostensibly written by "Two Tramps," and the other by H. C. Irwin. Here Wilde considered the permissibility of poetic borrowing. By using language pulled directly

130. The source in question is Ernest Lefébure, *Embroidery and Lace: Their Manufacture and History from the Remotest Antiquity to the Present Day—a Handbook for Amateurs, Collectors, and General Readers*, trans. Alan S. Cole (London: H. Grevel, 1888). Wilde's review, "A Fascinating Book," appeared in *Woman's World* 2, no. 1 (December 1888): 53–56; in *Journalism Part II*, ed. Stokes and Turner, 7:88–96; and sections of the review reappear in *The Picture of Dorian Gray*, ed. Bristow, 3:406.

131. Cf. "Experience, the name men give to their mistakes," *Vera*, in *Collected Works*, 2:173, and "Experience was of no ethical value. It was merely the name men gave to their mistakes," in *The Picture of Dorian Gray*, ed. Bristow, 3:48, 3:219. The aphorism recurred again in *Lady Windermere's Fan* (1892):

> CECIL GRAHAM That is a great error. Experience is a question of instinct about life. I have got it. Tuppy hasn't.
> Experience is the name Tuppy gives to his mistakes. That is all.
> LORD AUGUSTUS *looks round indignantly*
> DUMBY Experience is the name every one gives to their mistakes.

Lady Windermere's Fan, ed. Ian Small, 2nd ed. (London: A and C Black, 2002), 67. For a discussion of this habit of Wilde's as "self-plagiarism," see Josephine M. Guy, "Self-Plagiarism, Creativity and Craftsmanship in Oscar Wilde," 6–23. The concept of "self-plagiarism" has enjoyed wide currency in the scholarly world since the 1990s, where it continues to define the unacknowledged recycling of research in a redundant manner. Richard A. Posner observes that "self-copying becomes fraudulent and therefore plagiaristic only when the author represents his latest work to be newly composed when in fact it is a copy of an earlier work of his that readers may have read" (*The Little Book of Plagiarism* [New York: Pantheon, 2007], 43).

from the "Chatterton" notebook, he took the "two tramps" to task for conflating the "defensible pilfering from hen roosts" with the "indefensible pilfering from poets."[132] The lines that caused offence read as follows: "And builded him a pyramid, four square, / Open to all the sky and every wind."[133] The echo from Tennyson's famous "Ode on the Death of the Duke of Wellington" (1852) was loud and clear. "We feel," Wilde wrote in the *Pall Mall Gazette*, "that as bad as poultry-snatching is, plagiarism is worse. 'Facilis descensus Averno!' From highway robbery and crimes of violence one sinks gradually to literary petty larceny."[134] Earlier in his review, Wilde had excused the authors, even praised them, for trying to "annex the domain of the painter" through their aesthetic choices in paper color and binding, but here he suggested that plagiarism was a transgression far worse than that.[135] One reason was, although the appropriation of colors from the painters led to beauty in the finished product, the plagiarized lines simply resulted in terrible poetry. This contrast was heightened through Wilde's positive assessment of Irwin's collection, which, as he put it, "gains her colour effect from the poet not from the publisher."[136] In Irwin's poems, Wilde certainly witnessed traces of Matthew Arnold's works, but he nonetheless praised Irwin for "studying a fine poet without stealing from him, a very difficult thing to do, and though many of the reeds through which he blows have been touched by other lips, yet he is able to draw new music from them."[137] In other words, even when learning lessons from a master it was the case that the epigone might transform evident echoes of his idol into innovative art.

132. Wilde, "The Poets' Corner," in *Journalism Part I*, ed. Stokes and Turner, 6:96.

133. Wilde, 'The Poets' Corner," in *Journalism Part I*, ed. Stokes and Turner, 6:96. Cf. "O fallen at length that tower of strength / Which stood four-square to all the winds that blow" (*The Poems of Tennyson*, ed. Christopher Ricks, 2nd ed., 3 vols. [Harlow: Longman, 1989], 2:483).

134. Wilde, "The Poets' Corner," in *Journalism Part I*, 6: 96. The Latin translates as "easy is the descent," and it comes from Virgil *Aeneid* 6.126. Wilde's phrasing bears some resemblance to Brander Matthews's comment in "The Ethics of Plagiarism," which appeared in the October 1886 issue of *Longman's Magazine*: "All who desire to uphold the honour of literature, and to see petty larceny and highway robbery meet with their just punishment, are concerned that the charge shall not be idly brought or carelessly answered" (8 [1886]: 633). We discuss the phrasing that Wilde imported from the "Chatterton" notebook into this review earlier in this chapter (167–68).

135. Wilde, "The Poets' Corner," in *Journalism Part I*, ed. Stokes and Turner, 6:96.

136. Wilde, "The Poets' Corner," in *Journalism Part I*, ed. Stokes and Turner, 6:96.

137. Wilde, "The Poets' Corner," in *Journalism Part I*, ed. Stokes and Turner, 6:97. On this aspect of Wilde's review, Jerome H. Buckley, "Echo and Artifice: The Poetry of Oscar Wilde," *Victorian Poetry* 28 (1990): 19.

One of Wilde's last, and most fascinating, engagements with plagiarism occurred in a series of letters published in the *Pall Mall Gazette* under the heading "The Ethics of Journalism." The episode began on 5 August 1894, with the
publication of a poem, "The Shamrock," in the *Weekly Sun*, which the paper erroneously attributed to Wilde.[138] Soon thereafter, the poem was reprinted in the
New York Sun, where an alert reader recognized the poem as one that "Helena
Calahan" had previously published, and he demanded an explanation from
Wilde in a letter to the London paper. The *Weekly Sun's* editor, T. P. O'Connor
(whose publication Wilde clearly disliked), pressed Wilde for a response, which
came in a letter the following month to the *Pall Mall Gazette*.[139] Wilde noted
the ridiculousness of the situation. He faced an accusation of plagiarism from
an editor who had published a poem under his name without having verified
the authorship of the work, much less having asked for the (ostensible) author's
permission to publish it. Wilde referred to "The Shamrock" derisively as "some
doggerel verses," which raised the serious question of authorial and editorial
taste in addition to the "ethics of modern journalism."[140]

A letter of rebuttal from the *Weekly Sun's* assistant editor quickly appeared
in the *Pall Mall Gazette*. By prefacing his comments first with the acknowledgment that the editors "regret exceedingly the suggestion of plagiarism," the
editor explained the circumstance of the attribution: the poem had arrived in
the mail with a letter ascribing it to Wilde, and so the *Weekly Sun* published it
under Wilde's name. Perhaps because of the impeachability of this explanation,
the editor then pivoted to debates about taste, alternately defending the poem's
"melodic charm" and "pure and exalted patriotism" and suggesting that the
editors' willingness to attribute the poem to Wilde was an act of generosity:
"So conspicuous, indeed, was its elevation of tone that we were reluctant to
believe it could have been the product of a mind like Mr. Oscar Wilde's, and
were driven to take refuge in the charitable belief that it belonged to the period

138. For a discussion of the events surrounding "The Shamrock," see Wilde, *Decorative
Art in America*, ed. Richard Butler Glaenzer (New York: Brentano's, 1906), 265–67.

139. Wilde realized that there was little point in sending out review copies of the French
edition of *Salomé* (1893) to reviewers who were likely to express hostility toward his work;
in early February 1893, he informed his publisher, John Lane, "Pray remember it was
agreed that no copy of *Salomé* is to be sent either to the *National Observer* or to Mr.
O'Connor's *Sunday Sun*" (*Complete Letters*, 547). One of Wilde's archenemies, W. E.
Henley, edited the *National Observer*.

140. Wilde, "The Ethics of Journalism," "To the Editor of the *Pall Mall Gazette*," *Pall
Mall Gazette*, 20 September 1894: 3; in *Collected Works*, 14:172; and in *Complete Letters*,
611.

of a forgotten and generous youth."[141] A final missive from Wilde closed the conversation. He critiqued the *Weekly Sun* for sloppy editorial practices and blurring the boundaries between ethics and taste. If, he maintained, the paper actually believed the "fifth-rate verses" to be his, its staff would have asked his permission to publish.[142] "No respectable editor," wrote Wilde (himself a former periodical editor), "would dream of printing and publishing a man's work without first obtaining his consent."[143]

We take from this episode a snapshot of Wilde's position in the press. Since Wilde had long been a target for charges of plagiarism, the unscrupulous *Weekly Sun* suspended editorial integrity in order to catalyze once more a dated public conversation about his artistic inferiority. Moreover, in keeping with the jokes in *The Poet and the Puppets* about Wilde's national origins, the assistant editor's letter intimated that the author's Irish background should be considered the source of this embarrassment. It is remarkable, even amid all of this sniping, that in the *Weekly Sun's* letter to the *Pall Mall Gazette*, in which the assistant editor admitted his fault and apologized for accusing Wilde of plagiarism, a postscript serves as an unabashed advertisement for his own newspaper: "We are giving a number of letters bearing upon 'The Shamrock' in our next issue, together with the text of the poem and a letter from its actual author."[144] Such a self-serving apology, clearly enough, hones the belief that certain areas of the late Victorian press had little to lose when intervening in polemics about literary plagiarism.

Wilde's immersion in these debates about patently derivative, visibly unoriginal, and downright plagiaristic writing might give the mistaken impression that this controversy was especially pertinent to him. Yet public discussions about literary writers' unauthorized borrowing from other sources circulated as actively in the nineteenth century as they had done in the years leading up to the "Statute of Anne"—or the first English law of copyright ownership—in 1709. As Richard Terry ably demonstrates, after Ben Jonson first articulated the idea of "plagiary" in *The Poetaster* (1601) the term took some time before it sharp-

141. [Anon.,] "The Ethics of Journalism," *Pall Mall Gazette*, 22 September 1894: 3; and in Wilde, *Complete Letters*, 614. Millard observes that "The Shamrock" was reprinted, with Wilde's name, in the Manchester *New Weekly: A Journal with Illustrations*, 11 August 1893, 3 (Mason [Millard], *Bibliography*, annotated copy, 3 vols., 1: facing 162, Clark Library PR5822 A1M64bi 1914a).

142. Wilde, "The Ethics of Journalism," "To the Editor of the *Pall Mall Gazette*," 25 September 1894: 3; in *Collected Works*, 14:173; and in *Complete Letters*, 614.

143. Wilde, *Collected Works*, 14:173, and *Complete Letters*, 614.

144. "The Ethics of Journalism," *Pall Mall Gazette*, 22 September 1894: 3; the postscript is reprinted in Wilde, *Decorative Art in America*, ed. Glaenzer, 267.

ened in definition, eventually finding its clearest focus in Samuel Johnson's *Dictionary* (1755): "Pla'giarism . . . Theft; literary adoption of the thoughts or works of another."[145] Then again, as Walter Arthur Copinger pointed out in his standard Victorian textbook on the topic, it was Johnson who immediately recognized the difficulties in establishing plagiarism as a crime, as we can see from these sage words in *The Rambler* (1751): "As not every instance of similitude can be considered as a proof of imitation, so not every imitation ought to be stigmatized as plagiarism. The adoption of a noble sentiment, or the insertion of a borrowed ornament, may sometimes display so much judgment as will almost compensate for invention; and an inferior genius may, without any imputation of servility, pursue the path of the ancients, provided he declines to tread in their footsteps."[146] Copinger drew on Johnson's thoughtful *Rambler* essay to

145. Richard Terry, *The Plagiarism Allegation in English Literature from Butler to Sterne* (Basingstoke: Palgrave Macmillan, 2012), 18, 20. "Plagiary" appears in two places in Ben Jonson, *Poetaster, or, The Arraignment*, in *The Devil is an Ass and Other Plays*, ed. Margaret Jane Kidnie (Oxford: Oxford University Press, 2000), 49, 77. Samuel Johnson has two entries on "plagiarism" in his *Dictionary of the English Language: In Which the Words are Deduced from Their Originals, and Illustrated in Their Different Significations by Examples from the Best Writers, to Which are Prefixed, a History of the Language, and an English Grammar*, 2 vols. (London: W. Strahan, 1755), 2: unpaginated:

> Pla'giarism. n. s. [from *plagiary*] Theft; literary adoption of the thoughts or works of another.
>
> With great impropriety, as well as *plagiarism*, they have most injuriously been transferred into proverbial maxims.   *Swi.*
>
> Pla'giary. n. s. [from *plagium*, Lat.]
> 1. A thief in literature; one who steals the thoughts or writings of another.
>
> The ensuing discourse, lest I chance to be traduced for a *plagiary* by him who had played the thief, was one of those that, by a worthy hand, were stolen from me.   *South.*
>
> Without invention, a painter is but a copier, and a poet but a *plagiary* of others; both are allowed sometimes to copy and translate.   *Dryden's Dufresnoy.*
> 2. The crime of literary theft. Not used.
>
> *Plagiary* had not its nativity with printing, but began when the paucity of books scarce wanted that invention.   *Brown.*

146. Samuel Johnson, "The Criterions of Plagiarism," No. 143, *The Rambler*, ed. W. J. Bate and Albrecht B. Strauss, *The Yale Edition of the Works of Samuel Johnson*, 23 vols. to date (New Haven: Yale University Press, 1958 and continuing) 4:401; quoted in Walter Arthur Copinger, *The Law of Copyright, in Works of Literature and Art, Including that of Drama, Engraving, Music, Sculpture, Painting, Photography, and Ornamental and Useful Design, together with International and Foreign Copyright, with the Statutes Relating thereto, and References to the English and American Decisions* (London: Stevens and Haynes, 1870), 101.

bracket a "very delicate" question about imputed plagiarism: "What degree of imitation constitutes an infringement of the copyright of a particular composition?" As he saw it, there are plentiful examples in classical literature where a "strong likeness" exists between different writers, even if there is no "identity" between them.[147] By this, he meant that evident similitude between literary works, even when it indicated that considerable imitation had taken place, did not necessarily evince the callowness of theft. On this basis, had those commentators who made allegations against Wilde taken him to court, they would not have succeeded in prosecuting him for infringing copyright. This was as true of Whistler's unlikely charge that Wilde had broken the American "law of '84" as it was with regard to suing for literary plagiarism in England and Wales.

It was the test of piracy (i.e., the unauthorized reproduction of an existing work), and not plagiarism, that stood as the main focus in literary discussions about violations of copyright on both sides of the Atlantic. As Eaton S. Drone observed in the 1879 edition of his respected treatise on copyright law, "Piracy is the use of literary property in violation of the legal rights of the owner."[148] Cases such as *Dickens v. Lee* (1844), in which Charles Dickens filed a bill of complaint in order to restrain the defendant from publishing an abridgment (or, to use the fraudster's term, a "reoriginated" version) of *A Christmas Carol* (1843), remained touchstones for lawyers in Wilde's time. The wholesale lifting of complete passages, no matter how much they were abridged, thus formed the basis of the crime. Where cases against piracy proliferated in the lead-up to both the Berne Convention (1886) in Europe and the Chace Act (1891) in the United States, both of which extended the provisions that preserved international copyright, charges of plagiarism alone seldom resulted in lawsuits, largely because the supposed act of theft remained mired in questions relating to literary imitation, as well as debates about the stock nature of certain scenes, settings, and plot devices. In Drone's view, plagiarism differed from piracy because in itself it did not violate the law; he saw it as "a moral but not necessarily a legal wrong."[149] In other words, visible borrowing from another source did not break the law, because "the plagiarist falsely offers as his own what he has taken from the writings of another"; "the pirate," Drone adds, "may or may not do this."[150] To this day, lawyers take Drone's definition as a starting point in their analyses

147. Copinger, *The Law of Copyright*, 98.
148. Eaton S. Drone, *A Treatise on the Law of Property in Intellectual Productions in Great Britain and the United States: Embracing Copyright in Works of Literature and Art, and Playright in Dramatic and Musical Compositions* (Boston: Little, Brown, 1879), 383.
149. Drone, *A Treatise on the Law of Property*, 383.
150. Drone, *A Treatise on the Law of Property*, 383.

of plagiarism. They maintain that plagiarism is broader than the infringement of copyright because it can involve reproducing ideas, replicating forms of expression, or repeating small quantities of material that copyright law does not cover.[151]

For these reasons, Wilde's contemporaries looked on plagiarism as a somewhat intractable, if widespread, problem. As Andrew Lang astutely put it in 1887, plagiarism as a crime was paradoxically "easy to prove, and almost impossible to commit."[152] Seldom, in Lang's view, did one find acts of "perfect plagiarism": "the claiming of a work of art which belongs to another man."[153] Finding little solace in the courts, writers took to the press, airing their accusations of plagiarism with vigor. Even in this regard, however, the Victorians were scarcely original. Terry writes that trading accusations of plagiarism was a common authorial practice from at least Chatterton's own time, a "stock form of slander through which authors could needle one another"; desire to insult, Terry explains, rather than concerns about professional liability, underscored most public complaints.[154]

By and large, the courts concentrated on instances of unauthorized copying of such features as maps, diagrams, and lists of information. At the end of the nineteenth century, Augustine Birrell asserted that the cases that he grouped under the category of "literary larceny" mostly related to "disputes between book-makers and rival proprietors of works of reference."[155] As a consequence, charges of literary plagiarism mostly fueled vendettas about the rights and wrongs of borrowing from recognizable sources. This point became contentious when authors stated in their defense that they were only doing what countless writers had done in the past—namely, draw on and reuse the potted wisdom and familiar plots that their precursors had readily exploited. Charles Reade, whose name recurs with frequency in discussions of Victorian plagiarism, endured many public quarrels about his shameless appropriations of other people's works.

---

151. See, for example, Laurie Stearns, "Copy Wrong: Plagiarism, Process, Property, and the Law," in Lise Buranen and Alice Roy, eds., *Perspectives on Plagiarism and Intellectual Property in the a Post Modern World* (Albany: State University of New York Press, 2003), 5–17.

152. Andrew Lang, "Literary Plagiarism," *Contemporary Review* 51 (1887): 832.

153. Lang, "Literary Plagiarism," 833.

154. Richard Terry, "'In Pleasing Memory of All He Stole': Plagiarism and Literary Detection, 1747–1785," in Paulina Kewes, ed., *Plagiarism in Early Modern England* (Basingstoke: Palgrave Macmillan, 2003), 182.

155. Augustine Birrell, *Seven Lectures on the Law and History of Copyright in Books* (London: Cassell, 1899), 171. Birrell's preferred term is "literary larceny"; he does not refer to plagiarism.

As reported by John Coleman, the outraged Reade defended himself by exaggerating the basic principles that Johnson had acknowledged, if with some not entirely deserving self-esteem:

> "Plagiarist," he roared, crushing the paper in his fist and striding up and down. "Of course I am a plagiarist, Chaucer was a plagiarist, Shakespeare was a plagiarist, Molière was a plagiarist. We all plagiarise, all except those d— —d idiots who are too asinine to profit by learning from the works of their superiors!
>
> Surely to God every blockhead out of a lunatic asylum (except these idiots) must know, that, since Homer's time, all authors have parodied his incidents and paraphrased his sentiments. Molière 'took his own where he found it.' 'The thief of all thieves was the Warwickshire thief,' who stole right and left from everybody; but then he 'found things lead and left them gold.' That's the sort of thief I am!"[156]

That Shakespeare borrowed profusely from other sources was an unexceptional contention in the nineteenth century. Emerson, in his famous essay on the Bard, reminded his readers that in 1821 Edmond Malone had recorded that "out of 6,043 lines in the first, second, and third parts of Henry VI, 1,771 were written by others preceding Shakespeare, 2,373 by him on the foundation laid by his predecessors, and 1,899 were entirely his own."[157]

In the 1880s, American drama critic Brander Matthews, who forced attention on what he discerned as Reade's borrowings, remarked that the only way to

---

156. John Coleman, *Charles Reade as I Knew Him* (London: Traherne, 1903), 246–47. Robert Macfarlane contends that "it was Reade, more than any other prose writer of the second half of the century except perhaps Wilde, who would energize discussions of plagiarism and originality," and he points out the ways in which Reade maintained scrapbooks, dating from 1858–1859, containing manuscript entries and newspaper clippings. In later life, as Macfarlane shows, Reade created "his own compendium of 'plagiarism' from canonical writers" (*Original Copy: Plagiarism and Originality in Nineteenth-Century Literature* [Oxford: Oxford University Press, 2007], 135–36, 148). The ironies involved in Reade's prominence as a much-accused plagiarist and public champion of copyright reform are explored in Thomas Mallon, *Stolen Words: Forays into the Origins and Ravages of Plagiarism* (New York: Ticknor and Fields, 1989), 41–88. Mallon has little to say about Wilde's position as a plagiarist (see 25–26).

157. Edmond Malone, "A Dissertation of the Three Parts of King Henry VI," in *The Plays and Poems of Shakespeare: With the Corrections and Illustrations of Various Commentators —Comprehending a Life of the Poet, and an Enlarged History of the Stage*, 21 vols. (London: F. C. and J. Rivington, 1821), 18:572; cited in Ralph Waldo Emerson, "Shakespeare, or the Poet," in *Representative Men: Seven Lectures*, ed. Wallace E. Williams and Douglas Emory Wilson, *Collected Works*, 4:112.

resolve the widespread disputes about genuine instances of plagiarism was to follow this rule: "It is plagiarism for an author to take anything from another author and reproduce it nakedly; but it is not necessarily plagiarism if he re-clothes it and dresses it up anew."[158] By bearing such arguments in mind, James Orrock, in the 1888 "opusculum" he published with the Sette of Odd Volumes, the antiquarians' and bibliophiles' club that started in 1878, dwelt on the matter with the following words: "Let us continue our repeats and plagiarisms when the works are precious; and study deeply and assimilate all that is excellent in those of gifted men."[159] In the end, instead of contending that such "repeats" were fundamentally criminal in intent, Orrock adverted to Joshua Reynolds, who had remarked in his *Discourses* (1769–1790) that it was time to "dispel this phantom of inspiration" and admit that an artist "must be as necessarily an imitator of the works of *other* painters" as he is of nature.[160] Taken together, these various late Victorian interventions reveal that the question of whether literary plagiarism might prove criminal was not entirely clear-cut. Even if all of these commentators concurred with Matthews that plagiarism was in principle an "ugly crime," they also knew that the inevitable tendency among writers to borrow and imitate, as well as to take recourse to similar sources, often made it hard distinguish what was strictly derivative from what was indisputably original in an author's work.[161]

Modern scholars, however, have tended to address the charge that Wilde in-

158. Brander Matthews, "The Ethics of Plagiarism," 628–29. Matthews comments that "Reade's incorporation of fragments of the 'dialogues' of Erasmus in the 'Cloister and the Hearth' . . . was a proper and even a praiseworthy use of pre-existing material," while "some of his 'Hard Cash' was filched from the coffers of the 'Pauvres de Paris' of MM. Brisebarre and Nus" ("The Ethics of Plagiarism," 629). Reade's popular novels *The Cloister and the Hearth: A Tale of the Middle Ages* and *Hard Cash: A Matter-of-Fact Romance* had appeared in 1863 and 1864, respectively.

159. James Orrock, *Repeats and Plagiarisms in Art, 1888* (London: privately published, 1889), 33. Orrock's pamphlet is based on the talk he delivered to the Sette of Odd Volumes, Willis's Rooms, St. James's, on 4 January 1889.

160. Orrock, *Repeats and Plagiarisms in Art, 1888*, 33. Orrock's emphasis is his own. In "Discourse VI," 10 December 1774, Reynolds had remarked: "But to bring us entirely to reason and sobriety, let it be observed, that a painter must not only be of necessity an imi-tator of the works of nature, which alone is sufficient to dispel this phantom of inspiration, but he must be as necessarily an imitator of the works of other painters: this appears more humiliating, but it is equally true; and no man can be an artist, whatever he may suppose, upon any other terms" (*Discourses on Art*, ed. Robert R. Wark [San Marino, CA: Hunting-ton Library, 1959], 95–96).

161. Matthews, "The Ethics of Plagiarism," 629.

dulged in plagiarism with less flexibility than Victorian legal theorists, perhaps because their own research emerged in a climate where intense discussions about academic dishonesty among educators had since the 1980s been at the center of extensive debate on scholarly ethics. In the twenty-first century, as Richard A. Posner observes, the allegation of plagiarism "is considered by most writers, teachers, journalists, scholars, and even members of the general public to be the capital intellectual crime"; it is a crime, he contends, that can result in public embarrassment and humiliation, if not completely ruined careers.[162] Moreover, the criticism that has developed around Wilde's supposedly extravagant delight in stealing from other writers has not always addressed the fact that during the Victorian period, the law found it near impossible to establish plagiarism as a felony. And, more than any other document in Wilde's canon, his notes on Chatterton's life have struck modern critics as the example par excellence of his supposedly unscrupulous tendency to steal from other people's literary property.

Plagiarism, which for Victorians was a highly visible but largely nonactionable phenomenon, can at times give the impression that it has always been guided by calculated concealment or downright stealth, in ways that set out to deceive an unsuspecting readership. Yet this viewpoint is hardly pertinent to the "Chatterton" notebook. Given the obvious nature of the inclusions from both Wilson's and Masson's volumes noted above, it should not surprise us that these sources have long been properly attributed because their origins were well known. An auction catalogue from 1919 noted the biographical clippings in the document: "Essay on Chatterton, written partly in pencil and partly in ink, in a quarto exercise book. About 70 pages of Manuscript, interspersed with printed cuttings from Lives of Chatterton by Daniel Wilson and David Masson. 1886."[163] This particular catalogue entry included a facsimile of the handwritten first page, along with the following notation: "An Important Unpublished Manuscript, apparently intended for the 'Century Guild Hobby Horse' (see Stuart Mason's Bibliography of Oscar Wilde, pages 13 and 14). It would be a fascinating undertaking to prepare this manuscript for publication. In addition to the complete and consecutive passages there are numerous notes and suggestions which it was obviously Wilde's intention to incorporate into the complete work."[164] As the listing makes evident, Stuart Mason (the pen name of Christopher Sclater Millard) was the first person to suggest the idea that the notebook's

162. Posner, *The Little Book of Plagiarism*, 107.

163. [Anon.,] *The Library of Herschel V. Jones* (New York: Anderson Galleries, 1919), 228.

164. *The Library of Herschel V. Jones*, 227–28.

contents were ultimately intended for submission to the *Century Guild Hobby Horse*. Millard, however, did not offer a physical description of the notebook or its contents. His comments simply observed that the presumptive article for the Century Guild's journal did "not appear ever to have been published": "Portions of it exist in manuscript, but except for the introductory passage . . . the essay is in fragmentary state. It seems probable that it was originally prepared for delivery as a lecture."[165] Millard's phrasing suggests that he believed the notebook to contain portions of the eventual article, and, although he indicates the likelihood that it would have been linked to the lecture, his wording does not imply that the document records the talk that Wilde delivered at the Birkbeck Literary and Scientific Institution.

Neither did Rodney Shewan, who in 1983 advanced one of the most detailed readings of Wilde's interest in Chatterton to date. To Shewan, the crucial aspect of the notebook is the way it reveals Wilde grappling with the problem of where biography should stand in relation to any appreciation of an artist's work: "One is sometimes tempted | to wish," Wilde writes on one of the notebook's earliest pages, "that all art were | anonymous" (Appendix A, f.2ʳ [335]).[166] Yet, as Shewan observes, Wilde has to concede that on some occasions, such as the story of Chatterton, "criticism must take account | of history and physiology in order | to understand the work of art" (Appendix A, f.4ʳ [337]). When later critics turned attention to the notebook it was not this kind of observation that struck them as significant. Instead, a decade afterward, Merlin Holland looked on the notebook as the inescapable, even shame-inducing, reminder of his paternal grandfather's most problematic behavior.[167] Holland found it "profoundly disturbing" to see the clipped pages of Wilson's and Masson's volumes pasted into the notebook, and he rejected the idea that the notebook was intended to be "a simple *aide-mémoire*," on the grounds that Wilde had "actually fitted his own manuscript" around the printed excerpts.[168] Certainly, Holland was dismayed with the find, but while he granted that Wilde "was clearly going to use several thousand words of someone else's research in his piece" on Chatterton, he did

165. Mason [Millard], *Bibliography*, 13.

166. Rodney Shewan discusses this part of the "Chatterton" notebook in *Oscar Wilde: Art and Egotism*, 73.

167. Holland, "Plagiarist, or Pioneer?" 203.

168. Holland, "Plagiarist, or Pioneer?" 203. What shocked Holland even more than the telltale signs of plagiarism was the "mutilation" of the books themselves; however, it is—as we note above—not entirely unheard of to cut up a printed volume for inclusion in a scrapbook.

not take a stand on the notebook's relationship either to the lecture or to the promised essay.

In 1987, however, Ellmann, who quoted the concluding passage on f.82^r, had already resolutely referred to the document as Wilde's "lecture notes."[169] Ellmann might have been influenced by the fact that the first comment Wilde recorded in the notebook consists of these two words: "Previous lectures" (Appendix A, f.1^v [333]). Wilde followed this comment with these words: "Romantic movement" (Appendix A, f.1^v [333]). These jottings marked points of connection with what we presume could have been his talks titled "Dress," "The Mission of Art in the Nineteenth Century," and "The Value of Art in Modern Life," which he had delivered at eighteen different venues in England and Ireland in 1885 or, perhaps more probably, his San Francisco lecture titled "The Irish Poets and Poetry of the Nineteenth Century," the themes of which, including the influence of Ossian and the concept of a Romantic poetry, are directly relevant to Chatterton. A decade after Ellmann's assertion, Lawrence Danson restated the belief that the notebook was the record of the lecture. More to the point, in his view the notebook revealed, as it did to Holland, the alarming extent of Wilde's plagiarism. Danson finished his commentary on Wilde's apparent recklessness with some wistfulness: "It would be nice to think that this was merely a source-book, but Wilde's finicky alterations of a word here or a phrase there suggest that it is the text of the lecture pretty much as he delivered it, with notes to himself about subjects to elaborate either extempore during delivery or later in revision."[170]

Most treatments of the "Chatterton" notebook have followed Ellmann, Guy, and Danson by referring to the notebook unequivocally as a lecture, despite the stylistic dullness, not to say considerable length, of many of the excerpts Wilde duly clipped and pasted.[171] In addition to his edits on the clipped sections, other notebook elements that might be regarded as evidence that Wilde intended to present the contents as a finished product include his self-referential comments (Appendix A, f.4^r) on the reasons he turns to Chatterton's biography—"in going

169. Ellmann, *Oscar Wilde*, 284.

170. Lawrence Danson, *Wilde's Intentions: The Artist in His Criticism* (Oxford: Oxford University Press, 1997), 90.

171. See, for example, Josephine M. Guy and Ian Small, *Oscar Wilde's Profession: Writing and the Culture Industry in the Late Nineteenth Century* (Oxford: Oxford University Press, 2000), 271, and K. K. Ruthven, *Faking Literature* (Cambridge: Cambridge University Press, 2001), 140. Saint-Amour writes that he finds Danson's argument "persuasive" (*The Copywrights*, 251, n. 31), as does Macfarlane (*Original Copy*, 190–91). Other critics have taken Guy's and Danson's assertions that the "Chatterton" notebook is Wilde's lecture on trust: Florina Tufescu, *Oscar Wilde's Plagiarism*, 14–15; and Thomas Wright, *Oscar's Books* (London: Chatto and Windus, 2008), 41.

over the details | of the life of this marvellous | boy I do so not to mar the | perfect joy and loveliness of his | song"—or the reasons he plans to quote lines from Arnold—"I | venture to quote his sonnet to | Shakespeare" (Appendix A, f.3ʳ [336]). Yet these locutions could just as easily be addressed to a reader as a listener, and they may suggest that Wilde was thinking of constructing a paper on Chatterton as a dialogue such as we find in "The Decay of Lying." Further, such self-referential positioning ceases after the notebook's opening pages. By the sixth folio, coherent prose gives way to truncated notes, and it seems equally unlikely that Wilde would have read aloud his own incomplete phrases and that he would have delivered to his audience the minutiae contained in the clippings from Wilson and Masson.

The relationship between Wilde's notebook on Chatterton and the public presentation of this research is best elucidated in an article on the lecture on Chatterton that Wilde delivered at Bournemouth on Saturday, 7 April 1888. A report in the *Poole and Dorset Herald* summarizes Wilde's presentation and demonstrates that he adopted at least some of the formulations he developed or transcribed in the notebook. "In the lecture," we learn, Wilde spoke of "the marvellous boy in literature . . . who was the direct precursor of Coleridge and Keats, and from whom we might trace all the modern romantic movement in literature."[172] This is a phrase, as we have shown, that he more than likely adopted from Watts's 1880 essay, but it is an idea that had—by 1886—gained significant currency.[173] In a footnote in his *Essays on Poetry and Poets*, which Wilde had reviewed for the *Pall Mall Gazette*, Roden Noel writes that since having written his own essay on Chatterton in 1872, he has read Watts's essay and "must advert, with entire agreement, to his contention that Chatterton may be named father of the romantic movement in England, both in point of matter and manner."[174] J. C. Shairp was even quicker to adopt the idea, remarking in 1881 that Chatterton "has been truly said to be the father of the new Romantic school."[175]

Other details of the Bournemouth lecture in the newspaper, though, are

172. [Anon.,] *Poole and Dorset Herald*, 12 April 1888, 6.

173. See Introduction (15–16) and chapter 3, the section titled "Watts, Rossetti, and Chatterton: 'The New Romantic School,'" 149–59.

174. Noel, *Essays on Poetry and Poets*, 43.

175. J. C. Shairp, "English Poetry in the Eighteenth Century," *Princeton Review* 14 (July 1881): 49. Shairp cites "a recent critic," presumably Watts. And in an 1886 poem on Chatterton's death, William Stenhouse described the young poet as "Founder and Father of the New Romaunt," and insisted in a footnote: "The obligations of English Poetry to Chatterton, as the Father of the New Romantic School, which superseded the artificial and the classical, have never been fully acknowledged." "The Death of Chatterton," in *Poems, Songs, and Sonnets* (London: Simpkin, Marshall, 1886), 63.

unequivocally traceable to Watts's essay: the reporter observes that when Wilde addressed "the question as to whether we ought to regard Chatterton as a clever forger,—a man who wanted to take people in,—or whether we were to regard him as a great artist, [he] said he was convinced that the latter was the right view to take."[176] The framing of this question certainly echoes Watts's construction of the issue. But even here, when Wilde might appear to be plagiarizing Watts blatantly, the deviations from Watts's discussion are telling. After posing the question of whether Chatterton should be understood as a criminal or an artist, Watts writes that even "if the latter supposition is the true one"—that is, if it was Chatterton's blinding artistic or dramatic drive and not his criminal predilections that inspired his Rowley forgeries—"it does not, to be sure, excuse the delinquencies" that shocked Walpole in particular.[177] From Watts's perspective, acknowledging that there might be an aesthetic component of the poet's forged work "explains an apparent anomaly in Nature" and thus "clears Nature" of fault for creating a man in whom artistry is allied with tolerance of duplicity.[178] As we can see from the brief article in the *Poole and Dorset Herald*, Wilde diverges from Watts on this point. According to the published account, Wilde certainly repeats almost verbatim Watts's line that "[Chatterton] had all the artist's desire for perfect representation, and if perfect representation demanded forgery he needs must forge"; but, importantly, instead of supporting Watts's view that artistic desire mitigates the poet's criminality, Wilde rejects the charge of criminality altogether. In Wilde's mind, Chatterton was not motivated by a desire to "take people in" (a description, incidentally, not present in Watts's essay).[179] Neither was Chatterton culpable of any "delinquencies." To the contrary, Wilde suggests that Chatterton forged the Rowley poems "not to reveal himself, but to give pleasure to others."[180]

    Whether Wilde acknowledged Watts as his source for some of his ideas and phrasing is not recorded in the brief report. Watts clearly paid close attention to others adopting his ideas on Chatterton. In his September 1886 review of Noel's *Essays on Poetry and Poets*, Watts notes somewhat sarcastically that Noel "sometimes (as in the matter of Chatterton and the Romantic movement) does [one] the honour [of adopting]" one's own words.[181] Watts was also outspoken about

176. [Anon.,] "Lecture by Oscar Wilde," 6.

177. Watts, "Thomas Chatterton," in *The English Poets*, ed. Ward, 3:405.

178. Watts, "Thomas Chatterton," in *The English Poets*, ed. Ward, 3:405.

179. [Anon.,] "Lecture by Oscar Wilde," 6.

180. [Anon.,] "Lecture by Oscar Wilde," 6. This phrasing is different from that in the notebook (Appendix A, f.75' [403]) and from Watts's phrasing.

181. [Theodore Watts,] "Literature," *Athenæum* 3073 (1886): 361.

Wilde's derivativeness. While he ultimately came to view *The Ballad of Reading Gaol* and *De Profundis* with great esteem, Watts felt that Wilde's verses "were almost entirely imitative and derivative" and that his essays were "no doubt, very brilliant and full of many literary graces; but here again every thought in them has been derived from some previous writer, French or English."[182] If Watts's opinion of Wilde's literary merits was relatively low, he nonetheless enjoyed socializing with him, remarking that Wilde excelled even George Meredith in being "the most brilliant talker of his day": "In his writing," Watts wrote, Wilde "plagiarized unblushingly, but his talk was often original."[183] It seems unlikely that, had Wilde attempted to pass off Watts's recognizable ideas and phrasing as his own and without leave to do so, Watts would have maintained cordial relations with a so-called plagiarist. That Wilde invited Watts to participate in the scheme to erect a memorial to Chatterton in late 1886 suggests that the Bristol poet was a topic of shared interest for the writers. Moreover, the fact that Watts remained on social terms with the Wilde family through the summer of 1887 (at least) indicates that the well-attended Birkbeck lecture on Chatterton did not tread too heavily, or without attribution, on Watts's well-known work on the poet.[184]

No known accounts of the 1886 Birkbeck lecture exist that might indicate the level of similarity between the two outings. The *Poole and Dorset Herald* article, however, shows that Wilde's Bournemouth lecture in 1888 drew explicitly from lines written in his "Chatterton" notebook. Yet such information hardly suggests that each and every sentence found in this document made up the lecture that Wilde gave in both of these presentations. In fact, the *Poole and Dorset Herald* account makes it plainly evident that Wilde did not read the "Chatterton" notebook verbatim to his audience. Nevertheless, once several modern scholars concurred that the whole notebook constituted a plagiarized lecture, they determined the reasons why Wilde had filched his materials in such a brazen manner. In their search for answers, these critics tended to fall into two camps. The first set comprised those who ascribed the borrowings to the exigencies of financial pressure and the demanding schedule of periodical writing. Guy, for example, concluded that Wilde was "lacking inspiration and under pressure to produce copy"; in her view, he "expanded new works by incorporating passages from old ones, presumably in the hope that his readers would not notice."[185]

182. Hake and Compton-Rickett, *The Life and Letters of Theodore Watts-Dunton*, 1:177.
183. Hake and Compton-Rickett, *The Life and Letters of Theodore Watts-Dunton*, 1:180.
184. See Wilde, "To Herbert P. Horne," 13 December 1886, in *Complete Letters*, 290, and see our chapter 3, n. note 170 (150).
185. Josephine M. Guy, "Oscar Wilde's Self-Plagiarism: Some New Manuscript Evidence," *Notes and Queries* 52 (2005): 485.

The second grouping featured those researchers who regarded plagiarism as a necessary, if early, step on the road to Wilde's full artistic expression. Michael Patrick Gillespie, for instance, framed "borrowing and even mimicking" as one "important element of Wilde's sense of the creative act" during the early stages of his career.[186]

Still other critics, in turn, have contended that Wilde's lecture (which, they have presumed, is what we find in the notebook) embraced Chatterton as a means of explaining his own mode of artistic production. In other words, it became possible to account for Wilde's affinity for Chatterton through his desire to find an artistic model whose creative process would have endorsed or excused his own (equally unseemly) practices. From this perspective, since Chatterton was a beloved hero of the Romantics, it follows that Wilde maintained an enhanced attraction to the "marvellous Boy." As a consequence, Robert Macfarlane, who appears not to have consulted the document, asserts that the plagiarized lecture on Chatterton "in a way defended the methods which had been used to produce it."[187] Wilde, as Macfarlane sees it, "wished to create a theoretical context within which his own plundering raids on the tradition could be understood as radically creative"; as a result, Wilde plundered not only tradition but also Chatterton's persona along with the biographies of the eighteenth-century poet.[188]

There can be no doubt that Wilde's inquiries into Chatterton's life helped shape the future direction of his oeuvre, since the exploration of the relationships between crime and creation, originality and derivativeness underscores nearly all of the works Wilde produced in the years following the notes he took on Chatterton. But, as we explore in the following chapters, Wilde's interest is not merely egocentric, constructed around the creation of a defensive posture that would justify his own literary misdeeds. The opposite, we argue, is true: Wilde's studied investment in understanding the life and works of Chatterton forms the foundation for his staggeringly original approaches to literary criticism and fiction. Once we reject the idea that the "Chatterton" notebook is evidence of an embarrassing, if characteristic, instance of literary laziness and recognize instead that the document functioned as a repository of research

186. Michael Patrick Gillespie, *Oscar Wilde and the Poetics of Ambiguity* (Gainesville: University Press of Florida, 1996), 21. See also Shewan: "Far from being devoid of ideas, [Wilde's *Poems* (1881)] prefigures much of his mature work. Even the plagiarism serves an implicit subjective purpose" (*Oscar Wilde: Art and Egotism*, 7).

187. Macfarlane, *Original Copy*, 191.

188. Macfarlane, *Original Copy*, 192.

and a testing ground for ideas and phrasing, the significance of Chatterton for Wilde in the 1880s becomes apparent. Just as Chatterton's creative impulse became central to the late nineteenth-century understanding of Romanticism, so too did Wilde's engagement with Chatterton become central to his understanding of the generations of artists whom he most admired, and in whose wake he saw himself and his work.

5

Wilde, Forgery, and Crime: "Pen, Pencil and Poison," "The Decay of Lying," and the Short Fiction

In the "Chatterton" notebook, which served as a crucible for the formation of Wilde's artistic and authorial sensibilities at the end of the 1880s, Wilde certainly refined his understanding of the Romantic past and the impact of that past on late Victorian arts. Yet his engagement with the critical formation of Romanticism reveals only one aspect of the notebook's generative quality and its reach. Wilde's research on Chatterton transforms the shape and direction of the writings he produced after making his 1886 presentation at Birkbeck. Even though Wilde had long expressed fascination with transgressions of the law in plays such as *Vera* (1880) and the unfinished *Cardinal of Avignon* (c. 1882), his inquiries into Chatterton's career mark the moment his attention was for the first time fixed on the paradoxical links between the creation of unsurpassed beauty and unrepentant acts of fabrication: not just creating forgeries but also fabricating lies, performing roles, and donning masks. Here we begin with a dazzling group of works that Wilde composed in the period immediately following the "Chatterton" lecture and continuing through 1889: one of the most productive years in Wilde's professional life.

Taken together, *The Happy Prince, and Other Tales* (1888), "Pen, Pencil and Poison" and "The Decay of Lying" (both 1889, revised 1891), and *Lord Arthur Savile's Crime and Other Stories* (1891) reveal the manner in which Wilde's comprehension of art had, in light of the "Chatterton" notebook, become closely connected with the imaginative bravura that the Bristol poet demonstrated in his magnificent Rowley poems. The same is true of "The Portrait of Mr. W.H." (1889, revised c. 1891), which is so fully steeped in Wilde's engagement with the contexture of eighteenth-century forgery that we have devoted chapter 6 entirely to its discussion. These writings demonstrate the range of ideas Wilde cultivated about artful criminality: from the rollicking endorsement of unabashed deviance in "Pen, Pencil and Poison," to the dialogic reasoning of the positive value of lying in "The Decay of Lying," to the depiction in his stories of the ways that artifice can encourage affection and even altruism. In other words, this impressive body of essays and fiction from the late 1880s advances the unyielding belief that no moral system or rule of law should regulate and restrict the creative imagination.

"EXPRESSION BY PEN OR POISON": THOMAS GRIFFITHS WAINEWRIGHT'S ART OF FORGERY

The best starting point for understanding Wilde's fascination with forgery after he finished the "Chatterton" notebook is "Pen, Pencil and Poison." This spirited essay, which first appeared in Frank Harris's *Fortnightly Review* in January 1889, considers the extraordinary career of a notorious murderer (the first to administer strychnine to his victims). In a brazen discussion—which engages in a complicated dialogue with the prose writings of Swinburne, De Quincey, and Pater—Wilde signals an initial move toward establishing himself as a serious critic. Wilde's analysis seeks to explain his claim that Wainewright possessed (in a phrase drawn from Pater's 1876 essay "Romanticism") "an extremely artistic temperament," one that was so great that it excelled in many different areas of creative activity.[1] As Wilde drolly puts it, Wainewright was not "merely a poet and a painter, an art-critic, an antiquarian, and a writer of prose, an amateur of beautiful things, and a dilettante of things delightful, but also a forger of no mean or ordinary capabilities, and as a subtle and secret poisoner almost without rival in this or any other age."[2] Yet Wilde also acknowledges that to appreciate the poisoner's astounding career, one must confront the challenging view that Wainewright's heinous acts might have been just as artful as his abilities as a writer of fine prose and as a painter of admired portraits. As Wilde recognized, there was nothing especially novel about this provocative hypothesis. It took

1. Pater, "Postscript," in *Appreciations* (London: Macmillan, 1889), 245. Pater's "Postscript" first appeared as "Romanticism," *Macmillan's Magazine* 35 (1876): 64–70.

2. Wilde, "Pen, Pencil and Poison: A Study," *Fortnightly Review* 45, no. 265 (January 1889): 41–54. Reprinted as "Pen, Pencil, and Poison" on the contents page of *Intentions* (London: James Osgood, 1891), 49–75; and reprinted as "Pen Pencil and Poison" in *Criticism: Historical Criticism, Intentions, The Soul of Man*, ed. Josephine M. Guy, *The Complete Works of Oscar Wilde*, 7 vols. to date (Oxford: Oxford University Press, 2000 and continuing), 4:105. Guy follows the unpunctuated representation of the title at the start of Wilde's essay in *Intentions*, 49.

its cue from De Quincey's well-known essay "On Murder Considered as One of the Fine Arts" (1827), which in turn remarks that the most revered source for conjuring this idea is Aristotle, who, in the *Metaphysics*, reminds us of the idiom χλεπτην τέλειον ("the perfect thief").[3]

By the time he was sentenced, Wainewright's onetime associates knew that he had used *nux vomica* (apparently stored in one of his bejeweled rings) to finish the lives of three women relatives. These family members resided with him at the finely appointed Linden House, Turnham Green, which he inherited from his uncle (whom he may also have poisoned) in 1828.[4] Wainewright's mother-in-law and her daughters, Helen Abercromby and Madeleine Abercromby, were poisoned after he had taken out excessive insurance policies on the lives of his sisters-in-law. With the proceeds from insurance fraud and other misappropriated funds, Wainewright unconscionably supported his indulgent way of life and lavishly decorated this beautiful home. According to the main source that Wilde used for much of his biographical information on Wainewright, there was another victim, an unnamed "Norfolk gentleman," who also succumbed to the dandy's adept acts of poisoning.[5] Even though some insurers, after much legal wrangling, eventually refused to pay Wainewright on grounds of suspicion, he was never charged with the murders. To him, however, these deaths were less a source of shame than pride, since he freely admitted to the

3. Thomas De Quincey, "On Murder Considered as One of the Fine Arts," *Blackwood's Edinburgh Magazine* 20 (1827): 199–213; reprinted in *Articles from the* Edinburgh Evening Post, Blackwood's Edinburgh Magazine, *and the* Edinburgh Literary Gazette, 1826–1829, ed. David Groves and Grevel Lindop, *The Works of Thomas De Quincey*, gen. ed. Lindop, 21 vols. (London: Pickering and Chatto, 2000), 6:115. De Quincey also praises the art of the murderer in "On the Knocking at the Gate in *Macbeth*," when he writes of John Williams, the presumed perpetrator of the Ratcliffe Highway murders, "it is unreasonable to expect all men to be great artists, and born with the genius of Mr. Williams." *London Magazine* 8 (October 1823): 353, reprinted in *The Works of Thomas De Quincey*, ed. Lindop, 3:151.

4. Walter Thornbury, in a biographical sketch of Wainewright in *All the Year Round*, intimates that the death of Wainewright's uncle was itself suspect: "His death occurred after a very short illness, and during a visit paid him by Wainewright and his wife, who was there confined of her first . . . child. It was not exactly apoplexy, nor was it heart disease; but then even doctors are somewhat puzzled by organic complications" ("Old Stories Re-told: Thomas Griffiths Wainewright [Janus Weathercock], The Poisoner," *All the Year Round*, 5 January 1867: 36).

5. Wilde's main source for details about Wainewright's career was Carew Hazlitt's lengthy "Introduction," in Wainewright, *Essays and Criticisms*, ed. W. Carew Hazlitt (London: Reeves and Turner, 1880). Carew Hazlitt discusses the mysterious "Norfolk gentleman" on liv–lvi.

murders when visitors, including Dickens, witnessed him languishing at New-gate. (W. Carew Hazlitt, whose biography Wilde drew upon, mentions that during his exile in France, the criminal Wainewright committed to a "Diary, where he had placed on record, with perfect satisfaction and even zest, the method employed in his various operations.")[6] Charged with the forgery of sig-natures, Wainewright narrowly escaped execution before he was put aboard the convict ship *Susan*, which took him to Hobart, Tasmania, where he died ten years afterward. In the end, Wainewright received the reprieve of transportation largely because the Bank of England, under political pressure at the time, had no wish to sentence to death a man for forgery when the press had mounted a staunch campaign against such an immoderate punishment for what was a bureaucratic crime.

In what ways, then, were the suicidal Chatterton and the murderous Waine-wright entwined in Wilde's imagination? And what is the precise link between Wilde's "Chatterton" notebook and "Pen, Pencil and Poison"? To begin with, the subjects of both works were forgers, executing different varieties of such deceit for similar ends. Chatterton's fakes were exclusively literary acts of de-ception that he carried out in part to reap financial rewards, with very mixed success. The extravagant Wainewright's forgeries counterfeited signatures so that he could gain access to moneys tied up in a family trust. Despite their very different milieus, these forgers were also connected through a network of literary figures. As the grandson of Ralph Griffiths, who founded the eminent *Monthly Review* in 1749, Wainewright was a descendant of a literary elite that enjoyed fame from the mid-eighteenth century onward; he was also a gifted art critic and talented painter, who came to notice in the distinguished *London Magazine* and the Royal Academy at roughly the same time he began defraud-ing the trust fund in the early 1820s. At the bustling *London Magazine*, where he published under eccentric pen names (including "Janus Weathercock" and "Cornelius Van Vinkbooms"), Wainewright joined a remarkable ensemble of writers who made their mark during the reign of George IV: Thomas Carlyle, John Clare, Thomas De Quincey, William Hazlitt, Thomas Hood, and Leigh Hunt. Keats, too, was part of this circle; in 1821, he published "Sonnet—A Dream" in the journal. Many of these figures belonged to the Romantic tra-dition that Wilde had strongly identified with since his time at Oxford. Not surprisingly, this coterie expressed interest in Chatterton. The esteemed Dante

6. Carew Hazlitt, "Introduction," in Wainewright, *Essays and Criticisms*, lxx. This "diary" has not resurfaced. Carew Hazlitt claims that Wainewright's French employers seized this document, which came into the hands of "an agent from the life offices" (lxx).

scholar H. F. Cary, for example, contributed a detailed assessment of the Bristol poet's career to the journal in 1824. Struck by the youthful irreligion, profaneness, and ribaldry of the forger's later poetry, Cary concludes that he "cannot conceive that with a faculty so highly imaginative" Chatterton "could long have continued an unbeliever, or, perhaps, that he could ever have been so in his heart."[7] In Cary's mind, Chatterton's forgeries were ultimately excusable, since the teenage poet provided a "portentous example of the dangers to which an inexperienced youth, highly gifted by nature, is exposed, when thrown into the midst of greedy speculators."[8]

As we explain in chapter 2, there was some dissent among these ranks. William Hazlitt devoted parts of two of his 1818 lectures to a critical assessment of Chatterton's life and works, in which he claimed that, even if Chatterton "did not shew extraordinary powers of genius," it was nonetheless true that the teenage poet "performed wonders" with "extraordinary precocity."[9] Such measured remarks, as we observe above, may well have caused so much disappointment in Keats that he responded by dedicating *Endymion* (1818) to Chatterton. Keats's enthusiasm was certainly shared by many Victorian readers. Noticeably, when the editor of Wainewright's works—William Hazlitt's grandson, W. Carew Hazlitt—prepared the famous 1818 lectures for a new 1869 edition, he reorganized the book's table of contents to reflect Chatterton's ascendancy in the popular imagination. In the original edition, the table of contents recorded only the names of the lectures; William Hazlitt mentions Chatterton at the end of Lecture VI, "On Swift, Young, Gray, Collins, &c.," and at the start of Lecture VII, "On Burns, and the Old English Ballads." In his later edition, Carew Hazlitt divided those two lectures into four in the table of contents: "On Gray, Swift, Young, and Collins," "On Chatterton," "On Burns," and "On the Old English Ballads." While the lectures themselves retain the original breaks and numbering, the running head "On Chatterton" begins on the last page of the lecture titled "Swift, Young, and Gray" and continues through the first six pages of the one titled "On Burns."[10] Other than updating the original "On the Living Poets" to "On the Modern Poets," Carew Hazlitt's addition of Chatterton is the only change that he made to the organization of his distinguished ancestor's lectures.

7. [H. F. Cary,] "The Life of Chatterton," *London Magazine* 9 (1824): 638.

8. [Cary,] "The Life of Chatterton," 638.

9. William Hazlitt, "On Swift, Young, Gray &c.," *Lectures on the English Poets* (London: Taylor and Hessey, 1818), 243. For our discussion of Hazlitt's comments in chapter 2, see 82–83.

10. See Hazlitt, *Lectures on the English Poets, and the English Comic Writers*, ed. William Carew Hazlitt (London: Bell and Daldy, 1869), 163–69.

There was another connection with the circle around the *London Magazine* that might have drawn Wilde's attention to Wainewright's art criticism, forgeries, and murders: the journal formed a nexus, from which springs a genealogy of critics traceable from Wainewright and Charles Lamb to Pater and Swinburne. "Charles Lamb," Wilde observes, "speaks of 'kind, light-hearted Wainewright,' whose prose is 'capital.'"[11] Lamb, who distinguished himself through the essays he published in the *London Magazine* under the pen name "Elia," expressed great enthusiasm for Wainewright's finely honed criticism. (Lamb died before Wainewright's conviction and was thus not privy to his later downfall.) In 1822, when he uttered concern that Wainewright might depart from the magazine, Lamb appealed to its publisher, J. A. Hessey: "Above all what is become of Janus Weathercock—or by his worse name of Vink—something? He is much wanted. He was a genius of Lond. Mag."[12] In the following year, when Wainewright announced his farewell to this eminent publication, he singled out "the whimsical, the pregnant, the 'abundant joke-giving' Elia" as a colleague who "spoke flatteringly of Janus . . . as of one not absolutely inefficient, not the worst of Periodical scribblers."[13] Pater's 1878 essay on Lamb, whom he held in high regard, pays particular respect to Elia's wide-ranging artistic skills, in ways that bear close comparison with Wilde's comments on Wainewright. "What has not been observed so generally as the excellence of his literary criticism," Pater observes about the praise Lamb's writings have won, is that "Charles Lamb is a fine critic of painting also."[14] In every way, Lamb's prose style struck Pater as exemplary: "In the making of prose he realises the principle of art for its own sake, as completely as Keats in the making of verse."[15] In similar vein, Wilde detected preeminence in Janus Weathercock's art criticism: "The conception of making a prose-poem out of paint," he remarks of Wainewright's description

11. Wilde, "Pen, Pencil and Poison," in *Criticism*, ed. Guy, 4:107. Wilde is quoting from Lamb's correspondence in Carew Hazlitt's "Introduction" to Wainewright, *Essays and Criticisms*, xxx. A slightly different version of Lamb's letter appears in "To Bernard Barton," 2 September 1823, *The Letters of Charles Lamb, to Which Are Added Those of His Sister, Mary Lamb*, ed. E. V. Lucas, 3 vols. (London: J. M. Dent and Methuen, 1935), 2:394.

12. Charles Lamb, "To. J. A. Hessey," 15 April 1822, in *Letters*, 2:323.

13. [Thomas Griffiths Wainewright,] "Janus Weatherbound; or, the Weathercock Steadfast for Lack of Oil: A Grave Epistle," *London Magazine* 7 (1823): 45–52; in Wainewright, *Essays and Criticisms*, 308. Wainewright's quoted phrase comes from Leigh Hunt, "To Charles Lamb," in *Foliage: or, Poems Original and Translated* (London: C. and J. Ollier, 1818), cviii.

14. Pater, *Appreciations*, 113. Pater's essay originally appeared as "The Character of the Humourist: Charles Lamb," *Fortnightly Review* n.s. 24 (1878): 466–74.

15. Pater, *Appreciations*, 112.

of Giulio Romano's *Cephalus and Procris*, "is excellent."[16] And Wainewright composed his criticism, as Josephine Bauer observes in her fine history of the *London Magazine*, with an accomplished stylishness that owed much to his deliberate copying of Sterne. Wainewright's "cultivated eccentricities"—"his 'sentimentalities,' his breaking off and using sometimes four or five rows of as-terisks, his leaving unfinished fragments of thoughts, his juxtaposing of genuine pathos with absurd comicality, his innuendo"—were all evocative of Sterne's beloved persona, Yorick.[17]

Wilde, who dwells on Wainewright's outstanding critical faculties, stresses that those gifts were not lost on Wainewright's contemporaries such as Lamb. To be sure, in later years some members of this literary group, including "Barry Cornwall" (Bryan Waller Procter) and Thomas Noon Talfourd (Lamb's biog-rapher), found much to despise in Wainewright's fall from grace. Yet his ad-versaries acknowledged that during his heyday as Janus Weathercock—this resident art critic who wrote with great authority on Italian masters such as Giorgione—was, as De Quincey recognized, "not merely a copier from books."[18] Wainewright was, without question, an original thinker. Besides De Quincey's thoughtful 1848 commentary, two subsequent studies sought to provide readers with a balanced evaluation of Wainewright's considerable achievements. Both of these commentaries pointed out that Janus Weathercock contributed posi-tively to the valuation of artists and their work. In *William Blake, "Pictor Igno-tus"* (1863), Alexander Gilchrist found in Wainewright "real literary merit and originality; in a vein of partly feigned coxcombry and flippant impertinence, of wholly genuine sympathy with art (within orthodox limits), and recognition of the real excellencies of the moderns."[19] Gilchrist warmly acknowledged the critic's efforts to support the impecunious and misunderstood Blake by pur-chasing rare copies of the poet's illustrated books, including *Songs of Innocence and Experience* (1798). In 1868, when Swinburne wrote an extended essay on Blake, he too devoted several pages to Wainewright, only part of which directly addressed Wainewright's role in Blake's career. Attentive to Gilchrist's remark,

16. "Pen, Pencil and Poison," in *Criticism*, ed. Guy, 4:113.

17. Josephine Bauer, *The London Magazine, 1820–29*, Anglistica I (Copenhagen: Rosenkilde and Bagger, 1953), 167. In Sterne's *Life and Opinions of Tristram Shandy, Gentleman* (1759–1767), Parson Yorick is the character that readers have most commonly identified with Sterne himself.

18. [Thomas De Quincey], "Charles Lamb and His Friends," *North British Review* 10 (1848): 204.

19. Gilchrist, *William Blake, "Pictor Ignotus": With Selections from His Poems and Other Writings*, 2 vols. (London: Macmillan, 1863), 2:278.

Swinburne took it upon himself to amplify Wainewright's distinction by going so far as to suggest that Janus Weathercock was the finest art critic prior to John Ruskin: "Another worthy of notice here was, until our own day called forth a better, the best English critic on art; himself, as far as we know, admirable alike as a painter, a writer, and a murderer."[20] In the phrase that Wilde adapted for the title of his essay, Swinburne asserted that Wainewright's expert "hand was never a mere craftsman's," whether it held "pen . . . palette or . . . poison."[21] Swinburne's dispassionate appraisal of Wainewright's skills in prose, on canvas, and in poisoning powerfully shaped the direction of Wilde's essay.

The writings of Lamb, Pater, and Swinburne show that Wainewright's best biographer, Jonathan Curling, is not entirely correct when he claims that Wilde "was the first writer" to regard this criminal "as a man, not a monster, and, to omit the pious reprobations with which all other authors hitherto had justified themselves."[22] Yet, at the same time, Curling's comments alert us to the highly charged rhetoric that certain reporters had used when discussing the fate of Janus Weathercock. In his 1867 contribution to Dickens's *All the Year Round*, Walter Thornbury could scarcely contain himself when he asserted that Wainewright was a "monster egotist": "one of the most cruel, subtle, and successful secret murderers since the time of the Borgias."[23] Such contempt paved the way for Carew Hazlitt to declare sensationally, in his edition of Wainewright's contributions to the *London Magazine*, that his subject "was a villain of the true melodramatic stamp, but a thousand times more devilish and dangerous than any hero of melodrama."[24] Even after Wilde had advanced the dauntless view that Wainewright's career demonstrated that "there is no essential incongruity between crime and culture," those Victorian critics who were absorbed in debates on social Darwinism turned to Janus Weathercock as a glaring example of a regressive human type. In his classic study, *The Criminal* (1890), Havelock Ellis chose Wainewright as a "perfect picture of the instinctive criminal in his most highly developed shape" that "every one would be willing to

20. Algernon Charles Swinburne, *William Blake* (London: John Camden Hotten, 1868), 67.

21. Swinburne, *William Blake*, 68.

22. Jonathan Curling, *Janus Weathercock: The Life and Times of Thomas Griffiths Wainewright, 1794–1847* (London: Thomas Nelson, 1938), 10.

23. [Thornbury], "Old Stories Re-told," 39. John Camden Hotten similarly called Wainewright a "monster" whose "end . . . was in keeping with his tragic career" ("Introduction: Wainewright, the Poisoner," in Charles Dickens, *Hunted Down: A Story* [London: John Camden Hotten, 1870], 27). Hotten's edition was unauthorized.

24. Carew Hazlitt, "Introduction," in Wainewright, *Essays and Criticisms*, lxxvii.

accept."[25] Slightly later, in a work that exerted popular influence on public understandings of humankind's degeneration, Max Nordau asserted that Wilde's decision to make Wainewright the subject of a "very affectionate biographical treatise" was a plain indication of nothing less than Wilde's own "immorality, sin and crime."[26]

Nordau's observation startles in its presumptuousness, distracting attention from the primary connection that drove Wilde's writing on Chatterton and Wainewright: namely, how the deft criminality of forgery spurs the brilliant creativity of art. As we have explained, the intersection of forgery and artistry provides the vital link in Wilde's thought between the "marvellous Boy" and the legendary murderer. Yet it is also plain that in "Pen, Pencil and Poison" Wilde considers the work of a forger whose behavior, unlike Chatterton's, was literally criminal, even if its performance was dazzlingly clever. Wilde takes a considered look at the potentially troubling ways in which a poisoner might have been as adroit in his practices of murder as he was at writing criticism. More to the point, Wilde insists that Wainewright's outlandish crimes cannot be held against his artistry. "The fact of a man being a poisoner," he riskily asserts, "is nothing against his prose."[27] As his impenitent discussion unfolds, Wilde puts increasing pressure on the view that Wainewright was indeed "a man of culture," one for whom "painting was the first art that fascinated him," before he "sought to find expression by pen or poison."[28] Had Wainewright, Wilde contends in his concluding review of his talented subject's career, lived in an earlier era renowned for its tyrannical killers—such as imperial Rome, the Italian Renaissance, or seventeenth-century Spain—hardly anyone one in late Victorian times would pass judgments on his crimes. "Nobody," Wilde maintains, "with the true historical sense ever dreams of blaming Nero, or scolding Tiberius or censuring Caesar."[29] Wilde states that the only reason many of his peers and predecessors have cared "to distribute their praise and blame with the solemn complacency of a successful schoolmaster" is because Wainewright's outrageous wrongdoings remain within living memory.[30] "It is," he comments wryly in the earliest version of this essay, "impossible not to feel prejudice against a man who might have poisoned one's own grandmother."[31]

25. Havelock Ellis, *The Criminal* (New York: Scribner and Welford, 1890), 17, 12.
26. Max Nordau, *Degeneration* (New York: D. Appleton, 1895), 320.
27. "Pen, Pencil and Poison," in *Criticism*, ed. Guy, 4:121.
28. "Pen, Pencil and Poison," in *Criticism*, ed. Guy, 4:106.
29. "Pen, Pencil and Poison," in *Criticism*, ed. Guy, 4:121.
30. "Pen, Pencil and Poison," in *Criticism*, ed. Guy, 4:121.
31. "Pen, Pencil and Poison," in *Criticism*, ed. Guy, 4:121.

Such remarks have struck several modern critics, somewhat like Nordau, as evidence of Wilde's exceptionally strong personal identification with Wainewright's barefaced criminality. This line of thinking has some similarities to the arguments of scholars who claim that Wilde's "Chatterton" notebook provides proof of his tendency to plunder other critics' property. To Ellmann, for example, "Pen, Pencil and Poison" "is closest to Wilde's social presentation of himself."[32] In Ellmann's view, this study of Janus Weathercock intimates Wilde's self-fashioning as a deceptive figure that reveled in "inveterate artificiality," as a duplicitous man who had begun mingling in an "underworld of people who pretended to be what they were not."[33] For many reasons, Ellmann's remark is surprising, not least because Wainewright—as Carew Hazlitt observes—hardly held back in his "unblushing avowal of atrocities."[34] Such comments indicate that Wainewright flaunted his wrongdoing.

Other commentators on Wilde's essay have found several different reasons for casting its contents in almost wholly negative terms. Ian Small, for instance, has suggested that this exuberant discussion of Wainewright's career is to some degree criminal in itself, because Wilde apparently goes out of his way to conceal his main authority, Carew Hazlitt's 1880 edition of Wainewright's *Essays and Criticisms*: "Most of the evidence suggests that Wilde wanted to hide this particular source of information, and here his debt is not acknowledged. (An acknowledgment of sorts does occur very near the end of the essay where Wilde describes himself as being 'indebted' to Hazlitt's book for 'many of the facts' of the essay, and begrudgingly confesses that the work was 'quite invaluable in its way.' But this is only an extreme example of a systematic strategy to discredit all familiar forms of authority in *Intentions*.)"[35] Small's assertion that "Pen, Pencil and Poison" constitutes a further addition to Wilde's supposedly plagiarized canon looks somewhat odd, since Wilde scarcely hides or mystifies Carew Hazlitt as his main source. In any case, just as we find in published accounts of Chatterton's life, the many biographies of Wainewright are themselves peppered with unacknowledged borrowings; Carew Hazlitt cites some, though by no means all, of his sources. The same is true of popular histories of Wainewright, such as Thornbury's in *All the Year Round*.

32. Ellmann, *Oscar Wilde* (New York: Alfred A. Knopf, 1988), 299.
33. Ellmann, *Oscar Wilde*, 299.
34. Carew Hazlitt, "Introduction," in Wainewright, *Essays and Criticisms*, lxv.
35. Ian Small, "Intertextuality in Pater and Wilde," in "Essays & Poems: In Memory of Ian Fletcher, 1920–1988," *English Literature in Transition, 1880–1920*, special series, no. 4 (1990): 62–63.

Meanwhile, Josephine M. Guy has followed Small's other negative interpretations of "Pen, Pencil and Poison" by focusing on the purportedly satirical
implications that result from the echoes of Pater's works that arise in Wilde's
essay. She insists that Wilde's painstaking evocation of key phrases from Pater's
writings reveals that this is an insubordinate work that goes out of its way to
mock this critical master, down to the smallest and most personal detail. Certainly, there are audible echoes of Pater's essays in many parts of Wilde's discussion. Perhaps the most obvious resonance of Pater's critical voice occurs when
Wilde observes that in the guise of Janus Weathercock, the critic Wainewright
"concerned himself primarily with the complex impressions produced by a
work of art, and certainly the first step in aesthetic criticism is to realize one's
own impressions."[36] This sentence, which emphasizes independence of mind,
resounds with a well-known formulation in Pater's famous "Preface" to *Studies
in the History of the Renaissance*: "In æsthetic criticism the first step towards seeing one's object as it really is, is to know one's own impression as it really is, to
discriminate it, to realise it distinctly."[37] Moreover, it is not only Wilde's phrasing but also the subjects that absorbed Wainewright's attention that remind us
of Pater's essays on early modern culture. "He writes," Wilde observes of Janus
Weathercock, "about La Gioconda, and early French poets and the Italian Renaissance."[38] Since these are three topics that take up the larger part of Pater's
famous critical volume, Wilde here implicitly extends Swinburne's assertion
about Wainewright's great critical stature by implying that Janus Weathercock
anticipated Pater by more than half a century.

Wilde, as Guy shows, pursues the connection between Wainewright and
Pater much further, though she concludes that Wilde's studied allusions have
a satirical edge. Besides Wilde's overt evocations of *Studies in the History of
the Renaissance*, she detects some less explicit touches that suggest to her that
"Pen, Pencil and Poison" amounts to an impertinent "witty attack" on Pater.[39]
She notes, for instance, Wilde's attention to Wainewright's love of "Elizabethan translations of *Cupid and Psyche*, and the *Hypnerotomachia*, and book-
bindings, and early editions, and wide-margined proofs."[40] Such volumes not
only echo details in chapters of Pater's novel, *Marius the Epicurean* (1885), but

36. "Pen, Pencil and Poison," in *Criticism*, ed. Guy, 4:109.

37. Pater, *The Renaissance: Studies in Art and Poetry, the 1893 Text*, ed. Donald L. Hill
(Berkeley: University of California Press, 1980), xx.

38. "Pen, Pencil and Poison," in *Criticism*, ed. Guy, 4:108.

39. Guy, "Introduction," in *Criticism*, ed. Guy, 4:xxxii.

40. "Pen, Pencil and Poison," in *Criticism*, ed. Guy, 4:108.

also—from Guy's perspective—suggest "Pater's love of fine books and early editions," which was well known to those who had visited his rooms at Brasenose
College.[41] Furthermore, in her view, Wilde's suggestion that Wainewright "reminds us of Julien Sorel" bears a passing resemblance to an allusion to Pater's
comment in "Style" on Stendhal's *Le rouge et le noir* (1830)—which features
this entrancing protagonist—as one of the finest models of European prose.[42]
For Pater, since Stendhal's great novel remains independent "of all removable
decoration," it ranks as a perfect "composition utterly unadorned."[43] Yet, as one
reflects on these small but telling references, it is not necessarily the case that
they amount to an expression of Wilde's hostility to Pater. Wilde's invocation
of Sorel might equally signal his affinity with, and not antipathy toward, Pater's
views on the French novelist and his character. Wilde wholeheartedly agreed
with Pater about the greatness of Stendhal's novel, though Wilde's delight in
the novelist long precedes his acquaintance with Pater or Pater's works. According to the American poet and novelist Vincent O'Sullivan, Wilde counted
Sorel as one of his "two favourite characters" since boyhood.[44] More particularly, there are other specifics that possibly imply that Wilde might be making
some light-hearted jibes at aspects of Pater's tastes in decor. "He had," Wilde
writes of Wainewright, "that curious love of green, which in individuals is always the sign of a subtle artistic temperament."[45] Very possibly, Guy infers, this
"curious love" conjures the "pale green tint" that Edward Manson recalls on
the paneling of Pater's college rooms.[46] (One might, too, be tempted to find
male homoeroticism encoded in what was also a fashionable color in interior
decoration.)[47] Further still, it may appear that Wilde seeks to implicate Pater in

41. Guy, "Commentary," in *Criticism*, ed. Guy, 4:419.

42. Wilde, "Pen, Pencil and Poison," in *Criticism*, ed. Guy, 4:107.

43. Pater, *Appreciations*, 15–16. "Style" first appeared in the *Fortnightly Review* 44, no.
264 (December 1888): 728–43.

44. Vincent O'Sullivan, *Aspects of Wilde* (London: Constable, 1936), 36.

45. "Pen, Pencil and Poison," in *Criticism*, ed. Guy, 4:108.

46. Guy, "Commentary," in *Criticism*, ed. Guy, 4:417. Guy is referencing Edward Manson, "Recollections of Walter Pater," *Oxford Magazine* 25 (1906): 61.

47. Sally-Anne Huxtable observes that the "Green Dining Room" (or "Morris Room"),
which Morris, Marshall, Faulkner and Co. designed for the South Kensington Museum,
"was the first 'Aesthetic interior,' the room that launched a thousand (or so) green walls of
the 1870s and 1880s. . . . [I]t was this room which started the craze for muted 'Art' colours,
the 'Greenery-Yallery' tints, later satirized so famously in Gilbert and Sullivan's *Patience*
(1881)" ("Re-reading the Green Dining Room," in Jason Edwards and Imogen Hart, eds.,
Rethinking the Interior, c. 1867–1896 [Farnham: Ashgate, 2010], 37). In the late nineteenth
century, the idea that green carnations signaled male homosexuality is best known from

Wainewright's passion for feline companions. As Wilde observes, Wainewright "was extremely fond of cats": a small feature that perhaps evokes the fact that in his prose, as well as in his home life, Pater valued animals.[48]

By bearing this host of details in mind, Guy suggests that Wilde's essay is a crafty "double portrait" that deliberately affiliates Pater—through the various personalized touches—with the immorality of Wainewright's crimes.[49] Yet it is also, we believe, correspondingly possible to infer that Wilde's strategy is to associate Pater with the high caliber of Wainewright's critical prose. On different grounds, Horst Schroeder has also questioned the plausibility of Guy's claim. Schroeder determines that it is unlikely that "this most sensitive of sensitive men would have remained on speaking terms with Wilde, if he had felt himself caricatured in Wilde's essay."[50] The fact that Wilde's relations with Pater remained cordial suggests that "Pen, Pencil and Poison" had no negative impact on the significant intellectual relationship between the two men. Later, Wilde reviewed Pater's *Appreciations* (1889) in glowing terms, ones that elicited a kindly response: Wilde's "pleasantly written, genial, sensible, criticism," Pater wrote, had given him "very great pleasure."[51] Pater's generous statement is in line with an anecdote that Wilde's friend O'Sullivan recollected in the 1930s: "Once at Oxford [Wilde] came upon Pater brooding over an article which attempted to turn into ridicule his essay on Charles Lamb. The article was entitled: 'Lamb—and Mint Sauce,' and was written, according to Wilde, by H. D. Traill, a writer of considerable repute."[52] "Wilde," O'Sullivan adds, "was dumbfounded. He said

---

Robert Hichens's satire on the intimacy between Oscar Wilde and Alfred Douglas, *The Green Carnation* (London: W. Heinemann, 1894).

48. "Pen, Pencil and Poison," in *Criticism*, ed. Guy, 4:108.

49. Guy, "Introduction," in *Criticism*, ed. Guy, 4:xxii.

50. Horst Schroeder, "Volume IV of the OET Edition of *The Complete Works of Oscar Wilde*: III. 'Pen, Pencil and Poison,'" *The Wildean* 36 (2010): 32.

51. Walter Pater, "To Oscar Wilde," 22 March 1890, in *Letters of Walter Pater*, ed. Lawrence Evans (Oxford: Clarendon Press, 1970), 109. Wilde praised Pater's *Imaginary Portraits* (1887) in a review, "Mr. Pater's Imaginary Portraits," *Pall Mall Gazette*, 11 June 1887: 2–3; in *Journalism Part I*, ed. John Stokes and Mark W. Turner, *The Complete Works of Oscar Wilde*, 7 vols. to date (Oxford: Oxford University Press, 2000 and continuing), 6:178–80.

52. O'Sullivan, *Aspects of Wilde*, 12. Robert Seiler has informed us that T. H. S. Escott, the former editor of the *Fortnightly Review*, also observed that a "well-known nineteenth-century journalist made Pater's appreciation of Charles Lamb the theme of some writing entitled 'Charles Lamb and Culture Sauce'" ("Walter Pater and Other Memories," *The Bookman's Journal and Print Collector* 10 [1924]: 111). We have been unable to trace any satirical works by Traill or another writer that have either of these titles.

his estimate of Pater as a man altered from that moment. 'Just imagine! Pater! I could not conceive how one could be Pater and yet be susceptible to the insults of the lowest kind of journalism.'"[53]

An altogether stronger argument for understanding Wilde's deliberate evocation of Paterian ideas in the context of Wainewright's criminal career is one that Megan Becker-Leckrone has proposed. In her view, Wilde's ingenious essay urges "not only that we evaluate Wainewright's crimes from the same critically disinterested stance from which we would otherwise consider his artistic creations, but also, paradoxically, that we might perhaps view the aestheticist endeavour itself as a kind of 'crime'—one Wilde portrays as provocative, daring, but also dangerous, even 'deadly.'"[54] This insight suggests that Wilde's turn to Wainewright indicates not so much his intention to deride Pater or to glorying in transgressive behavior as his serious interest in developing the stakes of what *Studies in the History of the Renaissance* characterized as "æsthetic criticism" as an art form.[55] In many ways, the reflections on Wainewright's critical gifts in "Pen, Pencil and Poison" have much to say about Wilde's self-fashioning as an "æsthetic critic" who is acknowledging Pater's lead, if taking it in a direction that Pater—who hardly advocated crime—did not anticipate. The essay, from what evidence we have, struck no one as an offensive attack either on Pater or on any of the sources Wilde had used.

Wilde's motivation for writing "Pen, Pencil and Poison" remains unclear. Little information on its composition history has survived. We can reasonably conjecture that Wilde composed the essay in November and December 1888, immediately preceding its January 1889 publication in the *Fortnightly*. Given Wilde's correspondence of the period, he appears to have worked on it at the same time as "The Decay of Lying"; both pieces, in any case, were published in the same month. Henry Lucy had written a positive notice of "Pen, Pencil and Poison" for *Punch*, where he good-humoredly described it as "not too De Quincey-ish, but just De Quincey-ish enough."[56] In a note of thanks to Lucy, Wilde suggests "The Decay of Lying" was "so much the better of the two" essays, and he proceeded to ask Lucy for his "views on [the] new theory of art con-

53. O'Sullivan, *Aspects of Wilde*, 12. O'Sullivan adds that Wilde "always professed a great admiration for Pater's books," though for "the man he seemed to have the slightly contemptuous pity of one who lives in the sight of the public, despises it, and dominates it easily, for another who dreads the public and is morbidly sensitive to its hostility" (12).

54. Megan Becker-Leckrone, "Wilde and Pater's Strange Appreciations," *Victoriographies* 1 (2011): 105.

55. Pater, *The Renaissance*, xix.

56. [Henry Lucy,] "Our Booking Office," *Punch*, 5 January 1889: 12.

tained in it."[57] Even if Wilde might have preferred "The Decay of Lying," the
notices for both of these contributions to noteworthy journals were nonetheless
quite positive. Reviews of "Pen, Pencil and Poison" labeled it "entertaining" and
"interesting," perhaps because it addressed a figure whose notoriety remained
current at the time.[58]

The subject was topical. Although Wainewright had not, like Chatterton,
experienced ongoing revivals by subsequent generations of artists and poets,
his staggering biography had certainly kept his name alive in the cultural consciousness. Such was the spot Wainewright seems to have held in Wilde's circle at Oxford in the 1870s. In his diary, fellow undergraduate J. E. Courtenay
Bodley recorded attending a dinner at which a friend "was as usual full of chaff
about the Wainwright [sic] case."[59] The following day, Bodley played a practical
joke on Wilde, leaving fish heads wrapped in newspapers in his rooms; Wilde
riposted that he dropped them "stealthily in the Cherwell, feeling quite like
Wainewright."[60] Those who were newly accused of embezzlement by forgery
or murder by poisoning were also frequently compared to Wainewright in the
press, which confirmed his reputation altogether more on the basis of his criminal activity (poison) than for his writing (pen) or his art (pencil).

It is worth dwelling a little more on Wilde's title. Once again, it involved
Wilde's imprecise use of "inverted commas" (i.e., quotation marks) that we discuss in the previous chapter. Besides stating that "with pen, with palette, or with
poison, [Wainewright's] hand was never a mere craftsman's," Swinburne repeats this serial formulation twice more in *William Blake*. He describes Wainewright as "admirable alike as a painter, a writer, and a murderer" and then as
"an artist in words, in oils, and in drugs."[61] Such formal repetition underscores
the leveling effect of Swinburne's approach: murderer is an occupation analogous to painter and writer; drugs are an artistic medium parallel to words and

57. Wilde, "To Henry Lucy," c. 5 January 1889, in *The Complete Letters of Oscar Wilde*,
ed. Merlin Holland and Rupert Hart-Davis (London: Fourth Estate, 2000), 384.

58. "The Reviews for January," *Pall Mall Gazette*, 2 January 1889: 7; "Magazines (Fourth
Notice)," *Aberdeen Journal*, 14 January 1889: 7; and "Literary Notes, News, and Echoes,"
Pall Mall Gazette, 5 January 1889: 1.

59. 5 December 1875, Diary of John Edward Courtenay Bodley, Bodleian Library, Special Collections, MS. Eng. Misc. e. 460, 55ᵛ.

60. 6 December 1875, Diary of John Edward Courtenay Bodley, Bodleian Library, Special Collections, MS. Eng. Misc. e. 460, 55ᵛ. In Shane Leslie's *Memoir of John Edward
Courtenay Bodley*, this entry is excerpted and Leslie has added a parenthetical—"(the
murderer)"—to Wainewright's name ([London: Jonathan Cape, 1930], 26). Ellmann also
cites the entry, including (erroneously) Leslie's parenthetical comment (*Oscar Wilde*, 60).

61. Swinburne, *William Blake*, 67, 69.

oils; and poison is a tool comparable to a pen and a palette. Yet Wilde remodels Swinburne's expressions for the purpose of a very different kind of critique. He certainly draws upon Swinburne for the governing topos of pen, pencil, and poison, just as he relies on Carew Hazlitt for the biographical facts; but the balance of Wilde's essay reflects not just his wry humor but also his concomitant efforts to consider Wainewright as a model for the Paterian aesthetic critic.

Unfortunately, Wilde's wit is so mordant, and his tone so dry, that it is at times easy to miss the biting humor involved in modeling Wainewright's activities along explicitly Paterian lines. Especially amusing are Wilde's observations about the manner in which Wainewright expresses his love of the countryside in his exquisite critical prose. Wilde quotes a passage where Janus Weathercock depicts his springtime experience of the countryside through an artist's lens: "The polyanthus glowed in its cold bed of earth, like a solitary picture of Giorgione."[62] Wainewright saw "on the horizon's edge" a "light, warm, film of misty vapour, against which the near village, with its ancient stone church, shewed sharply out with blinding whiteness."[63] "I thought," he remarks, "of Wordsworth's *'Lines Written in March.'*"[64] Aesthetic in every way, Janus Weathercock has a highly refined perception of precisely the nature that Wordsworth famously celebrates in *Lyrical Ballads* (1798). Yet, as Wilde insists, there is nothing morally pure about Wainewright's devotion to Giorgione, Wordsworth, or the glorification of the natural world: "Like most artificial people," Wilde writes, "[Wainewright] had a great love of nature."[65] And, just so we cannot fail to miss Wilde's satirical point, he adds: "We must not forget that the cultivated young man who penned these lines, and who was so susceptible to Wordsworthian influences, was also, as I said at the beginning of this memoir, one of the most subtle and secret poisoners of this or any age."[66] Regenia Gagnier counts among a handful of scholars who have grasped the caustic joke underlying this sharp formulation: "Wilde builds a case through irony," she ob-

---

62. "Janus Weathercock" [Wainewright], "Sentimentalities on the Fine Arts: No. III," *London Magazine* 1 (1820): 401–8; in *Essays and Criticisms*, 35; quoted in "Pen, Pencil and Poison," in *Criticism*, ed. Guy, 4:115. This quotation also serves as one of Wilde's many passing allusions to Pater's writings. Pater wrote enthusiastically of "The School of Giorgione," *Fortnightly Review* n.s. 22 (1877): 526–38; the essay was first reprinted in *The Renaissance: Studies in Art and Poetry*, 3rd ed. (London: Macmillan, 1888), 135–61.

63. "Janus Weathercock," "Sentimentalities on the Fine Arts: No. III," in *Essays and Criticisms*, 37, 36; quoted in "Pen, Pencil and Poison," in *Criticism*, ed. Guy, 4:115.

64. "Janus Weathercock," "Sentimentalities on the Fine Arts: No. III," 36; quoted in "Pen, Pencil and Poison," in *Criticism*, ed. Guy, 4:115.

65. "Pen, Pencil and Poison," in *Criticism*, ed. Guy, 4:115.

66. Wilde, "Pen, Pencil and Poison," in *Criticism*, ed. Guy, 4:115.

serves, "against specialization (including a specialized 'art world'), the division of labor, scientific standards, and . . . journalism."[67] It is not surprising, then, that Wilde includes in his essay a version of the line commonly repeated in biographical sketches of Wainewright: the heartless quip that killing his lovely young sister-in-law "was a dreadful thing to do, but she had very ugly ankles."[68] In that unforgettable phrase, all three of Wainewright's identities—critic, aesthete, and murderer—provocatively commingle. Throughout the essay, Wilde underscores Wainewright's immense critical faculties as an aesthete, and he consistently links them to this figure's remarkable personality: "Art's first appeal is neither to the intellect nor to the emotions, but purely to the artistic temperament"; "he deals with his impressions of the work as an artistic whole, and tries to translate those impressions into works, to give, as it were, the literary equivalent for the visual and mental effect."[69]

The upshot of "Pen, Pencil and Poison" is similar to the overall conclusion that Wilde draws about Chatterton in the notebook. In the case of Chatterton, forgery was a constitutive part of his artistic ability (as Watts said, "he needs must forge").[70] Here, however, Wilde completely avoids the idea that an artist's crimes prove excusable or understandable. Instead, he pursues the unremorseful belief that Wainewright's admirably "intense personality" was "created out of sin."[71] In other words, in this daring essay Wilde goes so far as to suggest that criminality, whether murderous or otherwise, hastens artistic creativity. This was the kernel of a theory that he continued to explore from different perspectives in several other powerful works at this time.

"THE VERY BASIS OF CIVILIZED SOCIETY": WILDE'S "DECAY OF LYING"

In "The Decay of Lying," the vigorous dialogue that Wilde published in the well-regarded *Nineteenth Century* in January 1889, he again takes up the

67. Regenia Gagnier, *Idylls of the Marketplace: Oscar Wilde and the Victorian Public* (Stanford, CA: Stanford University Press, 1986), 36.

68. "Pen, Pencil and Poison," in *Criticism*, ed. Guy, 4:119. Wilde changed Carew Hazlitt's version of "thick legs" to "thick ankles" ("Introduction," in Wainewright, *Essays and Criticisms*, lxix).

69. "Pen, Pencil and Poison," in *Criticism*, ed. Guy, 4:109, 111.

70. Watts, "Thomas Chatterton," in T. Humphry Ward, ed., *The English Poets: Selections with Critical Introductions*, 4 vols. (London: Macmillan, 1880), 3:405. We discuss Watts's comment about Chatterton in chapter 4 (178–81).

71. "Pen, Pencil and Poison," in *Criticism*, ed. Guy, 4:120.

connections between crime and art in order to expand the arguments that developed from his fascination with Chatterton's forgeries, propelling them into
an unorthodox theory of artistic creation. The main speaker, Vivian, builds
arguments in support of his thesis, which he repeats throughout the dialogue:
"Life imitates art far more than Art imitates Life."[72] Vivian's general proposition, which he unfolds to his at times slow-witted interlocutor Cyril, is that the
best art hardly copies, through a process of transparent mimesis, the apparently
stable bedrock of reality. Instead, art at its finest is generated from the imagination of the artist and exerts an imaginative hold over its captivated audience.
For the most part, great art will break "from the prison-house of realism" and
"run to greet" and "kiss" the "false, beautiful lips" of "the liar": the figure, Vivian asserts, who stands at "the very basis of civilized society."[73] This "liar"—a
creator of magnificent fictions that have no bearing on recognizable moral
truths—is eminently the "founder of social intercourse."[74] Averse to the Philistinism attached to provable facts, this "cultured and fascinating" personage has
enchanted his listeners since time immemorial: it was he "who first, without
ever having gone out to the rude chase, told the wondering cave-men at sunset
how he had dragged the Megatherium from the purple darkness of its jasper
cave."[75] Furnished with such Homeric language, this entrancing "liar," even
if he has no firsthand experience of the heroic actions he recounts, possesses a
unique ability to inspire.

If art has a relationship to reality, it is a causal relationship. Thus, as Vivian
proceeds to explain, when dismal art comes into circulation, such as in the form
of popular Victorian "penny dreadfuls" featuring criminals like Jack Sheppard,
its effect on unsuspecting readers can have wretched consequences. The objection is aesthetic, not moral: "The most obvious and vulgarest form in which this
is shown is in the case of silly boys who," once they have digested these silly tales
about criminal heroes, "pillage the stalls of unfortunate apple-women, break
into sweet-shops at night, and alarm old gentlemen who are returning home
from the city by leaping on them in suburban lanes, with black masks and
unloaded revolvers."[76] Aesthetically, to Vivian these are the ugliest of crimes,
since they simply count as the most mindless; they are purely derivative. "The
boy-burglar," he states, in a sentence that clinches his main point, "is simply

72. Wilde, "The Decay of Lying," *Nineteenth Century* 25, no. 143 (January 1889): 35–56;
in *Criticism*, ed. Guy, 4:90, 94, 102.

73. "The Decay of Lying," in *Criticism*, ed. Guy, 4:88.

74. "The Decay of Lying," in *Criticism*, ed. Guy, 4:88.

75. "The Decay of Lying," in *Criticism*, ed. Guy, 4:88.

76. "The Decay of Lying," in *Criticism*, ed. Guy, 4:91.

the inevitable result of life's imitative instinct."[77] This kind of petty thief, Vivian maintains, personifies modern "Fact, occupied as Fact usually is, with trying to reproduce Fiction."[78] Artless in the extreme, this thug's lack of imagination finds itself "repeated on an extended scale throughout the whole of life."[79]

A willing audience can be equally in thrall to good art and to bad. Vivian drives home this idea through anecdotes about acquaintances who, when they recognize themselves in fictional characters, were powerless to avoid repeating the actions depicted in *Vanity Fair* (1847–1848) or *Strange Case of Dr. Jekyll and Mr. Hyde* (1886). He states that it is the lack of imagination that these individuals evince, rather than the moral acceptability (or unacceptability) of the fictional acts they replicate, that renders them failures. In Vivian's view, the most powerful fiction can thus have a profound effect on human history, which remains indebted to the glorious work of the sociable "liar." Wilde heightens the provocativeness of this claim by choosing as examples novelists typically characterized as realists. Vivian insists that "the Nihilist, that strange martyr who has no faith," was "invented by Tourgénieff, and completed by Dostoieffski."[80] These Russian authors gave life to the figure, and did not simply record his existence. "The nineteenth century, as we know it," Vivian further declares, "is largely an invention of Balzac," the great novelist who conjured the social panorama in the countless fictions making up *La comédie humaine* (1830–1848).[81] Such reasoning runs counter to Balzac's own declaration that he was merely a secretary, recording the events of the world as they occurred.[82] Vivian playfully, and perhaps paradoxically, suggests that Balzac's best quality was his Romanticism, and that his work became realist only as a consequence of the nineteenth century following the outlines set forth in his novels. George Meredith, whom Cyril has already upheld as another example of the realist novelist, receives only oblique praise from Vivian, whose strongest endorsement takes this wry form: "Whatever he is, he is not a realist."[83] In Vivian's view, Meredith is also, like Balzac, best characterized as a Romantic: "By deliberate choice he has made himself a romanticist."[84] Here, then, for Wilde the spirit of Romanticism

77. "The Decay of Lying," in *Criticism*, ed. Guy, 4:92–93.

78. "The Decay of Lying," in *Criticism*, ed. Guy, 4:92.

79. "The Decay of Lying," in *Criticism*, ed. Guy, 4:92.

80. "The Decay of Lying," in *Criticism*, ed. Guy, 4:92.

81. "The Decay of Lying," in *Criticism*, ed. Guy, 4:92.

82. "La Société française allait être l'historien, je ne devais être que le secrétaire" ("French Society would be the historian; I should only be the secretary"). Honoré de Balzac, "Avant propos," *La comédie humaine* (Paris: Furne, 1842), 14.

83. "The Decay of Lying," in *Criticism*, ed. Guy, 4:82.

84. "The Decay of Lying," in *Criticism*, ed. Guy, 4:82.

is not a temporal quality but rather an aspect of the creative imagination. Further, the imaginative untruths in which art necessarily trades are not in any manner corrupting. Instead, art—as it disobeys viewing reality in the plainest factual terms—becomes the medium through which the historical world might be creatively reinvented. "No great artist," Vivian elaborates later on, "ever sees things as they really are. If he did, he would cease to be an artist."[85]

As a consequence, Vivian urges Cyril—who eventually picks up the drift of Vivian's somewhat Socratic arguments—that the time has come to "revive this old art of Lying."[86] To be sure, there are, as Vivian says, contemptible forms of lying, such as those that support "a monthly salary . . . in Fleet Street," home of the English newspaper industry whose debased journalistic practices in distorting the truth Wilde never ceased to deplore.[87] By stark contrast, however, there is in Vivian's view an unquestionably pure form of lying: "Lying for its own sake"—a statement that resonates with Wilde's longtime espousal of *l'art pour l'art*. The supreme type of lying—the "highest development" of this practice that "is absolutely beyond reproach"—is "Lying in Art."[88] On this view, "Lying" turns its back on crude mimesis, has no truck with vulgar "Realism," and never once returns to "Life and Nature."[89] In many ways, such elevated "Lying" brings "Romance" back to the world, just as it sets "Romanticism"—as Vivian conclusively remarks—"in front of Life."[90] By this late point in Wilde's dialogue, it has become patently clear that when "Lying" shapes the highest imaginative endeavors, "Facts will be regarded as discreditable" and "Truth will be found mourning over her fetters."[91]

Echoes from the "Chatterton" notebook are plain in Wilde's essay. First, in "The Decay of Lying" the Romantic spirit connects with the artistry of the lie, a conception likely informed by Chatterton's influence. The poet's creation of Rowley was the height of lying for the sake of art, at least from the perspective of Watts, Wilde, and other believers. Nonbelievers such as Walpole, or those who fail to recognize the imaginative power of the Rowley poems, must rely on very different (and inferior) definitions of creativity or artistry. In his notebook, Wilde dwells on Chatterton's encounter with Walpole more than other episodes in the young man's life, and much of this content is recorded in Wilde's hand. Walpole at first warmly embraced Chatterton's beseeching offer

85. "The Decay of Lying," in *Criticism*, ed. Guy, 4:97.
86. "The Decay of Lying," in *Criticism*, ed. Guy, 4:100.
87. "The Decay of Lying," in *Criticism*, ed. Guy, 4:101.
88. "The Decay of Lying," in *Criticism*, ed. Guy, 4:101.
89. "The Decay of Lying," in *Criticism*, ed. Guy, 4:102.
90. "The Decay of Lying," in *Criticism*, ed. Guy, 4:101, 102.
91. "The Decay of Lying," in *Criticism*, ed. Guy, 4:101.

of Rowley's poetry; it was not until the older author had, as Wilde records, "sub-mitted the Rowley | poems to some of his friends | who were doubtful of their | authenticity" (Appendix A, f.50^r [382]) that this potential patron harshly rescinded his offer of help. This fact checking, then, appears to have overruled Walpole's initial response to Rowley's poetry. Walpole's behavior provoked, as we note in chapter 1, extensive debate in the decades following Chatterton's death. Wilde, in light of Daniel Wilson's study, turned again to Coleridge for a poetic assessment: "O ye who honour the | name of man rejoice | that this Walpole is | called a Lord" (f.51^v [383]), Coleridge wrote to Cottle, with seething sarcasm.[92] If Walpole had failed to recognize the value of Chatterton's verse, or let historical fact curb his enthusiasm for the young poet, Wilde joined Watts in offering a powerful corrective. Later in the notebook, in an adaptation of Watts's phrases, Wilde observes that even if "Chatterton | may not have had the moral | conscience which is Truth to Fact— | . . . he had the artistic conscience | which is truth to Beauty" (f.75^r [403]). Such a conscience, which embraced forgery, created the "pure artist" (f.75^r [403]), leaving "truth to Fact" no match for "truth to Beauty."

It is noticeable, too, that after Wilde has pasted a clipping from Wilson's *Chatterton* that discusses the young poet's impulse to rush into composition after "prolonged reveries," he inserts in the margin—in a large bold hand—the name "Plato" (f.8^r [341]). As we suggest in chapter 4, this reference may well refer to Socrates's accounts of different types of poetic rhapsody. Yet it is also worth bearing in mind that Vivian informs Cyril: "Lying and poetry are arts— arts, as Plato saw, not unconnected with each other—and they require the most careful study, the most disinterested devotion."[93] Vivian's point resonates with the tenth book of Plato's *Republic* where we encounter the lesson that the interlocutor has learned from Socrates's teaching: "The imitator or maker of the image knows nothing of true existence; he knows appearances only."[94] Such instructive wisdom imparts the knowledge that stands at the core of both the "Chatterton" notebook and "The Decay of Lying": namely, that the greatest art emerges not from the truthful recordation of reality but in representational deceptions, fabrications, and fictions. In the case of the Bristol poet, such artistic

92. From the unpublished prefatory note to "Monody on the Death of Chatterton." See Cottle, *Early Recollections: Chiefly Relating to the Late Samuel Taylor Coleridge, during His Long Residence in Bristol*, 2 vols. (London: Longman, Rees, 1837), 1:35–36. Cf. Daniel Wilson, *Chatterton: A Biographical Study* (London: Macmillan, 1869), 185.

93. "The Decay of Lying," in *Criticism*, ed. Guy, 4:76.

94. Plato, *The Republic*, in *The Dialogues of Plato, Translated into English with Analyses and Introductions*, ed. B[enjamin] Jowett, 2nd ed., 5 vols. (Oxford: Clarendon Press, 1875), 3:496.

fictions and literary forgeries took the powers of Plato's understanding of the imitative arts to their creative apogee.

"ALL OTHERS ARE COUNTERFEITE": WILDE'S SHORT FICTION

If "The Decay of Lying" is the apotheosis of Wilde's prose criticism, its treatment of the significance of lying illuminates his fiction of the period, in which traces of Chatterton's legend can certainly be found. Beginning in the spring of 1887, Wilde published a series of short stories, his first forays into fiction, which would culminate in 1891 with the single-volume edition of his only novel, *The Picture of Dorian Gray*. Even "The Happy Prince," the titular tale of Wilde's 1888 collection of fairy stories, recalls elements of Wilde's researches into Chatterton's career: the Prince—who happens to be the once gorgeously bejeweled and gilded statue of a young boy—stands high atop a column overlooking a town, until the mayor orders the statue be pulled down because of its shabby appearance (Figure 11). Such destruction echoes the removal of the towering Bristol memorial to Chatterton, with its small statue of the standing boy-poet placed on a high column (see Figure 9 [106]), which occurred at the behest of the city's disapproving rector. Further, the Prince's physical shabbiness has arisen from his generosity; in one of several episodes that reveal his self-sacrificing kindness, he orders a migrating swallow to strip the statue's shell of its gems and gold leaf and to give the riches to the townspeople in great need. Among the recipients of one jewel is a starving writer, a "young man in a garret."[95] The Prince describes his vision of this struggling artist: "He is leaning over a desk covered with papers, and in a tumbler by his side there is a bunch of withered violets. His hair is brown and crisp, and his lips are red as a pomegranate, and he has large and dreamy eyes. He is trying to finish a play for the Director of the Theatre, but he is too cold to write any more. There is no fire in the grate, and hunger has made him faint."[96] In the fable, the Prince's intervention saves the impoverished young writer from misery in his attic, and the writer's first response to the surprise gift suggests that his resemblance to Chatterton extends

95. "The Happy Prince," in *The Happy Prince, and Other Tales* (London: David Nutt, 1888), reprinted in *The Collected Works of Oscar Wilde*, ed. Robert Ross, 14 vols. (London: Methuen, 1908), 10:175.

96. "The Happy Prince," in *Collected Works*, 10:176. Geoff Dibb cites this quotation and notes the similarity between the "young man in a garret" and Chatterton. *Oscar Wilde, a Vagabond with a Mission: The Story of Wilde's Lecture Tours of Britain and Ireland* (London: Oscar Wilde Society, 2013), 212.

beyond lodging and poverty: "'I am beginning to be appreciated,' he cried; 'this is from some great admirer. Now I can finish my play.'"[97] A lack of appreciation, it seems, weighed heavier on the writer's mind than hunger or cold. Despite having rescued art in addition to life, the Prince is ruthlessly cast aside by the citizenry once he has given away his riches. Yet, at the end of the story, he is elevated to heaven. In this way, "The Happy Prince" rewrites with fairy-tale simplicity the role of Walpole (as failed patron) and Chatterton (as doomed poet), thus reminding readers of the importance of both artistic creation and the support of that creation. Further, by invoking Chattertonian figures in both the benefactor (as the small statue atop a column) and the artist (as a writer starving in a garret), Wilde subtly reinscribes Chatterton within a genealogy of artistic donors and recipients, each requiring the other.

The short fiction that Wilde wrote for adults during this period similarly touches on the themes that animated his research on Chatterton, especially characters and scenes from the young Bristol poet's career. The first of these stories to be published was "The Canterville Ghost," which appeared in Alsager Vian's fashionable *Court and Society Review* in February 1887, three months after Wilde delivered his lecture on Chatterton at the Birkbeck Institution. The same publication, which included fiction by Robert Louis Stevenson and George Moore, ran "Lord Arthur Savile's Crime: A Story of Cheiromancy" over the course of three issues in May that year. Also appearing in May 1887 was "Lady Alroy," later retitled "The Sphinx without a Secret," which Edmund Yates published in *World* (the same magazine that carried Wilde's epistolary feud with Whistler). The following month, *World* ran another of Wilde's stories, "The Model Millionaire." Uniting this group of works is a marked interest in the relationship between appearance and actuality, between artifice and sincerity, between the authentic and the counterfeit. Wilde collected all of these ingenious works of short fiction in *Lord Arthur's Savile's Crime and Other Stories*, which the new but short-lived publisher Osgood, McIlvaine issued in 1891.[98] They remain some of Wilde's most critically neglected works.

In the longest of these stories, "The Canterville Ghost"—itself a curious blend of lively satire and high Gothic sentiment—a centuries-old phantom is thwarted in his repeated attempts to spook the nouveau riche Americans who

---

97. "The Happy Prince," in *Collected Works*, 10:177.

98. The 1891 volume contains some noteworthy revisions to the stories. In "The Canterville Ghost," for example, Wilde added the subtitle "A Hylo-Idealistic Romance"; see Josephine M. Guy, "An Allusion in Oscar Wilde's 'The Canterville Ghost,'" *Notes and Queries* 45, no. 2 (1998): 224.

Figure 11. Walter Crane, illustration for "The Happy Prince" from Oscar
Wilde, *The Happy Prince and Other Tales* (London: David Nutt, 1888),
frontispiece. Image courtesy of William Andrews Clark Memorial Library,
University of California, Los Angeles. PR5818. H251 1888a.

have just taken possession of Canterville Chase, an ancestral English home.
Not only is the ghost a sad representation of his former self (condemned to
starve in a hidden room in the manor by the brothers of his wife, whom he
murdered in 1575), but his role within the house is purely one of embarrassingly
creaking performances. Through his clumsy theatrics, the ghost adopts over-
wrought characters (such as "Jonas the Graveless, or the Corpse-Snatcher of
Chertsey Barn" and "Reckless Rupert, or the Headless Earl") to try to scare the

American Otis family with the same old tricks that he had successfully used for generations. Alas, the recently installed Americans are quite canny themselves at playing their own newfound roles in the household, and they call the ghost's bluff by offering disarmingly practical advice to him—on how, for example, best to oil his clanking chains so as not to disturb their peace—and creating more convincing apparitions than the ghost himself ever could muster. When the Canterville Ghost encounters what he believes to be another apparition, he slinks off to his room in terror: "Never having seen a ghost before, he naturally was terribly frightened."[99] But in the light of day, he realizes that what he saw was not a phantom at all, only a bed curtain that the two Otis boys had rigged to look like a specter. In the story's most overt echo of Chatterton's fanciful fifteenth-century orthography, the Otis boys adorn their scarecrow ghost with a placard quaintly addressed to "Ye Olde Ghoste"; their cheeky script looks and sounds like "Rowleyese": "Ᵽe Onſie True anð Originaſe Spook. / Beware of Ᵽe Imᵼ itationes. / Aſſ otḥers are Counterfeite."[100] Here, then, a group of young, uncouth Americans have forged a peculiarly archaic English in order to fool a ghost who has haunted the Chase for hundreds of years.

Yet not all of the Otises treat the Canterville Ghost in a belittling manner. Toward the end of the tale, one of their much kinder offspring has the resource-fulness to manipulate the past so that the miserable ghost is freed from the ancient curse that has imprisoned him in this ancestral pile. Virginia, the charming fif-teen-year-old Otis daughter, accurately deciphers an old-fashioned six-line poem that is (somewhat in the style of a Rowley manuscript on vellum) "painted in curious black letters" on the library wall and proves "difficult to read."[101] She also prompts the ghost to tell her his story and agrees to travel with him to the site of his death, venturing into unknown times of yore. Together, she and the phantom slip back to an era that remains teasingly inscrutable to the reader. Yet one thing is sure on her return to the present. She has achieved a magical and rewarding transformation. In exchange for her willingness to enter quite literally into the spirit of this ancestral past and then eliminate the curse, Virginia finally receives the gratitude of the ghost, the Canterville jewels, a husband and title, and the praise of Wilde's approving narrator. In many ways, Virginia's ultimate fortune stems from her adept creative skills in projecting herself into a distant history that obviously belongs to the spellbinding world, not of dull authentic facts but

99. Wilde, "The Canterville Ghost," *Court and Society Review* 4, no. 138 (February 1887): 183–86, no. 139 (March 1887): 207–11; in *Collected Works*, 7:88.

100. "The Canterville Ghost," in *Collected Works*, 7:88.

101. "The Canterville Ghost," in *Collected Works*, 7:103.

of supernatural fiction. She demonstrates the imaginative capacity to rewrite history, in a manner that bears some resemblance to the talented forger who can refashion the historical record and create in turn beauty out of misery.

What is unusual about Virginia's imaginative flair for interpreting ancient texts and showing such sympathy with the ancient past, however, is that it stems from her assertive femininity. It does not take much to see that "The Canterville Ghost" brings together two important strands of Wilde's thought in the late 1880s. On the one hand, Virginia's imaginative correction of the patriarchal sins of the past speaks to the art of forgery. On the other hand, it also articulates a current of feminism that was becoming increasingly prominent in areas of Wilde's works. Not surprisingly, critics have largely understood "The Canterville Ghost" in light of Wilde's sustained efforts to put pressure on normative gender roles; he was, as Maureen O'Connor observes, undertaking the editorship of *The Lady's World* around this time, which he transformed in name to *The Woman's World*: a decisive change, which the novelist Dinah Mulock Craik recommended, that aimed to emphasize the political seriousness of this new editorial venture.[102] To support her point, O'Connor seizes upon one of the ghost's comments to show Wilde's shrewd sexual-political critique. When young Virginia points out that the ghost is cursed to haunt the manor because he murdered his wife, he scoffs in reply: "Well, I quite admit it . . . but it was a purely family matter, and concerned no one else."[103] Similarly, when Virginia chides him with her "sweet Puritan gravity," he doubles down: "My wife was very plain, never had my ruffs properly starched, and knew nothing about cookery."[104] O'Connor regards these comments as the ghost's attempt to establish "an equivalence between sex and cooking. . . . Lacking physical or domestic attractions, her existence was negligible."[105] She argues that "the unconscious-seeming ease with which wife-murder can facilitate comedy is an oblique yet devastating indictment."[106] To be sure, this is true. But it is also worth bearing in mind that the ghost's remarks wickedly evoke some of the best-known phrases of Thomas Griffiths Wainewright, whose cruel quip ascribing the murder of his sister-in-law to her ugly ankles proved such a durable punch line.

102. Maureen O'Connor, "The Spectre of Genre in 'The Canterville Ghost,'" *Irish Studies Review* 12, no. 3 (2004): 329–38. Ellmann remarks that Craik, who contributed to the new journal shortly before her death, advised Wilde to change the title to *The Woman's World* (*Oscar Wilde*, 292).

103. "The Canterville Ghost," in *Collected Works*, 7:99.

104. "The Canterville Ghost," in *Collected Works*, 7:99–100.

105. O'Connor, "The Spectre of Genre," 334.

106. O'Connor, "The Spectre of Genre," 334–35.

The droll humor of "The Canterville Ghost" arises in part from the ghost's unapologetic levity when he recounts his many grisly conquests: the murders, suicides, and madness that his age-old haunting has inspired. Further, the mordant wit derives from the detached conscientiousness that he brings to his many roles: the "Headless Earl" might require an "extremely difficult 'make up,'" but his artistry demands it.[107] In "The Canterville Ghost," then, there are glimpses of Chatterton's forgery, with the young upstart Americans' fooling the English old guard, as well as Virginia's imaginative ability to enter into and reframe the historical record. Moreover, the story reminds us of those questions about the pressing distinction between aesthetic and ethical concerns that Wilde unravels in his treatment of Wainewright's impeccable wrongdoings.

Both of these themes are revisited in "Lord Arthur Savile's Crime," this time rendered through the idiom of palmistry, another contemporary fad that had a prominent performative element that laid it open to accusations of fraud. This fairly novel pseudo-science, whose modern origins derive from Captain Casimir Stanislas D'Arpentigny's *La chirognomie* (1839), taught techniques that interpreted the inevitability of one's personality and destiny as manifest on the body. Cheiromancy, one of the favored 1880s terms for this type of inquiry into the promises written on the palm, was certainly on Wilde's mind at the time he gave his Chatterton lecture at the Birkbeck Institution. Wilde was friendly with a leading cheiromantist Edward Heron-Allen, whose immensely popular *Manual on Cheirosophy* (1885) showed his prodigious skills as a polymath who was equally at home in classical literature, the history of physiognomy, and Herbert Spencer's sociology.[108] Both men belonged to the Sette of Odd Volumes, an all-male antiquarians' and bibliophiles' club based in London, which began in 1878. This club, whose most active early "brothers" included the publisher and bookseller Bernard Quaritch, issued its quaintly styled pamphlet-length "opuscula" on a regular basis, and on occasion the members reveled in furnishing eccentric, somewhat Chattertonian, titles for their ventures into the more obscure reaches of erudition.

Heron-Allen's earliest contribution to what became a canon of almost two

---

107. "The Canterville Ghost," *Collected Works*, 7:92.

108. In addition to his expertise in cheiromancy, Heron-Allen was an accomplished translator of poetry; he completed a new edition of Omar Khayyám's *Rubáiyat* in 1898. The full title is *A Manual of Cheirosophy: Being a Complete Practical Handbook of the Twin Sciences of Cheirognomy and Cheiromancy, by Means Whereof the Past, the Present, and the Future May Be Read In the Formations of the Hands, Preceded by an Introductory Argument Upon The Science of Cheirosophy and Its Claims To Rank as a Physical Science*, 10th ed. (London: Ward, Lock, 1885).

hundred works that appeared through the 1930s was the forerunner of his widely circulated 1885 *Manual*. It bears a title and author's name that look as if they have been gleaned from one of the sources that Chatterton invented for the imaginary Rowley: *Codex Chiromantiae: Being a Compleate Manualle of ye Science and Arte of Expoundynge ye past, ye Presente, ye Future, and ye Charactere, by ye Scrutinie of ye Hande, ye Gestures thereof, and ye Chirographie*, by Bro[the]r. Ed[ward]. Heron-Allen, Necromance unto ye Sette of Odd Volumes, author of "A lyttel boke of Chyromancie" and Joint Author of "Chiromancy or the Science of Palmistry"—*Codicillus I, Chirognomy*. To add further scholarly distinction to this short but informative study, Heron-Allen proceeded to publish two further "opuscula" to accompany *Codex Chiromantiae: Appendix A, Dactylomancy, or, Finger-ring Magic, Ancient, Mediaeval, and Modern* (1883); and *Appendix B, A Discourse Concerning Autographs and Their Significations* (1886).[109] Heron-Allen enjoyed growing celebrity for his handbooks on palmistry. He undertook a lecture tour of the United States, where he introduced his brand of "cheiromancy." Wilde used this opportunity to ask Heron-Allen to offer "Lord Arthur Savile's Crime" to a newspaper syndicator in Philadelphia.[110]

Their friendship became clear in Heron-Allen's drawing of Wilde's palm that appeared in the New York *Daily Graphic* only weeks before the Chatterton lecture. In this feature, Heron-Allen provides his assessment of Wilde's hand by calling it "peculiar" before noting that its size indicates "a keen analytical power," while its lines mark his "extraordinary brain power and profound scholarship" as well as his "great power of expression."[111] Although palmistry appealed to many people who wished to understand (as the elaborate subtitle of Heron-Allen's *Manual* puts it) "the past, the present, and the future" of their unfolding lives, there was clearly an interest in what its techniques might reveal

109. Heron-Allen makes a friendly remark about Oscar Wilde, in connection with collecting handkerchiefs, as well as a comment on Wilde's upright style in writing the capital letters *I* and *H*, which for Heron-Allen displays "a higher and more precise nature to the artistic intellect, and increases the poetic faculty" (in *Codex Cheiromantiae: Appendix B, A Discourse Concerning Autographs and Their Significations* [London: Sette of Odd Volumes, 1886], 12, 34).

110. See Wilde, "To Edward Heron-Allen," 17 October 1887, *Complete Letters*, 328. The connection between Wilde and Heron-Allen would be reinforced when *Lippincott's* ran an article by Heron-Allen on cheiromancy in the same issue as *The Picture of Dorian Gray*: "The Cheiromancy of To-Day: The Evolution of an Occult Science," *Lippincott's Monthly Magazine* 46, no. 271 (July 1890): 102–11.

111. [Anon.,] "Hand Reading," *Daily Graphic*, 17 November 1886: 124–25; reprinted in Joan Navarre, "Oscar Wilde, Edward Heron-Allen, and the Palmistry Craze of the 1880s," *English Literature in Transition, 1880–1920* 54, no. 2 (2011): 177–79.

about exceptional or unique individuals such as Wilde. At the same time, however, the American press readily equated "cheiromancy" with the kinds of charlatanism that had made Wilde a repeated figure of fun during his North American lecture tour, when he sought to bring aestheticism to the ignorant masses. One dismissive American newspaper announced that the arrival of spurious palmistry signaled the welcome death of aestheticism (and with it, the voice of Wilde): "Æstheticism has died quietly away, and the voice of Oscar Wilde is no more heard in the land. Languishing and sighing over sunflowers, and the slow rolling of eyes over dreadfully crude pictures, are no longer fashionable. 'Too too utterly utter,' as a pet phrase has followed 'quite too awfully awful' to partial oblivion. Society is crazy over art no longer, but has taken to palmistry. Those young persons who dressed in a curious fashion, and threw themselves into elaborate postures, and seemed terribly sad all the live-long day, now take their friends into the shadow of the window curtains and read their fortunes."[112] Happily for Wilde, his voice was irrepressible, since he readily devised an ingenious plot from this fad.

"Lord Arthur Savile's Crime" features the inelegantly named Mr. Podgers ("pet cheiromantist" to Lady Windermere), who reads the palm of her nephew, Lord Arthur Savile. In Savile's hand, a deeply troubled Podgers foresees the inevitable crime of murder. Not wanting to sully his pending wedding or the honor of his fiancée, Savile chooses to forestall marriage to the woman he loves, believing he must perpetrate the crime that Podgers suggests he will inevitably commit. Savile's duty, framed in this way, becomes, not avoiding homicide, but instead carrying out a murder as quickly and with as few repercussions as possible: "Life to him," Wilde's narrator writes, "meant action, rather than thought."[113] In this ingenious story, avoiding the expression of his personality (as recorded in his palm) is thus not an option; murder is not an impediment to Lord Savile's personality—it is merely a momentary obstacle to wedded bliss. In some respects, his predicament reminds us of Theodore Watts's memorable account of Chatterton's hunger for forgery. If, Wilde's story suggests, murder is the only way for Savile to achieve the happily married life he hopes for, then he "needs must forge" the atrocity of murder.

Equating eventual happiness with inevitable murder generates some of the biting humor of the piece, as does Savile's ineptitude, when his earnest attempts to doff family members (by poison and then by bomb) fail to work. When Savile

112. "A New Society Craze," *The Shields Daily Gazette*, 18 September 1886: 4.

113. Wilde, "Lord Arthur Savile's Crime," *Court and Society Review* 4, no. 149 (11 May 1887): 447–50; 4, no. 150 (18 May 1887): 471–73; 4, no. 151 (25 May 1887): 495–97; in *Collected Works*, 7:28.

finally does fulfill the promise written in his hand by surreptitiously flinging Podgers into the Thames (an act that officials deem to be suicide), he also realizes the promise of the narrative, with a tidy Wildean twist. Although Lady Windermere concludes by the story's end that Podgers was a fraud, his death ensures that, at least in one reading, the cheiromantist's inauthentic art still had the prophetic power this pseudo-science professed. In other words, Podgers's fraudulent palmistry inspires in Lord Arthur criminal actions that result—so far as his marital prospects are concerned—in perfect happiness.

When Wilde included "Lord Arthur Savile's Crime" in his 1891 volume of short fiction, he noticeably revised the story's subtitle from "A Study in Cheiromancy" to "A Study in Duty." This important shift is of a piece with the ideas about forgery that Wilde had developed between 1887 and 1891. As Joan Navarre notes, "an ancient axiom informs all studies of cheiromancy: 'Know Thyself.'"[114] If one understands the study of the lines of the hand as an indicator of one's identity, then the revision of "cheiromancy" to "duty" reflects a transition from divination or study to obligation or action. It is a shift Wilde discusses overtly—if not in relation to palmistry—in his 1891 essay "The Soul of Man under Socialism." There, in describing his utopian vision, he similarly argues for a transformation of knowledge into existence or action: "'Know thyself' was written over the portal of the antique world. Over the portal of the new world, 'Be thyself' shall be written."[115]

The other two short stories from 1887—"The Model Millionaire" and "The Sphinx without a Secret"—are slighter, yet they share with "The Canterville Ghost" and "Lord Arthur Savile's Crime" an interest in the performance of one's duty and in the power of false representations. In the first, a wealthy aristocrat poses as a beggar and rewards the generosity of a man who offers him charity. In the second, a man falls in love with a woman who seems to have a hidden secret life but may in fact be only acting as if she did. It is no wonder that Wilde's work drew comparison with Stevenson's novella *Strange Case of Dr. Jekyll and Mr. Hyde*, which was published in early 1886.[116] But Wilde's

114. Navarre, "Oscar Wilde, Edward Heron-Allen, and the Palmistry Craze of the 1880s," 175. Heron-Allen gives pride of place to the Greek tag ΓΝΩΘΙ ΣΕΑΤΟΝ ("Know Thyself") in *A Manual of Cheirosophy*, 79.

115. Wilde, "The Soul of Man under Socialism," *Fortnightly Review* n.s. 49 (February 1891): 292–319, in *Criticism*, ed. Guy, 4:240.

116. William Sharp wrote about "Lord Arthur Savile's Crime" upon its publication in 1891: "This story is an attempt to follow in the footsteps of the author of *New Arabian Nights*. Unfortunately for Mr. Wilde's ambition, Mr. Stevenson is a literary artist of rare originality. Such a story as this is nothing if not wrought with scrupulous delicacy of touch. It is, unfortunately, dull as well as derivative" ("New Novels," *Academy*, 5 September 1891: 194). *The Picture of Dorian Gray* drew similar responses.

fascination with the blurring between action and personality was less grounded in the supernatural or in the psychical than Stevenson's disturbing narrative of dual identities and random homicide. Instead, his fiction was vested in the defiant inventiveness of the artistic consciousness, which sometimes could go to extreme lengths to conjure historical possibilities that had no basis in reality. This powerful instinct to disconnect the artistic impulse from moral duty in the name of taking actions that can realize one's independent vision gains its fullest expression in the remarkable story about forgery that Wilde placed in *Blackwood's Edinburgh Magazine:* "The Portrait of Mr. W.H."

6

FORGING LITERARY HISTORY: "THE PORTRAIT OF MR. W.H."

Without question, it is in Wilde's most ingenious short fiction, "The Portrait of Mr. W.H.," that his fascination with Chatterton's foundational role in the history of literary forgery reaches its summit. This brilliant, deeply learned story engages with the enduringly fraught critical debates that stemmed from the late eighteenth century about the mysterious identity of the individual mentioned in the cryptic initials of the dedication to the 1609 edition of Shakespeare's Sonnets: "TO. THE. ONLIE. BEGETTER. OF. | THESE. INSVING. SONNETS. | Mʳ. W.H." Much of Wilde's finely researched narrative pivots on the perilous consequences of a young man's obsessive desire to prove that "W.H." stands for the initials of "Willie Hughes": "the boy-actor of Shakespeare's plays."[1] Significantly, the theory of Willie Hughes was not in any way new when Wilde composed his tale, though it was hardly central to the wide-ranging discussion of this contentious topic among Victorian Shakespeare scholars. Although "The Portrait" never reveals the fact, the view that "W.H." indicated a young male actor named Will Hughes—as we explain in further detail below—originated with two individuals who were deeply involved in proving the inauthenticity of the Rowley poems. Thomas Tyrwhitt and Edmond Malone, who found much to admire in Chatterton's inventiveness, were the first scholars of Shakespeare to venture the sexually controversial and historically questionable idea that these initials belonged the Bard's young male object of passionate desire.

One of the major turning points in Wilde's story occurs with the death of Cyril Graham—the young man obsessed with proving that "W.H." was Willie Hughes—who commits suicide upon the exposure of his quite plausible forgery

1. Wilde, "The Portrait of Mr. W.H.," in *The Soul of Man under Socialism and Selected Critical Prose*, ed. Linda Dowling (Harmondsworth: Penguin Books, 2001), 41.

of a portrait of the beloved "Mr. W.H." Importantly, even though Chatterton's name appears only twice in the narrative, this act of self-murder alone suggests that the contours of the young Bristol poet's career powerfully shape aspects of Wilde's "Portrait." More to the point, Chatterton's crucial role in the history of literary forgery from the 1760s onward informs many sections of the tale. "The Portrait of Mr. W.H." offers a critical perspective on the powerful force that Chatterton's legacy exerted on the enduring controversies surrounding the series of significant Shakespeare forgeries that developed from the 1790s, perpetuated by the likes of William-Henry Ireland and John Payne Collier. Time and again, these scandals harshly divided the various believers and unbelievers in these numerous spurious documents, ones that repeatedly underwent painstaking scholarly scrutiny.

In order to dramatize the extraordinary presence that the history of literary forgery maintains in this story, in "The Portrait of Mr. W.H." Wilde invents an engaging narrator who excels at becoming just the kind of "liar" who uses fiction to substantiate the belief that the "artistic conscience" is related to the noble pursuit of equating—as he states in the "Chatterton" notebook—"truth to Beauty" and nothing else (Appendix A, f.75^r [403]). In other words, this narrative voice puts into fictional practice what Vivian in "The Decay of Lying" outlines theoretically. This ingenious short fiction fuses two strains of thought that Wilde brings to the fore in the outstanding essays he produced after completing his extensive research in the "Chatterton" notebook: it combines the criminal impulse that fuels creativity in "Pen, Pencil and Poison" with the esteemed acts of fabricating the truth that Vivian lauds in "The Decay of Lying." Further, Wilde's "Portrait" marks a concerted return to the subject of Shakespeare, whose writings he had initially explored at length in the first long essay he published in a major journal, "Shakespeare and Stage Costume," which originally appeared in the prestigious *Nineteenth Century* in May 1885. Later collected as "The Truth of Masks" in *Intentions* (1891), this essay reveals the extent of Wilde's early engagement with the trend toward archaeological stage design that enjoyed such vogue in many later Victorian productions of Shakespeare's works as well as modern plays on ancient subjects. Yet Wilde's "Portrait" diverges from this earlier endorsement of the archaeological reconstruction of the historical past in his contemporaries' theatrical productions. Whereas the 1885 essay focuses attention on the crucial role that archaeology—the excavation of historical truths—plays in grounding an appreciation of Shakespeare's world, "The Portrait" challenges the very notion of empirical, historical truths by exposing the intense desire and psychical investment that underscores our apperception of works of art.

LITERARY FORGERY CONTRA ARCHAEOLOGICAL HISTORY

Wilde's discovery of Chatterton helps explain a noticeable transformation that took place in his thinking during the 1880s about the artistic representation of the past, a transformation that is evident in Wilde's transition away from the commitment to archaeological accuracy that he articulated in "Shakespeare and Stage Costume." An informative essay that shows Wilde's deep acquaintance with the London theater during this decade, "Shakespeare and Stage Costume" closely examines the antiquarian impulse evident in current productions of Shakespeare's plays, as well as in very recent historical dramas, such as W. G. Wills's *Claudian* (1883). At its best, Wilde maintains, such archaeology "enables us to see a Greek dressed like a Greek, and an Italian like an Italian."[2] Precise attention to period detail, he contends, spares us the "stifling atmosphere of anachronisms" in which our "inartistic grandfathers" dwelt complacently.[3] Wilde maintains that great stage designers, such as his friend E. W. Godwin ("one of the most artistic spirits of this century in England"), have ensured that audiences no longer endure witnessing "Lady Macbeth in a large crinoline."[4] At the same time, Wilde scarcely wants this kind of historical authenticity to become didactic. He insists that alertness to period specificity in the theater should never indulge in "priggish pedantry," such as one might find in a "dreary lecture and a set of grimy casts."[5] Instead, he asserts that the evocation of past cultures in a dramatic setting will only become "really delightful when transfused into some form of art."[6] The finest archaeology thus evinces the artistic spirit when it departs from "mere science for the antiquarian"; in the early modern period when workmen dug up Roman sarcophagi, their findings provided their culture with "a means by which they could touch the dry dust of antiquity into the very breath and beauty of life."[7] The value of such "archaeology," Wilde proceeds to add, therefore "depends entirely on how it is used, and only an artist can use it."[8] Godwin, for Wilde, is indubitably the supreme exponent of the ways that

2. Wilde, "The Truth of Masks," in *Criticism: Historical Criticism, Intentions, The Soul of Man*, ed. Josephine M. Guy, *The Complete Works of Oscar Wilde*, 7 vols. to date (Oxford: Oxford University Press, 2000 and continuing), 4:218. "The Truth of Masks" is a revised version of "Shakespeare and Stage Costume," *Nineteenth Century* 17 (1885): 800–818. We note below any relevant changes between the 1885 and 1891 texts.

3. "The Truth of Masks," in *Criticism*, ed. Guy, 4:218.

4. "The Truth of Masks," in *Criticism*, ed. Guy, 4:216, 218.

5. "The Truth of Masks," in *Criticism*, ed. Guy, 4:216.

6. "The Truth of Masks," in *Criticism*, ed. Guy, 4:217.

7. "The Truth of Masks," in *Criticism*, ed. Guy, 4:215.

8. "The Truth of Masks," in *Criticism*, ed. Guy, 4:218.

archaeology can be transformed into distinguished art. The fact that in 1884 Godwin decorated the interior of Wilde's outwardly ordinary-looking home on Tite Street, Chelsea, says much about the close affinities between the two men.

By comparison, "The Portrait of Mr. W.H." shows little interest in upholding the belief that any kind of art might once and for all conjure an entirely convincing aura of archaeological or historical verisimilitude. To the contrary, the story exposes the frantic desires that can impel individuals to go to extraordinary lengths to fabricate the past, often through their compulsion to excavate any evidence that will suit their obsessive purposes. This fanatical impulse, as we discover very early in the story, characterizes the phenomenon of literary forgery, and this fascination with faking historical documents, we maintain, stems from Wilde's sustained engagement with Chatterton. It is not unreasonable to assert that Wilde's inquiries into the career of the "marvellous Boy" enabled him to make a decisive break with the literal-minded kinds of truth claims that scholars often associated with archaeological discoveries. As Iain Ross reminds us, this was the era when Heinrich Schliemann's excavations at Mykenai and Hissarlik aimed to divulge the literal reality of the *Iliad*. Such objectives became prominent in Wilde's classical education, especially when he was under the tutelage of J. P. Mahaffy at Trinity College Dublin during the early 1870s. Not only did Wilde take an archaeological tour of Greece with Mahaffy in April 1877; from 1879 to 1885, Wilde also subscribed to the Hellenic Society, known for its archaeological reports. Until the period just after "Shakespeare and Stage Costume" first appeared, Wilde—as Ross helpfully observes—used his time as a reviewer to "give judicious approval to archaeologically informed productions" on the stage.[9]

One of Wilde's later reviews evinces the reasons why he eventually abandoned archaeological claims on historical veracity. By 1888, in the last piece he ever wrote on the topic, Wilde turned to archaeology not so much for the "absolutely scientific demonstration" of the past it could provide, as for the "kind of artistic instinct" that evoked in him a "real romantic interest."[10] In his thoughtful reflections on W. J. Stillman's *On the Track of Ulysses* (1888), Wilde finds himself enchanted by this American author's imaginative theory that the Venus of Melos (the "marble mutilated goddess whom Gautier loved, to whom

9. Iain Ross, *Oscar Wilde and Ancient Greece* (Cambridge: Cambridge University Press, 2012), 100.

10. [Wilde,] "Venus or Victory?" *Pall Mall Gazette*, 24 February 1888: 2–3; in *Journalism Part II*, ed. John Stokes and Mark W. Turner, *The Complete Works of Oscar Wilde*, 7 vols. to date (Oxford: Oxford University Press, 2000 and continuing), 7:70, 68.

Heine bent his knee") is the "Victory without Wings that once stood in the little chapel outside the gates of the Acropolis at Athens."[11] Whether such a theory is correct remains beside the point for Wilde. He made much the same observation in "Pen, Pencil and Poison" when he commented on the dandyish Wainewright's aesthetic tastes: "He saw that in decorating a room, which is to be, not a room for show, but a room to live in, we should never aim at any archaeological reconstruction of the past, nor burden ourselves with any fanciful necessity for historical accuracy."[12] Slightly later, in "The Critic as Artist" the speaker Gilbert intensifies Wilde's earlier claims on the artistic role that archaeology plays in our living knowledge of the past. Gilbert attributes value not so much in archaeology's empirically accurate recovery of the past (such as we might witness in stage design) as in the inspiring critical capacity the discipline possesses to represent the dynamic coming-into-being of a bygone age (such as we might imagine when there is "no record," since the "history is either lost or was never written"):

> Criticism can re-create the past for us from the very smallest fragment of language or art, just as surely as the man of science can from some tiny bone, or the mere impress of a foot upon a rock, re-create for us the winged dragon or Titan lizard that once made the earth shake beneath its tread, can call Behemoth out of his cave, and make Leviathan swim once more across the startled sea. Prehistoric history belongs to the philological and archaeological critic. It is to him that the origins of things are revealed. The self-conscious deposits of an age are nearly always misleading. Through philological criticism alone we know more of the centuries of which no actual record has been preserved, than we do of the centuries that have left us their scrolls. It can do for us what can be done neither by physics nor metaphysics. It can give us the exact science of mind in the process of becoming. It can do for us what History cannot do.[13]

Such phrasing shows that by the late 1880s, Wilde believed that the active spirit of the archeological critic involved reinventing the dynamic cultural energies of the past in a manner that differed profoundly from the collection of dry facts from calcified, formal records.

11. "Venus or Victory?" in *Journalism Part II*, ed. Stokes and Turner, 7:68.
12. Wilde, "Pen, Pencil and Poison," in *Criticism*, ed. Guy, 4:108. Wilde adds, however, that Wainewright enjoyed such accuracy on the stage: "In everything connected with the stage, for instance, he was always extremely interested, and strongly upheld the necessity for archaeological accuracy in costume and scene-painting" (*Criticism*, ed. Guy, 4:113).
13. Wilde, "The Critic as Artist," in *Criticism*, ed. Guy, 4:201–2.

Arguably, it was Wilde's discovery of Chatterton that provided him at last with the critical understanding that our conceptions of the past are most instructively understood through the kind of "artistic instinct" that generated forgeries as great as the Rowley poems. It is a sign of the distance that Wilde's took from aspects of his 1885 essay "Shakespeare and Stage Costume" that he added a disclaimer when he reprinted it six years later as "The Truth of Masks" in *Intentions.* Toward the very end of his discussion, he offers this volte-face: "Not that I agree with everything I have said in this essay. There is much with which I entirely disagree."[14] By turning now to "The Portrait," we can see that the study of Chatterton's forgeries and the ensuing history of fakes attributed to the Bard enabled Wilde to adopt an approach toward the historical universe that Shakespeare inhabited that was very different from the archaeological one he valued in "Shakespeare and Stage Costume."

This shift was of unquestionable importance to Wilde. He clearly held the intellectual achievement of his "Portrait" in high regard, since he revised the first text that he published so comprehensively that its second version amounted to almost twice its original length. The first version appeared in the largely conservative *Blackwood's Edinburgh Magazine* in July 1889. It seems that Wilde sent it there because he thought the subject would have appeal to a journal that had over the years published several appraisals of the lively critical debates surrounding the identity of the Dark Lady and the "master mistress" of Shakespeare's Sonnets.[15] He drafted the much longer version promptly after *Black-*

14. "The Truth of Masks," in *Criticism*, ed. Guy, 4:228.

15. Wilde submitted his "Portrait" to William Blackwood at *Blackwood's Edinburgh Magazine* in April 1889, and he received an acceptance in the later part of May that year. (It appears that Frank Harris, at the *Fortnightly*, had rejected it.) Blackwood expressed delight in the "playful ingenuity" of the "Shakespearean theory" that Wilde sets forth (*The Complete Letters of Oscar Wilde*, ed. Merlin Holland and Rupert Hart-Davis [London: Fourth Estate, 2000], 398, 400). The Sonnets, as Shakespeare's readers know well, present a male poetic speaker who has two objects of love. The one is the figure critics call the Dark Lady, whom the speaker often associates with the color black (e.g., in Sonnet 127, "my mistress' eyes are therefore raven black"). The other is the poetic voice's male object of desire or veneration, known in Shakespeare's Sonnet 20 as the "master mistress" (*Shakespeare's Sonnets*, ed. Katherine Duncan-Jones, The Arden Shakespeare, 3rd series [London: Thomas Nelson, 1997], 369, 151). In the mid-1880s, *Blackwood's* published anonymously two articles by George Macaulay on the Sonnets, which set forth (somewhat pedantically) the theory that Dante is the so-called "other poet" or "Muse" mentioned in Sonnets 78 to 86 (see *Shakespeare's Sonnets*, 267, 269, 275, 281): "New Views of Shakespeare's Sonnets: The 'Other Poet' Identified," *Blackwood's Edinburgh Magazine* 135 (1884): 727–60; and "New Views of Shakespeare's Sonnets: The 'Other Poet' Identified," *Blackwood's Edinburgh Magazine* 137 (1885): 774–800.

wood's published the first text.[16] The expanded version, which adds considerably more historical information to the narrative, remained—for reasons that we explain below—unpublished in Wilde's lifetime. Our comments focus on the later, much longer text, which finally appeared posthumously in 1921, since this version of the "Portrait" draws more decisively on the "Chatterton" notebook and the post-Chatterton debates about literary forgery than its altogether more succinct predecessor.

TYRWHITT, MALONE, AND "WILLIE HUGHES": THE HISTORY OF A THEORY

At the start of "The Portrait of Mr. W.H.," Wilde's first-person narrator (who never reveals his identity) recalls an enthralling conversation he enjoyed with an after-dinner companion about the "question of literary forgeries."[17] This gentleman recounts the evening when, in phrases that recall Wilde's "Chatterton" notebook, he and his friend George Erskine reflected on three memorable forgers who became infamous in the late eighteenth century: Macpherson, Ireland, and Chatterton. "With regard to the last," the narrator observes, "his so-called forgeries were merely the result of an artistic desire for perfect representation."[18] He proceeds to comment that no one should censure Chatterton for creating brilliant counterfeits, since we cannot "quarrel with an artist for the conditions in which he chooses to present his work."[19] To dispute Chatterton's imaginative gifts on such unsteady grounds, he says, would be "to confuse an ethical with an aesthetical problem."[20] From the narrator's perspective, the point of Chatterton's forgeries is that they prove that "all Art" is "to a certain degree a mode of

16. Wilde described his intention to expand the story in a letter to Blackwood on 10 July 1889 (*Complete Letters*, 407), and Charles Ricketts's *Recollections* records discussions with Wilde that reveal that the revision was well under way by autumn 1889 (*Oscar Wilde: Recollections* [London: Nonesuch Press, 1932], 35–38). See also Horst Schroeder's discussion of the composition history: *Oscar Wilde, The Portrait of Mr. W.H.: Its Composition, Publication and Reception* (Braunschweig: Technische Universität Carolo-Wilhelmina zu Braunschweig, 1984), 22–26.

17. "The Portrait of Mr. W.H.," ed. Dowling, 33.

18. "The Portrait of Mr. W.H.," ed. Dowling, 33. This phrasing echoes Theodore Watts's description of Chatterton's artistic impulse: Chatterton "was so dominated . . . by the artist's yearning to represent, that, if perfect representation seemed to him to demand forgery, he needs must forge"("Thomas Chatterton," in T. Humphry Ward, ed. *The English Poets: Selections with Critical Introductions by Various Writers*, 4 vols. [London: Macmillan, 1880], 3:405). Wilde transcribes these lines in the notebook on f.75^r (Appendix A, 403).

19. "The Portrait of Mr. W.H.," ed. Dowling, 33.

20. "The Portrait of Mr. W.H.," ed. Dowling, 33.

acting, an attempt to realize one's own personality on some imaginative plain out of reach of the trammelling accidents and limitations of real life."[21] Here the echoes of Wilde's notes on Theodore Watts's remarks about Chatterton are especially perceptible: "All great artists | have personality as well as | perfection in their manner" (Appendix A, f.78ʳ [406]). Yet in "The Portrait of Mr. W.H." what is different from the notebook is Wilde's development of an explicit theory of performance—"a mode of acting"—with which to understand the shaping, if not staging, of a beautiful forged identity. Appositely, in order to develop this theory, Wilde focuses attention on the historical world of the theater through the lens of narrative fiction.

The subsequent story transforms into an intriguing discussion that concentrates, not explicitly on Macpherson, Ireland, and Chatterton (though their background presence as forgers remains highly influential), but on the tragic career of Cyril Graham: Erskine's friend who resorted to forgery to prove his belief that "W.H." stood for the initials of Willie Hughes. Even though Wilde informed his editor at *Blackwood's* that his "Portrait" contained "an entirely new view on the subject of the identity of the young man to whom the sonnets are addressed," it was the case that for more than a century the theory Cyril advanced had intermittently arisen in discussion of the Sonnets, although critics had seldom regarded the hypothesis with seriousness.[22] The theory originated with Chatterton's earliest editor, Tyrwhitt, who hazarded to the eminent Shakespeare scholar Malone the view that "W.H." was Will Hughes. And of course it was Malone who had earlier written approvingly of the ingenious boy from Bristol whose Rowley forgeries impressed him. In 1780, when he issued his immensely detailed two-volume critical supplement to Samuel Johnson and George Steevens's 1765 edition of Shakespeare's works, Malone commented:

> Mr. Tyrwhitt has pointed out to me a line in the twentieth Sonnet, which inclines me to think that the initials W.H. stand for W. Hughes. Speaking of this person, the poet says he is—
> "A man in *hew* all *Hews* in his controlling—"
> so the line is exhibited in the old copy. The name *Hughes* was formerly written *Hews*. When it is considered that one of these Sonnets is formed entirely on a play on our authour's Christian name, this conjecture will not appear improbable.—To this person, whoever he was, one hundred and twenty six of

21. "The Portrait of Mr. W.H.," ed. Dowling, 33.

22. Wilde, "To William Blackwood," April 1889, in *Complete Letters*, 398. Later, Wilde suggested to Blackwood that similar wording should be in an advance notice for his story in the *Athenæum*; see "To William Blackwood," c. 12 June 1889, in *Complete Letters*, 402.

the following poems are addressed; the remaining twenty-eight are addressed to a lady.[23]

The suggestion that Shakespeare's desire might be focused on a male object almost immediately generated resistance, as we can witness in later critics' efforts to initiate alternative theories that would return the poet's desire to a heteronormative tradition. One especially loud voice of protest was George Chalmers's, whose 1797 "Apology for the Believers in the Shakspeare Papers" was only the first of many attempts to overturn the Willie Hughes theory. In his exhaustive discussion, Chalmers remarked that Malone appeared ignorant of the basic fact "that Elizabeth was often considered as a man," since writers frequently referred to her as "Prince" (as in the Latin *princeps*), and, in Bacon's case, "a *Prince*, unparalleled among women."[24] As S. Schoenbaum has observed, the absurdity of this approach to the Sonnets deepens when we grasp that Chalmers not only "arrives at the conclusion that in these poems Shakespeare addresses the Queen" but also "urg[es] upon her the duties of marriage and procreation."[25] "That Elizabeth," Schoenbaum observes, "was then in her sixties does not bother Chalmers, who does not pretend to be a biologist."[26] Undeterred, two years later the headstrong Chalmers committed an additional six hundred pages to the wholesale condemnation of Tyrwhitt and Malone, while also indicting Johnson's coeditor Steevens for making the preposterous assumption

23. The bulk of these comments first appeared in [Edmond Malone,] *Supplement to the Edition of Shakspeare's Plays Published in 1778 by Samuel Johnson and George Steevens: Containing Additional Observations, to which Are Subjoined the Genuine Poems of the Same Author, and Seven Plays that Have Been Ascribed to Him; with Notes by the Editor and Others*, 2 vols. (London: C. Bathurst, and Others, 1780), 1:579. The text we have cited appears in *The Plays and Poems of William Shakspeare in Ten Volumes: Collated Verbatim with the most Authentick Copies, and Revised; with the Corrections and Illustrations of Various Commentators; to Which are Added, an Essay on the Chronological Order of His Plays; An Essay Relative to Shakspeare and Jonson; A Dissertation on the Three Parts of King Henry VI; an Historical Account of the English Stage; and Notes by Edmond Malone*, 10 vols. (London: H. Baldwin for J. Rivington and Sons, 1790), 10:191.

24. George Chalmers, *An Apology for the Believers in the Shakspeare-Papers, Which Were Exhibited in Norfolk-Street* (London: Thomas Egerton, 1797), 51–52. Chalmers is referring to Bacon's comments on Elizabeth in "Of the Advancement of Learning" (1695), where Bacon comments: "This Ladie was endued with learning in her sexe singular; and grace even amongst masculine Princes' (*The Two Books of Francis Bacon: Of the Proficience and Advancement of Learning, Divine and Humane* [London: Henrie Tomes, 1605], 1:35ᵛ).

25. S. Schoenbaum, *Shakespeare's Lives*, new ed. (Oxford: Clarendon Press, 1991), 168.

26. Schoenbaum, *Shakespeare's Lives*, 168.

that 126 of Shakespeare's Sonnets were "addressed to a male object."[27] This conclusion had dismayed its own author; Steevens reported that it provoked in him "an equal mixture of disgust and indignation."[28] For Chalmers, such a reaction evinced the "impure minds" that encouraged scholars to promote the idea that Shakespeare may have adored a young man.[29] Chalmers's conclusion—that Shakespeare remains captivated by none other than the princely Elizabeth—might have been an attempt to preclude outraged responses.[30] Yet scholars remained incensed, though for other reasons. In 1837, for instance, the seasoned Shakespeare scholar James Boaden, in a pamphlet dedicated to discovering the true identity of "W.H.," deemed Chalmers's assertions a "monstrous absurdity."[31]

In the meantime, the focus on "W.H." steadily shifted away from the offending idea that this figure was someone as lowly as the hypothetical Will Hughes. Gerald Massey, who had little time for Tyrwhitt and Malone's conjecture, thought Henry Wriothesley, Earl of Southampton—to whom Shakespeare dedicated two of his poems—"was the lord of Shakespeare's love."[32] Edward

27. George Steevens, *Supplement to the Edition of Shakspeare's Plays Published in 1778 by Samuel Johnson and George Steevens*, 2 vols. (London: C. Bathhurst, and Others, 1780), 1:596; quoted in George Chalmers, *A Supplemental Apology for the Believers in the Shakspeare-Papers: Being a Reply to Mr. Malone's Answer, Which Was Early Announced, but Never Published: With a Dedication to George Steevens, F.R.S. S.A. and a Postscript to T. J. Mathias, F.R.S. S.A. the Author of the Pursuits of Literature* (London: Thomas Egerton, 1799), 55.

28. Steevens, *Supplement to the Edition of Shakspeare's Plays Published in 1778*, 1:596.

29. Chalmers, *A Supplemental Apology*, 55, 63.

30. Chalmers, *A Supplemental Apology*, 56.

31. James Boaden, *On the Sonnets of Shakespeare: Identifying the Person to Whom They Are Addressed; and Elucidating Several Points in the Poet's History* (London: Thomas Rodd, 1837), 4. Boaden, after sifting much evidence, concludes: "Shakespeare addressed 126 of these Sonnets to Mr. WILLIAM HERBERT, subsequently third Earl of Pembroke" (34). Boaden does not engage with the Willie Hughes theory. In 1870, Henry Brown agreed that Herbert has the "honour of claiming the friendship of Shakespeare" (*The Sonnets of Shakespeare Solved, and the Mystery of His Friend, Love, and Rivalry Revealed* [London: John Russell Smith, 1870], iii).

32. Gerald Massey, *Shakspeare's Sonnets Never before Interpreted: His Private Friends Identified, together with a Recovered Likeness of Himself* (London: Longmans, Green, 1866), 49. Massey acknowledges but does not find any interest in the Willie Hughes theory (4). Massey reprinted an enlarged version of his commentary in two editions: *The Secret Drama of Shakespeare's Sonnets, with the Characters Identified* (London: privately printed, 1872; London: Kegan Paul, Trench, 1888).

Dowden, in his 1881 edition of the Sonnets, quoted Tyrwhitt and Malone's arguments from Nathan Drake's 1817 study. Dowden also paid little heed to the Willie Hughes theory, since he pointed out that "the Italics and capital letter" for *Hews* "suggested to Tyrwhitt that more is meant here than meets the eye."[33] (As Dowden observes, there are many other nouns, such as "Rose," that take a capital in the 1609 Quarto.) Equally, Charles Mackay cast the Willie Hughes theory aside in an 1884 article; he noted that some writers, whom he describes as "more egregious simpletons" than those arguing for either Southampton or the other likely candidate, William Herbert, 3rd Earl of Pembroke, "imagined . . . that the hero of the Sonnets was one William Hughes, whom nobody had ever heard of at the time, and whom nobody has ever heard of since."[34] By contrast, as Wilde's fictional Erskine makes clear, Cyril Graham contended that no poet "would have dreamed of addressing William Herbert, Earl of Pembroke, as Mr. W.H."[35] Correspondingly, it was simply absurd in Cyril Graham's view to imagine that the Earl of Southampton (who "was not beautiful") required any "entreaties to marry," since this noble "became at a very early age the lover of Elizabeth Vernon."[36] All of this information about the contenders for the real Mr. W.H. makes one point plain. By dismissing Pembroke and Southampton

33. *The Sonnets of William Shakespere*, ed. Edward Dowden (London: Kegan Paul, Trench, 1881), 207.

34. Charles Mackay, "A Tangled Skein Unravelled: On the Mystery of Shakespeare's Sonnets," *Nineteenth Century* 16 (1884): 238–63. Mackay prefers Pembroke as the most likely candidate for "W.H." To this day, Southampton remains one of the two most favored possibilities for "W.H.," not least because Shakespeare dedicated both *Venus and Adonis* (1593) and *The Rape of Lucrece* (1594) to him. Boaden and, before him, James Heywood Bright were the first scholars to advance William Herbert's case in the *Gentleman's Magazine* (1832). Thomas Tyler, who found the earl to be "the one answer of any probability," proved his greatest advocate in the 1880s and 1890s ("Introduction," in *Shakspere's Sonnets: The First Quarto, 1609—A Fac-simile in Photo-Lithography* [London: C. Praetorius, 1886], iv). Shakespeare's 1623 First Folio is dedicated to both William Herbert and his brother Philip. Modern critics continue to debate the identity of "W.H." In the New Arden edition of the Sonnets, Duncan-Jones states: "It is most improbable that [Shakespeare] would have wished the book to be dedicated, sentimentally, to some obscure actor or sea-cook (the mythical 'Willie Hughes'), or a penniless kinsman (his infant nephew William Hart, or his presumed brother-in-law William Hathaway)—least of all to 'William Himself' or 'William [S]h[akespeare]'"; in her view, the main candidate is Herbert (*Shakespeare's Sonnets*, 57).

35. "The Portrait of Mr. W.H.," ed. Dowling, 39.

36. "The Portrait of Mr. W.H.," ed. Dowling, 39.

and harking back to Tyrwhitt's original proposition, Wilde's fictional "Portrait" fearlessly revived what had in its time been a sensitive and questionable polemic.

To be sure, a handful of other late Victorian writers entertained the possibility of Willie Hughes. In the most exhaustive later treatment of the topic, Samuel Butler remained convinced that Tyrwhitt and Malone made a "very plausible conjecture" when they deduced that this figure was a boy actor; yet though he examined the historical records of various persons named William Hughes, even he could find no evidence of a young man who might explain the true identity of "W.H."[37] Since Butler does not mention "The Portrait of Mr. W.H.," it was left to Alfred Douglas in 1933 to keep a "considerable part of Wilde's theory alive" while making it congruent "with the theory of Samuel Butler."[38] "If he was an actor," Douglas speculates about the apparently attractive "W.H.," "it is perfectly certain that, at the age which I have conjectured for him, and with the appearance and smooth-cheeked beauty which Shakespeare ascribes to him, he would have acted the female parts in the plays produced in his company."[39] As we can see, the very idea that Shakespeare's beloved "W.H." was a man (whether an earl or a boy actor) had touched a nerve ever since Malone advertised Tyrwhitt's suggestion. Objections to the kind of indecency that Steevens found in the Sonnets continued throughout the nineteenth century. Perhaps the most notorious objection was the one that the distinguished historian Henry Hallam made in 1837 when he regretfully declared that it was "impossible not to wish that Shakespeare had never written them": this disdainful comment left such a deep impression on subsequent readers that Wilde's narrator observes that Hallam's contumely identified qualities that were both "dangerous" and "unlawful" in the Sonnets.[40]

37. Samuel Butler, *Shakespeare's Sonnets: Reconsidered, in Part Rearranged with Introductory Chapters, Notes, and a Reprint of the Original 1609 Edition* (London: A. C. Fifield, 1899), 114–15. The debate about "W.H." remained active in the 1890s. The theater critic William Archer presented evidence to disprove Southampton's candidacy for "W.H." in "Shakespeare's Sonnets: The Case against Southampton," *Fortnightly Review* n.s. 62 (1897): 817–34. In response, Sidney Lee adduced evidence to rebut the idea that Pembroke was "W.H." and claimed that it was "to Southampton that Shakespeare addressed such of the Sonnets as can be positively credited with a genuinely autobiographic significance" ("Shakespeare and the Earl of Pembroke," *Fortnightly Review* n.s. 63 [1898]: 223).

38. Alfred Douglas, *The True History of Shakespeare's Sonnets* (London: Martin Secker, 1933), 41.

39. Douglas, *The True History of Shakespeare's Sonnets*, 40–41.

40. Henry Hallam, *Introduction to the Literature of Europe in the Fifteenth, Sixteenth and Seventeenth Centuries*, 4 vols. (London: John Murray, 1837), 3:500. "The Portrait of Mr. W.H.," ed. Dowling, 68.

WILDE'S "PORTRAIT," SHAKESPEARE, AND FORGERY AFTER CHATTERTON: WILLIAM-HENRY IRELAND

The sexual sensitivity attached to Tyrwhitt's theory of Willie Hughes was inextricably linked with Malone's legendary name. Malone, who engaged deeply with Tyrwhitt on Chatterton's Rowley poems, was also central to the next major controversy about literary fakes to emerge in English cultural history, which shifted emphasis away from the "marvellous Boy" to a young man who tried his hand at counterfeiting previously unknown works by Shakespeare. The remarkable scandal in question, which began in 1794, featured the forgeries of nineteen-year-old William-Henry Ireland, whose handiwork included faking several dubious texts he impudently attributed to the Bard. None of this teenager's remarkable exploits, which scarred his career forever afterward, had any connection with the identity of Shakespeare's "onlie begetter" in the dedication to the 1609 edition of the Sonnets. But, crucially for Wilde's "Portrait," this teenage forger's literary misadventures demonstrate the extraordinary legacy of the Bristol poet. Ireland's startling attempt to convince the world that formerly undiscovered works that Shakespeare composed (including two lost plays) had been languishing for centuries at a private residence in the metropolis was inspired directly by Chatterton. Ireland's implausible forgeries not only attracted immense attention in their time but also resonated loudly in later decades, when intense debates about the textual editing of Shakespeare's oeuvre revived concerns over forgery. William-Henry's Shakespearean fakes were themselves rooted in this young man's fascination with Chatterton's Rowley poems. Although it dated from the mid-1790s, the legend of William-Henry Ireland was very much alive during Wilde's career, not least because his exploits stood at the head of a history of much-debated literary impostures that generations of forgers audaciously attributed to the Bard.

The hullabaloo around William-Henry Ireland began when his father—the readily hoodwinked and immensely self-important engraver and vendor of prints, as well as bumptious Shakespeare enthusiast, Samuel Ireland—became convinced that his seemingly dull-witted son had miraculously discovered a trove of genuine Shakespeare manuscripts from a mysterious gentleman, always known simply as "Mr. H." The enterprising youngster did his utmost to slake his credulous father's thirst for just these kinds of supposedly authentic materials. In the summer of 1793, William-Henry had accompanied his fanatical parent on a tour through Shakespeare's hometown of Stratford-upon-Avon and the surrounding countryside. Obsessively, Samuel Ireland made drawings of locations linked with Shakespeare's life, obtained souvenirs such as the "bugle purse" that the Bard supposedly gave to his beloved Anne Hathaway, and managed to search (though fruitlessly) for family papers at Clopton House, where Shakespeare's granddaughter Elizabeth Nash had resided. Such enthusiasm, as Doug Stewart has shown, derived from the fact that during the late eighteenth century "a full-blown Cult of Shakespeare" had emerged, largely at the behest of actor-manager David Garrick, whose naturalistic acting style ensured that audiences flocked to see him at Drury Lane during the twenty-nine years (1747–1776) he performed there.[41] Especially after the success of the Shakespeare Jubilee that he organized in 1769, Garrick, whose memorable redactions of Shakespeare's plays involved many cuts and additions to tragedies such as *Romeo and Juliet*, added the previously neglected *Taming of the Shrew* and *Antony and Cleopatra*, among other plays, to the repertory. Since this was also the era when Samuel Johnson and George Steevens issued their imposing edition of Shakespeare's works, cultural interest in the Bard was more intense than ever before. As commentators on Samuel Ireland have observed, even William-Henry, whose intellectual powers were limited at best, quickly grasped that fraudsters effortlessly conned his susceptible parent. Samuel Ireland proved only too willing to believe the dupers who claimed that the objets trouvés they presented to him had an intimate link with Shakespeare's career.

Ireland's forgeries, which his father willfully or otherwise never suspected, began with a deed from Shakespeare and John Heminge (the actor and financial manager of the King's Men) to Michael Fraser and his spouse. William-Henry Ireland, who was (like Chatterton) apprenticed to an attorney, had acquaintance with legal documents involved in the exchange of property, and he had access to reproductions of documents from Shakespeare's era in the rare volumes accessible through his father's well-kept library. Cunningly, he devised a recipe to create ink that looked antiquated, and he tried to make the script appear ancient by darkening it next to a flame. (On occasion, the pages looked unbelievably scorched.) Among the other legal items he forged was a deed of gift from Shakespeare to an imaginary ancestor, calculatedly named W. H. Ireland, dating from the early seventeenth century. This concocted deed, which is similar in spirit to the heraldic blazon that Chatterton presented to the bookseller Bur-

---

41. Doug Stewart, *The Boy Who Would Be Shakespeare: A Tale of Folly and Forgery* (Cambridge, MA: Da Capo Press, 2010), 61. As we observe in our annotations to the "Chatterton" notebook (n. 168, 397), Masson suggests that it was "not likely that [Chatterton] missed the opportunity of seeing Garrick in *Hamlet* at the Drury Lane on the 2d of May" (David Masson, *Chatterton: A Story of the Year 1770*, 2nd ed. [London: Macmillan, 1874], 140).

gum, declared that Shakespeare had generously left his treasured manuscripts to a fictitious contemporary, Ireland, together with his heirs. This truly fanciful document was a brilliant stroke, since it managed to delude William-Henry's self-deceiving father into believing that the Ireland clan had close genealogical bonds with the Bard. In this factitious document, where Shakespeare thanks the imaginary Ireland for saving him from drowning, the influence of Chatterton is clear. A diluted type of Rowleyese emerges in the eccentric (faintly Chaucerian) orthography: "I WILLIAM SHAKSPEARE . . . doe make ande ordeyne thys as ande for mye deede of Gyfte for inn as muche as life is mouste precyouse toe alle menne soe shoulde bee thatte personne who att the peryle of hys owne shalle save thatte of a fellowe Createure."[42]

If William-Henry derived his spellings from Chatterton's Rowley, he based the wording on a facsimile that appeared in Malone's ten-volume 1790 edition of *Plays and Poems of Shakspeare*. One of the smaller items, the execrable "Verses to Anna Hatherrewaye," defines the clear limitations of William-Henry's misguided Chattertonian ambitions, as we can see from the opening—dishearteningly insipid—stanza:

> Is there inne heavenne aught more rare
> Thanne thou sweete Nymphe of Avon fayre
> Is there onne Earthe a Manne more trewe
> Thanne Willy Shakspeare is toe you[43]

Later, an increasingly confident William-Henry became more ambitious in creating fakes of this kind. Such items include his annotations and insertions in what he purported to be Shakespeare's hand in the 1592 edition of Roger Cotton's *Direction to the Waters of Lyfe*. (One of the inserted handwritten slips states: "a mere | reptyle | withoute | thynne helpe | O myghtye Godde.")[44] His greatest imposture was arguably a lost tragedy, the 2,800-line *Vortigern* (culled from his father's copy of Shakespeare's best-known source, Holinshed's *Chronicles*, and completed hastily in two months), which—at Samuel Ireland's urging

42. "Deed of Gift to Ireland," in *Miscellaneous Papers and Legal Instruments under the Hand and Seal of William Shakspeare: Including the Tragedy of* King Lear, *and a Small Fragment of* Hamlet, *from the Original MSS*, ed. Samuel Ireland (London: Cooper and Graham, 1796), unpaginated.

43. "Verses to Anna Hattherewaye," *Miscellaneous Papers and Legal Instruments under the Hand and Seal of William Shakspeare*, unpaginated.

44. Roger Cotton, *A Direction to the Waters of Lyfe* (London: Gabriell Simson and William White, 1592), inserted between 2^v and 3^r, Clark Library PR2950 C85. It is not clear what year this forgery dates from.

—eventually opened, if for a disastrous single night, at Drury Lane on 2 April 1796. A further lost Shakespeare play, *Henry II*, followed.

The unsuspecting but unstoppably self-important Samuel Ireland exhibited some of the earliest of these dismal forgeries at his home on Norfolk Street for more than a year, and he proudly invited literary men to inspect them, though it is notable that the authoritative Malone decided to keep away. At the end of 1795, the conceited engraver published his hefty edition of *Miscellaneous Papers and Legal Instruments under the Hand and Seal of William Shakspeare*, including a lost version of *The Tragedye of Kynge Leare*, along with a fragment of a work that William-Henry, in a moment of Chattertonian excess, titled *Hamblette*. (*Kynge Leare*, it must be said, contains numerous wild instances of Rowleyan orthographic superfluity. When Edgar approaches the blind Gloucester, the earl declares himself to be "Oune poore ande unneforretunate Baggare."[45] There are many other longer and much sillier examples.) In the preface to these smugly edited documents, Samuel Ireland declared: *"These Papers can be no other than the production of Shakspeare himself."*[46] Such staunch assertiveness rested on the support that the engraver had mustered through managing to persuade a notable group of literary people—including (amazingly) James Boswell, Herbert Croft, and Hannah More—to sign, in February 1795, a "Certificate of Belief" in the veracity of his recently acquired Shakespeare papers. (He imposed a second such certificate when dissent began to stir among the ranks.) He even obtained an audience at Carlton House with the Prince of Wales, who, by all accounts, responded courteously—if somewhat unenthusiastically—toward the purported authenticity of the documents. From this point on, a throng of harshly critical voices, including his onetime supporter Boaden's, entered the fray by decrying these impostures. The most imposing voice of opposition was Malone's.

In large part, Malone stood in the best position to show the influence that Chatterton's forgeries had exerted on the altogether inferior ones that William-Henry Ireland contrived; his *Inquiry into Certain Miscellaneous Papers and Legal Instruments* (1796) offered a sustained indictment of Ireland's productions. In this anonymous work, as Peter Martin notes, Malone pursues an unyielding "prosecution of a literary felony."[47] Early in the *Inquiry*, Malone states

45. *The Tragedye of Kynge Leare*, in *Miscellaneous Papers and Legal Instruments under the Hand and Seal of William Shakspeare*, 117.

46. *Miscellaneous Papers and Legal Instruments under the Hand and Seal of William Shakspeare*, vi.

47. Peter Martin, *Edmond Malone, Shakespearean Scholar: A Literary Biography* (Cambridge: Cambridge University Press, 1995), 196.

that he will begin by concentrating on the matter of "ORTHOGRAPHY" that he had already pointedly explored fourteen years earlier with regard to the Rowley poems: "In the Chattertonian Controversy, in order to ascertain the spuriousness of the poems attributed by the youth, Thomas Chatterton, to Thomas Rowley, the author of one of the earliest pamphlets that appeared on that subject, produced numerous specimens of really ancient poetry, which when contrasted with the verses of the pseudo-bard of the fifteenth century proved, with irresistible force, that the author of those specimens, and of the pretended ancient reliques, could not have lived within the same period."[48] Malone observes that both Thomas Warton and Thomas Tyrwhitt had "produced many additional and incontrovertible proofs of that forgery."[49] Yet where Malone found in the Rowley poems evidence of literary genius, he detected nothing of merit in William-Henry's misguided efforts. Besides bemoaning the ridiculous orthography, Malone expressed despair at the young forger's ignorance of many different conventions, from the handwriting practices of Shakespeare's era to the proper modes of address to different ranks of aristocrat. Such "nonsensical and unintelligible trash" proved too much for him to bear.[50]

Malone's adamant *Inquiry* was well timed. It appeared two days before the theatrical premiere of the ludicrously worded *Vortigern* provoked much hilarity among its players and the restive audience. Since the play sold in handsome numbers (five hundred copies) just before its one and only abysmal performance, readers were prepared for what became a catastrophic production, from which the acquisitive Samuel Ireland had hoped to reap substantial profits. The distinguished actor John Philip Kemble tried to lend some solemnity to the terrible verse. But his stern delivery of an embarrassing line in act 4—"And when this solemn mockery is o'er"—sealed the fate of this appalling drama.[51]

48. [Edmond Malone,] *An Inquiry into the Authenticity of Certain Miscellaneous Papers and Legal Instruments, Published Dec. 24, MDCCXCV, and Attributed to Shakspear, Queen Elizabeth, and Henry, Earl of Southampton* (London: T. Cadell Jr. and W. Davies, 1796), 31–32.

49. [Malone,] *An Inquiry into the Authenticity of Certain Miscellaneous Papers and Legal Instruments*, 32.

50. [Malone,] *An Inquiry into the Authenticity of Certain Miscellaneous Papers and Legal Instruments*, 131.

51. W. H. Ireland, *Vortigern: An Historical Play, with an Original Preface. Represented at the Theatre Royal, Drury Lane, on Saturday, April 2, 1796, as a Supposed Newly-Discovered Drama of Shakspeare* (London: J. Thomas, 1832), 51. William-Henry Ireland recalls the crowd's response to Kemble's delivery of this line: "Having, in the course of his part, arrived at the anxiously expected line, he delivered it in an exceedingly pointed manner;

As George Bernard Shaw's journalism reveals, as late as 1887 the reaction to Kemble's delivery of that unfortunate line was still cited as the example par excellence of an actor and an audience scorning an atrociously bad play.[52]

In the first of two detailed rebuttals to Malone's *Inquiry*, an indignant Samuel Ireland concluded that he had rallied more than sufficient evidence to prove that "the world" would vindicate the authenticity of these documents: "I have laid the merits of my cause, before that tribunal, which will not suffer the voice of truth to be overwhelmed and extinguished."[53] Soon afterward, William-Henry expressed astonishment at Malone's critique, if for very different reasons. His 1796 confession doubtless made him into an embarrassing scapegrace, but in it he wonders, not unreasonably, why Malone should have written such a "tedious epistle" of "upwards of four hundred pages" if the great Shakespeare scholar sincerely believed that the forgeries were at base both "weak, and poorly contrived."[54] Among the other main defenders was Francis Webb, a military man who wrote floridly about the reasons why we should excuse the conspicuous "errors and omissions" in Ireland's documents, since they were "such as might be expected of a man of a warm temper, impetuous and prompt genius."[55] Yet the evidence kept building against Samuel Ireland's case. Boaden declared that the most problematic aspect of the forgeries was the orthogra-

---

when, of course, a deafening clamour reigned throughout one of the most crowded houses ever recollected in theatrical history, which lasted for several minutes. Upon a hearing being at length obtained, instead of taking up the following line of the speech in rotation, Mr. Kemble reiterated the above line with an expression the most pointedly sarcastic and acrimonious it is possible to conceive. The result was, from that moment so deafening became the uproar produced by conflicting applause and disapproval, that not one syllable more of the play was rendered intelligible" ("Preface," vi).

52. Bernard Shaw's "In Five Acts and in Blank Verse," a review of three plays, notes about a line in one of these dramas: "In actual performance that line might bring down the house, very much as it was brought down by Kemble's delivery of 'And when this solemn mockery is o'er' in Ireland's 'Vortigern'" (*Pall Mall Gazette*, 14 July 1887: 3; in *Bernard Shaw's Book Reviews*, ed. Brian Tyson [University Park: Pennsylvania State University Press, 1991], 296).

53. Samuel Ireland, *An Investigation of Mr. Malone's Claim to the Character of Scholar, or Critic, Being an Examination of His Inquiry into the Authenticity of the Shakspeare Manuscripts* (London: R. Faulder, and Others, 1796), 153.

54. William-Henry Ireland, *An Authentic Account of the Shaksperian Manuscripts* (London: J. Debrett, 1796), 26.

55. "Philalethes" [Francis Webb], *Shakspeare's Manuscripts, in the Possession of Mr. Ireland, Examined, Respecting the Internal and External Evidences of Their Authority* (London: J. Johnson, 1796), 13.

phy, since it "brought to the recollection the only typographic parallel in the forgeries of Chatterton."[56] Moreover, he found many other points to criticize, especially the "modern colouring of diction and flow of language."[57]

Out of good conscience, William-Henry eventually went into print asking naively for "favor and forgiveness," since all he had done was indulge in the "act of a boy"; after causing a great deal of embarrassment, he hoped to clear his father's name of "the odium" that had come to surround his handiwork.[58] But, even though Samuel Ireland acknowledged his son's published confession, which appeared in late 1796, when he died in 1800 he still refused to believe that this cache of documents was in any respect counterfeit, largely because he could not acknowledge that William-Henry possessed the talent to compose such works. (As William-Henry recorded five years after his father's death, it was somewhat galling to learn that his fanatical parent "was as fully convinced as that he then had existence that [his son] never could have produced" these items.[59] The same was true of Mrs. Freeman, the housekeeper, who may have been William-Henry's biological mother. She declined to countenance the unacceptable idea that the twenty-year-old had any literary ability.) In part to redeem his sullied reputation, as well as to display his ingenuity, in 1805 William-Henry produced yet another volume in which he confessed to his each and every act of forgery, this time in much more illuminating detail. In this second confession, he recalls how strongly as a depressed teenager he once identified with Chatterton, after he had read Croft's captivating *Love and Madness*: "I used frequently to envy his fate, and desire nothing so ardently as the termination of my existence in a similar cause."[60]

From that point forward during William-Henry's teenage years, the Chatterton legend maintained the firmest grip on his fertile imagination. In late 1796, when he broke from London to escape his irascible father, William-Henry duly made a pilgrimage to Chatterton's birthplace. So great was his fascination with the young Bristol poet that he went so far as to visit the Muniment Room at

56. James Boaden, *A Letter to George Steevens, Esq. Containing a Critical Examination of the Papers of Shakspeare: Published by Mr. Samuel Ireland, to Which are Added, Extracts from Vortigern* (London: Martin and Bain, 1796), 14.

57. Boaden, *A Letter to George Steevens, Esq.*, 42.

58. Ireland, *An Authentic Account of the Shaksperian Manuscripts*, 1.

59. *The Confessions of William-Henry Ireland: Containing the Particulars of His Fabrication of the Shakspeare Manuscripts, together with Anecdotes and Opinions (Hitherto Unpublished) of Many Distinguished Persons in the Literary, Political, and Theatrical World* (London: Ellerton and Byworth, 1805), 260.

60. *The Confessions of William-Henry Ireland*, 11.

St. Mary Redcliffe, where he spent time confiding with Chatterton's now aging sister: "As to his person, his sister said that he was thin of body, but neatly made; that his features were by no means handsome, and yet, notwithstanding, the *tout-ensemble* was striking; which arose, she conceived, from the wonderful expression of his eyes, and more particularly of the left eye, which, to use her own words, seemed at times, from its brilliancy, 'to flash fire.'"[61] William-Henry adds that the sister regretted the rumors that suggested her brother had been "partial to the society of abandoned women."[62] Since he had gone to such lengths to emulate his idol (one "who, had he lived, would have undoubtedly ranked with the first men of genius that have graced our isle"), William-Henry proceeded to visit an unnamed bookseller "in a bye street" who recalled how Chatterton "perused . . . promiscuously works on religion, history, biography, poetry, heraldry—and, in short, the most abstruse treatises on every subject."[63]

By taking the young Bristol poet's career as his leading example, William-Henry Ireland ultimately tried to do for William Shakespeare what Thomas Chatterton had with altogether greater success done for Thomas Rowley. Ireland's literary legacy, however, was entirely different from the splendid one of the "marvellous Boy." Despite the protestations in his 1805 *Confessions* ("I did not intend injury to any one"; "I really injured no one"; "I did not produce the papers from any pecuniary motives"), he remained an object of contempt for decades to come.[64] Around 1830, a middle-aged William-Henry had a contretemps outside a London bookshop with the now elderly Boaden. As their conversation turned to the forgeries, Boaden expostulated: "You must be aware, sir, of the enormous crime you committed against the divinity of Shakspeare. Why, the act, sir, was nothing short of sacrilege; it was precisely the same thing as taking the holy chalice from the altar, and ******* therein!!!!"[65] Mockingly, William-Henry found himself unable to stifle a "burst of laughter."[66] His recollections show that, even in later life, he suffered from no small amount of arrogance with regard to his literary skills, which he exercised in many later publications, including the volume titled (with unintentional irony) *Neglected Genius*, which contains his poetic tribute to Chatterton. In the end, all William-Henry wanted posterity to acknowledge was that his counterfeited

61. *The Confessions of William-Henry Ireland*, 16.
62. *The Confessions of William-Henry Ireland*, 16.
63. *The Confessions of William-Henry Ireland*, 17, 18–19.
64. *The Confessions of William-Henry Ireland*, 301.
65. W. H. Ireland, "Preface," in *Vortigern*, xiii.
66. Ireland, "Preface," in *Vortigern*, xiii.

works were aimed solely at "the permanent gratification of beholding a father happy."[67]

After his parent's demise, William-Henry moved restlessly between England and France in a series of attempts to sustain a literary career, in which he continued to publish original works and translations from the French at a remarkable pace. Seldom, it seems, did William-Henry seek to conceal his infamy. Patricia Pierce reveals that by 1830 he had printed a prospectus for a memoir presumptuously called *Shakespeare Ireland's Seven Ages.*[68] Equally inept was the title he gave to his biography of his good friend the actress Mrs. Jordan, who had offered him financial assistance in times of need. He chose to publicize the career of this well-known star of Drury Lane as *The Great Illegitimates!! Public and Private Life of that Celebrated Actress, Miss Bland, otherwise Mrs. Ford, or, Mrs. Jordan, Late Mistress of H.R.H. the D. of Clarence, Now King William IV* (1832). Not surprisingly, given its breathtaking lack of tact, this title was withdrawn from sale almost immediately after it appeared. As Nick Groom reminds us, Ireland produced much more than his Shakespeare and related forgeries, though little scholarship has since the time of Montague Summers's *Gothic Quest: A History of the Gothic Novel* (1938) paid much attention to this author's wealth of fiction, in addition to his poetic works, such as *Neglected Genius*: "Ireland," Groom writes, "is potentially as remarkable as Chatterton, though his works lie idle and uncollected and probably no one has yet read the whole lot."[69] Forgery alone defined Ireland's reputation in Victorian Britain, in an emphatically negative manner.

In 1859, C. Mansfield Ingleby looked back at the disgraced author of *Vortigern* as "perhaps, the most accomplished liar that ever lived."[70] Fifteen years later, the American scholar who established the Riverside Shakespeare, Richard Grant White, furnished an introduction for the reprint of William-Henry's *Confessions*, in which White reminds readers that it was largely Malone's work that revealed to the crowd at Drury Lane that *Vortigern* was indeed a "ridiculous sham."[71] By the time Wilde embarked on his tale about Shakespearean

67. Ireland, "Preface," in *Vortigern*, xiii.

68. Patricia Pierce, *The Great Shakespeare Fraud: The Strange, True Story of William-Henry Ireland* (Stroud: Sutton, 2004), 220.

69. Nick Groom, *The Forger's Shadow: How Forgery Changed the Course of Literature* (London: Picador, 2002), 220.

70. C. Mansfield Ingleby, *The Shakespeare Fabrications, or, the MS. Notes of the Perkins Folio Shown to Be of Recent Origin, with an Appendix on the Authorship of the Ireland Forgeries* (London: John Russell Smith, 1859), 101.

71. Richard Grant White, "Introduction," in *The Confessions of William-Henry Ireland*, ed. White (New York: James W. Bouton, 1874), xii.

forgery, the tide had turned entirely against the young attorney's apprentice who had sought, as best he could, to emulate Chatterton. Yet, as White's edition shows, interest in this curious phenomenon remained high, not least because the "question of literary forgeries" persisted with continued strength in the later nineteenth century, especially with regard to Shakespeare's works.

"The Portrait of Mr. W.H." therefore developed at a time when the ninety-year-old scandal about Ireland remained very much alive among scholars of Shakespeare's oeuvre. William-Henry's identification with Chatterton might have had little impact on his reputation among the critics, but it helped ensure that, when the Chatterton revival was well under way in the 1880s, his association with the "marvellous Boy" would bring him once again to public consciousness. The novelist and editor James Payn did his part to keep attention focused on Ireland's disreputable career by using it as the basis for his 1884 novel *The Talk of the Town*, which starred a William Henry Erin as a thinly veiled version of Ireland, and included an acrostic on Chatterton penned by this young protagonist, which was clearly a play on William-Henry's feeble verse on the Bristol poet in *Neglected Genius*.[72] It is certainly clear from one of Vivian's passing references to modern fiction in "The Decay of Lying" that Wilde thought little of Payn's novels ("James Payn is an adept in the art of concealing what is not worth finding").[73] But *The Talk of the Town* suggests that, although Ireland was undoubtedly a second-rate forger and poet (his works failing miserably to convince and failing aesthetically, since they were clumsy imitations of Shakespeare and Chatterton), his irrepressible character remained a source of fascination.

All of this information about the legacy of William-Henry Ireland's ill-fated exploits shows that in "The Portrait of Mr. W.H." Wilde's appeal to Tyrwhitt's theory of a young man named Hughes is rooted in several historically connected debates about Shakespeare's sexuality and about literary forgery. To begin with, the speculation about Shakespeare's "male object" in the Sonnets involves two of the scholars who were central to strengthening Chatterton's legacy in the late eighteenth century. Second, the implicit references to Tyrwhitt and Malone address their close involvement in exposing both the young Bristol poet's and William-Henry Ireland's respective forgeries. By virtue of these two sets of debates, Wilde's informed story is situated in a firmly established

72. Originally serialized in the *Cornhill*, which Payn edited from 1883 to 1896, with illustrations by Harry Furniss from July 1884 onward, *The Talk of the Town* subsequently appeared in a two-volume edition by Smith, Elder, and Co. and a single-volume edition by Chatto and Windus in 1885. See our discussion of William-Henry Ireland's poem on Chatterton in chapter 1 (82).

73. Wilde, "The Decay of Lying," *Criticism*, ed. Guy, 4:77–78.

tradition of literary fakes, in which competing camps rallied their vying sets of evidence to prove or disprove the genuineness of these documents.

It is therefore no accident that near the start of "The Portrait" Wilde's narrator mentions Macpherson, Chatterton, and Ireland all in one breath. Chatterton (who read deeply in *Ossian*) and (his admittedly far less gifted imitator) Ireland frame the fascinating career of another forger, who emerges in the narrative in the guise of the fictional Cyril Graham, Erskine's deceased friend from Eton and Cambridge days. As Erskine says, Cyril—although "a capital rider and a capital fencer"—remained "effeminate . . . in some things," not least, it seems, because he "was always dressing up and reciting Shakespeare."[74] Such a synthesis of masculine and feminine qualities made Cyril into a rare individual, one who embodied those attributes he appears to have discerned in the Willie Hughes of his passionate imagining. Not unlike Wainewright, Cyril declaimed at the university debating society that it was "better to be good-looking than to be good."[75]

JOHN PAYNE COLLIER, THE SECOND FOLIO, AND EDITORIAL FORGERY

With this background in place, Erskine recounts Cyril's well-developed theory of "W.H.": a theory supposedly based entirely on the internal evidence supplied by Shakespeare's Sonnets. By echoing Mackay's objection and anticipating Butler's, Erskine articulates the "one flaw in the theory": he "refused to be convinced till the actual existence of Willie Hughes, a boy-actor of the Elizabethan stage, had been placed beyond the reach of doubt or cavil."[76] Although their researches of parish registers and birth records yielded no evidence (this was the kind of detail that skeptics of the Willie Hughes theory routinely remarked upon), Cyril commissioned a remarkable fake portrait: a full-length depiction of a young Elizabethan man, which Cyril hoped would at last settle the enigmatic identity of Shakespeare's treasured "master mistress." Cyril, we learn, went to extreme lengths in order to convince himself that the male object of desire mentioned in a playful line from the Sonnets—"a man in hue" with "all 'hues' in his controlling"—was indeed Willie Hughes.[77] To strengthen his point, Cyril arranged for the model to rest one of his hands on a volume bearing the famous inscription: "TO. THE. ONLIE. BEGETTER. OF. | THESE. INSVING.

74. "The Portrait of Mr. W.H.," ed. Dowling, 36.
75. "The Portrait of Mr. W.H.," ed. Dowling, 36.
76. "The Portrait of Mr. W.H.," ed. Dowling, 44.
77. "The Portrait of Mr. W.H.," ed. Dowling, 44. The line from Sonnet 20 reads: "A man in hue, all hues in his controlling" (*Shakespeare's Sonnets*, 151).

SONNETS. | M^r. W.H." Once he had taken delivery of the picture, Cyril deceived Erskine by claiming he had found it "nailed to the side of an old chest that he had bought at a farmhouse" in Shakespeare's native Warwickshire.[78] (It is almost as if Cyril wished to produce an archaeological relic to substantiate his belief.) When he first saw the artwork, Erskine read "gold uncial letters on the faded *bleu de paon*" that spelled out "Master Will Hewes."[79] Erskine, it appears, would have remained wholly convinced of Cyril's discovery had he not been disabused when he stumbled across a near-copy by an artist in London. "I went off at once to Cyril's chambers," Erskine reveals, "waited there for three hours before he came in, with that horrid lie staring me in the face."[80] No sooner had Erskine challenged Cyril than his friend protested: "I did it purely for your sake."[81] Tragically, after their "fearful quarrel," Erskine learned that Cyril had committed suicide.[82] This quick succession of episodes, which we discover close to the beginning of Wilde's story, makes one irony glaringly clear: Erskine perpetrated the very form of brutal censure against Cyril that most Victorians believed had sent young Chatterton to an early grave.

Cyril's stunning forged portrait, which reminds us of the motives that inspired Chatterton's remarkable Rowley poems and William-Henry Ireland's less-than-competent fakes, serves as a powerful device whose exposure as a fraud hardly forestalls what becomes a dynamic plot that features several unexpected reversals. To begin with, the forgery inspires the narrator to convince himself that Cyril's theory about the true identity of "Mr. W.H." was not fake but utterly plausible. The narrator divulges that he desired to believe that "each poem seemed . . . to corroborate Cyril Graham's theory."[83] Willie Hughes became such "an ever-dominant personality" in the narrator's imagination that he was compelled to assemble masses of historical information in the hope that he would find "absolute verification."[84] Yet, at the same time, the narrator freely admits that he knew all along that he was deceiving himself, much in the manner of a forger. "One evening," he recalls, "I thought I had really discovered Willie Hughes in Elizabethan literature."[85] His source, he claims, was Thomas Knell's account of the last days of the Earl of Essex, in which a musician named

78. "The Portrait of Mr. W.H.," ed. Dowling, 44.
79. "The Portrait of Mr. W.H.," ed. Dowling, 44.
80. "The Portrait of Mr. W.H.," ed. Dowling, 46.
81. "The Portrait of Mr. W.H.," ed. Dowling, 46.
82. "The Portrait of Mr. W.H.," ed. Dowling, 46.
83. "The Portrait of Mr. W.H.," ed. Dowling, 49.
84. "The Portrait of Mr. W.H.," ed. Dowling, 58, 70.
85. "The Portrait of Mr. W.H.," ed. Dowling, 69.

William Hewes entertained his master. As the narrator quickly acknowledges, however, no matter how much he would like to have relied on Knell's commentary, it remained questionable to do so: "Lord Essex died in 1576, when Shakespeare was but twelve years of age."[86] "It was impossible," he concludes, "that his musician could have been the Mr. W.H. of the Sonnets."[87] Regardless of how readily he understood that his evidence was deficient, he nonetheless resolved to construct "a little book with fine vellum leaves and damask silk cover" to collect "such information" as he could about the young men who performed in Elizabethan theater companies.[88]

As he details the vast quantities of evidence that he commits to this antiquated document, the narrator begins to bear an uncanny resemblance to Chatterton, who fashioned his Rowley manuscripts on exactly the same obsolete material, which the churchwardens at St. Mary Redcliffe had stored in the Muniment Room. His eagerness to emulate Cyril Graham's fabrication of the past brings to mind William-Henry Ireland's impulse to follow Chatterton. Furthermore, the narrator's exacting inquiries prompt one to recall Chatterton's raids on both Bailey's and Kersey's historical dictionaries in order to make Rowley's fifteenth-century English sound genuine. In one sentence after another, Wilde's storyteller lists the wealth of references he had unearthed about boy actors in Shakespeare's time, with the aim of writing a persuasive history that would finally reveal "their true relations to the drama."[89] "I seemed to know them all: Robin Armin, the goldsmith's lad who was lured by Tarlton to go on the stage: Sandford, whose performance of the courtesan Flamantia Lord Burleigh witnessed at Gray's Inn: Cooke, who played Agríppina in the tragedy of *Sejanus*: Nat. Field, whose young and beardless portrait is still preserved for us at Dulwich, and who in *Cynthia's Revels* played the 'Queen and Huntress chaste and fair': Gil. Carie, who, attired as a mountain nymph, sang in the same lovely masque Echo's song of mourning for Narcissus."[90] This is only the start of an exhaustive list, which also shows that Wilde himself had undertaken not a small measure of research to assemble this array of intriguing historical facts.

Curiously, much of Wilde's plentiful information about boy actors came from an authority whose reputation had, by the 1880s, been linked for thirty years with an unusual variety of fakery: one that further complicates the connections between "The Portrait of Mr. W.H.," on the one hand, and the history

86. "The Portrait of Mr. W.H.," ed. Dowling, 69.
87. "The Portrait of Mr. W.H.," ed. Dowling, 69.
88. "The Portrait of Mr. W.H.," ed. Dowling, 70.
89. "The Portrait of Mr. W.H.," ed. Dowling, 70.
90. "The Portrait of Mr. W.H.," ed. Dowling, 70–71.

of literary forgery, on the other hand. Wilde accessed details about these young players through one of Shakespeare editor John Payne Collier's most imposing critical works: the revised edition of *The History of English Dramatic Poetry to the Time of Shakespeare: And Annals of the Stage to the Restoration* (1879). (The original edition of Collier's weighty *History* had appeared in 1831. The revised 1879 edition contained as an addendum the slightly emended text of Collier's *Memoirs of the Principal Actors in the Plays of Shakespeare* [1846].) By 1889, when Wilde's story was first published, Collier had been dead for six years. This prolific scholar of early modern English texts, whose eight-volume edition of the *Works of William Shakespeare* (1842–1844) established him as a leading authority at midcentury, went to his grave with a reputation tarnished by the discovery of his use of forged documents in his scholarship and editorial work. It was only in the 1850s, after Collier had firmly established his status as a revered Shakespeare expert, that several of his antagonistic contemporaries detected his editorial misdeeds. Collier's extensive editorial emendations to Shakespeare's work relied on spurious, hand-corrected manuscripts which he claimed to have found or purchased, but which he might in fact have fabricated himself. In their exhaustive study of Collier's sedulous deceptions, Arthur Freeman and Janet Ing Freeman explore the editor's long-undetected feats of "editorial or commentarial fraud."[91] They state that his surreptitious tampering with the historical and textual record involved "the fabrication or forgery of citations and sources, alternative readings with a bogus cachet, old provenance, [and] reports of 'lost' texts and the like."[92] In the case of the *History of English Dramatic Poetry*, they point out at least fifteen definite impostures in the first edition, which include "inventions pure and simple for which no documentary evidence survives" and "fabrications for which evidence, in the form of physical forgeries, is cited by Collier and remains extant."[93] One of the representative "inventions" is the substantial "Ballade in Praise of London Prentices, and What They Did at the Cock-Pit Playhouse in Drury Lane," which purportedly comes from an unattributed "contemporary MS" and describes an incident in 1617 when a mob invaded a theater. The Freemans observe that such made-up ballads had been a staple part of the literary history of forgery ever since Thomas Percy came under attack (wrongly, as it turned out) for allegedly inventing a portion of the contents of his *Reliques of English Poetry*. Similarly, Collier's otherwise

91. Arthur Freeman and Janet Ing Freeman, *John Payne Collier: Scholarship and Forgery in the Nineteenth Century*, 2 vols. (New Haven: Yale University Press, 2004), 1:179.
92. Freeman and Freeman, *John Payne Collier*, 1:179.
93. Freeman and Freeman, *John Payne Collier*, 1:193.

imposing edition of the *Works of William Shakespeare* contains some bogus annotations supposedly found in a First Folio of Shakespeare's works (1623) held at Bridgewater House.

But, in an editorial career that gave Collier access to countless rare manuscripts held at private libraries, these infractions were nothing compared to his later determination to impose upon the world his professed discovery of a heavily annotated Second Folio (1632) that contained corrections, in a mid-seventeenth-century hand, of countless evident misprints. Generally known as the "Perkins Folio" (since it was inscribed "Tho. Perkins, | his Booke"), this document came to public attention in early 1852 when Collier placed two pieces in the prestigious *Athenæum* about his acquisition of this previously unknown document. In his "Early Manuscript Emendations of Shakespeare's Text," Collier recalls the original reason for his purchase of this volume from a London bookseller, who, we are told, knew nothing at all about the immense value of the extensively marked-up contents. For practical purposes, Collier claims, he had bought this "much-thumbed, abused, and imperfect copy" to replace "some missing leaves" in another Second Folio he already owned.[94] Collier recounts expressing his immense surprise when he first opened this inferior-looking book: "Then it was that I for the first time remarked that the folio of 1632 which I had bought from Mr. Rodd contained manuscript alterations of the text as it stood printed in that early edition. These alterations were in an old hand-writing—probably not of a later date than the Protectorate,—and applied (as I afterwards found, on going through the volume here) to every play. There was hardly a page without emendations of more or less importance and interest,—and some of them appeared to me highly valuable. The punctuation, on which of course so much of the author's meaning depends, was corrected in, I may say, thousands of places."[95]

This letter produced a stream of correspondence to the *Athenæum*'s offices, and it generated such interest that Collier permitted the Perkins Folio to be consulted on several occasions by members of the recently founded Shakespeare Society and the Society of Antiquaries before he handed it to his publisher as a supplement for a fresh edition of the *Works*. Those individuals who managed to peruse the Perkins Folio would have seen that there were thousands of emendations in the apparently seventeenth-century hand of the man Collier called the "Old Corrector." Such interventions, on which Collier had expended the best part of two years, evidently aimed at producing a much more

94. John Payne Collier, "Early Manuscript Emendations of Shakespeare's Text," *Athenæum* 1266 (31 January 1852): 142.

95. Collier, "Early Manuscript Emendations of Shakespeare's Text," 142.

sophisticated type of editorial forgery than anything William-Henry Ireland had ever accomplished. Collier certainly knew of Ireland's limitations, since he possessed Malone's personal annotated copy of the *Inquiry* into the highly questionable *Miscellaneous Papers* that created such a stir in 1795. Yet at least one modern scholar of Collier's career remains unconvinced that this Victorian editor of Shakespeare would have expended such large quantities of time on fabricating "thousands of worthless changes."[96] Such a view reveals that the industrious Collier's extraordinary transgressions can test the credulity even of literary historians who study the art of forgery in good faith.

Not long after he proudly made his findings known in the *Athenæum*, Collier published, initially for members of the Shakespeare Society, his hefty 550-page *Notes and Emendations to the Text of Shakespeare's Plays* (1852), in which his desire to trump previous editors of the Bard's works becomes patently clear. In one instance, Collier adopts a marginal notation from the Perkins Folio to revise a line in *Coriolanus*, substituting "woolless" for "woolvish" before asking the credulous reader, "Can there be an instant's hesitation about it?"[97] The rhetorical force of his question suggests that no one was likely to quibble with such evident common sense. Collier, however, appears not to have fully anticipated the savage opposition that his so-called discoveries would roundly meet. His eagerness to discover if he could maintain copyright over these emendations hardly fostered a climate of good will. At the same time, he was determined to see if he could include these findings in a fresh edition of Shakespeare's works for the eminent publisher John Murray. As the Freemans show, the critically sharp John Gibson Lockhart, once he had reviewed the "Collier trouvaille" for John Murray, sensed that it was a "fabrication," though he did not allege that Collier himself was the author of such fakery.[98] It took until the following year before rival editors, who had been making their way through the innumerable changes attributed to the "Old Corrector," began to attack Collier, not for the offense of forgery but for proving so gullible to someone else's crimes. Among the earliest enemies to enter the fray was Samuel Weller Singer, whose own

96. Dewey Ganzel, *Fortune and Men's Eyes: The Career of John Payne Collier* (Oxford: Oxford University Press, 1982), 340. Freeman and Freeman persistently draw into question the scholarly authority and critical conclusions of Ganzel's study; see, for example, *John Payne Collier*, 1:371, 372, 505–8.

97. Collier, *Notes and Emendations to the Text of Shakespeare's Plays: From Early Manuscript Corrections in a Copy of the Folio, 1632, in the Possession of J. Payne Collier, Forming a Supplementary Volume to the Works of Shakespeare by the Same Editor, in Eight Volumes, Octavo* (London: Whittaker, 1853), xii.

98. John Gibson Lockhart, "To John Wilson Croker," c. 18–21 March 1852, in Freeman and Freeman, *John Payne Collier*, 1:594.

contributions to a much reprinted and revised edition of *The Dramatic Works of Shakespeare* dated back to 1826. "It would not be the first time," Singer expostulates near the start of his prefatory remarks, "that such knavish ingenuity has misled a well-trained Shakesperian antiquary and commentator" as Collier; "witness the Ireland forgeries," he proceeds to add, "which, clumsy as they were, had numerous believers and apologists."[99] In similar mood, Alexander Dyce, who had already published an extensive list of objections to Collier's 1842–1844 edition of the *Works*, also had a vested interest in drawing up lines of disagreement with the *Notes and Emendations*, since he was preparing his own edition of Shakespeare's works for the respected house of Edward Moxon. Dyce's highly critical *A Few Notes on Shakespeare* followed Singer's volume in 1853.

Such was the furor that sprang from the Perkins Folio that it spawned a sizable literature that caught the attention of editors based as far afield as Germany and the United States. Yet it was not until 1855 that Andrew Brae, an antiquarian hailing from Leeds, boldly accused Collier of "downright forgery."[100] In *Literary Cookery*, which presents the text of a strongly worded letter that the *Athenæum* declined to print, Brae had not a scrap of hard evidence on which to support his case, since he was not able to consult the Perkins Folio, which Collier had handed over (and most probably sold) to his patron, the Duke of Devonshire. Yet Brae's hunch proved right. By 1859, seven years after Collier had parted with the Perkins Folio, the duke's heir agreed to allow specialists at the British Museum to inspect this annotated copy of the Second Folio. Once he had subjected its contents to scrutiny, the Assistant Keeper of Manuscripts, N. E. S. A. Hamilton, divulged his conclusions to the *Times*: "I now come to the most astounding result of these investigations, in comparison with which all other facts concerning the corrected folio become insignificant. On a close examination of the margins they are found to be covered with an infinite number of faint pencil-marks and corrections, in obedience to which the supposed old corrector has made his emendations. These pencil corrections have not even the pretence of antiquity in character or spelling, but are written in a bold hand of the present century."[101] Although Collier defended himself in the *Times* ("I

---

99. Samuel Weller Singer, *The Text of Shakespeare Vindicated from the Interpolations and Corruptions Advocated by John Payne Collier, Esq., in His Notes and Emendations* (London: William Pickering, 1853), vi.

100. Andrew Brae, *Literary Cookery, with Matter Attributed to Coleridge and Shakespeare: A Letter Addressed to "The Athenaeum"* (London: John Russell Smith, 1855), 1.

101. N. E. S. A. Hamilton, "To the Editor of *The Times*," *Times* [London], 2 July 1859: 12; reprinted in Hamilton, *An Inquiry into the Genuineness of the Manuscript Corrections in Mr. J. Payne Collier's Annotated Shakspere, Folio, 1632: And of Certain Shaksperian Documents Likewise Published by Mr. Collier* (London: R. Bentley, 1860), 135.

never made a single pencil mark on the pages of the book, excepting crosses, ticks, or lines, to direct my attention to particular emendations"), he was coming ever closer to falling prey to the charge that Brae had ventured in 1855: namely, the emendations in the Perkins Folio were Collier's own furtive handiwork.[102] To be sure, Alexander Rivington rallied to Collier's defense: "Spots of corrosion eaten into the paper and ink [of the annotations to the Perkins Folio] . . . prove its antiquity," and thus—in Rivington's view—"prove at least that the hands of Mr. Collier had nothing to do with its manufacture."[103] But few others were convinced.

By 1861, after plenty of further exchanges in the press about Collier's findings, Ingleby—who by then had examined not only the Perkins Folio but also other documents on which Collier based his editorial endeavors—issued *A Complete View of the Shakspere Controversy, Concerning the Authenticity and Genuineness of Manuscript Matter Affecting the Works and Biography of Shakspere, Pub. by Mr. J. Payne Collier as the Fruits of his Researches.* In this unforgiving volume, Ingleby went much further than his previous claim that just as "knowledge of old orthography" had settled "the case of the Rowley and Ireland *Fabrications,*" so too should attention to modern spelling practices have shown that a "test-word (or test-phrase)" would reveal that the marginal comments did not derive from the seventeenth century.[104] Ingleby charged ahead by commenting on "the *extraordinary* resemblance between Mr. Collier's writing and that of the 'old corrector.'"[105] By the time he reaches Collier's 1841 edition of the memoirs of Edward Alleyn (one of Queen Elizabeth I's favorite actors), Ingleby insists that the "List of Players" appended to a 1604 letter from the Council of the City of London to the Lord Mayor has so much circumstantial evidence against its authenticity that it looked likely to have originated with none other than Collier himself. (Noticeably, in Wilde's story Erskine recalls consulting the Alleyn manuscripts at Dulwich to see if they contained any mention of Willie Hughes in order to "put the whole matter beyond reach of doubt.")[106] Ingleby knew he had to set out these devastating charges in the firmest detail, very much in the

102. Collier, "To the Editor," *Times* [London], 7 July 1859: 9.

103. "Scrutator" [Alexander Rivington], *Strictures on Mr. N.E.S.A. Hamilton's Inquiry into the Genuineness of the MS. Corrections in Mr. J. Payne Collier's Annotated Shakespeare Folio, 1632* (London: John Russell Smith, 1860), 25–26.

104. Ingleby, *The Shakspeare Fabrications,* 1.

105. Ingleby, *A Complete View of the Shakspere Controversy, Concerning the Authenticity and Genuineness of Manuscript Matter Affecting the Works and Biography of Shakspere, Pub. by Mr. J. Payne Collier as the Fruits of his Researches* (London: Nattali and Bond, 1861), 175. Emphasis in the original.

106. "The Portrait of Mr. W.H.," ed. Dowling, 43.

style that Malone had done throughout his *Inquiry*. Most important for Wilde's "Portrait" was Ingleby's pronounced sense of the difficulty of convincing critics that forgery had taken place when an individual might be prejudicially disposed to believe that this type of literary deceit could never have occurred:

> That a case like the present, which rests entirely on circumstantial evidence, should affect all minds alike, is not to be expected. No evidence of a literary forgery has ever been found "as subtle as Arachne's woof." There has ever been some "orifex," through which a crotchetty, partial, or sceptical mind might escape the necessity of conviction. After the forgeries of Macpherson, Chatterton, and Ireland, there remained critics who having committed themselves to an opinion in favour of the authenticity or genuineness of the matter to which spuriousness was imputed, held with consistent tenacity to their original opinion, even after the spuriousness had been established beyond a rational doubt.[107]

The very fact that much of Wilde's story pivots on each character's extreme shift between belief and unbelief in Cyril's theory of Willie Hughes addresses the irrational pattern of hyperbolic responses that Ingleby rightly identifies in the irascible debates that raged around the *The Works of Ossian*, the Rowley poems, and the wretched *Vortigern*.

In his defense, Collier pieced together a long study titled *Trilogy* that examined the extent to which one of his critics—his former friend turned adversary Dyce—had, in an eight-volume 1859 edition of Shakespeare's works, made use of the very corrections present in the Perkins Folio that he had elsewhere decried. (Dyce's edition, in the subtitle, stated that his text was "regulated by the folio of 1632.") Dyce had initially preserved the "woolvish tongue" that appears in the First Folio text of *Coriolanus*. As Collier had observed in his *Notes and Emendations*, the "Old Corrector" ventured "woolless togue." Dyce, Collier remarks, finally capitulated to this emendation. As one of Collier's interlocutors declares in the critical dialogues that make up *Trilogy*: "Now, owing to your corrected

107. Ingleby, *A Complete View of the Shakspere Controversy*, 2. Ingleby's reference comes from *Troilus and Cressida*, act 5, scene 2: "the spacious breadth of this division / Admits no orifex for point as subtle / As Arachne's broken woof to enter." "Orifex" is orifice. (*Troilus and Cressida*, ed. David Bevington, The Arden Shakespeare, 3rd series [Walton-on-Thames, Surrey: Thomas Nelson, 1998], 324.) Later in his study, Ingleby returns to these lines from Shakespeare's play because they provide an example of the kind of obscurity he believes the "impatient . . . Englishman" would like to have rephrased so that they make clear sense without hitch or halt" (9, 10). He believes that the emendations in the Perkins Folio provide "too great a comfort" for readers who find the original published text too taxing (10).

and much abused folio, 'woolless togue' must inevitably stand as the language of Shakespeare."[108] (Modern editors have remained unconvinced about Collier's suggestion that the adjective should be "woolless," though they have accepted Malone's proposed contraction of "tongue" into "toge.")[109] Yet, on some other matters, Collier proved more persuasive in the longer run. Active in his retirement, in 1875 he issued an edition of the anonymous *Edward III*, which he believed should be attributed to Shakespeare—a view that one substantial recent study of this historical drama has vigorously supported.[110]

At the time Wilde composed "The Portrait," Collier's standing therefore remained very mixed. In a letter to William Bell Scott, for example, Dante Gabriel Rossetti remarked on their differences of opinion about Collier's career: "You seem very confident as to Collier's right in that Perkins folio business. . . . I must

108. John Payne Collier, *Trilogy: Conversations between Three Friends on the Emendations of Shakespeare's Text Contained in Mr. Collier's Corrected Folio, 1632, and Employed by Recent Editors of the Poet's Works*, 3 vols. (London: T. Richards, 1874), 3:18.

109. In the orthography of the Second Folio (1632), the phrase is "Woolvifh gowne"; and in the Third Folio (1664), it is "Woolvifh gown," which recurs in the Fourth Folio (1685) (*Mr. William Shakespeares Comedies, Histories and Tragedies, Published According to the True Originall Copies: The Second, Third, and Fourth Folios in Facsimile*, 3 vols. [Cambridge: D. S. Brewer, 1985] 1:41, 2:600, 3:268). Collier agreed with Malone's reading that "toge" was the correct noun, which he printed in *The Works of Shakespeare: The Text Regulated by the Recently Discovered Folio of 1632, Containing Early Manuscript Emendations with a History of the Stage, a Life of the Poet, and an Introduction to Each Play, to Which are Added Glossarial and Other Notes and the Readings of Former Editions* (New York: Redfield, 1853), 606. Malone justified "toge" because "tongue" was "a very natural error for a compositor to fall into" (*The Plays and Poems of William Shakspeare: In Sixteen Volumes; Collated Verbatim with the Most Authentick Copies, and Revised: With the Corrections and Illustrations of Various Commentators; to Which Are Added, an Essay on the Chronological Order of his Plays; an Essay Relative to Shakspeare and Jonson; a Dissertation on the Three Parts of King Henry VI, an Historical Account of the English Stage*, ed. Malone, 16 vols. [Dublin: John Exshaw, 1794], 10:190). In his edition of the play, Philip Brockbank presents the phrase as "wolvish toge" (since it is "worn by Coriolanus as the fabled wolf wears sheep's clothing"; *Coriolanus*, ed. Brockbank, The Arden Edition of the Works of William Shakespeare [London: Methuen, 1976], 185). R. B. Parker agrees (*Coriolanus*, ed. Parker, The Oxford Shakespeare [Oxford: Clarendon Press, 1994], 237), as do Lee Bliss (*Coriolanus*, ed. Bliss, updated ed. [Cambridge: Cambridge University Press, 2010], 187), and Peter Holland (*Coriolanus*, ed. Holland, The Arden Shakespeare: Third Series [London: Bloomsbury, 2013], 258). In the original orthography, the phrase is "Wooluifh tongue." William Shakespeare, *The Tragedie of Coriolanus*, in *The Norton Facsimile of the First Folio of Shakespeare*, ed. Charlton Hinman, 2nd ed. (New York: Norton, 1996), 628.

110. See Eric Sams, *Shakespeare's Edward III* (New Haven: Yale University Press, 1996).

say that a careful reading of the correspondence *convinced* me (though to my great astonishment) that Collier was a trickster."[111] He proceeded to point out that one or two of the emendations seemed either "unaccountable" or "bold & most dubious."[112] In the following year, an obituary in the *Academy* gave a fair impression of Collier's troubling legacy. By 1883, when Collier passed away, the respected journal—even though it proved unwilling to revive the thirty-year-old "throwing about of brains" about the Perkins Folio—nonetheless took care to note that whenever one consulted works such as the *History of English Dramatic Poetry*, it was vital to exercise caution so that one might "distinguish what is genuine and trustworthy."[113] Meanwhile, in the *Bibliographer* Henry Wheatley concluded: "There can be no doubt that all Collier's work must be gone over again by others before it can be used with any satisfaction."[114] Such observations reveal that Collier went to his grave as an untrustworthy source. Commentators linked his disputed scholarship to the long-exposed frauds associated with Macpherson, Chatterton, and Ireland. It thus makes sense, in a story that begins by recalling the best-known figures in the history of literary fakes, that Wilde's narrator adopts some of his materials from Collier's contentious work. More interestingly, the storyteller of "The Portrait" in some respects emulates Collier by intermittently elaborating several imaginary details about numerous boy actors, which appear neither in this editorial forger's *History* nor in the various other sources on which Wilde drew.

If we return to the list of boy players that the narrator committed to his Chatterton-like "little book with fine vellum leaves and damask silk cover," we glean historical information—much of it derived from Collier—about the following individuals: Robin Armin, Sandford, Cooke, Nat. Field, Gil. Carie, Parsons, Will. Ostler, George Vernon, Alick Gough, Barrett, Dicky Robinson, Salathiel Pavy, Arthur Savile, Stephen Hammerton, Hart, and Kynaston. For most of these young men, the narrator provides either an unattributed quotation or an anecdotal fragment; he never divulges the precise origins of the evidence he had preserved from "the scanty record of their lives."[115] Moreover, the narrator

111. Dante Gabriel Rossetti, "To William Bell Scott," 4 July 1874, *The Correspondence of Dante Gabriel Rossetti*, ed. William E. Fredeman, 9 vols. (Cambridge: D. S. Brewer, 2002–2010), 6:506.

112. Rossetti, "To William Bell Scott," 4 July 1874, in *Correspondence*, 6:506.

113. "Obituary: J. Payne Collier," *Academy*, 29 September 1883: 214.

114. Henry Wheatley, *Notes on the Life of J. P. Collier; with a Complete List of His Works, and an Account of Such Shakespeare Documents as Are Believed to Be Spurious* (London: Elliot Stock, 1884), 51. This pamphlet reprints Wheatley's reflections on Collier's life that had appeared in the *Bibliographer* (1883–1884).

115. "The Portrait of Mr. W.H.," ed. Dowling, 70.

has a habit of occasionally tampering with the information Collier presents in the 1879 edition of his *History*. Here and there, he simply conjures something fanciful. Some of these lesser and greater deviations from an already disputed historical record then proceed in the spirit of Collier's willful "editorial and commentarial fraud." In a sense, these emendations, both large and small, bear more than a passing resemblance to forgeries modeled on Collier's specific type of commentarial counterfeiting.

Armin, whose first name happens to be Robert, not Robin, features more prominently than any other of the many boy actors mentioned in Collier's *History*, and it is clear that the narrator's reference to this "goldsmith's lad" who was "lured by *Tarlton* to go on stage" elaborates Wilde's source, where Collier simply remarks that all we learn from the volume titled *Tarlton's Jests* (1613) is that "[Robert] Tarlton prophesied that Armin should be his successor in clown's parts."[116] Meanwhile, Collier's *History* reveals that Sandford in "Mr. W.H." is in fact Sandfort. In Wilde's story, we learn that this young man's "performance of the courtesan Flamantia Lord Burleigh witnessed at Gray's Inn": a fact that appears in the cast list that Collier reproduces from the Lansdowne MSS.[117] By comparison, Wilde's narrator deviates slightly from Collier when he speaks of Cooke, "who played Agríppina in [Jonson's] tragedy of *Sejanus*."[118] In his *History*, it is worth noting, Collier reports: "We cannot assert positively, with Chalmers, that 'he acted as a woman in . . . *Sejanus*.'"[119] Yet, Collier adds, there is enough evidence "to make it probable that [Cooke] was Agríppina."[120] Similar license appears in Wilde's "Portrait" with regard to Nat. Field, who "played the 'Queen and Huntress chaste and fair'" in Jonson's *Cynthia's Revels*.[121] All Collier provides is a comment that affirms: "We are entitled, perhaps, to assume, from the place his name occupies, that Field was then the leading actor of the

116. "The Portrait of Mr. W.H.," ed. Dowling, 70. John Payne Collier, *The History of English Dramatic Poetry from to the Time of Shakespeare: And Annals of the Stage to the Restoration*, 2nd ed., 3 vols. (London: G. Bell, 1879), 3:412. Horst Schroeder has traced this and most of the succeeding references to boy actors to Wilde's sources; see *Annotations to Oscar Wilde, "The Portrait of Mr. W.H."* (Braunschweig: privately printed, 1986), 31–36.

117. "The Portrait of Mr. W.H.," ed. Dowling, 71; and Collier, *History of English Dramatic Poetry*, 1:260.

118. "The Portrait of Mr. W.H.," ed. Dowling, 71.

119. Collier, *History of English Dramatic Poetry*, 3:405–6.

120. Collier, *History of English Dramatic Poetry*, 3:405.

121. "The Portrait of Mr. W.H.," ed. Dowling, 71.

company."[122] With regard to Gil. Carie, Collier includes his name in a list of performers in the Children of the Revels.[123] Wilde's suggestion, however, that this particular young man—"attired as a mountain nymph"—also appeared in the "same lovely masque" performing "Echo's song for Narcissus" is not evident in the *History*, although Collier comments extensively on productions featuring boy actors in this drama.[124] Of "Parsons," Wilde's narrator tells us, he was "the Samalcis of the strange pageant of *Tamburlaine*."[125] Metaphorically, this is possibly true, since Parsons took the role of a hermaphrodite in a production of Christopher Marlowe's tragedy; the doubly sexed Samalcis—a legendary beauty—does not, however, appear in this famous play.[126]

The narrator's information about two boy actors whom King James favored at the time also deviates slightly from Collier's record, as well as from historical plausibility. The narrator claims, for example, that Will Ostler "accompanied King James to Scotland."[127] Collier, although he mentions this player, nowhere substantiates any such assertion, and, in any case, as Schroeder observes, this young man had been dead for three years by the time the monarch took the King's Men to Scotland in 1617.[128] As far as George Vernon is concerned, the *History* states that a 1629 royal warrant shows that there was nothing special in the fact that this young man—"to whom the King sent a cloak of scarlet cloth, and a cape of crimson velvet"—received this allowance, since His Majesty dispensed it to the other players in the King's Men.[129] At the same time, the remark that Alick Gough (whom Collier names Alexander) played "Cænis, Vespasian's concubine," in Philip Massinger's *Roman Actor* (1626) is correct.[130] The same is true of John Barret (said to be "Barrett" in the "Portrait") who took the lead

---

122. Collier, *History of English Dramatic Poetry*, 3:427–28.

123. Collier, *History of English Dramatic Poetry*, 1:341; 3:428.

124. "The Portrait of Mr. W.H.," ed. Dowling, 71; see, for example, Collier, *History of English Dramatic Poetry*, 3:427. Schroeder suggests that the narrator's elaboration may owe something to Amy Strachey's description of the roles boy actors took in *Cynthia's Revels* ("The Child-Players of the Elizabethan Stage," *The Woman's World* 2, no. 1 [1888]: 491; *Annotations*, 33).

125. "The Portrait of Mr. W.H.," ed. Dowling, 71.

126. Collier, *History of English Dramatic Poetry*, 3:206–7.

127. "The Portrait of Mr. W.H.," ed. Dowling, 71.

128. Schroeder, *Annotations*, 33.

129. "The Portrait of Mr. W.H.," ed. Dowling, 71; and Collier, *History of English Dramatic Poetry*, 1:450.

130. Collier, *History of English Dramatic Poetry*, 3:474.

in Nathaniel Richards's *Messalina* (c. 1634–1636).[131] Similarly, Wilde's narrator plucks information about Dicky Robinson—"a member of Shakespeare's company . . . who was known for his exquisite taste in costume, as well as for his love of woman's apparel"—directly from Collier's *History*.[132]

Much of the remaining information about boy actors in Wilde's "Portrait" derives from John Addington Symonds's *Shakspeare's Predecessors in the English Drama* (1884), a source the narrator is careful to cite. Symonds, who trained in classics at Oxford, was a prolific author whose works Wilde often drew upon for factual material while remaining sharply critical of some of the judgments he found in them. Although Wilde would have obviously known about Salathiel Pavy, "whose early and tragic death Jonson mourned in one of the sweetest threnodies," from this writer's famous poetic epitaph, it is still the case that when the narrator mentions this child performer he is largely following Symonds, who quotes at length from Jonson's poem and refers to it as a "beautiful elegy."[133] The situation is similar with the reference to Hammerton, "a most noted and beautiful woman-actor": this is a direct quotation from Symonds's commentary.[134] Yet the subsequent remark that this actor's "pale oval face with its heavy-lidded eyes and somewhat sensuous mouth looks out from a curious miniature of the time" appears to be a commentarial addition.[135] Meanwhile, Hart, whose "first success" involved playing "the Duchess in the tragedy of [James Shirley's] *The Cardinal* [1641]," appears, in this exact phrasing, in Symonds's study.[136]

The remaining two boy actors—"Arthur Savile" and "Kynaston"—emerge in other sources. The first appears in an 1875 edition of Shackerley Marmion's complete works, where we discover that one Arthur Savill played "Quartilla, Gentlewoman to Triphœna," in the comedy *Holland's Leaguer* (1631), and Collier mentions this actor's name in passing as one of six who "performed the

131. See Collier, *History of English Dramatic Poetry*, 2:29.

132. "The Portrait of Mr. W.H.," ed. Dowling, 71; Collier, *History of English Dramatic Poetry*, 3:475–76.

133. "The Portrait of Mr. W.H.," ed. Dowling, 71; and John Addington Symonds, *Shakspeare's Predecessors in the English Drama* (London: Smith, Elder, 1884), 301. Strachey also quotes Jonson's fine poem ("The Child-Players," 492). Wilde mentions Jonson's poem in "The Children of the Poets," *Pall Mall Gazette*, 14 October 1886, 5; reprinted in *Journalism Part I*, ed. Stokes and Turner, 6:99.

134. "The Portrait of Mr. W.H.," ed. Dowling, 71; and Symonds, *Shakspeare's Predecessors*, 299.

135. "The Portrait of Mr. W.H.," ed. Dowling, 71.

136. "The Portrait of Mr. W.H.," ed. Dowling, 71; and Symonds, *Shakspeare's Predecessors*, 298.

female characters" in this drama.[137] By comparison, the information about Edward Kynaston—whose career lasted for more than forty years—departs somewhat from a further source Wilde most likely used, John Doran's comprehensive study of the Restoration stage, *"Their Majesties' Servants"* (1850), though the narrator's comments on this famous actor's "white hands and amber-coloured hair," which "seem[s] to have retarded by some years the introduction of actresses upon our stage," appears to be Wilde's invention.[138]

This mass of details makes one point evident: in recalling the facts he consigned to this vellum-leaved book, Wilde's narrator remained reasonably close to the historical record while inserting some commentarial emendations of his own. And, for the most part, these Collier-like touches intensified the implicit homoerotic aspects of these boy actors' lives, especially when one reads of the intimacy that two of them supposedly enjoyed in King James's company. Moreover, in the paragraphs that follow, the narrator shows that cross-dressing on the early modern stage openly challenged the binary gender constructions that conscribed beauty, intellect, purity, or passion to "the mere accident of sex." Instead, and as made plain when a Willie Hughes or another attractive boy playing "Rosalind dons doublet and hose," on the Elizabethan stage, gender is returned to its proper place: the realm of "imaginative insight and creative energy."[139] By repudiating both Symonds's negative view that on stage "hobbledehoys 'squeaked' out the pathos of Desdemona and Juliet's passion," and the famous actress Helena Faucit's belief that Shakespeare requires our pity because inept boy actors "marred, misrepresented, [and] spoiled" the Bard's finest female cre-

---

137. *The Dramatic Works of Shackerley Marmion*, ed. James Maidment and W. H. Logan (Edinburgh: W. Paterson, 1875), 6; and Collier, *History of English Dramatic Poetry*, 1:451. It is perhaps an interesting coincidence that the title character of "Lord Arthur Savile's Crime" (1887) bears the same name.

138. Wilde's text runs as follows: "and Kynaston, of whom Betterton said 'it has been disputed among the judicious, whether any woman could have more sensibly touched the passions,' and whose white hands and amber-coloured hair seem to have retarded by some years the introduction of actresses upon our stage" (71). This wording modifies the source he likely used: "So exalted was [Kynaston's] reputation, 'that,' says Downes, 'it has since been disputable among the judicious, whether any woman that succeeded him so sensibly touched the audience as he" (John Doran, *"Their Majesties' Servants": Annals of the Stage, from Thomas Betterton to Edmund Kean*, ed. and rev. Robert Lowe, 3 vols. [London: J. C. Nimmo, 1888], 1:74). Doran's study, which first appeared in 1850, was reprinted several times in the nineteenth century. Schroeder, who provides this source, attributes Doran's quotation to John Downes, *Roscius Anglicanus, or, an Historical View of the Stage, from 1660 to 1706* (1708), 19, which appeared in facsimile reprint from J. W. Jarvis in 1886.

139. "The Portrait of Mr. W.H.," ed. Dowling, 73.

ations, the narrator maintains that these "lads and young men . . . suggested a new and delightful type of girlhood or of womanhood."[140] In making this bold claim, the narrator clears the ground to show that the boys in Shakespeare's theater, given their evident gifts as performers, were not simply attractive to men; this statement also suggests that masculinity and femininity were much more fluid than historians might imagine them to have been in the theatrical culture of the King's Men. He comments that the demand for young boys with fine looks and exquisite voices was so great in Shakespeare's day that—as a then newly discovered petition to the Star Chamber had shown—three men waylaid a "boy walking . . . quietly to Christ Church cloister one morning."[141] And, as Wilde's narrator proceeds to observe, if good-looking young men were not forced through abduction onto the stage, they adopted female parts because the Crown subjected them into playing such roles. We learn, for example, that Nathaniel Giles—one of the three men who kidnapped the chorister—served as Queen Elizabeth's chief commissioner, and it was he who supplied the Globe Theatre "with personable and graceful lads for the playing of female parts."[142] All of these comments provide a plausible context for the narrator to grasp in detail "the social position and early life of Willie Hughes before Shakespeare had met with him."[143] By this point, given the license with which he has treated an already questionable authority such as Collier, the storyteller reveals that he molded his evidence so that he could concoct what promised to be a plausible historical setting for his ultimate forgery: none other than Willie Hughes, the fictitious identity of the supposedly real "Mr. W.H."

THE ULTIMATE SHAKESPEAREAN FORGERY: "MR. W.H."

Determined to verify everything he could about the milieu in which "Mr. W.H." must surely have thrived, Wilde's impassioned narrator embarked on an elaborate historical fantasy in which Willie Hughes transformed into an entrancing figure through an imaginative tale that rendered the boy actor's character in-

140. Symonds, *Shakspeare's Predecessors*, 298; Lady Helena Saville Faucit Martin, *On Some of Shakespeare's Female Characters: Ophelia, Portia, Desdemona, Juliet, Imogen, Rosalind, Beatrice, Hermione*, 3rd ed. (London: Blackwood, 1888), 4; and "The Portrait of Mr. W.H.," ed. Dowling, 73.

141. "The Portrait of Mr. W.H.," ed. Dowling, 74. Wilde is alluding here to James Greenstreet's discovery of *Star Chamber Proceedings, Elizabeth*, Bundle C46, No. 39, *Clifton v. Robinson and Others*, Public Record Office, reported in *Athenæum* 3224 (10 August 1889): 203–4.

142. "The Portrait of Mr. W.H.," ed. Dowling, 75.

143. "The Portrait of Mr. W.H.," ed. Dowling, 75.

creasingly romantic: "I began to think of him not as the delicate chorister of a Royal Chapel, not as a petted minion trained to sing and dance in Leicester's stately masque, but as some fair-haired English lad whom in one of London's hurrying streets, or in Windsor's green silent meadows, Shakespeare had seen and followed, recognizing the artistic possibilities that lay hidden in so comely and gracious a form."[144] Yet, as the exuberant syntax shows, the colorful story the narrator conjured for "Mr. W.H." had become so embellished that it entirely lost what little hold it once had on amassing empirical proof to substantiate the truth of Cyril Graham's theory. As his wording reveals, he had distorted the task of "absolute verification" into one that pursued—as he imagined Shakespeare having done—the "artistic possibilities" of the Willie Hughes legend.[145]

This was a project that Wilde endorsed when he discussed the work of a long-standing friend who had completed a set of remarkable statues in honor of the Bard. Several months before the publication of "Mr. W.H.," Wilde praised the artist Lord Ronald Gower's monument to Shakespeare in Stratford-upon-Avon because it embraced the imaginative potential inspired by fictional characters. In his remarks, which the local press recorded in detail, Wilde noted that it was rare "that a sculptor passed beyond the imitative faculty and tried to mirror in marble and bronze the great creations of a great mind."[146] Shirking the base demands of naturalism, Gower's monument featured a brooding Hamlet, a distraught Lady Macbeth wringing her hands, a rotund Falstaff, and Prince Hal trying on his father's crown: characters striking attitudes in what Wilde enthusiastically described as "a moment of artistic revelation."[147] This effort to "produce such an ideal, imaginary, and poetic work of art" signaled for Wilde "a new birth of art taking place in England."[148] When the narrator in "The Portrait of Mr. W.H." vivifies the figure of Willie Hughes, it is an artistic and critical act that assuredly resembles Gower's efforts. In this regard, Wilde had begun to take up the kind of challenge that countless nineteenth-century artists, biographers, and dramatists faced when they sought to imagine not only the life that Chatterton led but also what the young poet looked like. Since nobody had depicted Chatterton in his own time, the most lasting image of the "marvellous Boy" was of course the Victorian one that Henry Wallis immortalized in the figure of George Meredith: a young man gorgeously half-draped

144. "The Portrait of Mr. W.H.," ed. Dowling, 76.
145. "The Portrait of Mr. W.H.," ed. Dowling, 70.
146. "Unveiling of the Gower Memorial at Stratford," *Birmingham Daily Post*, 11 October 1888: 5.
147. "Unveiling of the Gower Memorial," 5.
148. "Unveiling of the Gower Memorial," 5.

over a disheveled bed in what was supposed to be the forlorn poet's dismal London garret.[149]

In any case, we know that Wilde's storyteller had for some time been aware that he was engaging in nothing other than the forging of a factitious image for Willie Hughes. As we note above, the narrator admits that "absolute verification" might not be within his reach, since he has already confessed—given the lack of "the proofs, the links"—that he "could never readily attain" what he wanted.[150] The problem, as the narrator eventually recognized, was that his deepening immersion in the Shakespearean world of his own imagining brought before his mind a phantasmagoria that reflected not so much the hypothetical presence of "Mr. W.H." as his own projection of highly personal desires and passions onto the sixteenth-century universe he had researched in detail. "I was deciphering," he explains, "the story of a life that had once been mine, unrolling the record of a romance that, without my knowing it, had coloured the very texture of my nature."[151] Yet, instead of pausing over his intimate investment in realizing the truth of "Mr. W.H.," this chronicler of daydreams continued to spin tales of how his imagined Willie Hughes must have performed: "The very words that came to the actors' lips were wrung out of his pain. Their false tears were of his shedding."[152] In other words, the narrator's act of forgery threw his imagination into such a vivid past that he savored for some time the experience that accompanies the creative universe of any great work of fiction: Coleridge's famous theorization of the willing suspension of disbelief.[153]

Unpredictably, "The Portrait of Mr. W.H." hardly reaches a point of neat resolution when Wilde's narrator finally recognizes that his projections are in essence his own agonized performance of a desire to uphold a highly questionable theory through an extravagant—and, for quite a while, spellbinding—fiction. The moment he eagerly committed his theory to paper and sent it to Erskine, he suddenly suffered a "curious reaction" that gave away his "capacity for belief."[154]

149. For a discussion of Henry Wallis's famous painting, see our comments in chapter 2 (85–88).

150. "The Portrait of Mr. W.H.," ed. Dowling, 70.

151. "The Portrait of Mr. W.H.," ed. Dowling, 91.

152. "The Portrait of Mr. W.H.," ed. Dowling, 90–91.

153. Coleridge devised this term in a discussion of his and Wordsworth's *Lyrical Ballads* (first edition, 1798). See *Biographia Literaria*, 2 vols. (London: Rest Fenner, 1817), 2:2; in *Biographia Literaria, or Biographical Sketches of My Literary Life and Opinions*, ed. James Engell and W. Jackson Bate, *The Collected Works of Samuel Taylor Coleridge*, 16 vols., Bollingen Series LXXV (Princeton: Princeton University Press, 1969–2002), 7.2:6 Cf. *Lectures 1808–1819: On Literature*, ed. by R. A. Foakes, *Collected Works of Samuel Taylor Coleridge*, 5.2:266.

154. "The Portrait of Mr. W.H.," ed. Dowling, 94.

"Perhaps," he reflects, "the mere effort to convert any one to a theory involves some form of renunciation of the power of credence."[155] In the end, he recognized that his immense effort to transmit his evidence as an unassailable truth was simply the outcome of an exhausted passion. Certainly, the troubled history of forgery reveals that the art of fakery suffers greatest exposure when counterfeiters take their handiwork to the most strenuous lengths. Chatterton, Ireland, Collier: each of the names in turn bears witness to the perils involved in their exhaustive efforts to fabricate the past. Moreover, in each case these forgers' personal mission became one of public scandal. To Wilde's shattered narrator, the very idea of attempting to influence another led to "giving away what is most precious to one's self," and the lack of integrity in this act resulted in such fatigue that all he could do was capitulate to the fact that Willie Hughes was simply a "mere myth": one that prompted the narrator to wonder why Cyril Graham's forgery had "so deeply stirred" in him the desire to believe in it.[156] "To the present day," he remarks, "I cannot understand the beginning or the end of this strange passage in my life," so volatile had the experience of forgery been.[157]

Yet, in what becomes an unanticipated pattern, no sooner did the narrator come across Erskine in Central London than he discovered that his friend believed faithfully in all of the information received through the mail; in other words, the narrator's account moved Erskine to conclude that "Cyril Graham's theory" was "absolutely proved."[158] So urgent was Erskine in endorsing the theory that he was "determined to do justice to Cyril Graham's memory."[159] All of the male characters in this triangle—the narrator, Cyril, and Erskine—were, to some degree, occupying one another's past and present roles. By turns, each figure went through a frenetic process of passionately believing and then abruptly disbelieving in "Mr. W.H." As we have shown, this pattern habitually accompanied the troubled history of literary forgery in Britain.

This abrupt movement between extremes of belief and disbelief becomes glaringly obvious when we discover that in a letter Erskine informed the narrator "he had tried in every way to verify the Willie Hughes theory, and had failed."[160] As a consequence, Erskine declared that he had resolved to do, in an act of tragic mimicry, exactly what Cyril Graham had done: take his own life, in a manner that once more bears the weight of Chatterton's legend. But we

155. "The Portrait of Mr. W.H.," ed. Dowling, 94.
156. "The Portrait of Mr. W.H.," ed. Dowling, 94, 95.
157. "The Portrait of Mr. W.H.," ed. Dowling, 95.
158. "The Portrait of Mr. W.H.," ed. Dowling, 97.
159. "The Portrait of Mr. W.H.," ed. Dowling, 98.
160. "The Portrait of Mr. W.H.," ed. Dowling, 98.

learn that the moment the narrator reached Erskine's family home, to which he rushed upon receiving this letter, he realized that he had been completely wrong to assume that this friend had committed suicide. "Suicide," the doctor at the home responded: "Poor Erskine did not commit suicide. He died of consumption. He came here to die."[161] Ultimately, Erskine's declaration of dying for a theory was itself a carefully enacted forgery: one that was "actuated by a desire to reconvert" the narrator to an influential hypothesis about "Mr. W.H."[162] Fittingly enough, the story ends with Erskine's mother presenting the teller of this tragic tale with a gift: the forged portrait that Cyril tried to pass off as the original depiction of Willie Hughes. Wilde's narrator no longer has any interest in telling anyone about the "true history" of this fine artwork, which his friends believe must be "not a Clouet, but an Ouvry."[163] The culminating point of the story therefore resides in the idea that it should not matter whether a work of art, if well done, is forged or not, since "the Willie Hughes theory of Shakespeare's Sonnets"—as "The Portrait of Mr. W.H." has demonstrated—has an artistic power all of its own.[164] In other words, what matters in the end is the inspiring performance of the forgery (its elaborate staging), not what it tries to prove as the literal truth.

The stimulating thought of fabricating a history for Willie Hughes proved so captivating to Wilde that he himself was driven to devise, in a sense, a forgery of a forgery: this time by arranging for the creation of a copy of the imaginary fake he had conjured for Cyril Graham. After finishing his story, Wilde commissioned his friend Charles Ricketts to create a portrait of "Mr. W.H." along just those lines that the Old Etonian had desired. (This picture, which hung in Wilde's home at Tite Street, was sold at the bankruptcy auction, and has been missing ever since it passed into the hands of a London bookseller. On receiving the portrait, Wilde amusingly informed Ricketts: "It is not a forgery at all; it is an authentic Clouet of the highest *artistic* value.")[165] For a while, Ricketts considered publishing an edition of Wilde's story, one that considerably

161. "The Portrait of Mr. W.H.," ed. Dowling, 99.

162. "The Portrait of Mr. W.H.," ed. Dowling, 100.

163. "The Portrait of Mr. W.H.," ed. Dowling, 101. Horst Schroeder points out that Wilde probably meant an "Oudry," since this painter's work is described as "a Frenchman of the school of Clouet II" who painted Mary, Queen of Scots (Review of the Stuart Exhibition, *Athenæum* 3199 [16 February 1889]: 220; quoted in Schroeder, *Oscar Wilde, The Portrait of Mr. W.H.*, 11).

164. "The Portrait of Mr. W.H.," ed. Dowling, 101.

165. Wilde, "To Charles Ricketts," undated, in *Complete Letters*, 412. This letter was probably written in late 1889. Clouet was a sixteenth-century painter of miniatures.

expanded the version that *Blackwood's* had published, through his upcoming venture into fine printing, the Vale Press. But this idea came to nothing. In the end, the extended version of "The Portrait," which Wilde completed in the early 1890s, went to Elkin Mathews, although this arrangement proved to be an uncomfortable one. Wilde had already issued some of his works with the partnership that John Lane had with Mathews; together, the two publishers had reissued Wilde's *Poems* in 1892, with a fresh binding that Ricketts designed, and they issued *The Sphinx* (1894), which also featured Ricketts's outstanding design work. For reasons that remain unclear, even though in 1893 Mathews and Lane announced that a single-volume edition of what had become a novella was forthcoming, no such version of "The Portrait" emerged before Wilde's trials.

Scholars have rightly inferred that the scarcely disguised male homoerotic content of Wilde's story gave Mathews considerable unease. Mathews determined, in Lane's words, not to publish it "at any price."[166] (In any case, the delay in producing the longer text of "The Portrait of Mr. W.H." occurred when Mathews and Lane were ending their joint publishing enterprise.) Modern queer approaches have been usefully informed by studies in the history of sexuality that see Wilde's "Portrait" as a strategic and tactful response to the Labouchere Amendment to the eleventh section of the 1885 Criminal Law Amendment Act, which placed a wholesale ban on sexual relations between men, whether in public or in private. (This was the extremely prohibitive law under which Wilde received the maximum sentence.) Yet, as William A. Cohen has shown, it would be mistaken to assume that Wilde's "Portrait" provides "an unequivocal affirmation of homoeroticism," for reasons that are not purely connected with the fact that any manifesto in favor of love between men would prove impossible—given the hostile legal climate—to make public.[167] Cohen's point is that it remains misleading to assume that the story supports the modern

166. John Lane, "To Oscar Wilde," 7 September 1894, in *Complete Letters*, 607. Several days earlier, aware that Mathews and Lane were breaking up their partnership, Wilde had offered Lane to publish his plays and Mathews "Mr. W.H." ("To John Lane," 3 September 1894, in *Complete Letters*, 606).

167. William A. Cohen, *Sex Scandal: The Private Parts of Victorian Fiction* (Durham, NC: Duke University Press, 1996), 212–13. By comparison, Richard Halpern remarks upon the silence around sodomy that we find in Wilde's "Portrait"; Halpern observes Cyril Graham's "portrait embodies the silence that is the beyond of representation. And just as the portrait tries to fill the flaw or hole in Cyril's theory but fails, so the word 'sodomy' tries but fails to fill the void of speech that surrounds and conjures it" (*Shakespeare's Perfume: Sodomy and Sublimity in the Sonnets, Wilde, Freud, and Lacan* [Philadelphia: Univer-

presumption that Wilde stands "as the foundation upon which modernist gay self-identification is built," since "The Portrait" keeps exposing (among other things) the idea that "W.H." was Shakespeare's male object of desire as a theoretical fake. Moreover, the structure of the story makes it patently clear that Cyril Graham, Erskine, and the narrator are never simultaneously brought into any conceivable kind of mutual intimacy through the elaborate Willie Hughes theory. Their unquestionable orientation toward the erotic attractiveness of the beautiful male is always mediated through an elusive (because entirely imaginary) figure that answers to the initials "W.H." For this reason, as our chapter has tried to show, it is not so much the male object that codes the scarcely concealed homoeroticism of this story as the repeated acts of forgery themselves, which pass in turn from Cyril Graham to Erskine to the narrator. On this view, the patterns of homosexual attraction that suffuse many parts of the narrative remain intimately connected with the transmission of an imaginative longing to prove the truth that "W.H." was a boy actor; it is in this longing, one that can at last tire of its ambitions to fabricate the truth, where the homoerotic desire of Wilde's "Portrait" resides.

"The Portrait of Mr. W.H." therefore does nothing to suggest that the narrator's passion for "Mr. W.H." expressed a longing for the *physical* sexual intimacy between men that the brutal 1885 law proscribed. In 1889, Wilde's readers thought the same. The *Pall Mall Gazette*, for example, praised the "wonderful ingenuity" of Wilde story, while stating that the "article will amuse, if it does not convince, every student of Shakespeare."[168] The *Graphic*, too, amiably noted the "pleasant fictional guise" in which Wilde advanced "a new theory of Shakespeare's Sonnets."[169] Noticeably, as Schroeder observes, only one review thought *Blackwood's* had stepped out of line by printing a story with such a "very unpleasant" subject, and the *Scots Observer*—which had Wilde's future archenemy, W. E. Henley, at the helm—deemed the work "out of place . . . in

---

sity of Pennsylvania Press, 2002], 52). More recently, James Campbell has written of the patterns of "homoerotic spiritual procreation" that we find in "W.H."; Campbell sees the transmission of the theory of Willie Hughes between Cyril Graham, Erskine, and the narrator as the form of a powerful "sexual gnosis" that does not operate according to a hetero-reproductive logic ("Sexual Gnosticism: The Procreative Code of 'The Portrait of Mr. W.H.," in Joseph Bristow, ed., *Wilde Discoveries: Traditions, Histories, Archives* [Toronto: University of Toronto Press, 2013], 176). These queer analyses tend not to emphasize the history of forgery that informs Wilde's story.

168. "Literary Notes, News and Echoes," *Pall Mall Gazette*, 29 June 1889: 1.

169. "Magazines," *The Graphic*, 6 July 1889, 30.

any popular magazine."[170] For the most part, however, the main point of debate about Wilde's 1889 text of "The Portrait" was whether there was credibility in the Willie Hughes theory. The *Daily News*, for instance, maintained that since the "truth is that people only guess at William Herbert as the Mr. W.H. of the sonnets . . . Mr. Oscar Wilde's guess is perhaps quite as plausible."[171]

What remains crucial about male homoeroticism in "The Portrait," which seemed not to offend most of its early readers, is its status as a stigmatized form of desire that has throughout cultural history inspired the finest art. Such homosexual love, which the narrator identifies in the Neoplatonism of the Renaissance, involved "a kind of mystic transference of the expressions of the physical sphere to a sphere that was spiritual."[172] Thoughtfully worded formulations like this one show, as the storyteller asserts, that the passion that the noble Shakespeare had for the imaginary Willie Hughes was hardly based in "gross bodily appetite."[173] In order to create a firm connection between Socrates's reflections on the disciplined desire of the ἐραστής (*erastes*) for the ἐρώμενος (*eromenos*), on the one hand, and the amative emotional universe that Shakespeare inhabited, on the other hand, Wilde's plentiful additions to the 1889 text turn to Marsilio Ficino's 1492 translation of Plato's *Symposium* as a touchstone for comprehending a genealogy of writings that uphold the prophetess Diotima's claim that male "friends are married by a far nearer tie than those who beget mortal children."[174] By carefully maintaining his focus on the philosophical and spiritual supremacy of the intimacy between male friends, the narrator remarks that a truly distinguished European intellectual tradition—which includes Christopher Marlowe, Francis Bacon, Michael Angelo, Montaigne, Philip Sidney, Richard Barnfield, and Johann Joachim Winckelmann—has long elevated male friendship above procreation. This wealth of sources, some of them revealing the lasting influence of Pater's *Renaissance* on Wilde's creativity, provides the cue for the narrator to observe that "in Willie Hughes, Shakespeare found . . . the visible incarnation of his idea of beauty."[175] No sooner has he made this assertion than he draws directly from the "Chatterton"

170. *World*, 10 July 1889, 29. "The Magazines," *Scots Observer* 2, no. 33 (6 July 1889): 193. Schroeder, *Oscar Wilde, The Portrait of Mr. W.H.*, 14.

171. [Andrew Lang,] *Daily News* (London), 29 June 1889, in Stuart Mason [Christopher Sclater Millard], *Bibliography of Oscar Wilde* (London: T. Werner Laurie, 1914), 6.

172. "The Portrait of Mr. W.H.," ed. Dowling, 66.

173. "The Portrait of Mr. W.H.," ed. Dowling, 66.

174. "The Portrait of Mr. W.H.," ed. Dowling, 65.

175. "The Portrait of Mr. W.H.," ed. Dowling, 69.

notebook: "It is not too much to say that to this young actor . . . the Romantic Movement of English Literature is largely indebted."[176]

In the notebook, it is of course Chatterton who memorably stands as "the father of the | Romantic movement in England" (Appendix A, f.5ʳ [338]). Why, then, has the focus of Wilde's erudite story shifted this claim onto the ultimately unknowable Willie Hughes? The answer lies in at least two ideas about young male artists that Wilde had traced earlier in his career. Clearly, "The Portrait of Mr. W.H." suggests that the "Romantic Movement of English Literature" finds its origins in the figure of male embodiment of an "idea of beauty." This view is entirely consistent with Wilde's first conceptions of Keats: "It is in Keats," we recall Wilde observing in his 1882 lecture "The English Renaissance of Art," "that one discerns the beginning of the artistic renaissance of England."[177] Wilde built this assertion on his initial perception that the author of *Endymion* was a captivating icon of male splendor that could be best understood through one of Renaissance artist Guido Reni's renditions of St. Sebastian: "a lovely brown boy, with crisp, clustering hair and red lips."[178] By comparison, in Chatterton, Wilde had discovered a forger of unknown appearance who was interested, not in self-revelation, but in dramatic invention: "his aim was not to reveal | himself but to give pleasure—an | artist of the type of Shakespeare | and Homer—" (f.76ʳ [404]). By the time we reach "Mr. W.H." this powerful conception of the inspired young male artist who creates the "Romantic Movement" has transmuted into the "visible incarnation" of a beautiful idea that stirred "Romantic" figures such as Shakespeare. On this basis, from the Renaissance onward, all efforts that artists have made to realize this highest form of male-incarnated beauty have been necessarily thwarted, since their desire to forge it has repeatedly demonstrated the intensity of their great artistic striving. Here, then, the multiple connotations of "forge" become energized: the fabrication of a desired object and the fraudulent appropriation of the persona of someone other than oneself. These are dual definitions that have apparently been in use since the word entered the English language. In a sense, Wilde shows that all artistic creation is an act of forgery: an idea that animates nearly all of his prose of the period. All things considered, "The Portrait of Mr. W.H." situates itself in an ongoing "Romantic Movement" that continues to forge beauty in imaginary male guises. This was the decisive breakthrough that Wilde had originally made in the "Chatterton" notebook.

176. "The Portrait of Mr. W.H.," ed. Dowling, 69.

177. Wilde, "The English Renaissance of Art," in *The Collected Works of Oscar Wilde*, ed. Robert Ross, 14 vols. (London: Methuen, 1908), 14:249.

178. Wilde, "The Tomb of Keats," in *Journalism Part I*, ed. Stokes and Turner, 6:12. We discuss this passage in chapter 2 (137).

In many ways, Wilde's "Portrait" emphasizes the purely aesthetic and almost spiritual quality of male same-sex desire by representing heterosexual eroticism in stark contrast as expressly carnal, especially in relation to the sonnets about the "dark woman who, like a shadow or thing of evil omen, came across Shakespeare's great romance, and for a season stood between him and Willie Hughes."[179] Noticeably, it is the Dark Lady (as most commentators on the Sonnets style her) who eventually arouses "physical passion" in the poet.[180] Once the narrator reads that she is, promiscuously, "the bay where all men ride" in Sonnet 137, he recognizes this poem belongs to the part of the sequence where Shakespeare's voice has to contend with the fact that the Dark Lady has some control over the "master mistress" of his passion.[181] Yet here, too, the fiction-making power of forgery also comes to the fore. Noticeably, it is in this part of the Sonnets that the narrator discovers Shakespeare's most perfect skills, since it is when the poet "offers to mortgage his very life and genius to her if she will but restore to him that 'sweetest friend' of whom she had robbed him" that we find the greatest art.[182] In Sonnet 147, the narrator admires the passionate energy in the poetic voice's ability to "forge . . . false words of love."[183] Not only does the poet in this sonnet "lie . . . to her"; he also "tells her that he lies": "I have sworn thee fair, and thought thee bright, / Who art as black as hell, as dark as night."[184] As we can see, this triumph in expressing falsehood is what secures the exquisite status of this artwork. On this view, those sonnets addressed to the hellish Dark Lady are Shakespeare's supreme fictions. With regard to "that great Sonnet upon Lust" (Sonnet 129), which begins "Th' expense of spirit in a waste of shame," Wilde's narrator reminds us that no one less than Theodore Watts—who wrote influentially about Chatterton in 1880—remarked that this account of the poet's desire for the Dark Lady amounts to "the greatest sonnet ever written."[185] The point is surely a crucial one, since it once more brings to mind the belief that the most moving art stems from feelings that remain purely

---

179. "The Portrait of Mr. W.H.," ed. Dowling, 78.

180. "The Portrait of Mr. W.H.," ed. Dowling, 79.

181. "The Portrait of Mr. W.H.," ed. Dowling, 80; *Shakespeare's Sonnets*, 389.

182. "The Portrait of Mr. W.H.," ed. Dowling, 80.

183. "The Portrait of Mr. W.H.," ed. Dowling, 80.

184. "The Portrait of Mr. W.H.," ed. Dowling, 80; *Shakespeare's Sonnets*, 411.

185. "The Portrait of Mr. W.H.," ed. Dowling, 80; *Shakespeare's Sonnets*, 373. Theodore Watts declared that Sonnet 129 was "the greatest sonnet not only in the English language, but in the world" (Review of *The Sonnets of John Milton*, ed. Mark Pattison, *Athenæum* 2914 [1 September 1883]: 264). Watts's comments were reprinted in William Sharp, "Introductory Note," in *The Songs, Poems, and Sonnets of William Shakespeare*, ed. Sharp [London: W. Scott, 1888], 35).

performative: "At random," as Sonnet 147 declares, "from the truth vainly express'd."[186]

Wilde's "Portrait of Mr. W.H." redirects the vexed history of forging Shakespeare's works to the advent of the "Romantic movement" he earlier identified with Chatterton. Where Ireland and Collier transmuted the Bard's works into different kinds of literary fraud, Wilde's story reorients this intense desire to create fakes of Shakespeare by following the young Bristol poet's inspiring example. Further, Wilde's rehabilitation of Shakespearean forgery follows a lead that two of Chatterton's finest readers, Tyrwhitt and Malone, first suggested. In the process, Wilde's dynamic "Portrait" shifts the "Romantic" image of the young male artist away from the imagery he initially associated with Keats and the sensibility that he later found in the inspiring Rowley poems to the "master mistress" that captivated Shakespeare's heart in the Sonnets.

Ultimately, the task that this extraordinary story undertakes is to trace the origins of Romanticism back to the elusive figure of "W.H.": an object that becomes the venue for the most extravagant and decidedly homoerotic fiction of them all. By 1889, it is Willie Hughes who has become the "perfect representation" (f.75^r [403]) that Chatterton sought to create through his imaginary Rowley. And, in that respect, it is the memory of Chatterton's forgeries that guides the narrator's longing to fabricate the history of a Renaissance boy actor. In the end, even if the narrator admits that the extravagant concoction of "Mr. W.H." has been implausible all along, he also acknowledges—while he remains staring at Cyril Graham's ingeniously forged portrait—that there is a "great deal to be said for the Willie Hughes theory of Shakespeare's Sonnets."[187] There certainly is, since the theory of "W.H." that developed in the eighteenth century generated in Wilde's expert story an exemplary Shakespearean forgery that remains faithful to the decidedly "Romantic" tradition that the "marvellous Boy" Chatterton had begun.

186. *Shakespeare's Sonnets*, 411.
187. "The Portrait of Mr. W.H.," ed. Dowling, 101.

Conclusion

WILDE'S WRITINGS AND CHATTERTON'S REPUTATION: THE FIN DE SIÈCLE AND BEYOND

Wilde's "Chatterton" notebook not only marked a decisive moment of transition in his maturing success; it also coincided with what was arguably the zenith of Chatterton's literary legacy. By the spring of 1895, the respective reputations of the eighteenth-century Bristol poet and his late Victorian admirer could not have reached a higher pitch. At the time, Wilde—who at this point had firmly established his name as one of London's greatest dramatists—had two fine society comedies commanding the West End stage. Even if the play opened on 1 January to somewhat mixed reviews, the negative attacks that several respected commentators made on the hallmark "Oscar Wildeisms" and "Oscarisms" in *An Ideal Husband* hardly diminished its commercial success.[1] Six weeks later, *The Importance of Being Earnest* was greeted with great applause at the St. James's Theatre, although critics still varied in their opinions about the value of the exceptionally amusing "pure and undiluted Wildese" that all of his characters uttered in each scene.[2] On the evening of 18 February, Wilde, flush from the rapturous premiere of *Earnest,* made a visit to his cherished friend Charles Ricketts at Beaufort Street, London. In the 1930s, Ricketts recollected that during this visit Wilde urged him to publish, under the auspices of the newly founded Vale Press, a volume of Chatterton's poetry: "'You must of course bring out a Chatterton' . . . 'Rossetti was right; Chatterton was the founder of our romantic

1. Clement Scott, "The Playhouses," *Illustrated London News,* 12 January 1895: 35; and "A.B.W." [A. B. Walkley], Review of *An Ideal Husband,* in *Speaker,* 12 January 1895: 43–44; reprinted in Karl Beckson, ed., *Oscar Wilde: The Critical Heritage* (London: Routledge and Kegan Paul, 1970), 178–79.

2. [Anon.,] "The Importance of Being Oscar," *Truth,* 21 February 1895: 464–65; reprinted in Beckson, ed. *Oscar Wilde: The Critical Heritage,* 192.

school.' [Wilde] quoted some lines [by Chatterton] and said 'These might be by Keats.'"[3]

Later that evening, an episode occurred that precipitated the drastic series of events through which Wilde's meteoric rise as a dramatist was quickly met with an unexpected and devastating fall: Wilde received at the Albermarle Club what Ricketts recalled was "the insulting postcard that led to the 'Oscar Wilde Case.'"[4] The offending item was the notoriously misspelled calling card from the Marquess of Queensberry. As we mention in our Introduction, the irascible aristocrat accused Wilde of "Posing as Somdomite." This insulting document was the last straw of several unseemly affronts that the marquess had made against Wilde in both public places and the privacy of the writer's home. The allegation that Wilde had posed as a sodomite stemmed from his intimate involvement with the marquess's youngest son, Lord Alfred Douglas. It was at the start of March that Wilde—at Douglas's urgent prompting—hastily pursued what turned into a perilous libel suit against a titled man who appointed a formidable defense team. By 3 April, Wilde stood in the dock at the Old Bailey weathering a fierce cross-examination from Edward Carson, who had been one of his peers at Trinity College Dublin. Much to Wilde's surprise, he discovered that the defense wanted him to be answerable for the seemingly questionable morality of works such as "The Portrait of Mr. W.H." "I believe," Carson pronounced, "that you have written an article pointing out that Shakespeare's sonnets were sodomitical."[5]

Yet such allegations were nothing compared with the vitriol that Carson reserved for the 1890 text of Wilde's only novel, *The Picture of Dorian Gray*, which had appeared—to the consternation of some quarters of the British press—to be a thinly veiled celebration of male homoeroticism.[6] Carson interrogated Wilde about the revisions the author had made in the 1891 single-volume edition

3. Charles Ricketts, *Oscar Wilde: Recollections by Jean Paul Raymond and Charles Ricketts* (London: Nonesuch Press, 1932), 41. Wilde also seemed eager for Ricketts to issue the extended version of "The Portrait of Mr. W.H."; Ricketts did his best to explain that his purpose was "to issue the English classics and some minor poets, Vaughan, Suckling, Herbert, and Crashaw" (41). It appears that Wilde was very unhappy at this response, and Ricketts then agreed to issue "Mr. W.H." "at some distant date" (42).

4. Ricketts, *Oscar Wilde: Recollections*, 43.

5. Merlin Holland, *Irish Peacock and Scarlet Marquess: The Real Trial of Oscar Wilde* (London: Fourth Estate, 2003), 93.

6. For the hostile reviews of the version of *The Picture of Dorian Gray* that appeared in *Lippincott's Monthly Magazine* in July 1890, see Beckson, ed., *Oscar Wilde: The Critical Heritage*, 67–75.

that expanded and transformed the scandalous version that the transatlantic American monthly *Lippincott's* originally issued. Wilde admitted that he had rewritten parts of the narrative. "It had been pointed out to me," Wilde told the court, "not by any newspaper criticism or anything, but by the only critic of this century I set high, Mr. Walter Pater, he had pointed out to me that a certain passage was liable to misconstruction."[7] "In what respect?" Carson inquired. "In the respect that it would convey the impression that the sin of Dorian Gray was sodomy."[8] Such an admission unfortunately capitulated to Carson's persistent line of questioning, which sought to make it plain that aspects of Wilde's writings were—to recall the lurid epithet that recurred in these exchanges— "sodomitical." Once it became clear that the defense had additional stores of incriminating evidence, in the shape of carefully tracked-down information about Wilde's contacts with blackmailers, prostitutes, and cross-dressing partygoers in London's queer subculture, his lawyers advised him to withdraw his suit. This outcome bankrupted Wilde. Overnight, the Crown made the unprecedented move of pursuing Wilde for committing acts of "gross indecency" according to the eleventh section of the Criminal Law Amendment Act (1885). On 25 May 1895, after two messy trials, Wilde was sent down for two years with hard labor in solitary confinement. On his release in May 1897, when Wilde moved in exile through France and Italy under the pseudonym Sebastian Melmoth, Ricketts counted among the handful of loyal friends who remained in contact with him. The artist furnished the design for Wilde's last original work, *The Ballad of Reading Gaol*, which Leonard Smithers issued in 1898.

This turn of legal events has prompted scholars to reflect on what it might say about Wilde's character. Ellmann, in his influential biography, paints a picture in which this episode reveals that Wilde displayed an "inclination to betray himself"—an idea that Wilde explores in the early poem "Humanitad"—even if this disposition was not "thoroughgoing."[9] In "Humanitad," Wilde's desperate speaker strives to discover where truth resides in nature, only to sense humankind's profound alienation from the universe in which it dwells: "we / Lords of the natural world are yet our own dread enemy."[10] To be "purely human," in this poem, means that "we are but crucified," betrayed very much in the

7. Holland, *Irish Peacock and Scarlet Marquess*, 79.

8. Holland, *Irish Peacock and Scarlet Marquess*, 79.

9. Richard Ellmann, *Oscar Wilde* (New York: Alfred A. Knopf, 1988), 440.

10. Wilde, "Humanitad," in *Poems and Poems in Prose*, ed. Bobby Fong and Karl Beckson, *The Complete Works of Oscar Wilde*, 7 vols. to date (Oxford: Oxford University Press, 2000 and continuing), 1:104. "Humanitad" first appeared in *Poems* (London: David Bogue, 1881), 203–29.

manner of Jesus Christ.[11] Bearing these lines in mind, Ellmann asserts that Wilde "thought of self-betrayal as proceeding in surges, after which there would be recoveries."[12] On this view, Wilde "fulfilled his own half-wish to kill the success he loved."[13] Ellmann's perspective on the singularly misjudged libel suit extends what he has already stated about Wilde's fascination with Chatterton as one of several "analogues to his own new mode of life."[14] Chatterton, it seems, counted among one of the "new variations of his poem 'Humanitad'; the young man destroying himself by his own lasting song was like the nightingale in his new fairy tale, 'The Nightingale and the Rose,' who puts her breast against the thorn, until, by her death agony, a rose is born."[15] Wilde's discovery of Chatterton therefore forms part of a much larger pattern where the author's highly aestheticized propensity for finding examples of humanity's self-betrayal appealed to ineradicable, treacherous energies. Such an argument detects the same tragic flaw reappearing everywhere in Wilde's life and art. This persistent line of inquiry provides little room for imagining that Wilde's discovery of the Bristol poet might have had rather different implications for those works that the courts in 1895 wished to expose for their presumed criminal intent.

Yet, as we have aimed to show, Wilde's identification with Wordsworth's "marvellous Boy" was not necessarily the outgrowth of any self-destructive urge that we might detect in his behavior. In the remainder of this Conclusion, we consider the enduring artistic significance that the Rowley poems had in relation to Wilde's mature writings, ones that engage explicitly with forgery and fakery, especially with regard to questions about a character's authentic identity. Our juxtaposition of *The Picture of Dorian Gray*, with its tragically deceptive protagonist, and *The Importance of Being Earnest*, with its comic confounding of assumed names, suggests that the art of forgery remained a central, though unresolvable, preoccupation in Wilde's works after he published "The Portrait of Mr. W.H." We then consider the rather different fate of Chatterton's reputation beyond the fin de siècle. Even though twentieth-century scholarship on the young poet increased considerably in authority and reliability, it emerged during a period when there was lessening cultural interest in the figure that the late Victorian critics had placed at the head of the Romantic school. Seldom do current accounts of English Romanticism pay much attention to Chatterton's

11. Wilde, "Humanitad," in *Poems and Poems in Prose*, ed. Beckson and Fong, 1:104.

12. Ellmann, *Oscar Wilde*, 440.

13. Ellmann, *Oscar Wilde*, 440.

14. Ellmann, *Oscar Wilde*, 284.

15. Ellmann, *Oscar Wilde*, 285. Wilde's story "The Nightingale and the Rose" appeared in *The Happy Prince, and Other Tales* (London: David Nutt, 1888), 25–41.

defining role in shaping that movement. In the meantime, it took until Ellmann's imposing biography before Wilde's scholarly reputation—which had long been eclipsed by the shame and scandal attached to his trials and imprisonment—eventually put the Irish writer's name squarely within the canon of modern English literature. As knowledge of Wilde's life has subsequently increased, one point has become especially clear to us. Wilde dedicated considerable time to tracing the development of Romanticism because he strove to understand his place in English literary history. As he tracked that history back to Chatterton, he extended in his writings the powerful discovery that there were immense creative possibilities in the art of forgery.

ADVANCED BUNBURYISTS: WILDE'S FORGED IDENTITIES AFTER "MR. W.H."

As we explain in chapter 6, Wilde's "Portrait of Mr. W.H." inhabits a complex series of forged networks that link authors across time and literary conventions, and it further establishes fresh connections between the counterfeit artifacts that emerged in a tradition that started with James Macpherson's *Works of Ossian* and Chatterton's Rowley poems, and finished with the fictional Cyril Graham's forged portrait of Shakespeare's "onlie begetter." These resonant connections inform the writings that Wilde composed at his creative peak: *The Picture of Dorian Gray* and his society plays of the early 1890s. In her astute study of "The Portrait of Mr. W.H.," Aviva Briefel considers an additional network that arises from the intricate turn of events in this novella. Briefel claims that the forged portrait that Cyril Graham commissioned of "Mr. W.H." is the nexus of a male homosocial network. "Rather than using the fake as an object of disavowal," she writes, Wilde "positions it [the portrait] as a forthright enabler of male intimacy," one that "has the power to mesmerize and satisfy its viewer completely."[16] This suggestive idea drives at the heart of why the forged work is so compelling: it is an object that aims to satiate perfectly a desire that most likely cannot be otherwise fulfilled, whether through an absence of historical evidence (as in the case of the forged portrait of Willie Hughes) or owing to the presence of restrictive social mores or even laws punishing homosexual desire (the 1885 Criminal Law Amendment Act). Briefel focuses on the aspect of connoisseurship that underscores the characters' analysis and appreciation of the forged portrait. In her view, theirs is an interpretive mode that serves as the

16. Aviva Briefel, *The Deceivers: Art Forgery and Identity in the Nineteenth Century* (Ithaca, NY: Cornell University Press, 2006), 75.

basis for their shared interest, and thus represents a conduit for their intimate same-sex relationships. Yet we have suggested that the falseness of the beautiful forged object is not necessarily a disavowal of an otherwise unrepresented homoeroticism. Instead, we argue, the faking of Cyril Graham's portrait of "W.H." remains central to its status as a supreme work of art.

In "The Portrait of Mr. W.H.," and in many other works Wilde completed in the early 1890s, the forged object is one example of a true inventiveness that is both artful and aesthetic. Here, then, we discover the imprint of Chatterton, the creator who "needs must forge" (Appendix A, f.75ʳ [403]), not because any socially proscribed desire compels him to create fakes, but because the art he wishes to fashion requires that remarkable imaginative impulse. For both Erskine and the unnamed narrator of Wilde's "Portrait," their belief in the theory of Willie Hughes depends upon their faith in the veracity of the narrative that Cyril had told about the painting of "W.H." Endless searches through the historical record never bear fruit; the true Willie Hughes is never identified. Yet, by setting in motion the events that definitively shaped the lives (and sometimes the deaths) of three men, the impact of the Willie Hughes in the faked likeness is almost the same as if he had been real. In the broadest sense, Cyril, Erskine, and the narrator reenact the activities of those generations of literary scholars who sought to prove whether Rowley existed. Like these male characters, such scholars searched archives and scrutinized the intricate details of the supposed fifteenth-century manuscripts. The proof that finally put the question to rest did not arrive until 1871 when Walter W. Skeat published his edition of the Rowley poems. But by that time the inspiring impression that Chatterton's verse and his forged inventions had left on subsequent poets and scholars was unmistakable. During the fin de siècle, the fact that Rowley was Chatterton's invention had simply become beside the point. As Vivian suggests in "The Decay of Lying," life imitates art far more than art ever imitates life.

At greater length than ever before, Wilde addressed the value of the well-crafted lie and the tendency of life to follow the direction of art or artifice in *The Picture of Dorian Gray*. With a title that echoes "The Portrait of Mr. W.H.," *The Picture of Dorian Gray* also reiterates the plot and topics of the shorter fiction: a male homosocial triad of connoisseurs invested in the creation of a portrait and the person it depicts are caught up in events which that artwork precipitates, and the lives of two of the three men consequently come to an end. Briefel classifies Basil Hallward's portrait of Dorian Gray as a "fake," and she contends that Dorian Gray's attempts to "separate himself from the portrait lead him to take on its appearance."[17] This, from her perspective, becomes an exercise that

17. Briefel, *The Deceivers*, 179.

proves futile, since these attempts only further integrate Dorian Gray's tragic fate with the fate of his portrait.[18] But, in contradistinction to Briefel's claim, it is the case that within the diegesis the painting is not (even metaphorically) a forgery: it is neither an image that someone other than its painter purports to have created nor a picture illustrating someone different from its sitter. Instead, this artwork is a contemporary likeness that bears an uncannily high degree of verisimilitude to the captivating youthfulness of its male subject. The supernatural economy that affects the painting—which becomes, of course, increasingly ugly as Dorian commits more and more crimes, even as Dorian himself retains his youth and beauty—renders the image ever more true to life. Only when he has committed homicide does Dorian Gray finally confront the grotesqueness of the hidden-away portrait, which is now "more loathsome, if possible, than before."[19] In a final moment of anagnorisis, he recognizes that he has conducted his long career of appalling misdeeds "for curiosity's sake" in the name of the "denial of the self."[20] At the very instant that he stabs the unsightly painting, which has borne witness to his horrifying crimes, he dies "withered, wrinkled, and loathsome of visage."[21] In an equally startling reversal, the portrait correspondingly returns to its original form: a pristine image of Dorian Gray in "his exquisite youth and beauty."[22]

Where, then, might the Chattertonian art of forgery lie in *The Picture of Dorian Gray*? There are several scenes that resonate with Chatterton's legacy. Take, for example, Sibyl Vane, the young actress in the second-rate theater whose Shakespearean performances temporarily captivate Dorian Gray. As he informs his friend, Lord Henry Wotton: "She was the loveliest thing I have ever seen in my life."[23] It is Sibyl's "consummate art-instinct" that inspires the superficially youthful and seemingly innocent protagonist.[24] Infatuated, Dorian Gray believes that her perfect role-playing will "make the world as mad" as it has made him.[25] But the precise moment he experiences a "very complex passion" for her, Sibyl Vane undergoes an altogether different transformation.[26] She loses the thrill of Shakespeare's words and her ability to portray them when she be-

18. Briefel, *The Deceivers*, 179.

19. Wilde, *The Picture of Dorian Gray: The 1890 and 1891 Texts*, ed. Joseph Bristow, *The Complete Works of Oscar Wilde*, 7 vols. to date (Oxford: Oxford University Press, 2000 and continuing), 3:359. We are quoting from the 1891 text.

20. *The Picture of Dorian Gray*, ed. Bristow, 3:356.

21. *The Picture of Dorian Gray*, ed. Bristow, 3:359.

22. *The Picture of Dorian Gray*, ed. Bristow, 3:357.

23. *The Picture of Dorian Gray*, ed. Bristow, 3:213.

24. *The Picture of Dorian Gray*, ed. Bristow, 3:217.

25. *The Picture of Dorian Gray*, ed. Bristow, 3:217.

26. *The Picture of Dorian Gray*, ed. Bristow, 3:219.

lieves that hers is an authentic romance with the man she misleadingly knows only as "Prince Charming." This is a sad state of affairs, not just because Dorian Gray is hardly a fairy-tale prince. Once Lord Henry accompanies him to witness her glory, her performance disintegrates miserably because she presumes it is she and not her character that is in love. In *Romeo and Juliet*, she delivers the dialogue "in a thoroughly artificial manner": "It took the life away from the verse. It made the passion unreal."[27] For Sibyl, the reality that derives from artistic skill is not authentic emotion. Yet her terrible performance shows that the only way to sustain the illusion of authenticity is through the techniques in performance that she has rejected. As a result, we recognize that the reality that art may brilliantly conjure derives its power far more from its practices in fabricating feeling than from the free and spontaneous expression of emotion.

At the same time, the narrative suggests that art cannot serve as an instruction manual that provides consumerist subjects with a ready-made repertoire of elegant thoughts and gracious feelings. This point becomes evident in an earlier chapter where Dorian Gray adopts the "yellow book" that Lord Henry has given him.[28] This volume, which features a "certain young Parisian, who spent his life trying to realize in the nineteenth century all the passions and modes of thought that belonged to every century but his own," inspires Dorian Gray's artistic choices and tastes.[29] "The hero," Wilde's narrator remarks, "in whom the romantic and scientific temperaments were so strangely blended, became to him a kind of prefiguring type of himself."[30] Even more unnervingly, "the whole book seemed to him to contain the story of his own life, written before he had lived it."[31] In many respects, Dorian Gray recalls those characters described in "The Decay of Lying"—the Kensington governess and Mr. Hyde—who recognize a parallel to their own lives in novels and then find themselves drawn into a life imitating the narratives they have read, powerless to change the course of events predetermined by the plot. Wilde attributes these dynamics to "life's imitative instinct," which he distinguishes from "imagination," which is "essentially creative" and always "seeks for a new form."[32] Dorian Gray's greatest fault

27. *The Picture of Dorian Gray*, ed. Bristow, 3:239.

28. *The Picture of Dorian Gray*, ed. Bristow, 3:274. This "yellow book" (the color suggests it is French) is implicitly J.-K. Huysmans' anti-realist *À rebours* (1884); the title is usually translated into English as *Against Nature*.

29. *The Picture of Dorian Gray*, ed. Bristow, 3:274.

30. *The Picture of Dorian Gray*, ed. Bristow, 3:276.

31. *The Picture of Dorian Gray*, ed. Bristow, 3:276.

32. Wilde, "The Decay of Lying," in *Criticism: Historical Criticism, Intentions, The Soul of Man*, ed. Josephine M. Guy, *The Complete Works of Oscar Wilde*. 7 vols. to date (Oxford: Oxford University Press, 2000 and continuing), 4:91.

may be that he is derivative in a purely reactionary, unimaginative way. It is not that he has creatively forged a powerfully original identity that has absorbed the finest lessons from either Lord Henry's aesthetic criticism or Hallward's portraiture. Neither has he perfected an inspired art of lying. Instead, Dorian Gray exists in a world of hazardously preserved and belated imitations: a heartless mimesis that displays no ingenuity, only cunning deception and downright criminality. One might therefore think of Dorian Gray as the inversion of Chatterton, whose Rowley poems had at one time mistakenly appeared to hostile critics as the sign of the poet's innate delinquency. Everything in Dorian Gray's world is an uninventive "echo of someone else's music"—as the whimsical Lord Henry, from whom Wilde's protagonist unthinkingly imbibes so much, puts it with such calculated irony.[33]

Since they address the duplicity and hypocrisy of British high society, and since they draw on a rich tradition of satirical drama and farce, Wilde's fin-de-siècle society plays explore the friction between artificiality and veracity. At the time of their writing, Wilde's extramarital intimacy with Douglas came ever closer to exposure, and the threat of this type of scandal surfaces at different points in these dramas. If the tidy resolutions of *Lady Windermere's Fan* (1892) and *An Ideal Husband* excuse dishonesty (insofar as they are the sole route to securing a desired outcome: Robert Chiltern's political office, Lord Goring's marriage, and the restoration of the Windermeres' social status quo), in *Earnest* the entire plot turns on the hilarious creation and uncovering of false identities. Jack Worthing forges a doppelgänger: a fictitious brother Ernest, whom he visits whenever he wishes to escape his tedious life in the country. Likewise, the London-based Algernon Moncrieff has devised a similar fraud, although on this occasion his alibi takes the form of an imaginary companion, Bunbury. As modern critics have observed, Bunbury—whom Algernon declares is an "incomparable expression"—serves with great versatility not only as a proper name but also as a noun ("Bunburyist"), a verb ("Bunburyed," "Bunburying"), and an adjective for items of clothing ("Bunbury suits").[34] By occupying all these parts of speech, Bunbury therefore operates as the generic signifier of any fictive persona that anyone might adopt for his or her personal grammar so that an individual might resist the repressive demands of social decorum and thus enjoy an otherwise prohibited existence. In Algernon's case, his obligations to disappear from his domineering aunt to visit his absent friend Bunbury have been cultivated over many years. Jack has gone even further by commissioning calling cards and

33. *The Picture of Dorian Gray*, ed. Bristow, 3:182.

34. Wilde, *The Importance of Being Earnest*, ed. Russell Jackson, New Mermaids (London: Ernest Benn, 1980), 13, 14, 16, 40.

a cigarette case for his alter ego, Ernest. Such details bear some resemblance to the significance of objects—such as parchment manuscripts and painted portraits—that Thomas Chatterton and Cyril Graham needed to sustain their respective phantom creations.

Yet the eventual revelation of these forgeries hardly alienates the two men from each other. When Jack reveals that his name is not Ernest, Algernon replies: "You have always told me it was Ernest. I have introduced you to every one as Ernest. You look as if your name was Ernest. You are the most earnest-looking person I ever saw in my life. It is perfectly absurd your saying that your name isn't Ernest."[35] As we can see, Jack's fraud leaves Algernon bemused, not angry. His baffled reaction to Jack, and their ensuing conversation, shows that the revelation has not weakened but enhanced their bond. Both of them turn out to be resourceful Bunburyists—a fact that Algernon concedes he had "always suspected."[36] Meanwhile, the plot in which they have performed these elaborate fabrications proves to be even more ingenious than either of them could ever have predicted. The lies that were necessary to procure their short-term desires—including Jack's story that he was named Ernest and Algernon's story that he was Jack's brother—turn out to be true. Simultaneously, Jack's forced and ostensibly painful statement of truth—"I have no brother at all. I have never had a brother in my life"—transpires as patently false.[37] As Christopher Craft observes, the play's "deepest insistence is that individual and collective identities are based upon, and secured by, the most arbitrary of constructs"—namely, those of language.[38] To render Jack's fiction legitimate, the family must, like the scholars trying to verify Thomas Rowley and Willie Hughes, turn to the written record, which is exactly what they do. In the final scene, Jack scours the army lists for names of people who actually *were:* "Mallam, Maxbohm, Magley . . . Markby, Migsby, Mobbs."[39] Only when he discovers "Moncrieff! . . . Ernest John" will the happy ending ensue.[40] And, as Craft shrewdly perceives, only at that moment do the coded suggestions that buttressed the comic coincidences become explicable, thus allowing a heteronormative marriage plot to bring the action to a close. The amusing conclusion thus puts the teasing homoerotic insinuations between Jack, Algernon, and Algernon's forged friend, Bunbury,

35. *The Importance of Being Earnest*, ed. Jackson, 12.
36. *The Importance of Being Earnest*, ed. Jackson, 13.
37. *The Importance of Being Earnest*, ed. Jackson, 76.
38. Christopher Craft, "Alias Bunbury: Desire and Termination in *The Importance of Being Earnest*," *Representations* 31 (1990): 22.
39. *The Importance of Being Earnest*, ed. Jackson, 103.
40. *The Importance of Being Earnest*, ed. Jackson, 103.

in fictional suspension. From one perspective, it looks as if the real world of the play has simply mimicked fiction. Yet from another, the comedy shows that fiction must remain intact for real life to continue. Wilde developed this insight from a suggestion that originated in the "Chatterton" notebook, where he carefully noted, along with Watts, the demands of "perfect representation" for the true artist (Appendix A, f.75ʳ [403]). In Chatterton's Rowley poems, Wilde discovered consummate art that strove to invent, not imitate, reality. This was a dazzling achievement that inspired Wilde's sophisticated dialogues, aesthetic theories, demanding fiction, and sparkling dramas, which he completed during the most intense period of his professional life, from the late 1880s to the mid-1890s.

CHATTERTON, THE 1890s, AND HIS TWENTIETH-CENTURY AFTERLIFE

As his conversation with Ricketts shows, Wilde's enthusiasm for Chatterton, which spurred the Vale Press edition, remained unabated during the 1890s. Wilde also made his passion for the Bristol poet clear in an 1894 interview with the *Theatre*. The journal, which kept a close critical eye on the London stage, sent a staff member to meet with Wilde at Babbacombe, the seaside retreat where Constance Wilde's family owned a gracious home, and where he composed *A Woman of No Importance* and *Lady Windermere's Fan*. Wilde held forth with his opinions on an array of authors. Shelley, he stated, was "a magnificent genius" who was nevertheless "too ethereal"; Tennyson was a "supreme artist"; and those who preferred H. Rider Haggard to R. L. Stevenson were simply "insane."[41] In the same discussion, Wilde revived his penchant for extolling the virtues of minor criminals, including smugglers (he was "very sorry Smugglers have gone out of fashion"), pirates ("very fine fellows"), and burglars (for whom he feels "considerable sympathy").[42] (Babbacombe is on the Devon coast, which historically has links with pirates and wreckers.) In this witty conversation about great writers and petty criminals, Wilde reserved his superlative for Chatterton, whose life, Wilde said, was "the most tremendous tragedy in history."[43]

Even after Wilde had endured eighteen months of solitary confinement, Chatterton still served as one of his touchstones. As we have noted, Chatterton's

---

41. Percival Almy, "New Views of Oscar Wilde," *Theatre* (March 1894): 120, 121.
42. Almy, "New Views of Oscar Wilde," 124.
43. Almy, "New Views of Oscar Wilde," 121.

name appears among the list of works Wilde requested while in Reading Gaol, and Wilde cites Chatterton's "Excelente Balade of Charitie" in the long prison letter which he completed toward the end of his sentence, and which, in 1905, Robert Ross named *De Profundis*. Although he was forty-two years old on his release, the pecuniary destitution and loneliness he suffered in Paris made his desperate plight—in the eyes of one of his contemporaries—resemble that of the teenage Chatterton. His earliest biographer, Robert Harborough Sherard, thought the shabby room at the Hotel d'Alsace, where Wilde expired in late 1900, resembled Chatterton's Holborn lodgings: "All was faded and threadbare. The impression was that of poverty masquerading at comfort. Chatterton's garret in Brook Street must have presented a sight less poignant."[44] This allusion suggests the rich associations of the young poet's name. Not only, then, was Chatterton Wilde's poetic forebear, but Chatterton's life story, especially its distressing end, also appears to have anticipated Wilde's demise from brain disease.

Chatterton's name became a resonant point of reference for other writers associated with Wilde's circle. This was especially true of the Rhymers' Club, whose attendees included Arthur Symons and Wilde. This all-male gathering, which met mostly at the Cheshire Cheese public house off Fleet Street, produced two important anthologies in the early 1890s, and it served as a platform for several noteworthy poets to launch their careers. In 1894, Ernest Rhys, who went on to edit the popular Everyman series for Dent, published a poem that recounts a country boy making a visit to a bookstore on Brooke Street, London, where he serendipitously sees an edition of the Rowley poems in an "open window" that "kept / Old books in rare display."[45] The watchful vendor apprehends the speaker: "''Twas Brook Street,' said he, 'saw him die, / Old Holborn knew him well.'"[46] Mindful of the throngs that pass along the busy street, the speaker concludes with a brief "Requiem" where he says it is "well" that Chatterton "sleeps" in this bustling modern city.[47] According to Victor Plarr, another prominent Rhymer, his colleague Ernest Dowson, who died aged thirty-two at Sherard's home at Catford, was "becoming almost as famous as that earlier unhappy poet who by self-destruction set apart his life-story in the sorrowful annals of litera-

---

44. Robert Harborough Sherard, *Twenty Years in Paris: Being Some Recollections of a Literary Life* (London: Hutchinson, 1905), 448.

45. Ernest Rhys, "Chatterton in Holborn," *A London Rose and Other Rhymes* (London: Elkin Mathews and John Lane, 1894), 13.

46. Rhys, "Chatterton in Holborn," 14.

47. Rhys, "Chatterton in Holborn," 15.

ture."[48] Plarr further suggests that Dowson embraced the comparison during his lifetime, since this gifted Decadent poet chose to take up lodgings in the Featherstone Buildings on High Holborn because "of poor Chatterton's supposed residence there long ago."[49]

In the meantime, the painful loss of Chatterton still served as a warning toward those who disregarded poetic genius. Edward Dowden, one of Wilde's first professors at Trinity College Dublin, made this point. Dowden, whose research on Shakespeare has some bearing on "The Portrait of Mr. W.H.," maintained a tangled relationship with Wilde. Although Dowden was one of the sponsors of Lady Wilde's annuity from the Royal Literary Fund, he was also the only person who refused W. B. Yeats's request for a letter of sympathy for Wilde on the eve of his trial.[50] Certainly, Dowden praised the real "literary talent" demonstrated in Wilde's 1881 *Poems*, but he also remained concerned that Wilde's "want of sincerity, and of original power of thought and feeling will condemn him to be only a phantasm."[51] To Dowden, Chatterton was a much better example of the artist. Almost ten years after Wilde's death, Dowden wrote a poem, "Prologue to Maurice Gerothwohl's Version of Vigny's 'Chatterton,'" where the speaker warns the "world of men" that by sacrificing the poet, they disinherit themselves.[52] Wilde's presence lingered in Dowden's family, if in a manner that helped shape Wilde's reputation along very different lines. Dowden's daughter, Hester Travers Smith, was a noted spiritualist who channeled Wilde's spirit and transcribed the messages she claimed he communicated through a Ouija board. Her transmission of Wilde's wisdom from beyond the grave, particularly his views on modernist writers, appeared in 1924. Travers Smith's shaky sense of literary history led to some rather surprising moments in her mediumship. She wrote automatically at Wilde's otherworldly behest: "The only mind I have entered into which appeals to my literary sense is John Galsworthy. He is my successor, in a sense. He is the aristocrat in literature, the man who takes joy

48. Victor Plarr, *Ernest Dowson 1888–1897: Reminiscences, Unpublished Letters, and Marginalia* (New York: Laurence J. Gomme, 1914), 9.

49. Plarr, *Ernest Dowson*, 104.

50. See *The Complete Letters of Oscar Wilde*, ed. Merlin Holland and Rupert Hart-Davis (London: Fourth Estate, 2000), 364–66; and William Butler Yeats, *Autobiographies*, ed. William H. O'Donnell and Douglas N. Archibald, *The Works of W. B. Yeats*, 13 vols. (New York: Macmillan and Scribner's, 1989–2008), 3:224.

51. Edward Dowden, *The Letters of Edward Dowden* (London: Dent, 1914), 178.

52. Edward Dowden, *Poems* (London: Dent, 1914), 218. Gerothwohl's version of the play was, as Dowden's title suggests, based on Vigny's and first performed in 1909. See H. J. Eldredge, *The Stage Cyclopaedia* (London: "The Stage," 1909), 74.

in selection, as our poor friend Shaw never did."[53] On James Joyce's *Ulysses*, Wilde's ghost opined: "It gives me the impression of having been written in a severe fit of nausea. . . . [H]ere we have the heated vomit continued through the countless pages of this work."[54] What remains significant about *Psychic Messages from Oscar Wilde* is not so much the literary preferences that Travers Smith attributes to the posthumous Wilde as her bold initiative to forge his spiritual presence. No matter how effete her channeling of Wilde's supernatural wit (at one point her automatic pencil jots down the words "vulgarity always begins at home"), her eagerness to relay these psychic messages belongs to a broader cultural wish to reanimate his spirit.[55]

The 1910s and 1920s marked an era when Wilde's spectral presence started to haunt twentieth-century culture in other ways. In the years leading up to World War I, several events ensured that Wilde's legacy returned to public attention. To begin with, news reports circulated around the libel trial that Alfred Douglas took out against Arthur Ransome, Ransome's publisher, and the Times Book Club for issuing *Oscar Wilde: A Critical Study* (1912). This impressive volume, which was the first significant appraisal of Wilde's career, caused offense because it insinuated that the unpublished portion of *De Profundis* was addressed to Douglas. Simultaneously, fanciful stories about Wilde's life and legend began to flow. The most extreme ones divulged that he had escaped burial. His nephew by marriage, Fabian Lloyd, capitalized on his uncle-in-law's fame through a report stating that Wilde had absconded to India. Lloyd told this tall tale when Wilde's remains were about to be moved from the undistinguished burial site in suburban Bagneux to the controversial modernist monument at Père Lachaise that Jacob Epstein had designed. (The installation of Epstein's striking sphinx, whose sculpted testicles delayed the unveiling of the tomb, was a sure sign that Wilde's memory was proving irrepressible.) Lloyd bet ten thousand francs that the soon-to-be exhumed coffin "held nothing but paving stones, cotton wool, and a large glass jar, which in turned [held] a manuscript by Wilde, entitled 'Amen,' with subtitles, 'A Comedy' and 'A Tragedy.'"[56] By this point, Lloyd had done much more than simply provoke the press. He had also become a dab hand at fabricating forgeries of Wilde's works. Lloyd—poet, boxer, and Dada performance artist, who went by the names of Arthur Cravan,

53. Hester Travers Smith, *Psychic Messages from Oscar Wilde* (London: T. Werner Laurie, 1924), 23; the American edition appeared as *Oscar Wilde from Purgatory: Psychic Messages* (New York: H. Holt, 1926).

54. Travers Smith, *Psychic Messages from Oscar Wilde*, 39.

55. Travers Smith, *Psychic Messages from Oscar Wilde*, 11.

56. This report appeared widely in the United States press; see, for example, "Says Oscar Wilde Is Alive and Well," *Ogden Standard* (Ogden City, UT), 3 November 1913: 10.

Dorian Hope, and Sebastian Hope—produced some of the most elaborate imitations of Wilde's bold Greek hand, if in an implausible mauve-colored ink.[57] One of the reasons for such forgeries related to Wilde's rising stock in the auction market. Even in recent years, salerooms and book fairs have been disappointed to discover that manuscripts that promised to command very high prices are fakes.[58] Such evidence suggests that quite early in the twentieth century Wilde's works, along with his life story—which began to emerge in film adaptations, stage plays, poetry, and novels—already commanded the imaginative hold over British audiences that Chatterton's memory had enjoyed during the Victorian age.

Wilde's legend ascended in tandem with the noticeable decline in Chatterton's reputation. Certainly, some authors continued to find inspiration in Chatterton's legend. J. M. Barrie, after hearing David Masson lecturing on the Bristol poet in the 1880s at the University of Edinburgh, imagined feeling that he was "meant to be a Chatterton, but greater."[59] Several minor poets—Mackenzie Bell, Elihu Vedder, and Ernest Druce—perpetuated the well-worn legend in verses dedicated to or inspired by the "marvellous Boy."[60] Yet, with the turn of the century, his name also became linked with thwarted promise, and, increasingly, he began to appear too antiquated to have much relevance to the mod-

57. The Clark Library houses eighty items that have been attributed to Fabian Lloyd; these manuscripts, which are carefully executed, are based on Wilde's works (W6721M C697). Another famous forgery from this period purports to be a previously undiscovered play by Wilde: "Mrs. Chan-Toon" [Mabel Wodehouse-Pearse], "For the Love of the King: A Burmese Play in Three Acts and Nine Scenes," *Hutchinson's Magazine* 5, no. 28 (1921): 349–55; this appeared in a single volume, Oscar Wilde, *For Love of the King: A Burmese Masque* (London: Methuen, 1922), before it was exposed as an imposture. Even though Wodehouse-Pearse did not know Wilde, Travers Smith reports Wilde stating that he "had the honour of her acquaintance some years ago" (*Psychic Messages from Oscar Wilde*, 10). For more on these forgeries, see Joseph Bristow, "Introduction," in Bristow, ed., *Oscar Wilde and Modern Culture: The Making of a Legend* (Athens: Ohio University Press, 2008), 32–35, and Gregory Mackie, "Forging Oscar Wilde: Mrs. Chan-Toon and *For Love of the King*," *English Literature in Transition, 1880–1920* 54, no. 3 (2011): 267–88.

58. On the apparently forged documents that appeared at the New York Antiquarian Book Fair in 2007, see Anthony Gardner, "The Oscar Wilde Forgeries," http://www.anthony gardner.co.uk/features/oscar_wilde.html.

59. J. M. Barrie, *An Edinburgh Eleven: Pencil Portraits from College Life* (London: Hodder and Stoughton, 1896), 22.

60. Mackenzie Bell, "The Boy Thomas Chatterton to Himself," *Pictures of Travel and Other Poems* (Boston: Little, Brown, 1898), 68–69; Ernest Druce, Sonnet XXX, *Sonnets to a Lady* (London: J. Long, 1908), 49–51; and Elihu Vedder, *Doubt and Other Things* (Boston: Porter Sargent, 1922), 270. A sarcastic poem on Walpole precedes Vedder's hymn to Chatterton.

ern age. In his *Study of British Genius* (1904), sexologist Havelock Ellis cites Chatterton as an exemplar of premature demise: he is the only "man of genius" on Ellis's list of "eminent persons" to have died under the age of twenty.[61] Not surprisingly, Gerard Manley Hopkins's friend Digby Mackworth Dolben, the French experimental poet Rimbaud, and the good-looking sonneteer of valiant Englishness Rupert Brooke were all compared to Chatterton because their early deaths curtailed their immense potential.[62] By 1907, the Bristol Museum of Antiquities—acknowledging that a "life which came to such an untimely end has been told so often that no repetition of its sad details is needed here"—published a catalogue of the autograph manuscripts by Chatterton that it had acquired over the years.[63] Even though, it observes, "many years ago a number of manuscripts found its way to the British Museum," it remains the case that Bristol, "being Chatterton's birthplace, is the natural depository of such relics as are available."[64] It is almost as if the museum had become a shrine to a disappearing legend.

Still, Chatterton every now and again retained some association with the image of the unacknowledged wunderkind. That he remained a figure of interest, especially for young people, is evident in two sets of tobacco cards produced by Phillips cigarettes. In the "Famous Boys" series from 1924, Chatterton was featured as the first of twenty-five cards; many of the young men featured, including Prince Arthur and "Casabianca" (the boy who stood on the burning deck, in Felicia Hemans's famous 1826 poem), seemed to earn their fame through an early and dramatic death. "In desperation at his poverty," we read in the biography on the back of the Chatterton card, the young poet "poisoned himself," and "the promising life of this poetic genius ended early in tragedy."[65] These ciga-

61. Havelock Ellis, *A Study of British Genius* (London: Hurst and Blackett, 1904), 174.

62. [Anon.,] "The Poems of Digby Mackworth Dolben," *Athenæum* 4558 (6 March 1915): 207; Osbert Burdett, "A Life of Thomas Chatterton'" *Saturday Review*, 8 November 1930: 604; Herbert S. Gorman makes the link in "Arthur Rimbaud, Who Could Supersede Himself," *New York Times Book Review*, 21 December 1924: 20; and [Anon.,] "Book Notes," *New York Times*, 9 October 1931: 27.

63. W. R. Barker, ed., *A Catalogue of the Autograph Manuscripts and Other Remains of Thomas Chatterton Now in the Bristol Museum of Antiquities* (Bristol: Bristol Art Gallery, 1907), [3].

64. Barker, *A Catalogue of the Autograph Manuscripts and Other Remains of Thomas Chatterton*, [3].

65. "Chatterton," in "Famous Boys," no. 1 of 24, c. 1924, George Arents Collection, New York Public Library, Arents Cigarette Cards 730. In 1936, Chatterton was again featured in a Phillips card series, "Famous Minors," though in that instance the biography omitted any mention of suicide. "Thomas Chatterton," no. 29 of fifty in the "Famous Minors" series, c. 1936, New York Public Library, Arents Cigarette Cards 791.

rette cards, though, mark an unusual modern instance of a popular reference to Chatterton's legacy. In 1934, the English writer Clemence Dane—perhaps best known for her girls' school story *Regiment of Women* (1917)—completed a musical verse play based on Chatterton's life, *Come of Age* (1934), with Richard Addinsell. Yet this production closed after a few days in New York. It is perhaps a sign that Chatterton's life story had a loosening grip on the popular imagination that Dane—whose earlier dramatic work had been successfully adapted for film—found that *Come of Age* would not translate into cinema.[66] The only film about Chatterton we have located is a German made-for-television one broadcast in 1970. (Other Romantic poets have fared better, as we can see from Julien Temple's *Pandaemonium* [2000], which finds roles not only for Byron, Coleridge, and the Wordsworths but also for Southey and his family.) The most recent work to bring Chatterton's career into modern performance is German composer Matthew Pintscher's opera, which premiered at the Dresden Semperoper in 1998.

Complicating matters in the twentieth century was an increasing unsteadiness in Chatterton's literary reputation. Ricketts's glorious Vale Press edition of the Rowley poems did much to restore a measure of scholarly accuracy to Chatterton's texts, especially in light of the insensitive modernizations of the faux-antique spellings that had attracted attention in the 1870s.[67] But there was one further unsuccessful attempt at modernizing the Rowley poems. In 1906, Henry D. Roberts followed Skeat by stripping the Rowley poems of their original orthography and glosses. In his preface to his two-volume edition, Roberts explains his reasoning: "A reference to the 1777 edition, or to the manuscripts at the British Museum and elsewhere, will show that the poems as written are unintelligible to the majority of readers."[68] It is, he contends, "more advisable, for the better knowledge of the works of the poet, that they should be rewritten."[69] Yet, even on this basis, Roberts could take his modernization only so far. *Ælla*, for example, posed noticeable challenges. In the original Rowley poem, we discover these lines: "Pardon, yee Graiebarbes, gyff I saie, onwise / Yee are, to stycke so close and bysmarelie / To hystorie."[70] Here is Roberts's rewriting:

---

66. Dane's play, *A Bill of Divorcement* (1921), was adapted for silent cinema in 1922; ten years later it was adapted again in George Cukor's film, starring Katharine Hepburn and John Barrymore.

67. See our discussion of the Vale Press's edition of Chatterton's Rowley poems in chapter 1 (75–78).

68. Henry D. Roberts, "Preface," in *The Complete Poetical Works of Thomas Chatterton*, ed. Roberts, 2 vols. (London: George Routledge and Sons, 1906), 1:x.

69. Roberts, "Preface," in *The Complete Poetical Works of Thomas Chatterton*, 1:xi.

70. *Ælla*, in *The Complete Works of Thomas Chatterton*, ed. Donald S. Taylor and Benjamin B. Hoover, 2 vols. (Oxford: Clarendon Press, 1971), 1:177.

"Pardon, ye graybeards, if I say, unwise / Ye are to stick so close and bysmarelie / To history."[71] Unable to accommodate either "curiously" or "steadfastly" in the redrafted lines, Roberts requires his readers to consult his glossary for the modern meaning of the adverb.[72] Such a maneuver, besides disturbing Chatterton's prosody, defeats Roberts's aims. Not surprisingly, in his review of this edition, art for art's sake champion Symons—who became prominent in his theorization of literary Decadence in the 1890s—recalled the "almost faultless" Vale Press volumes.[73] In phrasing that echoes Theodore Watts's essay on Chatterton, Symons declares: "In Chatterton the whole modern romantic movement begins, consciously and as a form of achieved art."[74] Fortunately, in Symons's view, Roberts's confused editing would not undermine the fidelity that the Vale Press edition showed toward Tyrwhitt's 1777 text. As he points out, even if one could not afford the exclusive Vale Press volumes, Sidney Lee's "cheap edition," which reprinted Chatterton's "miscellaneous poems" and Rowley poems in line with reliable texts, promised to make a valuable canon of poetry available to a fresh audience.[75]

Yet, despite the appearance of fresh editions, opinion about Chatterton's poetic achievement had already begun to shift. In a discussion of M. E. Hare's 1911 Clarendon edition of Chatterton's poems, the *Saturday Review* claimed that the "essence of [Chatterton's] fame lies in the fascination of his personality for the sympathetic spirits of the romantic revival," though not in the quality of his poetry: "Intrinsically, the value of Chatterton as poet has always been exaggerated."[76] Hare's edition understandably prompted John M. Ingram, who had for years sought to stabilize the record of Chatterton's life, to defend the "genius" of the Rowley poems. But Ingram himself at this time faced critique for participating in the legend making, rather than the serious critical study, of the poet.

71. *Ælla*, in *The Complete Poetical Works of Thomas Chatterton*, ed. Roberts, 2:17. Roberts maintains Chatterton's original orthography in the title of this poem.

72. *The Complete Poetical Works of Thomas Chatterton*, ed. Roberts, 2:210.

73. Arthur Symons, "Causerie of the Week: Chatterton and his Editors," *Speaker*, 19 May 1906: 164.

74. Symons, "Causerie," 164.

75. Symons, "Causerie," 164; *The Poems of Thomas Chatterton*, ed. Sidney Lee, 2 vols. (London: Methuen, 1906).

76. [Anon.,] "The Rowley Poems of Thomas Chatterton," *Saturday Review*, 1 June 1912: 689. Thomas Chatterton, *The Rowley Poems*, ed. M. E. Hare (Oxford: Clarendon Press, 1911). Hare used the third edition of Tyrwhitt's *Poems, Supposed to Have Been Written at Bristol, by Thomas Rowley, and Others, in the Fifteenth Century . . .* (London: T. Payne, 1778) as his copy text.

A commentator on Ingram's *The True Chatterton: A New Study from Original Documents* (1910) registered the dwindling interest in the poet's writings: "In anthologies we may search for [Chatterton's] name in vain, but in the hagiology of literature it shines as bright as any."[77] Even Sidney Lee, in his affordable 1906 edition, admitted: "Opinions differ as to the literary value of Chatterton's work."[78] After World War I, which witnessed young men dying before their time on a scale that most likely obscured the tragedy of Chatterton's early death, efforts to honor his suicide diminished. Only occasionally were additions made to the scholarly record.[79] Among these sources, E. H. W. Meyerstein's scholarship was paramount, since it drew upon newly available techniques to expand the scope of literary biography, providing additional nuance to Chatterton's well-trodden life story.[80] It was Meyerstein, for example, who initiated chemical analysis to determine that Chatterton's final effects contained traces of opium, and not merely arsenic: a discovery that confirmed "the belief that Chatterton took the drug to alleviate his suffering, either before or immediately after the arsenic" that killed him.[81] Part of Meyerstein's bequest was to establish the annual Chatterton Lecture at the British Academy. Since 1955, this event has featured a presentation on English poetry by an early career scholar. The Chatterton Lecture is perhaps the only enduring tribute that acknowledges the Bristol poet's legacy to the literary history of the nation.

A midcentury lull in Chatterton studies followed Meyerstein's own death, which lingered until Richard Holmes published his fine 1970 discussion of the ways in which, "with Chatterton, it has always tended to be the completed ges-

77. [Anon.,] "Apparent Failure," *Academy*, 30 July 1910: 106.

78. Sidney Lee, "Introduction," in *The Poems of Thomas Chatterton*, ed. Lee, 1:ix.

79. Charles Edward Russell, *Thomas Chatterton, the Marvelous Boy: The Story of a Strange Life 1752–1770* (New York: Moffat, Yard, 1908); John Henry Ingram, *The True Chatterton: A New Study from Original Documents* (London: T. F. Unwin, 1910); Edward Ball, *The Life of Thomas Chatterton* (London: G. Bell and Sons, 1912); John Henry Ingram, *Chatterton and his Poetry* (London: G. G. Harrap, 1916); Esther Parker Ellinger, *Thomas Chatterton: The Marvelous Boy* (Philadelphia: University of Pennsylvania Press, 1930); John Cranstoun Nevill, *Thomas Chatterton* (London: F. Muller, 1930); Ernst Penzoldt, *The Marvellous Boy*, trans. Eleanor Woolf and John Tounstine (London: Harcourt Brace, 1931); Donald S. Taylor, *Thomas Chatterton's Art: Experiments in Imagined History* (Princeton: Princeton University Press, 1978); Louise J. Kaplan, *The Family Romance of the Imposter-Poet Thomas Chatterton* (New York: Atheneum, 1988).

80. E. H. W. Meyerstein, *A Life of Thomas Chatterton* (New York: Charles Scribner's Sons, 1930). Meyerstein frequently contributed to the *Times Literary Supplement* and other periodicals with addenda to the biography.

81. [Anon.,] "New Light on the Death of Chatterton" *Times* (London), 29 May 1947: 7.

ture of the life which produced the writing, and not the writing alone, that has exercised the greatest fascination and influence on others."[82] Yet the following year the perceived scholarly neglect of Chatterton underwent a welcome transformation. In 1971, Donald S. Taylor and Benjamin B. Hoover brought out their excellent, bicentenary textual edition of Chatterton's works from Clarendon Press.[83] This authoritative edition, however, is out of press today, and extra-library copies remain scarce. Taylor and Hoover's *Complete Works* nonetheless sparked further important inquiries into the poet. Louise J. Kaplan's psychoanalytic study, *The Family Romance of the Imposter-Poet Thomas Chatterton* (1988), seeks to connect his forgeries with his psychology.[84] Kaplan explores Chatterton's revival of William Canynges as an attempt to recuperate the paternal relationship he lacked in his own life. Certainly, Ian Haywood's *Making of History* has resuscitated Chatterton as a subject of serious literary study, but his has been a somewhat isolated voice, even though the scholarly field of English Romanticism has remained a juggernaut.[85] Nick Groom, who has also published with great authority on Chatterton, admitted in 1999: "Chatterton's iconicity has eclipsed his very work as a writer."[86]

If Chatterton's star in the academy is debatably lower than it ought to be, he has still proved a figure of interest for several artists. Outside academic circles, fictionalizations in the tradition of Herbert Croft's *Love and Madness* have appeared occasionally.[87] The best known of these is Peter Ackroyd's *Chatterton*

82. Richard Holmes, "Thomas Chatterton: The Case Re-Opened," *Cornhill* 176 (1970): 206.

83. Thomas Chatterton, *The Complete Works of Thomas Chatterton*, ed. Donald S. Taylor and Benjamin B. Hoover, 2 vols. (Oxford: Clarendon Press, 1971).

84. Louise J. Kaplan, *The Family Romance of the Imposter-Poet Thomas Chatterton* (New York: Atheneum, 1988).

85. Ian Haywood, *The Making of History: A Study of the Literary Forgeries of James Macpherson and Thomas Chatterton* (London: Associated University Press, 1987).

86. Nick Groom, "Introduction," in Groom, ed., *Thomas Chatterton and Romantic Culture* (Basingstoke: Macmillan, 1999), 5. See also Groom, "'I am Nothing': A Typology of the Forger from Chatterton to Wilde," in Francis O'Gorman and Katherine Turner, eds., *The Victorians and the Eighteenth Century: Reassessing the Tradition* (Aldershot: Ashgate, 2004), 203–22.

87. Examples include Ernest Lacy's one-act play *Chatterton* in *Plays and Sonnets* (Philadelphia: Sherman, 1900) and his full-length play *The Bard of Mary Redcliffe* (Philadelphia: Sherman, 1916), Francis William Grattan's dramatization *Thomas Chatterton, the Marvelous Boy in the Foes and Woes of a Poet* (Astoria, NY: J. Falez Odewadell, 1918), F. C. Owlett's *Chatterton's Apology* (Hoddesdon, Herts.: Thomas Knight, 1930), and Neil Bell's *Cover His Face: A Novel of the Life and Times of Thomas Chatterton, the Marvel-*

(1987), which intersects multiple plots across time—including stories featuring Chatterton, Meredith, and Wallis, and a contemporary poet—to examine the stability of identity and authorship.[88] Ackroyd's *Chatterton,* and the press it received (the novel was shortlisted for the Booker Prize), helped bring the young poet again into public view. *Chatterton* followed Ackroyd's *Last Testament of Oscar Wilde* (1983), a work that applies a Chattertonian title to an account of Wilde's last years in Paris. In this fictionalized autobiography, Ackroyd's Wilde mentions Chatterton on two occasions, in a manner that echoes Sherard's account of Wilde's final days. *The Last Testament of Oscar Wilde* secured for Ackroyd the 1984 Somerset Maugham Award. Both *Chatterton* and *The Last Testament of Oscar Wilde* not only draw plentifully on biographical details of the two artists but also—unlike the literary nonfiction that Ackroyd has also excelled in writing—depart from fact in order to explore notions of creativity and authenticity.

Ackroyd's fictional narratives, although in some respects traditional in the sense of Croft's melding of biographical fact with imagined events, nevertheless exemplify the completion of the shift in interest from Chatterton's poetry to Chatterton the poet, or even, more specifically, Chatterton the suicidal teenager.[89] That shift is nowhere clearer than in Chatterton's absence from one of the most important arbiters of the literary canon: the anthology aimed at undergraduates enrolled in North American survey courses. If the reviewer of Ingram's biography bemoaned in 1910 that one searched in vain for Chatterton's name in literature anthologies, the situation in our own time is little improved. These days, despite the palpable influence he exerted on writers such as Scott, Keats, and Wordsworth, and regardless of the value that many others from Samuel Johnson to Dante Gabriel Rossetti placed upon the "marvellous Boy," Chatterton has never made an appearance in all nine iterations of the most comprehensive of college anthologies of British literature from W. W. Norton, which now span more than half a century.[90] The same is true of the "Roman-

lous Boy of Bristol (London: Collins, 1943). Ernst Penzoldt's popular *Der arme Chatterton* (Leipzig: Insel, 1928) was translated from the German by Eleanor Woolf and John J. Tounstine (London: Harrap, 1931).

88. Peter Ackroyd, *Chatterton* (London: Hamish Hamilton, 1987).

89. Serge Gainsbourg's late 1960s pop song "Chatterton" opens with the line "Chatterton suicide," and lists the poet among Van Gogh, Schumann, and others who made attempts on their lives.

90. The most recent iteration is Stephen Greenblatt et al., eds., *Norton Anthology of English Literature,* vol. 2, 9th ed. (New York: Norton, 2012).

tics and Their Contemporaries" volume in the fifth edition of the increasingly influential Longman anthology of British literature, as well as the Broadview volumes on the Restoration and the eighteenth century and on the "Age of Romanticism."[91] But, then, as the editors of these volumes readily acknowledge, their selections are based on works that have entered a literary canon that has necessarily taken its present shape in light of changing cultural tastes and institutional preferences. Several different reasons account for the absence of not only Chatterton but also other poets—ones who commanded considerable respect in their time, such as Thomas Campbell, Samuel Rogers, and Thomas Moore—from the pages of these important anthologies.

Efforts to memorialize Chatterton in more concrete forms have fared only marginally better. A blue plaque adorns the modern bank building that stands in London at Brooke Street, Holborn, on the site of the house in which Chatterton died. In Bristol, Chatterton remains a proud son of the city. St. Mary Redcliffe, the church in which the poet first encountered the medieval documents that would inspire his best work, at first refused a memorial to Chatterton on the grounds that his suicide rendered him unsuitable for commemoration. These days a modest plaque now hangs in the south transept of the church, close to Canynges's imposing tomb, and reads simply "Thomas Chatterton | of this parish | 1752–1770 | Poet." The whereabouts of the cenotaph, which fell into disrepair and was dismantled in the 1960s, however, remain unknown. According to a 1967 article in the Bristol *Evening Post*, upon the dismantling of the cenotaph the city had plans to ensure that the "stiff little figure holding its scroll of poetry [would] be preserved by the City Museum in a suitable niche."[92] Apparently, the "suitable niche" did not transpire. A February 1987 newspaper story on the resident of Chatterton's birthplace describes "an eroded statue locked away awaiting a decision as to its future" and features a photograph of the "the head of the neglected statue of Thomas Chatterton, now crumbling in the back garden."[93] This is the last record we have been able to locate of the monument.

What once was Pile Street, the site of the school and adjoining house where Chatterton was born, is now Redcliffe Way. Changes to the roadways required

91. Joseph Black et al., eds., *Broadview Anthology of British Literature*, vols. 3–4, 2nd ed. (Calgary: Broadview, 2010); and David Damrosch et al., eds., *Longman Anthology of British Literature*, vol. 2, 5th ed. (Harlow: Pearson Longman, 2012).

92. Marjorie Wilding, "Monument Fight Lost," *Evening Post* (Bristol), 20 April 1967: 10.

93. James Belsey, "Living in the Home of that 'Marvellous Boy,'" unknown source. Clipping hand-dated "Feb 87," in a twentieth-century scrapbook, Bristol Record Office #40704/box 4/5).

the removal and rebuilding of the schoolhouse façade and house in the 1930s, and during the Second World War the property sustained damage as part of the Bristol blitz.[94] Today, although the Grade II–listed building still stands in the shadow of St. Mary Redcliffe, it lies in disrepair, its gardens overgrown, the façade marked with graffiti, the two plaques noting Chatterton's significance situated next to garish alarm signs warning trespassers to keep away. Yet in the face of this appalling neglect in Chatterton's hometown, the University of Bristol has for more than ten years been the home of the Thomas Chatterton Society, which came into being on the 250th anniversary of his birth.

By contrast, Wilde's reputation—especially when we bear in mind that Sherard once recalled his former friend's decline as similar to Chatterton's—could not have made a more inspiring recovery in both popular culture and the scholarly world. By 1954, he received his very own blue plaque at his family home on Tite Street. And in 1995 a second one was unveiled, though, given the outbursts of homophobia that erupted in that decade, it was promptly defaced the next day. Academically, too, every student on those survey courses is more than likely to know something not just about Wilde's imprisonment but also his works. The weighty ninth edition of the Norton Anthology reprints the whole of *The Importance of Being Earnest*. These developments form but one part of the ongoing effort to comprehend the full scope of Wilde's considerable literary achievements in his own comparatively short life. We hope that *Oscar Wilde's Chatterton* augments our growing knowledge of a major writer who had good reasons to dedicate his remarkable energies to the study of English literary history, the emergence of Romanticism, and the tantalizing art of forgery.

94. "Buildings in Bristol of Architectural or Historic Interest Damaged or Destroyed by Enemy Action, 1940–1942," *Transactions of the Bristol and Gloucestershire Archeological Society* 65 (1944): 171.

Editorial Introduction to
Appendixes A and B

APPENDIX A: WILDE'S "CHATTERTON" NOTEBOOK

In our transcription of the "Chatterton" notebook, which is held in the William Andrews Clark Memorial Library at the University of California, Los Angeles (Wilde W6721M3 E78 [1886?] Bound), we have striven to present the contents as faithfully as possible, reflecting their unique formal characteristics. It is the only known manuscript featuring Wilde's work on Thomas Chatterton and is titled simply "Chatterton" on the top of the second folio (Figure 12). With marbleized board covers, the notebook features ninety-four quarto (7" × 9" or 18 cm × 22.6 cm) leaves of unlined cream paper; eighty-two of those leaves include some content, while the final twelve leaves are left blank. No page numbers appear in the notebook, either by Wilde or by any later archivist, and previous scholarship on the notebook conforms to no standard pagination. On the inside cover, there are two handwritten notes in pencil, which record the following: "Cuttings from | (1) Chatterton: A Biographical Study by Daniel Wilson, LLD. | London, 1869. | (2) Chatterton: A Story of the Year 1770. By David Masson | 1874. pp. 58–119." Beneath there is a yellow-colored sticker that begins with the call number, and states "Wilde, Oscar | [Essay on Chatterton] (2440) | W. S. Lewins: 1952." (The number 2440 refers to the listing of this item in John Charles Finzi, *Oscar Wilde and His Literary Circle: A Catalog of Manuscripts and Letters in the William Andrews Clark Memorial Library* [Berkeley and Los Angeles: Published for the Library by the University of California Press, 1957].) On the first recto leaf, there is a pasted-in clipping from a sale catalog, which includes the following note in pencil: "Anderson Gall. | May 13, 1919 | $315.^{00} | [illegible words]." The clipping contains the following printed text:

UNPUBLISHED MANUSCRIPT BY OSCAR WILDE

832. WILDE (OSCAR). Essay on Chatterton, written partly in pencil and partly in ink, in a quarto exercise book. About 70 pages of Manuscript, interspersed with printed cuttings from Lives of Chatterton by Daniel Wilson and David Masson. 1886

An Important Unpublished Manuscript, apparently intended for the "Century Guild Hobby Horse" (see Stuart Mason's Bibliography of Oscar Wilde, pages 13 and 14). It would be a fascinating undertaking to prepare this manuscript for publication. In addition to the complete and consecutive passages there are numerous notes and suggestions which it was obviously Wilde's intention to incorporate in the complete work.[1]

The clipping comes from the sale dedicated to *English Literature from London: To Be Sold on the Afternoons and Evenings of Tuesday and Wednesday, May 13th and 14th, 2.30 and 8.15 O'CLOCK* (New York: Anderson Galleries, 1919). As this entry states, Stuart Mason (the professional name of Christopher Sclater Millard) had knowledge of the manuscript. Mason assumes in his 1914 *Bibliography of Oscar Wilde* that the notebook provided the basis of an essay that Wilde was preparing for the *Century Guild Hobby Horse*. He remarks that "the article does not appear ever to have been published," though "portions of it exist in manuscript," by which he means the notebook.[2] Underneath the pasted-in clipping, there is a further note in pencil: "James Drake, May 1952, $375.00."

Placed as a loose leaf inside the "Chatterton" notebook is a detailed typewritten (undated) note on letterhead from the offices of James F. Drake, which sold the manuscript to Wilmarth S. Lewis (not Lewins, as the pasted-in yellow sticker states) in 1952. Drake furnished the following information:

CHATTERTON AND WALPOLE

WILDE (OSCAR). Autograph Manuscript. About 70 pages, in ink and pencil, interspersed with printed clippings from biographies of Chatterton by Daniel Wilson and David Masson, in a quarto exercise book. N.d. (c. 1886).

A very interesting and important unpublished rough draft, including many notes for projected expansion of the text, of an essay on Thomas Chatterton. Apparently originally intended to be used as notes for a lecture, announcement was made in the October 1886 number of "The Century Guild Hobby

---

1. Anderson Galleries, *English Literature from London: To Be Sold on the Afternoons and Evenings of Tuesday and Wednesday, May 13th and 14th, 2.30 and 8.15 O'CLOCK* (New York: Anderson Galleries, 1919), 228.

2. Stuart Mason [Christopher Sclater Millard], *Bibliography of Oscar Wilde* (London: T. Werner Laurie, 1914), 13.

Horse" that "Mr. Oscar Wilde's article on Chatterton has been unavoidably postponed until the January number" (See Mason Bibliography of Wilde, pp. 13, 14, where the introductory part of the essay is quoted). However, Wilde never completed the essay and it has remained unpublished.

Wilde devotes nine pages to the well known story of Chatterton's relations with Horace Walpole. Chatterton's first letter to Walpole is copied in Wilde's own hand. The remainder of the part of the essay dealing with Walpole, excepting only printed copies of Walpole's reply to Chatterton's first letter and Chatterton's note of July 24 demanding an explanation of Walpole's failure to return his manuscripts, is in Wilde's autograph.

The essay concludes with a sonnet to Chatterton by Wilde which is also apparently unpublished. Both essay and sonnet are highly laudatory in tone asserting that Chatterton was the precursor of the Romantic Movement in English poetry and comparing him with such giants of literature as Shakespeare and Milton.

Drake's account appears to have been pitched to Lewis, a distinguished scholar, who had begun publishing his magisterial *Yale Edition of Horace Walpole's Correspondence* in 1937.

A short article in *Mecurius Redivivus: Being an Occasional News-Letter from the William Andrews Clark Memorial Library* reveals how Wilde's "Chatterton" notebook made its way from Lewis's private library at Farmington, Connecticut, to the Clark's premises in the Adams District of Los Angeles:

Wilde vs. Walpole

Last spring the Clark Library had its first visit from that great scholarly bookman, Wilmarth S. Lewis of Farmington, Connecticut, whose Yale Walpole is one of the noblest literary monuments of all time. Those who read the profile of "Lefty" Lewis in the *New Yorker*, the pictorial spread on his work in *Life*, and his own witty book called *Collector's Progress*, know that he has an undisputed priority on Walpoleana wherever it turns up on the market. His magnetic charm has even extracted items from libraries which hitherto thought their treasures had come to stay. Our custodianship of the Clark treasures was not put to the test, for Lewis did not find any Walpoleana on West Adams which was not already represented at Farmington.

That is not, however the point of this story; *this* is the point. Lewis saw our Oscar Wilde collection and was impressed by its width and depth, so that when he returned home he wrote us a letter in which he confessed to having recently bought Oscar Wilde's 75 pages of unpublished notes for a lecture on Chatterton and Horace Walpole. Lewis went on to say, "It is hard to determine the relative claims in such a case: Wilde versus Walpole-Chatterton, but I have tried to do so, and I think the Wilde interest of this manuscript is perhaps the greater. So—at the risk of appearing quixotically generous—I'll offer it to you what I paid for it."

It would have been churlish to refuse this generous offer. We promptly accepted it, and are happy now to record this unselfish act of "Lefty" Lewis. It confirms our faith in bookish people as being among the nicest people on earth. And a library such as the Clark, magnetized more and more by its potent books and manuscripts, draws such people from near and far.[3]

Starting with the first recto leaf, we number each folio of the notebook, designating the recto (ʳ) and the verso (ᵛ). Since it is not practical to reprint the numerous blank pages in the notebook, we have identified their locations within round parentheses.

Much of the fascination with the "Chatterton" notebook is attributable, as the handwritten notes inside in the front cover suggest, to Wilde's inclusion of printed pages from two biographies of Chatterton: Daniel Wilson's *Chatterton: A Biographical Study* (1869) and David Masson's *Chatterton: A Story of the Year 1770* (1874). Sections from pages cut out of these books are pasted into the

---

3. Anonymous, "Wilde vs. Walpole," *Mercurius Redivivus: Being an Occasional News-Letter from the William Andrews Clark Memorial Library at 2205 West Adams Boulevard in the City of Los Angeles* 1 (Autumn 1952): 5. The author of this piece is more than likely Lawrence Clark Powell, director of the Clark Library, who corresponded with Lewis on 21 November 1952, thanking the collector for his "generosity in letting us acquire the Wilde lecture" (Clarkive Post-1934, Correspondence, 1944–1958, I-Magee, Box 6). The publications mentioned in this article that relate to Lewis's career are "Life Explores World's Finest Walpole Library," *Life*, 23 October 1944: 116–17; Geoffrey T. Hellman, "The Steward of Strawberry Hill I," *New Yorker*, 6 August 1949: 26–38; Hellman, "The Steward of Strawberry Hill II," *New Yorker*, 13 August 1949: 31–38; and Lewis, *Collector's Progress* (New York: Knopf, 1951). Susan Odell Walker, head of Public Services at the Lewis Walpole Library, shared correspondence that shows that Marston E. Drake, on behalf of James F. Drake Inc., offered Wilmarth S. Lewis the "Chatterton" notebook on 11 April 1952. On 8 May that year, Marston E. Drake followed up with an inquiry about Lewis's level of interest in the manuscript: "I have several clients to quote it to who are very much interested in Wilde." The exchange with Lewis confirms that he purchased the notebook from James F. Drake Inc. for $375 in May 1952. On 9 July 1952, Lawrence Clark Powell, director of the Clark Library, wrote to Lewis thanking him for the kind offer to sell the notebook: "Drake should be ashamed of himself for not having first offered us the Wilde ms.!" Lewis, who received $375 from Powell, dispatched the manuscript to the Clark Library on 11 July 1952. We quote these materials courtesy of the Lewis Walpole Library, Yale University.

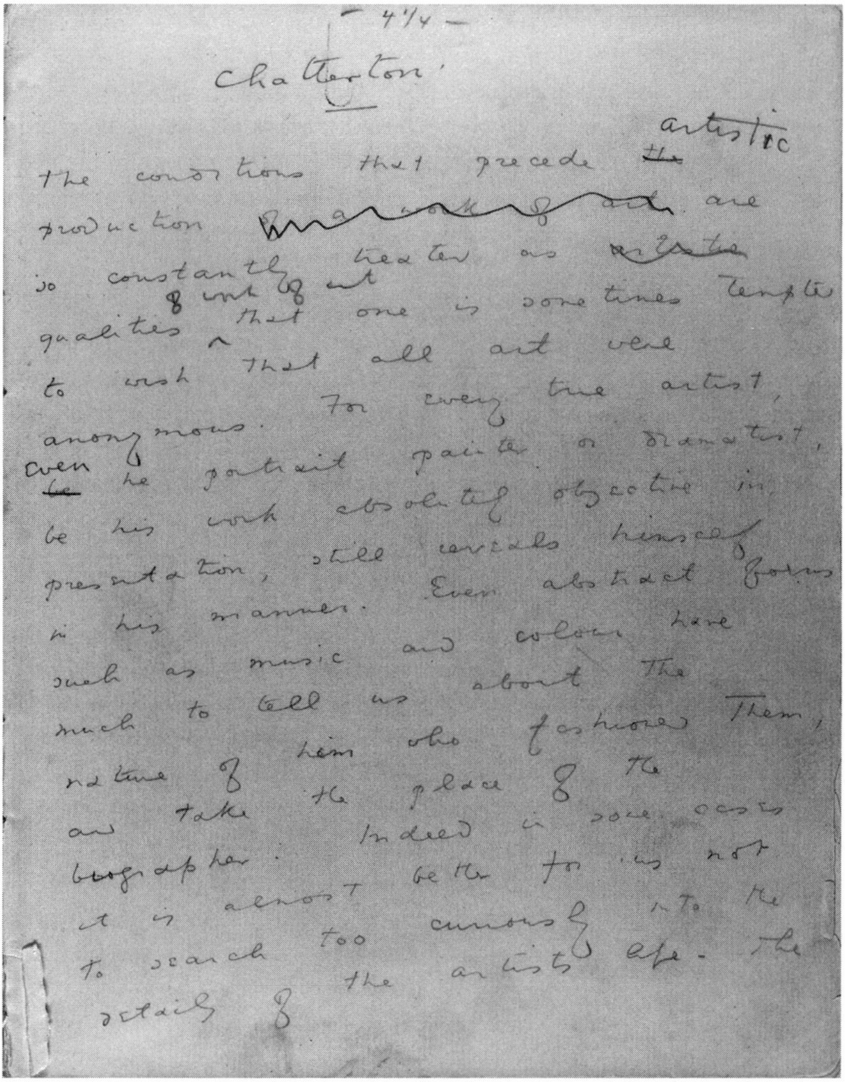

— 4/4 —

Chatterton

the conditions that precede the artistic production ~~of a work of art~~ are so constantly treated as ~~artistic~~ qualities of work of art that one is sometimes tempted to wish that all art were anonymous. For every true artist, even be he portrait painter or dramatist, be his work absolutely objective in presentation, still reveals himself in his manner. Even abstract forms such as music and colour have much to tell us about the nature of him who fashioned them, and take the place of the biographer. Indeed in some cases it is almost better for us not to search too curiously into the details of the artist's life. The

Figure 12. Oscar Wilde, "Chatterton" Notebook, f.2r, autograph manuscript. Image courtesy of William Andrews Clark Memorial Library, University of California, Los Angeles. Wilde W6721M3 E78 [1886?] Bound.

notebook, often with multiple clippings pasted on a single notebook page. We have collated all of the clippings in the notebook with these two volumes. It will quickly become apparent that most of Wilde's cuttings draw from factual biographical information, re-reported details, and quotations from Chatterton's original writing. All of the pages from Wilson or Masson included in the notebooks are, to some degree, trimmed; most of Wilde's clippings from Wilson's study omit entirely the marginal notes and the running heads from the original. In some cases, as on f.35ʳ (368–69), Wilde abuts clippings from the recto and verso of the same folio of one of the books, indicating that he must have used two copies in the creation of his notebook. In other cases, as in f.54ʳ (384–86 [see Figure 14]), Wilde jigsaws together clippings from both Wilson's and Masson's books to achieve a seamless rendering of text; in the noted case, Wilde reproduces Chatterton's "Last Will and Testament," recorded verbatim by both Wilson and Masson.

Contents of the printed clippings are represented as blocks of text enclosed within square brackets in a font that reproduces, as faithfully as possible, the typeface of the original publications, allowing readers to distinguish readily those lines written by Wilde from the clippings. We have maintained the original line breaks and alignment of the sources and, where footnotes were included in the original clippings, we have reproduced those footnotes *within* the brackets. Additional formatting, including indentation, italics, underlining, and small caps, is also reproduced from the originals. Page numbers for the printed excerpts are given in notes. In instances where Wilde has hand-transcribed or paraphrased text from Wilson, Masson, Watts, or others, we offer notes (introduced with "Cf.") that include the pertinent text and pagination from the sources.

On many of the pasted-in clippings, Wilde has struck part or all of the text; his method for striking sections varies widely, sometimes with a simple X marked through an entire paragraph, and in other instances with a series of hash marks that covers nearly the entire section. All instances of printed excerpts with text thus marked are rendered with the text ~~struck through~~. See Figure 13 for an example of such an instance.

Sections of text in Wilde's own hand are reproduced with the line breaks of the original manuscript, and we have tried to maintain, as far as possible, the vertical alignment (see Figures 13 and 14). In places where Wilde has provided revisions to the printed excerpts or comments in the margins, we have reproduced the location of his notations as faithfully as possible, and have rendered lines that he has crossed out with the text ~~struck through~~. The majority of Wilde's writing is in pencil, though there are a few insertions written in black ink; these insertions are identified in notes. We believe these comments were additions made after the initial penciled writing.

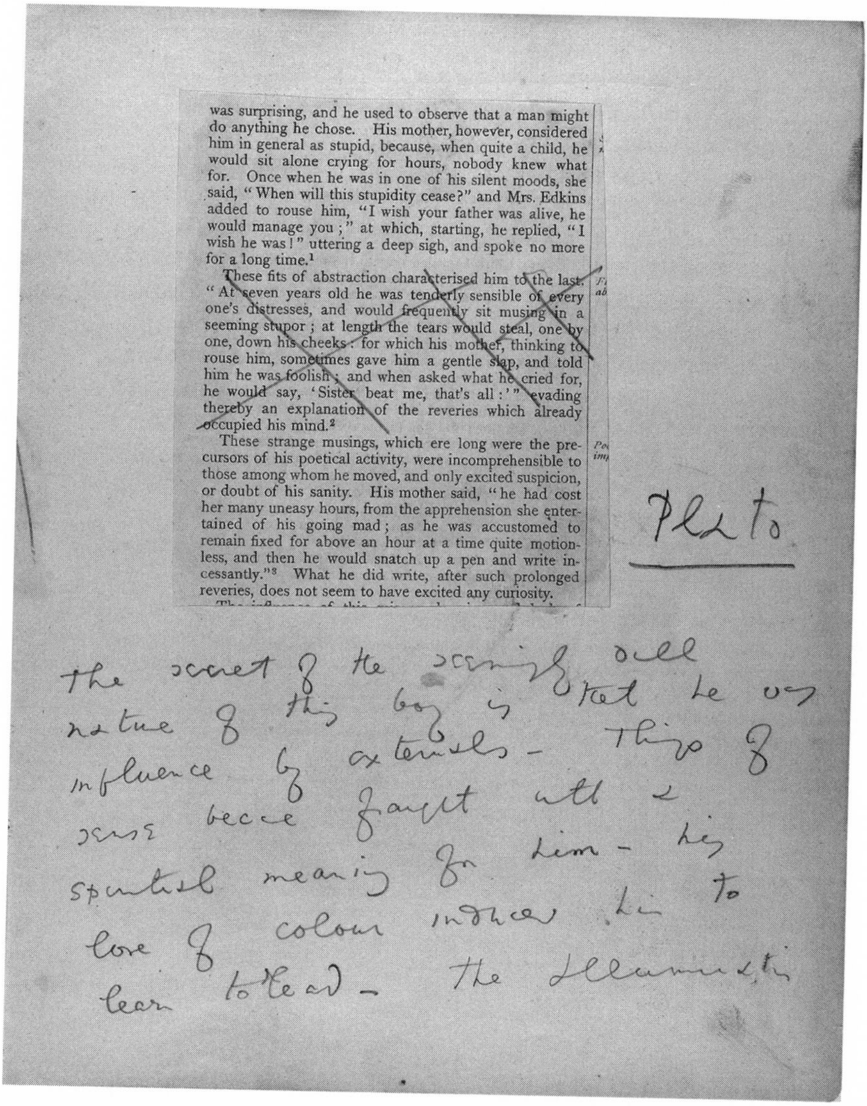

was surprising, and he used to observe that a man might do anything he chose. His mother, however, considered him in general as stupid, because, when quite a child, he would sit alone crying for hours, nobody knew what for. Once when he was in one of his silent moods, she said, "When will this stupidity cease?" and Mrs. Edkins added to rouse him, "I wish your father was alive, he would manage you;" at which, starting, he replied, "I wish he was!" uttering a deep sigh, and spoke no more for a long time.[1]

These fits of abstraction characterised him to the last. "At seven years old he was tenderly sensible of every one's distresses, and would frequently sit musing in a seeming stupor; at length the tears would steal, one by one, down his cheeks: for which his mother, thinking to rouse him, sometimes gave him a gentle slap, and told him he was foolish; and when asked what he cried for, he would say, 'Sister beat me, that's all:'" evading thereby an explanation of the reveries which already occupied his mind.[2]

These strange musings, which ere long were the precursors of his poetical activity, were incomprehensible to those among whom he moved, and only excited suspicion, or doubt of his sanity. His mother said, "he had cost her many uneasy hours, from the apprehension she entertained of his going mad; as he was accustomed to remain fixed for above an hour at a time quite motionless, and then he would snatch up a pen and write incessantly."[3] What he did write, after such prolonged reveries, does not seem to have excited any curiosity.

Plato

the secret of the seemingly dull nature of this boy is that he was influenced by externals — things of sense became fraught with a spiritual meaning for him — his love of colour induced him to learn to read — the Illuminati

Figure 13. Oscar Wilde, "Chatterton" Notebook, f.8ʳ, autograph manuscript with printed excerpt from Daniel Wilson's *Chatterton: A Biographical Study* (London: Macmillan, 1869), p. 9. Image courtesy of William Andrews Clark Memorial Library, University of California, Los Angeles. Wilde W6721M3 E78 [1886?] Bound.

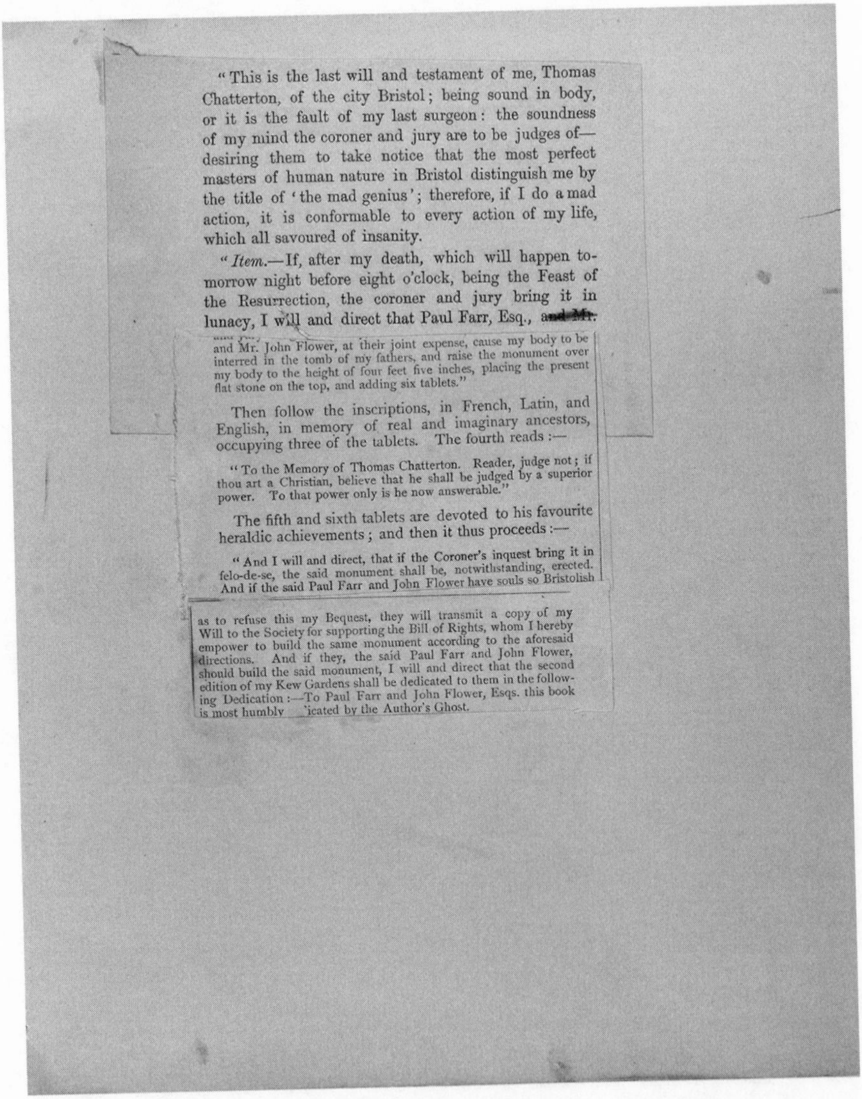

"This is the last will and testament of me, Thomas Chatterton, of the city Bristol; being sound in body, or it is the fault of my last surgeon: the soundness of my mind the coroner and jury are to be judges of—desiring them to take notice that the most perfect masters of human nature in Bristol distinguish me by the title of 'the mad genius'; therefore, if I do a mad action, it is conformable to every action of my life, which all savoured of insanity.

"*Item.*—If, after my death, which will happen to-morrow night before eight o'clock, being the Feast of the Resurrection, the coroner and jury bring it in lunacy, I will and direct that Paul Farr, Esq., and Mr.

and Mr. John Flower, at their joint expense, cause my body to be interred in the tomb of my fathers, and raise the monument over my body to the height of four feet five inches, placing the present flat stone on the top, and adding six tablets."

Then follow the inscriptions, in French, Latin, and English, in memory of real and imaginary ancestors, occupying three of the tablets. The fourth reads :—

"To the Memory of Thomas Chatterton. Reader, judge not; if thou art a Christian, believe that he shall be judged by a superior power. To that power only is he now answerable."

The fifth and sixth tablets are devoted to his favourite heraldic achievements ; and then it thus proceeds :—

"And I will and direct, that if the Coroner's inquest bring it in felo-de-se, the said monument shall be, notwithstanding, erected. And if the said Paul Farr and John Flower have souls so Bristolish

as to refuse this my Bequest, they will transmit a copy of my Will to the Society for supporting the Bill of Rights, whom I hereby empower to build the same monument according to the aforesaid directions. And if they, the said Paul Farr and John Flower, should build the said monument, I will and direct that the second edition of my Kew Gardens shall be dedicated to them in the following Dedication :—To Paul Farr and John Flower, Esqs. this book is most humbly   'icated by the Author's Ghost.

Figure 14. Oscar Wilde, "Chatterton" Notebook, f.54^r, with printed excerpts from Daniel Wilson's *Chatterton: A Biographical Study* (London: Macmillan, 1869), pp. 241–42, and David Masson's *Chatterton: A Story of the Year* 1770 (London: Macmillan, 1874), p. 78. Image courtesy of William Andrews Clark Memorial Library, University of California, Los Angeles. Wilde W6721M3 E78 [1886?] Bound.

Wilde's hand is marvelously readable (see Figure 15). In the manuscript, as in many manuscripts from the same period, Wilde often uses the Greek alpha (α) in place of the letter "a"; we have rendered these instances with a roman "a." He often used the Greek high dot to mark separation between sentences, and we have maintained this punctuation in the transcription. Distinguishing between Wilde's capital and lowercase letters can, in some cases, be difficult: he will often dot a capital "I," for example. When letters with ambiguous capitalization appear at the start of a sentence, or in a title of a work, we capitalize the letters in our transcription.

There are relatively few nontextual markings in the manuscript. Unlike Wilde's other notebooks, which sometimes feature doodles or drawings, the "Chatterton" notebook contains only one figure, on f.32^r (365). Other flourishes of Wilde's pen are typeset here to approximate their appearance in the original, including underlined and double-underlined words, slashes, and separators.

As the notebook bears no date, we must rely on circumstantial evidence to estimate its composition as being between summer 1886 and spring 1888. Wilde's burgeoning interest in Chatterton coincides largely with his early interactions with the members of the Century Guild. He began his acquaintance with Herbert Horne in June 1886, and published his first (and ultimately, his only) article in the *Century Guild Hobby Horse* the following month.[4] We have collated the "Chatterton" notebook with Wilde's contemporary reviews, which frequently drew on phrasing developed in the notebook, and have noted the references accordingly; such moments are helpful in dating the notebook's creation. Phrases from the notebook appear, for example, in "Miner and Minor Poets," a review published in the *Pall Mall Gazette* on 1 February 1887, suggesting that Wilde was still relying on the contents of the notebook for his writing in the months following his November 1886 Birkbeck lecture. His final lecture, delivered in April 1888 in Bournemouth, was on Chatterton, so it is likely that he would have returned to the notebook again. As we observe above, notations and edits to the notebook made in black ink appear to be additions introduced after the earlier, pasted and penciled contributions, although it is impossible to tell conclusively how much time had passed in the interim, and since no records of the Birkbeck lecture have yet been identified, no collation can be done to clarify the chronology.

Toward the completion of our editing, we were able to consult Geoff Dibb's transcription of the "Chatterton" notebook, which appears as "Appendix G"

---

4. Wilde invited Horne to tea at his home in a letter dated 23 June 1886; see *The Complete Letters of Oscar Wilde*, ed. Merlin Holland and Rupert Hart-Davis (London: Fourth Estate, 2000), 282–83. "Keats' Sonnet on Blue" appeared in the July 1886 issue of the *Century Guild Hobby Horse* 1, no. 3 (July 1886): 82–86.

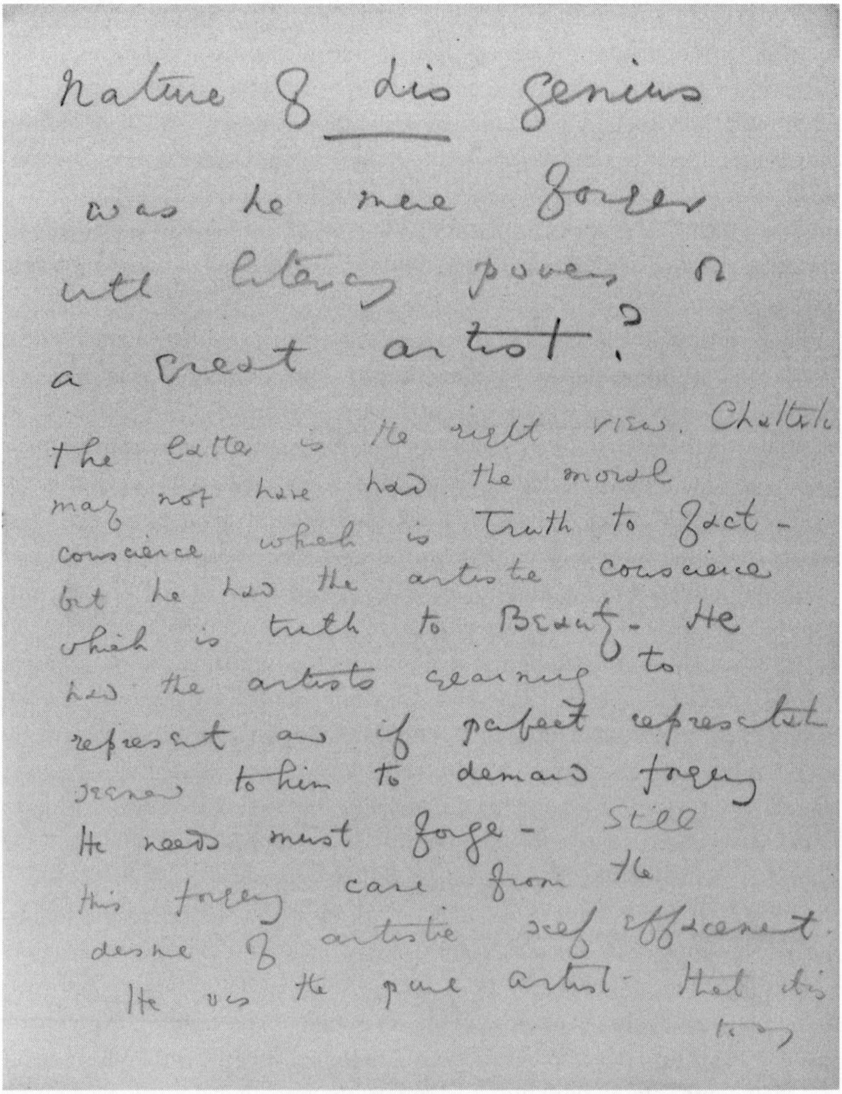

Nature of his genius

was he mere forger
with literary power, or
a great artist?

The latter is the right view. Chatterton
may not have had the moral
conscience which is Truth to fact —
but he had the artistic conscience
which is truth to Beauty. He
had the artists yearning to
represent and if perfect representation
seemed to him to demand forgery
He needs must forge — still
this forgery came from the
desire of artistic self effacement.
He was the pure artist — that is
to say

Figure 15. Oscar Wilde, "Chatterton" Notebook, f.75ʳ, autograph manuscript. Image courtesy of William Andrews Clark Memorial Library, University of California, Los Angeles. Wilde W6721M3 E78 [1886?] Bound.

in his 2013 study, *Oscar Wilde, a Vagabond with a Mission: The Story of Oscar Wilde's Lecture Tours of Britain and Ireland*. If readers care to consult the holograph reproduction of the "Chatterton" notebook, which is available through Gale Cengage's *British Literary Manuscripts Online, c. 1660–1900*, they will discover that there are many divergences between the presentation of our textual edition in Appendix A below and Dibb's transcription of the document, which he has titled "Chatterton: Essay and Lecture."[5] In an introductory comment, Dibb explains that the notebook constitutes an "important and intriguing piece of work," which he has chosen to reproduce "because, although it began as an essay for the *Century Guild Hobby Horse*, it was then abandoned and used by Wilde as a supporting text for his lecture *Chatterton*."[6] Presumably, in an attempt to make the notebook accessible, Dibb presents Wilde's at times fragmentary handwritten notes and the numerous clippings in largely continuous prose. In order to differentiate between Wilde's notes and the clippings, Dibb represents Wilde's own holograph in bold typeface, Wilde's manuscript copy from his sources in bold italic typeface, and the cut-and-pasted sections from both Wilson's and Masson's studies in ordinary typeface. For the most part, Dibb chooses not to reproduce the line breaks and high dots in Wilde's handwritten notes. Neither does Dibb provide precise page references for the clippings that Wilde cut and pasted from Wilson's *Chatterton* and Masson's *Chatterton: A Story of the Year 1770*. Nor does Dibb record the footnotes that appear in Wilson's study. Further, his transcription provides no sense of the foliation of the document. Throughout Dibb's representation of the "Chatterton" notebook, it remains impossible to comprehend the full scope of Wilde's deletions and insertions in Wilde's own handwritten notes and in the clippings from both Wilson's and Masson's respective books. Further, Dibb has inserted Matthew Arnold's sonnet on Shakespeare into the transcription, when this poem is only referenced in the notebook.[7]

Dibb's method of presentation, while producing a readable text, does not do justice to this complicated document. There are places where his transcription stands at odds with Wilde's handwriting. Let us give two examples. One of the

5. The Gale Cengage database can be consulted through http://gdc.gale.com/products/british-literary-manuscripts-online-c.-1660-1900/.

6. Geoff Dibb, "Appendix G—Chatterton: Essay and Lecture," in *Oscar Wilde, a Vagabond with a Mission: The Story of Oscar Wilde's Lecture Tours of Britain and Ireland* (London: Oscar Wilde Society, 2013), 295. As we explain above, we believe that there is no evidence to suggest that the notebook began as the basis for an essay that subsequently became a lecture.

7. See Dibb, *Oscar Wilde, a Vagabond with a Mission*, 296–97. Cf. f.3^r (336).

most noticeable differences between Dibb's transcription and our own appears on f.75^v. Dibb transcribes Wilde's important engagement with a comment from Watts's 1880 essay on Chatterton as follows:

> There was something in him of 'the yearning of great *Vishnu* to create a world.'?
> He loved to let his intellect play—to separate the artist from the man.

The notes that he has reproduced in this order are on different pages and in different media (pen on f.75^v and pencil on f.76^r). The text reads as follows on f.75^v: "there was something in him | of 'the yearning of great | ? <u>Vishnu</u> to create a world'— | ——— | yet a distinctive note | of his own—" (404). For some reason, Dibb has split this continuous note into two, placing Wilde's adaptation of Watts ("the yearning of great | ? <u>Vishnu</u> to create a world") immediately before the notes that begin "He loved to let his intellect play—," and end with "Macpherson, Ossia" (in the "Chatterton" notebook the final "n" is missing), and positioning the (mistranscribed) phrase "Yet a destructive note of his own" after the (also mistranscribed) "Ossian." As one can see, Dibb represents the final words of this comment as "a destructive note of his own."[8] In this part of the notebook, Wilde has quoted (as Dibb acknowledges) one of Watts's striking observations about Chatterton. Yet, in the final seven words, whose writing in black ink suggests they were added at a later stage to the mostly penciled notes, the phrase that Wilde has employed is clearly "a distinctive note of his own." What struck Wilde as quintessentially significant about Chatterton was this young author's ability to learn from predecessors and inject his distinctive originality into the body of English writings that make the Rowley poems, in particular, such a triumph of art. Elsewhere, on f.61^r Dibb suggests that Wilde has written "Sir Herbert Crofts visits" before the clipping where Masson quotes from Croft's *Love and Madness*. In our view, there is no mistaking that Wilde's note should read: "Sir Herbert Crofts writes." ("Crofts," which is Wilde's misspelling, stands for "Croft.") We are not sure why Dibb should have misconstrued Wilde's generally legible Greek hand in this way.

Elsewhere, Dibb has chosen to transpose other portions of the notebook, in a manner that once again places them out of sequence. One such transposition occurs on f.51^v and f.52^r. On f.51^v Wilde made this note from Wilson's study about the comment that Coleridge inserted into the preface to the famous "Monody on the Death of Chatterton," which Joseph Cottle first recorded in 1837:

8. Dibb, "Appendix G," in *Oscar Wilde, a Vagabond with a Mission*, 326–27.

Coleridge
O ye who honour the
name of man rejoice
that this Walpole is
    a
called ^ Lord (383)

This note appears before the next following handwritten observation, which quotes and then comments upon a passage from Wilson's *Chatterton*:

on his return he found on his
table what seemed to him a
"singularly impertinent letter"
but what seems to us rather
spirited and manly. (383)

The quoted remark comes of course from Walpole, which Wilson includes in his commentary on the correspondence between the young Bristol poet and the aristocrat. Thereafter, Wilde has pasted in a clipping from Masson's *Chatterton: A Story of the Year 1770*, in which Chatterton famously reproaches Walpole, on 25 July 1769: "I cannot reconcile your behavior to me with the notions I once entertained of you. I think myself injured, Sir." (Wilde's clipping reproduces the whole letter.) Underneath the cut-and-pasted text of this epistle, Wilde adds this comment:

Walpole accordingly
returned the M.SS·
Chattertons dream of
a real Canynge
   was <u>over</u>. (384)

As we point out, the "dream of a real Canynge" is a phrase that largely derives from Wilson's *Chatterton*, as does the epithet "spirited."

Dibb places these folios in the following order, using the typographic distinctions we have explained above:

. . . **On his return he found on his table what seemed to him a "singularly impertinent letter" but what seems to us rather spirited and manly:**

Sir,—I cannot reconcile your behavior with the notions I once entertained of you. I think myself injured, sir; and did you not know my circumstances, you would not dare to treat me thus.

I have sent twice for a copy of the manuscripts;—no answer from you. An explanation or excuse for your silence would oblige

Thomas Chatterton.

July 24th

Walpole accordingly returned the M.S.S. Chatterton's dream of a real Canynge was over.

Coleridge:
O ye who honour the Name of man rejoice that this Walpole is called a Lord.[9]

We reproduce this passage from Dibb's transcription at such length because it provides a revealing instance of the extent to which he makes it hard to grasp not only the order but also the sources that appear in these notes. To begin with, Dibb's placement of Wilde's note on Coleridge's remark gives the impression that the comment from the preface to the "Monody on the Death of Chatterton" concludes, rather than frames, the well-known letter in which Chatterton expresses a sense of injury to Walpole. More to the point, Dibb's use of bold typeface obscures the places where words and phrases such as "singularly impertinent letter," "spirited," and "dream of a real Canynge" originate. This problem is all the more pressing because the notebook reveals how carefully Wilde was working with his sources, especially with regard to the powerful analysis that Wilson's *Chatterton* offered him.

We hope that Appendix A will disambiguate many of those areas of the notebook that Dibb has transcribed in his chosen manner. We have annotated both Wilde's manuscript notes and clippings as fully as possible, with the aim of illuminating not only the sources that Wilde used but also those sources that Wilson and Masson employed in researching Chatterton's life and works. Such references demonstrate how well researched Wilson's *Chatterton*, in particular, was for its time.

APPENDIX B: WILDE'S NOTES ON DANTE GABRIEL ROSSETTI'S *BALLADS AND SONNETS* (1881)

Five unnumbered, undated, handwritten foolscap sheets comprise a set of notes on Dante Gabriel Rossetti's *Ballads and Sonnets* held in the William Andrews Clark Memorial Library at the University of California, Los Angeles

9. Dibb, "Appendix G," in *Oscar Wilde, a Vagabond with a Mission*, 319.

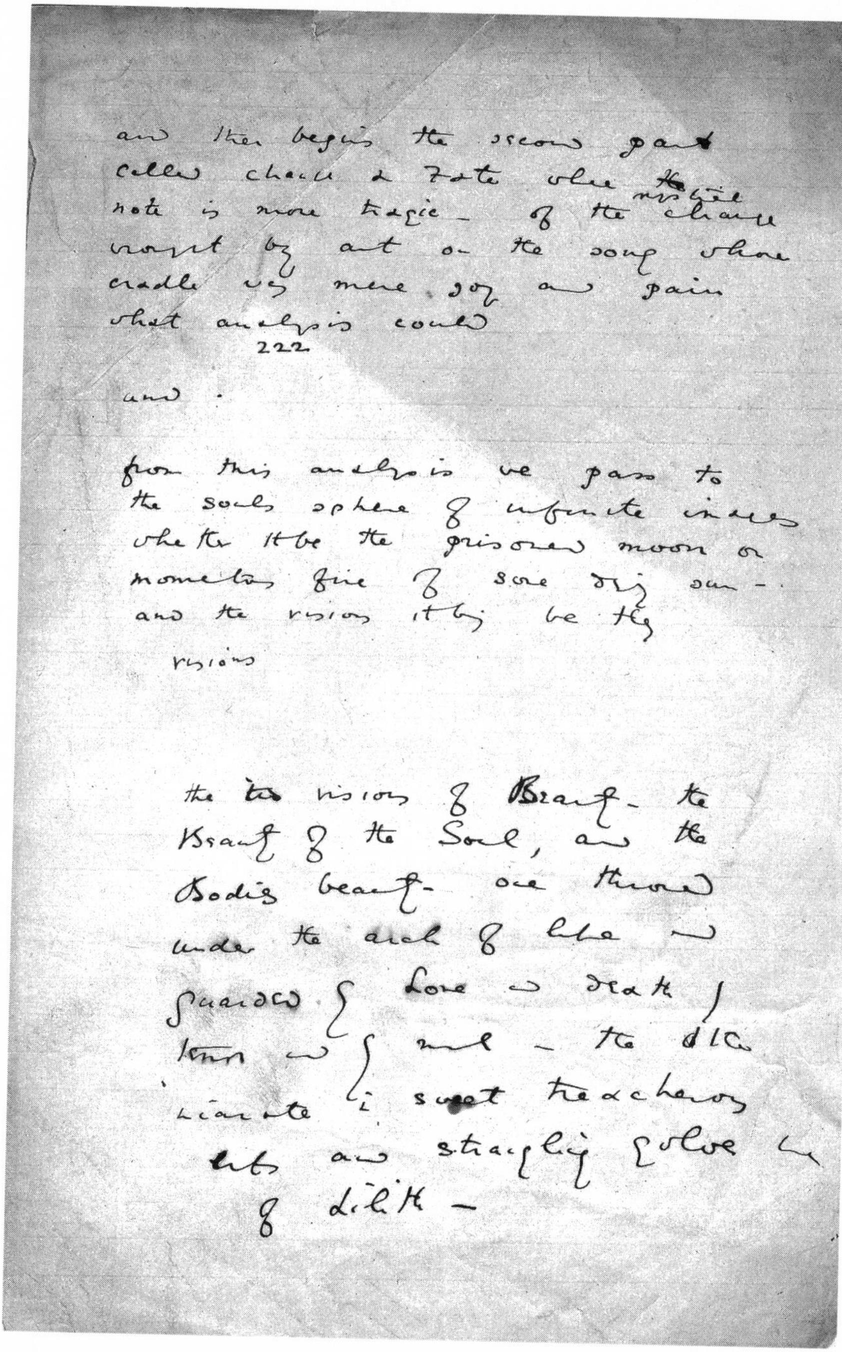

Figure 16. Oscar Wilde, Notes on Dante Gabriel Rossetti's *Ballads and Sonnets* (1881), f.3ʳ, autograph manuscript. Image courtesy of William Andrews Clark Memorial Library, University of California, Los Angeles. W6721M3 D758 [188–?].

(Wilde W6721M3 D758 188-?). Rossetti's volume appeared in 1881 and includes the sonnet on Thomas Chatterton that Wilde transcribed on the final page of his "Chatterton" notebook, a fact that, when taken together with the thematic resonance between the notebook and the Rossetti notes, makes definitive dating of the notes difficult. Wilde certainly could have encountered *Ballads and Sonnets* at the time of its original publication and produced the notes at any point thereafter; it seems possible, though, that Wilde might have returned to the volume closer to the time of the composition of the "Chatterton" notebook, especially given the terms he uses to describe Rossetti's work, which center repeatedly on the notion of a "romantic school" (f.1^v, f.5^r [412, 415]). Then again, the fact that these notes do not mention either the sonnet dedicated to Chatterton or the sonnet "Tiber, Nile, and Thames," which alludes to Chatterton, perhaps points to a date closer to the time when Rossetti's volume first appeared in 1881.[10] Although the notes seem to function as a draft, and include page references from *Ballads and Sonnets*, no publication of a review resulted from them.

Since the pages are not numbered or dated, and since it is hard to discern a likely order from the notes' contents, the pagination remains arbitrary. We have given each folio a number for ease of reference. It is clear that the pages have been removed from a notebook—with a torn margin indicating the bound edge—and we have thus designated them recto (^{r}) and verso (^{v}). Wilde used black ink throughout. There are several ink smudges and blots on what appears to be a very hastily written document. In several places, Wilde's usually legible hand proves very hard to interpret, as one can readily see in Figure 16 (which reproduces f.3^r [413–14]). A single doodle from f.1^v is included in our transcription. Such doodles, especially ones featuring a rapidly sketched profile, are not unusual in Wilde's notebooks.[11]

We apply the same approach to transcription and rendering of Wilde's notes on Rossetti as we do to the "Chatterton" notebook. Line breaks and alignment have been retained, and deleted words are rendered ~~struck through~~. Illegible words are noted in brackets; questionable words are followed by a question mark in brackets [?]. The notes have been collated with *Ballads and Sonnets*, and we include the original text wherever relevant, along with page references, in our notes.

10. We discuss both "Five English Poets: I. Chatterton" and "Tiber, Nile, and Thames" in chapter 4 (184).

11. On Wilde's habitual doodling, see John Paul Riquelme, "Oscar Wilde's Anadoodlegram: A Genetic, Performative Reading of *An Ideal Husband*," in Joseph Bristow, ed., *Wilde Discoveries: Traditions, Histories, Archives* (Toronto: Toronto University Press, 2013), 289–314.

Appendix A

The "Chatterton" Notebook

{1ʳ}

(For handwritten notes and other documentation not by Wilde on this page, see Editorial Introduction [317–20].)

{1ᵛ}[1]

Previous lectures[2]

Romantic movement—

first in <u>poetry</u>

Chatterton— Coleridge— Keats[3]

=

---

1. Entire page is in black ink. As we explain in our Editorial Introduction, the larger proportion of the "Chatterton" notebook is written in pencil (322); any notes made in pen are recorded here.

2. Reference to previous lectures is unclear; Wilde might be referring to his own series of lectures, which—in this season—addressed "various matters appertaining to aesthetics" (*Northern Echo*, 7 October 1886: 2), including "Dress," or the previous lectures in the series at the Birkbeck Literary and Scientific Institute. If the note was added prior to his April 1888 Bournemouth lecture on Chatterton, it could refer to his previous lectures at Bournemouth. During 1885 and 1886, Wilde's main lecture topic was "Dress," although he also gave talks titled "The House Beautiful," "The Value of Art in Modern Life," and "Personal Impressions of America." For further information, see Geoff Dibb, *Oscar Wilde, a Vagabond with a Mission: The Story of Oscar Wilde's Lecture Tours of Britain and Ireland* (London: Oscar Wilde Society, 2013), 190–91, 214.

3. Cf. Theodore Watts: "And when we consider the influence Coleridge himself had upon the English romantic movement generally, and especially upon Shelley and Keats, and the enormous influence these latter have had upon subsequent poets, it seems impossible to refuse to Chatterton the place of the father of the New Romantic school" (Theodore Watts, "Thomas Chatterton," in *The English Poets: Selections with Critical Introductions by Various Writers, and a General Introduction by Matthew Arnold*, ed. Thomas Humphry Ward, 4 vols. [London: Macmillan, 1880], 3:401). Cf. f.5ʳ (338) where Wilde traces the lineage from Chatterton to William Blake (1757–1827), Samuel Taylor Coleridge (1772–1834), and John Keats (1795–1821).

language— expression. instrument
technical process precedes arts.[4]

cf.[5]

Emerson   =
A man is only half himself,
the other ꝑ half is his expression.[6]
he reveres men of genius because
they are more himself than he
is—[7]

                =

Son of a poor widow — a
boy— who began to write at
12— and died at 17 —
matured genius—

And greet with smiles the young-eyed poesy
All deftly masked as hoar antiquity.[8]

                =

---

4. Cf. Wilde's essay "Keats' Sonnet on Blue": "In the case of poetry, as in the case of the other arts, what may appear to be simply technicalities of method are in their essence spiritual, not mechanical." *Century Guild Hobby Horse* 1, no. 3 (July 1886): 83–84, in Oscar Wilde, *Journalism Part I*, ed. John Stokes and Mark W. Turner, *The Complete Works of Oscar Wilde*, 7 vols. to date (Oxford: Oxford University Press, 2000 and continuing), 6:84.

5. This word is ambiguous; it could also read as "of" before "technical" (in the line above).

6. "The man is only half himself, the other half is his expression" (Ralph Waldo Emerson, *Essays: Second Series*, ed. Alfred R. Ferguson and Jean Ferguson Carr, *The Collected Works of Ralph Waldo Emerson*, 10 vols. [Cambridge, MA: Belknap Press of Harvard University Press, 1971–2013], 3:4). Emerson (1803–1882) was an important point of reference for Wilde; see, for example, "The Critic as Artist" (1890, revised 1891), in *Criticism: Historical Criticism, Intentions, The Soul of Man*, ed. Josephine M. Guy, *The Complete Works of Oscar Wilde*, 4:143.

7. "The young man reveres men of genius, because, to speak truly, they are more himself than he is" (Emerson, *Essays: Second Series*, 3:5).

8. Coleridge first wrote his "Monody on the Death of Chatterton" in 1790 and revised the poem throughout his life. E. H. Coleridge notes that "the Monody numbered 107 lines in 1794, 143 in 1796, 135 in 1797, 119 in 1803, 143 in 1828, 154 in 1829, and 165 lines in 1834" (*The Complete Poetical Works of Samuel Taylor Coleridge*, ed. E. H. Coleridge, 2 vols. [Oxford: Clarendon Press, 1912], 1:125). The lines Wilde quotes did not appear in the poem's first publication, which was included in an edition of Chatterton's Rowley poems (*Poems, Supposed to Have Been Written at Bristol, by Thomas Rowley and Others, in the Fifteenth Century*, ed. Lancelot Flower [Cambridge: B. Flower, 1794), xxv–xxviii); Coleridge added these as lines 132–33 in *Poems on Various Subjects* (London: C. G. and J. Robinsons: Bristol: J. Cottle, 1796), 10. In the final, 1834 version, they appear as lines 154–55:

And greet with smiles the young-eyed POESY
All deftly mask'd, as hoar ANTIQUITY.

(*Poetical Works*, 3 vols. [London: W. Pickering, 1834], 1:12, in *Poetical Works I: Poems (Reading Text): Part 1*, ed. J. C. C. Mays, *The Collected Works of Samuel Taylor Coleridge*, 22 vols., Bollingen Series LXXV [Princeton: Princeton University Press, 1969–2002], 16.1.1:144). See I. A. Gordon, "The

{2^r}

— 4 ¼ —
Chatterton
———

the conditions that precede[9] ~~the~~ artistic

production ~~of a work of art~~[10] are

so constantly treated as ~~artistic~~
     of work of art
qualities ^ that one is sometimes tempted

to wish that all art were

anonymous.[11] For every true artist,
Even
~~be~~ he portrait painter or dramatist,

be his work absolutely objective in

presentation, still reveals himself

in his manner.[12] Even abstract forms

such as music and colour have

much to tell us about the

nature of him who fashioned them,

Case-History of Coleridge's *Monody on the Death of Chatterton*," *Review of English Studies* 18, no. 9 (January 1942): 49–71.

9. Cf. Wilde's "Keats' Sonnet on Blue": "It shows us the conditions that preceded the perfected form" (in *Journalism Part I*, ed. Stokes and Turner, 6:84).

10. These words are struck in black ink.

11. Cf. Wilde's "Miner and Minor Poets," a review of Joseph Skipsey's *Carols from the Coal-Fields*, published in the *Pall Mall Gazette*, 1 February 1887: 5: "The conditions that precede artistic production are so constantly treated as qualities of the work of art itself, that one is sometimes tempted to wish that all art were anonymous" (in *Journalism Part I*, ed. Stokes and Turner, 6:120).

12. A variation of this sentence also appears in Wilde's later review of Harry Quilter's *Sententiæ Artis: First Principles of Art for Painters and Picture Lovers*: "That there is a difference between colour and colours, that an artist, be he portrait-painter or dramatist, always reveals himself in his manner, are ideas that can hardly be said to occur to [Quilter]" ("A 'Jolly' Art Critic," *Pall Mall Gazette*, 18 November 1886: 6, in *Journalism Part I*, ed. Stokes and Turner, 6:109.)

and take the place of the

biographer. Indeed in some cases

it is almost better for us not

to search too curiously into the

details of the artists life. The

{2ᵛ}

(page blank)

{3ʳ}

incompleteness of Keats' life for
instance blinds many of his critics
to the perfection of his songs[13]— and
it is well on the whole that
we know so little about Shakespeare.
Mʳ· Mathew Arnold has so well
expressed in verse what I am
trying to convey in prose that I
venture to quote his sonnet to
Shakespeare.[14]

---

13. Cf. Wilson: "The pleasure derived from the intense poetic spirit with which the verse of Keats is inspired is ever mingled with the regretful thought that we possess only the creations of his immature genius" (Daniel Wilson, *Chatterton: A Biographical Study* [London: Macmillan, 1869], 318).

14. "Shakspeare" by Matthew Arnold (1822–1888); this sonnet was first published in 1849:

Others abide our question. Thou art free.
We ask and ask: Thou smilest and art still,
Out-topping knowledge. For the loftiest hill
That to the stars uncrowns his majesty,
Planting his stedfast footsteps in the sea,
Making the Heaven of Heavens his dwelling-place,
Spares but the cloudy border of his base
To the foil'd searching of mortality:
And thou, who didst the stars and sunbeams know,
Self-school'd, self-scann'd, self-honour'd, self-secure,
Didst walk on Earth unguess'd at. Better so!
All pains the immortal spirit must endure,
All weakness that impairs, all griefs that bow,
Find their sole voice in that victorious brow.

("A." [Matthew Arnold,] *The Strayed Reveller, and Other Poems* [London: B. Fellowes, 1849], 50.)

{3ᵛ}

(page blank)

{4ʳ}

Yet there are cases where the nature
of the artist is so bound up
with the nature of the man, that
art criticism must take account
of history and physiology in order
to understand the work of art.[15]
And this is specially so in the
case of Chatterton — Without a full
comprehension of his life the secret
of his literature is not revealed.[16]
And so in going over the details
of the life of this marvellous
boy[17] I do so not to mar the
perfect joy and loveliness of his
song by any overemphasis of the
tragedy of his death, but simply
to enable us to understand
the curious form he used, and to
appreciate an art that to many
        may seem an anachronism.

{4ᵛ}[18]

<u>Bristol</u> city built by
merchants —
Cathedral.

————

15. Cf. Wilde's "Miner and Minor Poets": "Yet there are certain forms of art so individual in their utterance, so purely personal in their expression, that for a full appreciation of their style and manner some knowledge of the artist's life is necessary" (*Pall Mall Gazette*, 1 February 1887: 5, in *Journalism Part I*, ed. Stokes and Turner, 6:120).

16. Cf. Watts: "The circumstances attending the production of such purely objective and impersonal poetry as the Rowley Poems were so exceptional that, unlike the poetry of Keats—unlike any other purely artistic poetry—it must be read entirely in connexion with the poet's life" ("Thomas Chatterton," in *The English Poets*, ed. Ward, 3:404).

17. William Wordsworth (1770–1850) wrote of "Chatterton, the marvellous Boy, / The sleepless Soul that perished in his pride" in "Resolution and Independence" (lines 43–45) (*Poems, in Two Volumes and Other Poems, 1800–1807*, ed. Jared Curtis [Ithaca, NY: Cornell University Press, 1983], 125).

18. All lines on this page are written in black ink.

{5ʳ}

Thomas Chatterton the father of the
Romantic movement in literature, the
precursor of Blake, Coleridge and
Keats,[19] the greatest poet of his time,
was born on the 20th November
1752· in the house adjoining the
Pyle Street School in Bristol. The
house is still standing—
A posthumous child. his father having
died three months previously.—
His father not the sexton— though
that office for some centuries had
been hereditary in his family
　　Character of his father—
　　　　a subchaunter in the cathedral—
fond of music and wrote glees—[20]
fond of poetry— of magic— deeply
read in Cornelius Agrippa—
an antiquarian — collected Roman
　　　　　　　　coins—[21]

{5ᵛ}

(page blank)

{6ʳ}

dissipated[22] and reckless Bohemian—
an old relative said of him "he
talked little, was very absent in
company, and used often to walk
by the river side, talking to himself,
and flourishing his arms about"—[23]

---

19. Cf. f.1ᵛ (333–34).

20. *glees:* "A musical composition, of English origin" (OED).

21. Cf. Wilson: "'Old C. was not a little inclined to a belief in magic, and was deeply read in Cornelius Agrippa' . . . he appears to have had a great love for antiquities. He had formed a collection of
several hundred Roman coins" (*Chatterton: A Biographical Study*, 5). Heinrich Cornelius Agrippa
(1486–1535): German occult writer, theologian, astrologer, and magician, known for *De occulta
philosophia libri tres* (1526–1527).

22. Wilson describes Chatterton's father as a "dissipated lover of song" (*Chatterton: A Biographical
Study*, 5).

23. Cf. Wilson: "His abilities appear to have been far above his associates, and accompanied by
some eccentricities suggestive of inherited peculiarities of his posthumous child. An old female relative said of him: 'He talked little, was very absent in company, and used very often to walk by the river
side, talking to himself, and flourishing his arms about'" (*Chatterton: A Biographical Study*, 5–6).

His mother

———

    gentle and kindly— married at
18. was just of age at birth of
her son— described by an old
servant of her daughter as "attery"
a word used in the north of Scotland
as equivalent to fretful.[24]

Eccentricity of the father became genius
in the son,[25] from his mother he
inherited his nervous temperament.

{6ᵛ}

(page blank)

{7ʳ}

not a precocious ~~boy~~ child·
"dull in learning, not knowing
many letters at four years old"[26]
At five he was sent back from
the Pyle Street School as an
incorrigible dunce[27]—To Cromek, a
London engraver we owe the
preservation of many details about
him— especially of the information
derived from Mrs Edkins.—[28]

---

24. Cf. Wilson: "As Molly Hayfield, an old servant of Mrs. Newton characterised her, 'attery,' a word used in the north of Scotland as equivalent to fretful" (*Chatterton: A Biographical Study*, 6–7).

25. Wilson notes: "All that is known" of Chatterton's father "reveals glimpses both of genius and an unwonted range of pursuits not greatly dissimilar to those of the son" (*Chatterton: A Biographical Study*, 5).

26. Wilson, *Chatterton: A Biographical Study*, 10.

27. Cf. Wilson: "The impatient teacher remanded him to his mother as an incorrigible dunce" (*Chatterton: A Biographical Study*, 7-8).

28. Cf. Wilson: "Mr. R.H. Cromek, a London engraver . . . employed himself in the early part of the present century in accumulating information concerning Chatterton, which he did not live to reduce to form. But to him we are indebted for the valuable though undigested notes of Mr. George Cumberland . . . and especially for the information derived from Mrs. Edkins" (*Chatterton: A Biographical Study*, 8). Robert Hartley Cromek (1770–1812) was a well-known art dealer, engraver, and publisher in London. Cromek provided George Cumberland with notes on Chatterton's early life in 1808; as Wilson notes, these finally appeared as "Appendix A," in John Dix, *The Life of Thomas Chatterton, Including His Unpublished Poems and Correspondence* (London: Hamilton, Adams, 1837), 299–31.

[She appears to have resided with Mrs. Chatterton, assisting her as a sempstress, and thus enjoyed the most favourable opportunities for studying the disposition and habits of the boy. She was present at his birth, and was wont to speak of him tenderly as her foster-child. "Many," she says, "were the uneasinesses that his singularities cost his mother; and until he was six years and a half old, they thought he was an absolute fool."[1] But this hasty conclusion seems to have been mainly based on his distaste for the rudimentary studies of a child's schooling. One of his sister's earliest remembrances of him was his "thirst for preeminence. Before he was five years old he would always preside over his playmates as their master, and they his hired servants." His foster-mother also states: he was so ingenious when a child, that if anything got out of order he was always set to mend it, and generally succeeded, to the admiration of his mother; when older, his ingenuity in the mechanic arts

[1]Dix's Life, App. p. 314][29]

{7ᵛ}

(page blank)

{8ʳ}

[was surprising, and he used to observe that a man might do anything he chose. His mother, however, considered him in general as stupid, because, when quite a child, he would sit alone crying for hours, nobody knew what for. Once when he was in one of his silent moods, she said, "When will this stupidity cease?" and Mrs. Edkins added to rouse him, "I wish your father was alive, he would manage you;" at which, starting, he replied, "I wish he was!" uttering a deep sigh, and spoke no more for a long time.[1]

~~These fits of abstraction characterised him to the last.~~
~~"At seven years old he was tenderly sensible of every~~
~~one's distresses, and would frequently sit musing in a~~
~~seeming stupor; at length the tears would steal, one by~~
~~one, down his cheeks: for which his mother, thinking to~~
~~rouse him, sometimes gave him a gentle slap, and told~~

---

29. Wilson, *Chatterton: A Biographical Study*, 8.

~~him he was foolish; and when asked what he cried for,~~
~~he would say, 'Sister beat me, that's all.'"~~ ~~evading~~
~~thereby an explanation of the reveries which already~~
~~occupied his mind.~~[2]

These strange musings, which ere long were the precursors of his poetical activity, were incomprehensible to
those among whom he moved, and only excited suspicion,
or doubt of his sanity. His mother said, "he had cost
her many uneasy hours, from the apprehension she entertained of his going mad; as he was accustomed to
remain fixed for above an hour at a time quite motion-   <u>Plato</u>
less, and then he would snatch up a pen and write incessantly."[3] What he did write, after such prolonged
reveries, does not seem to have excited any curiosity.][30]

the secret of the seemingly dull
nature of this boy is that he was
influence by externals— Things of
sense became fraught with a
spiritual meaning for him—his
love of colour induced him to
learn to read— The illumination[31]

{8ᵛ}

(page blank)

{9ʳ}

of an old French M.S.S. of music

fascinated him— also a black
                       born in a classical age[32]
letter Bible[33]— ^ cradled in

---

30. Wilson, *Chatterton: A Biographical Study*, 9. Wilson's footnotes, omitted from Wilde's clipping, read as follows: "[1] Dix's Life, App. p. 310."; "[2] Ibid. p. 314."; "[3] Mrs. Stockwell, Dix, App. p. 300."
The marginal reference to Plato may relate to Socrates's reflections on poetic rhapsody in both *Ion*
and *Phaedrus* (see our discussion in chapter 4 [184–85]).

31. Cf. Watts: "In his childhood, so occupied was Chatterton's mind by the impression upon it of
the external world through the senses, that for a long time it refused to be distracted by the common
processes of education. Up to about his seventh or eighth year he could not be taught his letters, and
even then this was effected through his delight in colour" ("Thomas Chatterton," in *The English
Poets*, ed. Ward, 3:404.)

32. Insertion is written in black ink.

33. Cf. Watts: "He 'fell in love' with the illuminated letters upon an old piece of French music;
and afterwards 'took to' the picturesque characters of a black letter Bible, and so learned to read"
("Thomas Chatterton," in *The English Poets*, ed. Ward, 3:404).

medieavelisms. From this began

to improve. "At ~~seven~~ eight

years of age so eager for books

that he read from the moment

he waked which was early

until he went to bed, if they

would let him.[34]

> [~~affectionate, and with peculiarly winning ways when he~~
> ~~had an object to gain.~~
>
> His delight was to lock himself up in his little attic,
> with his books, papers, and drawing materials. He
> appears to have had an intuitive taste for drawing, as
> for so much else that was strange for his years; and
> there also, before long, he is found with his parchments,
> "great piece of ochre in a brown pan, pounce bags full
> of charcoal dust, which he had from a Miss Sanger, a
> neighbour; also a bottle of black-lead powder, which
> they once took to clean the stove with, and made him
> very angry." So at length his mother carried off the
> key, lest he should hurt his health in this dusty old garret,
> from whence, after long abstinence, he was wont to
> emerge, begrimed with the traces of his antiquarian
> handicraft. Thus excluded from his favourite haunt,
> "he would come to Mrs. Edkins and kiss her cheek,
> and coax her to get it for him, using the most persuasive
> expressions to effect his end."]][35]

Appearance[36]

---

34. Cf. Wilson: "The mother's apprehensions about her strange child were thus gradually dissipated. 'At seven he visibly improved, to her joy and surprise, and at eight years of age he was so eager for books, that he read from the moment he waked, which was early, until he went to bed, if they would let him'" (*Chatterton: A Biographical Study*, 10).

35. Wilson, *Chatterton: A Biographical Study*, 12. Wilson's footnote, omitted from Wilde's clipping, reads, "¹ Mrs. Edkins, Dix's Life, App. p. 313."

36. Chatterton was never painted in his lifetime, and almost no information about his physical appearance survives. Nevertheless, the influence of an early spurious portrait of the poet in profile,

{9ᵛ}

(page blank)

{10ʳ}

two great influences of his
childhood— St. Mary Redcliffe
and the Canynge M.S.S.

———

St Mary Redcliffe one of the loveliest
specimens of parochial architecture
in[37] England.

> [England; and its elevated site on the "cliff" greatly
> adds to the effect of a building which has excited the
> admiration of successive generations. William of Wor-
> cester, Camden, Fuller, and many another worthy of
> later centuries, have lavished their praises on its stately
> tower, richly groined and many-windowed avenues of
> nave, choir, transepts, and Lady Chapel. But when the
> child-poet yielded to its aesthetic influences, the taste for
> such memorials of ancient piety was at its lowest ebb;
> ~~though ere long the first glimmerings of that renewed~~
> ~~appreciation for medieval art were discernible, which has~~
> ~~culminated in our own day in a revival of much else~~
> ~~more fitly pertaining to the same "good old times."~~
> But the imaginative boy anticipated this medieval passion,
> and lived apart in an olden world of ideal perfection.
> "This wonder of mansyons," he exclaims, in one of his
> early utterances from behind the antique mask which he
> so speedily assumed, "was ybuildenne bie the nowe
> Mastre Canynge, of whych need no oder to bie said
> botte see ytte and bee astonyed. Ytte was deyned bie
> Johne a Shaillinger, a Bristowe manne borne; who yn
> the sayde chyrche wyll shewe hys Reede for aye: each
> one pyllare stondynge as a letterre in hys blase."
> This idea of fame reaching far into the coming time
> was strong within him even as a child; and it grew and

---

along with the sensation caused by Wallis's painting of the dying Chatterton, kept the figure of the boy alive in the public imagination. Purists objected to such depictions: Wilde protested the inclusion of a bas-relief of Chatterton in the proposed Bristol memorial, and Dante Gabriel and William Michael Rossetti maintained a lively correspondence about the questionable authenticity of purported portraits. See our discussion in chapter 4 (187–88).

37. Cf. Wilson: "St. Mary Redcliffe is justly regarded as one of the finest specimens of parochial church architecture in . . ." (*Chatterton: A Biographical Study*, 13).

took its strange shape as he made himself familiar with the ancient dwellers in Redclilffe Church: pondering over the beautiful altar-tomb of William Canynge and his wife Joan, ~~with its laudatory epitaph in prose and verse, the addition of a later age~~; or studying the quaint sculpture of the nameless occupant of an adjoining tomb, where the reputed purse-bearer of the old merchant and church-builder lies, with an angel supporting his head, and at his feet his dog with a huge bone in its paws. Near by a plain slab, decorated only with a large knife and strainer, records in antique characters a prayer for the soul of one faithful servitor, supposed to have been his cook; another slab, with incised cross, is dedicated to his reputed brewer; while on an adjoining][38]

{10^v}

(page blank)

{11^r}

[altar-tomb reposes a nameless ecclesiastic commonly regarded as the same "riche merchant of Bristowe," in his later character as Dean of Westbury.

Thus on every hand the boy found that old generation reposing there in dignified contrast to the men of his own day. Nor was he wholly limited to Canynge and his times. Under the great window of the north transept lies the effigy of a mailed knight, cross-legged after the fashion of an old crusader; supposed to represent Robert de Berkeley, Lord of Bedminster and Redcliffe, whose armorial bearings, along with those of the Beauchamps, Montacutes, and other benefactors of the church, are sculptured on bosses in the north aisle of the nave. Other benefactors are commemorated in like heraldic fashion, in sculpture or painted glass; and in earlier times the windows were rich with the blazonry of the Cradocks, Sturtons, Says, Fitzwarrens, Rivers, and others, who claimed a share in the exequies and requiems

---

38. Wilson, *Chatterton: A Biographical Study*, 14. Chatterton presented the historical figure he called William Canynge (strictly speaking, William II Canynges [c. 1399–1474]) as Rowley's patron. Five times mayor and three times member of Parliament for Bristol, the wealthy merchant Canynges was a major patron of the city who did much to help restore the Church of St. Mary Redcliffe after it suffered storm damage in 1446. "Bristowe" is Chatterton's rendition of the ancient name for Bristol.

for founders and benefactors. Everywhere walls and floor were enriched, as they still are, with graven brasses of ancient knights and dames, chief justices, and civic dignitaries, of the times of the Roses; judges and magnates of the Tudors and Stuarts; and on one of the pillars, the armour and banners of Admiral Sir William Penn, father of the more celebrated founder and legislator of Pennsylvania.

Such were the chosen associates of Chatterton's boyhood, in whose company many a pleasant hour was dreamt away, until that old past, with its knights, priests, and merchant princes, became for him the world of realities in which alone he willingly dwelt.

> "So the foundations of his mind were laid.
> In such communion, not from terror free,
> While yet a child, and long before his time,
> Had he perceived the presence and the power
> Of greatness; and deep feelings had impressed
> Great objects on his mind, with portraiture
> And colour so distinct, that on his mind
> They lay like substances, and almost seemed
> To haunt the bodily sense."][39]

Of the church itself Chatterton
wrote many lovely lines of wh.
       they are patently[?] the best.

{11ᵛ}

    (page blank)

{12ʳ}

> ["Thou seest this mastery of a human hand,
>   The pride of Bristowe and the western land;
>   Yet are the builder's virtues much more great,
>   Greater than can by Rowley's pen be scann'd.
>   Thou seest the saints and kings in stony state,
>   That seem with breath and human souls dispand;
>   As 'pared to us enseem these men of slate,
>   Such is great Canynge's mind when 'pared to God elate."][40]

---

39. Wilson, *Chatterton: A Biographical Study*, 15. Verse is Wordsworth, *The Excursion: Being a Portion of The Recluse, a Poem* (1814), Book First ("The Wanderer"), lines 132–39. Wilson slightly changes Wordsworth's text; cf. *The Excursion: Being a Portion of The Recluse, a Poem*, 2nd ed. (London: Longman, Hurst, Rees, Orme and Brown, 1820), 10, in *The Excursion*, ed. Sally Bushell, James A. Butler, and Michael C. Jaye (Ithaca, NY: Cornell University Press, 2007), 52–53.

40. Quoted in Wilson, *Chatterton: A Biographical Study*, 143. Wilson comments that this stanza typifies the way that the Church of St. Mary Redcliffe "is the theme of repeated versification, in

[St. Mary Redcliffe forms, accordingly, the centre around which revolve all the quaint, fanciful, and richly poetic phases of the Rowley fiction. The hold it retained on his imagination repeatedly manifests itself even in his latest London correspondence; as in his letter to Cary, in ~~defence of his "Kew Gardens" satire, and its panegyric on Allen, a Bristol organist, whom he had pronounced "divine."~~ "Step into Redcliffe Church," he exclaims, "look at the noble arches, observe the symmetry, the regularity of the whole; how amazing must that idea be which can comprehend at once all that magnificence of architecture. Do not examine one particular beauty, or dwell upon it minutely; take the astonishing whole into your empty pericranium, and then think what the architect of that pile was in building, Allen is in music." When he wrote this he seemed to be absorbed in the excitement of London, and the politics of the day. But the moment his thoughts reverted to Bristol and its church, the old feelings revived. It was the cradle of his inspiration, and the cynosure of all his latest fancies. Within its charmed precincts he passed at will into another life, and his antique dreams became credible and true. In all his guisings and literary masquerades, the same antique realism predominates. He lives in the middle of that fifteenth century in which lived William Canynge as merchant, mayor, church-builder, priest, and dean; and revels in fancy amid the noble doings of this hero of his romantic dream. With this key to the plot, the Rowley manuscripts acquire a consistent unity, imperfect as they are.][41]

And what are the Rowley
manuscripts—

---

which [the church's] praises and those of its reputed builder are livingly set forth" in the Rowley poems (*Chatterton: A Biographical Study*, 143). Here and throughout, Wilson has modernized Chatterton's text. Wilson writes in his preface: "Excepting in one or two brief extracts, designedly selected to illustrate the disguise of the poet, I have, in the following pages, modernised the spelling of the poems, and even replaced coined or obsolete words by the equivalents furnished in Chatterton's own foot-notes, where this could be done without marring the rhythm of the passages quoted" (*Chatterton: A Biographical Study*, x). Taylor and Hoover title the piece "Stay curious Traveller and pass not bye," in "A Discourse on Brystowe by Thos. Rowleie wrotten and gotten at the Desire of Wm: Canynge, Esq.," lines 199–206, in *The Complete Works of Thomas Chatterton*, ed. Donald S. Taylor and Benjamin B. Hoover, 2 vols. (Oxford: Clarendon Press, 1971), 1:99.

41. Wilson, *Chatterton: A Biographical Study*, 135.

{12ᵛ}

(page blank)

{13ʳ}

[Over the north porch of St. Mary Redcliffe—rebuilt on the site of an earlier structure, and traditionally affirmed to have been completed at the cost of William Canynge, merchant, and mayor of Bristol in the reigns of Henry VI. and Edward IV.,—there is a chamber, designated in][42]

[ancient deeds the Treasury House, in which lay, deposited in six or seven oaken chests, the charters and title-deeds of the church, including documents of a still earlier date than the present noble edifice. Among those was one large, iron-bound coffer secured with six locks, designated in a deed of the fifteenth century, "William Canynge's chest in the treasury-house of the church of the Blessed Mary of Redcliffe."[1] Such receptacles for the safe-keeping of the holy vessels, vestments, charters, and service-books, are still common in old churches, and are frequently ornamented with iron scroll-work, or wrought in carved panelling ~~according to the style of the con-~~ ~~temporary architecture~~. But Master Canynge's coffer was long guarded with peculiar jealousy, as in the days when it held the treasures of the old merchant. Two of its six keys were entrusted to the vicar and procurator of the church, two to the mayor, and one each of the churchwardens: whereby it is no marvel that by and by they nowhere could be found. An impatient vestry wanted access to certain deeds; and so, about the year 1730[2] the locks, not only of Mr. Canynge's coffer, but of all the chests, were forced, the deeds relating to the church property removed, and the remaining papers and parchments exposed to neglect, because the vestry attorney could not read them, and they seemed valueless as title-deeds of any church estates.[3]

The actual worth of the ancient documents to the ignorant custodians to whom they were now abandoned, was simply the material on which they were engrossed. The muniment room was accessible to the sexton and

---

[1] Barrett's History, p. 576][43]

---

42. Wilson, *Chatterton: A Biographical Study*, 20.

43. Wilson, *Chatterton: A Biographical Study*, 21. Wilson is referencing William Barrett, *The History and Antiquities of the City of Bristol; comp. from Original Records and Authentic Manuscripts, in*

{13ᵛ}

(page blank)

{14ʳ}

[his family, and its contents were turned to account as mere waste paper. Some of the old documents were even employed to wipe church candlesticks, and many more were carried off for equally vile uses.[1] But the most unscrupulous plunderer was the old sexton's heir, Thomas Chatterton, father of the poet, who found he could turn them to account in various ways in the parish Free School. From time to time, accordingly, bundles of the parchments were removed; until at length, summoning to his aid a posse of the schoolboys, he carried off a large basketful, and deposited the spoils in a cupboard of the school-room for common use.

Primers and copy-books were thenceforth furnished with wrappers that would now be worth more than any volume they could cover. Twenty Bibles presented to the boys by the ~~Rev. John Gibb~~, Vicar of St. Mary Redcliffe prior to 1744, were covered with the old parchments; and when the death of the schoolmaster necessitated his widow's removal from Pyle Street, in 1752, there still remained so large a stock that she emptied the school-room cupboard "partly into a large deal box where her husband used to keep his clothes, and into a square box of a smaller size." The ample receptacles indicate the abundance of the antique store, after all the depredations it had suffered at the hands of her husband and his pupils. It is inconceivable, indeed, that the box-loads still remaining were all parchments. The greater part were probably the ordinary parish registers, accounts,

---

Public Offices or Private Hands; Illustrated with Copper-Plate Prints (Bristol: W. Pine, 1789). Wilson's additional footnotes, omitted from the clipping, read as follows: "[2] Dr. Gregory says (Life, p. xxiv.) 'about the year 1727.' Mr. Barrett gives the date 1748, in a letter to Dr. Ducarel of Doctors' Commons, in 1772 (Gent. Mag. vol. lvi. p. 460). But the old Vicar, Mr. Gibb, whose school Bibles were covered with the parchments, was succeeded by Mr. Thomas Broughton in 1744. The date should probably be 1735. In the following year the first of the old documents, hereafter referred to, was produced at a meeting of the Society of Antiquaries."; "[3] Barrett, Gent. Mag. vol. lvi. p. 460." Wilson is referencing G[eorge]. Gregory, *The Life of Thomas Chatterton, with Criticisms on His Genius and His Writings, and a Concise View of the Controversy Concerning Rowley's Poems* (London: G. Kearsley, 1789), and "Original Correspondence on the Discovery of Rowley's Poems," *Gentleman's Magazine* 56 (1786): 361–62, 460–64, 544–47, 580, and 859–60. As Wilson notes, this correspondence includes Bristol surgeon William Barrett, antiquary Andrew Coltée Ducarel, and others.

&c., usually found in such repositories: but still including curious, and probably valuable deeds.

Old parchments were thus more abundant in the poor widow's house than ordinary paper: "some being turned into thread-papers, some into patterns, some into dolls," and applied to other equally mean uses.[2] In all probability, Chatterton's first efforts with the pencil and pen were scrawled on the margins of deeds in imitation of]⁴⁴

{14ᵛ}

(page blank)

{15ʳ}

[characters engrossed in the time of the Plantaganets, or when Occleve and Lydgate were feebly reechoing Chaucer's rhythm. Thus the child, who acquired his first knowledge of letters from the illuminated capitals of an ancient music-book, and learned their use in the pages of an old black-letter Bible, was familiar from infancy with a medieval palæography and the aspect of antique parchments. ~~Mrs. Phillips remembers that when his mother's thread-papers were found to be of such material he said they belonged to Redcliffe Church, and intimated his intention of informing his uncle, the sexton.¹ Bryant, an early champion of the authenticity of the fifteenth-century Rowley and his poems, assigns the discovery of the antique thread-papers to the period of Chatterton's entering the office of Mr. Lambert. But the date rests on the authority of statements chiefly furnished by Mr. William Smith fully fifteen years after that event; and is contradicted by various independent proofs of his familiarity with the spoils of Canynge's coffer before he entered Colston's Hospital: apart from the more conclusive fact that he produced some of his Rowley MSS. while still a Bluecoat boy.~~⁴⁵

The antique poems had no doubt made some progress, and the romance begot in the strange reveries of the

---

44. Wilson, *Chatterton: A Biographical Study*, 22. Wilson's footnotes, omitted from Wilde's clipping, read as follows: "¹ Letter of Rev. John Chapman, Gent. Mag. vol. lvi. p. 361."; "² Mr. William Smith, Milles's Rowley, p. 13." Wilson is referencing [Thomas Chatterton,] *Poems, Supposed to Have Been Written at Bristol, in the Fifteenth Century, by Thomas Rowley,* ed. Jeremiah Milles (London: T. Payne, 1782).

45. These lines are struck in black ink with a large X.

young dreamer was assuming shape and consistency,
before an actual Thomas Rowley, priest and poet of the
olden time, was called into being as their assigned author.
The Rowley romance has been realized in the purlieus
of St. Mary Redcliffe, by the child-poet, in very early
years. But, to his simple unimaginative mother, his
reveries were suggestive rather of defective intellect
than poetic inspiration. Hence he learned to conceal
his poetical recreations as reprehensible, if not altogether
criminal indulgences. With a strength of filial attach-
ment which never failed him, he nevertheless cherished
his most familiar thoughts in his own breast: until we
have to note among his many ~~singular~~ characteristics, a][46]

singular secretiveness[47] and love

of mystery—

{15ᵛ}

(page blank)

{16ʳ}

Admitted into Colston's Hospital
on 3ʳᵈ· of August 1760,
sort of Blue Coat school—
cf. Charles Lamb & Coleridge—[48]

at first delighted— thinks he
would there get all the learning
he wanted— but soon seemed
hurt— as he said "he could not
learn so much at school as
he could at home"[49]

---

46. Wilson, *Chatterton: A Biographical Study*, 23. The word "singular" is struck in black ink. Wilson's footnote, omitted from Wilde's clipping, reads, "¹ Mrs. Jane Phillips, Dix, App. p. 303."

47. Cf. Wilson: "secretiveness altogether remarkable" (*Chatterton: A Biographical Study*, 24).

48. Wilson compares the "simple curriculum" of the Bluecoat school to the "ample provisions of Edward the Sixth's foundation . . . in which Charles Lamb [1775–1834], and another 'inspired charity boy,' Coleridge, shared to such good purpose" (*Chatterton: A Biographical Study*, 29).

49. Cf. Wilson: "he was at first greatly elated at his election, 'thinking he should there get all the learning he wanted; but soon he seemed much hurt, as he said: he could not learn so much at school as he could at home'" (*Chatterton: A Biographical Study*, 29). Wilson's source for the quotation is "Dix, App. p. 314."

Consciousness of aims and
power beyond those of the
other boys was even now
manifesting itself— [50]

{16ᵛ}

(page blank)

{17ʳ}

> [~~even now manifesting itself in the boy.~~ As a mere child
> he had shown a thirst for preeminence; claimed to
> take the lead among his playmates; ~~began to talk to his~~
> ~~mother and sister of the good things in store for them~~
> ~~when he grew up and was able to repay their kindness;~~
> and already indulged in dreams of future fame. While
> still very young, a manufacturer of earthenware undertook
> to present Mrs. Chatterton's children with specimens of
> his art, and asked the boy what device he would have
> upon his. "Paint me," he replied, "an angel, with wings
> and a trumpet, to trumpet my name over the world."
>
> It is not to be wondered that to such a child, Colston's
> Hospital should prove distasteful. Instead of wandering
> at pleasure about St. Mary Redcliffe, or musing over its
> monuments till he dreamt of himself as the monk-poet
> of the days when it was in building, he had to submit
> to the actual durance of a modern Bluecoat monk. The
> absence of all means of retirement must have been no
> less irksome to him than the inadequacy of the instruc-
> tion received. ~~The unvarying routine of a common~~
> ~~school education was only relieved by the catechising and~~
> ~~church services of Sundays and saints' days. The~~
> ~~school hours were in the morning, from seven till noon;~~
> ~~and from one till five in the afternoon. During the~~
> ~~shorter winter days they did not enter the school-room~~
> ~~till eight, and left at four. But throughout the year they~~
> ~~were required to be in bed by eight;~~[1] ~~so that, with the~~
> ~~additional time for meals, the moments snatched for such~~
> ~~communings with his own thoughts as the young poet~~
> ~~craved must have been scanty enough.~~[51] This may well
> account for his sister's remark, that he became gloomy

---

50. Cf. Wilson: "The consciousness of powers and aims far beyond those of his fellows was even now manifesting itself in the boy" (*Chatterton: A Biographical Study*, 29–30).

51. Lines on this page are struck in pencil.

from the time he began to learn.[2] All his bright anticipa-
tions of getting the knowledge he craved had vanished;
and he instinctively longed to return to his own little
study, and his solitary musings in Redcliffe Church.

But no impediments could shut out the eager youth
from the acquisition of knowledge. By his tenth year he

[1]*Bristoliensis,* Gent. Mag. vol. xlviii. p. 403.
[2] Mrs. Newton's Letter, Croft, p. 162.][52]

{17ᵛ}

(page blank)

{18ʳ}

[was perusing all the books accessible to him; and
expending the little pocket-money his mother allowed
him in hiring others from a lending library. Then, too,
brief hours of release from the noisy playground and the
unattractive studies of the school recurred at frequent
intervals. Each Saturday brought about its precious
half-holiday; and, like its great London prototype, the
Bristol Bluecoat School held the saints' days of the
Anglican Calendar in becoming reverence. On those
welcome occasions the boys were emancipated from the
hospital bounds from noon till eight in the evening; and
then Chatterton hastened home to the happy solitude of
the attic he had appropriated as his study under his
mother's roof. Each Saturday, says Mrs. Edkins, he was
always at home, returning punctually a few minutes after
the clock struck twelve, to get to his little room and shut
himself up. There were deposited his own little stock
of books, parchments, and all the materials already in
use by him in the first efforts of his antique muse. His
scheme of a series of poems to be produced under the
guise of an ancient poet-monk was already in embryo;
and he would lock himself in his favourite retreat, and
frequently remain there without food the whole day: till
his mother became alarmed for his health; and wonder
grew into doubt and suspicion at his strange proceedings,

52. Wilson, *Chatterton: A Biographical Study,* 30. Wilson is referencing "Bristoliensis," "On Row-
ley's Poems and Chatterton," *Gentleman's Magazine* 48 (September 1778): 403, and Herbert Croft,
Love and Madness: In a Series of Letters, One of Which Contains an Original Account of Chatterton
(London: G. Kearsley, 1786).

the apparatus, the parchments, both plain and written, "and the begrimed figure he always presented when he came down at tea-time, his face exhibiting many stains of black and yellow. All these circumstances began to alarm them; and," as Mrs. Edkins relates, "when she could get into his room, she would be very inquisitive, and peep about at everything. Once he put his foot on a parchment on the floor to prevent her from taking it up, saying, 'you are too curious and clear-sighted, I wish you would bide out of the room; it is my room.' To this she replied it was only a general lumber-room, and that she wanted some parchments, some of his old Rowley's, to make thread-papers of;" —for already he had familiarised those at home with his imaginary monk,— "but he was offended,]⁵³

{18^v}

(page blank)

{19^r}

[and would not permit her to touch any of them, not even those that were not written on. But at last, with a voice of entreaty, he said, 'Pray don't touch anything here,' and seemed very anxious to get her away."¹

At other times, it was only by entreaty, or threats to force the door, that he could be induced to unlock it; and then, as Mrs. Edkins described it, he sat surrounded by the strange materials of his antique art: his ochre, charcoal, pen and pencils, the little square deal table covered with letters, papers, and parchments in utmost confusion, and all round the room a complete litter of parchments. His hands and face betrayed, as usual, the nature of his work. But it has been too hastily assumed that the boy was systematically engaged in the conversion of modern parchments into spurious antiques. His antique poems became, ere long, voluminous enough; but as to the spurious parchments, all he ever produced could have been manufactured in a few days. But he was a self-taught draughtsman; delighted in realizing to the eye his fancies of the long-vanished architecture of the Bristowe, of Ælla, Canynge, and Rowley: as in the elaborate elevations of the Bristowe

---

53. Wilson, *Chatterton: A Biographical Study*, 31.

Castle of A.D. 1138, gravely reproduced with accompanying ground-plans, in Barrett's "History," as "engraved from drawings on vellum preserved to this day."
Such drawings are spoken of as numerous. His uncle
Phillips had some; Barrett and Catcott obtained others.
His relative Mr. Stephens, Mr. Palmer, Mr. Richard
Smith and others, had many of his heraldic drawings;
and Mrs. Edkins, in describing to Mr. George Cumberland "the old deeds that came from the muniment room,
which were used indiscriminately for any purpose," adds,
"there were many of them covered with strange figures
of men's heads, &c., on the backs," which she supposes
were his drawing. It may be assumed, therefore, that
the half-holidays of the Bluecoat boy were more frequently spent in gratifying his artistic and antiquarian
tastes—in recreating, in such visible form, his concep-

[1] Mrs. Edkins, Dix, p. 313][54]

{19ᵛ}

(page blank)

{20ʳ}

[tions of the past—than in manufacturing professed
originals of his Rowley poems. Such spurious antiques
belong altogether to a later period, after the poems
themselves had been produced, and the originals were
called for by Barrett and others.

In every step of Chatterton's brief career we meet
with surmises and suspicions of his contemporaries,
dealt with at a subsequent period as facts. Towards
the close of his residence in Colston's Hospital, where
we know some of his Rowley poems were written, he
was observed to seclude himself more than ever in his
little study. When Mrs. Edkins narrated this to Mr.
Cumberland long afterwards, she entertained no doubt
that he was then assiduously labouring at the Rowley
manuscripts. But this was an after-thought. So little
did even the mother and other nearest relations comprehend the strange boy, that when he was nearly fourteen
years of age they became apprehensive "lest he should

---

54. Wilson, *Chatterton: A Biographical Study*, 32.

be doing something improper, knowing his want of
money and ambition to appear like others;" but the only
idea they could conjure up to account for his recluse
habits was, "that these colours were to colour himself,
and that, perhaps, he would join some gipsies one day
or other, as he seemed so discontented with his station
in life."[1]

Sometimes, however, especially in the earlier period
of his residence in the Bluecoat School, he would spend
his holidays in his mother's company, writing "on the
seat of the schoolroom window, which was high, and to
accomplish which he was obliged to stand on a chair.
If any of his mother's pupils interrupted him, he would
get down from it in a great rage, and strike them to
make them quiet. Occasionally his mother would take
the children into an upper room when he was thus
engaged, that he might not be disturbed."[2] It was not
therefore from an unsocial disposition, or any undue
secretiveness, but from the natural craving of the young
poet for silence in his hours of inspiration that he]

[1] Mrs. Edkins, Dix, App. p. 314. [2] Dix's Life, p. 15.][55]

learned to court the privacy
of his little study—[56]

{20ᵛ}

(page blank)

{21ʳ}

began to write poetry when only
~~eleven~~ 10 years old— His first
poem religious— Christ's Coming—
published in Felix Farley's Journal[57]

---

55. Wilson, *Chatterton: A Biographical Study*, 33.

56. Cf. Wilson: "learned to court the privacy of his little study" (*Chatterton: A Biographical Study*, 34).

57. Cf. Wilson: "It appears to have been in his eleventh year that Chatterton took to writing verse; and at that same early age he made his first public appearance as a poet. . . . But the researches of Mr. W. Tyson . . . have led to the discovery of one of the poetical productions referred to by Mrs. Newton, in *Felix Farley's Journal*, of the earlier date of January 8, 1763, when he was only ten years of age. . . . At the same time he also wrote the following little piece, entitled 'On the Last Epiphany; or, Christ's Coming to Judgment'" (*Chatterton: A Biographical Study*, 34). Established in 1752, *Felix Farley's Advertiser* became *Felix Farley's Bristol Journal* three years later; it merged with the *Bristol Times* in 1853. "On the Last Epiphany, or Christ Coming to Judgment" appeared in *Felix Farley's Bristol Journal*, 8 January 1763, and is reprinted in Dix, "Appendix B: Chatterton's First Poetical Production,"

"He had been gloomy, his sister
remarked, from the time he had
begun to learn— but was more
cheerful after he began to write
poetry[58]— then we find him
coming forward as the
champion of Mediaevalism—
and satirising the churchwardens[59]
for desecrating the graveyards—

{21^v}

(page blank)

{22^r}

(page blank)

{22^v}

(page blank)

{23^r}

[Chatterton now gave full play to his intellectual powers. His reading was pursued with unwearied zeal; and
the usher reported that he made rapid progress in arith-
metic. Between his eleventh and twelfth years, as his
sister reports, "he wrote a catalogue of the books he
had read, to the number of seventy. History and
divinity were the chief subjects;" and these, as his
schoolmates informed her, he retired to read at the
hours allotted for play.[1] Ere long, also, the elder poets
were lovingly studied. Chaucer was his special favourite.
The motto to his "Epistle to Mastre Canynge" is taken
from Barbour's "Bruce;" his MSS. in the British Museum
include an extract from "Piers Ploughman," though elsewhere he ascribes its authorship to Chaucer. His own
writings furnish evidence of his familiarity with Shakespeare, Milton, Dryden, Prior, Cowley, and Gray; Pope
and Thomson were studied with care; and Churchill became his favourite model as a satirist. It was probably

---

in *The Life of Thomas Chatterton*, 323. Taylor and Hoover list this poem among "Works of Doubtful
Authenticity" (*Complete Works of Thomas Chatterton*, 2:688, 1138–39).

58. Cf. Wilson: "'He had been gloomy,' his sister says, 'from the time he began to learn; but we
remarked he was more cheerful after he began to write poetry'" (*Chatterton: A Biographical Study*, 35).

59. Cf. Wilson: "It was in the following December that the unpopular churchwarden of St. Mary
Redcliffe became the butt of [Chatterton's] satirical muse" (*Chatterton: A Biographical Study*, 35).

for modern authors such as those that he resorted to the
circulating library; while private collections chiefly supplied the rarer folios and quartos of Hall, Hollingshed,
Camden, Stowe, Weever, and the like historical, heraldic,
and antiquarian works, which furnished delightful occupation for the play-hour.][60]

We hear of him reciting poems
to his friends on the school steps,
and satirising the masters in
verse— though to one master
he was particularly attached—
<u>Phillips</u>— a poet of a minor
order—[61]

{23ᵛ}

(page blank)

{24ʳ}

Before he was twelve years old
he had conceived the idea of
a series of antique poems, ascribed
to the imaginary Thomas Rowley a
monk of the 15ᵗʰ century—[62]
Thistlethwaite a school fellow
tells us the following story—
"Going down Horse-Street
near the school, one day
during the summer of 1764, I
accidentally met with Chatterton.
Entering into conversation with
him,[63]

---

60. Wilson, *Chatterton: A Biographical Study*, 36. Wilson's footnote, omitted from Wilde's clipping, reads "¹ Croft, p. 162." Wilson, here and elsewhere, quotes from Croft, *Love and Madness*, 1786.

61. Cf. Wilson, *Chatterton: A Biographical Study*, 37–38. The English poet Ambrose Philips
(1674–1749) is best known for the attacks that Henry Carey (1687–1743) and Alexander Pope (1688–
1744) made on his "Namby-Pamby" (i.e., excessively sentimental) verse.

62. Cf. Wilson: "The orphan charity boy, with only such common English education as the Bluecoat School afforded, had already, in his twelfth year, conceived the idea of a series of antique poems,
ascribed to the imaginary Thomas Rowley, a monk of the fifteenth century" (*Chatterton: A Biographical Study*, 41).

63. Cf. Wilson: "[Thistlethwaite's] account is as follows: 'Going down Horse street, near the
school, one day during the summer of 1764, I accidentally met with Chatterton. Entering into conversation with him . . .'" (*Chatterton: A Biographical Study*, 41).

{24ᵛ}

(page blank)

{25ʳ}

[he informed me that he was in possession of certain old MSS. which had been deposited in a chest in Redcliffe Church, and that he had lent some or one of them to Phillips. Within a day or two after this, I saw Phillips, and repeated to him the information I had received from Chatterton. Phillips produced a MS. on parchment or vellum, which I am confident was *'Elinoure and Juga,'* a kind of pastoral eclogue, afterwards published in the *Town and Country Magazine*.

Different manuscript copies exist of some of Chatterton's larger antique poems, showing that they were carefully elaborated, and underwent repeated revisions ere he recongised them as complete; but this eclogue, or rather ballad, is only known as it appeared in the *Town and Country Magazine* for May 1769, under the title "Elinoure and Juga: written three hundred years ago by T. Rowley, secular priest."

Two tearful maidens, the nut-brown Elinoure and fair Juga, sit by the banks of the river Rudborne, near St. Albans, bewailing the perils of their absent knights, both of whom prove to have fallen, fighting for the White Rosé, in the old wars of York and Lancaster. ~~The language and orthography are of the affected Chaucerian character which formed the disguise of all the Rowley poems; but it is curious to catch in its stanzas echoes of the polished quatrains of Gray's "Elegy," then in the first blush of its popularity. Slightly modernised, two of its stanzas thus present the maidens interchanging their plaints:~~

JUGA.
"Sisters in sorrow, on this daisied bank,
    Where melancholy broods, we will lament;
Bewet with morning dew and even dank;
    Like levind oaks in each the other bent;
    Or like forletten halls of merriment,
Whose ghastly mitches hold the train of fright,
Where lethal ravens bark, and owlets wake the night.

ELINOURE.
No more the miskynette shall wake the morn,
　　The minstrel dance, good cheer, and morris play;][64]

[No more the ambling palfry and the horn
　　Shall from the lessel rouse the fox away;
　　I'll seek the forest all the live-long day;
　　All night among the graved church-glebe will go,
　　And to the passing sprites lecture my tale of woe."[65]

~~The stanzas given here are modernized in spelling;~~
~~and if in addition to this the small sprinkling of obsolete~~
~~or coined words were replaced by their modern equiva-~~
~~lents in the footnotes—e.g. forletten, forsaken; mitches,~~
~~ruins; lessel, forest, or bush,—the whole would be restored~~
~~to the language of the eighteenth century. Here and~~
~~there, indeed, the line would require modification where~~
~~the modern equivalent in the footnote differs in accent~~
~~or number of syllables; and not infrequently a rich allite-~~
~~ration would be lost: as in the replacement of levynde~~   bagpipe
~~by blasted; chyrche-glebe, by churchyard; forletten by~~
~~forsaken; and miskynette by its interpretation of a small][66~~

{25ᵛ}

(page blank)

{26ʳ}

many such poems he no doubt
read to his schoolfellows, but his
first real attempt at deception
was the great De Bergham
Pedigree—
　　Mr· Henry Burgum a
Bristol worthy and pewterer by
trade had a shop on the
road between the School and
Chatterton's home— He was a
man who had tried to

---

64. Wilson, *Chatterton: A Biographical Study*, 42.

65. "Elinoure and Juga," lines 15–28. See *Complete Works of Thomas Chatterton*, ed. Taylor and Hoover, 1:292–93.

66. Wilson, *Chatterton: A Biographical Study*, 43. The word "bagpipe" that Wilde adds in the margin is the final word of Wilson's last sentence, which awkward cutting has made barely legible on the printed clipping. Sections marked for deletion are struck with a large X.

educate himself late in life —
was fond of music

{26ᵛ}

(page blank)

{27ʳ}

one Saturday half holiday
in the spring of 1767· Chatterton
paid a visit to the shop of
this worthy pewterer and informed
him that he had discovered
among the ancient parchments
of Redcliffe Church an heraldic
blazon of the De Bergham
arms, and a pedigree which
proved his descent from some
of the noblest families in
England. Burgum was filled
with delight and[67]

{27ᵛ}

(page blank)

{28ʳ}

[craved sight of the wondrous pedigree; and within a few days was presented with the De Bergham quarterings blazoned on an old piece of parchment about eight inches square, and a first instalment of the pedigree itself, in Chatterton's own handwriting, copied into a book in which he had already transcribed portions of antique verse with this title: "Poems by Thomas Rowley, Priest of St. John's, in the City of Bristol, containing The Tournament, an Interlude, and a piece by Canynge, called the Gouler's Requiem."

From this pedigree it appeared that Mr. Burgum's ancestor, Simon de Seyncte Lyze, *alias* Senliz, came into England with the Conqueror, married Matilda, daughter of Waltheof, Earl of Northumberland, and in 1075,

---

67. Cf. Wilson: "On a Saturday half-holiday, as we may presume, — at latest in the spring of 1767, — Chatterton paid a visit to the shop of Mr. Burgum . . . and delighted the pewterer with the announcement that he had discovered among the ancient parchments of Redcliffe Church an heraldic blazon of the De Bergham arms, and had a pedigree at home which proved his descent from some of the noblest families in England" (*Chatterton: A Biographical Study*, 55).

after the execution of the Earl for high treason, obtained
a deed of gift of Bergham Castle, with the title of Earl of
Northampton. The document in which this, and much
else of the like kind, was set forth, bore this heading in
large text: "Account of the family of the De Berghams,
from the Norman Conquest to this time; collected from
original Records, Tournament Rolls, and the Heralds of
March and Garter's Records, by Thomas Chatterton."
The arms alone claimed to be of ancient authority. Nevertheless the sources of the family pedigree are of the most
indisputable character. Marginal references abound, with
such authorities as the "Roll of Battle Abbey;" "Ex
stemma fam. Sir Johan de Leveches," "De Lee," &c.;
Stowe, Ashmole, Collins, Dugdale, Rouge Dragon, Garter,
Norroy, and, better than all, "Rowley's MSS." ~~Mr. Wil-
cox, a critical editor, was sorely aggrieved by supposed
reference to oral charters, where the marginal note
appealed, in a common enough abbreviation, to the originals: e.g. "Oral Ch. from Hen. II. to Sir Ino. De
Bergham." But, in truth, the references are, in many
cases, as apocryphal as the pedigree itself; though not
without some interesting traces of the unwonted range
of study in which the boy delighted.~~

~~The pedigree is also garnished with sundry scraps of
heraldic Latin, adapted from Weaver, and other sources]~~[68]

{28ᵛ}

(page blank)

{29ʳ}

By a brilliant if somewhat
daring act of imagination

> [Chatterton had contrived to fit into the
> De Bergham pedigree a learned record of one of the
> pewterer's ancestors, who in the 24th year of the reign
> of Henry VI. obtained a patent for the use of alchemy,
> whereby this philosophic metallurgist was to transmute
> the inferior metals into gold or silver. There was a
> delicate flattery in this discovery, that working in the
> baser metals was an honourable art pertaining to the

68. Wilson, *Chatterton: A Biographical Study*, 56. Lines on this page are struck in cross-hatched pencil marks.

Burgums as a hereditary chartered right. Immediately following this comes another paragraph, no less apt and curious. Thomas de Asheton, the old alchemist, left issue four sons, of whom, according to the De Bergham pedigree, the second was "Edward Asheton, of Chatterton ~~in Com. Lanc.~~ in the right of his wife, the daughter and heir of Radcliffe de Chatterton of Chatterton, the heir-general of many families." The name is sufficently suggestive ~~to the reader~~ now, though Mr. Burgum doubtless passed over it without thought of its bearing any reference to his humble protégé. RADCLIFFE DE CHATTERTON! There is a volume of poetical romance crowded into the very name. It is an epitome of the whole biography of the inspired charity boy.

The delight of the glorified pewterer on the acquisition of his patent of nobility may be imagined. His aspiring partner had already achieved notoriety by more than one notable deed, duly set forth ere long in Chatterton's satirical effusions; but here was he, without effort of his own, exalted to an equality with the proudest peer of the realm. The first act of the ennobled tradesman was to present the discoverer of his pedigree with five shillings. The sum, though but poor largess from the hands of a De Bergham of Norman lineage, was probably a greater amount than the young herald had ever before possessed; and its acceptance cost him no scruples, either then or afterwards. It figures at a later date, among other counts in the satirical indictment against Burgum and others, appended to his Will, where he exclaims:—][69]

{29ᵛ}

(page blank)

{30ʳ}

["Burgum, I thank thee, though hast let me see
That Bristol has impressed her stamp on thee;
Thy generous spirit emulates the Mayor's;
Thy generous spirit with thy Bristol pairs.
Gods! what would Burgum give to get a name,
And snatch his blundering dialect from shame!
What would he give to hand his memory down
To time's remotest boundary? A crown!"][70]

---

69. Wilson, *Chatterton: A Biographical Study*, 58.

70. "[Will]," lines 9–16. See *Complete Works of Thomas Chatterton*, ed. Taylor and Hoover, 1:501.

But this was an after-thought, if not a mere piece of satirical exaggeration, when he had exchanged the Blue-coat school for an attorney's office; and experience had given him further insight into the value of money. At the time it was given, Burgum's crown-piece amply rewarded the genealogist, for what I conceive to have been no more, at first, than a roguish experiment on the credulity of the pewterer. ~~That this was the case finds confirmation from another of the boy's heraldic jests. Mr. Richard Smith, a relative both of the Catcotts and Smiths who figure so prominently in connexion with Chatterton, has recorded some interesting reminiscences of him. "Two of my paternal uncles," he says, "were his constant playmates; three of my maternal uncles were very intimate with him; and to this list may be added an aunt and my own father. Every one of these he by turns laughed at, ridiculed, censured, and, with the exception of the female, satirised most unmercifully, and abused most grossly."~~[1] ~~Aunt Martha, a venerable spinster, described by her nephew as "one of those pious and wise women yclept 'old maids,'" appears to have better appreciated the young scapegrace than others who were made the butts of his jests. She told her nephew that "young Chatterton was a sad wag of a boy, and always upon some joke or another." The old lady incurred his displeasure by taking him to task for some of his misdeeds, whereupon he revenged himself by forwarding to her "a scolding epistle," enclosed in which was her coat of arms, surrounded by a garter, and surmounted, for crest, by what its inheritor describes as a queer-looking flower, tinted~~][1] gules, with a

scroll over it, labelled The
Rose of Virginity![2]
          For heraldry Chatterton

{30ᵛ}

architecture, music, painting,
sculpture— antiquarian

---

71. Wilson, *Chatterton: A Biographical Study*, 59. Lines on this page are struck in a large figure of eight in black ink. Wilson's footnote, omitted from Wilde's clipping, reads, "¹ Gent. Mag. N.S. vol. x. p. 603." Wilson's source is [Richard Smith,] "Anecdotes of Chatterton and His Associates," *Gentleman's Magazine* n.s. 10 (1838): 603–7.

72. *gules*: "Red, as one of the heraldic colours" (OED). Cf. Wilson: "gules, with a scroll over it, labelled, 'The Rose of Virginity!'" (*Chatterton: A Biographical Study*, 60).

like Scott, like Scott cd.
make the dry bones live—
_____ 73

{31ʳ}

had a great passion— The
one decorative art whose
tradition is unbroken was
full of wonder for him—
among the M.S.S. at the
British Museum is an
elaborate piece of blazonry
with nine shields— intended
for an imaginary genealogy
of the Chattertons—⁷⁴

> [It was with Chatterton's heraldry, as with his antique
> prose and verse: a vein of earnestness is inextricably
> blended with what, in other respects, appears as palpable
> fraud. We are reminded of the boy and the visionary
> dreamer, in the midst of his most elaborate fictions, till
> it becomes a puzzle to determine how much of self-
> deception and how much actual belief were blended with the
> humour of the jest."]⁷⁵

{31ᵛ}

(page blank)

{32ʳ}

Bristol Patrons ·

George Catcott.⁷⁶

---

73. These lines are written in black ink. Cf. Ezekiel 37:3–4: "And he said unto me, Son of man, can these bones live? And I answered, O Lord GOD, thou knowest. Again he said unto me, Prophesy upon these bones, and say unto them, O ye dry bones, hear the word of the LORD."

74. Cf. Wilson: "Among the MSS. in the British Museum is an elaborate piece of blazonry of nine distinct shields, executed by him as the first materials for an imaginary genealogy of the Chattertons" (*Chatterton: A Biographical Study*, 64).

75. Wilson, *Chatterton: A Biographical Study*, 65.

76. Chatterton had entrusted some of the Rowley manuscripts to George Catcott (1729–c. 1802); Catcott was an ardent defender of Rowley's authenticity. His name is mentioned frequently in both Wilson's and David Masson's respective studies; see, for example, f.19ʳ, f.30ʳ, and f.55ʳ. See our discussion in chapter 1 (51–70).

Doctor Barrett— surgeon &
antiquarian[77]

—

<u>1767</u>.[78] went to lawyers office
1ˢᵗ July. Mʳ· Lambert—
very unhappy—[79]

 [80]

Opening of Bridge
Second Forgery—

{32ᵛ}

(page blank)

{33ʳ}

The Rowley Romance.[81]

—

great recreation of the past[82]— an
Elaborate historical novel.

objective power—

=

> [~~Saxon of his monk-poet, Turgot. In reality, his antique~~
> ~~prose and verse work out an historical romance of Bris-~~
> ~~towe in the olden time, exhibiting in the grouping of its~~
> ~~characters the graphic fullness of the novelist, and in many~~
> ~~of its passages not a little dramatic power as well as tender~~
> ~~lyrical sweetness.~~
>
> Thomas Rowley, a native of Somersetshire, and a
> zealous Yorkist,[1] of the times when the Red and the
> White Roses were the badges of party strife in England,
> was priest of St. John's, in the city of Bristol, in the year
> 1465. From early years he had borne the most intimate
> relations with the Canynges' family. He and William,

---

77. "surgeon & antiquarian" in black ink.

78. Top underline is written in pencil; bottom underline is written in black ink.

79. Wilson discusses Chatterton's employment as a scrivener to Bristol attorney John Lambert in *Chatterton: A Biographical Study*, 93–114.

80. Figure drawn in black ink.

81. "The Rowley Romance" is the title of chapter VIII in Wilson, *Chatterton: A Biographical Study*, 129–60.

82. Cf. Wilson: "The pomp of heraldry had a fascinating charm for Chatterton; and the intricacies of its symbolic ramifications evidently furnished a favourite recreation, in which he could live over again that heroic past" (*Chatterton: A Biographical Study*, 63).

the second son of John Canynge, a youth of cunning
wit,—as we learn from the "Lyfe of W. Canynge," one of
the Chatterton MSS.,—improved their lear together, under   were educated
the care of the Carmelite brothers, in the old priory which   by
once occupied the site of Colston's School. In fact,
they were Bristol Bluecoat boys of the good old times.
"Here," says Rowley, "began the kindness of our lives;
our minds and kinds were alike, and we were always
together." William's father loved him not as he did his
brother Robert, because, while the latter was a man after
his own heart,—greedy of gain and sparing of alms,—
William was courteous and liberal in word and deed.
But both father and brother died the same year, leaving
William to inherit their great wealth; and about the
same time his old school-mate, Thomas Rowley, took
holy orders, and was made his chaplain and confessor.
A brief extract from the good priest's account of his
friend and benefactor will serve to illustrate the quaint
graphic style of the narrative: — "Master Roberte, by
Master William's desyre, bequeathed me one hundred
marks; I sent to thank Master William for his mickle
courtesie, and to make tender of myselfe to him.
'Fadre,' quod he, 'I have a crotchett in my brayne
that will need your aide.' 'Master William,' said I, 'if
you command me I will go to Roome for you.' 'Not
so farr distant,' said he; 'I ken you for a mickle learned

¹ *Vide* notes to Balade of Charitie]⁸³

{33ᵛ}

(page blank)

{34ʳ}

[priest; if you will leave the parysh of our Ladie,¹ and
travel for mee, it shall be mickle to your profits.' I
gave my hands, and he told mee I must goe to all the
abbies and pryorys, and gather together auncient draw-
yngs, if of anie account, at any price. Consented I to
the same, and pursuant sett out the Mundaie following
for the Minister of our Ladie and Saint Goodwyne, where
a drawing of a steeple, contryvd for the belles when
runge to swaie out of the syde into the ayre, had I
thence. It was done by Syr Symon de Mambrie, who,

---

83. Wilson, *Chatterton: A Biographical Study*, 136.

in the troublesome rayne of Kyng Stephen, devoted himself, and was shorne."

    In like fashion the good priest continues to collect
valuable drawings and manuscripts for Master Canynge,
and to partake liberally of his bounty. But the death of
the latters ~~his~~ tenderly loved wife, Johanna, in child-bearing, leaves
him widowed and childless; and he thenceforth devotes
himself to the patronage of art, letters, and all good
works. Then did his nobleness shine forth to the world.][84]

[The Sir William Canynge of the Rowley Romance
is himself a man of letters, an artist, and even at times
a poet, devoted to all liberal tastes, and especially to
architecture; and he gathers around him a group of
kindred spirits. There is his friend, Carpenter, Bishop
of Worcester, not incapable of penning a stanza at times:
as appears from an inscription affixed to the cover of an
old mass book, which Chatterton was able to recover for
Mr. Barrett with Rowley's aid.[1] Maystre John a Iscam,
Canon of St. Augustine's Abbey, — himself a poet,—also
bears his part, on more than one occasion, in the dramatic
performances at the Rudde House; and wins the special
commendation of Maistre Canynge, in the character of
"Celmonde," when Rowley acts "Ælla" in his own
"Tragycal Enterlude." In a letter of Rowley to his
brother-poet, he thus jestingly invites him to become
verse-monger to a niggard patron of the muse: "I haveth
metten wythe a syllie knyghte of twayne hondreth poundes
bie the yeere. 'God's nayles,' quod hee, 'leave oute mie
scarlette and ermine doubtlette, I know nete I love better
than vearses. I woulde bestowe rentalls of golde for rolles
of hem.' ~~'Naie, quod I, 'I bee notte a vearse-monger;~~
~~goe to the Black Fryer Mynsterre yn Brystoew wheere the~~
~~Freeres rhyme to the swote smelle of the gowtes, theere~~
~~maie you deale maiehappe.' 'Now, Johan, wylle you~~
~~stocke yis Worscypfulle knyghte wythe somme Ballet~~
~~oune Nellye and Bellie? You quotha naie—botte bee~~
~~here bie twa daies, we shall have an Entyrlude to plaie~~
~~whyche I haveth made, wherein three kynges will~~
~~smeethe~~][85]

---

84. Wilson, *Chatterton: A Biographical Study*, 137. Wilson's footnote, omitted from Wilde's clipping, reads, "[1] From this it may be inferred that Chatterton originally purposed to represent Rowley
as parish priest of St. Mary Redcliffe."

85. Wilson, *Chatterton: A Biographical Study*, 138. Wilson's footnote, omitted from Wilde's clip-

{34ᵛ}

(page blank)

{35ʳ}

[Sir Thybbot Gorges, a neighboring knight of ancient family, contributes to the "Tragycal Enterlude" one of the minstrels' songs, as his quota of verse; enacts the character of "Hurra" the Dane, among the Rudde House amateurs; and pledges, in surety of a liberal benefaction towards the rebuilding of Redcliffe Church, certain jewels of great value. The group is completed by Sir Allan de Vere, Mastre Edwarde Canynge, and others: knights, aldermen, and minstrels; among whom we may specially picture to ourselves John a Dalbenie,—a citizen fond of wordy strife, and prone to mar the pleasant gatherings at the Rudde House by intruding politics into that haunt of the Muses;—who is twitted by the host in this epigrammatic fashion:—

> "Johne makes a jarre boute Lancaster and Yorke;
> Bee stille gode manne, and learne to mynde thie worke."

The old merchant prince of Bristowe, the centre of this group, formed in the estimation of Dean Milles,— most enthusiastic among the early champions of the ancient Rowley,—a parallel to Mæceneas with his three friends, Virgil, Horace, and Varus. To him Rowley sends his verses from time to time, ever sure of some liberal acknowledgement in return. At times the real author expressed under this guise his own estimate of some of those wondrous creations of his muse, given away, or requited by the niggard dole of Catcott or Barrett; for his chief antique productions figure in Rowley's narrative with their becoming reward. "I sent him," writes the good priest, "my verses touching his church, for which he did send me mickle good things;" and again: "I have Master Cannings my Bristow tragedy, for which he gave me in hands twentie pounds, and did praise it more than I did think myself did deserve; for I can say in troth I was never proud of my verses since I did read Master Chaucer; and now haveing nought to do, and not][86]

---

ping, reads, "¹ Works, iii, p. 312." Wilson is referencing *The Works of Thomas Chatterton, Containing His Life by G[eorge]. Gregory, D.D., and Miscellaneous Poems*, ed. Joseph Cottle and Robert Southey, 3 vols. (London: T. N. Longman and O. Rees, 1803).

86. Wilson, *Chatterton: A Biographical Study*, 139.

[wyling to be ydle, I went to the minister of our Ladie and Saint Goodwin, and there did purchase the Saxon manuscripts, and sett myself diligently to translate and worde it in English metre, which in one year I performed, and styled it the Battle of Hastyngs. Master William did bargyin for one manuscript, and John Pelham, an esquire, of Ashley, for another. Master William did praise it muckle greatly, but advised me to tender it to no man, beying the menn whose name were therein mentioned would be offended. He gave me 20 markes, and I did goe to Ashley, to Master Pelham, to be payd of him for the other one I left with him. But his ladie being of the family of the Fiscamps, of whom some things are said, he told me he had burnt it, and would have me burnt too, if I did not avaunt. Dureing this dinn his wife did come out, and made a dinn, to speake by a figure, would have over sounded the bells of our Ladie of the Cliffe; I was fain content to get away in a safe skin."][87]

{35ᵛ}

(page blank)

{36ʳ}

all the Chatterton antique poems
are connected with the Rowley
circle—
the wonderful song to Ælla
Lorde of the Castle of Bristowe
is Rowley's own composition, sent
to Lydgate the Laureate of
Henry VI. in answer to a
friendly challenge—
So marvellous is this
Ode that one cannot
pass it without quotation.[88]

{36ᵛ}

(page blank)

---

87. Wilson, *Chatterton: A Biographical Study*, 140.
88. Wilson describes these events in *Chatterton: A Biographical Study*, 147–48.

{37^r}

[antique or modern rival:—

"Oh thou, or what remains of thee,
    Ælla, the darling of futurity,
Let this, my song, bold as thy courage be,
    As everlasting to posterity!

"When Dacia's sons, whose hair of blood-red hue,
Like kingcups bursting with the morning dew,
        Arranged in drear array,
        Upon the lethal day,
Spread far and wide on Watchet's shore:
        Then didst thou furious stand,
        And by thy valiant hand
Besprenged all the meads with gore.

    "Drawn by thine anlace[1] fell,
    Down to the depths of hell
        Thousands of Dacians went;
    Bristowans, men of might,
    Ydared the bloody fight,
        And acted deeds full quaint.

    "Oh thou, where'er—thy bones at rest—
    Thy spirit to haunt delighteth best;
Whether upon the blood-imbrued plain,
    Or where thou kenst from far
    The dismal cry of war,
Or seest some mountain made of corse of slain;
    Or seest the hatchèd[2] steed
    Yprancing on the mead,
And neigh to be among the pointed spears;][89]

    [Or in black armour stalk around
    Embattled Bristowe, once thy ground,
And glow ardúrous[1] on the castle-stairs;
    Or fiery round the minster glare:
    Let Bristowe still be made thy care.
Guard it from foemen and consuming fire;
    Let Avon's stream encirc it round,
    Ne let a flame enharm the ground,
Till in one flame all the whole world expire."[90]

This episode of a poetical challenge and rejoinder
between the Laureate of Henry VI. and the imaginary

---

89. Wilson, *Chatterton: A Biographical Study*, 148. Wilson's footnotes, omitted from Wilde's clipping, read as follows: "[1] *Anlance*, sword."; "[2] *Hatchèd*, covered with achievements." The verse is Chatterton's "Songe toe Ella," lines 1–27; see *Complete Works of Thomas Chatterton*, ed. Taylor and Hoover, 1:61–62.

90. "Songe toe Ella," lines 28–36, in *Complete Works of Thomas Chatterton*, ed. Taylor and Hoover, 1:62.

Rowley is completed by a transcript of commendatory verses, by Lydgate, in which, after glancing at the great poets of elder times, he concludes by saying that now "in these mokie days" Chaucer lives over again in every line that Rowley writes."][91]

The fragmentary Tragedy of Godwin
also, is supposed to have been
acted by Canygyne and Rowley
at the Rudde House and[92]

{37^v}

(page blank)

{38^r}

contains this fine Ode to
Liberty· one of the noblest of our
martial lyrics—[93]

["When Freedom, drest in blood-stained vest,
 To every knight her war-song sung,
Upon her head wild weeds were spread,
 A gory anlace by her hung.
  She danced on the heath;
  She heard the voice of Death;
Pale-eyed Affright, his heart of silver hue,
 In vain assailed her bosom to acale.[1]
She heard unflemed[2] the shrieking voice of woe,
 And sadness, in the owlet, shake the dale.
  She shook the burled[3] spear;
   On high she jeste[4] her shield;
  Her foemen all appear
   And flie along the field.
Power, with his heafod straught[5] into the skies,
 His spear a sunbeam and his shield a star;
~~Alike twae bredying gronfyres[6] rolls his eyes;~~
 ~~Chafts with his iron feet and sounds to war.~~
  ~~She sits upon a rock;~~
   ~~She bends before his spear;~~
  ~~She rises from the shock,~~
   ~~Wielding her own in air.~~
~~Hard as the thunder doth she drive it on;~~

---

91. Wilson, *Chatterton: A Biographical Study,* 149. Wilson's footnote, omitted from Wilde's clipping, reads "[1]*Arderous,* burning."

92. Cf. Wilson on "The Tragedy of Goddwyn": "The cast of the piece distributes its characters among the select amateurs of the Rudde House theatricals: the author undertaking 'Harolde,' and Canynge himself 'King Edwarde.' This tragedy exists only as a fragment" (*Chatterton: A Biographical Study,* 149.)

93. Cf. Wilson: "This ode . . . indeed may claim its place among the finest martial lyrics in the language" (*Chatterton: A Biographical Study,* 150).

~~Wit skilly wimpled[7] guides it to his crown;~~
~~His long sharp spear, his spreading shield, is gone;~~
~~He falls, and falling rolleth thousands down.~~
~~War, gore-faced War, by Envy burl'd arist,~~
~~His fiery helm ynodding to the air,~~
~~Ten bloody arrows in his straining fist——"][94]

The Battle of Hastings, as I
before noticed, was supposed to
the work of Turgot, a Saxon
monk of the 10th century, and
to have been translated by Rowley[95]

{38[v]}

superb ballad on the death

of Sir Charles Bawdin —

The feathered songster Chanticleere

Had wound his bugle horn,

And low the early villagers

The coming of the morn
         ruddy
Kind Edward saw the ~~coming~~ streaks

of light eclipse the grey,

And heard the raven's croaking throat

Proclaim the fated day.
  =[96]

---

94. Wilson, *Chatterton: A Biographical Study*, 150. These lines are struck in black ink with a large X. "Goddwyn: A Tragedie," lines 196–224; see *Complete Works of Thomas Chatterton*, ed. Taylor and Hoover, 1:304–5. Wilson's footnotes, omitted from Wilde's clipping, read as follows: "[1] *Acale*, freeze"; "[2] *Unflemed*, undismayed."; "[3] *Burled*, pointed."; "[4] *Jeste*, raised."; "[5] *Heafod straught*, head stretched."; "[6] *Brendyng gronfyres*, flaming meteors."; "[7] *Wimpled*, covered."

95. Cf. Wilson: "The history of 'The Battle of Hastings' has already been given. . . . It is professedly the work of Turgot, a Saxon monk, of the tenth century; which, as already narrated, Rowley set himself to translate with all diligence" (*Chatterton: A Biographical Study*, 151.)

96. Lines are written in black ink. Wilson records these two stanzas of the ballad in *Chatterton: A Biographical Study*, 85. "The Death of Sir Charles Baldwin," lines 1–8; see *Complete Works of Thomas Chatterton*, ed. Taylor and Hoover, 1:6–7.

{39^r}^{97}

How charming are these two
stanzas from it.

> ["White as the chalky cliffs of Britain's isle,
>   Red as the highest coloured Gallic wine,
> Gay as all nature at the morning smile:
>   Those hues with pleasaunce on her lips combine,
>   Her lips more red than summer evening skyne,
> Or Phœbus rising in a frosty morn;
>   Her breast more white than snow in fields that lyen,
> Or lily lambs that never have been shorn:
> Swelling like bubbles in a boiling well
> Or new-burst brooklets gently whispering in the dell.
>
> "Brown as the filbert dropping from the shell,
>   Brown as the nappy ale at Hocktide game,
> So brown the crooked rings that featly fell
>   Over the neck of the all-beauteous dame.
>   Grey as the morn before the ruddy flame
> Of Phœbus' charriot rolling thro' the sky;
>   Grey as the steel-horn'd goats Conyan made tame:
> So grey appear'd her featly sparkling eye;
>   Those eyne that did oft mickle pleased look
> On Adhelm, valiant man, the virtues' doomsday book."]^{98}

> [~~"As Elynour by the green lessel²~~ ~~was setting,~~
>   ~~As from the sun's heatè she harried,~~
> ~~She said, as her white hands white hosen were knitting,~~
>   ~~What pleasure it is to be married!~~]^{99}

> [~~"My husband, Lord Thomas, a forrester bold,~~   and
>   ~~As ever clove pin, or the basket,~~   this charming
> ~~Does no cherysaunces¹ from Elynour hold,~~   ballad is
>   ~~I have it as soon as I ask it.~~   from the
>   pen of
> ~~"When I lived with my father in merry Clowdell,~~   Sir Tybbot
>   ~~Tho' 'twas at my lief to mind spinning,~~   Gorges—
> ~~I still wanted something, but what ne could tell,~~
>   ~~My lord father's barbed hall had ne winning.~~
>
> ~~"Each morning I rise, do I set my maidèns,~~
>   ~~Some to spin, some to curdel, some bleaching;~~
> ~~If any, new entered, do ask for my aidens,~~
>   ~~Then swythen² you find me a teaching.~~

---

97. Wilde's comment in the right margin is struck with a single vertical line in black ink.

98. Wilson, *Chatterton: A Biographical Study*, 153. "The Battle of Hastynges [II]," lines 401–20; see *Complete Works of Thomas Chatterton*, ed. Taylor and Hoover, 1:79–80.

99. Wilson, *Chatterton: A Biographical Study*, 165. Wilson's footnote, omitted from Wilde's clipping, reads, "² *Lessel*, arbour." For Wilde's comment, cf. Wilson: "A ballad, ascribed to the pen of Syr Thybbot Gorges" (*Chatterton: A Biographical Study*, 165). The poem is "Anodher Mynstrelles Songe, bie Syr Thybbot Gorges," from *Ælla*, lines 326–29; see *Complete Works of Thomas Chatterton*, ed. Taylor and Hoover, 1:187.

"Lord Walter, my father, he loved me well,
    And nothing unto me was needing;
But should I again go to merry Clowdell,
    In soothen 'twould be without redeyng.³

"She said, and Lord Thomas came over the lea,
    As he the fat deerkins was chaceing;
She put up her knitting, and to him went she:
    So we leave them both kindly embracing."]¹⁰⁰

{39ᵛ}

(page blank)

{40ʳ}

Many other charming stories of
Canynge appear in the Rowley
M.S·S· such as his account
of his masonic lodge opened
on the vigil of Epiphany 1432
with his address on the value
of the fine arts and their
application to trade to a
chapter composed of 27 Friars
16 gentlemen and three
brother aldermen, in which
this sly touch of humour
betrays the modern Rowley's
hand— "I did speak of
the use of the Arts to
improve the trade. The¹⁰¹

{40ᵛ}

(page blank)

{41ʳ}

Friars did enlarge, the
gentlemen attend, and the

---

100. Wilson, *Chatterton: A Biographical Study*, 166. "Anodher Mynstrelles Songe, bie Syr Thybbot Gorges," from *Ælla*, lines 330–49; see *Complete Works of Thomas Chatterton*, ed. Taylor and Hoover, 1:187–88. Wilson's footnotes, omitted from Wilde's clipping, read as follows: "¹ *Cherysaunces*, comforts."; "² *Swythen*, immediately."; "³ *Redeyng*, wisdom." Excerpt is struck with a large X in black ink.

101. Cf. Wilson: "The old merchant writes to his friend and confessor an account of his masonic lodge opened on the vigil of Epiphany, 1432, with his address on the value of the fine arts in their application to trade, to a chapter composed of seven-and-twenty friars, sixteen gentlemen, and three brother aldermen, in which this sly touch of humour betrays the modern Rowley's hand: 'I dyd speak of the use of the Artes to improve the trade. The . . .'" (*Chatterton: A Biographical Study*, 154).

Council men fell asleep."¡[102]
The collection of letters closes
with a panygeric of Canynge
by Rowley— "As a learned
wisacre he excelled in all
things. As a poet and
a painter he was great.
With him I lived at
Westbury six years before
he died, and be now
hasting to the grave
          myself— So ends[103]

{41ᵛ}

(page blank)

{42ʳ}

this marvellous romance
which Chatterton not only
wrote but lived—[104] It is his
own story— but he had
not yet <u>found</u> his <u>Canynge</u>—[105]

His attempts to gain a
publisher and a patron.
          =
His first attempt was upon
Dodsley the publisher of
Pall Mall the author of
some literary trifles and
the founder of the Annual
Register. One morning[106]

---

102. Cf. Wilson: "Freeres did enlarge, the gentlemen attende, and the Councylmen felle asleepe!" (*Chatterton: A Biographical Study*, 154).

103. Cf. Wilson: "The collection of letters closes with an editorial colophon from Rowley's pen, setting forth the virtues of his revered patron: 'As a leorned wyseager he excelled ynne all thynges. As a poette and peyncter he was greete. Wythe hym I lyved at Westburie sixe yeeres before he died, and bee nowe hasteynge to the grave mieselfe.' So ends . . ." (*Chatterton: A Biographical Study*, 155).

104. Cf. Wilson: "this ingenious romance, which Chatterton not only wrote but lived" (*Chatterton: A Biographical Study*, 155).

105. Wilson clearly articulates the idea that Chatterton was looking for a modern-day Canynge. Chapter IX of *Chatterton* is titled "The Modern Canynge" and contains these lines: "The dream of Chatterton's life, I doubt not, was the realization of some modern Mæcenas—the Canynge of his fancy,—by whom his genius was to be recognised" (*Chatterton: A Biographical Study*, 163).

106. Cf.: "His first attempt was upon Dodsley, the publisher of Pall Mall, the brother and succes-

{42ᵛ}

(page blank)

{43ʳ}

in December 1768 the worthy
publisher finds among his letters
one from Bristol— addressed in a
small neat hand and worded as
follows.
                    Bristol. Dec. 21, 1768.
Sir.
    I take this method to inform
you that I can procure copies of
several ancient poems, and an
interlude, perhaps the oldest
dramatic piece extant, wrote by
one Rowley, a priest of
Bristol who lived in the reigns
of Henry VI. and Edward IV.
    If these pieces will be of
service to you, at your
command copies shall be
sent to you by your

{43ᵛ}

(page blank)

{44ʳ}

        most obedient servant
                    D. B.
Please direct to D. B. to be left
with Mr. Thomas Chatterton
Redcliffe Hill· Bristol.[107]

—

sor in business of the more celebrated Robert Dodsley, the author of the 'Muse in Livery,' and other
trifles of some note in their day, and the projector, along with Burke, of the *Annual Register*" (David
Masson, *Chatterton: A Story of the Year 1770*, 2nd ed. [London: Macmillan, 1874], 56). James Dodsley
(1724–1797) was a bookseller based in Pall Mall, London.
    107. Cf. Masson: "one morning towards the Christmas of 1768, the worthy publisher . . . finds
among his letters one from Bristol, addressed in a neat small hand, and worded as follows [quotes

Dodsley probably answered this
for among his papers was
found this other letter from
Chatterton.[108]

["Bristol, *Feb.* 15, 1769.

"Sir,— Having intelligence that the tragedy of *Ælla*
was in being,[109] after a long and laborious search I was so
happy as to attain a sight of it. I endeavoured to
obtain a copy of it to send you; but the present
possessor absolutely denies to give me one, unless I give
him one guinea for a consideration. As I am unable
to procure such a sum, I made a search for another
copy, but unsuccessfully. Unwilling such a beauteous
piece should be lost, I have made bold to apply to you.
Several gentlemen of learning who have seen it join
with me in praising it. I am far from having any mer-
cenary views for myself in the affair; and, was I able,
would print it at my own risk. It is a perfect tragedy][110]

{44ᵛ}

(page blank)

{45ʳ}

[—the plot clear; the language spirited; and the songs
(interspersed in it) flowing, poetical, and elegantly
simple; the similes judiciously applied, and, though
wrote in the age of Henry VI., not inferior to many
of the present age. If I can procure a copy, with or
without the gratification, it shall be immediately sent
to you. The motive that actuates me to do this is to
convince the world that the monks (of whom some

---

letter in its entirety]" (*Chatterton: A Story of the Year 1770,* 57). Wilson also quotes the letter in *Chat-terton: A Biographical Study,* 163–64. See "To J[ames]. Dodsley, 21 December 1768," in *Complete Works of Thomas Chatterton,* ed. Taylor and Hoover, 1:157. The initials "D.B." stood for "Dunhelmus Bristoliensis." Chatterton first signed himself with this name when he submitted his forged "Bridge Narrative" to *Felix Farley's Bristol Journal* in September 1768 (published 1 October 1768); see *Complete Works of Thomas Chatterton,* ed. Taylor and Hoover, 1:56.

108. Cf. Masson: "In reply to this, Dodsley probably sent an intimation to the effect that he would be glad to see the poems . . . for the following letter, turned up long afterwards . . . among the loose papers in Dodsley's counting house" (*Chatterton: A Story of the Year 1770,* 57).

109. Wilde has underscored these words in pencil.

110. Masson, *Chatterton: A Story of the Year 1770,* 58. "To James Dodsley, 15 February 1769," "To J[ames]. Dodsley, 21 December 1768," in *Complete Works of Thomas Chatterton,* ed. Taylor and Hoover, 1:171–72.

have so despicable an opinion) were not such block-
heads as generally thought, and that good poetry might
be wrote in the dark days of superstition, as well as
in these more enlightened ages. An immediate answer
will oblige. I shall not receive your favour as for
myself, but as your agent.

"I am, sir, your most obedient servant,

"Thomas Chatterton.

"P.S.—My reason for concealing my name was lest
my master (who is now out of town) should see my][111]

[~~*THE ATTORNEY'S APPRENTICE OF BRISTOL 59*~~ [112]

letters, and think I neglected his business. Direct for
me on Redcliffe Hill.

(Here followed an extract from the tragedy, as a
specimen of the style.)

"The whole contains about one thousand lines. If it
should not suit you, I should be obliged to you if you
would calculate the expenses of printing it, as I will
endeavour to publish it by subscription on my own
account.

"*To* Mr. James Dodsley, *Bookseller, Pall Mall,
London.*"[113]

This ~~clumsy~~ attempt to extract a guinea from the
publisher ~~(Chatterton had probably just finished his
own manuscript of AElla, and did not like the notion
of copying out so long a poem on mere chance) very
naturally~~ failed.[114] Mr. Dodsley did not think the
speculation worth risking a guinea on; and "*Ælla, a
Tragycal Enterlude, or Discoorseynge Tragedie, wrotten
by Thomas Rowllie; plaiedd before Mastre Canynge, atte
hys Howse, nempte the Rodde Lodge*" remained useless
among Chatterton's papers.][115]

---

111. Masson, *Chatterton: A Story of the Year 1770*, 58. "To James Dodsley, 15 February 1769," "To
J[ames]. Dodsley, 21 December 1768," in *Complete Works of Thomas Chatterton*, ed. Taylor and
Hoover, 1:172.

112. Wilde has struck in black ink the header in this clipping from Masson, *Chatterton: A Story of
the Year 1770*, 59.

113. "To James Dodsley, 15 February 1769," in *Complete Works of Thomas Chatterton*, ed. Taylor
and Hoover, 1:72–73.

114. Lines are struck in pencil.

115. Masson, *Chatterton: A Story of the Year 1770*, 59.

{45ᵛ}

(page blank)

{46ʳ}

Chatterton however was undaunted.
The next person he tried was
Mʳ· Horace Walpole—
        The son of the great
minister of the First and Second
Georges— Walpole was devoted
to arts and letters— Had
a taste for medievalism—
made Strawberry Hill into a
pseudo Gothic Palace,
and had published in 1764
his Castle of Otranto—
supposed to be a translation
by William Marshall of
an old Italian story —[116]

{46ᵛ}

(page blank)

{47ʳ}

To him accordingly Chatterton
addressed the following note—
        Bristol. March 25. Corn St.
Sir.
        Being versed a little in
antiquities I have met with
several curious manuscripts,
amongst which the following
may be of service to you
in any future edition of your
truly entertaining anecdotes of
painting. In correcting the

---

116. Cf. Masson: "Chatterton was not daunted" (*Chatterton: A Story of the Year* 1770, 59); and Wilson: "This son of the great minister of the first and second Georges, though he did not abjure politics, made art and letters the real business of his life. . . . He, too, had his dream of mediæval art, and realized it in costly, if not very tasteful fashion, by converting his cottage at Strawberry Hill, Twickenham, into a pseudo-Gothic Aladdin's palace" (*Chatterton: A Biographical Study*, 169–70). Cf. Wilson on *The Castle of Otranto* (1764) by Horace Walpole (1717–1797) "This marvellous story made its first appearance in 1764 . . . professedly as a translation by one William Marshall, from an Italian MS." (*Chatterton: A Biographical Study*, 170).

mistakes (if any) in the
notes you will greatly
oblige your most humble
servant
Thomas Chatterton[117]

{47ᵛ}

(page blank)

{48ʳ}

Appended to this letter was a
most picturesque account of
the Rise of Painting in England—
as well as some specimens of
Rowley poetry—[118]

Walpole was completely taken in
and replied in the following letter[119]

[~~reply~~[120]

"ARLINGTON ST., *March* 28, 1769.

"Sir,—I cannot but think myself singularly obliged
by a gentleman with whom I have not the pleasure of
being acquainted, when I read your very curious and
kind letter, which I have this minute received. I give
you a thousand thanks for it, and for the very obliging
offer you make of communicating your manuscript to me.
What you have already sent me is valuable, and full
of information; but, instead of correcting you, Sir, <u>you
are far more able to correct me</u>.[121] I have not the happiness of understanding the Saxon language, and, without
your learned notes, should not have been able to comprehend Rowley's text.

"As a second edition of my *Anecdotes* was pub-

---

117. Both Masson (*Chatterton: A Story of the Year 1770*, 60) and Wilson (*Chatterton: A Biographi-cal Study*, 172) reprint the letter in its entirety. See "To Horace Walpole, 25 March 1769," in *Complete Works of Thomas Chatterton*, ed. Taylor and Hoover, 1:258.

118. Cf. Masson: "Appended to this short note were several pages of antique writing, entitled 'The Ryse of Peyncteyne in England'" (*Chatterton: A Story of the Year 1770*, 60). See "The Ryse of Peync-teynge, yn Englande, wroten bie T. Rowleie. 1469 for Mastre Canynge," in *Complete Works of Thomas Chatterton*, ed. Taylor and Hoover, 1:259–62.

119. Cf. Masson: "Walpole was completely taken in" (*Chatterton: A Story of the Year 1770*, 62).

120. This deletion is in pencil.

121. Wilde has underlined in pencil this line in the printed text.

lished last year, I must not flatter myself that a third will be wanted soon; but I shall be happy to lay up any notices you will be so good as to extract for me, and send me at your leisure; for, as it is uncertain when I may use them, I would by no means borrow or detain your MSS.

"Give me leave to ask you where Rowley's poems are to be found. I should not be sorry to print them, or at least a specimen of them, if they have never been printed.

"The Abbot John's verses that you have given me are wonderful for their harmony and spirit, though there are some words that I do not understand. You][122]

{48ᵛ}

(page blank)

{49ʳ}

[do not point out exactly the time when he lived, which I wish to know, as I suppose it was long before John van Eyck's discovery of oil-painting; if so, it confirms what I have guessed, and hinted in my *Anecdotes,* that oil-painting was known here much earlier than that discovery or revival.

"I will not trouble you with more questions now, Sir; but flatter myself, from the urbanity and politeness you have already shown me, that you will give me leave to consult you. I hope, too, you will forgive the simplicity of my direction, as you have favoured me with none other.

"I am, Sir, your much obliged and obedient servant,
            "HORACE WALPOLE.
"P.S.—Be so good as to direct to Mr. Walpole, Arlington Street."][123]

Chatterton wrote back frankly[124]
to Walpole that he was the
son of a poor widow, and
a clerk to an attorney—

---

122. Masson, *Chatterton: A Story of the Year 1770,* 62. See "From Horace Walpole, 28 March 1769," lines 1–21, in *Complete Works of Thomas Chatterton,* ed. Taylor and Hoover, 1:262–63.

123. Masson, *Chatterton: A Story of the Year 1770,* 63. See "From Horace Walpole, 28 March 1769," lines 21–36, in *Complete Works of Thomas Chatterton,* ed. Taylor and Hoover, 1:263.

124. "frankly" is written over a lighter, illegible word.

but that he desired to
take up literature— and enclosed
some specimens of the great
treasures of old poetry
found in his native Town.[125]

{49ᵛ}

(page blank)

{50ʳ}

Walpole's tone at once changed.[126]
He wrote back to Chatterton
that he advised him against
taking up literature, and that
he had submitted the Rowley
poems to some of his friends
who were doubtful of their
authenticity.

Chatterton replied in a
bitter letter. He reiterated
his claims of the genuineness
of his Rowley M.S.S. but
proceeds to say "though I
am but sixteen years of
age I have lived long[127]

{50ᵛ}

(page blank)

{51ʳ}

enough to ~~know~~ see that Poverty
attends literature. I am
obliged to you, Sir, for your
advice, and will go a little

---

125. Cf. Wilson: "betrayed by his courtesy into a candour that only required the long-coveted friendly response to be converted into an ingenuous confession of his deception,—he threw himself on the generosity of his correspondent. 'Chatterton,' says Walpole, 'informed me that he was the son of a poor widow, who supported him with great difficulty; that he was a clerk or apprentice to an attorney, but had a taste and turn . . .' He then referred to the great treasures of ancient poetry discovered in his native city, of which he enclosed specimens" (*Chatterton: A Biographical Study*, 178).

126. Cf. Wilson: "The change which this confession and appeal produced on the tone of Walpole's letters was only too marked" (*Chatterton: A Biographical Study*, 179).

127. Cf. Wilson: "Chatterton replied, in what Walpole characterises as a peevish letter, reiterating the genuineness of the antique poems, and concluding thus: 'Though I am but sixteen years of age, I have lived long . . .'" (*Chatterton: A Biographical Study*, 179–80).

beyond it by destroying all
my useless lumber of literature
and never using my pen
again but in Law.[128]
His great hope had
failed him.[129]
A week later he
applied for the return of his
papers[130]— Walpole paid
no attention and went off
to Paris[131]

{51ᵛ}

Coleridge
O ye who honour the

name of man rejoice

that this Walpole is
    a
called ^ Lord[132]

{52ʳ}

on his return he found on his
table what seemed to him a
"singularly impertinent letter"
but what seems to us rather
spirited and manly.[133]

---

128. Cf. Wilson: ". . . enough to see that poverty attends literature. I am obliged to you, sir, for your advice, and will go a little beyond it, by destroying all my useless lumber of literature and never using my pen again but in law" (*Chatterton: A Biographical Study*, 180). "To Horace Walpole, 8 April 1769," lines 7–10, in *Complete Works of Thomas Chatterton*, ed. Taylor and Hoover, 1:271.

129. Cf. Wilson: "His great hope had failed him" (*Chatterton: A Biographical Study*, 180).

130. Cf. Wilson: "A week later he again wrote requesting the return of his papers" (*Chatterton: A Biographical Study*, 180).

131. Cf. Wilson: "To Walpole it was, indeed, a matter of the utmost insignificance. But to Chatterton it involved a harsh waking from the dream of a lifetime. To Paris, accordingly, Walpole went" (*Chatterton: A Biographical Study*, 180).

132. Cf. Wilson: "'Oh ye who honour the name of Man,' wrote the indignant Coleridge, 'rejoice that this Walpole is called a Lord'" (*Chatterton: A Biographical Study*, 185). Coleridge made the sarcastic comment in a prefatory note to his "Monody on the Death of Chatterton," which was never published but recounted in a letter to Joseph Cottle. See Cottle, *Early Recollections; Chiefly Relating to the Late Samuel Taylor Coleridge, during His Long Residence in Bristol*, 2 vols. (London: Longman, Rees, 1837), 1:35–36.

133. Cf. Wilson: "and on his return found on his table the following spirited, but, as it appeared to him, 'singularly impertinent letter':—" (*Chatterton: A Biographical Study*, 180).

["SIR,— I cannot reconcile your behavior to me with the notions I once entertained of you. I think myself injured, Sir; and, did you not know my circumstances, you would not dare to treat me thus. I have sent twice for a copy of the MSS.; no answer from you. An explanation or excuse for your silence would oblige

"THOMAS CHATTERTON.

"*July* 24."][134]

> Walpole accordingly
> returned the M.SS·
> Chattertons dream of
> a real Canynge
> was over—.[135]

{52ᵛ}

spoke casually
to one of his friends—

{53ʳ}

The effect on Chatterton—
   Satire.
   political letters—

   —

moody, and subject to fits
of despair— contemplates
Suicide and drew up
this extraordinary document
now in the Bristol
Museum.

{53ᵛ}

(page blank)

{54ʳ}

["This is the last will and testament of me, Thomas Chatterton, of the city Bristol; being sound in body,

---

134. Masson, *Chatterton: A Story of the Year 1770*, 68. Wilson also records the letter (*Chatterton: A Biographical Study*, 180). See also *Complete Works of Thomas Chatterton*, ed. Taylor and Hoover, 1:340.

135. Cf. Wilson: "The fancy that Horace Walpole was to prove the Mæcenas of the poet had thus been dissipated beyond recall. . . . One can see in stray allusions to his plans and hopes, that he had been looking earnestly into the uncertain future, revolving many schemes for emancipation, and falling back on his old dream of a Canynge worthy of the true Rowley; and now came this harsh awakening to the truth" (*Chatterton: A Biographical Study*, 189–90).

or it is the fault of my last surgeon: the soundness
of my mind the coroner and jury are to be judges of—
desiring them to take notice that the most perfect
masters of human nature in Bristol distinguish me by
the title of 'the mad genius'; therefore, if I do a mad
action, it is conformable to every action of my life,
which all savoured of insanity.

"*Item.* — If, after my death, which will happen to-
morrow night before eight o'clock, being the Feast of
the Resurrection, the coroner and jury bring it in
lunacy, I will and direct that Paul Farr, Esq., and Mr.]¹³⁶

[and Mr. John Flower, at their joint expense, cause my body to be
interred in the tomb of my fathers, and raise the monument over
my body to the height of four feet five inches, placing the present
flat stone on the top, and adding six tablets."

Then follow the inscriptions, in French, Latin, and
English, in memory of real and imaginary ancestors,
occupying three of the tablets. The fourth reads:—

"To the Memory of Thomas Chatterton. Reader, judge not; if
thou art a Christian, believe that he shall be judged by a superior
power. To that power only is he now answerable."

The fifth and sixth tablets are devoted to his favourite
heraldic achievements; and then it thus proceeds:—

"And I will and direct, that if the Coroner's inquest bring it in
felo-de-se, the said monument shall be, notwithstanding, erected.
And if the said Paul Farr and John Flower have souls so Bristolish]¹³⁷

[as to refuse this my Bequest, they will transmit a copy of my
Will to the Society for supporting the Bill of Rights, whom I hereby
empower to build the same monument according to the aforesaid
directions. And if they, the said Paul Farr and John Flower,
should build the said monument, I will and direct that the second
edition of my Kew Gardens shall be dedicated to them in the follow-

---

136. Masson, *Chatterton: A Story of the Year 1770*, 78. The final two words of the excerpt are struck
heavily in pencil. See ["Will,"] lines 63–73, in *Complete Works of Thomas Chatterton*, ed. Taylor and
Hoover, 1:502–3.

137. Wilson, *Chatterton: A Biographical Study*, 241. Wilson cites ["Will,"] lines 74–77, 93–95, and
100–102; see *Complete Works of Thomas Chatterton*, ed. Taylor and Hoover, 1:503–4.

ing Dedication:— To Paul Farr and John Flower, Esqs. this book is most humbly dedicated by the Author's Ghost.][138]

{54ᵛ}

(page blank)

{55ʳ}

[following dedication: 'To Paul Farr and John Flower, Esqrs., this book is most humbly dedicated by the Author's Ghost.'[139]

"*Item.*— I give all my vigour and fire of youth to Mr. George Catcott, being sensible he is most in want of it.

"*Item.*— From the same charitable motive, I give and bequeath unto the Rev. Mr. Camplin, sen., all my humility. To Mr. Burgum all my prosody and grammar, likewise one moiety of my modesty; the other moiety to any young lady who can prove, without blushing, that she wants that valuable commodity. To Bristol all my spirit and disinterestedness, parcels of goods unknown on her quays since the days of Canning and Rowley. ('Tis true, a charitable gentleman, one Mr. Colston, smuggled a considerable quantity of it; but, it being proved that he was a Papist, the worshipful society of aldermen endeavoured to throttle him with the oath of allegiance.)[140] I leave also my religion to Dr. Cutts Barton, Dean of Bristol, hereby empowering the sub-sacrist to strike him on the head when he goes to sleep in church. My powers of utterance I give to the Rev. Mr. Broughton, hoping he will employ them to a better purpose than reading lectures on the immortality of the soul. I leave the Rev. Mr. Catcott some little of my free-thinking, that he may put on spectacles of reason, and see how vilely he is duped in believing the Scriptures literally. (I wish he and his brother George would know how far I am their real enemy: but I have an unlucky way of raillery; and, when the

---

138. Wilson, *Chatterton: A Biographical Study*, 242. The last lines are repeated in the following excerpt, in Masson's telling. See ["Will,"] lines 103–10, in *Complete Works of Thomas Chatterton*, ed. Taylor and Hoover, 1:504.

139. Lines struck in pencil, in wavy lines.

140. Lines struck in heavy, cross-hatched pencil marks.

strong fit of satire is upon me, I spare neither friend nor foe. This is my excuse for what I have said of them elsewhere.) I leave Mr. Clayfield the sincerest][141]

{55ᵛ}

(page blank)

{56ʳ}

[thanks my gratitude can give; and I will and direct that, whatever any person may think the pleasure of reading my works worth, they immediately pay their own valuation to him, since it is then become a lawful debt to me, and to him as my executor in this case.

"I leave my moderation to the politicians on both sides of the question. I leave my generosity to our present right worshipful mayor, Thomas Harris, Esq. I give my abstinence to the company at the Sheriff's annual feast in general, more particularly the aldermen.

"*Item.*—I give and bequeath to Mr. Matthew Mease a mourning ring with this motto, 'Alas, poor Chatterton!' provided he pays for it himself. *Item.*— I leave the young ladies all the letters they have had from me, assuring them that they need be under no apprehensions from the appearance of my ghost, for I die for none of them. *Item.*—I leave all my debts, the whole not five pounds, to the payment of the charitable and generous Chamber of Bristol, on penalty, if refused, to hinder every member from a good dinner by appearing in the form of a bailiff. If, in defiance of this terrible spectre, they obstinately persist in refusing to discharge my debts, let my two creditors apply to the supporters of the Bill of Rights. *Item.*—I leave my mother and sister to the protection of my friends, if I have any.

"Executed, in the presence of Omniscience, this 14ᵗʰ of April, 1770.

"Thomas Chatterton."][142]

---

141. Masson, *Chatterton: A Story of the Year 1770*, 80. See ["Will,"] lines 108–35, in *Complete Works of Thomas Chatterton*, ed. Taylor and Hoover, 1:504.

142. Masson, *Chatterton: A Story of the Year 1770*, 81. See ["Will,"] lines 135–61, in *Complete Works of Thomas Chatterton*, ed. Taylor and Hoover, 1:504–5.

To this is added the endorsement
"All this wrote between 11 and
2 o'c Saturday in the
utmost distress of mind,
April 14$\underline{th}$ [143]

{56^v}

(page blank)

{57^r}

There is also with it an

apostrophe to Catcott.[144]

Thy friendship never cd. be dear to me,

Since all I am is opposite to thee,

If ever obligated to thy purse,

Rowley discharges all my first chief

             curse.

For had I never known the antique lore,

I ne'er had ventured from my peaceful shore,
      the
To be ^ wreck of promises and hopes,

A boy of Learning, and a Bard of

             Tropes,

But happy in my humble sphere,

           had moved,

---

143. Cf. Wilson: "Such is Chatterton's will, to which is added the endorsement: 'All this wrote between 11 and 2 o'clock, Saturday, in the utmost distress of mind, April 14" (*Chatterton: A Biographical Study*, 243). See ["Will,"] epigraph, in *Complete Works of Thomas Chatterton*, ed. Taylor and Hoover, 1:501.

144. Cf. Wilson: "and he bitterly exclaims in the apostrophe to Catcott:—" (*Chatterton: A Biographical Study*, 240).

Untroubled, unrespected,

unbeloved![145]

{57ᵛ}

(page blank)

{58ʳ}

About the same time in another
letter he writes "I abominate
the Muses and their works—
they are the nurses of
poverty and insanity"—
These lines on suicide also
show his despair, though
dated 1769.[146]

["Since we can die but once, what matters it
If rope, or garter, poison, pistol, sword,
Slow-wasting sickness, or the sudden burst
Of valve-arterial in the noble parts,
Curtail the miseries of human life?
Tho' varied is the cause, the effect's the same;
All to one common dissolution tends."][147]

and his friends became
alarmed— Mʳ· Lambert

---

145. ["Will,"] lines 27–36. Wilson gives the lines as follows (*Chatterton: A Biographical Study*, 241):

Thy friendship never could be dear to me,
Since all I am is opposite to thee;
If ever obligated to thy purse,
Rowley discharges all: my first, chief curse;
For had I never known the antique lore,
I ne'er had ventured from my peaceful shore,
To be the wreck of promises and hopes:
A Boy of Learning, and a Bard of Tropes;
But happy in my humble sphere had moved,
Untroubled, unrespected, unbeloved.

Cf. the text of this poem in *Complete Works of Thomas Chatterton*, ed. Taylor and Hoover, 1:501–2; there are several noticeable differences from Wilson's presentation of the text.

146. Cf. Wilson: "Mr. Cottle gives an extract from another written to Mr. Baster about the same time, in which he curses the Muses, exclaiming: 'I abominate them and their works. They are the nurses of poverty and insanity'" (*Chatterton: A Biographical Study*, 237).

147. Wilson, *Chatterton: A Biographical Study*, 235. The poem is Chatterton's "Sentiment" (at times also titled "Suicide"), in *Complete Works of Thomas Chatterton*, ed. Taylor and Hoover, 1:446.

found on his desk a
    letter addressed to M^r [148]

{58^v}

(page blank)

{59^r}

Clayfield threatening suicide—
and forwarded it to M^r·
Barrett who at once sent
for Chatterton and remonstrated
with him— the next day
he received the following
letter—[149]

> ["SIR, — Upon recollection I don't know how Mr. Clayfield could come by his letter; as I intended to have given him a letter, but did not. In regard to my motives for the supposed rashness, I shall observe that I keep no worse company than myself. I never drink to excess; and have, without vanity, too much sense to be attached to the mercenary retailers of iniquity. No! it is my pride, my damn'd, native, unconquerable pride, that plunges me into distraction. You must know that 19-20ths of my composition is pride. I must either live a slave, a servant; have no will of my own, no sentiments of my own which I may freely declare as such; or die! —perplexing alternative. But it distracts me to think of it. I will endeavour to learn humility, but it cannot be here. What it will cost me on the trial Heaven knows!
>
>   "I am, your much obliged, unhappy, humble Servant,
>   "T. C."][150]

In a short time his
indentures were cancelled
and he started for
London.[151]

---

148. Cf. Wilson: "Mr. Lambert . . . found on his clerk's writing-desk . . . a letter addressed to his friend Mr." (*Chatterton: A Biographical Study*, 236).

149. Cf. Wilson: "Clayfield, stating his distresses, and that on the receipt of that letter he should be no more. Mr. Lambert, in alarm, despatched the letter, not to Mr. Clayfield, but to Mr. Barrett . . . [who] sent 'immediately for Chatterton'" (*Chatterton: A Biographical Study*, 236).

150. Wilson, *Chatterton: A Biographical Study*, 236. "To [William] Barrett, [February or March 1770]," in *Complete Works of Thomas Chatterton*, ed. Taylor and Hoover, 1:494.

151. Cf. Wilson: "The indentures which bound him to the attorney were forthwith cancelled, and within six days thereafter he was writing his first London letter to his mother" (*Chatterton: A Biographical Study*, 246).

{59ᵛ}

(page blank)

{60ʳ}

never to see Bristol again.
His first letter is full of
~~high spirits~~ enthusiasm—
he writes,
    London April 26.
       1770.

                 ["~~London, *April 26th, 1770.*~~
    ~~"Dear Mother, Here I am, safe and in high~~
~~spirits. To give you a journal of my tour would not~~
~~be unnecessary. After riding in the basket to Brisling~~
~~ton, I mounted the top of the coach, and rid easy,~~
~~and was agreeably entertained with the conversation~~
~~of a Quaker *in dress*, but little so in personals and~~
~~behaviour. This laughing Friend, who is a carver,~~
~~lamented his having sent his tools to Worcester, as~~
~~otherwise he would have accompanied me to London.~~][152]

    [~~I left him at Bath; when, finding it rained pretty~~
~~fast, I entered an inside passenger to Speenhamland,~~
~~the half-way stage, paying seven shillings. 'Twas~~
~~lucky I did so, for it snowed all night, and on Marl-~~
~~borough Downs the snow was near a foot high.~~
    ~~"At seven in the morning I breakfasted at Speen-~~
~~hamland, and then mounted the coach-box for the~~
~~remainder of the day, which was a remarkable fine~~
~~one. Honest Gee ho complimented me with assuring~~
~~me that I sat bolder and tighter than any person who~~
~~ever rid with him. Dined at Stroud most luxuriously~~
~~with a young gentleman, who had slept all the pre-~~
~~ceeding night in the machine, and an old mercantile~~
~~genius, whose school-boy son had a great deal of wit,~~
~~as the father thought, in remarking that Windsor was~~
~~as old as *our Saviour's time.*~~][153]

---

152. Masson, *Chatterton: A Story of the Year 1770*, 106. These lines are struck in black ink. See "To Sarah Chatterton, 26 April 1770," lines 1–7, in *Complete Works of Thomas Chatterton*, ed. Taylor and Hoover, 1:510–11.

153. Masson, *Chatterton: A Story of the Year 1770*, 107. These lines are struck in black ink with a large X. See "To Sarah Chatterton, 26 April 1770," lines 7–20, in *Complete Works of Thomas Chatter-ton*, ed. Taylor and Hoover, 1:511.

{60^v}

(page blank)

{61^r}

["~~Got into London about five o'clock in the evening.~~
~~Called upon Mr. Edmunds, Mr. Fell, Mr. Hamilton,~~
~~and Mr. Dodsley. Great encouragement from them;~~
~~all approved of my design. Shall soon be settled.~~
~~Call upon Mr. Lambert; show him this; or tell him,~~
~~if I deserve a recommendation, he would oblige me to~~
~~give me one: if I do not, it will be beneath him to~~
~~take notice of me. Seen all aunts, cousins all well~~
~~and I am welcome. Mr. T. Wensley is alive, and com-~~
~~ing home.~~ Sister, grandmother, &c. &c. &c., remember.

"I remain your dutiful son,

T. CHATTERTON"][154]

Lodging with a plasterer in
Shoreditch of the name of
Walmsley, with whom resided
an aged relative a M^{rs}.
Ballance—[155]

Sir Herbert Crofts[156] writes—

["The man and woman where he first lodged are still
(1780) living in the same house. He is a plasterer.
They, and their nephew and niece (the latter about as
old as Chatterton would be now, the former three years
younger), and Mrs. Ballance—who lodged in the house
and desired them to let Chatterton, her relation, live][157]

{61^v}

(page blank)

---

154. Masson, *Chatterton: A Story of the Year 1770*, 107. These lines are struck in black ink with a large X; it appears likely that Wilde intended to strike the entire excerpt. See "To Sarah Chatterton, 26 April 1770," lines 21–31, in *Complete Works of Thomas Chatterton*, ed. Taylor and Hoover, 1:511.

155. Cf. Wilson: "[Chatterton] made his way to Mr. Walmsley's, a plasterer in Shoreditch, where a relative, Mrs. Ballance, lodged" (*Chatterton: A Biographical Study*, 248).

156. Wilde, both here and on f.62^r (393), misspells the last name of Herbert Croft.

157. Masson, *Chatterton: A Story of the Year 1770*, 116. Masson introduces the quotation as follows: "The following is an extract from Sir Herbert's *Love and Madness*, embodying all he could gather about Chatterton from this source:—."

{62ʳ}

[_____ SHOREDITCH _____ 117

there also—have been seen. The little collected from them you shall have in their own words....

"Mrs. Ballance says he was as proud as Lucifer. He very soon quarrelled with her for calling him 'Cousin Tommy,' and asked her if she ever heard of a poet's being called *Tommy;* but she assured him that she knew nothing of poets, and only wished he would not set up for a gentleman. Upon her recommending it to him to get into some office, when he had been in town two or three weeks, he stormed about the room like a madman, and frightened her not a little by telling her that he hoped, with the blessing of God, very soon to be sent prisoner to the Tower, which would make his fortune. He would often look steadfastly in a person's face, without speaking, or seeming to see the person, for a quarter of an hour or more, till it was quite frightful; during all which time (she supposes from what she has since heard) his thoughts were gone about something else. . . . He frequently declared that he should settle the nation before he had done: but how could she think that her poor cousin Tommy was so great a man as she now finds he was? His mother should have written word of his greatness, and then, to be sure, she would have humoured the gentleman accordingly.

"Mr. Walmsley observed little in him, but that there was something manly and pleasing about him, and that he did not dislike the wenches.

"Mrs. Walmsley's account is, that she never saw any harm of him—that he never *mislisted* her, but was always very civil whenever they met in the house by accident; that he would never suffer the room in which][158

{62ᵛ}

(page blank)

{63ʳ}

> and
>
> he used to read ^ write to be swept,

---

158. Masson, *Chatterton: A Story of the Year 1770*, 117.

because he said poets hated brooms.

that she told him she did not

know anything poet-folks were

good for but to sit in a dirty

cap and gown in a garret

and at last be starved—

that during the nine weeks

he was at her house he

never stayed out after the

family hours except once

when he did not come home

all night, and how she

heard been poeting a song

about the streets.[159]

{63ᵛ}

(page blank)

{64ʳ}

the niece says, for her part
she always took him more for
a mad boy than for anything
else, he would have such
flights and vagaries— that but
for his face and her knowledge

---

159. Cf. Masson: "he used to read and write to be swept, because, he said, poets hated brooms; that she told him she did not know anything poet-folks were good for, but to sit in a dirty cap and gown in a garret, and at last to be starved; that during the nine (?) weeks he was at her house, he never stayed out after the family hours except once, when he did not come home all night, and had been, she heard, *poeting* a song about the streets" (*Chatterton: A Story of the Year 1770*, 118; emphasis in the original).

of his age she should never
have thought him a boy he
was so manly and so much
himself. That he never
touched meat, and drank
only water, and seemed to
live on the air. That he
was good-tempered and
agreeable, but sadly
proud and haughty—
      nothing was too good[160]

{64ᵛ}

(page blank)

{65ʳ}

for him, nor was anything to be
too good for his grandmother
mother and sister hereafter—
that he used to sit up
almost all night reading
and writing— and that her
brother said he was afraid
to lie with him— for, to
be sure, he was a spirit,
and never slept. For he
never came to bed till
it was morning, and then
for what he saw never
closed his eyes— [161]

{65ᵛ}

(page blank)

---

160. Cf. Masson: "The Niece says, for her part, she always took him more for a mad boy than anything else, he would have such flights and *vagaries*; that, but for his face, and her knowledge of his age, she should never have thought him a boy, he was so manly, and *so much himself* . . . that he never touched meat, and drank only water, and seemed to live on the air. . . . The Niece adds that he was good-tempered, and agreeable, and obliging, but sadly proud and haughty; nothing was too good" (*Chatterton: A Story of the Year 1770*, 118; emphasis and ellipsis in the original).

161. Cf. Masson: "for him; nor was anything to be too good for his grandmother, mother, and sister, hereafter. . . . That he used to sit up almost all night, reading and writing; and that her brother said he was afraid to lie with him—for, to be sure, he was a *spirit*, and never slept; for he never came to bed till it was morning, and then, for what he saw, never closed his eyes" (*Chatterton: A Story of the Year 1770*, 118; ellipsis and emphasis in the original).

{66ʳ}

> ["The Nephew (Chatterton's bed-fellow during the
> first six weeks he lodged there) says that, notwithstand-
> ing his pride and haughtiness, it was impossible to help
> liking him; that he lived chiefly upon a bit of bread, or
> a tart, and some water—but he once or twice saw him
> take a sheep's tongue out of his pocket;[162] that Chatterton,
> to his knowledge, never slept while they lay together;
> that he never came to bed till very late, sometimes three
> or four o'clock, and was always awake when he (the
> nephew) waked, and got up at the same time, about
> five or six; that almost every morning the floor wa [*sic*]
> covered with pieces of paper not so big as sixpences,
> into which he had torn what he had been writing
> before he came to bed."][163]

———

In his letter to his mother
he had stated he was going
to see Dodsley, Edmunds.
Hamilton, and Fell—[164]
  Of Dodsley we have
already spoken— Edmunds
was Editor of Middlesex
Journal— Hamilton of

{66ᵛ}

(page blank)

---

162. These lines are struck in black ink, with a check mark or accidental pen mark in the right margin.

163. Masson, *Chatterton: A Story of the Year 1770*, 119.

164. Cf. Wilson, quoting Chatterton's letter to his mother: "Got into London about five o'clock in the evening; called upon Mr. Edmunds, Mr. Fell, Mr. Hamilton, and Mr. Dodsley" (*Chatterton: A Biographical Study*, 248). The letter is reproduced in *Complete Works of Thomas Chatterton*, ed. Taylor and Hoover, 1:510–11. Taylor and Hoover observe: "All four men were editors; three had printed C[hatterton] contributions already. William Edmunds edited the Patriot weekly, the *Middlesex Journal* [1769–84], which published C's Decimus letters; he was imprisoned in May 1770, after which Archibald Hamilton, Sr., took over the paper . . . Isaac Fell, editor of *The Freeholder's Magazine* [1769–70], a patriot monthly, published C's political verse . . . Archibald Hamilton Jr. editor of *The T[own] & C[ountry]M[agazine]*[1769–96], published C's miscellaneous stuff" (2:1065). "James Dodsley (1724–97), publisher, also edited the *Annual Register* [1758–continuing], which printed several of C's pieces" (2:914).

{67ʳ}

Town and County[165] magazine and
Fell of the Freeholders Mag.
an ardent Wilkite[166]
At first Chatterton jubilant.
"I am familiar with the
Chapter Coffee House he
writes and know all the
geniuses there"[167]— Wilkes, he
tells us, had desired to know
him— he gets to know
Beckford— goes to theatres
Garrick acting Hamlet—
    Addison's Cato—[168]

{67ᵛ}

Sketch of
English Politics
    here
                    [169]

---

165. The title is *Town and Country Magazine*. The same error appears on f.70ʳ (399).

166. Radical journalist and politician John Wilkes (1725–1797) fought the Middlesex election in 1757 on the grounds that voters, not the House of Commons, should determine their representatives. Lord Mayor of London, William Beckford (1709–1770) founded the *Middlesex Journal* to support Wilkes's ongoing political campaign. We discuss Chatterton's engagement with Wilkite politics in chapter 1 (41–42).

167. Cf. Wilson from Chatterton's letter: "What a glorious prospect! Mr. Wilkes knew me by my writings, since I first corresponded with the booksellers here. . . . He affirmed that what Mr. Fell had of mine could not be the writings of a youth; and expressed a desire to know the author. . . . I am quite familiar at the Chapter Coffee-house, and know all the geniuses there" (*Chatterton: A Biographical Study*, 262). Masson records the letter (*Chatterton: A Story of the Year 1770*, 145–46). See "To Sarah Chatterton, Thomas Cary, and Others, 6 May 1770," lines 12–14, in *Complete Works of Thomas Chatterton*, ed. Taylor and Hoover, 1:560.

168. Masson records social and theatrical events that occurred during Chatterton's stay in London, so that "readers may the more easily fill out the picture for themselves" of Chatterton's experience (*Chatterton: A Story of the Year 1770*, 137). Masson offers no evidence that Chatterton attended these events, however. Referring to the list of events, he writes: "It was into the midst of such incidents as these, episodic as they were to the two great topics of Wilkes and the Constitution and the growing disaffection of the American Colonies, that Chatterton transferred himself by his removal from Bristol to London. . . . If he did not go to see Addison's tragedy of *Cato* at Covent Garden on the 30th of April, it is not likely that he missed the opportunity of seeing Garrick in *Hamlet* at Drury Lane on the 2d of May" (*Chatterton: A Story of the Year 1770*, 140). Joseph Addison (1672–1719) is perhaps best known today for his essays and his contributions to the *Spectator* (1711–1712), which he founded with Richard Steele (1672–1729). Addison's play *Cato: A Tragedy* premiered in 1713 to immediate success; its subject is Cato the Younger, whose fidelity to the Roman Republic and resistance to the tyranny of Caesar's rule made him a hero to eighteenth-century revolutionaries. The play ends with Cato's suicide.

169. This phrase is scrawled diagonally across the page in large letters.

{68ʳ}

Brooke Street. Mʳˢ. Angel
a dressmaker— Sir Herbert
Crofts was never able to
see her, but he found a
neighbor of hers— Mʳˢ.
Wolfe a barbers wife
who spoke of Chattertons
proud and haughty spirit
adding that he appeared to
her and to Mʳˢ. Angell
as if born for something
great" —[170] there was also
     one Cross an
               apothecary[171]

{68ᵛ}

(page blank)

{69ʳ}

who had a great liking of
Chatterton and found his
conversation, as he told
Warton— very captivating,
a little infidelity excepted[172]

————

When Beckford died he
was perfectly frantic and
out of his mind and
said he was ruined—[173]
     Lost by his death   1.11.6

---

170. Cf. Wilson: "Mrs. Wolfe, the wife of a barber in Brooke street, spoke of his proud and haughty spirit, and added that he appeared to both her and Mrs. Angel as if born for something great" (*Chatterton: A Biographical Study*, 301).

171. Cf. Wilson: "In Brooke Street, Holborn, within a few doors of Mrs. Angel's, was the shop of Mr. Cross, an apothecary" (*Chatterton: A Biographical Study*, 291).

172. Cf. Wilson: "[Cross] afterwards told Mr. Warton that he found his conversation most captivating. in spite of the occasional intrusion of deistical opinions" (*Chatterton: A Biographical Study*, 291).

173. Cf. Wilson: "Mrs. Ballance told Sir Herbert Croft, 'when Beckford died, he was perfectly frantic, and out of his mind; and said that he was ruined'" (*Chatterton: A Biographical Study*, 266).

Gained by writing on
      him   5.5-0
Am glad he is dead
      by   3.13.6[174]

{69ᵛ}

(page blank)

{70ʳ}

Gets despondent in July
Ballad of Charity—
rejected by the Town and
County magazine

⸺

<u>Read</u>

{70ᵛ}

a friend who was with him ·
helped him out, and laughing
congratulated him on the resurrection
of genius— Chatterton replied with
a sad smile, "my dear friend, I
feel the sting of a speedy dissolution—
I have been at war with the grave
for some time, and find it is not so
easy to vanquish as I imagined. We
can find an asylum from every creditor
but that"—[175]

---

174. Cf. Wilson:

	£ s. d.	£ s. d.
Lost by his death on this Essay. . . .		1 11 6
Gained in Elegies. 2 2 0		
" Essays.	3 3 0	
	5 5 0	
Am glad he is dead by.	£3 13 6	

(*Chatterton: A Biographical Study*, 267). See also "A Briton. To Lord North. The Moderator No. 1. Probus. To the Earl of Bute. Decimus. To the King. Probus. 2d to the Lord Mayor. Decimus (or Probus). To C. Jenkinson, Esq. The Moderator. To Lord North," in *Complete Works of Thomas Chatterton*, ed. Taylor and Hoover, 2:774.

175. Written in black ink. Cf. Wilson: "He was accompanied by a friend, who, as he helped him out again, jestingly congratulated him on the happy resurrection of Genius; but Chatterton, taking him by the arm, replied, with a sad smile: 'My dear friend, I feel the sting of a speedy dissolution. I have been at war with the grave for some time, and find it is not so easy to vanquish as I imagined. We can find an asylum from every creditor but that'" (*Chatterton: A Biographical Study*, 297). Wilson references Dix, *Life of Thomas Chatterton*, 290.

{71^r}

on 15th August writes
desponding letter to his
mother— and tells strange
story of his falling into
X[176]

a grave in a churchyard.[177]

———

Barrett refuses certificate

———

Finally Friday 24th Aug.
M^{rs}. Wolfe tells us that
M^{rs}. Angell told her
that "as she knew he
had not eaten anything
for 2 or 3 days[178]

{71^v}

(page blank)

{72^r}

she begged he would take
dinner with her, but he was
offended at her expressions
which seemed to hint he
was in want and assured
her (though his looks
showed him to be 3 parts
starved) that he was
not hungry[179]— on Saturday

---

176. Written in black ink.

177. Cf. Wilson: "There is indeed a story told, in more than one form, of a still later letter received by his mother, in which he stated that, wandering a few days before in some London churchyard, he was so lost in thought that he did not perceive a newly opened grave until he fell into it. According to Mr. Dix's version, it occurred in St. Pancras Churchyard, and within three days of his death" and "In [this letter] he had narrated the incident of his stumbling into an open grave. . . . The letter was written about the 15th or 16th of August" (*Chatterton: A Biographical Study*, 297–98). According to Taylor and Hoover, the letter is lost. See "To Sarah Chatterton [c. 20 August 1770]," in *Complete Works of Thomas Chatterton*, ed. Taylor and Hoover, 2:778.

178. Cf. Wilson: "After his death, [Mrs. Angel] told her neighbor, Mrs. Wolfe, that, 'as she knew he had not eaten anything for two or three days'" (*Chatterton: A Biographical Study*, 302). Wilson cites Croft as his source (*Love and Madness*, 219).

179. Cf. Wilson: "she begged he would take some dinner with her on the 24th of August; but he was offended at her expressions, which seemed to hint that he was in want, and assured her—though

25th August found dead.
the room covered
with scraps of paper — [180]

{72^v}

(page blank)

{73^r}

no notice at the time.
in October Cary's
Elegy in Town & County
mag:[181]

April 23. 1771.
First Academy Dinner.
Goldsmith tells
about poems — and said
he believed in them.
S · Johnson laughs at
him:[182] Walpole hears

{73^v}[183]

X   X   X

[~~able apprehension of being called upon to refund
the money should their modern origin be substantiated.~~[184]
Boswell has preserved a lively account of the interview of Catcott with Dr. Johnson, when the latter visited Bristol in 1776. "On Monday, April 29th," writes
Boswell, "he and I made an excursion to Bristol, where

---

his looks showed him to be three-parts starved, — that he was not hungry" (*Chatterton: A Biographical Study*, 303). Wilson cites Croft as his source (*Love and Madness*, 219).

180. Cf. Masson: "On . . . Saturday the 25th of August . . . [Chatterton's] room was broken open and he was discovered lying dead, having swallowed arsenic in water. 'His room, when they broke it open, after his death,' says Sir Herbert Croft, 'was found, like the room he quitted at Mr. Walmsley's, covered with scraps of paper'" (*Chatterton: A Story of the Year 1770*, 249; Croft, *Love and Madness*, 222).

181. Cf. Wilson: "In the October number of the *Town and Country Magazine* following [Chatterton's] death . . . [Thomas Cary] contributed an Elegy to the memory of Chatterton with the signature T.C." (*Chatterton: A Biographical Study*, 271).

182. Wilson cites Walpole's recollection of what is believed to be the first dinner at the Royal Academy: "Dr. Goldsmith attracted the attention of the company by his account of a marvellous treasure of ancient poems lately discovered at Bristol, and got laughed at by Dr. Johnson for his enthusiastic belief in them" (*Chatterton: A Biographical Study*, 289–90).

183. This rare pasted clipping on a verso glosses the narrative alluded to on the opposite page.

184. Lines are struck with vertical wavy lines in pencil.

I was entertained with seeing him inquire, upon the spot,
into the authenticity of Rowley's poetry. George Catcott,
the pewterer, attended us at our inn, and with a trium-
phant air of lively simplicity, called out, 'I'll make Dr.
Johnson a convert.' Dr. Johnson, at his desire, read
aloud some of Chatterton's fabricated verses, while
Catcott stood at the back of his chair, moving himself
like a pendulum, and beating time with his feet, and now
and then looking into Dr. Johnson's face, wondering
that he was not yet convinced. Honest Catcott seemed
to pay no attention whatever to any objections, but
insisted, as an end of all controversy, that we should go
with him to the tower of St. Mary Redcliffe, and view
with our own eyes the ancient chest in which the manuscripts were found. To this Dr. Johnson good-naturedly
agreed; and, though troubled with a shortness of
breathing, laboured up a long flight of steps, till we came
to the place where the wondrous chest stood. 'There,'
said Catcott, with a bouncing, confident credulity, 'there
is the very chest itself.' After this ocular demonstration
there was no more to be said."][185]

{74[r]}

of Chatterton's death.[186]
<u>1776</u> Jonson and
Boswell visit Bristol
see <u>Catcott</u> see opp.

—

1777 · Tyrwhitt[187]
1782. Mills
            controversy[188]

---

185. Wilson, *Chatterton: A Biographical Study*, 88.

186. Wilson cites Walpole's conversation with Goldsmith at the Royal Academy dinner: "'I told Dr. Goldsmith,' says Walpole, 'that [the novelty of Chatterton's Rowley poems] was none to me, who might, if I had pleased, have had the honour of ushering the great discovery to the learned world. But though [Goldsmith's] credulity diverted me, my mirth was soon dashed; for on asking about Chatterton, he told me that he had been in London, and had destroyed himself'" (*Chatterton: A Biographical Study*, 290).

187. [Thomas Chatterton,] *Poems, Supposed to Have Been Written at Bristol by Thomas Rowley, and Others, in the Fifteenth Century*, ed. Thomas Tyrwhitt (London: T. Payne, 1777).

188. Wilde misspells Milles's last name. As we discuss in chapter 1 (56–57), Tyrwhitt adopted a dispassionate perspective on whether the Rowley poems were authentic fifteenth-century works or forgeries, while Milles defended their historical genuineness.

{74^v}

(page blank)

{75^r}

Nature of his genius

———

was he mere forger
with literary powers or
a great artist?[189]
the latter is the right view. Chatterton
may not have had the moral
conscience which is Truth to Fact—
but he had the artistic conscience
which is truth to Beauty. He
had the artists yearning to
represent and if perfect representation[190]
seemed to him to demand forgery
He needs must forge[191]— Still
this forgery came from the
desire of artistic self effacement.[192]
He was the pure artist— that it is
to say

---

189. Cf. Watts: "What was the nature of the man? Do these Rowley poems show the vitalising power which only genius can give? and if they do, was Chatterton's impulse to exercise that power the impulse of the dramatic poet having 'the yearning of the Great Vish'nu to create a world'? or, was it that of the other class of artists, whose skill lies in 'those more facile imitations of prose, promissory notes,' among whom Horace Walpole would place him? For neither the assailants nor the defenders of Chatterton's character seem to see that between these two conclusions there is no middle one" ("Thomas Chatterton," in *The English Poets*, ed. Ward, 3:405).

190. Cf. Wilde's "Portrait of Mr. W.H.": "[Chatterton's] so-called forgeries were merely the result of an artistic desire for perfect representation" ("The Portrait of Mr. W.H.," in *The Soul of Man under Socialism and Selected Critical Prose*, ed. Linda Dowling [Harmondsworth: Penguin Books, 2001], 33).

191. Cf. Watts: "Either Chatterton was a born forger, having, as useful additional endowments, poetry and dramatic imagination almost unmatched among his contemporaries, or he was a born artist, who, before mature vision had come to show him the power and the sacredness of moral conscience in art, was so dominated by the artistic conscience—by the artist's yearning to represent, that, if perfect representation seemed to him to demand forgery, he needs must forge" ("Thomas Chatterton," in *The English Poets*, ed. Ward, 3:405).

192. Cf. Watts: "showing that power of artistic self-effacement" ("Thomas Chatterton," in *The English Poets*, ed. Ward, 3:403).

{75ᵛ}

there was something in him
of "the yearning of great
? <u>Vishnu</u>[193] to create a world" —[194]

——

yet a distinctive note
of his own —[195]

{76ʳ}

his aim was not to reveal
himself but to give pleasure— an
artist of the type of Shakespeare
and Homer— as opposed to Shelley
or Petrarch or Wordsworth[196]— He was
essentially a dramatist and
claimed for the artist freedom of
mood[197]— He saw the realm of
the imagination differed from the

---

193. The question mark and the double underscore beneath "Vishnu" are in pencil.

194. Written in black ink. Cf. Watts: "was Chatterton's impulse to exercise that power the impulse of the dramatic poet having 'the yearning of the Great Vish'nu to create a world'?" ("Thomas Chatterton," in *The English Poets*, ed. Ward, 3:405). Watts cites the *Padma-Puran'a*. The 1860 *Chambers's Encyclopedia* includes the following in its entry on "Trimúrti": "The *Padma-Puran'a*, which, being a Puran'a of the Vaishn'ava sect, assigns to Vishn'u the highest rank in the T., defines its character in the following manner: 'In the beginning of creation, the great Vishn'u, desirous of creating the whole world, became threefold: creator, preserver, and destroyer'" ([London: W. and R. Chambers, 1867], 813). Watts was fond of the phrase, and used it in his "Poetry" entry in both the *Encylopædia Britannica*, 25 vols. ([New York: H. G. Allen, 1888–1890], 19:264) and in a review of H. A. Page's *Thoreau, His Life and Aims: A Study* (*Athenæum* 2610 [3 November 1877]: 563).

195. Written in black ink.

196. The distinction between Homer and Shakespeare, on the one hand, and Percy Bysshe Shelley (1792–1822), Petrarch (1304–1374), and Wordsworth, on the other hand, resembles Watts's observations in "Poetry": "Allowing, however, for all the potency of external influences, we shall not be wrong in saying that of poetic imagination there are two distinct kinds—(1) the kind of poetic imagination seen at its highest in Æschylus, Sophocles, Shakespeare, and Homer, and (2) the kind of poetic imagination seen at its highest in Pindar, Dante, and Milton, or else in Sappho, Heine, and Shelley. The former, being in its highest dramatic exercise unconditioned by the personal or lyrical impulse of the poet, might perhaps be called absolute dramatic vision; the latter, being more or less conditioned by the personal or lyrical impulse of the poet, might be called relative dramatic vision" ("Poetry," in *Encyclopædia Britannica*, 19: 263).

197. Cf. Wilde's "The Poets' Corner," a review of *Low Down: Wayside Thoughts in Ballad and Other Verse* by "Two Tramps" and *Rhymes and Renderings* by H. C. Irwin. Of the tramp, Wilde writes: "He if any one should possess that freedom of mood which is so essential to the artist, for he has no taxes to pay and no relations to worry him." Wilde's comments on Irwin also resonate with Chattertonian themes: "It is easy to see that Mr. Irwin is a fervent admirer of Mr. Matthew Arnold. But he is in no sense a plagiarist. He has succeeded in studying a fine poet without stealing from him, a very difficult thing to do" (*Pall Mall Gazette*, 27 September 1886: 5; in *Journalism Part I*, ed. Stokes and Turner, 6:95, 96–97).

realm of fact. He loved to let
his intellect play— to separate
the artist from the man— this
explains his extraordinary
versatility—he cd. write polished
lines like Pope, satire like
Churchill— Philippics like
Junius— fiction like Smolletts.
   Gray, Collins, Macphersons
        Ossia .[198]

{76ᵛ}

(page blank)

{77ʳ}

also his statements
   that "He is a poor ~~artist~~
author who cannot write
on both sides".[199] and this
curious note found in his
papers—

   "In a dispute concerning the
character of David, it was argued
that he must be a holy man
from the strain of piety that
breathes through his whole works—
Being of a contrary opinion
and knowing that a great
genius can affect anything,
endeavoured in the foregoing
poems to represent an
   enthusiastic Methodist"[200]

---

198. Cf. Wilson: "There is surely something very noteworthy in the versatility thus manifested at so early an age. . . . Chameleon-like, he catches the satiric vein of [Charles] Churchill [1732–1764]; the envenomed prejudice of Wilkes; and the lofty-toned, yet narrow, bitterness of Junius [the unknown writer who published under that name in the *Public Advertiser* between 1769 and 1772]. He assumes, not unsuccessfully, the rough vigour of [Tobias] Smollett [1721–1771]; apes at times the r[h]ythmical niceties and the antithesis of Pope, or the polished grace of [Thomas] Gray [1716–1771] and [William] Collins [1721–1759]; or, in the guise of a Saxon monk, rivals the Gaelic Ossian [rendered into English by James Macpherson (1736–1796)], in his heroic affectations" (*Chatterton: A Biographical Study*, 261).

199. Both Wilson (*Chatterton: A Biographical Study*, 264) and Masson (*Chatterton: A Story of the Year* 1770, 184) quote the "both sides" comment.

200. Cf. Wilson: "In a dispute concerning the character of David, it was argued that he must be a holy man from the strain of piety that breathes through his whole works. Being of a contrary opinion,

{77^v}

(page blank)

{78^r}

important [illeg.]—
   "a great genius can <u>affect</u>
   anything"—
no lyrical egotism—[201]

Romantic Movement
   (1) <u>Form</u>.
           All great artists
      have personality as well as
      perfection[202] in their manner.
           What seems technical
      is really spiritual—[203]
      lyrical octosyllabic movement

_____

           Scott stole from Coleridge[204]
      Coleridge got from Chatterton—

{78^v}

(page blank)

{79^r}

what Coleridge claimed as a
new principle in poetry— the
anapaestic variations in

_____

and knowing that a great genius can affect everything; endeavouring in the foregoing poems to repre-sent an enthusiastic Methodist" (*Chatterton: A Biographical Study*, 245). Since Wilson notes that he has corrected Cottle's "effect" to "affect," it appears that he is citing *Works of Thomas Chatterton*, ed. Cottle and Southey, 3:447–48.

   201. Cf. Watts: "a producer, that is to say, of work purely artistic and in its highest reaches unadul-terated by lyric egotism" ("Thomas Chatterton," in *The English Poets*, ed. Ward, 3:403).

   202. Cf. Wilde, "The Soul of Man Under Socialism" (1891): "From the point of view of subject, a healthy work of art is one the choice of whose subject is conditioned by the temperament of the artist, and comes directly out of it. In fine, a healthy work of art is one that has both perfection and personality." In *The Soul of Man under Socialism*, ed. Dowling, 146. See also Josephine M. Guy's dis-cussion of Wilde's treatment of "personality" in Rossetti: "'Trafficking with Merchants for His Soul': Dante Gabriel Rossetti among the Aesthetes," *Proceedings of the British Academy* 105 (199): 171–86.

   203. Cf. 1^v (334).

   204. Cf. Watts on Chatterton's influence: "as to the romantic form, it is a matter of familiar knowl-edge, for instance, that the lyric octo-syllabic movement of which Scott made such excellent use in *The Lay of the Last Minstrel*, and which Byron borrowed from him, was originally borrowed (or rather stolen) by Scott from Coleridge" ("Thomas Chatterton," in *The English Poets*, ed. Ward, 3:401).

correspondence with some transition
in the nature of the imagery or
passion — was in reality
Chattertons —[205]	Influence of
Chatterton seen in Coleridges
Kubla Khan[206] a Christabel
   in Keats Eve of St. Agnes —[207]

———

Feeling —
        music and painting are
the romantic arts — Poetry
has both — colour and
new melody — also

{79ᵛ}

(page blank)

{80ʳ}

1 medievalism
2 love of nature
  (1) variety of life — sympathy with
      passion — sensuous imagery —
      for <u>images</u> as opposed to ideas
      continuity of English poetry —
      Chaucer[208] — Spenser — Chatterton
      Coleridge — Keats — Tennyson[209] —
      Morris[210]
  (2) <u>nature</u> — quote.

---

205. Cf. Watts: "With regard to octo-syllabics with anapaestic variations, it may be said no doubt that some of the miracle-plays (such as *The Fall of Man*) are composed in this movement, as is also one of the months in Spenser's *Shepherd's Calendar;* but the irregularity in these is, like that of the Border ballads, mostly the irregularity of makeshift, while Chatterton's *Unknown Knight,* like *Christabel,* and like Goethe's *Erl King,* has several variations introduced (as Coleridge says of his own) 'in correspondence with some transition in the nature of the imagery or passion.' The 'new principle,' in short, was Chatterton's" ("Thomas Chatterton," in *The English Poets,* ed. Ward, 3:402).

206. Cf. Watts: "Again, in the mysterious suggestiveness of remote geographical names . . . the world-involving echoes of [Coleridge's] *Kubla Khan* [published 1816] seem to have been caught from such lines as these in Chatterton's African eclogue *Narva and Mored*" ("Thomas Chatterton," 3:402).

207. Cf. Watts: "It is difficult to express in words wherein lies the entirely spiritual kinship between Chatterton's *Ballad of Charity* and Keats's *Eve of St. Agnes* [1820], yet I should be sceptical as to the insight of any critic who should fail to recognise that kinship" ("Thomas Chatterton," in *The English Poets,* ed. Ward, 3:402).

208. Geoffrey Chaucer (c. 1343–1400); see f.15ʳ (349), f.23ʳ (356), and f.37ʳ (371).

209. Alfred Tennyson (1809–1892), poet laureate from 1850 onward.

210. William Morris (1834–1896), Pre-Raphaelite poet, designer, and socialist.

{80ᵛ}

(page blank)

{81ʳ}

What do we learn?
    Can only be understood by
being enjoyed—
Not "criticism of life—
but it is the ideal
not the realistic artist who
expresses his age—
mist of familiarity makes
this obscure to us
                    Shelley[211]

{81ᵛ}

(page blank)

{82ʳ}

Picture of Rossetti in the
House—
With Shakespeare's manhood at a boys wild heart
Through Hamlets doubt to Shakespeare near allied
And kin to Milton through his Satan's pride
At Deaths sole door he stooped and craved a dart
And to the dear new bower of Englands art
Even to that shrine Time else had deified
The unuttered heart that seared against his side
Drove the fell point and smote lifes seals apart

Thy nested homeloves, noble Chatterton
The angel trodden stair thy soul could trace
Up Redcliffe spire, and in the worlds armed space

---

211. Shelley uses the phrase "mist of familiarity" at least twice. The essay "On Life," which first appeared in the *Athenæum* in 1832, opens: "Life and the world, or whatever we call that which we are and feel, is an astonishing thing. The mist of familiarity obscures us from the wonder of our being"; later in the essay, Shelley offers a spirited defense of the imaginary over the actual. In a letter of 27 September 1819 to Leigh Hunt, Shelley praises Boccaccio: "What descriptions of nature are those in his little introductions to every new day! It is the morning of life stripped of that mist of familiarity which makes it obscure to us" (Percy Bysshe Shelley, *Essays, Letters from Abroad, Translations and Fragments*, ed. Mary Shelley, 2 vols. [London: Edward Moxon, 1840], 1:223, 2:228). Cf. n. 80 in chapter 4 (184) for an additional discussion of Shelley's use of "mist of familiarity." On this folio, Wilde has placed a diagonal line under "Shelley."

Thy gallant swordplay: these to many a one
Are dear for ever—as thy grave unknown,
And love-dream of thine
           unrecorded <u>face</u>[212]

{82ᵛ–94ᵛ}

  (blank pages)

---

212. Pre-Raphaelite poet Dante Gabriel Rossetti (1828–1882) first published his sonnet to Thomas Chatterton in *Ballads and Sonnets*:

With Shakespeare's manhood at a boy's wild heart,—
Through Hamlet's doubt to Shakespeare near allied,
And kin to Milton through his Satan's pride,—
At Death's sole door he stooped and craved a dart;
And to the dear new bower of England's art,—
Even to that shrine Time else had deified,
The unuttered heart that soared against his side,—
Drove the fell point and smote life's seals apart.

Thy nested home-loves, noble Chatterton;
The angel-trodden stair thy soul could trace
Up Redcliffe's spire; and in the world's armed space
Thy gallant sword-play:—these to many an one
Are sweet for ever; as thy grave unknown
And love-dream of thine unrecorded face.

(London: Ellis and White, 1881, 333)

Cf. Wilde's notes on Rossetti's *Ballads and Sonnets* in Appendix B (411–15).

Appendix B

NOTES ON DANTE GABRIEL ROSSETTI'S
BALLADS AND SONNETS (1881)

{1ʳ}

the very sweetness and simplicity
of the vision affecting us like the
tenderness of Aeschylus, and like
Dante's tenderness. 323[1]

in such lines as

~~all so~~

golden king[2] 181	
deep in the[3]	218
an osier odoured[4]	174
o'er water daisies[5]	182

---

1. Wilde's numbers here and throughout refer to page numbers in *Ballads and Sonnets* (London: Ellis and White, 1881). "Spring," a pastoral sonnet, is featured on p. 323.

2. From "Silent Noon," Sonnet XIX in *The House of Life*: "All round our nest, far as the eye can pass, / Are golden kingcup-fields with silver edge" (ll. 5–6, *Ballads and Sonnets*, 181).

3. No lines on p. 218 include the words "deep in the." The reference could be, like the previous citation, from "Silent Noon": "Deep in the sun-searched growths the dragon-fly / Hangs like a blue thread loosened from the sky" (ll. 9–10, *Ballads and Sonnets*, 181).

4. "The Lovers' Walk," Sonnet XII in *The House of Life*: "An osier-odoured stream that draws the skies / Deep to its heart; and mirrored eyes its eyes" (ll. 4–5, *Ballads and Sonnets*, 174).

5. "Gracious Moonlight," Sonnet XX in *The House of Life*: "O'er water-daisies and wild waifs of Spring" (l. 9, *Ballads and Sonnets*, 182).

the cuckoo throb[6]   226

one might almost think that

Perdita[7] spake here, and[?] these three

lines from 201[8]

seem like some lost revel from
As You Like It

{1ᵛ}

        like another great leader
of the romantic school
he has become a classic
in his lifetime: and remains for
younger workers in song the most
splendid and perfect model:
        because
splendid ~~and~~ unattainable: ~~he by~~

great brotherhood with all
other beautiful work which is
note of genius, and that perfect
indivisible individuality wh. is
genius itself—

        the passion which they
reveal and so by revelation
make mysterious—[9]

sacramental view of
life—their noble deification—

the shrill voice of envy and folly
busies[?] in
before such work is its[?] must be
silent—and this London

6. "Ardour and Memory," Sonnet LXIV in *The House of Life:* "The cuckoo-throb, the heartbeat of the Spring" (l. 1, *Ballads and Sonnets*, 226).

7. Perdita is a heroine of Shakespeare's *Winter's Tale*.

8. *Ballads and Sonnets* (201) features "Sleepless Dreams," Sonnet XXXIX of *The House of Life*.

9. The small ink doodle that appears in the left margin of the page could be a profile of Rossetti.

{2ʳ; right bottom corner is torn}

       the not completed thought
as contrasted artistic completeness of the
worksmanship which expresses it, affecting
one like a deferred resolution in
Beethoven—

   getting in there the quintessential
   music of out words, ~~which~~
         cadenced wonders
   are hidden to ordinary workers.

    Il n'y a rien said Gautier[10]
      and Mr. Rossetti
   he has the perfect articulateness
   of the real artist—

     affects one with the
   sense of working in a very
   precious material.

{3ʳ}

and then begins the second part
called Change & Fate[11] where ~~the~~
       mystical
note is more tragic—of the change
wrought by art on the song whose
cradle was mere joy and pain[12]
what analysis could
   222
and •

---

10. Théophile Gautier's preface to his novel *Mademoiselle de Maupin* (1835) serves as a manifesto for *l'art pour l'art*. Wilde's notation recalls two of the boldest statements from the preface: "Il n'y a de vraiment beau que ce qui ne peut server à rien; tout ce qui est utile est laid" ("There is nothing truly beautiful except for that which serves no purpose; everything that is useful is ugly") and "Rien de ce qui est beau n'est indispensable à la vie" ("Nothing that is beautiful is not essential to life") [Paris: Charpentier, 1875], 21).

11. Part II of *The House of Life*, "Change and Fate," indeed begins on p. 222.

12. The octet of Sonnet LX of *The House of Life*, "Transfigured Life," describes the shift in a child's appearance: when very young, it reveals "the father's with the mother's face combin'd" (l. 3), but as the child enters adulthood, "in the blended likeness now we find / A separate man's or woman's countenance" (ll. 7–8). The sestet begins, "So in the Song, the singer's Joy and Pain, / Its very parents, evermore expand / To bid the passion's fullgrown birth remain, / By Art's transfiguring essence subtly spann'd" (ll. 9–12, *Ballads and Sonnets*, 222).

from this analysis we pass to
the souls sphere of infinite images[13]
whether it be the prisoned moon or
momentous fire of some dying sun—[14]
and the vision itself[?] be they
                    visions

the two visions of Beauty—the
Beauty of the Soul, and the
Bodies beauty[15]—one throned
under the arch of life and
guarded by Love and death[16] /
terror[?] and by soul — the [illegible]
incarnate in sweet treacherous
            [illegible] and strangling golden hair[17]
                    of Lilith—[18]

{4[r]}

giving that homage which only poets can
give to poets, the homage of one King
to another King—

the strength and splendour of his
own dominant personality.

            where the splendour & str. of the
            verse mocks the weakness,
            and the immortal kills[?] the
            Death •

                    ————
                    ————

13. Sonnet LXII of *The House of Life*, "The Soul's Sphere": "Lo! the soul's sphere of infinite images!" (l. 8, *Ballads and Sonnets*, 224).

14. "The Soul's Sphere": "Some prisoned moon in steep cloud-fastnesses,— / Throned queen and thralled; some dying sun whose pyre / Blazed with momentous memorable fire" (ll. 1–3, *Ballads and Sonnets*, 224).

15. "Soul's Beauty" is Sonnet LXXVII and "Body's Beauty" is Sonnet LXXVIII of *The House of Life* (*Ballads and Sonnets*, 239–40).

16. "Soul's Beauty": "Under the arch of Life, where love and death, / Terror and mystery, guard her shrine, I saw / Beauty enthroned" (ll. 1–3, *Ballads and Sonnets*, 239).

17. Sonnet LXXVIII of *The House of Life*, "Body's Beauty": "And round his heart one strangling golden hair" (l. 16, *Ballads and Sonnets*, 240).

18. "Body's Beauty" centers on Lilith's seduction of Adam (*Ballads and Sonnets*, 240).

{5^r}

it's possible to make
of Wordsworth, of Byron even, selections
~~beatific~~
but ~~Mr. Rossetti's work~~ from the   vision

of the [~~illegible~~] beatific damozel[19] leaning
out through the gold bars of heaven,
to the "hand heart handselled in
a lovers hand[20] which ends this volume
there is nothing that is not perfect,
                    does
nothing that is   not bear the impress of

the hand of a great master, and by
such sealing give warrant to its.
                         one other it
own grandeur. Like another

leader of a romantic school — the author
of L'annee terrible[21] he has become
a classic —

                              diverse
                    the unity of the ^ message of art
whether borne on the spiritual wings of
song, or visually transfigured in the
gorgeousness of colour and august
glory of design which mark the
paintings of DGR.

                    He who gives another
                    freedom to Art finds[?] it with
                    another law •

---

19. Rossetti's poem "The Blessed Damozel" was published in *The Germ* in 1850 and repeatedly revised. It is the basis for his painting (1875–1878) of the same title.

20. "La Bella Mano (For a Picture)": "O hand! heart-handsel'd in a lover's hand" (l. 15, *Ballads and Sonnets*, 335).

21. Victor Hugo's volume of poetry *L'année terrible* (1872) addresses the Siege of Paris, 1870–1871.

BIBLIOGRAPHY

"A.B.W." [A. B. Walkley.] Review of *An Ideal Husband. Speaker*, 12 January 1895: 43–44.

———. Review of *Lady Windermere's Fan. Speaker*, 27 February 1892: 257–58.

Ackroyd, Peter. *Chatterton*. London: Hamish Hamilton, 1987.

Almy, Percival. "New Views of Oscar Wilde." *The Theatre* 23 (March 1894): 119–27.

Anderson, Anne. "Oscar's Enemy . . . and Neighbour: 'Arry' Quilter and the 'Gospel of Intensity.'" *The Wildean* 27 (2005): 39–54.

Anderson Galleries. *English Literature from London: To Be Sold on the Afternoons and Evenings of Tuesday and Wednesday, May 13th and 14th, 2.30 and 8.15 o'CLOCK*. New York: Anderson Galleries, 1919.

Anonymous. "Apparent Failure." *Academy*, 30 July 1910: 106–7.

———. "Art Notes." *Liverpool Mercury*, 3 June 1884: sec. 5.

———. "The Banquet to Mr. Barrett." *The Era*, 14 August 1886: 13.

———. "Bell and Skeat's Chatterton." *Saturday Review*, 3 April 1875: 447–48.

———. "Book Notes." *New York Times*, 9 October 1931: 27.

———. "Chatterton." *Saturday Review*, 21 January 1899: 85–86.

———. "Chatterton Memorials." *Bristol Mercury*, 4 November 1887: 3.

———. "Chatterton: Or, the Rowley Romance." *Tinsley's Magazine* 14 (1874): 382–97.

———. "The Cheiromancy of To-Day: The Evolution of an Occult Science." *Lippincott's Monthly Magazine* (July 1890): 102–11.

———. *City Petitions, Addresses, and Remonstrances &c., Commencing in the Year MDC-CLXIX, and Including the Last Petition for the Burial of the Rt. Hon. the Earl of Chatham in St. Paul's Cathedral with his Majesty's Answers, also Mr. Alderman Beckford's Speech to the King, on the Twenty-Third of May, 1770*. London: David Steel, 1778.

———. "Commonplace-Books." *Chambers's Journal* 849 (3 April 1880): 216–17.

———. "Contents of No. IV." *Century Guild Hobby Horse* 1, no. 4 (October 1886): 122. Ohio State University Special Collections Library SPEC.RARE.CMS.59.

———. "The Country Gentleman." *Agricultural Journal* (13 November 1886): 1464.

———. "Current Literature." *Daily News* (London), 27 March 1875: 2.

——. "The Drama." *Westminster Review* 137 (1892): 476–80.

——. "Eleanor and Juga: Modernised from Rowley's Poems." *Bath Chronicle*, 10 October 1872: 4.

——. "Elinour and Juga: Modernized from Chatterton." *European Magazine and London Review* 18 (September 1790): 224–25.

——. "The Ethics of Journalism." *Pall Mall Gazette*, 22 September 1894: 3.

——. *An Examination of the Poems Attributed to Thomas Rowley and William Canynge with a Defence of the Opinion of Mr. Warton.* Sherborne: R. Goadby; London: R. Baldwin, 1782.

——. "From Our London Correspondent." *Manchester Guardian*, 14 June 1888: 5.

——. "Hand Reading." *Daily Graphic*, 17 November 1886: 124–25.

——. "Imaginary Plagiarism." *The Era*, 22 October 1892: 15.

——. "The Importance of Being Oscar." *Truth*, 21 February 1895: 464–65.

——. "Impression de Gaiety Théâtre (by Ossian Wilderness)." *Punch*, 8 April 1882: 168.

——. "Interesting Literary Discovery." *Edinburgh Evening News*, 7 June 1879: 4.

——. "January Magazines." *Leeds Mercury*, 30 December 1885: 6c.

——. "Lecture by Oscar Wilde." *Poole and Dorset Herald*, 12 April 1888: 6.

——. *The Library of Herschel V. Jones.* Auction Catalogue of the Anderson Galleries. New York: privately printed, 1919.

——. "*Life* Explores World's Finest Walpole Library." *Life*, 23 October 1944: 116–17.

——. "Literary, Music, and Drama." *Sheffield and Rotherham Independent*, 24 July 1886: 3.

——. "Literary Notes." *Pall Mall Gazette*, 6 March 1884: 6.

——. "Literary Notes and Gossip." *Glasgow Herald*, 28 March 1896: 9.

——. "Literary Notes, News, and Echoes." *Pall Mall Gazette*, 5 January 1889: 1.

——. "Literary Notes, News, and Echoes." *Pall Mall Gazette*, 29 June 1889: 1–2.

——. "Literature." *Bristol Mercury, and Western Counties Advertiser*, 9 December 1871: 6.

——. "London Gossip." *Northern Evening Mail* (Hartlepool), 10 June 1879: 4.

——. "*Lyrical Compositions Selected from the Italian Poets; with Translations* by James Glassford." *Edinburgh Review* 84, no. 169 (July 1846): 102–16.

——. "Magazines (Fourth Notice)." *Aberdeen Journal*, 14 January 1889: 7.

——. "Magazines." *The Graphic*, 6 July 1889: 31, 33.

——. "The Magazines." *Scots Observer*, 6 July 1889: 193–94.

——. "The Memorial to the Men of Letters of the Lake District." *Century Guild Hobby Horse* 1, no. 5 (January 1887): 41–44.

——. "Minor Notices." *The Literary World* 18, no. 8 (April 1887): 123.

——. "Mr. Oscar Wilde on Dress." *Freeman's Journal and Daily Commercial Advertiser*, 6 January 1885: 7.

——. "Mr. Oscar Wilde's Lecture on Dress." *Bath Chronicle and Weekly Gazette*, 23 October 1884: 7.

——. "Mr. Oscar Wilde's Poems." *Spectator*, 13 August 1881: 1048–50.

——. "New Light on the Death of Chatterton." *Times* (London), 29 May 1947: 7.

——. "New Pieces Produced at the Provincial Theatres, from December 1884, to End of November, 1885." *The Era Almanack and Annual* (1886): 70–74.

——. "A New Society Craze." *The Shields Daily Gazette*, 18 September 1886: 4.

——. "News of the Day." *Birmingham Daily Post*, 31 January 1887: 4.

——. "Notice of Lecture." *The Morning Post*, 20 November 1884: 2.

——. "Obituary: J. Payne Collier." *Academy*, 29 September 1883: 214.

——. "Occasional Notes." *Edinburgh Evening News*, 20 March 1884: 2.

——. "Oscar Wilde's Lecture: A Large Audience Listens to the Young Æsthete." *New York Times*, 10 January 1882: 5.

——. "Ossian Savage's New Play." *The Ephemeral* 1 (May 1893): 3–4.

——. "Ossian (with Variations): The Son of Ia-Cultcha." *Punch*, 11 March 1882: 117.

——. "Our London Letter," *Northern Echo*, 7 October 1886: 2.

——. "The Poetical Works of Thomas Chatterton, with an Essay on the Rowley Poems." *Athenæum* 2302 (9 December 1871): 749–50.

——. "The Poems of Digby Mackworth Dolben." *Athenæum* 4558 (6 March 1915): 207–8.

——. "Preface." In *Fragments of Ancient Poetry, Collected in the Highlands of Scotland, and Translated from the Galic or Erse Language* by [James Macpherson], iii–viii. Edinburgh: J. Hamilton and G. Balfour, 1760.

——. "Recent Poetry." *Saturday Review*, 23 July 1881: 117–18.

——. "The Regeneration of Our National Poetry." *Athenæum* 627 (November 1839): 824–27.

——. "Report." In *Transactions of the Ossianic Society, for the Year 1853*. Dublin: Printed under the Direction of the Council, 1853.

——. Review of *The English Poets*, ed. T. Humphry Ward, *Vol. III, Addison to Blake*; *Vol. IV, Wordsworth to Dobell. Athenæum* 2778 (22 January 1881): 127–29.

——. Review of *Lady Windermere's Fan. Black and White*, 27 February 1892: 264.

——. Review of the Stuart Exhibition. *Athenæum* 3199 (16 February 1889): 219–21.

——. "The Reviews for January." *Pall Mall Gazette*, 2 January 1889: 7.

——. "The Rowley Poems of Thomas Chatterton." *Saturday Review*, 1 June 1912: 689–90.

——. "The Royal Academy: Exhibition the Eighty-Eighth." *Art Journal* 18 (June 1856): 161–74.

——. "Ryde." *Portsmouth Evening News*, 3 December 1886: 2.

——. "Says Oscar Wilde Is Alive and Well." *Ogden Standard* (Ogden City, UT), 3 November 1913: 10.

——. "Unveiling of the Gower Memorial at Stratford." *Birmingham Daily Post*, 11 October 1888: 5.

——. Untitled. *Daily News* (London), 25 November 1886: 6.

——. "Value of Art in Modern Life." *Freeman's Journal and Daily Commercial Advertiser*, 7 January 1885: 5.

——. "Wilde vs. Walpole." *Mercurius Redivivus: Being an Occasional News-Letter from the William Andrews Clark Memorial Library at 2205 West Adams Boulevard in the City of Los Angeles* 1 (Autumn 1952): 5.

——. "Wilson Barrett as Chatterton." *The Era*, 31 May 1884: 10.

——. "Wilson Barrett as Chatterton." *The Era*, 7 June 1884: 11.

Archer, William. "Robert Louis Stevenson at 'Skerryvore.'" *Critic: Weekly Review of Literature and the Arts* 201 (5 November 1887): 225–27.

———. "Shakespeare's Sonnets: The Case against Southampton." *Fortnightly Review* n.s. 62 (1897): 817–34.

Arnold, Matthew. "Byron." *English Literature and Irish Politics*. In *The Complete Prose Works of Matthew Arnold*. Edited by R. H. Super. Vol. 9, 217–37. Ann Arbor: University of Michigan Press, 1973.

———. *Culture and Anarchy*. London: Smith, Elder, 1869.

———. *Culture and Anarchy with Friendship's Garland and Some Literary Essays*. In *The Complete Prose Works of Matthew Arnold*. Edited by R. H. Super. Vol. 5. Ann Arbor: University of Michigan Press, 1965.

———. *English Literature and Irish Politics*. In *The Complete Prose Works of Matthew Arnold*. Edited by R. H. Super. Vol. 9. Ann Arbor: University of Michigan Press, 1973.

———. "On the Study of Celtic Literature." *Lectures and Essays in Criticism*. In *The Complete Prose Works of Matthew Arnold*. Edited by R. H. Super. Vol. 3, 291–386. Ann Arbor: University of Michigan Press, 1962.

———. "Shakespeare." In *The Poems of Matthew Arnold*. Edited by Kenneth Allott and Miriam Allott, 38–40. Harlow: Longman, 1979.

——— [A]. "Shakspeare." In *The Strayed Reveller, and Other Poems*, 50. London: B. Fellowes, 1849.

———. "Shelley." *The Last Word*. In *The Complete Prose Works of Matthew Arnold*. Edited by R. H. Super. Vol. 9, 305–27. Ann Arbor: University of Michigan Press, 1977.

Bacon, Francis. *The Two Books of Francis Bacon: Of the Proficience and Advancement of Learning, Divine and Humane*. London: Henrie Tomes, 1605.

Baines, Paul. *The House of Forgery in Eighteenth-Century Britain*. Aldershot: Ashgate, 1999.

Ball, Edward. *The Life of Thomas Chatterton*. London: G. Bell and Sons, 1912.

Balzac, Honoré de. "Avant propos." *La comédie humaine*. Vol. 1. Paris: Furne, 1842.

Barker, W. R., ed. *A Catalogue of the Autograph Manuscripts and Other Remains of Thomas Chatterton Now in the Bristol Museum of Antiquities*. Bristol: Bristol Art Gallery, 1907.

Barrett, William. *The History and Antiquities of the City of Bristol; comp. from Original Records and Authentic Manuscripts, in Public Offices or Private Hands; Illustrated with Copper-Plate Prints*. Bristol: W. Pine, 1789.

Barrett, William, et al. "Original Correspondence on the Discovery of Rowley's Poems." *Gentleman's Magazine* 56 (1786): 361–62, 460–64, 544–47, 580, 859–60.

Barrie, J. M. *An Edinburgh Eleven: Pencil Portraits from College Life*. London: Hodder and Stoughton, 1896.

Baudelaire, Charles. *La Fanfarlo*. In *Petits poèmes en prose: Les paradis artificiels*. Paris: Michel Lévy Frères, 1869.

Bauer, Josephine. *The London Magazine, 1820–29*, Anglistica I. Copenhagen: Rosenkilde and Bagger, 1953.

Beatty, Bernard. "The Form of Oscar: Wilde's Art of Substitution." *Irish Studies Review* 11 (2003): 33–49.

Becker-Leckrone, Megan. "Wilde and Pater's Strange Appreciations." *Victoriographies* 1 (2011): 96–123.

Beckson, Karl, ed. *Oscar Wilde: The Critical Heritage*. London: Routledge and Kegan Paul, 1970.

[Bell, Edward]. "The Life of Thomas Chatterton." In *The Poetical Works of Thomas Chatterton*. Edited by W. W. Skeat. Vol. 1, xiii–cvii. London: Bell and Daldy, 1871.

Bell, Mackenzie. *Pictures of Travel and Other Poems*. Boston: Little, Brown, 1898.

Bell, Neil. *Cover His Face: A Novel of the Life and Times of Thomas Chatterton, the Marvellous Boy of Bristol*. London: Collins, 1943.

Bendz, Ernst. *Notes on the Literary Relationship between Walter Pater and Oscar Wilde*. Helsinki: Aktiebolaget Handelstryckeriet, 1912.

Bennett, Andrew. *Romantic Poets and the Culture of Posterity*. Cambridge: Cambridge University Press, 1999.

Birrell, Augustine. *Seven Lectures on the Law and History of Copyright in Books*. London: Cassell, 1899.

Black, Joseph, et al., ed. *Broadview Anthology of British Literature*. Vols. 3–4. 2nd ed. Calgary: Broadview, 2010.

Blair, Ann M. *Too Much to Know: Managing Scholarly Information before the Modern Age*. New Haven: Yale University Press, 2010.

[Blair, Hugh?]. "Appendix." In *The Works of Ossian, the Son of Fingal, Translated from the Galic Language by James Macpherson*. 3rd ed. London: T. Becket and P. A. Dehondt, 1765.

Blau, Heinrich. *Thomas Chatterton: Tragödie in vier Akten*. London: Hirschfeld Bros., 1887.

Bloom, Harold. *The Anxiety of Influence: A Theory of Poetry*. New York: Oxford University Press, 1973.

Boaden, James. *A Letter to George Steevens, Esq. Containing a Critical Examination of the Papers of Shakspeare: Published by Mr. Samuel Ireland, to Which are Added, Extracts from Vortigern*. London: Martin and Bain, 1796.

———. *On the Sonnets of Shakespeare: Identifying the Person to Whom they Are Addressed; and Elucidating Several Points in the Poet's History*. London: Thomas Rodd, 1837.

Bodley, John Edward Courtenay. Diary. Bodleian Library Special Collections, MS. Eng. Misc. e. 460.

Boswell, James. *Boswell's Life of Johnson, together with Boswell's Journal of a Tour of the Hebrides and Johnson's Diary of a Journey into North Wales*. Edited by George Birkbeck Hill. Revised by L. F. Powell. 6 vols. Oxford: Clarendon Press, 1934–1950.

Brae, Andrew. *Literary Cookery, with Matter Attributed to Coleridge and Shakespeare: A Letter Addressed to "The Athenæum."* London: John Russell Smith, 1855.

Brewer, John. *Sentimental Murder: Love and Madness in the Eighteenth Century*. London: HarperCollins, 2004.

Briefel, Aviva. *The Deceivers: Art Forgery and Identity in the Nineteenth Century*. Ithaca, NY: Cornell University Press, 2006.

Bristol and Gloucester Archaeological Society. "Buildings in Bristol of Architectural or Historic Interest Damaged or Destroyed by Enemy Action, 1940–1942." *Transactions of the Bristol and Gloucestershire Archeological Society* 65 (1944): 167–74.

"Bristoliensis." "On Rowley's Poems and Chatterton." *Gentleman's Magazine* 48 (September 1778): 403.

Bristow, Joseph, ed. *Oscar Wilde and Modern Culture: The Making of a Legend.* Athens: Ohio University Press, 2008.

——. "Picturing His Exact Decadence: The British Reception of Oscar Wilde, 1900–1987." In *The Reception of Oscar Wilde in Europe.* Edited by Stefano-Maria Evangelista, 20–50. London: Continuum, 2010.

——, ed. *Wilde Discoveries: Traditions, Histories, Archives.* Toronto: University of Toronto Press, 2013.

Bronson, Bertrand. "Thomas Chatterton." In *The Age of Johnson,* 239–56. New Haven: Yale University Press, 1949.

Brooke, Charlotte. *Reliques of Irish Poetry, Consisting of Heroic Poems, Odes, Elegies, and Songs, Translated into English Verse, with Notes Explanatory and Historical; and the Originals in the Irish Character, to which is Subjoined an Irish Tale by Miss Brooke.* Dublin: George Bonham, 1789.

Brookfield, Charles H. E., and James Glover. *The Poet and the Puppets: A Travestie Suggested by "Lady Windermere's Fan."* In *Victorian Theatrical Burlesques.* Edited by Richard W. Schoch, 209–46. Aldershot: Ashgate, 2003.

Brown, Henry. *The Sonnets of Shakespeare Solved, and the Mystery of His Friend, Love, and Rivalry Revealed.* London: John Russell Smith, 1870.

[Browning, Robert]. Review of *Conjectures and Researches Concerning the Love Madness and Imprisonment of Torquato Tasso,* by Richard Henry Wilde. *Foreign Quarterly Review* 29, no. 58 (1842): 465–83.

——. *Browning's Essay on Chatterton.* Edited by Donald Smalley. Cambridge, MA: Harvard University Press, 1948.

Bryant, Jacob. *Observations upon the Poems of Thomas Rowley, in which the Authenticity of Those Poems is Ascertained.* London: T. Payne, T. Cadell, and P. Elmsley, 1781.

[Buchanan, Robert]. Review of Swinburne's *Poems and Ballads. Athenæum* 2023 (4 August 1866): 137–38.

Buckley, Jerome H. "Echo and Artifice: The Poetry of Oscar Wilde." *Victorian Poetry* 28, nos. 3–4 (1990): 19–31.

Bullock, William. *Catalogue of the Library of Valuable Books, Pictures, Portraits of Celebrities, Arundel Society Prints, Household Furniture, Carlyle's Writing Table, Chippendale and Italian Chairs, Etc., Which Will Be Sold by Auction, by Mr. Bullock . . . on Wednesday, April 24th 1895.* London: Bullock, 1895. Clark Library, PR5828 C357.

Burdett, Osbert. "A Life of Thomas Chatterton." *Saturday Review,* 8 November 1930: 604–6.

Burnand, F. C. *The Colonel.* Edited by Pierre Marteau. 2004. http://www.xix-e.pierre-mar teau.com/ed/colonel.html, n.p.

Butler, Samuel. *Shakespeare's Sonnets: Reconsidered, in Part Rearranged with Introductory Chapters, Notes, and a Reprint of the Original 1609 Edition.* London: A. C. Fifield, 1899.

Byron, George Gordon, Baron. *The Works of Lord Byron: With His Letters and Journals, and His Life.* Edited by Thomas Moore. 17 vols. London: John Murray, 1832–1833.

Caine, T. Hall. *Cobwebs of Criticism: A Review of the First Reviewers of the "Lake," "Satanic," and "Cockney" Schools.* London: Elliot, Stock, 1883.

——. *Recollections of Dante Gabriel Rossetti.* London: Elliot, Stock, 1882.

Campbell, James. "Sexual Gnosticism: The Procreative Code of "The Portrait of Mr. W.H." In *Wilde Discoveries: Traditions, Histories, Archives*. Edited by Joseph Bristow, 169–89. Toronto: University of Toronto Press, 2013.

Campbell, Thomas. *Specimens of the British Poets; with Biographical and Critical Notices and Essay on English Poetry*. 7 vols. London: John Murray, 1819.

Carroll, Lewis. *Through the Looking-Glass and What Alice Found There*. In *The Annotated Alice: Alice's Adventures in Wonderland and Through the Looking-Glass*. Edited by Martin Gardner. Definitive Edition. New York: W. W. Norton, 2000.

Carlyle, Thomas. "To Daniel Wilson." 10 January 1870. British Library, Add. MS 47867.

[Cary, H. F.]. "The Life of Chatterton." *London Magazine* 9 (1824): 631–38.

Cassidy, John A. *Robert W. Buchanan*. New York: Twayne, 1973.

———. "Robert Buchanan and the Fleshly Controversy." *PMLA* 67 (1952): 65–93.

Chalmers, Alexander. "The Life of Chatterton." In *The Works of the English Poets, from Chaucer to Cooper; Including the Series Edited with Prefaces, Biographical and Critical, by Dr. Samuel Johnson; the Additonal Lives, by Alexander Chalmers*. Vol. 15, 367–79. London: J. Johnson, 1810.

Chalmers, George. *An Apology for the Believers in the Shakspeare-Papers, Which Were Exhibited in Norfolk-Street*. London: Thomas Egerton, 1797.

———. *A Supplemental Apology for the Believers in the Shakspeare-Papers: Being a Reply to Mr. Malone's Answer, Which Was Early Announced, but Never Published: With a Dedication to George Steevens, F.R.S. S.A. and a Postscript to T. J. Mathias, F.R.S. S.A. the Author of the Pursuits of Literature*. London: Thomas Egerton, 1799.

Chaney, Edward, and Jane Hall. "Herbert Horne's 1889 Diary of His First Visit to Italy." *The Volume of the Walpole Society* 64 (2002): 69–125.

"Chan-Toon, Mrs." [Mabel Wodehouse-Pearse]. "For the Love of the King: A Burmese Play in Three Acts and Nine Scenes." *Hutchinson's Magazine* 5, no. 28 (1921): 349–55.

———. *For Love of the King: A Burmese Masque*. London: Methuen, 1922.

Chapman, John. "To Dr. Ducarel." In *Illustrations of the Literary History of the Eighteenth Century: Consisting of Authentic Memoirs and Original Letters of Eminent Persons, and Intended as a Sequel to the Literary Anecdotes*. Edited by John Nichols. Vol. 4, 571–72. London: Nichols, Son, and Bentley, 1822.

Charteris, Evan. *The Life and Letters of Sir Edmund Gosse*. New York: Harper and Brothers, 1931.

Chatterton, Thomas. "Chatterton's Will, 1770." In *A Supplement to the Miscellanies of Thomas Chatterton*. London: T. Becket, 1784.

———. *The Complete Poetical Works of Thomas Chatterton*. Edited by Henry D. Roberts. 2 vols. London: George Routledge and Sons, 1906.

———. *The Complete Works of Thomas Chatterton*. Edited by Donald S. Taylor and Benjamin B. Hoover. 2 vols. Oxford: Clarendon Press, 1971.

———. "The Execution of Sir Charles Baldwin." London: privately printed, 1772.

———. *The Poems of Thomas Chatterton*. Edited by Sidney Lee. 2 vols. London: Methuen, 1906.

———. *Poems, Supposed to Have Been Written at Bristol, by Thomas Rowley and Others, in the Fifteenth Century*. Edited by Lancelot Flower. Cambridge: B. Flower, 1794.

———. *Poems, Supposed to Have Been Written at Bristol, by Thomas Rowley, and Others, in the Fifteenth Century; the Greatest Part Now First Published from the Most Authentic Copies, with an Engraved Specimen of One of the MSS, to which Are Added, A Preface, an Introductory Account of the Several Pieces, and a Glossary.* Edited by Thomas Tyrwhitt. London: T. Payne, 1777.

———. *Poems, Supposed to Have Been Written at Bristol, by Thomas Rowley, and Others, in the Fifteenth Century: the Third Edition, to Which is Added an Appendix, Containing Some Observations upon the Language of These Poems; Tending to Prove That They Were Written, Not by Any Ancient Author, but Entirely by Thomas Chatterton.* London: T. Payne, 1778.

———. *The Poetical Works of Thomas Chatterton.* Edited by Walter W. Skeat. 2 vols. London: Bell and Daldy, 1871.

———. *The Poetical Works of Thomas Chatterton, with Notices of His Life, History of the Rowley Controversy, a Selection of His Letters, and Notes Critical and Explanatory.* Edited by C. B. Willcox. 2 vols. Cambridge: W. P. Grant, 1842.

———. *The Poetical Works of Thomas Chatterton, with Notices of His Life, History of the Rowley Controversy, a Selection of His Letters, Notes Critical and Explanatory, and a Glossary.* Edited by C. B. Willcox. 2nd ed. 2 vols. Boston: Little, Brown, 1857.

———. *The Rowley Poems.* Edited by M. E. Hare. Oxford: Clarendon Press, 1911.

———. *The Rowley Poems.* Edited by Richard Steele. 2 vols. London: Vale Press, 1898.

———. *The Works of Thomas Chatterton.* Edited by Joseph Cottle and Robert Southey. 3 vols. London: T. N. Longman and O. Rees, 1803.

"Chatterton, Thomas" [pseud.]. "The Jabberwock Traced to Its True Source." *Macmillan's Magazine* 25 (1872): 337–38.

Cieskowski, Krzysztof Z. "The Legend Makers: Chatterton, Wallis and Meredith." *History Today* 32, no. 11 (1982): 33–37.

Clare, John. *The Letters of John Clare.* Edited by Mark Storey. Oxford: Clarendon Press, 1985.

Clark, John. *An Answer to Mr. Shaw's Inquiry into the Authenticity of the Poems Ascribed to Ossian.* London: T. Longman and T. Cadell, 1781.

Cohen, William A. *Sex Scandal: The Private Parts of Victorian Fiction.* Durham, NC: Duke University Press, 1996.

Coleman, John. *Charles Reade as I Knew Him.* London: Traherne, 1903.

Coleridge, Samuel Taylor. *Biographia Literaria: or, My Literary Life and Opinions.* 2 vols. London: Rest Fenner, 1817.

———. *Biographia Literaria, or Biographical Sketches of My Literary Life and Opinions.* Edited by James Engell and W. Jackson Bate. In *The Collected Works of Samuel Taylor Coleridge.* Vol. 7. Bollingen Series LXXV. Princeton: Princeton University Press, 1983.

———. *Christabel: Kubla Khan, A Vision; The Pains of Sleep.* London: John Murray, 1816.

———. *The Complete Poetical Works of Samuel Taylor Coleridge.* Edited by E. H. Coleridge. 2 vols. Oxford: Clarendon Press, 1912.

———. "The Eolian Harp." In *Poems on Various Subjects.* London: C. G. and J. Robinsons, 1796.

———. *Lectures 1808–1819: On Literature.* Edited by R. A. Foakes. In *The Collected Works of Samuel Taylor Coleridge,* Vol. 7. Bollingen Series LXXV. Princeton: Princeton University Press, 1987.

———. "Monody on the Death of Chatterton." *Poetical Works II: Poems (Variorum Text): Part 1.* Edited by J. C. C. Mays. In *The Collected Works of Samuel Taylor Coleridge.* Vol. 16, 166–87. Bollingen Series LXXV. Princeton: Princeton University Press, 2001.

———. *Poetical Works.* 3 vols. London: W. Pickering, 1834.

———. *Poetical Works I: Poems (Reading Text): Part I.* Edited by J. C. C. Mays. In *The Collected Works of Samuel Taylor Coleridge.* Vol. 16. Bollingen Series LXXV. Princeton: Princeton University Press, 2001.

Collier, John Payne. "Early Manuscript Emendations of Shakespeare's Text." *Athenæum* 1266 (31 January 1852): 142–44.

———. *The History of English Dramatic Poetry to the Time of Shakespeare: And Annals of the Stage to the Restoration.* 2nd ed. 3 vols. London: G. Bell, 1879.

———. *Notes and Emendations to the Text of Shakespeare's Plays: From Early Manuscript Corrections in a Copy of the Folio, 1632, in the Possession of J. Payne Collier, Forming a Supplementary Volume to the Works of Shakespeare by the Same Editor, in Eight Volumes, Octavo.* London: Whittaker, 1853.

———. "To the Editor." *Times* (London), 7 July 1859: 9.

———. *Trilogy: Conversations between Three Friends on the Emendations of Shakespeare's Text Contained in Mr. Collier's Corrected Folio, 1632, and Employed by Recent Editors of the Poet's Works.* 3 vols. London: T. Richards, 1874.

Collins, Wilkie. *The Woman in White.* Edited by Maria K. Bachman. Peterborough, Ontario: Broadview Press, 2006.

Cook, Daniel. *Thomas Chatterton and Neglected Genius, 1760–1830.* Basingstoke: Palgrave Macmillan, 2013.

———. "Tyrwhitt's Rowley and Authorial Editing." *The Library: The Transactions of the Bibliographical Society* 11, no. 4 (2010): 447–67.

Cook, E. T. "An Art Critic and His Sententiæ." *Pall Mall Gazette,* 23 November 1885: 11–12.

Copinger, Walter Arthur. *The Law of Copyright, in Works of Literature and Art, Including That of Drama, Engraving, Music, Sculpture, Painting, Photography, and Ornamental and Useful Design, together with International and Foreign Copyright, with the Statutes Relating thereto, and References to the English and American Decisions.* London: Stevens and Haynes, 1870.

Cornwall, Barry [Bryan Waller Procter]. *Marcian Colonna: An Italian Tale with Three Dramatic Scenes and Other Poems.* London: John Warren and C. and J. Ollier, 1820.

Cottle, Joseph. *Early Recollections; Chiefly Relating to the Late Samuel Taylor Coleridge, during his Long Residence in Bristol.* London: Longman, Rees, 1837.

———. *Malvern Hills, with Minor Poems and Essays.* 4th ed. 2 vols. London: T. Cadell, 1829.

Cotton, Roger. *A Direction to the Waters of Lyfe.* London: Gabriell Simson and William White, 1592. Clark Library, PR2950 C85.

[Courthope, William John]. "The Latest Development of Literary Poetry: Swinburne—Rossetti—Morris." *Quarterly Review* 132 (1872): 59–84.

———. "Modern Culture." *Quarterly Review* 137 (1874): 389–415.

———. "The State of English Poetry." *Quarterly Review* 135 (1873): 1–21.

———. "Wordsworth and Gray." *Quarterly Review* 141 (1876): 104–36.

Cowley, Hannah. "A Monody." *Morning Post and Daily Advertiser*, 24 October 1778: 9.

Cox, R. G. "Victorian Criticism of Poetry: The Minority Tradition." *Scrutiny* 18 (1951): 2–17.

Craft, Christopher. "Alias Bunbury: Desire and Termination in *The Importance of Being Earnest*." *Representations* 31 (Summer 1990): 19–46.

Crane, Julie. "'Wandering between Two Worlds': The Victorian Afterlife of Thomas Chatterton." In *Romantic Echoes in the Victorian Era*. Edited by Andrew Radford and Mark Sandy, 27–37. Aldershot: Ashgate, 2008.

[Croft, Herbert]. *Love and Madness: In a Series of Letters, One of Which Contains the Original Account of Chatterton, a New Edition, Corrected*. London: G. Kearsley, 1786.

———. "A Letter from Denmark to Mr. Nichols, Printer of the *Gentleman's Magazine*, by the Rev. Sir Herbert Croft, Respecting an Unprovoked Attack Made upon Him during His Absence from England." *Gentleman's Magazine* 79 (1800): 99–104, 222–26, 322–25.

Curley, Thomas M. *Samuel Johnson, The Ossian Fraud, and the Celtic Revival in Great Britain and Ireland*. Cambridge: Cambridge University Press, 2009.

Curling, Jonathan. *Janus Weathercock: The Life and Times of Thomas Griffiths Wainewright, 1794–1847*. London: Thomas Nelson, 1938.

Dallas, E. S. *Poetics: An Essay on Poetry*. London: Smith, Elder, 1852.

[Dampier, Henry]. *Remarks upon the Eighth Section of the Second Volume of Mr. Warton's History of English Poetry*. London: T. Payne, 1778.

Damrosch, David, et al., eds. *Longman Anthology of British Literature*. 5th ed. Vol. 2. Harlow: Pearson Longman, 2012.

Danson, Lawrence. *Wilde's Intentions: The Artist in His Criticism*. Oxford: Oxford University Press, 1997.

Davis, John. *The Life of Thomas Chatterton*. London: T. Tegg, 1806.

De Quincey, Thomas. *Articles from the* Edinburgh Evening Post, Blackwood's Edinburgh Magazine, *and the* Edinburgh Literary Gazette, *1826–1829. The Works of Thomas De Quincey*. Edited by David Groves and Grevel Lindop. Vol. 4. London: Pickering and Chatto, 2000.

[———]. "Charles Lamb and His Friends." *North British Review* 10 (1848): 179–214.

[———]. "On Murder Considered as One of the Fine Arts." *Blackwood's Edinburgh Magazine* 20 (1827): 199–213.

[———]. "On the Knocking at the Gate in *Macbeth*." *London Magazine* 8 (October 1823): 353–56.

Dibb, Geoff. *Oscar Wilde, a Vagabond with a Mission: The Story of Wilde's Lecture Tours of Britain and Ireland*. London: Oscar Wilde Society, 2013.

Dickens, Charles. *Bleak House*. Edited by George Ford and Sylvère Monod. New York: Norton, 1977.

———. *The Letters of Charles Dickens*. Edited by Graham Storey and Kathleen Tillotson. The Pilgrim Edition. 12 vols. Oxford: Clarendon Press, 1965–2002.

Dix, John Ross. *The Life of Thomas Chatterton, Including His Unpublished Poems and Correspondence*. London: Hamilton, Adams, and Co., 1837.

Doran, John. *Their Majesties' Servants: Annals of the Stage, from Thomas Betterton to Edmund Kean*. Edited and revised by Robert Lowe. 3 vols. London: J. C. Nimmo, 1888.

Donoghue, Denis. "One Life Was Not Enough." *New York Times*, 17 January 1988, sec. 7.

Douglas, Alfred. *The True History of Shakespeare's Sonnets*. London: Martin Secker, 1933.

Dowden, Edward. *The Letters of Edward Dowden*. Edited by Elizabeth and Hilda Dowden. London: Dent and Sons, 1914.

——. *The Life of Percy Bysshe Shelley*. 2 vols. London: Kegan Paul, Trench, 1886.

——. *Poems*. London: Dent and Sons, 1914.

Downes, John. *Roscius Anglicanus, or, an Historical View of the Stage, from 1660 to 1706*. London: H. Playford, 1709.

Drone, Eaton S. *A Treatise on the Law of Property in Intellectual Productions in Great Britain and the United States: Embracing Copyright in Works of Literature and Art, and Playright in Dramatic and Musical Compositions*. Boston: Little, Brown, 1879.

Druce, Ernest. *Sonnets to a Lady*. London: J. Long, 1908.

Dryhurst, Nannie Florence. Letter to Alfred Robert Dryhurst, 22 November 1883. Clark Library, MS. 2013 010.

Dunn, Henry Treffry. *Recollections of Dante Gabriel Rossetti (Cheyne Walk Life)*. London: Elkin Mathews, 1904.

Eldredge, H. J. *The Stage Cyclopaedia*. London: "The Stage," 1909.

Ellinger, Esther Parker. *Thomas Chatterton: The Marvelous Boy*. Philadelphia: University of Pennsylvania Press, 1930.

Ellis, Havelock. *The Criminal*. New York: Scribner and Welford, 1890.

——. *A Study of British Genius*. London: Hurst and Blackett, 1904.

Ellmann, Richard. *Oscar Wilde*. New York: Alfred A. Knopf, 1988.

Elton, Oliver. *Survey of English Literature, 1780–1830*. 2 vols. London: Edward Arnold, 1912.

Emerson, Ralph Waldo. "The American Scholar." In *Nature, Addresses, and Lectures*. Edited by Robert E. Spiller and Alfred R. Ferguson. *The Collected Works of Ralph Waldo Emerson*. Vol. 1. Cambridge, MA: Belknap Press of Harvard University Press, 1971.

——. *Essays: Second Series*. Boston: Thurston, Torry, 1844.

——. *Essays: Second Series*. Edited by Alfred R. Ferguson and Jean Ferguson Carr. In *The Collected Works of Ralph Waldo* Emerson. Vol. 3. Cambridge, MA: Belknap Press of Harvard University Press, 1984.

——. "Self Reliance." In *Essays: First Series*. Edited by Joseph Ferguson, Alfred F. Carr, and Jean Ferguson. *The Collected Works of Ralph Waldo Emerson*. Vol. 2. Cambridge, MA: Belknap Press of Harvard University Press, 1980.

——. "Shakespeare, or the Poet." In *Representative Men: Seven Lectures*. Edited by Wallace E. Williams and Douglas Emory Wilson. *The Collected Works of Ralph Waldo Emerson*. Vol. 4. Cambridge, MA: Belknap Press of Harvard University Press, 1987.

Escott, T. H. S. "Walter Pater and Other Memories." *The Bookman's Journal and Print Collector* 10 (1924): 110–11.

Eyre-Todd, George. "Introduction." In *Poems of Ossian, Translated by James Macpherson*. Edited by G. Eyre-Todd, ix–lxix. London: Walter Scott, 1888.

Fawcett, Edgar. "To Oscar Wilde: On Receiving from Him a Book of His Poems." In *Song and Story: Later Poems*, 181. Boston: James R. Osgood, 1884.

Finney, Brian. *English Fiction since 1984*. Basingstoke: Palgrave Macmillan, 2006.

Finzi, John Charles. *Oscar Wilde and His Literary Circle: A Catalog of Manuscripts and Letters in the William Andrews Clark Memorial Library*. Berkeley: Published for the Library by the University of California Press, 1957.

Flaubert, Gustave. *Correspondance, deuxième série (1850–1854)*. Paris: Charpentier, 1889.

Fletcher, Ian. *Rediscovering Herbert Horne: Poet, Architect, Typographer, Historian*. Greensboro, NC: ELT Press, 1990.

Forman, Harry Buxton. *Poetry and Prose by John Keats: A Book of Fresh Verses and New Readings—Essays and Letters Lately Found—and Passages Formerly Suppressed*. London: Reeves and Turner, 1890.

Forman, M. Buxton. "Preface." In *Letters of Fanny Brawne to Fanny Keats, 1820–1824*. Edited by Fred Edgcumbe, v–vii. New York: Oxford University Press, 1937.

Freeman, Arthur, and Janet Ing Freeman. *John Payne Collier: Scholarship and Forgery in the Nineteenth Century*. 2 vols. New Haven: Yale University Press, 2004.

Fussell, Paul. *Theory of Prosody in Eighteenth-Century England*. New London: Connecticut College, 1954.

"G." "The Long Arm of Coincidence." *Scots Observer*, 6 October 1890: 410–11.

Gagnier, Regenia. *Idylls of the Marketplace: Oscar Wilde and the Victorian Public*. Stanford, CA: Stanford University Press, 1986.

Gainsbourg, Serge. "Chatterton." *Comic Strip*. Island Records, 1997.

Galton, Arthur. "Ancient Legends of Ireland by Lady Wilde." *Century Guild Hobby Horse* 1, no. 6 (April 1887): 67–74.

Ganzel, Dewey. *Fortune and Men's Eyes: The Career of John Payne Collier*. Oxford: Oxford University Press, 1982.

Gardner, Anthony. "The Oscar Wilde Forgeries." http://www.anthonygardner.co.uk/features /oscar_wilde.html.

Gardner, Averil. "'Literary Petty Larceny': Plagiarism in Oscar Wilde's Early Poetry." *English Studies in Canada* 8, no. 1 (1982): 49–61.

Gautier, Théophile. "Préface." In *Mademoiselle de Maupin*, 1–35. Paris: Charpentier, 1875.

———. "Reprise de Chatterton (en Décembre 1857)." In *Histoire du romantisme*, 152–61. Paris: Bibliothèque Charpentier, 1905.

———. *Histoire de l'art dramatique en France depuis vingt-cinq ans*. Brussels: Librarie Universelle, 1859.

George, William. *New Facts Relating to the Chatterton Family, Gathered from Manuscript Entries in a "History of the Bible," Which Once Belonged to the Parents of Thomas Chatterton the Poet and from Parish Registers*. Bristol: privately printed, 1883.

Gilbert, W. S. *Patience, Or, Bunthorne's Bride!* London: Chappell, 1882.

Gilchrist, Alexander. *William Blake, "Pictor Ignotus": With Selections from His Poems and Other Writings*. 2 vols. London: Macmillan, 1863.

Gillespie, Michael Patrick. *Oscar Wilde and the Poetics of Ambiguity*. Gainesville: University Press of Florida, 1996.

Gittings, Robert. "Keats and Chatterton." *Keats-Shelley Journal* 4 (1955): 47–54.

Glassford, James. *Chatterton's Ella, and Other Pieces Interpreted: Or, Selection from the Rowley Poems, in Modern Reading*. Edinburgh: privately printed, 1837.

Goethe, Johann-Wolfgang von. *Die Leiden des jungen Werthers*. Leipzig: Weygand, 1775.

Goodridge, John. *John Clare and Community.* Cambridge: Cambridge University Press, 2013.

Gordon, I. A. "The Case-History of Coleridge's *Monody on the Death of Chatterton.*" *Review of English Studies* 18, no. 69 (January 1942): 49–71.

Gorman, Herbert S. "Arthur Rimbaud, Who Could Supersede Himself." *New York Times Book Review,* 21 December 1924: 20.

Gosse, Edmund. *History of Eighteenth Century Literature, 1660–1780.* London: Macmillan, 1889.

———. "A Plea for Certain Exotic Forms of Verse." *Cornhill Magazine* 36 (1877): 53–71.

———. Review of *Letters of John Keats to Fanny Brawne. Academy,* 9 February 1878: 111–12.

Grattan, Francis William. *Thomas Chatterton, the Marvelous Boy in the Foes and Woes of a Poet.* Astoria, NY: J. Falez Odewadell, 1918.

Greenblatt, Stephen, et al., eds. *Norton Anthology of English Literature.* 9th ed. Vol. 2. New York: Norton, 2012.

Greene, Edward Burnaby. *Strictures upon a Pamphlet Intitled, Cursory Observations on the Poems Attributed to Rowley, a Priest of the Fifteenth Century, with a Postscript.* London: J. Stockdale, 1782.

Greenstreet, James. "Blackfriars Theatre in the Time of Shakespeare." *Athenæum* 3224 (August 1889): 203–4.

Gregory, G[eorge]. *The Life of Thomas Chatterton, with Criticisms of His Genius and Writings, and a Concise View of the Controversy Concerning Rowley's Poems.* London: G. Kearsley, 1789.

———. "Thomas Chatterton." In *Biographia Britannica; or, the Lives of the Most Eminent Persons Who Have Flourished in Great Britain and Ireland from the Earliest Ages, to the Present Times.* 2nd ed. Vol. 4, 573–619. London: Rivington, 1789.

Groom, Nick. "The Case against Chatterton's 'Lines to Walpole' and 'Last Verses.'" *Notes and Queries* 50 (2003): 278–80.

———. "The Death of Chatterton." In *From Gothic to Romantic: Thomas Chatterton's Bristol.* Edited by Alistair Heys, 116–26. Bristol: Redcliffe Press, 2005.

———. *The Forger's Shadow: How Forgery Changed the Course of Literature.* London: Picador, 2002.

———. "'I Am Nothing': A Typology of the Forger from Chatterton to Wilde." In *The Victorians and the Eighteenth Century: Reassessing the Tradition.* Edited by Francis O'Gorman and Katherine Turner, 203–22. Aldershot: Ashgate, 2004.

———. "Introduction." In *Thomas Chatterton and Romantic Culture.* Edited by Groom, 3–11. Basingstoke: Macmillan, 1999.

———. "Love and Madness: Southey Editing Chatterton." In *Robert Southey and the Contexts of English Romanticism.* Edited by Lynda Pratt, 19–36. Aldershot: Ashgate, 2006.

———. *The Making of Percy's Reliques.* Oxford: Clarendon Press, 1999.

———, ed. *Thomas Chatterton and Romantic Culture.* New York: St. Martin's; Basingstoke: Macmillan, 1999.

Gurley, E. W. *Scrapbooks and How to Make Them.* New York: The Authors' Publishing Company, 1880.

Guy, Josephine M. "An Allusion in Oscar Wilde's 'The Canterville Ghost.'" *Notes and Queries* 45, no. 2 (1998): 224–26.

——. "Introduction." In *Criticism: Historical Criticism, Intentions, The Soul of Man. The Complete Works of Oscar Wilde.* Vol. 4, xix–lxxxvi. Oxford: Oxford University Press, 2007.

——. "Oscar Wilde's Self-Plagiarism: Some New Manuscript Evidence." *Notes and Queries* 52, no. 4 (December 2005): 485–88.

——. "Self-Plagiarism, Creativity and Craftsmanship in Oscar Wilde." *English Literature in Transition, 1880–1920* 41, no. 1 (1998): 6–23.

——. "'Trafficking with Merchants for His Soul': Dante Gabriel Rossetti among the Aesthetes." *Proceedings of the British Academy* 105 (1999): 171–86.

Guy, Josephine M., and Ian Small. *Oscar Wilde's Profession: Writing and the Culture Industry in the Late Nineteenth Century.* Oxford: Oxford University Press, 2000.

Hackwood, Frederick William. *Notes of Lessons on Moral Subjects: A Handbook for Teachers in Elementary Schools.* London: T. Nelson and Sons, 1883.

Hake, Gordon. *Memoirs of Eighty Years.* London: Richard Bentley, 1892.

Hake, Thomas, and Arthur Compton-Rickett. *The Life and Letters of Theodore Watts-Dunton.* 2 vols. London: T. C. and E. C. Jack, 1916.

Hall, Mrs. S. C. *Pilgrimages to English Shrines.* London: Arthur, Hall, Virtue, 1850.

Hallam, Henry. *Introduction to the Literature of Europe in the Fifteenth, Sixteenth and Seventeenth Centuries.* 4 vols. London: John Murray, 1837.

Halpern, Richard. *Shakespeare's Perfume: Sodomy and Sublimity in the Sonnets, Wilde, Freud, and Lacan.* Philadelphia: University of Pennsylvania Press, 2002.

Hamilton, N. E. S. A. *An Inquiry into the Genuineness of the Manuscript Corrections in Mr. J. Payne Collier's Annotated Shakspere, Folio, 1632: And of Certain Shaksperian Documents Likewise Published by Mr. Collier.* London: R. Bentley, 1860.

——. "To the Editor of *The Times.*" *Times* (London), 2 July 1859: 12.

Hamilton, Walter. *The Aesthetic Movement in England.* London: Reeves and Turner, 1882.

Hardinge, George. *The Genius of Chatterton: An Irregular Ode, Written on the Supposition of His Being the Author of the Poems Attributed to Thomas Rowley in the Fifteenth Century.* London: T. Becket, 1788.

[Hardinge, George]. *Rowley and Chatterton in the Shades: or, Nugæ Antiquæ et Novæ—A New Elysian Interlude in Prose and Verse.* London: T. Becket, 1782.

Hardy, Thomas. *The Literary Notebooks of Thomas Hardy.* Edited by Lennart A. Björk. 2 vols. New York: New York University Press, 1985.

——. *A Pair of Blue Eyes. Tinsley's Magazine* 11 (1872–1873): 122–45, 242–62, 362–82, 482–500, 601–20; 12 (1873): ix–xxi, 122–42, 242–60, 362–82, 481–501, 602–20.

——. *A Pair of Blue Eyes.* 3 vols. London: Tinsley, 1873.

——. *The Woodlanders. Macmillan's Magazine* 54 (1886): 63–80, 81–99, 222–40, 301–20, 385–400, 466–80; 55 (1886–1887): 1–18, 81–96, 224–40, 306–20, 385–400, 407–28.

——. *The Woodlanders.* 3 vols. London: Macmillan, 1887.

Harmon, Maryhelen C. "Melville's 'Borrowed Personage': Bartleby and Thomas Chatterton." *ESQ: A Journal of the American Renaissance* 33, no. 1 (1987): 35–44.

Harris, Frank. *Contemporary Portraits.* London: Methuen, 1915.

Hayley, William. *An Essay on Epic Poetry; in Five Epistles, to the Revd. Mr. Mason with Notes.* London: J. Dodsley, 1782.

Haywood, Ian. *The Making of History: A Study of the Literary Forgeries of James Macpherson and Thomas Chatterton.* London: Associated University Press, 1986.

Hazlitt, W. Carew. "Introduction." In *Essays and Criticisms* by Thomas Griffiths Wainewright. Edited by W. Carew Hazlitt, ix–lxxxi. London: Reeves and Turner, 1880.

Hazlitt, William. *Lectures on the English Poets: Delivered at the Surrey Institution.* London: Taylor and Hessey, 1818.

——. *Lectures on the English Poets and the English Comic Writers.* Edited by William Carew Hazlitt. London: Bell and Daldy, 1869.

——. *The Selected Writings of William Hazlitt.* Edited by Duncan Wu. 9 vols. London: Pickering and Chatto, 1998.

Heath, George. *The History of Antiquities, Survey and Description of the City and Suburbs of Bristol; or Complete Guide.* Bristol: W. Matthews, 1797.

Hellman, Geoffrey T. "The Steward of Strawberry Hill I." *New Yorker*, 6 August 1949: 26–38.

——. "The Steward of Strawberry Hill II." *New Yorker*, 13 August 1949: 31–38.

Heron-Allen, Edward. "The Cheiromancy of To-Day: The Evolution of an Occult Science." *Lippincott's Monthly Magazine* 46, no. 271 (July 1890): 102–10.

——. *Chiromancy, or the Science of Palmistry.* London: Routledge and Sons, 1883.

——. *Codex Chiromantiae: Appendix A, Dactylomancy, or, Finger-ring Magic, Ancient, Mediaeval, and Modern.* London: Sette of Odd Volumes, 1883.

——. *Codex Chiromantiae: Appendix B, A Discourse Concerning Autographs and Their Significations.* London: Sette of Odd Volumes, 1886.

——. *Codex Chiromantiae: Being a Compleate Manualle of ye Science and Arte of Expoundynge ye past, ye Presente, ye Future, and ye Charactere, by ye Scrutinie of ye Hande, ye Gestures thereof, and ye Chirographie.* London: Sette of Odd Volumes, 1883.

——. *A Manual of Cheirosophy: Being a Complete Practical Handbook of the Twin Sciences of Cheirognomy and Cheiromancy, by Means whereof the Past, the Present, and the Future May Be Read in the Formations of the Hands, Preceded by an Introductory Argument upon the Science of Cheirosophy and Its Claims to Rank as a Physical Science.* 10th ed. London: Ward, Lock, 1885.

Herrick, Robert. *Hesperides.* Edited by Herbert Horne. London: Walter Scott, 1887.

Hewlett, Dorothy. *A Life of John Keats.* New York: Hurst and Blackwell, 1949.

Hichens, Robert. *The Green Carnation.* London: W. Heinemann, 1894.

Holland, Merlin. *Irish Peacock and Scarlet Marquess: The Real Trial of Oscar Wilde.* London: Fourth Estate, 2003.

——. "Plagiarist, or Pioneer?" In *Rediscovering Oscar Wilde.* Edited by George Sandulescu, 193–213. Gerrards Cross: Colin Smythe, 1994.

Hollingshead, John. *Gaiety Chronicles.* London: Archibald Constable, 1898.

Holmes, Richard. "Thomas Chatterton: The Case Re-Opened." *Cornhill* 178 (1970): 205–51.

Horne, Herbert. "A—Further—Meditation for His Mistress." *Century Guild Hobby Horse* 1, no. 2 (April 1886): 47.

——. "A Study of Certain Buildings Designed by Inigo Jones and yet Remaining in London." *Century Guild Hobby Horse* 1, no. 4 (October 1886): 123–39.

———. "Nescio quæ nugarum, No. I: At the Charterhouse." *Century Guild Hobby Horse* 1, no. 2 (April 1886): 77–79.

Horwood, A. J. "A Sonnet by Keats." *Athenæum* 2536 (3 June 1876): 764.

Hotten, John Camden. "Introduction: Wainewright, the Poisoner." In Charles Dickens, *Hunted Down: A Story*, 5–28. London: John Camden Hotten, 1870.

Howe, Percival P. *The Life of William Hazlitt.* New York: George H. Doran, 1922.

Hume, David. "Essay on the Genuineness of the Poems." In John Hill Burton. *Life and Correspondence of David Hume: From the Papers Bequeathed by His Nephew to the Royal Society of Scotland, and Other Original Sources.* 2 vols. 1:471–80. Edinburgh: W. Tait, 1846.

———. "To Hugh Blair, 19 September 1763." In *Report of the Committee of the Highland Society of Scotland Appointed to Inquire into the Nature and Authenticity of the Poems of Ossian.* Edited by Henry Mackenzie, 4–8. Edinburgh: A. Constable, 1805.

Hunt, Leigh. "To Charles Lamb." In *Foliage: or, Poems Original and Translated*, cviii–cxiv. London: C. and J. Ollier, 1818.

[———.] "Young Poets." *Examiner*, 1 December 1816: 761–62.

Hunt, William Holman. *Pre-Raphaelitism and the Pre-Raphaelite Brotherhood.* 2 vols. London: Macmillan, 1905.

Huxtable, Sally-Anne. "Re-reading the Green Dining Room." In *Rethinking the Interior, c. 1867–1896.* Edited by Jason Edwards and Imogen Hart, 25–40. Farnham: Ashgate, 2010.

Hyett, F. A., and W. Bazeley, eds. *Chattertoniana.* Gloucester: John Bellows, 1914.

Image, Selwyn. "On the Representation of the Nude." *Century Guild Hobby Horse* 1, no. 1 (January 1886): 8–13.

———. "On the Unity of Art." *Century Guild Hobby Horse* 1, no. 5 (January 1887): 2–8.

Ingleby, C. Mansfield. *A Complete View of the Shakspere Controversy, Concerning the Authenticity and Genuineness of Manuscript Matter Affecting the Works and Biography of Shakspere, Pub. by Mr. J. Payne Collier as the Fruits of His Researches.* London: Nattali and Bond, 1861.

———. *The Shakespeare Fabrications, or, the MS. Notes of the Perkins Folio Shown to Be of Recent Origin, with an Appendix on the Authorship of the Ireland Forgeries.* London: John Russell Smith, 1859.

Ingram, John H. "Chatterton and His Associates." *Harper's New Monthly Magazine* 67 (1883): 225–40.

———. *Chatterton and His Poetry.* London: G. G. Harrap, 1916.

———. "To the Editor." *Athenæum* 2825 (17 December 1881): 813.

———. *The True Chatterton: A New Study from Original Documents.* London: T. Fisher Unwin, 1910.

Ireland, Samuel. *An Investigation of Mr. Malone's Claim to the Character of Scholar, or Critic, Being an Examination of His Inquiry into the Authenticity of the Shakspeare Manuscripts.* London: R. Faulder, and Others, 1796.

———. *Miscellaneous Papers and Legal Instruments under the Hand and Seal of William Shakspeare: Including the Tragedy of King Lear, and a Small Fragment of Hamlet, from the Original MSS.* Edited by Samuel Ireland. London: Cooper and Graham, 1796.

Ireland, William-Henry. *An Authentic Account of the Shaksperian Manuscripts*. London: J. Debrett, 1796.

———. *The Confessions of William-Henry Ireland: Containing the Particulars of His Fabrication of the Shakspeare Manuscripts, together with Anecdotes and Opinions (Hitherto Unpublished) of Many Distinguished Persons in the Literary, Political, and Theatrical World*. London: Ellerton and Byworth, 1805.

———. *Neglected Genius: Illustrating the Untimely and Unfortunate Fate of Many British Poets, from the Period of Henry the Eighth to the Era of the Unfortunate Chatterton*. London: G. Cowie, 1812.

———. *Vortigern: An Historical Play, with an Original Preface. Represented at the Theatre Royal, Drury Lane, on Saturday, April 2, 1796, as a Supposed Newly-Discovered Drama of Shakspeare*. London: J. Thomas, 1832.

J.B. [Broughton, John]. "Preface." In *Miscellanies in Prose and Verse by Thomas Chatterton: The Supposed Author of the Poems Published under the Names of Rowley, Canning, &c.*, ix–xxiii. London: Fielding and Walker, 1778.

Jefferson, Thomas. *Jefferson's Literary Commonplace Book*. Edited by Douglas L. Wilson. Princeton: Princeton University Press, 1989.

Johnson, R. V. "Pater and the Victorian Anti-Romantics." *Essays in Criticism* 4 (1964): 42–57.

Johnson, Samuel. "The Criterions of Plagiarism. No. 143." In *The Rambler*. Edited by W. J. Bate and Albrecht B. Strauss. *The Yale Edition of the Works of Samuel Johnson*. Vol. 4, 393–401. New Haven: Yale University Press, 1979.

———. *Dictionary of the English Language: In Which the Words are Deduced from their Originals, and Illustrated in Their Different Significations by Examples from the Best Writers, to Which Are Prefixed, a History of the Language, and an English Grammar*. 2 vols. London: W. Strahan, 1755.

———. *A Journey to the Western Islands of Scotland*. London: W. Strahan and T. Cadell, 1775.

Jones, Henry Arthur [and Henry Herman]. "Chatterton." In *One-Act Plays for Stage and Study*. Edited by Zona Gale, 17–37. New York: Samuel French, 1943.

Jonson, Ben. *Poetaster, or, The Arraignment*. In *The Devil Is an Ass and Other Plays*. Edited by Margaret Jane Kidnie, 1–101. Oxford: Oxford University Press, 2000.

Jowett, Benjamin. *The Dialogues of Plato, Translated into English with Analyses and Introductions*. Translated by B. Jowett. 2nd ed. 5 vols. Oxford: Clarendon Press, 1875.

Kaplan, Louise J. *The Family Romance of the Impostor-Poet Thomas Chatterton*. New York: Atheneum, 1988.

Keats, John. *Complete Poems*. Edited by Jack Stillinger. Cambridge, MA: Harvard University Press, 1978.

———. *The Letters of John Keats, 1814–1821*. Edited by Hyder Edward Rollins. 2 vols. Cambridge, MA: Harvard University Press, 1958.

———. *Letters of John Keats to Fanny Brawne Written in the Years MDCCCXIX and MDCCCXX*. Edited by Harry Buxton Forman. London: Reeves and Turner, 1878.

———. *Life, Letters, and Literary Remains*. Edited by Richard Monckton Milnes. 2 vols. London: Edward Moxon, 1848.

——. *The Poetical Works and Other Writings of John Keats, Now First Brought together, Including Poems and Numerous Letters Not before Published.* Edited by Harry Buxton Forman. 4 vols. London: Reeves and Turner, 1883.

Knight, Joseph. *Life of Dante Gabriel Rossetti.* London: Walter Scott, 1887.

Knox, Vicesimus. *Essays Moral and Literary: A New Edition.* 2 vols. London: Charles Dilly, 1782.

Lacy, Ernest. *The Bard of Mary Redcliffe.* Philadelphia: Sherman, 1916.

——. *Chatterton.* In *Plays and Sonnets.* Philadelphia: Sherman, 1900.

Laing, Malcolm. "Preface." In *The Poems of Ossian, &c., Containing the Poetical Works of James Macpherson, Esq.* 3 vols., 1:vii–xvii. Edinburgh: A. Constable, 1805.

Lamb, Charles. *The Letters of Charles Lamb, to Which Are Added Those of His Sister, Mary Lamb.* Edited by E. V. Lucas. 3 vols. London: J. M. Dent and Methuen, 1935.

[Lang, Andrew]. Review of "The Portrait of Mr. W.H." *Daily News* (London), 29 June 1889: 1.

Lang, Andrew. "Literary Plagiarism." *Contemporary Review* 51 (1887): 831–40.

Lang, Cecil Y. "Swinburne on Keats: A Fragment on an Essay." *Modern Language Notes* 64 (1949): 168–71.

Last and Sons. Letter to the Editor of the *Pall Mall Gazette,* 19 November 1886. British Library, Add. MS 81648.

Le Gallienne, Richard. *The Romantic '90s.* New York: Doubleday, Page, 1925.

Lee, Sidney. "Shakespeare and the Earl of Pembroke." *Fortnightly Review* n.s. 63 (1898): 210–23.

Lefébure, Ernest. *Embroidery and Lace: Their Manufacture and History from the Remotest Antiquity to the Present Day—a Handbook for Amateurs, Collectors, and General Readers.* Translated by Alan S. Cole. London: H. Grevel, 1888.

Leslie, Shane. *Memoir of John Edward Courtenay Bodley.* London: Jonathan Cape, 1930.

Lewis, Lloyd, and Henry Justin Smith. *Oscar Wilde Discovers America (1882).* New York: Harcourt, Brace, 1936.

Lewis, Roger. "A Misattribution: Oscar Wilde's 'Unpublished Sonnet on Chatterton.'" *Victorian Poetry* 28, no. 2 (1990): 164–69.

Lewis, Wilmarth S. *Collector's Progress.* New York: Knopf, 1951.

Lloyd, Fabian. "Collection of Manuscript Letters, Essays, Poems, and Plays, Accompanied by Dealers' and Experts' Correspondence Regarding These Particular Manuscripts. 1887–1900." Clark Library, W6721M C697.

Lonsdale, Roger, ed. *The Poems of Thomas Gray, William Collins and Oliver Goldsmith.* London: Longman, 1969.

[Lucy, Henry]. "Our Booking Office." *Punch,* 5 January 1889, 12.

[Macaulay, George]. "New Views of Shakespeare's Sonnets: The 'Other Poet' Identified." *Blackwood's Edinburgh Magazine* 135 (1884): 727–60; 137 (1885): 774–800; 139 (1886): 327–50.

Macfarlane, Robert. *Original Copy: Plagiarism in Nineteenth-Century Literature.* Oxford: Oxford University Press, 2007.

Mackay, Charles. "A Tangled Skein Unravelled: On the Mystery of Shakespeare's Sonnets." *Nineteenth Century* 16 (1884): 238–62.

Mackenzie, Henry. *Report of the Committee of the Highland Society of Scotland Appointed to Inquire into the Nature and Authenticity of the Poems of Ossian.* Edinburgh: A. Constable, 1805.

Mackie, Gregory. "Forging Oscar Wilde: Mrs. Chan-Toon and *For Love of the King.*" *English Literature in Transition, 1880–1920* 54, no. 3 (2011): 267–88.

Mackmurdo, Arthur H. "The Guild Flag's Unfurling." *Century Guild Hobby Horse* 1 (1884): 2–13.

——. "Notes on the National Gallery: Giotto." *Century Guild Hobby Horse* 1, no. 1 (January 1886): 34–39.

Macpherson, James. "A Critical Dissertation on the Poems of Ossian, the Son of Fingal." In *The Works of Ossian, the Son of Fingal, Translated from the Galic Language by James Macpherson.* 3rd ed. Vol. 1, i–xlii. London: T. Becket and P. A. De Hondt, 1765.

——. *Fragments of Ancient Poetry, Collected in the Highlands of Scotland, and Translated from the Galic or Erse Language.* Edinburgh: J. Hamilton and G. Balfour, 1760.

——. *The Poems of Ossian and Related Works.* Edited by Hugh Gaskill. Edinburgh: Edinburgh University Press, 1996.

——. *Temora, An Ancient Epic Poem, in Eight Books: Together with Several Other Poems, Composed by Ossian, the Son of Fingal.* London: T. A. Becket and P. A. De Hondt, 1763.

Maitland, Thomas [Robert Buchanan]. "The Fleshly School of Poetry." *Contemporary Review* 18 (1871): 334–50.

Mallon, Thomas. *Stolen Words: Forays into the Origins and Ravages of Plagiarism.* New York: Ticknor and Fields, 1989.

Malone, Dumas. *Jefferson the Virginian.* In *Jefferson and His Time.* Vol. 1. Boston: Little, Brown, 1948–1981.

[Malone, Edmond]. *Cursory Observations on the Poems Attributed to Thomas Rowley, A Priest of the Fifteenth Century, with Some Remarks on the Commentaries on Those Poems, by the Rev. Dr. Jeremiah Milles, Dean of Exeter, and Jacob Bryant, Esq; and a Salutary Proposal Addressed to those Gentlemen.* London: J. Nichols, 1782.

Malone, Edmond. "A Dissertation of the Three Parts of King Henry VI." In *The Plays and Poems of Shakespeare: With the Corrections and Illustrations of Various Commentators—Comprehending a Life of the Poet, and an Enlarged History of the Stage.* Vol. 18, 553–97. London: F. C. and J. Rivington, 1821.

——. *An Inquiry into the Authenticity of Certain Miscellaneous Papers and Legal Instruments, Published Dec. 24, MDCCXCV, and Attributed to Shakspeare, Queen Elizabeth, and Henry, Earl of Southampton.* London: T. Cadell Jr. and W. Davies, 1796.

——, ed. *The Plays and Poems of William Shakspeare: In Sixteen Volumes; Collated Verbatim with the Most Authentick Copies, and Revised: With the Corrections and Illustrations of Various Commentators; to Which Are Added, an Essay on the Chronological Order of His Plays; an Essay Relative to Shakspeare and Jonson; a Dissertation on the Three Parts of King Henry VI, an Historical Account of the English Stage.* 16 vols. Dublin: John Exshaw, 1794.

——. *Supplement to the Edition of Shakspeare's Plays Published in 1778 by Samuel Johnson and George Steevens: Containing Additional Observations, to Which Are Subjoined the Genuine Poems of the Same Author, and Seven Plays That Have Been Ascribed to Him; with Notes by the Editor and Others.* 2 vols. London: C. Bathurst, and Others, 1780.

———. *The Works of Shakespeare: The Text Regulated by the Recently Discovered Folio of 1632, Containing Early Manuscript Emendations with a History of the Stage, a Life of the Poet, and an Introduction to Each Play, to Which Are Added Glossarial and Other Notes and the Readings of Former Editions.* New York: Redfield, 1853.

Manley, John Matthews. *English Prose and Poetry.* Boston: Ginn, 1916.

Manson, Edward. "Recollections of Walter Pater." *Oxford Magazine* 25 (1906): 60–61.

Marmion, Shackerley. *The Dramatic Works of Shackerley Marmion.* Edited by James Maidment and W. H. Logan. Edinburgh: W. Paterson, 1875.

Marsh, Jan. *Dante Gabriel Rossetti: Painter and Poet.* London: Weidenfeld and Nicolson, 1999.

———. "The Portrait: 'Dante Gabriel Rossetti' by Theodore Watts-Dunton." *National Portrait Gallery.* http://www.npg.org.uk/collections/search/portraitExtended/mw05468/Dante-Gabriel-Rossetti-Theodore-Watts-Dunton (accessed 25 May, 2013).

Martial [Marcus Valerius Martialis]. *Epigrammata.* Edited and translated by D. R. Shackleton Bailey. 3 vols. Stuttgart: Teubner, 1990.

Martin, Frederick. "Memoir." In *Poems of Thomas Chatterton.* Edited by Frederick Martin, ix–xlvi. London: Charles Griffin, 1865.

Martin, Helena Saville Faucit, Lady. *On Some of Shakespeare's Female Characters: Ophelia, Portia, Desdemona, Juliet, Imogen, Rosalind, Beatrice, Hermione.* 3rd ed. London: Blackwood, 1888.

Martin, Peter. *Edmond Malone, Shakespearean Scholar: A Literary Biography.* Cambridge: Cambridge University Press, 1995.

Mason, Stuart [Christopher Millard]. *Art and Morality: A Record of the Discussion Which Followed the Publication of "Dorian Gray."* 2nd ed. London: Frank Palmer, 1912.

———. *Bibliography of Oscar Wilde.* London: T. Werner Laurie, 1914.

———. *Impressions of America.* Sunderland: Keystone Press, 1906.

Massey, Gerald. *Shakspeare's Sonnets Never before Interpreted: His Private Friends Identified, together with a Recovered Likeness of Himself.* London: Longmans, Green, 1866.

———. *The Secret Drama of Shakespeare's Sonnets, with the Characters Identified.* London: privately printed, 1872; London: Kegan Paul, Trench, 1888.

Masson, David. *Chatterton: A Story of the Year 1770.* 2nd ed. London: Macmillan, 1874.

———. "Chatterton: A Story of the Year 1770." In *Essays Biographical and Critical: Chiefly on English Poets,* 178–345. Cambridge: Macmillan, 1856.

———. "Chatterton: A Story of the Year 1770." *Dublin University Magazine* 38 (1851): 1–17, 178–92, 420–35.

Matthews, Brander. "The Ethics of Plagiarism." *Longman's Magazine* (October 1886): 633.

McGann, Jerome J. "Infatuated Worlds." *London Review of Books* 16, no. 18 (22 September 1994): 6–7.

———. "The Infatuated Worlds of Thomas Chatterton." In *Early Romantics: Perspectives in British Poetry from Pope to Wordsworth.* Edited by Thomas Woodman, 233–41. Basingstoke: Macmillan, 1998.

Mendelssohn, Michèle. *Henry James, Oscar Wilde, and Aesthetic Culture.* Edinburgh: Edinburgh University Press, 2007.

Meyerstein, E. H. W. *A Life of Thomas Chatterton.* New York: Charles Scribner's Sons, 1930.

Milles, Jeremiah. "Preliminary Dissertation." In *Poems Supposed to Have Been Written at Bristol by Thomas Chatterton,* 1–32. London: T. Payne, 1782.

Mitchell, Rebecca N. "Robert Herrick, Victorian Poet: Christina Rossetti, George Meredith, and the Victorian Recovery of *Hesperides.*" *Modern Philology* 113, no. 1 (August 2015).

["M.M.D."]. "On the Genius of Spenser, and the Spenserian School of Poetry." *European Magazine and London Review* 82 (1822): 333–41, 431–40.

Moir, D. M. *Sketches of the Poetical Literature of the Past Half Century.* Edinburgh: William Blackwood, 1851.

Moore, Dafydd, ed. *Ossian and Ossianism.* 4 vols. London: Routledge, 2004.

[Mowbray, Morris]. "Thomas Chatterton." *Quarterly Review* 150 (1880): 78–110.

Murphy, J. D. "Additions and Corrections to Horst Schroeder's *Additions and Corrections to Richard Ellmann's* Oscar Wilde." *The Wildean* 24 (2004): 72–75.

Murray, Christopher D. "D. G. Rossetti, A. C. Swinburne and R. W. Buchanan: The Fleshly School Revisited, I and II." *Bulletin of the John Rylands Library* 65, no. 1 (1982): 206–32 and 65, no. 2 (1983): 176–207.

[Napier, Alexander]. "The Life and Works of John Keats." *Edinburgh Review* 162 (1885): 1–36.

Navarre, Joan. "Oscar Wilde, Edward Heron-Allen, and the Palmistry Craze of the 1880s." *English Literature in Transition, 1880–1920* 54, no. 2 (2011): 174–84.

Nevill, John Cranstoun. *Thomas Chatterton.* London: F. Muller, 1930.

Newbolt, Henry. *My World as in My Time.* London: Faber and Faber, 1932.

Noel, Roden. *Essays on Poetry and Poets.* London: Kegan Paul, Trench, 1886.

Nordau, Max. *Degeneration.* New York: D. Appleton, 1895.

North, Michael. "The Picture of Oscar Wilde." *PMLA* 125, no. 1 (2010): 185–91.

O'Connor, Maureen. "The Spectre of Genre in 'The Canterville Ghost.'" *Irish Studies Review* 12, no. 3 (2004): 329–38.

O'Kearney, Nicholas. "Introduction" to "The Battle of Gabhra: Garristown in the County of Dublin, Fought in A.D. 283." In *Transactions of the Ossianic Society, for the Year 1853.* Vol. 1., 9–67. Dublin: Printed under the Direction of the Council, 1854–1864.

[Oliphant, Margaret]. "Review of Wilson's *Chatterton.*" *Blackwood's Edinburgh Magazine* 107 (1870): 453–76.

Orrock, James. *Repeats and Plagiarisms in Art, 1888.* London: privately published, 1889.

O'Sullivan, Vincent. *Aspects of Wilde.* London: Constable, 1936.

Owlett, F. C. *Chatterton's Apology.* Hoddesdon, Herts.: Thomas Knight, 1930.

Pater, Walter. *Appreciations: With an Essay on Style.* London: Macmillan, 1889.

——. "The Character of the Humourist: Charles Lamb." *Fortnightly Review* n.s. 24 (1878): 466–74.

——. "Coleridge." In *The English Poets: Selections with Critical Introductions by Various Writers, and a General Introduction by Matthew Arnold.* Edited by Thomas Humphry Ward. Vol. 4, 102–54. London: Macmillan, 1880.

——. *Letters of Walter Pater.* Edited by Lawrence Evans. Oxford: Clarendon Press, 1970.

——. "On Wordsworth." *Fortnightly Review* n.s. 15, no. 88 (1874): 455–65.

——. *The Renaissance: Studies in Art and Poetry, The 1893 Text.* Edited by Donald L. Hill. Berkeley: University of California Press, 1980.

——. "Romanticism." *Macmillan's Magazine* 35 (1876): 64–70.

——. "The School of Giorgione." *Fortnightly Review* n.s. 22 (1877): 526–38.

——. "Shakespeare's English Kings." In *Appreciations: With an Essay on Style,* 192–212. London: Macmillan, 1889.

——. *Studies in the History of the Renaissance.* London: Macmillan, 1873.

Payn, James. *The Talk of the Town.* 2 vols. London: Chatto and Windus, 1885.

Pearson, Hesketh. *The Life of Oscar Wilde.* London: Methuen, 1946.

Penzoldt, Ernst. *Der arme Chatterton.* Leipzig: Insel, 1928.

——. *The Marvellous Boy.* Translated by Eleanor Woolf and John J. Trounstine. New York: Harcourt, Brace, 1931.

Percy, Thomas. *Reliques of Ancient English Poetry: Consisting of Old Heroic Ballads, Songs, and Other Pieces of Our Earlier Poets, (Chiefly of the Lyric Kind.) Together with Some Few of Later Date.* 3 vols. London: J. Dodsley, 1765.

Perkins, David. *Is Literary History Possible?* Baltimore: Johns Hopkins University Press, 1992.

Philalethes [Francis Webb]. *Shakspeare's Manuscripts, in the Possession of Mr. Ireland, Examined, Respecting the Internal and External Evidences of Their Authority.* London: J. Johnson, 1796.

Pierce, Patricia. *The Great Shakespeare Fraud: The Strange, True Story of William-Henry Ireland.* Stroud: Sutton, 2004.

Plarr, Victor. *Ernest Dowson 1888–1897, Reminiscences, Unpublished Letters, and Marginalia.* New York: Laurence J. Gomme, 1914.

Plato. *The Dialogues of Plato.* Translated by Benjamin Jowett. 2nd ed. 5 vols. Oxford: Clarendon Press, 1875.

Posner, Richard A. *The Little Book of Plagiarism.* New York: Pantheon, 2007.

Powell, Lawrence Clark. "To Wilmarth S. Lewis." 21 November 1952. Clarkive Post-1934. Correspondence, 1944–1958, I-Magee. Box 6.

Pressly, William L. *The Artist as Original Genius: Shakespeare's "Fine-Frenzy" in Late-Eighteenth-Century British Art.* Newark: University of Delaware Press, 2007.

Prior, Matthew. *The Literary Works of Matthew Prior.* Edited by H. Bunker Wright and Monroe K. Spears. 2 vols. Oxford: Clarendon Press, 1959.

Pye, Henry James. *Poems on Various Subjects.* 2 vols. London: J. Stockton, 1787.

Pyne, Evelyn. "A Poet's Death (Chatterton, August 1770)." In *A Poet in May,* 58–64. London: Kegan Paul, Trench, 1885.

Quilter, Harry. "Letter to the Editor." *Pall Mall Gazette,* 23 November 1885: 11.

——. *Sententiæ Artis: First Principles of Art for Painters and Picture Lovers.* London: Isbister, 1886.

Reynolds, Joshua. *Discourses on Art.* Edited by Robert R. Wark. San Marino, CA: Huntington Library, 1959.

Rhys, Ernest. *A London Rose and Other Rhymes.* London: Elkin Mathews and John Lane, 1894.

Richards, S. Wall. Letters to Oscar Wilde, 16 June 1887 and 16 March 1888. Clark Library. Wilde MS Box 74 Folder 8.

Richmond, John. "Prefatory Notice." In *The Poetical Works of Thomas Chatterton*. The Canterbury Poets, 7–29. London: Walter Scott, 1886.

Ricketts, Charles. *Oscar Wilde: Recollections by Jean Paul Raymond and Charles Ricketts*. London: Nonesuch Press, 1932.

Ricks, Christopher. *Allusion to the Poets*. Oxford: Oxford University Press, 2002.

Riquelme, John Paul. "Oscar Wilde's Anadoodlegram: A Genetic, Performative Reading of *An Ideal Husband*." In *Wilde Discoveries: Traditions, Histories, Archives*. Edited by Joseph Bristow, 289–314. Toronto: University of Toronto Press, 2013.

Ritson, Joseph. *Select Collection of English Songs*. 3 vols. London: J. Johnson, 1873.

Robinson, Mary. "The Poet: A Fragment." *Morning Herald and Daily Advertiser*, 11 October 1785: 10.

Roe, Nicholas. *John Keats: A New Life*. New Haven: Yale University Press, 2012.

Rogers, Robert, and Richard N. Ramsey. "Recent Studies in the Restoration and Eighteenth Century." *Studies in English Literature, 1500–1900* 12, no. 3 (Summer 1972): 567–90.

Ross, Iain. *Oscar Wilde and Ancient Greece*. Cambridge: Cambridge University Press, 2012.

Rossetti, Dante Gabriel. *Ballads and Sonnets*. London: Ellis and White, 1881.

———. *The Correspondence of Dante Gabriel Rossetti*. Edited by William E. Fredeman. 9 vols. Cambridge: D. S. Brewer, 2002–2010.

———. *Letters of Dante Gabriel Rossetti*. Edited by Oswald Doughty and John Robert Wahl. 4 vols. Oxford: Clarendon Press, 1965–1967.

———. "The Stealthy School of Criticism." *Athenæum* 2303 (16 December 1871): 792–94.

Rossetti, Dante Gabriel, and Hall Caine. *Dear Mr. Rossetti: The Letters of Dante Gabriel Rossetti and Hall Caine, 1878–1881*. Edited by Vivien Allen. Sheffield: Sheffield Academic Press, 2000.

Rossetti, William Michael. *Dante Gabriel Rossetti: His Family-Letters, with a Memoir*. Edited by William Michael Rossetti. 2 vols. London: Ellis and Elvey, 1895.

———. "Ford Madox Brown: Characteristics." *Century Guild Hobby Horse* 1, no. 2 (April 1886): 48–54.

———. *Life of John Keats*. London: Walter Scott, 1887.

Ruskin, John. *Notes on Some of the Principal Pictures Exhibited in the Rooms of the Royal Academy and the Society of Painters in Water-Colours: No. II—1856*. 6th ed. London: Smith, Elder, 1856.

Russell, Charles Edward. *Thomas Chatterton, the Marvelous Boy: The Story of a Strange Life 1752–1770*. New York: Moffat, Yard, 1908.

Ruthven, K. K. *Faking Literature*. Cambridge: Cambridge University Press, 2001.

Saint-Amour, Paul K. *The Copywrights: Intellectual Property and the Literary Imagination*. Ithaca, NY: Cornell University Press, 2003.

Saintsbury, George. *Historical Manual of English Prosody*. London: Macmillan, 1926.

Sams, Eric. *Shakespeare's Edward III*. New Haven: Yale University Press, 1996.

Saunders, Thomas Bailey. *The Life and Letters of James Macpherson, Containing a Particular Account of His Famous Quarrel with Dr. Johnson, and a Sketch of the Origin and Influence of the Ossian Poems*. London: Swan Sonnenschein, 1894.

Savu, Laura. *Postmortem Postmodernists: The Afterlife of the Author in Recent Narrative.* Cranbury, NJ: Associated University Presses, 2009.

Schlegel, Friedrich. *Dialogue on Poetry and Literary Aphorisms.* Translated by Ernst Behler and Roman Struc. University Park: Pennsylvania State University Press, 1968.

Schoenbaum, S. *Shakespeare's Lives.* New Edition. Oxford: Clarendon Press, 1991.

Schroeder, Horst. *Annotations to Oscar Wilde, "The Portrait of Mr. W.H."* Braunschweig: privately printed, 1986.

———. *Oscar Wilde, The Portrait of Mr. W.H.: Its Composition, Publication and Reception.* Braunschweig: Technische Universität Carolo-Wilhelmina zu Braunschweig, 1984.

———. "Volume IV of the OET Edition of *The Complete Works of Oscar Wilde:* III. 'Pen, Pencil and Poison.'" *The Wildean* 36 (2010): 28–60.

Scott, Clement. "The Playhouses." *Illustrated London News,* 12 January 1895: 35.

Scott, John. "Written after a Journey to Bristol." In *Poetical Works,* 223–27. London: J. Buckland, 1782.

Scott, Temple. "Mr. Charles Ricketts and the Vale Press." *Bookselling* 2 (1896): 501–12.

Scrutator [Alexander Rivington]. *Strictures on Mr. N. E. S. A. Hamilton's Inquiry into the Genuineness of the MS. Corrections in Mr. J. Payne Collier's Annotated Shakespeare Folio, 1632.* London: John Russell Smith, 1860.

Seiler, R. M., ed. *Walter Pater: The Critical Heritage.* London: Routledge and Kegan Paul, 1980.

Shairp, J. C. "English Poetry in the Eighteenth Century." *Princeton Review* 14 (July 1881): 30–50.

———. "Ossian." *Macmillan's Magazine* 24 (1871): 113–25.

Shakespeare, William. *Coriolanus.* Edited by Lee Bliss. Updated Edition. Cambridge: Cambridge University Press, 2010.

———. *Coriolanus.* Edited by Philip Brockbank. The Arden Shakespeare. London: Methuen, 1976.

———. *Coriolanus.* Edited by Peter Holland. The Arden Shakespeare. 3rd series. London: Bloomsbury, 2013.

———. *Coriolanus.* Edited by R. B. Parker. The Oxford Shakespeare. Oxford: Clarendon Press, 1994.

———. *King Henry VIII (All Is True).* Edited by Gordon McMullan. London: The Arden Shakespeare, 2000.

———. *Mr. William Shakespeares Comedies, Histories and Tragedies, Published According to the True Originall Copies: The Second, Third, and Fourth Folios in Facsimile.* 3 vols. Cambridge: D. S. Brewer, 1985.

———. *Plays and Poems of William Shakspeare in Ten Volumes: Collated Verbatim with the most Authentick Copies, and Revised; with the Corrections and Illustrations of Various Commentators; to Which are Added, an Essay on the Chronological Order of His Plays; An Essay Relative to Shakspeare and Jonson; a Dissertation on the Three Parts of King Henry VI; an Historical Account of the English Stage; and Notes by Edmond Malone.* 10 vols. London: H. Baldwin for J. Rivington and Sons, 1790.

———. *The Plays and Poems of William Shakspeare: In Sixteen Volumes; Collated Verbatim with the Most Authentick Copies, and Revised: With the Corrections and Illustrations of Various Commentators; to Which Are Added, an Essay on the Chronological Order of His Plays; an Essay Relative to Shakspeare and Jonson; a Dissertation on the Three Parts of King Henry VI, an Historical Account of the English Stage.* Edited by E. Malone. Dublin: John Exshaw, 1794.

——. *Richard II.* Edited by Charles R. Forker. The Arden Shakespeare. 3rd series. London: Thomson, 2002.

——. *Shakespeare's Sonnets.* Edited by Katherine Duncan-Jones. The Arden Shakespeare. 3rd series. London: Thomas Nelson, 1997.

——. *The Sonnets of William Shakespere.* Edited by Edward Dowden. London: Kegan Paul, Trench, 1881.

——. *The Tragedie of Coriolanus.* In *The Norton Facsimile of the First Folio of Shakespeare.* Edited by Charlton Hinman. 2nd ed., 617–46. New York: Norton, 1996.

——. *Troilus and Cressida.* Edited by David Bevington. The Arden Shakespeare. 3rd series. Walton-on-Thames, Surrey: Thomas Nelson, 1998.

——. *The Works of Shakespeare: The Text Regulated by the Recently Discovered Folio of 1632, Containing Early Manuscript Emendations with a History of the Stage, a Life of the Poet, and an Introduction to Each Play, to Which Are Added Glossarial and Other Notes and the Readings of Former Editions.* Edited by J. P. Collier. New York: Redfield, 1853.

Sharp, William. *Dante Gabriel Rossetti: A Record and a Study.* London: Macmillan, 1882.

——. "Introductory Note." In *The Songs, Poems, and Sonnets of William Shakespeare.* London: W. Scott, 1888.

——. "New Novels." *Academy,* 5 September 1891: 193–94.

——. *The Life and Letters of Joseph Severn.* London: Sampson Low, Marston, 1892.

Shaw, George Bernard. *Bernard Shaw's Book Reviews.* Edited by Brian Tyson. University Park: Pennsylvania State University Press, 1991.

——. "In Five Acts and in Blank Verse." *Pall Mall Gazette,* 14 July 1887: 3.

Shaw, William. *An Enquiry into the Authenticity of the Poems Ascribed to Ossian.* London: J. Murray, 1781.

Shelley, Percy Bysshe. *Essays and Letters.* Edited by Ernest Rhys. London: Walter Scott, 1887.

——. *Essays, Letters from Abroad, Translations and Fragments.* Edited by Mary Shelley. 2 vols. London: Edward Moxon, 1840.

——. *The Poetical Works of Percy Bysshe Shelley.* Edited by Mary Shelley. 2 vols. London: Edward Moxon, 1839.

——. *The Prose Works of Percy Bysshe Shelley.* Edited by H. Buxton Forman. 4 vols. London: Reeves and Turner, 1880.

——. *Shelley's Poetry and Prose.* Edited by Donald H. Reiman and Neil Fraistat. 2nd ed. New York: W. W. Norton, 2002.

Sherard, Robert Harborough. *The Real Oscar Wilde.* London: T. Werner Laurie, 1916.

——. *Twenty Years in Paris: Being Some Recollections of a Literary Life.* London: Hutchinson, 1905.

Sheridan, Richard B. *The School for Scandal.* Edited by F. W. Bateson. London: Ernest Benn, 1979.

Shewan, Rodney. *Oscar Wilde: Art and Egotism.* London: Macmillan, 1977.

Shields, Frederic. "Some Notes on Dante Gabriel Rossetti." *Century Guild Hobby Horse* 1, no. 4 (October 1886): 140–54.

Singer, Samuel Weller. *The Text of Shakespeare Vindicated from the Interpolations and Corruptions Advocated by John Payne Collier, Esq., in His Notes and Emendations.* London: William Pickering, 1853.

Skeat, Walter. "Preface." In *The Poetical Works of Thomas Chatterton.* 2 vols., ix–xi. London: Bell and Daldy, 1872.

Small, Ian. "Intertextuality in Pater and Wilde." In "Essays & Poems: In Memory of Ian Fletcher, 1920–1988." *English Literature in Transition, 1880–1920* special series, no. 4 (1990): 57–66.

[Smith, Richard]. "Anecdotes of Chatterton and His Associates." *Gentleman's Magazine,* n.s. 10 (1838): 603–7.

Southey, Robert. *The Life and Correspondence of Robert Southey.* Edited by Charles Cuthbert Southey. 6 vols. London: Longman, Brown, Green, and Longmans, 1849–1850.

———. *New Letters of Robert Southey.* Edited by Kenneth Curry. 2 vols. New York: Columbia University Press, 1965.

———. "Preface." In *The Works of Thomas Chatterton.* Edited by Joseph Cottle and Robert Southey. Vol. 1, n.p. London: T. N. Longman and O. Rees, 1803.

———. "To the Editor of the *Monthly Magazine.*" *Monthly Magazine* 8 (1799): 770–72.

———. *The Vision of Judgement.* London: Longman, Hurst, Rees, Orme, and Brown, 1821.

Stacey, Robert, and Elizabeth Hulse. *Sir Daniel Wilson: Ambidextrous Polymath.* Toronto: University of Toronto Press, 2001.

Stafford, Fiona. *Sublime Savage: James Macpherson and the Poems of Ossian.* Edinburgh: Edinburgh University Press, 1988.

Stearns, Laurie. "Copy Wrong: Plagiarism, Process, Property, and the Law." In *Perspectives on Plagiarism and Intellectual Property in a Post Modern World.* Edited by Lise Buranen and Alice Roy, 5–17. Albany: State University of New York Press, 2003.

Steele, Robert. Prospectus for *The Rowley Poems of Thomas Chatterton.* London: Vale Press, n.d. (c. 1898).

Steevens, George. *Supplement to the Edition of Shakspeare's Plays Published in 1778 by Samuel Johnson and George Steevens.* 2 vols. London: C. Bathhurst, and Others, 1780.

Stendhal [Henri Beyle]. *Racine et Shakespeare: Études sur le romantisme.* Nouvelle edition. Paris: Michel Lévy Frères, 1854.

Stenhouse, William. *Poems, Songs, and Sonnets.* London: Simpkin, Marshall, 1886.

Stewart, Douglas. *The Boy Who Would Be Shakespeare: A Tale of Folly and Forgery.* Cambridge, MA: Da Capo Press, 2010.

Stewart, Susan. *Poetry and the Fate of the Senses.* Chicago: University of Chicago Press, 2002.

Stoddard, R. H. "John Keats and Fanny Brawne." *Appleton's Journal* 4 (1878): 379–82.

Story, Somerville. *Twenty Years in Paris.* London: Alston Rivers, 1925.

Strachey, Amy. "The Child-Players of the Elizabethan Stage." *Woman's World* 2, no. 11 (1888): 490–94.

"S.W.A." [Robert Nares?]. "Eleanora and Juga." *Town and Country Magazine* (June 1769): 328–29.

Swinburne, Algernon Charles. "Charles Lamb and George Wither." *Nineteenth Century* 17, no. 95 (January 1885): 66–91.

——. *The Collected Poems of Algernon Charles Swinburne.* 6 vols. London: Chatto and Windus, 1904.

——. "The Leper." In *Poems and Ballads*, 137–43. London: John Camden Hotten, 1866.

——. *The Letters of Algernon Charles Swinburne, With Some Personal Recollections.* Edited by Thomas Hake and Arthur Compton-Rickett. London: John Murray, 1918.

——. *Miscellanies.* London: Chatto and Windus, 1886.

——. *Poems and Ballads.* London: John Camden Hotten, 1866.

——. "The Poems of Dante Gabriel Rossetti." *Fortnightly Review* n.s. 7, no. 41 (1870): 551–79.

——. "Sonnet: With a Copy of *Mademoiselle de Maupin*." In *Poems and Ballads*. 2nd series. London: Chatto and Windus, 1878.

——. *The Swinburne Letters.* Edited by Cecil Y. Lang. 6 vols. New Haven: Yale University Press, 1959–1962.

——. "Tennyson and Musset." *Fortnightly Review* n.s. 29, no. 170 (February 1881): 129–53.

——. *William Blake.* London: John Camden Hotten, 1868.

——. "Wordsworth and Byron." *Nineteenth Century* 15 (April 1884): 583–609; 15 (May 1884): 764–90.

Symonds, John Addington. *Fragilia Labilia.* Portland, ME: Thomas B. Mosher, 1902.

——. Review of *The Poetical Works of Thomas Chatterton. Academy* 2, no. 38 (December 1871): 549–50.

——. *Shakspeare's Predecessors in the English Drama.* London: Smith, Elder, 1884.

Symons, Arthur. "Causerie of the Week: Chatterton and His Editors." *Speaker* n.s. 14, no. 346 (19 May 1906): 163–64.

Taylor, Donald S. *Thomas Chatterton's Art: Experiments in Imagined History.* Princeton: Princeton University Press, 1978.

Taylor, John. "To the Editor." *Athenæum* 2824 (10 December 1881): 780.

Taylor, Una. *Guests and Memories: Annals of a Seaside Villa.* London: Humphrey Milford and Oxford University Press, 1924.

Tennyson, Alfred Lord. *The Poems of Tennyson.* Edited by Christopher Ricks. 2nd ed. 3 vols. Harlow: Longman, 1989.

Terry, Richard. "'In Pleasing Memory of All He Stole': Plagiarism and Literary Detection, 1747–1785." In *Plagiarism in Early Modern England.* Edited by Paulina Kewes, 181–200. Basingstoke: Palgrave Macmillan, 2003.

——. *The Plagiarism Allegation in English Literature from Butler to Sterne.* Basingstoke: Palgrave Macmillan, 2012.

Thomas, James. *The Art of the Actor-Manager: Wilson Barrett and the Victorian Theatre.* Ann Arbor, MI: UMI Research Press, 1984.

Thomas, W. Moy. "The Inquest on Chatterton." *Athenæum* 1571 (5 December 1857): 1518–19.

Thompson, Alfred. "The Bard of Beauty." *Time* 3 (September 1880): 95–97.

Thomson, Derick S. *The Gaelic Sources of Macpherson's Ossian.* Aberdeen University Studies, No. 130. Edinburgh: Oliver and Boyd, 1952.

Thornbury, Walter. "John Dix, the Biographer of Chatterton." *Notes and Queries* 4, no. 9 (April 1872): 294–96.

———. "Old Stories Re-told: Thomas Griffiths Wainewright [Janus Weathercock], The Poisoner." *All the Year Round*, 5 January 1867: 34–41.

Ting, Nai-Tung. "The Influence of Chatterton on Keats." *Keats-Shelley Journal* 5 (1956): 103–8.

Travers Smith, Hester. *Oscar Wilde from Purgatory: Psychic Messages.* New York: H. Holt, 1926.

———. *Psychic Messages from Oscar Wilde.* London: T. Werner Laurie, 1924.

Tufescu, Florina. *Oscar Wilde's Plagiarism: The Triumph of Art over Ego.* Dublin: Irish Academic Press, 2008.

Tyler, Thomas. "Introduction." In *Shakspere's Sonnets: The First Quarto, 1609 — A Facsimile in Photo-Lithography.* London: C. Praetorius, 1886.

[Tyrwhitt, Thomas]. "Preface." In *Poems, Supposed to Have Been Written at Bristol, by Thomas Rowley, and Others, in the Fifteenth Century; the Greatest Part Now First Published from the Most Authentic Copies, with an Engraved Specimen of One of the MSS, to Which Are Added, A Preface, an Introductory Account of the Several Pieces, and a Glossary* by Thomas Chatterton, v–xiv. London: T. Payne, 1777.

Vallance, Aymer. "Mr. Arthur H. Mackmurdo and the Century Guild." *Studio* 16, no. 73 (April 1899): 183–92.

Vedder, Elihu. *Doubt and Other Things.* Boston: Porter Sargent, 1922.

Wainewright, Thomas Griffiths. *Essays and Criticisms.* Edited by W. Carew Hazlitt. London: Reeves and Turner, 1880.

[Wainewright, Thomas Griffiths (pseud. Janus Weathercock)]. "Janus Weatherbound; or, the Weathercock Steadfast for Lack of Oil: A Grave Epistle." *London Magazine* 7 (1823): 45–52.

———. "Sentimentalities on the Fine Arts: No. III." *London Magazine* 1 (1820): 401–8.

Wallace, William. "Prolegomena." In *The Logic of Hegel: Translated from the Encyclopaedia of the Philosophical Sciences with Prolegomena*, xiii–clxxxiv. Oxford: Clarendon Press, 1874.

Walpole, Horace. *The Castle of Otranto: A Gothic Story.* 3rd ed. London: William Bathoe, 1766.

———. *A Letter to the Editor of the Miscellanies of Thomas Chatterton.* Strawberry Hill: privately printed, 1779.

———. *Letters of Horace Walpole, Earl of Orford.* 6 vols. London: Richard Bentley, 1840.

———. *The Yale Edition of Horace Walpole's Correspondence.* Edited by W. S. Lewis. 48 vols. New Haven: Yale University Press, 1937–1983.

Ward, Thomas Humphry, ed. *The English Poets: Selections with Critical Introductions by Various Writers, and a General Introduction by Matthew Arnold.* 4 vols. London: Macmillan, 1880.

Warner, Ferdinando. *Remarks on the History of Fingal, and Other Poems of Ossian: Translated by Mr. Macpherson.* London: H. Payne and W. Cropley, 1762.

Warton, Thomas, ed. *The History of English Poetry, from the Close of the Eleventh to the Commencement of the Eighteenth Century.* 4 vols. London: Dodsley, 1774.

Watry, Maureen. *The Vale Press: Charles Ricketts, a Publisher in Earnest*. New Castle, DE: Oak Knoll Press, 2004.

Watts, Theodore. "Poetry." In *Encylopædia Brittanica*. 9th ed. Vol. 19, 256–73. New York: H. G. Allen, 1890.

——. "Review of *The Sonnets of John Milton*." *Athenæum* 2914 (1 September 1883): 263–65.

——. "Thomas Chatterton." In *The English Poets: Selections with Critical Introductions by Various Writers, and a General Introduction by Matthew Arnold*. Edited by Thomas Humphry Ward. Vol. 3, 400–408. London: Macmillan, 1880.

——. "Thoreau, His Life and Aims: A Study." *Athenæum* 2610 (3 November 1877): 562–64.

——. "The Truth about Rossetti." *Nineteenth Century* 13 (1883): 404–23.

[——.] "Literature." *Athenæum* 3073 (18 September 1886): 361–63.

Wedmore, Frederick. "The Stage." *Academy*, 5 March 1892: 236–37.

Wellek, René. "The Concept of 'Romanticism' in Literary History." *Comparative Literature* 1, no. 1 (1949): 1–23.

Whalley, George. "England: Romantic — Romanticism." In *"Romantic" and Its Cognates: The European History of a Word*. Edited by Hans Eichner, 157–262. Toronto: University of Toronto Press, 1972.

Wheatley, Henry. *Notes on the Life of J. P. Collier; with a Complete List of His Works, and an Account of Such Shakespeare Documents as Are Believed to Be Spurious*. London: Elliot Stock, 1884.

Whistler, James Abbott McNeill. *The Gentle Art of Making Enemies*. New Edition. London: Heinemann, 1892.

——. "The Habit of Second Natures." *Truth*, 2 January 1890: 4–5.

——. "Tenderness in Tite Street." *World*, 25 February 1885: 14.

——. "To the Committee of the 'National Art Exhibition.'" *World*, 17 November 1886: 16.

Whistler, James McNeill, and Oscar Wilde. *Wilde v. Whistler*. London: privately printed, 1906.

Whitaker, John. "To Dr. Ducarel." In *Illustrations of the Literary History of the Eighteenth Century: Consisting of Authentic Memoirs and Original Letters of Eminent Persons, and Intended as a Sequel to the Literary Anecdotes*. Edited by John Nichols. Vol. 4, 855–57. London: Nichols, Son, and Bentley, 1817–1858.

White, Richard Grant. "Introduction." In *The Confessions of William-Henry Ireland*, vii–xxxi. New York: James W. Bouton, 1874.

Whittington-Egan, Molly. *Frank Miles and Oscar Wilde: "Such White Lilies."* High Wycombe: Rivendale Press, 2008.

Wilde, Constance. Autograph Album of Constance Wilde. British Library, Add. MS 81755.

Wilde, Jane Francesca. *Ancient Legends, Mystic Charms, and Superstitions of Ireland*. Boston: Ticknor, 1888.

——. *Lady Jane Wilde's Letters to Oscar Wilde, 1875–1895: A Critical Edition*. Edited by Karen Sasha Anthony Tipper. Lewiston, PA: Edwin Mellen Press, 2011.

Wilde, Oscar. "The Beauties of Bookbinding: Mr. Cobden-Sanderson at the Arts and Crafts." *Pall Mall Gazette*, 23 November 1888: 3.

——. "[ΓΛΥΚΥΠΙΚΡΟϛ ΕΡΩϛ]" ["Bittersweet Love"]. In *Poems and Poems in Prose*.

Edited by Bobby Fong and Karl Beckson. *The Complete Works of Oscar Wilde*. Vol. 1, 126–27. Oxford: Oxford University Press, 2000.

——. "The Canterville Ghost." In *Lord Arthur Savile's Crime and Other Prose Pieces*. Edited by Robert Ross. *The Collected Works of Oscar Wilde*. Vol. 7, 65–119. London: Methuen, 1908.

——. "The Canterville Ghost." *Court and Society Review* 4, no. 138 (February 1887): 183–86; no. 139 (March 1887): 207–11.

——. "A Cheap Edition of a Great Man." *Pall Mall Gazette*, 18 April 1887: 5.

——. "The Children of the Poets." *Pall Mall Gazette*, 14 October 1886: 5.

——. "The Close of the 'Arts and Crafts': Mr. Walter Crane's Lecture on Design." *Pall Mall Gazette*, 30 November 1888: 3.

——. *The Collected Works of Oscar Wilde*. Edited by Robert Ross. 14 vols. London: Methuen, 1908.

——. "Commonplace Book." Clark Library, Wilde W6721M3 C734 Boxed.

——. *The Complete Letters of Oscar Wilde*. Edited by Merlin Holland and Rupert Hart-Davis. London: Fourth Estate, 2000.

——. *The Complete Works of Oscar Wilde*. Series edited by Ian Small. Oxford English Texts. 7 vols. to date. Oxford: Oxford University Press, 2000 and continuing.

——. "The Critic as Artist." In *Criticism: Historical Criticism, Intentions, The Soul of Man*. Edited by Josephine M. Guy. *The Complete Works of Oscar Wilde*. Vol. 4, 123–206. Oxford: Oxford University Press, 2007.

——. *Criticism: Historical Criticism, Intentions, The Soul of Man*. Edited by Josephine M. Guy. *The Complete Works of Oscar Wilde*. Vol. 4. Oxford: Oxford University Press, 2007.

——. "The Decay of Lying." *Nineteenth Century* 25, no. 143 (January 1889): 35–56.

——. "The Decay of Lying." In *Criticism: Historical Criticism, Intentions, The Soul of Man*. Edited by Josephine M. Guy. *The Complete Works of Oscar Wilde*. Vol. 4, 72–103. Oxford: Oxford University Press, 2007.

——. *Decorative Art in America*. Edited by Richard Butler Glaenzer. New York: Brentano's, 1906.

——. "Endymion." In *Poems and Poems in Prose*. Edited by Bobby Fong and Karl Beckson. *The Complete Works of Oscar Wilde*. Vol. 1, 69–70. Oxford: Oxford University Press, 2000.

——. "The English Renaissance of Art." In *Miscellanies*. Edited by Robert Ross. *The Collected Works of Oscar Wilde*. Vol. 14, 241–78. London: Methuen, 1908.

——. "Ethics of Journalism." *Pall Mall Gazette*, 20 September 1894: 3.

——. "Ethics of Journalism." *Pall Mall Gazette*, 25 September 1894: 3.

——. "A Fascinating Book." *Woman's World* 2, no. 1 (December 1888): 53–56.

——. "The Garden of Eros." In *Poems and Poems in Prose*. Edited by Bobby Fong and Karl Beckson. *The Complete Works of Oscar Wilde*. Vol. 1, 128–35. Oxford: Oxford University Press, 2000.

——. "The Grave of Keats." In *Poems and Poems in Prose*. Edited by Bobby Fong and Karl Beckson. *The Complete Works of Oscar Wilde*. Vol. 1, 36. Oxford: Oxford University Press, 2000.

——. "The Grave of Shelley." In *Poems and Poems in Prose*. Edited by Bobby Fong and

Karl Beckson. *The Complete Works of Oscar Wilde*. Vol. 1, 43. Oxford: Oxford University Press, 2000.

———. "The Happy Prince." In *The Happy Prince, and Other Tales*, 1–24. London: David Nutt, 1888.

———. "The Happy Prince." In *A House of Pomegranates. The Happy Prince and Other Tales*. Edited by Robert Ross. *The Collected Works of Oscar Wilde*. Vol. 10, 167–83. London: Methuen, 1908.

———. "Helas!" In *Poems and Poems in Prose*. Edited by Bobby Fong and Karl Beckson. *The Complete Works of Oscar Wilde*. Vol. 1, 156–57. Oxford: Oxford University Press, 2000.

———. *A House of Pomegranates*. London: Osgood, McIlvaine, 1891.

———. "Humanitad." In *Poems and Poems in Prose*. Edited by Bobby Fong and Karl Beckson. *The Complete Works of Oscar Wilde*. Vol. 1, 92–104. Oxford: Oxford University Press, 2000.

———. *An Ideal Husband*. In *Two Society Comedies*. Edited by Russell Jackson and Ian Small. New Mermaids. London: Ernest Benn, 1983.

———. *The Importance of Being Earnest*. Edited by Russell Jackson. New Mermaids. London: Ernest Benn, 1980.

———. "In the Market Place." *Truth*, 9 January 1890: 51.

———. *Irish Poets and Poetry of the Nineteenth Century: A Lecture Delivered at Platt's Hall on Wednesday April Fifth, 1882*. Edited by Robert D. Pepper. San Francisco: Book Club of California, 1972.

———. "A 'Jolly' Art Critic." *Pall Mall Gazette*, 18 November 1886: 6.

———. *Journalism Part I*. Edited by John Stokes and Mark W. Turner. In *The Complete Works of Oscar Wilde*. Vol. 6. Oxford: Oxford University Press, 2013.

———. *Journalism Part II*. Edited by John Stokes and Mark W. Turner. In *The Complete Works of Oscar Wilde*. Vol. 7. Oxford: Oxford University Press, 2013.

———. "Keats' Sonnet on Blue." *Century Guild Hobby Horse* 1, no. 3 (July 1886): 82–86.

———. *Lady Windermere's Fan*. Edited by Ian Small. 2nd ed. London: A. and C. Black, 2002.

———. Letter to E. Cook. Undated (c. November 17, 1886). Eccles Bequest. British Library, Add. MS 81648.

———. "Lord Arthur Savile's Crime." *Court and Society Review* 4, no. 149 (11 May 1887): 447–50; 4, no. 150 (18 May 1887): 471–73; 4, no. 151 (25 May 1887): 495–97.

———. "Lord Arthur's Savile's Crime." In *Lord Arthur Savile's Crime and Other Prose Pieces*. Edited by Robert Ross. *The Collected Works of Oscar Wilde*. Vol. 7, 8–61. London: Methuen, 1908.

———. *Lord Arthur Savile's Crime and Other Stories*. London: James R. Osgood, 1891.

———. "Miner and Minor Poets." *Pall Mall Gazette*, 1 February 1887: 5.

———. "Mr. Morris on Tapestry." *Pall Mall Gazette*, 2 November 1888: 6.

———. "Mr. Pater's Imaginary Portraits." *Pall Mall Gazette*, 11 June 1887: 2–3.

———. "Mr. Pater's Last Volume." *Speaker*, 22 March 1890: 319–20.

———. "Mr. Whistler's Ten O'Clock." *Pall Mall Gazette*, 21 February 1885: 1–2.

———. "The New Helen." *Time: A Monthly Miscellany of Interesting and Amusing Literature* 1 (July 1879): 400–402.

——. "New Novels." *Pall Mall Gazette*, 28 October 1886: 4–5.

——. "The Nightingale and the Rose." In *The Happy Prince, and Other Tales*, 25–41. London: David Nutt, 1888.

——. Note-book Kept at Oxford. Clark Library, Wilde W6721M3 N9111 Bound.

——. Notes on Dante Gabriel Rossetti. Clark Library, Clark W6721M3 D758.

——. *Oscar Wilde's Oxford Notebooks: A Portrait of Mind in the Making*. Edited by Philip E. Smith II and Michael S. Helfand. New York: Oxford University Press, 1989.

——. *Oscar Wilde in America: The Interviews*. Edited by Matthew Hofer and Gary Scharnhorst. Urbana: University of Illinois Press, 2010.

——. "Pen, Pencil, and Poison." In *Intentions*, 59–94. London: James Osgood, 1891.

——. "Pen, Pencil and Poison: A Study." *Fortnightly Review* n.s. 45, no. 265 (January 1889): 41–54.

——. "Phrases, Aphorisms and Fragments of Verse." Clark Library, W6721 P576 Bound.

——. *The Picture of Dorian Gray*. Edited by Joseph Bristow. In *The Complete Works of Oscar Wilde*. Vol. 3. Oxford: Oxford University Press, 2005.

——. *Poems and Poems in Prose*. Edited by Bobby Fong and Karl Beckson. In *The Complete Works of Oscar Wilde*. Vol. 1. Oxford: Oxford University Press, 2000.

——. "The Poets' Corner." *Pall Mall Gazette*, 27 September 1886: 5.

——. "The Portrait of Mr. W.H." *Blackwood's Edinburgh Magazine* 146 (July 1889): 1–21.

——. "The Portrait of Mr. W.H." In *The Soul of Man under Socialism and Selected Critical Prose*. Edited by Linda Dowling, 31–102. Harmondsworth: Penguin Books, 2001.

——. "The Portrait of Mr. W.H." New York: Privately Printed for Mitchell Kennerley, 1921.

——. "Printing and Printers: Lecture at the Arts and Crafts." *Pall Mall Gazette*, 16 November 1888: 5.

——. "Puppets and Actors." *Daily Telegraph*, 20 February 1892: 3.

——. *Salomé: Drame en un acte*. Paris: Librairie de l'art independent; London: Elkin Mathews and John Lane, 1893.

——. *Salomé: Drame en un acte*. In *Plays I: The Duchess of Padua; Salomé: Drame en un acte; Salome: Tragedy in One Act*. Edited by Joseph Donohue. *The Complete Works of Oscar Wilde*. Vol. 5. Oxford: Oxford University Press, 2013.

——. *Salome*. Translated by Alfred Douglas. London: Elkin Mathews and John Lane, 1894.

——. "Sculpture at the 'Arts and Crafts.'" *Pall Mall Gazette*, 9 November 1888: 3.

——. "A 'Sentimental Journey' through Literature." *Pall Mall Gazette*, 1 December 1886: 5.

——. "Shakespeare and Stage Costume." *Nineteenth Century* 17, no. 99 (May 1885): 800–818.

——. "Sir Charles Bowen's *Virgil*." *Pall Mall Gazette*, 30 November 1887: 3.

——. "Some Literary Notes." *Woman's World* 2, no. 5 (March 1889): 277–80.

——. "Sonnet: On the Recent Sale by Auction of Keats's Love Letters." *Dramatic Review* 2, no. 52 (January 1886): 249.

——. *The Soul of Man under Socialism and Selected Critical Prose*. Edited by Linda Dowling. Harmondsworth: Penguin Books, 2001.

——. "The Tomb of Keats." *Irish Monthly*, 5 July 1877: 476–78.

———. "The True Function and Value of Criticism; with Some Remarks on the Importance of Doing Nothing: A Dialogue." *Nineteenth Century* 28, no. 161 (July 1890): 123–47; 28, no. 163 (September 1890): 435–59.

———. "The Truth of Masks." In *Criticism: Historical Criticism, Intentions, The Soul of Man.* Edited by Josephine M. Guy. *The Complete Works of Oscar Wilde.* Vol. 4, 207–28. Oxford: Oxford University Press, 2007.

———. "To Sarah Bernhardt." *World: A Journal for Men and Women* 10 (1879): 18.

———. "To the Painter." *World*, 25 February 1885: 14.

———. "Two Biographies of Keats." *Pall Mall Gazette*, 27 September 1887: 3.

———. "The Unity of the Arts: A Lecture and a Five O'Clock." *Pall Mall Gazette*, 12 December 1887: 13.

———. "Venus or Victory?" *Pall Mall Gazette*, 24 February 1888: 2–3.

———. *Vera; or, The Nihilists.* In *Salomé. A Florentine Tragedy. Vera.* Edited by Robert Ross. *The Collected Works of Oscar Wilde.* Vol. 2, 115–261. London: Methuen, 1908.

[Willcox, C. B.]. "The Life of Thomas Chatterton." In *Poetical Works of Thomas Chatterton, with Notices of His Life, History of the Rowley Controversy, a Selection of His Letters, and Notes Critical and Explanatory.* Edited by C. B. Willcox. Vol. 1, xvii–cl. Cambridge: W. P. Grant, 1842.

Williams, Helena Maria. "Sonnet to Expression." *Morning Herald and Daily Advertiser*, 17 September 1782: 18.

Wilson, Daniel. *Chatterton: A Biographical Study.* London: Macmillan, 1869.

Wise, Thomas J. "The Performance of Hellas." *Note-Book of the Shelley Society*, 134–36. London: Reeves and Turner, 1888.

Wolfson, Susan J. *Borderlines: The Shiftings of Gender in British Romanticism.* Stanford, CA: Stanford University Press, 2006.

———. *Formal Charges: The Shaping of Poetry in British Romanticism.* Stanford, CA: Stanford University Press, 1997.

Wordsworth, William. *The Excursion: Being a Portion of The Recluse, a Poem.* 2nd ed. London: Longman, Hurst, Rees, Orme and Brown, 1820.

———. *The Excursion.* Edited by Sally Bushell, James A. Butler, and Michael C. Jaye. Ithaca, NY: Cornell University Press, 2007.

———. *The Letters of Dorothy and William Wordsworth.* Edited by Ernest de Selincourt. 2nd ed. Edited by Mary Moorman and Alan G. Hill. 8 vols. Oxford: Clarendon Press, 1967–1993.

———. *Poems, in Two Volumes and Other Poems, 1800–1807.* Edited by Jared Curtis. Ithaca, NY: Cornell University Press, 1983.

———. "The Tables Turned; An Evening Scene, on the Same Subject" (1798). In *Lyrical Ballads and Other Poems, 1797–1800.* Edited by James Butler and Karen Green. *The Cornell Wordsworth.* 108–9. Ithaca, NY: Cornell University Press, 1992.

———. *Wordsworth, Last Poems, 1821–1850.* Edited by Jared Curtis. *The Cornell Wordsworth.* Ithaca, NY: Cornell University Press, 1999.

Wright, Thomas. *Oscar's Books.* London: Chatto and Windus, 2008. Also published as *Built of Books: How Reading Defined the Life of Oscar Wilde.* New York: Henry Holt, 2008.

Yearsley, Ann. "Elegy on Mr. Chatterton." In *Poems on Various Subjects, by Ann Yearsley, Milkwoman of Clifton, near Bristol; Being Her Second Work*, 168–72. London: G. G. J. and J. Robinson, 1787.

Yeats, William Butler. *Autobiographies*. Edited by William H. O'Donnell and Douglas N. Archibald. In *The Collected Works of W. B. Yeats*. Vol. 3. New York: Scribner, 1999.

Young, Edward. *Night Thoughts*. Edited by Stephen Cornford. Cambridge: Cambridge University Press, 1989.

Zola, Émile. *Les romanciers naturalistes*. Paris: Charpentier, 1893.

———. "M. H. Taine, Artiste." In *Mes haines: Causeries littéraires et artisteques*, 201–32. Paris: Charpentier, 1879.

INDEX

Note: Page numbers in *italics* refer to illustrations.